15536

IRISH PERSPECTIVES ON EC LAW

Edited by

MARY CATHERINE LUCEY

AND

CATHRINA KEVILLE

DUBLIN
ROUND HALL LTD
2003

Published in 2003 by
Round Hall Ltd
43 Fitzwilliam Place
Dublin 2
Ireland

Typeset by
Carrigboy Typesetting Services
Printed by
ColourBooks Ltd, Dublin

A CIP catalogue record for this book is available from the British Library

ISBN 1–85800–280–X

TABLE OF CONTENTS

FOREWORD

When delivering the decision of the Supreme Court, in April 1987, on the challenge brought by the late Mr Raymond Crotty to ratification of the Single European Act, Finlay C.J. said that the European

> "Community was . . . a developing organism with diverse and changing methods for making decisions and an inbuilt and clearly expressed objective of expansion and progress, both in terms of the number of its Member States and in terms of the mechanics to be used in the achievement of its agreed objectives."[1]

The same can be said with equal truth fifteen years later. Three new Member States have joined. More significantly, the intervening years have witnessed the adoption of three further treaties, the creation of the European Union, the establishment of a single currency and of Union citizenship as well as the common area of freedom, security and justice. These changes necessitated the expansion of Community and Union competence. Justice and Home Affairs policy moved to centre stage in a most striking way in the 1990s.

There are, nonetheless, some shadows on the x-ray. It has proved difficult to maintain unanimity among the Member States. Compromise, in the guise of "variable geometry", has accommodated opt-outs for one or other of the trio of the United Kingdom, Denmark or Ireland, for the single currency or the Schengen Agreement. More generally, there has been a move away from the Community method to intergovernmentalism.

Yet, change continues to take place at a rate which does not seem to diminish. I will cite three matters only. We are on the threshold of the greatest single enlargement of the Union. The accession of ten new Member States from central Europe, the Baltic and the Mediterranean, with at least ten new languages, will transform the character of the Union. To mention one simple problem, the Court of Justice will need to recruit twenty additional translators for each new language. The Giscard d'Estaing Convention on the Future of the European Union has begun to formulate proposals for the future shape of the Union. This will be followed by an Intergovernmental Conference, perhaps even during the Irish Presidency, and, no doubt, a further referendum. Even as I write, there is controversy surrounding Ireland's role in the Convention. An only slightly less momentous pending event is the coming into force of the European Arrest Warrant at the beginning of 2004. These events provide a backdrop to the current very welcome work on "Irish Perspectives on EC Law".

The Court of Justice, in its 1982 judgment in *AM & S v. Commission* stated that Community law "derives not only from the economic but also the legal

---

[1]   *Crotty v. An Taoiseach* [1987] I.R. 713, 770.

interpenetration of the Member States."[2] That legal interpenetration has not been entirely one way. Some familiar common law principles have found their way into Community law. Most notable of these is the great principle of *audi alteram partem*. It was said that "even God himself did not pass sentence upon Adam, before he was called upon to make his defence."[3] Advocate General Warner, the first U.K. Advocate General, deserves the credit for introducing this principle to Community law.[4]

In the main, however, the experience of the Irish courts has been one of deference, if not subservience, to the Court of Justice. Finlay C.J. pointed out in the *Crotty* case that "the decisions of the [Court of Justice] on the interpretation of the Treaty and on questions covering its implementation take precedence, in case of conflict, over domestic law and the decisions of national courts of Member States."[5]

I do not think it is seriously contested that, as the President of the Court of Justice, Gil Carlos Rodríguez Iglesias, stated recently, "the Court has made a decisive contribution to ensuring that the Union is a community, not just of national states but also of people, and one based on law." The Court has, in a judgment delivered on September 17, 2002, continued to give real effect to the right of Union citizens to reside freely in the Member States. It stated:

> "As regards, in particular, the right to reside within the territory of the Member States under Article 18(1) EC, that right is conferred directly on every citizen of the Union by a clear and precise provision of the EC Treaty . . . ."[6]

The present work comprises fifteen scholarly expositions of a wide range of European law topics with explanation of their relevance to Ireland. The subjects range from topics of a general or "horizontal" character, such as the principle of effectiveness (Cathrina Keville) and Judicial Review standards (Cathryn Costello) to specific "vertical" topics such as the Electronic Commerce Directive (Dermot Cahill) and Transfer of Undertakings (Cathy Maguire).

After thirty years of membership of the European Community and now the Union, it is interesting to recall some of the cases of the Court of Justice with Irish connections, on the one hand, and some European Community law cases decided by our own courts, on the other.

The field of equality law has been a particularly fruitful one. Ireland, of course, intervened (successfully, in limiting the retrospective effect of the judgment) in the celebrated case, concerning equal pay for air hostesses, of *Defrenne v. Sabena*,[7] but *Murphy v. Bord Telecom Eireann*,[8] also on equal pay

---

2   Case 155/79 *A M & S v. Commission* [1982] ECR 1575, para. 18.
3   *R v. University of Cambridge* [1723] 1 Str. 557.
4   Case C–17/74 *Transocean Marine Paint v. Commission* [1974] ECR 1063.
5   *Crotty v. An Taoiseach* [1987] I.R. 713, 769.
6   Case C–413/99 *Baumbast v. Secretary of State for Home Department*.
7   Case 43/75 [1976] ECR 455.
8   Case 157/86 [1988] ECR 673.

was a reference from an Irish court. The failure of the State to implement the social welfare equality Directives in a timely fashion produced a series of Irish references to the Court of Justice in the 1980s.[9] This sorry saga culminated in the comprehensive judgment of Miss Justice Carroll, awarding *Francovich* damages against the State in *Tate v. Minister for Social Welfare*.[10] This decision is an outstanding example of the legal interpenetration mentioned earlier. The Court had to fashion an Irish legal remedy to give effect to rights under Community law.

Another litigious saga was, and still is, the ice cream dispute, originally known as *HB v. Mars*. HB made freezer cabinets available without charge to retailers selling its ice creams on condition that they be used exclusively for the sale of those HB products. In March 1990, Mars asked the High Court for a declaration that the exclusivity requirement in HB's freezer-cabinet agreements was void as being contrary to competition law, specifically Articles 85 and 86 (now Articles 81 and 82) of the EC Treaty. HB applied for an interlocutory injunction to restrain Mars from using their freezers in March 1990. Lynch J. rejected Mars' defence. Keane J. also dismissed Mars' arguments in May 1992 and HB got a permanent injunction.[11] In the meantime, the Commission had commenced an investigation, on foot of a complaint from Mars, and ultimately made a decision in March 1998, which, in effect, demanded that HB desist from the activity that had been held lawful by the High Court. In July 1998, the Court of First Instance made an order suspending the Commission decision, pending the hearing of a full annulment action. Confronted with the apparent inconsistency between the results of the High Court action and the Commission decision, the Supreme Court, on Masterfoods' appeal, asked for guidance from the Court of Justice. The latter ruled in December 2000 that the national court should not proceed in the face of a contrary Commission decision.[12] There the matter stands. It has not yet reached resolution at either Community or national level, but the decision of the Court of Justice has been cited by the President of the Court as an important decision on the distribution of roles between the national courts and the Community courts.

There have been many other examples of Irish cases making a contribution to the development of Community law. It is presumably the absence of a land frontier, except with Northern Ireland, which is within a common travel area, that causes us to have so few cases concerning free movement of persons.

---

[9] Case 286/85 *McDermott & Cotter v. Minister for Social Welfare* [1987] ECR 1453; Case C–377/89 *Cotter & McDermott v. Minister for Social Welfare* [1991] ECR I–1155; Case C–208/90 *Emmott v. Minister for Social Welfare* [1991] ECR I–2467.
[10] [1995] 1 I.R. 418.
[11] *Masterfoods Ltd v. HB Ice Cream Ltd* [1993] I.L.R.M. 145.
[12] Case C–344/98 *Masterfoods Ltd v. HB Ice Cream Ltd* [2000] ECR I–11369.

Groener v. Minister for Education[13] is one. There the Court of Justice upheld, at least in principle, the right of Ireland to impose an Irish language test on a Dutch applicant for a teaching post.

It is obviously not possible for me to do justice to any extent to the many excellent contributions in the current volume. It will not be surprising, however, if I declare a special interest in Liz Heffernan's thorough and thoughtful piece on "Judicial Reform under the Treaty of Nice". Having had the honour of participating, with Judge John Cooke, as a member of the joint internal committee of the Court and the Court of First Instance in preparation for what became the Nice Treaty, I have to pay tribute to the accuracy and perspicuity of the author's comments. My interest in the topic may have distorted my judgement, but I could not help noting that the changes in the Community judiciary never rated even the slightest mention in the recent Nice Treaty referendum debate. At most, there was the occasional complaint of the transfer of yet more competences, of which changes to the Rules of Procedure of the Court is one example, to qualified majority vote.

The changes now made are not major. Most strikingly, the excellent work of the group which laboured under the chairmanship of former President Ole Due was entirely ignored.[14] One is left wondering whether there was any point in establishing such an expert group. None of the proposals for needed reform in the preliminary ruling procedure were adopted. Indeed, they had been discarded well before the final negotiations. I believe the stated average period for a preliminary ruling (nineteen months) is really a minimum in a case of any substance. In reality, it is very difficult to ask that parties to litigation interrupt the resolution of their dispute for such a lengthy period. I am personally in favour of two changes. First, the obligation of final instance courts to refer should be removed. These are the courts best fitted to inform themselves about the correct interpretation of Community law. They should be trusted to make a reference where there is real need or doubt or the point is important. Furthermore, it is notorious that there is serious variation in the current practice of such courts. In the event of serious abuse, the Commission could resort to an infringement action. Secondly, further consideration should be given to establishing a shorter, more informal method of providing answers to national courts. I believe Dr Temple Lang put forward the notion of a national Advocate General. Such an officer could provide the answer in clear cases and advise that there be a reference, if necessary.

I await with interest two developments. The Court of First Instance may finally be given competence to receive references for preliminary ruling. The Court of Justice has lost its former monopoly for the proposal of changes.

---

[13] Case 379/87 [1989] ECR 3967.
[14] Commission, *Report by the Working Group on the Future of the European Communities' Court System* (Brussels, 2000).

Thus it cannot block its sister Court from being given such competence. Secondly it will now be possible to dispense with the opinion of the Advocate General. As Liz Heffernan points out, the decision will be that of the Court. I am not convinced that this change is justified by the small number of uncontested infringement actions. They take very little time. It is possible that some reporting judges will be more disposed than others to propose bypassing the Advocate General. It is certain that some judges form a very firm view at an early stage of how a case should be decided. It is precisely in such cases that the Advocate General's Opinion may be of assistance to other members of the formation.

Finally, I wish to congratulate the editors and all the authors on their admirable work. It is gratifying to see that there is such a broad range of expertise in so many aspects of Community law.

MR JUSTICE NIAL FENNELLY
Supreme Court

PREFACE

This collection of essays on European Community law was compiled with the Irish legal community in mind and seeks to highlight issues of particular relevance and interest to that constituency.

The opening chapters examine general matters of overarching significance, namely, the principle of effectiveness and remedies, judicial review and judicial reform post-Nice. Discrete European Community laws or policies are considered in the ensuing chapters and include competition, telecommunications, environmental, contract, consumer rights, e-commerce, free movement of goods, transfer of undertakings, human rights, equality, free movement of persons and the rights of Third Country family members. Each author offers a considered personal view of the issues addressed. A notable feature of this collection is that the authors are drawn from both the academic and the practising legal communities.

While this collection is not intended to constitute a comprehensive textbook on European Union law it is hoped that the chosen combination of substantive and procedural/institutional topics makes this a unique and valuable work. As regards the taxonomy of European "Union" versus "Community" we chose the latter for the title on the basis that it is a more accurate description of the contents.

We are especially grateful to the authors for their contributions and sincerely thank them accordingly. We are honoured that Mr Justice Nial Fennelly furnished the generous foreword. We thank James Kingston for initially suggesting the idea of a compilation and for his subsequent support. Liz Heffernan gave us invaluable advice and assistance which we greatly appreciate. Finally, we express our gratitude to Round Hall and in particular to Thérèse Carrick, Orla Fee and David McCartney.

MARY CATHERINE LUCEY
CATHRINA KEVILLE
November 2002

TABLE OF CASES

English and Commonwealth Cases

European Cases and Opinions

TABLE OF LEGISLATION

Statutory Instruments

ENGLAND

Statutes

EUROPEAN CHARTERS, CONVENTIONS, DIRECTIVES AND TREATIES

Treaties

1. THE PRINCIPLE OF EFFECTIVENESS AND THE DEVELOPMENT OF A SYSTEM OF REMEDIES AT EUROPEAN COMMUNITY LAW

CATHRINA KEVILLE*

1.(1) INTRODUCTION

1.(1)(a) The useful effect of European Community (EC) law

Effet utile or the "useful effect" of Community law informs much of the jurisprudence of the European Court of Justice (ECJ).[1] The desire by the ECJ to transform what may have been seen by some as an abstract or even inchoate assortment of Community law rights into an enforceable and effective[2] corpus of laws has been assisted by a reliance on this principle as the rationale for extending or even creating Community law concepts.[3]

As is clear to anyone with even a rudimentary knowledge of EC law, the ECJ has not been hampered in the positive performance of its function by lack of specific Treaty competence.[4] Instead, judicial activism has led to the development of certain key concepts in EC law such as direct effect, supremacy, the interpretative obligation or indirect effect and state liability for non-implementation/non-observance of EC law.[5] These concepts have not merely facilitated but also compelled the observance and enforcement of EC law.[6]

---

* LL.B(DUB), LL.M (European Law), B.L. I wish to thank Fiona Kerins, B.L. who read this chapter. However, any errors remain my own.

[1] *i.e.* that E.C. law rights will be of practical significance to a plaintiff so that in the event of a breach of such rights, a plaintiff will have an effective remedy before the relevant domestic court.

[2] As is noted by Craig and de Búrca in *EU Law, Text, Cases and Materials*, (2nd ed), Chapter 5, p.213, "the fact that . . . provisions may be relied on before the national courts does not necessarily give proper effect to them unless adequate remedies and sanctions are also available for their enforcement."

[3] An early example of the ECJ's approach was set out in the seminal decision of Case 26/62 *Van Gend en Loos v. Nederlandse Administratie der Belastingen*, [1963] E.C.R. 1, where it is stated that "Article 12 [of the EC Treaty] must be interpreted as producing direct effect and creating individual rights which national courts must protect."; See below Kingston, chapter 12, para. 12.2.

[4] It is argued by John Temple Lang, below n.14, p.87, that Article 10 of the Treaty, whilst couched in general terms, in fact has provided a specific Treaty basis for certain developments in the case law of the ECJ including the principle that national courts have a duty to give "effective" protection to EC law rights.

They are devices by which the ECJ seeks to ensure the practical or useful effect of EC law.

Whilst the ECJ has been criticised for its judicial activism, it can be argued that its activity in the field of remedies is in response to the lack of legislation in this area.[7] Clearly, legislating for a system of harmonised remedies for breach of EC law would be an extremely onerous task involving consideration of public and private law remedies as well as the substance of such remedies and the procedural rules to be applied in such cases.[8] It is, therefore, unsurprising that it is the ECJ, arguably by default, which has been left with the task of creating, albeit on an ad hoc basis, remedies for breaches of EC law rights.

1.(1)(b) Role of national courts and Article 10 EC

Whilst the ECJ has developed the aforesaid concepts, the task of ensuring the useful effect of EC law rights for individual plaintiffs is ultimately one for the courts of the Member States, as:

> "It is the national courts which are the courts of general jurisdiction to apply Community Law wherever appropriate."[9]

By virtue of applying Community law to the actual cases which come before them, the national courts play a vital role in the judicial system of the Community as recognised by one commentator as follows:

---

5 See Craig and de Búrca, in EU Law, text, Cases and Materials (3rd ed), Chapters 5, 6 and 7.

6 The development of the law in this fashion was possible due to the purposive or teleological approach of the ECJ which is in contrast to the literal approach adopted generally by the Irish courts. It is arguable that the judicial activism of the ECJ has led to it acting outside of its powers and its approach has been criticised by certain commentators. See further H. Rasmussen, *On Law and Policy in the European Court of Justice* (Martinus Nijhoff, 1986).

7 Note that some harmonisation has been put in place by the public procurement Directives, *e.g.* the Remedies Directive No. 89/665 (1989) O.J. L395/33. The application of Order 84a, Rule 4 of the RSC, 1986 (as inserted by the Rules of the Superior Courts (No.4)(Review of the Award of Public Contracts) 1998 (S.I. No. 374 of 1998)) which was adopted to comply with Ireland's obligations under the aforesaid Directive, was discussed in a recent decision of the High Court in *Dekra Erin Teo v. Minister for Environment* [2002] 2 I.L.R.M. 30. It was submitted by the applicant, *inter alia*, that the three month time limit for challenging the award of public contracts as prescribed by the rule was *ultra vires* as it offended the principle of equivalence (discussed below at para.1.2.1). Whilst it was unnecessary for the trial judge to express a view on this point in order to arrive at his ultimate decision, he did find that there was no comparator for such an action in domestic law, breach of statutory duty being too wide and diffuse a comparison. He concluded by adopting the reasoning of Buxton L.J. in the case of *Matra Communications v. Home Office* [1999] 1 WLR 1646 and found that Order 84a, Rule 4 did not fall foul of the principle of equivalence.

8 See further F. Snyder, "The Effectiveness of European Community Law" (1993) 56 MLR 19, 50–3 and C. Himsworth, "Things Fall Apart: The Harmonisation of Community Judicial Protection Revisited" (1997) 22 ELRev. 291.

9 See Temple Lang, "Duties of National Courts Under Community Constitutional Law" [1997] ELRev. 3, p.5.

> "[I]t is national courts, not the Community courts which decide what the practical consequences are when a Member State fails to fulfil its obligations under Community Law. It is the national courts which decide whether a rule of national law should be regarded as inapplicable in individual cases or as effectively repealed, because it is inconsistent with Community Law. The jurisdiction of the Court of Justice is limited; it is the national courts which are the courts of general jurisdiction to apply Community Law whenever appropriate."[10]

Ultimately, it is the national courts which can decide whether Community law is applicable to a case or not and if they decide Community law is irrelevant, that is a decision against which there is no appeal to the ECJ.[11] Thus the system of EC law is a dependent legal system relying on each of the legal systems of the Member States for ultimate enforcement and application. A disadvantage of such a fragmented system of remedies is that differences in national systems will affect the extent to which individuals can in practice rely on rights derived from EC law.[12] However, national courts are bound by Article 10 (ex Article 5) of the EC Treaty to ensure the legal protection of rights which individuals derive from EC law.[13] Article 10 of the EC Treaty sets out as follows:

> "Member States shall take all appropriate measures whether general or particular, to ensure fulfillment of the obligations arising out of this Treaty or resulting from action taken by the Institutions of the Community. They shall facilitate the achievement of the Community's tasks. They shall abstain from any measure which could jeopardise the attainment of the objectives of the Treaty."[14]

1.(1)(c) Article 10 and new remedies[15]

Initially it seemed that the extent of the obligations imposed by Article 10 was for EC law rights to be protected by "existing national remedies enforced by domestic courts applying national rules of procedure."[16] Arguably, this is no

---

10 *ibid.*
11 As noted by Schermers and Waelbroek, *Judicial Protection in the European Union*, (6th ed), p.198, p.385.
12 As is noted by Snyder, above at n.8.
13 Case 33/76 *Rewe v. Landwirtschaftskammer Saarland* [1976] E.C.R. 1989, para 5. See below Lucey at para 4(2)(a).
14 See further on national courts and Article 10: M.Finlay and N.Hyland: "The Duties of Co-operation of National Authorities and Courts and Community Institutions under Article 10 EC." (2000) I.J.E.L. 267–289.
15 See the comments made by John Temple-Lang in "The Duties of Co-operation of National Authorities and Courts under Article 10 EC: Two More Reflections" (2001) 26 ELRev. 84, p.87 where he states that "Article 10 certainly seems to be the principal or only basis for judgments such as. . . . Francovich, Factortame and the principle that national courts have a duty to give effective protection to EC law derived rights."
16 Brealy and Hoskins, *Remedies in EC Law*, (2nd ed.), Chapter 6, para 1. They state further at p.105 as follows: "The duty of national courts to ensure the legal protection which individuals derive from Community law is unlikely to involve the invention of new

longer the case. The ECJ has intervened[17] in cases concerning both matters of national procedure and the provision of substantive remedies and, while it is true to say that it is the national courts which are charged with the application of Community law in the cases that come before them, it is the principles derived from the ECJ's jurisprudence which are applied by the national courts in a manner that would not have been available to them by virtue of purely national law. Many such departures from national law principles were fuelled by the principle of effectiveness.

It is submitted therefore that it is somewhat disingenuous of the ECJ to insist that it is the national courts which enforce Community law through national remedies and applying their own rules of procedure when that note clearly has not been the case in numerous decisions such as the first *Factortame* case,[18] where an Article 234 (ex Art. 177) preliminary reference by the House of Lords to the ECJ resulted in a situation where the House of Lords was obliged to grant an injunction suspending the application of an Act of Parliament, which had never occurred before due to the existence of a rule of U.K. constitutional law.[19] Wyatt and Dashwood[20] state that the proposition that national courts were not obliged to create new remedies for the purpose of implementing Community law is contradicted by the judicial development of the principle of state liability for breach of Community law.[21] In addition, they state that the above proposition "understates the effect to which Community law is capable of modifying the application of national procedures and remedies . . . the practical effect of which is to make available a remedy which if not new is at any rate something of a hybrid."[22]

---

remedies." This statement is supported by a quotation from the ECJ's judgment in Case 158/80 *Rewe v. Hauptzollamt Kiel* [1981] E.C.R. 1805 para 44, ". . . although the Treaty has made it possible in a number of instances for private persons to bring a direct action, where appropriate, before the Court of Justice, it was not intended to create new remedies in the national courts to ensure the observance of Community law other than those already laid down by national law."

[17] Such intervention being in the form of a preliminary ruling given by the ECJ on foot of a reference by a national court or tribunal made under Art. 234 of the EC Treaty.

[18] Case C–213/89 *R v. Secretary of State for Transport and Others ex parte Factortame* [1990] E.C.R. 1–2433.

[19] Indeed, it is arguable that by virtue of such intervention, Community law derived rights may well be better protected than national law derived rights. The reason the injunction in *Factortame* was granted was due to the fact that the principle of effectiveness of Community law required that Community law derived rights (albeit putative) should be protected in the interim pending the resolution of the substantive dispute. Had the rights at issue been purely domestic in nature, the injunctive relief would not have been available.

[20] *European Union Law*, (3rd ed), at p.197.

[21] Cases C–6 & 9/90 *Francovich and Bonifaci v. Italy* [1991] E.C.R. 1–5357.

[22] See above, n.20. Note also in this context the decision in the second *Simmenthal* case where the intervention of the ECJ resulted in the lower courts being imbued with a jurisdiction by virtue of EC law which they had not formerly possessed at national law. Case 106/77 *Amministrazione delle Finanze dello stato v. Simmenthal SpA* [1978] E.C.R. 629.

It is proposed, therefore, to demonstrate that the principle of effectiveness has had at least the following effects:

(1) It has resulted in the modification of the principle of national procedural autonomy to the extent that remedies have been made available to plaintiffs which, if not new, were either what could be described as hybrid or that such remedies were only made available due to the modification of national rules.

(2) It was central to the reasoning employed by the ECJ in their creation of a new remedy of state liability for breach of Community Law.[23]

1.(2) THE PRINCIPLE OF NATIONAL PROCEDURAL AUTONOMY

1.(2)(a) National procedural autonomy and the principles of equivalence and practical possibility

The decentralised mode of enforcement of EC law derived rights conforms, at least in theory, with the principle of national procedural autonomy which the ECJ has consistently emphasised in its judgments. In the *Rewe* case,[24] it was set out that it is for the "domestic legal system of each Member State to designate the Courts having jurisdiction and to determine the procedural conditions governing actions at law intended to ensure the protection of rights which citizens have from the direct effect of Community law."

The principle of procedural autonomy is qualified by the following:

(1) The principle of equivalence[25] or non-discrimination, *i.e.* that the same procedural treatment must be given to claims based on Community law as is given to claims based on domestic law.[26]

(2) The principle that applicable national procedural rules should not be such as to render in practice the exercise of Community law derived rights either impossible or excessively difficult.[27]

Initially it appeared that the ECJ was reluctant to intervene in the task of setting Community standards of judicial process,[28] which is demonstrated by

---

23 See the decision in *Francovich*, above at n.21.
24 Case 33/76 *Rewe-Zentralfinanz eG and Rewe-Zentral AG v. Landwirtschaftskammer fur das Saarland* [1976] E.C.R. 1989.
25 See the *Dekra* case, above at n.7.
26 *ibid.*
27 *ibid.* This early statement of "practical possibility" later evolved into the principle of effectiveness.
28 It is argued by Biondi, in "The European Court of Justice and Certain National Procedural Limitations" [1999] 36 CMLRev., p.1272, that the ECJ swings between intrusive investigation and a more restrained approach and he further states that "over-intrusive incursions into national procedural law risks upsetting the co-operation with national judges upon which Community law depends . . ." The ECJ has to strike a balance between ensuring the

the result in the *Comet* case,[29] where the plaintiff was able to show a good cause of action at EC law but his claim was ultimately thwarted due to the operation of national procedural rules.

1.(2)(b) Procedural autonomy v. adequate and effective protection of rights

There was a change of approach in a series of decisions where the ECJ shifted its emphasis. It moved away from the minimalist or non-interventionist approach to rights protection as demonstrated by the bare application of the two principles outlined above, to the principle that rights must be given adequate and effective protection even if such meant disapplying national rules[30] the operation of which would have denied such protection. The decisions in such cases have been well documented and analysed[31] and perhaps represented a high point of the interventionist approach of the ECJ in the area[32] from which there has been somewhat of a retrenchment in recognition of the fact that:

> "all procedural rules restrict to some extent the right of affected parties to rely
> on Community law and that the principle of effectiveness was not infringed by
> e.g. the laying down of reasonable periods of limitation of actions as well as
> time limits for complaints and legal actions as . . . normal procedural rules exist
> in all legal systems and which are justified by the mandatory requirements of
> legal certainty."[33]

In exceptional circumstances where national rules deprive a plaintiff of any remedy in respect of Community law rights, then such rules will not be applied.[34] Whilst it is legitimate for national limitation periods to limit the

---

effectiveness of Community law and the compliance of national courts with its judgments.

29 Case 45/76 *Comet v. Produktschap voor Siergewassen* [1976] E.C.R. 2043.

30 See most notably the decisions in Case 14/83 *Von Colson and Kamann v. Land Nordrhein-Westfalen* [1984] E.C.R. 1891, Case C–213/89 *R v. Secretary of State for Transport, ex parte Factortame Ltd. and Others* [1990] E.C.R. 1–2433, Case C–377/89, *Cotter and McDermott v. Minister for Social Welfare and Attorney General* [1991] E.C.R. 1–1155, Case C–208/90, *Emmot v. Minister for Social Welfare* [1991] E.C.R. 1–4269, Case C–271/91, *Marshall v. Southampton and South West Area Health Authority* 11 [1993] E.C.R. 1–4367 etc. Note also that sometimes there may be a difficulty in clearly distinguishing rules of procedure from rules of substance and further the way such rules are characterised can vary from Member State to Member State.

31 See Craig and de Búrca, above at n.2, pp.213–229, Wetherill and Beaumont, *EU Law*, (3rd ed.), pp.392–433.

32 Whilst the results of such cases were positive from the point of view of the principle of effectiveness, they introduced an element of uncertainty into national legal systems.

33 Schermers and Waelbrock, *Judicial Protection in the European Union*, (6th ed.), p.202, para. 395.

34 See *Emmot*, cited above at n.30. The *Emmot* decision was a demonstration of a "hard case" and has been distinguished to the point that the principle contained therein is now confined to the facts of the case. See decisions C–338/91 *Steenhorst-Neerings v. Bedrijfsvereniging voor Detailhandel, Ambachten en Huisvrouwen* [1993] E.C.R. 1–5475, C–410/92 *Johnson v. Chief Adjudication Officer* [1994] E.C.R. 1–5483, Case C–2/94, *Denkavit International v. Kamer von Koophandel en Fabrieken voor Midden-Gederland* [1996] E.C.R. 1–5063 and in

retroactivity of a claim, such rules cannot operate to "strike at the very essence of rights conferred by the Community legal order."[35]

1.(2)(c) *Peterbroek*[36] and *Van Schijndel*[37]: an uneasy balance

It seems now that the national courts are expected to perform a type of balancing exercise between the application of their own rules and the need to ensure the effectiveness of EC law rights.[38]

Sometimes, the ECJ is not consistent in its rulings in this area which was demonstrated by two apparently contradictory decisions, where the national rule at issue in each was one which imposed limits on the capacity of the domestic courts to raise points of Community law of their own motion. Whilst the ECJ held in *Van Schijndel* that the national rule was compatible with the exercise of the Community law right, the opposite finding was made in *Peterbroek*.[39]

1.(2)(d) Rule of reason approach

The ECJ did however formulate a type of rule of reason approach in these two decisions. This sets out that compliance with the principle of effectiveness must be measured by reference to the specific operation of the national rule in the circumstances of the individual case which involves an examination of the purpose or aim of the national rule weighed against how it operates to restrict the Community law right at issue.[40] Whilst this is a less heavy-handed approach

---

particular Case C–188/95 *Fantask v. Industtrimisteriet* [1998] 1 CMLR 473, where the E.C.J. decided that *Emmot* was a case decided on its own facts. In *Fantask*, the E.C.J. held that the Danish Government could rely on a five year limitation period for the recovery of debts even where a Directive had not been properly implemented but note also the decisions in C–246/96 *Magorrian and Cunningham*, [1997] E.C.R. 1–7153, Levez, discussed below at n.42 and Case C–78/98 *Preston v. Wolver Hampton Healthcare NHS Trust* [2000] E.C.R. 1–3201.

[35] See Magorrian, above at n.29, at para. 44 and referred to by Weatherill and Beaumont, above at n.31, at p.405. See below Costello, para. 2(2)(a)(ii) for a discussion of whether restrictive locus standi rules in relation to the operation of the EIA Directive may well run counter to the effective protection of Community rights in Ireland.

[36] Case C–312/93, *Peterbroeck, Van Campenhout & Cie v. Belgian State* [1995] E.C.R. 1–4599.

[37] Cases C–430, 431/93 *Van Schijndel & Van Veen v. Stichting Pensioen fonds voor Fysiotherapeuten* [1995] E.C.R. 1–4705.

[38] On this point, see Biondi, above at n.28, 1284, where it is suggested that the national courts should apply a type of "*Keck*" approach to the exercise, *i.e* certain procedural limitations which are not by their nature such as to prevent access to the full enjoyment of Community rights or to impede it more that it impedes the access of domestic rights do not come within the scope of community law. The decision in Keck is reported as Cases C–267 & 268/91 *Criminal Proceedings against Keck and Mithouard* [1993] E.C.R. 1–6097.

[39] For a more detailed analysis of these two cases see the discussion by R. Craufurd Smith, Remedies for Breaches of EU Law in National Courts: Legal Variation and Selection, in *the Evolution of EU Law*, (Craig and de Burca ed., Oxford, 1999) p.288, pp.315–316.

[40] See Biondi, above n.28, at p.1277 para. 2 for a criticism of this approach. In short, it is argued that it is somewhat unsatisfactory that the ECJ can refer to the principle of legal certainty in

on the part of the ECJ, lack of specific guidance as to how the national courts should operate this balancing exercise has resulted in a number of complex Article 234 references wherein the ECJ have engaged in an analysis of rules of national procedure[41] as well as examining the specific facts of the case before it.[42]

Whilst it is questionable whether the ECJ should be engaging in such activities in the context of Article 234 preliminary rulings, it seems that such will be unavoidable in view of this "rule of reason" approach which the ECJ itself has devised as a way of ensuring the application of the principle of effectiveness without unnecessarily impinging on the application of national procedural rules.[43] It is suggested by one commentator that such difficulties could be avoided by leaving the question of compatibility of national procedural rules with the principle of effectiveness of Community law to the national courts to decide.[44]

1.(3) POSSIBILITY OF DAMAGES FOR BREACH OF COMMUNITY LAW

1.(3)(a) A new Community remedy in damages – *Francovich* and *Brasserie du Pêcheur/Factortame III*

Whilst it is clear from the foregoing that the ECJ has intervened to modify the application of rules of national procedure, thus giving rise to remedies which

---

order to justify the operation of just about any domestic provision. It seems that a number of cases have been decided on this basis: C–188/95 *Fantask and Others*, [1997] E.C.R. 1–6783, C–114/95 and C115/95 *Texaco and Olieselskabet Danmark*, [1997] E.C.R. 1–4263, *Haahr Petroleum v. Abenra Havn and Others* [1997] E.C.R. 1–4085.

41 Italian repayment cases cited by Biondi, at n.5 of his article, above at n.28 for details. Note the difficulties for national courts in applying the principle of equivalence. By what criteria can a court decide if a domestic law right is similar to a European law right even if the court is supposed to have regard to the purpose and essential characteristics of the allegedly similar domestic action. What is to be done where there is no comparable domestic law (as in the *Dekra* case, it was conceded in that case that the principle of effectiveness was not infringed). Further, is it properly the role of the ECJ pursuant to an Art. 234 reference to be engaging in an analysis of domestic law rules?

42 Note in this context, Case C–326/96 *Belinda Levez v. TH Jennings (Harlow Pools) Limited* [1998] ECRI–7835, where the ECJ looked to the specific facts of the case, namely, the applicant was unaware of the extent of the discrimination against her due to the fact that her employer had deliberately misinformed her. The ECJ in this case held that the principle of effectiveness meant that national limitation periods could not apply in circumstances where their operation would enable the employer to benefit from his own deceit by defeating the applicant's claim.

43 This appears to be akin to a proportionality test. For a further discussion of proportionality as a general principle of EC law, see Craig and de Búrca, above at n.5, chapter 9, pp.371–377.

44 Biondi, above at n.28; this was the approach adopted by the ECJ in Case C–120/97, *Upjohn Ltd. v The Licensing Authority established by the Medicines Act, 1968 and Others* [1999] E.C.R. 1–233, where the ECJ when faced with a complex question concerning procedures in

would not have been available to a plaintiff at national law, it has also intervened in the domain of substantive remedies. The principle that a State must be liable for loss and damage caused to individuals as a result of a breach of Community law for which the State can be held responsible, was first formulated in the *Francovich* case.[45] This development largely came about due to the desire to make Community law effective.[46] The judgment also referred to the general obligation contained in Article 10 of the Treaty that Member States must take all appropriate measures to fulfil their obligations under the Treaty. The refined *Francovich* principle was in *Brasserie du Pêcheur/ Factortame III*[47] which made a distinction between where the State has a broad discretion to act and where it has a narrow discretion. In the former situation the test for recovery of damages would be more onerous, requiring a sufficiently serious breach by the Member State to give rise to a liability in damages.[48] The ECJ in making this finding looked, *inter alia*, to the criteria applied in relation to the non-contractual liability of the Community under Article 288 of the Treaty.[49]

After the decisions in *Francovich* and *Brasserie du Pêcheur/Factortame*, it is impossible for the ECJ to maintain the stance that Community law does not require the creation of new remedies by the courts. Perhaps what was meant by the ECJ was that Community law does not require the creation of new remedies by national courts for its enforcement whilst reserving to itself such a power[50] despite the fact that arguably this is not within the remit of the ECJ but is a matter for the Community legislature.

---

relation to the marketing of medicinal products simply stated that domestic procedures have to guarantee the full application of community rules. See below Costello, para 2.(2)(d)(i).

[45] Cases C–6&9/90, *Francovich v. Italy* [1991] E.C.R. 1–5357. For references to the many articles on this case, see Schermers and Waelbroeck, above at n.33, p.205.

[46] See Rachel Craufurd Smith, above at n.39, pp.302–307 who opines that the reasons for the decision in *Francovich* were, *inter alia*, to encourage timeous and correct implementation of Directives by Member States as well as providing an alternative enforcement mechanism to an action based on direct effect.

[47] Joined Cases C–46/93 & C–48/93 *Brasserie du Pêcheur SA v. Germany and R v. Secretary of State for Transport, ex parte Factortame Ltd. and others* [1996] E.C.R. 1–1029.

[48] This decision has been exhaustively discussed. For an analysis see, *inter alia*, Craig and de Búrca, above at n.5, Chapter 6, p.257–273.

[49] Case C–178–98, 188–190/94. Note the decision in *Dillenkofer v. Germany* [1996] E.C.R. 4845. In this case the ECJ held that the German government was liable for damages to German nationals who suffered loss as a result of the failure of the German government to implement the Package Holidays Directive. The ECJ in its judgment said that the question of whether damages arose for a breach of Community law by a Member State depended on the nature of the breach. In circumstances where no legislative discretion was given to the Member State and no choices had to be made with regard to the manner in which the directive be implemented, then the mere failure to comply with time limits, as in this case, could give rise to an action for damages, as the failure was of itself a sufficiently serious breach of EC law. This decision therefore suggests that the narrow discretion/wide discretion distinction is no longer relevant, rather the test is a global one of whether a "sufficiently serious" breach of EC law has been committed.

[50] As exercised in *Francovich*, above n.35.

The fact remains that this remedy is a judicial creation of the ECJ, the operation of which is then left to the national courts applying national laws on liability provided that such laws do not treat the European claim less favourably than a domestic claim and do not make it impossible or excessively difficult in practice to obtain compensation.[51]

1.(4) Application in Ireland of *Francovich*/*Brasserie du Pêcheur* Principle

1.(4)(a) *Tate v. Minister for Social Welfare*

In Ireland, the first application of the principle was in the case of *Tate v. Minister for Social Welfare*.[52] In brief, the claim in *Tate* related to Ireland's failure to properly implement the provisions of a Directive, the aim of which was to equalise social welfare payments between men and women. This failure meant that social welfare payments were not equalised from the due date intended by the Directive. Carroll J. in her judgment characterised the said failure as "a breach of duty to implement the Directive which approximates to a breach of constitutional duty" but interestingly from the procedural point of view, she held that the breach came within the term "tort" with the result that a six-year limitation period applied to claims thereunder within the Statute of Limitations Act, 1957, s.11(2).[53] Ultimately, damages were awarded to the plaintiffs equivalent to the payments made to married men in the same circumstances which had not been paid to the plaintiffs.

---

[51] *i.e.* the principles of equivalence and effectiveness. National rules which have been found incompatible with these requirements include making the right to recover compensation dependent on *e.g.* proof of misfeasance in public office or on proof of fault. Further, loss of profit as a head of damages could not be excluded at national law for an action based on breach of European Community law. See in this context the decision in Cases C–46/93 and C–48/93 *Brasserie du Pêcheur v. Factortame* [1996] E.C.R. 1–1029 and Case C–178–9 & 188–190/94 *Dillenkofer v. Germany* [1996] E.C.R. 1–4845. Other matters such as time limits for bringing claims are governed by national rules. See also in this context Cases C–94–95/95, *Bonifaci and Berto v. Istituto Nazionale della Previdenza Sociale* [1997] E.C.R. 1–3969, Case C–261/95 *Palmisani v. IPNS* [1997] E.C.R. 1–4025, Case C–375/95 *Maso and Ors v. IPNS* [1997] E.C.R. 1–4051 in relation to the interaction of the principle of state liability as *per Francovich*, with rules of national procedure.

[52] [1995] 1 I.R. 418. This case had been well documented elsewhere, see Scannell, Influence of Community Law, (2001) *Judicial Studies Institute Journal*, p.63 at p.99 and Finlay and Hyland, above at n.13, p.271.

[53] Such limitation, as already noted, is not inconsistent with the principle of effectiveness on the grounds that it merely limits claims rather than barring them absolutely. See in this context the case of *Steenhorst Neerings*, above at n.34.

1.(4)(b) *Emerald Meats v. Minister for Agriculture*

In *Emerald Meats v. Minister for Agriculture*[54] the plaintiff claimed that it was entitled to be included on a list of applicants for a GATT quota for the import of meat. The quota was to be allocated by the Commission rather than the Member States (as had formerly been the case.) The list was to be drawn up by the first named defendant in compliance with its obligations under a Community Regulation. Applicants would only qualify for a quota if they could show that they had imported GATT meat in the previous three years. The plaintiff was only included on the list in respect of meat imports for the year 1989. It claimed that it should also have been included on the list in respect of the years 1988 and 1987, on the basis that whilst it had not directly been awarded the quotas for those years, it had purchased such quotas from other meat processors and had imported GATT meat in the relevant years.

On this basis, the plaintiff sought various orders, including an order that the Minister comply with his obligations under the relevant regulation by including the plaintiff on the list of applicants to be forwarded to the Commission, as well as a declaration that the plaintiff was entitled to be considered as such an applicant (for a share in the quota) and that it was entitled to damages for breach of statutory duty and negligence. In the High Court, it was held by Costello J. that the plaintiff was entitled to damages against the Minister but that it was only entitled to special damages and not to general damages. Blayney J. (with whom Hamilton C.J. and Denham J. agreed) in the Supreme Court set out that the right to recover damages from a Member State for a breach of European Community law seems to be clearly recognised in the *Francovich* case. He then cited paragraphs 31–37 of the *Francovich* judgment and concluded that these principles must be applied by the courts of every Member State and that it was clear on that basis that the plaintiff was entitled to compensation from the State.

1.(4)(c) *Maxwell v. Minister for Agriculture*

In *Maxwell v. Minister for Agriculture,*[55] the case related to payments to producers of beef and veal who were in financial difficulties due to the BSE crisis. The Irish scheme was put into place to allocate the payments differentiated between producers who sold animals to factories within the State for slaughter and producers who exported animals live. The latter were restricted to claiming for 90 animals whereas no such restriction was placed on the former. McCracken J. found that such discrimination was not objectively justified and that even though he had not been addressed on what constituted a "sufficiently serious" breach, found that there had been such a

---

[54] [1997] 1 I.R. 1.
[55] [1999] 2 I.R. 474.

breach by the State of Article 40(3) of the EC Treaty which prohibits discrimination between producers or consumers within the Community. In so making this finding, he took into account the fact that the Irish scheme applied retrospectively which gave the applicant no opportunity to mitigate his loss and that the question of seriousness must be examined objectively. He further found that the applicant was entitled to damages on the basis of the test set out in *Brasserie du Pêcheur/ Factortame*.[56]

1.(4)(d) *Dublin Bus v. The Motor Insurers' Bureau of Ireland*

A decision of McMahon J. of the Circuit Court in the case of *Dublin Bus v. The Motor Insurers' Bureau of Ireland*[57] is also relevant in this context. It is an interesting application of the *Francovich* principle in that it was not the State but an emanation of the State[58] which was found liable in damages.

The case came before the Circuit Court by way of an appeal from the District Court against monetary decrees awarded to compensate for property damage suffered by the plaintiff. The case arose in circumstances where vehicles which were either stolen or taken without their owners consent had been crashed into buses, the property of the plaintiff/respondent.

The defendant/appellant in this case was the Motor Insurers' Bureau of Ireland (MIBI) whose function is, *inter alia,* to provide compensation for property damage suffered in certain circumstances. In order to guard against fraudulent claims, the agreement regulating the payment of such compensation contained the following provision:

> "The Liability of the MIBI for damage to property shall not extend to damage caused by a vehicle the owner or user of which remains unidentified or untraced."

It was argued by the appellant in this particular case that compensation would only be payable if both owner and user were identified and traced. The respondent submitted that compensation should be payable in the circumstances of the present case where only the owner of the vehicle had been identified and traced (but not the user).

This case is interesting from the point of view of EC law because the current version of the MIBI agreement was enacted to give effect to Directive

---

[56] See above at n.47.

[57] Circuit Court, unreported, McMahon J., October 29, 1999, unreported judgments (2000), Vol. 5, at 1786. Clearly being a decision of the Circuit Court it is subject to any subsequent conflicting decisions in the High or Supreme Courts.

[58] This concept originated in the Case C–152/84 *Marshall v. Southampton and South West Area Health Authority (No.1)* [1986] CMLR 688. An emanation of the State is every aspect of the State and every guise within which the State could be found to exist. The creation of this concept was an an attempt to broaden the category of defendants against whom the direct effect of a Directive could be asserted. By analogy, therefore, *Francovich* damages-type actions are also possible against emanations of the State.

84/5. The above clause, 7(2), was supposed to be a specific expression of the restriction on the liability of the MIBI permitted by the said Directive, Article 1.4 of which provides as follows:

> "Member States may limit or exclude payments of compensation by that body in the event of damage to property by an unidentified vehicle."

McMahon J. concluded fairly simply that the transposition into Irish law of the EC obligations was wrong or improper. He said that the Directive only allows an exception when the vehicle is unidentified. If the vehicle is identified, then no further enquiry in relation to the owner or the user of the vehicle is necessary and will not therefore be allowed within the national scheme. He further stated that had the Directive been properly implemented, the respondents would have recovered their property damage from the MIBI. Thus, under the dicta laid down in *Francovich*, the State are obliged to make good loss and damage suffered as a result of their failure to implement the relevant Directive properly or at all.

However, in the circumstances of the present case, the defendant/appellant was the MIBI. Therefore, the question to be determined was whether the loss sustained could be recovered from the MIBI as distinct from the State because the State had not been joined to the proceedings. In considering this issue, McMahon J. looked to the means by which the obligations contained in Directive 84/5 were transposed into Irish law *viz.* the 1988 MIBI agreement between the Bureau and the Minister for the Environment. He stated that the MIBI participated fully in drafting the agreement and appeared as a signatory to the agreement. On this basis, he concluded that the MIBI must be associated with the State in taking responsibility for the improper implementation of the Directive. The consequence for the MIBI was that they were, therefore, open to claims by individuals for the improper implementation of the Directive. Further, since the MIBI was responsible for the management and administration of the scheme, including the processing of claims thereunder, it is the party which "carries all litigation contemplated by the scheme."[59] As such, McMahon J. found that there can be little argument but that the MIBI is a public body, an emanation of the State which would make it liable for the failure to properly implement the Directive.

However, in holding that the MIBI was an emanation of the State, McMahon J. was not doing so for the purposes of allowing the plaintiff/ respondents to assert a right based on the direct effect of the Directive in question but in order to make the MIBI liable for the damage suffered by the plaintiff/ respondent based on the reasoning that the MIBI was responsible for the transposition of the Directive, (thereby endowing it with a species of legislative competence) and that the improper transposition of the Directive was a "sufficiently

---

[59] See judgment at p.1796.

serious" breach of EC law sounding in damages against the defendant in line with the decisions in *Francovich* and *Brasserie du Pêcheur*.[60]

Whilst the result of the case is commendable from the point of view of rendering rights derived from EC law effective, in line with the principle of effectiveness, it is arguable that this decision may have gone too far.[61] Further, it would not have been necessary to find that the MIBI was an emanation of the State had the State itself been joined to the proceedings.[62]

It seems that an inference to be drawn from the decision in *Dublin Bus* is that bodies classified as "emanations of the State" are now potential defendants under the conditions set out in *Francovich/Brasserie du Pêcheur*. However it is unlikely that there will be any further developments in rendering "emanations of the State" liable under the *Francovich/Brasserie du Pêcheur* cause of action due to the fact that any well-informed plaintiff would simply join the State to their proceedings or sue the State *simpliciter*.

1.(5) CONCLUSION

It is stated by one commentator[63] that "in effect a national court has a legal duty under Community law to create an effective remedy, both procedural and substantive if one does not already exist". This statement would appear to reflect a full application of the principle of effectiveness and has been borne out in some of the cases discussed in this article. However, case law has also demonstrated that on occasion, the application of the principle of effectiveness means the disapplication of rules of national procedure with an associated loss

---

[60] See above at n.47.

[61] An interesting U.K. decision found that the equivalent body in the U.K., the MIB was not an emanation of the State. *Mighell v. Reading and another* and *Evans v. Motor Insurers Bureau*, unreported, C.A., September 30, 1998, at p.17; Lord Shiemann in his judgment stated as follows: "The Bureau is not constitutionally an emanation of the State: it is a private law company. It is not functionally an emanation of the State: it acts on its own behalf in the commercial interests of its members not on behalf of the State or as a delegate of the state. It enters into commercial law private contracts with *inter alia* the Secretary of State. Similarly, when seeking to implement the second Directive in relation to uninsured drivers the Secretary of State chose to make use of the same private law mechanisms as before. The only capacity in which the Bureau has acted is as a private law entity and the only obligations which it has assumed have been private law contractual obligations. This cannot be said to be a situation where any public law relationship has come into existence."

[62] See Scannell, above, n.52 at p.86.

[63] Temple Lang, above at n.9, p.6.

[64] A further problem noted by Hoskins in "Tilting the Balance, Remedies and National Procedural Rules", [1996] EL Rev. 375–376 is that a finding that a national rule is unacceptable in one situation may have a serious knock-on effect within the legal system as a whole. He further states that a balance must be sought between the need to ensure the primacy of community law and the procedural effectiveness of litigation in the courts of the Member States.

of legal certainty[64] as well as procedural autonomy. Whilst it is true to say that new remedies have been made possible by the modification or even disapplication of rules of procedure in the past together with the development of the substantive remedy of damages against the State for failure to abide by its obligations under Community law, it seems that the ECJ is now taking a less interventionist approach.[65]

The application of the *Francovich/Brasserie du Pêcheur* principles are largely a matter for the national courts in line with their own rules of substance and procedure. Further, it is suggested that any balancing exercise between the application of the principles of equivalence and effectiveness and national procedural rules be a matter at first instance for the national courts who can resort to an Article 234 ruling if necessary. Whilst such a balancing approach appears to concede that there are limits to the possible uniformity of Community remedies given the existence of all the distinct legal systems, perhaps such a concession represents an acknowledgement by the ECJ of the limits of its powers. Of course, one cannot discount the possibility that sometime in the future the judicial quick-sands will shift again to produce another decision on the scale of *Factortame* or *Francovich* and the debate will begin anew.

---

[65] Although note the decision in Case C–453/99 *Courage Ltd. v. Crehan* [2001] ECRI–6297, where it was held that a rule of English law which does not allow a party to an illegal agreement to claim damages from the other party could in principle be disapplied, notwithstanding the implications of such a ruling for the principle of national procedural autonomy. This would be so on the basis of ensuring the full effectiveness of Article 85 (now 81) of the EC Treaty. However, national law could still deny such a remedy if the claimant was found to bear significant responsibility for the distortion of competition which was at issue in the case.

BIBLIOGRAPHY

Biondi, "The European Court of Justice and Certain National Procedural Limitations" [1999] CMLRev., p.1272.

Brealy and Hoskins, *Remedies in EC Law* (2nd ed.).

Cahill, Kennedy and Power (eds), *Applied European Law.*

Craig and de Búrca, *EU Law, Text, Cases and Materials* (2nd ed.).

——, *EU Law, Text, Cases and Material* (3rd ed.).

Craufurd Smith, *Remedies for Breaches of EU Law in National Courts: Legal Variation and Selection, in the Evolution of EU Law*, edited by Craig and deBurca.

Himsworth, "Things Fall Apart: The Harmonisation of Community Judicial Protection Revisited" (1997) 22 EL Rev. 291.

Finlay, and Hyland, "The Duties of Co-operation of National Authorities and Courts and Community Institutions under Article 10 EC" (2000) IJEL 267–289.

Hoskins, "Tilting the Balance, Remedies and National Procedural Rules" [1996] EL Rev. 375–376.

Rasmussen, *On Law and Policy in the European Court of Justice* (Martinus Nijhofen, 1986).

Scannell, "Influence of Community Law" (2001) *Judicial Studies Institute Journal*, p.63.

Schermers and Waelbroek, *Judicial Protection in the European Union* (6th ed.)

Snyder, "The Effectiveness of European Community Law" (1993) 56 MLR 19, 50–53.

Temple Lang, "Duties of National Courts Under Community Constitutional Law" [1997] EL Rev. 3.

Temple-Lang, "The Duties of Co-operation of National Authorities and Courts under Article 10 EC: Two More Reflections" (2001) 26 EL Rev. 84.

Wetherill and Beaumont, *EU Law* (3rd ed.).

2. EUROPEAN COMMUNITY JUDICIAL REVIEW IN THE IRISH COURTS – SCOPE, STANDARDS AND SEPARATION OF POWERS

CATHRYN COSTELLO*

2.(1) INTRODUCTION

The European Community (EC) has its own complex judicial system which aims to provide a comprehensive system of judicial remedies. The European Court of Justice (ECJ) has described the EC as "a Community based on the rule of law, inasmuch as neither its Member States nor its institutions can avoid a review of the question whether the measures adopted by them are in conformity with the basic constitutional charter, the Treaty."[1] Largely through the doctrines of direct effect[2] and supremacy[3] of Community law, as well as the later arrivals of indirect and incidental direct effect[4] and state liability in damages,[5] the Community legal order has taken on many of the features of a federal legal order, with a particularly strong legal armoury for ensuring Member State compliance with Community norms. Similarly, the Community institutions themselves are subject to judicial review.[6] The European legal subject is, at least according to the ECJ, well-armed.

---

* B.CL. (N.U.I.), LL.M. (College of Europe, Bruges), B.L. Lecturer in European Law, University of Dublin; Director, Irish Centre for European Law. I am grateful to Eoin O'Dell for his comments on this paper. All errors remain, of course, my own.
[1] Case 294/83 [1986] E.C.R. 1339, para. 23.
[2] Seminal direct effect cases include Case 26/62 *Van Gend en Loos v. Nederlandse Administratie der Belastingen* [1963] E.C.R. 1; Case 57/65 *Lutticke v. Hauptzollamt Saarlouis* [1966] E.C.R. 205; Case 2/74 *Reyners* [1974] E.C.R. 631; Case 36/74 *Walrave & Koch v. Union Cycliste Internationale* [1974] E.C.R. 1405; Case 43/75 *Defrenne v. Sabena* [1976] E.C.R. 455; Case 41/74 *Van Duyn v. Home Office* [1974] E.C.R. 1337.
[3] Case 6/64 *Costa v. ENEL* [1964] E.C.R. 585; Case 11/70 *Internationale Handelsgesellschaft* [1970] E.C.R. 1125.
[4] Case 80/86 *Kolpinghuis Nijmegen* [1987] E.C.R. 3969; Case C–106/89 *Marleasing v. La Comercial* [1990] E.C.R. I–4135; Case C–334/92 *Wagner-Miret* [1993] E.C.R. I–6911; Case C–168/95 *Criminal Proceedings Against Luciano Arcano* [1996] E.C.R. I–4705; Case C–194/95 CIA *Security SA v. Signalson SA* [1996] E.C.R. I–2201; Case C–443/93 *Unilever v. Central Foods*, September 26, 2000.
[5] Cases C–6/90 and C–9/90 *Francovich & Bonifaci v. Italy* [1991] E.C.R. I–5357; Case C–46/93 and C–48/93 *Brasserie du Pêcheur v. Germany; R v. Secretary of State for Transport ex parte Factortame* [1996] E.C.R. I–1029. See above Keville, para 1(3)(a).
[6] Core provisions are Article 230 (ex Article 173) EC (action for invalidity) and Article 288 (ex Article 215) EC (action for damages against the Community institutions).

However, this armoury is an ephemeral one, unless given substance in national courts. The ECJ emphasises the duties of national judges under Article 10 (ex Article 5) EC to give full effect to Community law,[7] yet unless these duties are taken seriously by national judges, the effectiveness of Community law is impaired. Thus, the realities of the decentralised legal order that is Community law must be scrutinised. In this vein, this chapter will examine the role of judicial review in the Irish courts in the context of Community law.[8] The purpose of this chapter is to examine the manner in which the national system of judicial review has adapted to Community law. In certain jurisdictions, the effect of Community law has been felt as a "big bang"[9] – the impact of the *Factortame*[10] judgment in the U.K. for example, altered irrevocably the British conception of parliamentary sovereignty. In the context of the robust tradition of judicial review in the Irish courts, the effects of Community law are less dramatic, but they are no less pervasive for that. In particular, the impact of the general principles of Community law will be considered.

This chapter considers two distinct areas where the Irish courts play a role in Community judicial review. Section 2.2 deals with the manner in which national rules on judicial review operate when an individual seeks to challenge a national act/measure, in light of a superior rule of Community law. Out of this potentially vast subject, four discrete aspects will be examined. First, an attempt will be made to delimit the scope of application of Community general principles 2(2)(a). Secondly, the interaction between national and EC precepts and grounds of review will be considered 2(2)(b). Thirdly, the impact of this decentralised administration on the domestic legislative/executive separation of powers will be examined 2(2)(c). Finally, the standard of review will be considered, and the extent to which Community law demands a particular standard of review will be canvassed 2(2)(d). In order to elucidate the standard of review issue, an overview of judicial reviews concerning the application of the Environmental Impact Assessment (EIA) Directive[11] will be provided.

Section 2.3 examines the manner in which judicial review operates when an individual seeks to challenge the validity of a Community Act in the Irish

---

[7]   For a full discussion of the various specific duties which have been held to derive from Article 10 EC see Temple Lang, "The Principle of Effective Protection of Community Law Rights" in *Judicial Review in European Union Law*, (O'Keeffe ed., Kluwer Law International, 2000), pp.236–274. See above Keville, para. 1(1)(c).

[8]   The phrase "judicial review" is employed in a relatively broad sense, meaning the procedure whereby public acts are challenged before national courts.

[9]   So described by Szyszczak, "Judicial Review of Public Acts" (1998) E.L.Rev 89.

[10] Case C–231/89 *R v. Secretary of State for Transport ex parte Factortame Ltd* (Factortame I) [1990] E.C.R. I–2433.

[11] Council Directive 91/11/EC amending Directive 85/337/EC on the Assessment of the Effects of Certain Public and Private Projects on the Environment [1997] O.J. L5; Council Directive 85/337/EC on the Assessment of the Effects of Certain Public and Private Projects on the Environment, [1985] O.J. L175/30.

courts. Indirect challenges to Community measures *via* national courts are crucial to access to Community justice. While there have been relatively few such references from the Irish courts, they nonetheless represent a key aspect of the Community role of national judges.

The overarching theme is, therefore, the disaggregation of the state brought about by Community law, and its impact for national judicial control mechanisms. The national executive, in particular, has various Community roles which alter its legal status. Indeed, the Community has been characterised as "a complex legislative machinery the executive branch of which are the Member States."[12] The decentralised administration of Community law is a reality, and yet rather an invisible one. As Dashwood has memorably put it:

> "The individual citizen . . . continues to experience government as, essentially a Member State phenomenon. Rules touching the lives of individuals in all kinds of ways may no longer be home-produced; but the consequences of the rules are exacted by officials with familiar accents and uniforms and owing their allegiance to political masters who are answerable through the national democratic process."[13]

Legally, however, those actors play a Community role also, which transforms the nature of judicial review.

2.(2) Judicial Review of National Norms in light of Community law

Students of elementary EC law become familiar with the Community law doctrines which govern the situation where an individual seeks to challenge a national law in light of Community law. The predominant concern in the foundational era of Community law was to establish the individual as a subject of Community law, with superior rights deriving directly from Community law, which could be enforced in national courts.[14] The starting point is of course the doctrine of direct effect, whereby most Community norms become justiciable at the national level.[15] According to the Community doctrine of supremacy, all national judges, however lowly in the national judicial hierarchy, are not merely entitled, but rather obliged, to set aside national law which conflicts with Community law.[16] Further tools have been developed to

---

[12] Green & Barav, "Damages in the National Courts for Breach of Community Law" [1986] Y.E.L. 55.

[13] Dashwood, "States in the European Union" (1998) 23 E.L.Rev. 201 at p.213.

[14] Some of the classic literature on this theme includes Stein, "Lawyers, Judges and the Making of a Transnational Constitution" [1981] A.J.I.L. 1; Weiler, "The Transformation of Europe", (1991) 100 *Yale Law Journal* 2403 or updated in Weiler, *The Constitution of Europe*, (Cambridge University Press, 1999).

[15] See above n. 2.

[16] Case 106/77 *Ammistrazione delle Finanze dello Stato v. Simmenthal* [1978] E.C.R. 629.

ensure effective enforcement. National procedural rules are constrained by the
twin Community law requirements of equality and efficacy.[17] There is a
general requirement to provide effective remedies, and a specific entitlement
to a remedy in damages against a Member State in certain circumstances.[18]
Interim relief must be made available.[19]

However, there is another pervasive feature of the Community legal order
which impacts on national enforcement mechanisms, namely the role of the
general principles of Community law. The general principles comprise a body
of unwritten public law, which has been fashioned by the ECJ, influenced to
varying degrees by national legal traditions. The outcome is, however, distinctly
communautaire.[20] The principles include the general principle of equal
treatment, the protection of fundamental rights, the principles of proportionality,
legal certainty, protection of legitimate expectation and the right to a fair
hearing. The general principles have various roles in relation to Community
measures; they are criteria for determining the validity of Community law,
they fill gaps in the Treaty, and they aid in the interpretation of Community
norms.

These Community general principles would operate in isolation from
national legal systems were it not for the fact that the ECJ has also extended
their application to national acts "within the scope of Community law." Thus,
when an individual challenges the legality of a national measure within the
scope of Community law, two sets of administrative laws form the basis for the
legal scrutiny of that act – national and Community. The ECJ has consistently
acknowledged the impact of the national legal milieu, noting that when
implementing Community law national authorities "act in accordance with the
procedural and substantive rules of their own national law".[21] Thus, national
measures implementing regulations are "governed by the public law of the
Member State in question."[22] The implications of this dual application are

---

[17] See for example, Case C–208/90 *Emmott v. Minister for Social Welfare* [1991] E.C.R. I–4269;
      Case C–271/91 *Marshall v. Southhampton and South West Area Health Authority* II [1993]
      E.C.R. I–4367. See above Keville, para. 1(2).
[18] See above n.5. See above Keville, para. 1(3).
[19] Case C–231/89 *R v. Secretary of State for Transport ex parte Factortame Ltd* (Factortame I)
      [1990] E.C.R. I–2433.
[20] While commentators have identified the French instrumentalist approach to judicial control
      as the primary influence, no one national legal culture is dominant. As Schwarze has stated:
      "Looking at the method chosen by the Court for developing a European administrative law,
      it becomes clear that the law of the Member States has served as a reservoir and source of
      knowledge. Using the method of an evaluative comparison of the national legal principles,
      the jurisdiction has regularly tried to find the solution that is most compatible with the legal
      order of Community law and that most closely corresponds to the functional capacity and the
      goals of the Community." Schwarze, Jurgen (ed), *Administrative Law under European
      Influence*, (Sweet & Maxwell/Nomos, 1996).
[21] Case C- 285/93 *Dominikanerinnen-Kloster Altenhohenau v. Hauptzollamt Rosenheim* [1995]
      E.C.R. I– 4069, para. 26; Case C–292/97 *Kjell Karlsson and others* [2000] E.C.R. I–2737.
[22] Case 230/78 *Eridania v. Minister for Agriculture and Forestry* [1979] E.C.R. 2749, para. 33.

legally significant. While there are similarities between the Community general principles and national principles, divergences are also apparent.[23]

A further factor in the Irish constitutional context is that the application of constitutional standards may be set aside by the provisions of Article 29.4.7 which provides:

> "No provision of the Constitution invalidates laws enacted, acts done or measures adopted by the State which are necessitated by the obligations of membership of the European Union or the Communities, or prevents laws enacted, acts done or measures adopted by the European Union or by the Communities or by the institutions thereof, or by bodies competent under the Treaties establishing the Communities, from having the force of law in the State."

Thus, the possibility emerges that national acts may be subject to Community principles alone, where they are "necessitated" by Community obligations, although the review will be conducted by national judges.[24]

2.(2)(a) General Principles of Community law – Scope of Application

The entire complexion of a judicial review action is changed once a Community aspect is established. Although the ECJ remains far from asserting a general power to scrutinise Member State measures for compliance with EC general principles, in a series of well-known cases[25] it has asserted its review jurisdiction over national measures within the field of EC law. Two main areas in which EC general principles bind national authorities are clear – firstly, where the Member State acts as the "agent" of the EC in the implementation of EC law[26] 2(2)(a)(i) and secondly, where the Member State is acting in derogation from one of the core economic freedoms which form the basis of the common market[27] 2(2)(a)(ii).

The rationale for the former type of review appears sound and reflects the reality of the decentralised administration of EC law. Review of national measures derogating from economic freedoms is more problematic. The apparent underlying rationale reflects the particular conception of the extent of EC competences. Once a national measure interferes with one of the economic freedoms, which are generally broadly defined, it is prima facie prohibited. In

---

[23] A comprehensive comparison is outside the scope of this chapter. For general treatises on Community general principles see Tridimas, *General Principles of EC Law*, (OUP, 1999); Usher, *General Principles of EC Law*, (Longman, 1998); Schwarze, *European Administrative Law*, (Sweet & Maxwell, 1992); Arnull, *The General Principles of EEC Law and the Individual*, (Palgrave-MacMillan, 1990).

[24] On Article 29.4.7 see below Lucey, para 4(2)(b).

[25] See, for example, Case 36/75 *Rutili* [1975] E.C.R. 1219; Cases 60 & 61/84 *Cinéthèque SA v. Fédération des Cinémas Français* [1985] E.C.R. 2605; Case 5/88 *Wachauf v. Germany* [1989] E.C.R. 2609; Opinion of Advocate General in Case C–159/90 *Society for the Protection of the Unborn Child (SPUC) v. Grogan* [1991] E.C.R. I–4685.

[26] For example, Case 5/88 *Wachauf v. Germany* [1989] E.C.R. 2609.

[27] For example, *Rutili*, Case C–260/89 *ERT* [1991] E.C.R. I–2925.

that instance, the Member State may invoke any of a number of grounds in order to justify the impugned measure. Typically the ECJ will scrutinise the measure not only as to the legitimacy of the aim pursued, but also as to the proportionality of the means employed. It is argued that the application of other Community general principles is also appropriate, as the Member State is operating entirely within the realm of EC law. Both of these situations are examined more closely below, and the question of whether further areas of national activity fall within the scope of Community law is addressed.

One complicating factor which may emerge in the future is the EU Charter of Fundamental Rights.[28] This instrument was solemnly declared by the Council, Commission and Parliament at Nice in December 2000. The aim of the instrument was to make the protection of fundamental rights in the Community legal order more visible. Although the legal status of the Charter has yet to be decided, it does contain provisions which set out its legal character, if it does become binding.[29] An examination of these makes it clear that the Charter does not purport to have as broad a scope of application as the existing unwritten general principles. Article 50(1) provides that:

> "[t]he provisions of this Charter are addressed to the institutions and bodies of the Union with due regard for the principle of subsidiarity and *to the Member State only when they are implementing Union law*. They shall therefore respect the rights, observe the principles and promote the application thereof in accordance with their respective powers."(emphasis added).

The drafting Convention had difficulties in agreeing when Member State acts would be subject to the Charter. In earlier versions, the words "implementation and application" were used. The Commission argues that the Article 49(1) reference to Member States "implementing" European law reflects the case law of the ECJ.[30] However, it is difficult to see how this is so. In fact, the phrase appears to under-represent the current state of EC law, as outlined below. If the Charter becomes legally binding, this issue is likely to require an early resolution to preclude the development of divergent Community lines of authority.

---

[28] See below Kingston para. 12(5).

[29] For a discussion of these so-called "horizontal clauses" see Liisberg, "Does the EU Charter of Fundamental Rights threaten the supremacy of Community law? (2001) C.M.L.Rev. 2001, at pp.1171–1199; Curtin & Van Ooik, "The sting is always in the tail: the personal scope of application of the EU Charter of Fundamental Rights" (2001) *Maastricht Journal of European and Comparative Law* 102–114; Hepple, "The EU Charter of Fundamental Rights" (2001) *Industrial Law Journal* 225–231; Garcia, *The General Provisions of the Charter of Fundamental Rights of the European Union* Jean Monnet Working Paper 4/02.

[30] European Commission Communication, *The Legal Nature of the EU Charter of Fundamental Rights of the European Union*, Brussels, October 11, 2000, para.5. Available at <http://europa.eu.int/comm/justice_home/unit/charte/pdf/com2000–644_en.pdf>.

2.(2)(a)(i) Member States as agents of Community Law

2.(2)(a)(i)(1) Member States implementing regulations

In *Wachauf* the ECJ stated that Community general principles (in that case fundamental rights principles) bind the Member States "when they implement Community rules" and that "the Member States must, as far as possible, apply those rules in accordance with those requirements."[31] Often, this Member State duty has been considered in the context of national implementation of regulations – the classic form of decentralised administration practised by the Community. Several such cases have arisen in the context of the administration of the Common Agricultural Policy. Thus, for example in *Bostock*,[32] the ECJ was called upon to examine whether Member State implementation of the milk quota scheme required a system of compensation. Similarly in *Demand*, again regarding milk quotas, the ECJ reiterated that when Member States make use of the power granted to them in a Community regulation, they must do so "in compliance with general principles and fundamental rights upheld in Community law by decisions of the Court of Justice."[33]

However, what is less clear is whether this duty also extends to situations where Member States give effect to Community law obligations, but in a sphere where they have greater discretion.

2.(2)(a)(i)(2) Member States implementing Directives

Regarding the implementation of Directives, this issue recently came before the ECJ for consideration in *Booker Aquaculture Ltd.*[34] The Court of Session in Edinburgh made a reference to the ECJ asking whether the relevant authorities, in implementing Directive 93/53/EEC,[35] were required to pay compensation for economic loss suffered. Advocate General Mischo cited Professor Bruno de Witte:

> "The question whether the *Wachauf* line (Member States are bound by Community fundamental rights when they implement EC law) also applies to the transposition and implementation of Directives (as opposed to the mere execution of regulations as in *Wachauf* and *Bostock*) remains unclear, it is difficult to see the justification for saying that, when implementing Directives,

---

[31] Case 5/88 [1989] E.C.R. 2609, para. 19.

[32] Case C–2/92 [1994] E.C.R. I–955.

[33] Case C–186/96 [1998] E.C.R. I–8529, para. 35.

[34] Joined Cases C–20/00 and C–64/00 *Booker Aquaculture Ltd v. The Scottish Ministers*, Opinion of Advocate General Mischo delivered on September 20, 2001. For a discussion of the Scottish decision and the AG's Opinion see O'Neill, "The Protection of Fundamental Rights in Scotland as a General Principle of Community Law – The Case of *Booker Aquaculture*" (2000) *European Human Rights Law Review* 18–32; and Beal, "Sauce for the goose, sauce for the cow, pig and fish?" (2002) I.C.C.L.R. 2002, 13(5), 192–201.

[35] Council Directive 93/53/EEC introducing minimum Community measures for the control of certain fish diseases [1993] O.J. L175/23.

the Member States are freed from their obligation to respect the fundamental rights enshrined in the Community legal order."[36]

In particular, de Witte points out that it has long been established that Directives should be interpreted in light of Community general principles.[37] Accordingly, he supports the application of general principles to Member State action in transposing Directives. This conclusion has been supported by the Opinion in *Booker Aquaculture*: "I will . . . take it for granted that . . . a Member State must respect fundamental rights when it implements a Directive."[38]

2.(2)(a)(i)(3) Member States fulfilling broad Community obligations

This conclusion seems a sensible one, and would seem to also apply to areas where Member States take other discretionary measures, pursuant to broad Community objectives. For example, it has been established that Member States are required to take action to prevent private barriers to the free movement of goods.[39] In this case, they are obliged to act on the basis of the general duty to achieve Community aims under Article 10 (ex Article 5) EC, read in conjunction with Article 28 (ex Article 30) EC on the free movement of goods. It is clear that in these circumstances Member States are implementing a Community obligation, but within a wide field of application. The *Booker* Opinion would seem to suggest that Community general principles also apply in these circumstances.

2.(2)(a)(ii) Member States derogating from Community obligations

2.(2)(a)(ii)(1) Derogating from Community internal market obligations

The second scenario concerns when Member States seek to apply national rules which derogate from Community law principles, in particular from any of the four freedoms. This scenario presupposes that a Member State will be found in violation of a Treaty provision, and then have recourse to some established justification for such violation. The Member State is in effect called upon to justify the measure on the basis of the permissible policy justification *and* Community general principles.[40]

Originally, in the *Cinéthèque*[41] case, the ECJ did not accept that this situation warranted the application of Community fundamental rights principles. Referring to the situation of derogating from Article 28 (ex Article 30)

---

[36] de Witte,"The past and future of the European Court of Justice in the protection of human rights", *EU and Human Rights* (Alston ed., Oxford University Press, 1999), pp.859 to 897.
[37] Case 222/84 *Johnston* [1986] E.C.R. 1651.
[38] Opinion, at para. 59.
[39] Case C–265/95 *Commission v. France* [1997] E.C.R. I–6959.
[40] See below Kingston para. 12(2)(b).
[41] Cases 60 and 61/84 *Cinéthèque SA v. Fédération Nationale des Cinémas Français* [1985] E.C.R. 2605.

EC, the ECJ stated that it had "no power to examine the compatibility with the European Convention of national law which concerns, as in this case, an area which falls within the jurisdiction of the national legislator."[42] However, subsequently in *ERT*[43] the ECJ extended its fundamental rights jurisdiction to just this situation, albeit without acknowledging the significant change in judicial stance.

In the wake of *Cinéthèque* and *ERT*, the question had been raised as to whether Community fundamental rights review also extended to situations where the Member State was not derogating on the basis of a ground explicitly recognised in the Treaty (such as Article 30 (ex Article 36) EC), but rather was invoking a mandatory requirement or overriding public policy objective.[44] It had been suggested that, in the latter scenario, the Member State was not actually in derogation from an obligation, but rather that there was no breach of the obligation in the first place. Any doubts to this effect were dispelled by *Familiapress*.[45] There the ECJ had to consider a Member State act which was an indistinctly applicable barrier to free movement of goods. In justification, the Member State invoked the mandatory requirement of maintaining press diversity. The ECJ also reviewed the Member State measure for fundamental rights compliance, in particular on the basis of Article 10 ECHR on freedom of expression.

The potential ramifications of this jurisprudence are best illustrated in the *SPUC* case.[46] AG Van Gerven found a violation of Community provisions on the free movement of services in the Irish abortion information prohibition. On that basis, as well as reviewing the policy justification for this ban, the AG also reviewed its compliance with Community general principles, in particular the right to freedom of expression. In contrast, the ECJ found no violation of the freedom to provide services, and so avoided becoming embroiled in a Community fundamental rights review of an Irish constitutional provision.[47] Later the Strasbourg Court of Human Rights found that the provisions did not in fact respect Article 10 of the ECHR on freedom of expression.[48]

---

[42] *Ibid.* at para. 26.

[43] Case C–260/89 *Elliniki Radiophonia Tileorassi* [1991] E.C.R. I–2925.

[44] According to the case of Case 120/78 *Rewe-Zentrale Ag v. Bundesmonopolverwaltug fur Branntwein (Cassis de Dijon)* [1979] E.C.R. 649, indistinctly applicable trade impeding measures may be justified according to mandatory requirements, i.e. non-exhaustive grounds of legitimate policy intervention, as well as the explicit grounds under Article 30 (ex Article 36) EC.

[45] Case C–368/95 *Vereinigte Familiapress Zeitungsverlags v. Heinrich Bauer Verlag* [1997] E.C.R. I–3689.

[46] Case C–159/90 *Society for the Protection of the Unborn Child (SPUC) v. Grogan* [1991] E.C.R. I–4685.

[47] For further discussion see Phelan, "Right to Life of the Unborn v Promotion of Trade in Services: The European Court of Justice and the Normative Shaping of the European Union" (1992) 55 M.L.R. 670.

[48] *Open Door and Dublin Well Woman Clinic*, judgment of October 29, 1992 Series A, No 246–A.

2.(2)(a)(ii)(2) Derogating from other Community obligations

While the *ERT*-type review is now well-established as regards internal market provisions, it is unclear just how far the underlying rationale extends. For example, does every national measure which may require scrutiny from a Community law point of view also have to comply with Community general principles? In the U.K., difficulties have arisen as to whether the general principles apply in such situations. The cases below illustrate these difficulties. These scenarios have yet to be ruled upon by the ECJ.

In *First City Trading*[49] the English High Court refused to apply the general principle of equal treatment in the following situation: a number of exporters of beef products challenged the legality of an emergency scheme adopted by the U.K. Government to provide financial assistance to the slaughtering industry, which had been badly affected by the BSE ban on beef exports and the ban on meat and bone meal in animal foodstuffs. The applicants argued that the scheme discriminated against exporters who did not possess slaughtering or cutting facilities. Laws J. held that the general principles had a much narrower scope of application than the EC Treaty itself. In order to invoke them it was necessary to show that the legislation adopted was strictly pursuant to Community law. The scheme was neither authorised nor required by Community law. The applicants had argued that the scheme did fall within the scope of Community law, on the basis that the scheme was adopted as a direct consequence of the EC ban. Tridimas agrees with the assessment of Laws J., but argues it should be applied cautiously, as "all national measures which are necessary for the application of [a Community] act fall within the scope of Community law, even if they are not expressly required by it."[50]

Subsequently in *British Pig Industry Support Group*[51] the question arose as to whether the principle of equal treatment applied to a decision of the U.K. government not to apply for authorisation to grant state aid for the pig industry, in the aftermath of the BSE crisis. The authorisation of such aid is required under Article 87 (ex Article 92) EC. Commission decisions on such applications are governed by the Community Guidelines on Aid in the Agriculture Sector.[52] Such applications had been made in relation to the beef industry. However, the pig industry had also suffered due to the meat and bone meal ban, which meant that piggeries had to pay for the removal of bone meal waste which had

---

[49] *R v. Ministry of Agriculture, Fisheries and Food, ex p.First City Trading Ltd.* [1997] 1 C.M.L.R. 250 (QBD.) For a comparative discussion of the case see Boyron, "General Principles of Law and National Courts: Applying a *Jus Commune*" (1998) E.L.Rev. 171–178. The case is also discussed by Tridimas, *General Principles of Community Law*, (OUP, 1999), pp.27–29.

[50] *ibid.* at 29.

[51] *R v. Ministry of Agriculture, Fisheries and Food, ex parte British Pig Industry Support Group*, NO. CO /0608/2000 (HCt, QBD), July 27, 2000. For a discussion of both cases, see Beal, above n.34.

[52] [2000] O.J. C28/02.

previously been a source of revenue. Thus, the applicants argued that authorisation should also be sought for the pig industry. *First City Trading* was cited by the Ministry as authority for the proposition that a notifiable state aid did not fall to be considered under the general principle of equal treatment. Richards J. disagreed on this interpretation of the case. Notably, he expressed "real doubts" about that authority and opined that as the lawfulness of state aid depends on Community law, it could be regarded as within the scope of Community law, notwithstanding the fact that it does not amount to the "implementation" of Community law. However, as on the facts there was no possible violation of the equal treatment principle, and no basis for compelling the Minister to seek authorisation for aid, the application was dismissed.

These particular issues have not been addressed by the ECJ, and although they are partly explicable by the English judiciary's reluctance to deal with such exacting grounds of review as that based on equal treatment, they do illustrate a genuine difficulty in delimiting the scope of Community law. If it is the case that derogations from Article 28 (ex Article 30) EC on the free movement of goods must be compatible with Community general principles, it is difficult in principle to exclude situations like that of state aid, where the Member State act would be unlawful but for Community authorisation.

2.(2)(a)(iii) Limits to the scope of application of the Community General Principles

In light of the apparently shifting line which delimits the scope of application of Community general principles, it might be wondered whether there are any determinable limits on their scope of application. While the limits are unclear, certain scenarios have been deemed outside the scope of Community law. For example, where an individual asserts a purely hypothetical link with the exercise of an economic freedom,[53] the situation will be deemed outside the scope of Community law.[54] Similarly, where national law prohibited an individual from planting an orchard in a national park, this curtailment of his land-use rights was deemed to be outside the scope of Community law. The national measure was not taken pursuant to or in derogation from a Community measure.[55] That the ECJ does scrutinise scenarios carefully is evident in *Maurin*.[56] There a trader charged with selling foodstuffs after the use-by date attempted to invoke the general principle of the right of defence. He argued that his situation was covered by Community law, as a Directive provided that the use-by date must be evident on packaging and required a Member State to

---

[53] Such as Article 39 (ex Article 48) EC on the free movement of workers.
[54] Case C–299/95 *Kremzow v. Austria* [1997] E.C.R. I–2629.
[55] Case C–309/96 *Annibaldi v. Sindaco del Comune di Guidonia and Presidente Regione Lazio* [1997] E.C.R. I–7493.
[56] Case C–144/95 [1996] E.C.R. I–2909.

prevent trade in goods that did not comply with that requirement. The Court noted that the Directive did not deal with the applicant's situation, namely selling goods which complied with the Directive beyond their marked use-by-date. As such, the situation was outside the scope of Community law.

However, this is not to suggest that the dividing line is static. Writing extra-curially, a member of the ECJ has advocated that the situation in the *Demirel* case be re-examined.[57] The case concerned the residence rights of the family members of a Turkish worker. The worker's right to reside in the EU derives from the Association Agreement between the EC and Turkey. However, that Agreement does not provide rights to family reunification for the migrant worker. The ECJ deemed the family's situation to be outside the scope of Community law. In contrast, Lenaerts argues that restrictions on family reunification are impediments to the movement of workers, and accordingly the issue should be regarded as within the scope of Community law, "even if no material provision of Community law refers expressly to that right."[58] The case illustrates that the breadth accorded to substantive Community rights will ultimately determine the scope of application of the general principles.

The high watermark as to the extension of the scope of Community general principles remains the Opinion of AG Jacobs in *Konstantinidis*.[59] He argued that simply being a Community national in another Member State should trigger the application of Community fundamental rights principles, regardless of whether the material situation was governed by Community law.[60] The ECJ did not follow the Opinion, preferring to address the issue from a substantive free movement of workers perspective. However, when one examines recent developments in relation to the development of non-discrimination on grounds of nationality, and the meaning of the "scope of Community law" in this context, such extension does not appear as fanciful as it once did.[61]

---

[57]   Case 12/86 *Demirel* [1987] E.C.R. 3719, discussed by Lenaerts, "Fundamental Rights in the European Union" (2000) E.L.Rev. 575, 592.

[58]   *ibid*. at 592.

[59]   Case C–168/91 *Konstantinidis v. Stadt Altensteig* [1993] E.C.R. I–1191.

[60]   "In my opinion, a Community national who goes to another Member State as a worker or a self-employed person under Article 48, 52 or 59 of the Treaty is entitled not just to pursue his trade or profession and to enjoy the same living and working conditions as a national of the host state; he is in addition entitled to assume that, wherever he goes to earn his living in the European Community, he will be treated in accordance with a common code of fundamental values, in particular those laid down in the ECHR. In other words, he is entitled to say "civis europeus sum" and to invoke that status in order to oppose any violation of his fundamental rights." Para. 46, Opinion.

[61]   Article 12 (ex Article 6) EC provides: "Within the scope of application of this Treaty, and without prejudice to any special provisions contained therein, any discrimination on grounds of nationality shall be prohibited." In Case C–85/96 *Martinez Sal*a [1998] E.C.R. I–2691; Case C–274/96 *Bickel and Franz* [1998] E.C.R. I–7637; Case C–184/99 *Rudy Grzelczyk v. Centre Public d'Aide Sociale d'Ottignes-Louvain-la-Neuve* (CPAS) [2001] ECR I–6193 the Court extended the scope of non-discrimination in novel ways, partly based on the citizenship provisions based in Article 17 (ex Article 8) EC. It may well be that the extensive application

Whether this is desirable is another matter. The application of Community general principles alongside those of national origin may provide added-value for litigants. However, as the next section demonstrates, the interaction between national and Community review has its own complications.

2.(2)(b) Interaction between national and Community review

The interaction of national and Community standards and grounds of review has led to some difficulties in the Irish courts. For some time it appeared as though Irish judges were employing the constitutional immunity provisions of Article 29.4.7 in a profligate manner, abnegating their constitutional role.[62] By interpreting the notion of "necessitated" broadly, national constitutional review was excluded. The application of Community general principles was often not considered. This left a potentially serious lacuna in legal protection.

However, two recent litigation sagas illustrate a change in judicial approach whereby national and Community grounds of review were pursued with equal vigour. While this is certainly to be welcomed, the protracted nature of the litigation in both cases is partly explicable by the complications arising when two sets of criteria for validity must be applied. In both cases national standards afforded "higher" standards of legal protections to the applicants, but the Community general principles were nonetheless considered. In a further welcome development, the Article 29.4.7 constitutional immunity emerged only when it was clear that Community law left no choice for the national authority.

2.(2)(b)(i) An uncertain start

In 1988 in *Lawlor v. Minister for Agriculture*[63] Murphy J. examined national implementing regulations[64] under the personal rights provisions of the Irish constitution. However, he then went on to suggest that the regulation was protected by Article 29.4.3 (now Article 29.4.7). Unfortunately, Murphy J. took an exceptionally wide view of what was "necessitated" by Community

---

of the general principle of non-discrimination in these cases is related to the peculiarities of these core provisions, rather than an expansion of the application of all general principles.

It should also be borne in mind that non-discrimination on grounds of nationality does not apply in "purely internal" situations. See Case 175/78, *R v. Saunders,* [1979] E.C.R. 1129; Cases 35 & 36/82, *Morson & Jhanjan v. Netherlands* [1982] E.C.R. 3723; Case C–370/90, *R v. Immigration Appeal Tribunal and Surinder Singh, ex parte Secretary of State for the Home Department* [1992] E.C.R. I–4265. The citizenship provisions have not affected this restriction. See Joined Cases C–64/96 and 65/96, *Land Nordrhein-Westfalen v. Uecker and Jacquet v. Land Nordrhein-Westfalen* [1997] E.C.R. I–3171. However, what constitutes a cross-border element will be easier to satisfy in light of Case C–60/00 *Carpenter v. Secretary of State for the Home Department,* July 11, 2002.

62 On Article 29.4.7 see below Lucey para 4(2)(b).
63 [1988] I.L.R.M. 400.
64 European Communities (Milk Levy) Regulations 1985.

obligations, extending the constitutional immunity to measures "consequent upon" membership, and "even where there may be a choice or degree of discretion vested in the State as to the particular manner in which it would meet the general spirit of obligations of membership." Such a wide immunity is neither necessary nor desirable. In *Condon*[65] the High Court further complicated the issues. Adopting a particularly confused analysis, Lynch J. reviewed the relevant Minister's implementation of a Community regulation[66] on the basis of constitutional standards, but then suggested that where discretionary implementation measures were reasonable, they are to be regarded as "necessitated" by Community membership and hence immune from constitutional scrutiny. Community general principles were not invoked in these cases. These cases exemplify the regrettable judicial tendency to avoid rigorous scrutiny of national implementing measures. However, *Duff* and *Bosphorus* illustrated a change in judicial approach.

2.(2)(b)(ii) Duff

The *Duff* saga[67] arose out of the interplay between two Community schemes, namely the milk quota regime and the agricultural modernisation scheme. Under the pertinent milk quota Regulation[68] dairy farmers were liable to a levy if they produced more than the allocated quota.[69] However, the Regulation allowed the distribution of additional quotas to certain farmers, including "development farmers" who had planned to increase output under the earlier agricultural modernisation scheme.[70] The Minister for Agriculture chose not to distribute additional quotas to the development farmers. These development farmers had adopted milk production development plans, and financed increased production by private borrowing and grants from the European Commission, administered by the Department of Agriculture. However, without additional quota allocation, they would be subject to levies if they reached the targets set out in the development plans.[71]

---

[65] *Condon v. Minister for Agriculture*, H.C., October 12, 1990 [1993] I.J.E.L. 151.

[66] Council Regulation (EEC) No 857/84 of March 31,1984 adopting general rules for the application of the levy referred to in Article 5c of Regulation (EEC) No 804/68 in the milk and milk products sector [1984] O.J. L90/13.

[67] High Court and Supreme Court reported at [1997] 2 I.R. 22; AG and ECJ at [1996] E.C.R. I–569; finally culminating in several judgments of Laffoy J. on the damages to be awarded to the plaintiffs March 25,1999, June 3,1999, August 11, 1999, August 24, 1999.

[68] Council Regulation (EEC) No 857/84 of March 31, 1984 adopting general rules for the application of the levy referred to in Article 5c of Regulation (EEC) No 804/68 in the milk and milk products sector [1984] O.J. L90/13.

[69] Properly called a "reference quantity." The colloquial term "quota" will be employed here.

[70] Council Directive 72/159/EEC on the modernization of farms O.J. [1972] L96/1. This initiated a scheme to restructure agriculture. In Ireland the Directive was administered by ACOT, a semi-state body.

[71] For a number of years the levies were not payable as Ireland had not reached its overall allocation of milk production. However, in the late 1980s and early 1990s, overall production

In the High Court, Murphy J. characterised the main legal issue as the extent of the Minister's discretion under the Regulation in relation to the allocation of additional quotas. He noted that such discretion was not unfettered, but rather that its exercise had to be based on national policy. Such a decision was reviewable only if it infringed the constitutional rights of the citizen or was shown to involve the abuse of function. The judge also examined the arguments based on Community general principles, albeit in a cursory manner.[72]

The approach of the Supreme Court was more alert to the Community issues and a number of questions were referred to the ECJ. The questions related to whether the regulation *required* Member States to allocate additional quotas to development farmers, or, alternatively, whether the general principles of Community law so required. If not, the Court asked whether the regulation was contrary to these general principles and hence invalid. The ECJ ruled that there was no obligation to grant development farmers additional reference quantities, and that the regulation was valid.[73] On return to the Supreme Court, it was noted that although the ECJ had not found a violation of the regulation, the Minister's conduct still fell to be scrutinised under national standards. In particular, Barrington J. referred to the Opinion of Advocate-General Cosmas[74] as evidence that the plaintiffs might have a remedy in national law, notwithstanding that there was no violation of Community law.

The Supreme Court split 3:2 as to whether the Minister's actions would be upheld as a matter of national law. Hamilton C.J. and Keane J. (dissenting) were in no doubt that the plaintiffs were morally entitled to an additional quota, but noted that their legal entitlement was to have their situation considered by the Minister. It was clear that the Minister had taken the situation of development farmers into account. His final decision not to allocate the additional quota was not irrational, and hence upheld. In contrast, the majority (O'Flaherty, Blaney and Barrington JJ.) focused on the detailed operation of the scheme. The Minister had originally intended to cater for development farmers, but to do so out of so-called "flexi-milk", that is, unused quotas that would become available during the year. However, the Regulation provided that the additional quotas were to be allocated out of the national

---

was such that development farmers, including the plaintiffs, became liable for large penalty levies (the so-called "milk superlevy").

[72] The issue of legitimate expectation was considered – citing Case 120/86 *Mulder v. Minister van Landbouw en Visserij* [1988] E.C.R. 2321. For a fascinating analysis of the content and impact of that decision see Sharpston, "Milk Lakes, SLOMS, and Legitimate Expectations – a Paradigm in Judicial Review" in *Judicial Review in European Union Law,* (O'Keeffe, ed., Kluwer Law International, 2000), pp.557–568.

[73] [1996] E.C.R. I–569.

[74] "[T]here is nothing to prevent such a requirement [to grant additional quotas to development farmers] from being founded on principles of national law which, in an appropriate case, may ensure greater protection in this respect than that afforded by the general principles applicable in the Community legal order." Opinion, para. 60.

reserve. When this was pointed out by the Commission, it was clear that there was no remaining quota that could be designated the national reserve. On this basis, it was held that the Minister had committed an error in law and accordingly put himself in a position where he could not exercise his discretion in favour of the development farmers. The legitimate expectations of those farmers as a matter of national law were also noted. The matter was remitted to the High Court to examine the claims of the applicants.[75]

The analysis of the majority of the Supreme Court is peculiar. The Minister had certainly made a mistake in his original interpretation of the Regulation. However, his error did not impinge upon the legal nature of his determination in relation to additional quotas. This remained a discretionary one, and his legal role was unaffected by this choice. It is also peculiar that the majority treat the issue of legitimate expectation as a peripheral one, rather than the basis for the decision. On the other hand, the minority judgments appear too deferential in their review, the tenor of Keane J.'s judgment suggesting that the Minister's decision is an entirely discretionary one, and consequently subject to only a deferential standard of review.

However, the significance of the case goes beyond the particular grounds on which it was decided. The case is an excellent illustration of the dual application of national and Community standards: here national standards providing a remedy where Community law found no violation.

2.(2)(b)(iii) Bosphorus

The dual application of Community and national law provided enhanced judicial protection in *Duff*. However, the situation will not always be so unproblematic. In certain instances, where the national implementing authority lacks all discretion, national constitutional standards may not be invocable. Such difficulties are illustrated by the on-going *Bosphorus* saga.

Two separate sets of judicial review proceedings arose out of the Minister's impounding of an aircraft, pursuant to an EC Regulation which had imposed sanctions against Serbia.[76] The craft was owned by Yugoslav airlines, but leased to Bosphorus, a Turkish airline. Murphy J. held that the action was disproportionate, as Bosphorus was an innocent party. The substantive case turned on the interpretation of Article 8 of the Regulation and the notion of

---

[75] Awards were made on the basis of this as a "mistake of law". However, O'Dell has argued that the correct basis for liability was the breach of legitimate expectation. O'Dell, Eoin, "Restitution" in *Annual Review of Irish Law 1997*, (Byrne & Binchy ed.), pp.619–623 and *Annual Review of Irish Law 1999*, (Byrne & Binchy ed.), pp.472–473. In the High Court, Laffoy J. noted that: "The concept of a remedy in the form of an award of damages for the consequences of a mistake of law is novel and its application rare, if not unique." (*Duff v. Minister for Agriculture*, H.C., March 25, 1999).

[76] Council Regulation (EEC) No. 990/93 of April 26, 1993 concerning trade between the European Economic Community and the Federal Republic of Yugoslavia (Serbia and Montenegro) [1993] O.J. L102/14.

"controlling interest" therein.[77] Murphy J. interpreted "interest" as "interest in possession" in light of the overall purpose of the regulation.[78]

The Minister then proceeded to take action under another provision of the Regulation, namely Article 1(e).[79] The aircraft had been maintained by an Irish state company, TEAM. Under the lease, maintenance was the joint responsibility of the Turkish lessor and the Yugoslav airline. Accordingly, the Minister decided that the maintenance constituted non-financial service to a Yugoslav company, in contravention of the Regulation. On this basis the aircraft was impounded a second time under Article 9 of the Regulation.[80] A second set of judicial review proceedings were taken. In January 1996, Barr J. found in favour of Bosphorus and again quashed the decision of the Minister.[81] The crucial issue was the delay in invoking Article 9. It was held that the Minister should have reviewed all relevant parts of the sanctions Regulation at the same time, within a reasonable time from the original impoundment in May 1993. Further breaches of fair procedures were also noted. The Minister then appealed to the Supreme Court, and applied for a stay of the High Court's order. The Supreme Court refused to grant the stay, as the balance of justice was in the airline's favour.[82] When the appeal on the merits came before the Supreme Court, it was held to be moot, as the applicant's lease had by then expired.[83]

Subsequently, the appeal to the Supreme Court against the original judicial review decision of Murphy J. came for hearing. On February 12, 1995, the Supreme Court referred questions to the ECJ on the interpretation of Article 8 of the Regulation. On April 30, 1996, AG Jacobs gave his Opinion. He disagreed with the High Court's narrow interpretation of the concept of controlling interest, and opined that the lessor's interest was sufficient to trigger the Regulation. On the issue of whether the property rights of Bosphorus had been interfered with, he conducted a detailed analysis of Community[84] and ECHR

---

[77] Article 8 provides: "All vessels, freight vehicles, rolling stock and aircraft in which a majority or controlling interest is held by a person or undertaking in or operating from the Federal Republic of Yugoslavia (Serbia and Montenegro) shall be impounded by the competent authorities of the Member States. Expenses of impounding vessels, freight vehicles, rolling stock and aircraft may be charged to their owners."

[78] [1994] 2 I.L.R.M. 551.

[79] Article 1(e) provided: "As from 26 April 1993, the following shall be prohibited: . . . . (e) the provision of non-financial services to any person or body for purposes of any business carried out in the Republics of Serbia and Montenegro."

[80] Article 9: "All vessels, freight vehicles, rolling stock, aircraft and cargos suspected of having violated, or being in violation of, Regulation (EEC) No 1432/92 or this Regulation shall be detained by the competent authorities of the Member States pending investigations."

[81] [1997] 2 I.R. 22.

[82] [1997] 2 I.R. 1.

[83] As described in the Admissibility Decision of the European Court of Human Rights, Application No. 45036/98, decided on September 13, 2001.

[84] Case 44/79 *Hauer v. Land Rheinland-Pfalz* [1979] E.C.R. 3727; Case C–280/93 *Germany v. Council* [1994] E.C.R. I–4973.

case law[85] and concluded that the interference with property rights, although grave, was justified by the general interest in stopping a devastating war. Similarly, the ECJ held that the action was not disproportionate, based on the "objective of general interest so fundamental to the international community", namely ending the Balkan conflict. After the ECJ's decision, on August 6, 1996 the Minister reinstated the impounding of the aircraft. On November 29, 1996 the Supreme Court delivered its judgment. On the basis of the ECJ's ruling, it simply noted that the Minister was bound to impound the aircraft under the terms of Article 8 of the Regulation.

The case illustrates that dual standards will not be applicable where no discretion is exercised by the national authority. Where Community law dictates a particular solution, then national constitutional standards are not applicable. This is so as a matter of Community law[86] and as a matter of Irish constitutional law, where the measure will benefit from the Article 29.4.7 immunity. The Irish court's use of the principle of proportionality was focused on the individual circumstances of the applicant and the grave losses it suffered, *vis-à-vis* the relatively small damage to the Yugoslav owner of the plane. In contrast, the ECJ's proportionality analysis was at a higher level of generality, focusing on the overriding importance of the objective of the sanctions, which outweighed the injury to the economic interests imposed. As the terms of the Regulation required the seizure in this case, there was no room for a proportionality analysis pertaining to the situation of the individual applicant.

While the ECJ's ruling may seem particularly harsh from an individual rights perspective, it was faithfully applied by the Supreme Court. However, a third jurisdiction has become involved since the Supreme Court's final ruling, namely the Strasbourg Court of Human Rights.[87] In September 2001, the case was declared admissible. It is noteworthy that in the admissibility decision, the Irish government argued that as the Regulation was self-executing and directly effective, a constitutional challenge was excluded by Article 29.4.7 of the Irish Constitution. Thus, it argued that the State was simply acting as the agent of the EC, and accordingly, the complaint should be treated as inadmissible. Any complaint should be directly against the EC institutions.[88] In contrast, the applicant argued that the application of the EC provisions by the Irish State was nonetheless subject to ECHR review, on the basis that the State still

---

[85] For example, *AGOSI v. U.K.*, judgment of October 24, 1986, Series A no. 108; *Air Canada v. U.K.*, May 5, 1995, Series A no 316–A.

[86] Case 11/70 *Internationale Handelsgesellschaft* [1970] E.C.R. 1125.

[87] Application no 45036/98, decided on September 13, 2001.

[88] The Strasbourg Court has admitted claims against Community acts only in limited circumstances. The leading case is *Matthews* 5 B.H.R.C. 686 (ECHR) where the Strasbourg Court suggested that it would scrutinise Community measures only where there was no avenue to challenge under Community law. For a discussion see Canor, "Primus Inter Pares. Who is the ultimate guardian of fundamental rights in Europe?" (2000) 25 E.L.Rev. 3.

retained a "residual human rights discretion." The applicant suggested, for example, that the implementation could have included provision for compensation.

The Strasbourg Court refused to address these issues at the admissibility stage, noting that they were closely bound up with the merits of the case. The impact of this case is far-reaching in light of the provisions of Article 29.4.7. Constitutional review of national measures "necessitated" by the obligations of EU membership is excluded. However, if the applicants' arguments are accepted, such national measures still remain to be scrutinised under the ECHR. While the Community principles are informed by the ECHR, there are key areas of divergence between Community fundamental rights general principles and the ECHR.[89] In light of the exclusion of national constitutional principles, Strasbourg principles may come to the fore.

2.(2)(c) Judicial review and the separation of powers

Much turns on the meaning of "necessitated" under Article 29.4.7. In the *Bosphorus* scenario, the seizure was explicitly required by the terms of the Regulation. Thus, as a matter of Community law it was "necessary". As such, the Irish government regarded it as "necessary" under the terms of Article 29. However, in the earlier cases, it was made clear that the term has an autonomous national law meaning. In the context of judicial review of separation of powers issues, this issue has come to the fore. The modification of the separation of powers has been described as "one of the most far reaching consequences to date of Ireland's EU membership."[90] A broad interpretation of "necessitated" has constitutionally facilitated this transformation, undermining the role of the Oireachtas in EC law-making. Thus, a feature of the EC's democratic deficit, namely the dominance of executive over legislative bodies, has been given a constitutional imprimatur by the Irish judiciary.

The starting point of the constitutional analysis is the *Meagher* decision of 1994.[91] The case concerned the constitutionality of the European Communities Act 1972, in particular its facilitation of the implementation of EC law by way

---

[89] For a discussion, see Lawson, "Confusion and Conflict? Diverging Interpretations of the European Convention on Human Rights in Strasbourg and Luxembourg" in *The Dynamics of the Protection of Human Rights in Europe: Essays in Honour of Henry G. Schermers* (Lawson & De Bloijs ed., 1994); Speilmann, "Human Rights Case Law in the Strasbourg and Luxembourg Courts: Conflicts, Inconsistencies and Complementarities" in *EU and Human Rights* (Alston ed., Oxford University Press, 1999), p.777; Costello, "The ECHR and EU Law", unpublished lecture, *ICEL Lecture Series on the ECHR*, March 20, 2001. (on file with the author). See below Kingston para. 12(4).

[90] Hogan & Schuster "Ireland" in *Administrative Law under European Influence* (Schwarze ed., Nomos Verlagsgesellschaft, 1996).

[91] *Meagher v. Minister of Agriculture* [1994] 1 I.L.R.M. 1. For critiques of the decision see Whelan, Note (1993) DULJ 152; Hogan & Whelan *Ireland and the European Union: Constitutional and Statutory Texts and Commentary*, (Sweet & Maxwell, 1995), pp.51–67 and Lucey below at para 4(2)(b).

of statutory instrument (S.I.). Also challenged was a particular exercise of this power whereby the Minister for Agriculture has implemented a number of Directives by S.I.[92] The contentious aspect of that implementation was the decision to extend the normal time-limit for prosecution of minor offences from 6 months to 2 years. The Directives did not explicitly require such a change. Under normal constitutional law principles, such a policy decision could not be made by way of S.I., but would rather require an Act of the Oireachtas.[93]

Thus, at issue was whether this decision, and indeed the entire apparatus of the 1972 Act, was necessitated by membership of the EU. If so, then they would benefit from constitutional immunity under Article 29.4.7 of the Constitution. The Supreme Court's approach was highly pragmatic, essentially finding that the volume of Community legislation "necessitated" an expedited form of implementation, thus justifying the 1972 Act mechanism. As to the particular implementation at issue, it was found that the decision to extend the time limit, although not explicitly required by the Directive (which was silent as to sanctions) was nonetheless required in order to ensure the effectiveness of the measure. As such it was "necessitated". The possibility was left open to challenge individual implementation measures in the future, based on the fact that they did contain a policy choice.[94] However, in the case itself, the Court took an expansive view of what was required by any given Directive, going

---

[92] Council Directive 81/602/EEC concerning the prohibition of certain substances having a hormonal action and of any substances having a thyrostatic action [1981] O.J. L222/32; Council Directive 81/851/EEC on the approximation of the laws of the Member States relating to veterinary medicinal products [1981] O.J. L317/1; Council Directive 86/469/EEC concerning the examination of animals and fresh meat for the presence of residues [1986] O.J. L275/36; and Council Directive 88/299/EEC on trade in animals treated with certain substances having a hormonal action and their meat, as referred to in Article 7 of Directive 88/146/EEC [1988] O.J. L128/36.

[93] The principle was set down in *Cityview Press v. An Comhairle Oiliuna* [1980] I.R. 381 and is based on Article 15(2)(1) of the Constitution ("sole and exclusive lawmaking power for the Oireachtas"). O'Higgins C.J. The leading passage reads as follows: "[T]he ultimate responsibility rests with the Courts to ensure that constitutional safeguards remain, and that the exclusive authority of the National Parliament in the field of law-making is not eroded by a delegation of power which is neither contemplated nor permitted by the Constitution. In discharging that responsibility, the Courts will have regard to where and by what authority the law in question purports to have been made. In the view of this Court, the test is whether that which is challenged as an unauthorised delegation of parliamentary power is more than a mere giving of effect to principles and policies which are contained in the statute itself. If it be, then it is not authorised; for such would constitute a purported exercise of legislative power by an authority which is not permitted to do so by the Constitution. On the other hand, if it be within the permitted limits – if the law is laid down in the statute and details only are filled in or completed by the designated Minister or subordinate body – there is no unauthorised delegation of legislative power."

[94] Denham J. in particular stated: "If the Directive left to the national authority matters of principle or policy to be determined then the "choice" of the Minister would require legislation by the Oireachtas. But where there is no case made that principles or policies have to be determined by the national authority, whether the situation is that the principles and

well beyond that which was required by the text itself. Thus, the indicators for the success of such challenges were poor.[95]

Such a challenge was brought more recently in *Maher*.[96] The applicants challenged a S.I.[97] which purported to implement the new EC milk quota regime.[98] The effect of the S.I. was that subject to certain exceptions, it was no longer possible for persons who were not actively engaged in milk production to transfer their quota with the land by way of sale or lease (except on renewal of a lease for an additional one-year period). On the expiry of a lease, the landowner would have to resume milk production. Otherwise the quota would have to be sold to the State at a fixed price, and then redistributed to active milk producers. The S.I. also provided for a "restructuring scheme" under which a quota holder could offer all or part of his or her quota to the purchaser of the milk in return for payment, with a maximum price to be determined by the Minister.

The applicants claimed that this was a form of compulsory acquisition without adequate compensation, which interfered with their property rights guaranteed by the Constitution. The applicants submitted that while the ECJ did not regard a milk quota as a property right,[99] that did not prevent a milk quota from being regarded as a property right under the provisions of Irish constitutional law. The applicants also argued that the S.I. was not necessitated by Ireland's membership of the European Union, and therefore was not covered by Article 29.4.7 of the Constitution. Thus, the exercise of the Minister's policy discretion was contrary to Article 15.2.1. In particular, they argued that the distribution of quotas to active milk producers was not required by the Community Regulation.

The High Court, *per* Carroll J., refused the application, holding that the milk quota was not "property" and that the choice in the S.I. was warranted by the governing EC Regulations. On appeal to the Supreme Court, the applicants argued that the High Court erred in finding that the Minister was merely executing principles and policies laid down in Community law. The Supreme Court (Keane C.J., Denham, Murphy, Murray and Fennelly JJ.), dismissed the appeal.

In a key respect, the decision represents a reconsideration of the *Meaghar* decision. The Supreme Court held that the choice of an S.I. rather than an Act

---

policies were determined in the Directive, then legislation by a delegated form, by regulation, is a valid choice."

[95] For a critique of the *Meagher* reasoning, see Hogan& Schuster "Report on Ireland" in *Administrative Law under European Influence,* (Schwarze ed., Nomos Verlagsgesellschaft, 1996), at pp.441–446.

[96] *Maher v. Minister for Agriculture, Food and Rural Development* [2001] 2 I.R. 139; [2001] 2 I.L.R.M. 481.

[97] European Communities (Milk Quota) Regulations 2000.

[98] Council Regulation (EC) No 1256/1999 amending Regulation (EEC) No 3950/92 establishing an additional levy in the milk and milk products sector [1999] O.J. L160/73.

[99] Case C–2/92 *R v. Ministry of Agriculture, ex parte Bostock* [1994] E.C.R. I–955.

of the Oireachtas as the method of implementation of the detailed rules set out in the Regulation, was not in any sense necessitated by the obligations of Community membership. However, it went on to hold that the choice of implementation by statutory instrument was valid in this particular case, as the Council Regulations were part of Irish law and could be regarded in the same way as an enabling statute of the Oireachtas.

The application of the *Cityview* test to the measures at issue warrants attention. In order to determine the extent of the principles and policies, the Court looked not only to the parent EC Regulation, but also to the EU Treaties, the objectives of the Common Agricultural Policy (CAP), and the general principles of Community law. Thus, having reviewed the legislative background, Fennelly J. concluded that the S.I. amounted to "a clear and explicit decision by the State to avail of the power given by Community law to break the link between land and milk quota."[100] There was no question but that the Minister's decision was a choice on his part, but this was characterised as the exercise of discretion "circumscribed by the objectives of the scheme authorising it."[101] In particular, Fennelly J. referred to the general principles of Community law and the Regulation itself as constraints on the extent of the policy choice.

Turning to the exceptions enshrined in the S.I., it becomes apparent just how wide the discretion was. Regulation 6, in particular, deals with transfers to family members.[102] In response to the argument that the exemption amounted to a policy choice not required by Community law, Fennelly J. referred to the "the social structure of agriculture" as being among the considerations relevant to the CAP under Article 33 (ex Article 39) EC. This included the family basis of farm ownership. The relaxation of the new provisions to facilitate family transactions accorded with the aim of taking into account the social structure of agriculture, an aim enshrined in Community law. The other exemptions were deemed to be in keeping with the main objective of encouraging transfers to active producers.

While the analysis is entirely correct from a Community law point of view in that the national implementation measure does indeed have to comply with those Community general principles, to apply this analysis to the deter-mination of the *Cityview* test is to muddy the waters. That the Member State must implement the Regulations in a manner compatible with Community law is clear. That these requirements act as a general constraint on the choice of domestic policy is also apparent. However, this is not to suggest that policy choice is altogether constrained, such that the implementation cannot be

---

[100] *Maher v. Minister for Agriculture, Food and Rural Development* [2001] 2 I.R. 139, at 257 *per* Fennelly J.
[101] *ibid.* at 258.
[102] Defined as spouses, parents, children, brothers, sisters, grandparents, grandchildren, uncles and aunts.

regarded as a matter of policy. Ireland had a policy choice to make in the implementation. That choice was for the Oireachtas under Article 15.2.1.

2.(2)(d) Standard of review

The previous sections are concerned with substantive issues that arise in judicial review, in particular when there are different grounds of review under national and Community principles. In the context of judicial review proceedings, the issue of the standard of review is ubiquitous. A deferential standard of review can render all but the most egregious decisions impervious to challenge. A very robust standard threatens to undermine the autonomy and efficiency of decision-makers. Courts do strike the wrong balance at times, keeping decision-makers to procedural rigours, but allowing the heart of the assessment to become rotten. This section examines whether the Community law context warrants a distinctive approach to the *standard* of review.

2.(2)(d)(i) The European case law

In principle, the ECJ has answered this question in the negative. However, its judgment warrants careful scrutiny as it provides the seeds for further re-visitation of the topic. The leading Community authority is *Upjohn*.[103] Upjohn Ltd brought proceedings in the English courts challenging the division of the U.K. Medicines Board's revocation of authorisation of one of its products. The pertinent Community Directives allowed such a withdrawal "where [a] product proves to be harmful in the normal conditions of use, or where its therapeutic efficacy is lacking, or where its qualitative and quantitative composition is not as declared."[104] On appeal, the Court of Appeal stayed the proceedings and referred questions to the ECJ for a preliminary ruling. The questions related to the proper standard of review, in particular whether the national court was obliged to revoke the licence if it concluded the grant was incorrect, or alternatively whether the grant should stand provided it was "a decision which the licensing authority could reasonably have reached on the material before it."

These questions went to the heart of the national court's role in judicial review proceedings. The Court began by reiterating that in the absence of Community rules:

> "[I]t is for the domestic legal system of each Member State to designate the courts and tribunals having jurisdiction and to lay down the detailed procedural rules governing actions for safeguarding rights which individuals derive from

---

[103] Case C–120/97 *Upjohn Ltd v. The Licensing Authority established by the Medicines Act 1968 and Others* [1999] E.C.R. I–223: see Breen, Note (1999) 4 *Bar Review* 351–352.

[104] Council Directive 65/65 on the approximation of provisions laid down by Law, Regulation or Administrative Action relating to proprietary medicinal products [1965] O.J. L22/369 and Second Council Directive 75/319 [1975] O.J. L147/13, as amended by Council Directive 83/570 [1983] O.J. L332/1.

Community law, provided, however, that such rules are not less favourable than those governing similar domestic actions (the principle of equivalence) and do not render virtually impossible or excessively difficult the exercise of rights conferred by Community law (the principle of effectiveness)."[105]

The Court then went on to state that it did not appear necessary that national courts be empowered:

"to substitute their assessment of the facts and, in particular, of the scientific evidence relied on in support of the revocation decision for the assessment made by the national authorities competent to revoke such authorisations."[106]

Interestingly, and in line with other areas of its jurisprudence, the Court drew an analogy with similar reviews of Community authorities, referring to its case law whereby:

"where a Community authority is called upon, in the performance of its duties, to make complex assessments, it enjoys a wide measure of discretion, the exercise of which is subject to a limited judicial review in the course of which the Community judicature may not substitute its assessment of the facts for the assessment made by the authority concerned. Thus, in such cases, the Community judicature must restrict itself to examining the accuracy of the findings of fact and law made by the authority concerned and to verifying, in particular, that the action taken by that authority is not vitiated by a manifest error or a misuse of powers and that it did not clearly exceed the bounds of its discretion."[107]

Thus, Community law did not demand more from national courts.[108] However, as always the Court did not grant *carte blanche* to national procedural rules, stating that it still had to be possible "to apply the relevant principles and rules of Community law when reviewing its legality."[109] This is a loaded caveat, for in the grounds of judicial review, Community general principles allow for a more searching substantive review than that traditionally available under common law principles.

2.(2)(d)(ii) Judicial Review and the EIA Directive in Ireland

In order to elucidate the operation of these principles, it is useful to look to an area of law where the national standard of review is traditionally deferential,

---

[105] Para.32, citing Case C–312/93 *Peterbroeck v. Belgian State* [1995] E.C.R. I–4599, paras 12 and 18 of the judgment in Case C–326/96 *Levez* [1998] E.C.R. I–7835.

[106] Para. 33.

[107] Para. 34, citing Joined Cases 56/64 and 58/64 *Consten and Grundig v. Commission* [1966] E.C.R. 299; Case 55/75 *Balkan-Import Export v. Hauptzollamt Berlin-Packhof* [1976] E.C.R. 19; para. 8, Case 9/82 *Delvaux v. Commission* [1983] E.C.R. 2379, para. 14; Case C–225/91 *Matra v. Commission* [1993] E.C.R. I–3203, paras 24 and 25; and Case C–157/96 *National Farmers' Union and Others* [1998] E.C.R. I–2211, para. 39.

[108] Para. 35.

[109] Para. 36.

and examine the manner in which Community law impacts on this standard. In the context of planning law, *O'Keeffe v. An Bord Pleanála*[110] provided that where discretionary determinations were made by expert planning bodies (planning authorities and An Bord Pleanála), the courts should not intervene unless the decision was irrational.[111] However, before such a deferential standard will apply, the nature of the body's discretion must be scrutinised. Where a Community measure is at issue, then its application is mandatory, and any discretion will be legally circumscribed. Consequently, the standard of review should be increased in order to verify application of the EC legal requirements.

In a trenchant critique of the Irish application of EC environmental law, Dillon has argued that the domestic approaches to judicial review have thwarted the full application of EC environmental law.[112] In relation to the Environmental Impact Assessment (EIA) Directive[113] she argues that "the Irish courts have . . . folded the Directive back into terms of national standards of review generally applicable to administrative decision-making on environmental issues. Even though the standards are notoriously deferential, the courts have not analysed the relationship between traditional standards of review and the context of this new European environmental law."[114] While the European Court has clarified the importance of Environment Impact Statements (EIS) in the context of developments which fall below the thresholds where EIS is mandatory, the Irish courts have until very recently treated this determination as a purely discretionary one, and refused to apply an appropriate standard of review.[115]

In *Kraijveld*[116] the European Court clarified that national administrative discretion in relation to the need for EIS in the sub-threshold category was fettered by the general requirements set down in the Directive. The implications for judicial review were spelled out by the Court:

> "[W]here Community authorities have, by Directive, imposed on Member States the obligation to pursue a particular course of conduct, the useful effect of such an act would be weakened if individuals were prevented from relying on it before their national courts, and if the latter were prevented from taking it

---

[110] [1993] I.R. 39.

[111] For a discussion see Hogan & Gwynn Morgan, *Administrative Law in Ireland*, (3rd ed., Round Hall Sweet & Maxwell, 1998), pp.643–644.

[112] Dillon, "The Mirage of EC Environmental Federalism in a Reluctant Member State Jurisdiction" (1999) N.Y.U. Envtl. L.J. 1.

[113] Council Directive 91/11 amending Directive 85/337 on the Assessment of the Effects of Certain Public and Private Projects on the Environment [1997] O.J. L5; Council Directive 85/337 on the Assessment of the Effects of certain Public and Private Projects on the Environment, [1985] O.J. L175/30. See below, Doyle, chapter 6.

[114] See Dillon, above n.112 at 26.

[115] See also to this effect MacEochaidh, "The application of the Environmental Impact Assessment Directive in Ireland" (2000) I.J.E.L. 4–22.

[116] Case 72/95 *Kraaijeveld BV v. Gedepudteerde Staten van Zuid-Holland* [1996] E.C.R. I–5403.

into consideration as an element of Community law in order to rule whether the
national legislature, in exercising the choice open to it as to the form and
methods of implementation, has kept within the limits of its discretion set out
in the Directive."[117]

Despite this clear indication, the Irish courts have failed to exercise robust
review over the exercise of discretion in this context. For example, in *Browne*[118]
the High Court stated that "there is no justification for the basic premise relied
on by the applicants which is that the need for an EIS with specific information
is a condition precedent to a valid application for planning permission."[119]
Accordingly, it was for the planning authority to decide whether the information provided in the EIS was sufficient, and whether the assessment based
on that information was correct.[120] In deferring to the expertise of the planning
authority, the Court rendered the Directive unenforceable. While a deferential
standard of judicial review is generally acceptable in reviewing discretionary
decisions of expert bodies,[121] what seems to be at issue here is the mischar-
acterisation of the decision as a discretionary one. Where the provisions of a
Directive are mandatory, as is the case with the EIA Directive, then its
application must be judicially controlled. The decision to apply the Directive
is patently a legal determination, quintessentially amenable to judicial review.

Subsequent case law on the Directive has only served to emphasise the
suspicion that its requirements are being taken less than seriously. For example
in *Lancefort*[122] a peculiar application of national *locus standi* rules[123] thwarted
the litigation of an important issue relating to the mis-transposition of the
Directive in Ireland. This same mis-transposition later became the subject of
infringement proceedings brought by the Commission under Article 226 (ex
Article 169) EC against Ireland.[124] Such a restrictive *locus standi* rule may
well run counter to the requirement of effective protection of Community
rights.[125] In *MacNamara*[126] the High Court refused to consider whether the

---

[117]   *ibid.* at p.5452.

[118]   *Browne v. An Bord Pleanála* [1989] I.L.R.M. 865.

[119]   *ibid.* at 875.

[120]   It was accepted that the provisions of the Directive were mandatory, but it was "solely for
        the planning authority to determine upon the sufficiency of any environmental impact study".
        ibid. at 875–76. This was approved and applied in *Murphy v. Wicklow County Council*, H.C.,
        December 13, 1999.

[121]   For a comparative discussion of this concept, see Delaney, *Judicial Review of Administrative
        Action*, (Round Hall Sweet & Maxwell, 2001), pp.8–13.

[122]   *Lancefort v. An Bord Pleanála* [1998] 2 I.L.R.M. 401.

[123]   On this point, see Simons, *"Lancefort v. An Bord Pleanála"* (1999) 5 I.P.E.L.J. 131.

[124]   Case C–392/96 *Commission v. Ireland* [1999] ECR I–5901.

[125]   For a discussion of the impact of Community law requirements on *locus standi* rules see
        Afilalo, *How Far Francovich? Effective Judicial Protection and Associational Standing to
        Litigate Diffuse Interests in the European Union* Harvard Jean Monnet Center Working
        Paper, 1/98. Available at <http://www.law.harvard.edu/programs/JeanMonnet/papers/
        papers98.html>.

[126]   *MacNamara v. Kildare County Council and Dublin County Council* [1996] 2 I.L.R.M. 339.

strict two-month time limit for bringing judicial review proceedings was adequate enforcement of the Directive. In *MacBride*[127] the High Court, *per* Quirke J., failed to appreciate the justiciability of Article 4(2) of the EIA Directive. In the Supreme Court the issue was avoided as the Court held that the requirements of the Directive had in fact been complied with.

Contrasting with these decisions is that of *O'Nuallain*[128] concerning the O'Connell Street Spike.[129] It was argued that the scale of the monument required an EIA. The High Court, *per* Smyth J., accepted this point. Notably, he reviewed the exercise of discretion on the part of the planning authority as to whether an EIS was required for the sub-threshold development, and decided that they had erred in their assessment that the project was not "likely to have significant effects on the environment." There is no doubt but that *O'Nuallain* is difficult to reconcile with the previous authorities.[130]

Whatever the explanation for this new found adherence to robust review,[131] the case throws into sharp relief the inadequacies of the previous judicial attitude. In refusing to acknowledge that the nature of the administrative discretion was altered by the Directive's requirements, the Irish courts previously thwarted the principle of effective enforcement of Community obligations. While *Upjohn* is in principle indulgent of deferential standards of review, this is clearly confined to expert determinations of fact. In the EIA cases, even where sub-threshold development is at issue, whether an EIA is required is a matter of Community law. It should be reviewed accordingly.

2.(3) CHALLENGING THE LEGALITY OF COMMUNITY ACTION

It is extraordinary given the Irish propensity to challenge public acts, that there have been so few preliminary references from the Irish Courts concerning the

---

[127] *MacBride v. Mayor. Alderman and Burgesses of Galway* [1988] 1 I.R. 485 (HCt); [1998] 1 I.R. 517 (SCt).

[128] 1999 No 154 JR (H.C., July 2, 1999) .

[129] The "Spike" was chosen as the winner in a competition for a Millenium Monument for Dublin's main thoroughfare, O'Connell St, which had long been acknowledged to be in need of urban regeneration. The site chosen was to replace a monument that had been destroyed in the 1960s.

[130] To this effect see Simons, "Planning Law" in *Annual Review of Irish Law 1999* (Byrne & Binchy eds., Round Hall Sweet & Maxwell, 2000), p.424.

[131] Simons suggests that the fact that the local authority official decided that the matter was to be determined under Part X may have meant that the matter never came before the Minister for decision. In the absence of such a decision, the High Court was required to determine the requirement itself, or remit the issue. *ibid.* Dillon cynically suggests that the change is due to the fact that "where the project involved a comparatively small amount of public money, and did not involve the rights of important property interests, the court had little trouble applying the EIA Directive in a manner that had been strenuously avoided in earlier cases." Dillon, "The Mirage of EC Environmental Federalism in a Reluctant Member State Jurisdiction" (1999) N.Y.U. Envtl. L.J. 1, at 58.

validity of Community measures. In this section the potential importance of such references will be explained.

2.(3)(a) The role of national courts in challenges to the validity of Community measures

The starting point for any discussion in relation to challenges to Community action is the cardinal principle of Community law that national courts may not declare Community acts invalid.[132] While it would be naïve to assume that national courts are never tempted to apply their own domestic standards to test the validity of Community measures,[133] that principle, a corollary of the doctrine of supremacy, is now well-established. How, then, is there a role for national courts in this area? The answer is the preliminary reference on validity.[134] On a reading of the text of Article 234 (ex Article 177) EC it appears that national courts, apart from courts against whose decisions there is no appeal, always have discretion whether to refer cases to the ECJ. However, the ECJ has provided a key limitation to this discretion, where questions of validity of EC law are concerned. Where a question of validity is raised in a national court, although the national judge may examine the measure, if she has doubts as to its validity, she is obliged to refer the issue to the ECJ.[135]

2.(3)(b) The importance of preliminary references on validity

The importance of preliminary references[136] on validity arises out of two factors. First, the peculiarities of the Community system of judicial review, are such that it is very difficult for individuals to challenge actions of general application directly before the ECJ. The text of the main provision governing such review, Article 230(4) (ex Article 173(4)) EC, makes it clear that it is only in limited circumstances that an individual may bring a direct challenge to the ECJ. In addition, the manner in which the provision has been interpreted and applied has led to a particularly restrictive understanding of *locus standi*.[137] In

---

[132] Case 314/85 *Foto-frost v. Hauptzollamt Lubeck-Ost* [1987] E.C.R. 4199.

[133] The German Constitutional Court has been most overt in asserting a residual power to scrutinise Community measures based on national standards. For a discussion see Kumm, "Who is the Final Arbiter of Constitutionality in Europe?: Three Conceptions of the Relationship Between the German Federal Constitutional Court and the European Court of Justice" (1999) C.M.L.Rev. 36 (1999) 351–386.

[134] Article 234(b) EC.

[135] Case 314/85 *Foto-Frost v. Hauptzollamt Lubeck-Ost* [1987] E.C.R. 4199. National courts may "consider the validity of a Community act and, if they consider the grounds put forward by the parties in support of invalidity are unfounded, or concludes that the measure is valid, they may reject them." Otherwise a preliminary reference must be made.

[136] On preliminary rulings see below Heffernan para. 3(3)(e).

[137] The seminal case is Case 25/62 *Plaumann v. Commission* [1963] E.C.R. 95, where the Court interpreted individual concern as relating to situation where measures affect individuals "by reason of certain attributes which are peculiar to them or by reason of circumstances in

certain areas, a softening of this approach has emerged,[138] but the hurdles are nonetheless insurmountable for many individual litigants. It has been stressed that the indirect route to challenge Community acts is a counterbalance to the restrictive Article 230(4) EC criteria.

In *Greenpeace*[139] the ECJ considered the argument that because the impugned decision could not be challenged in national courts, the applicant should, therefore, be granted standing under Article 230(4) EC. The Court rejected that argument on the facts, noting that the applicant had indeed brought national court proceedings.[140] In a subsequent case it was argued that it was possible to read the Court's analysis in *Greenpeace* as suggesting that an individual must be granted *locus standi* to challenge a Community measure directly where it was impossible to challenge the measure indirectly via proceedings before national courts.[141] While it remains to be seen whether this argument will be accepted, it nonetheless illustrates the importance of the preliminary reference on validity.

The second reason for the importance of such rulings relates to decen-tralised administration of Community law. Even if the *locus standi* criteria for direct challenges were expanded, many challenges would still arise in the context of national proceedings. As reiterated throughout this chapter, very often it is via national administration that individuals come into contact with Community law. Issues relating to actions of the national administration often raise questions as to the legality of national acts of implementation together with questions as to the basis of that action in Community law. It is appropriate in such cases that the dispute starts and finishes in a national court.

---

which they are differentiated from all other persons and by virtue of these factors distin-guishes them individually just as in the case of the person addressed." For a comprehensive critique of the restrictions on individual access to justice under Article 230(4) EC see Ward, *Judicial Review and the Rights of Private Parties in EC Law*, (OUP, 2000).

[138] Case C–358/89 *Extramet Industrie SA v. Council* [1991] E.C.R. I–2501; Case C–309/89 *Codorniu SA v. Council* [1994] E.C.R. I–1853.

[139] Case 321/95 P [1998] E.C.R. I–1651, at paras 32–34.

[140] *ibid.*

[141] This was the argument of the applicant in Case C–50/00 *UPA v. Council.* Advocate General Jacobs recently gave his Opinion (21 March 2002), taking this analysis as its starting point. However, he ultimately argues against reliance on national courts as the main conduit for challenges to Community acts. Rather he argues in favour of a radical re-interpretation of the concept of "individual concern" such that an applicant would be "individually concerned by a Community measure where the measure has, or is liable to have, a substantial adverse effect on his interests." (Opinion, para.102) Hot on the heels of this Opinion, came a judgment from the Court of First Instance going ever further. (Case T–177/01 *Jego-Quere et Cie SA*, May 3, 2002 " . . . a natural or legal person must be regarded as individually concerned by a Community measure of general application that concerns him directly if the measure in question affects his legal position, in a manner which is both definite and immediate, by restricting his rights or by imposing obligations on him." Para. 51. However, the ECJ's ruling in *UPA* (July 25, 2002) did not follow the Advocate General's opinion.

2.(3)(c) Preliminary references on validity from the Irish courts

An example of a reference on validity is *Duff*, considered above. The reference
in that case concerned not only the requirements of the Regulation at issue, but
also whether the Regulation itself was valid. It was entirely appropriate in the
circumstances that the consideration of the requirements of the general principles of Community law should require not only an examination of the proper
interpretation of the Regulation, but also its validity.[142] In contrast, in *Bosphorus*
there was no explicit challenge to the legality of the Regulation. Rather, it was
argued that fundamental rights general principles required an interpretation of
the measure which did not affect the applicant's property rights.

A further reference on validity was *Omega Air*.[143] This recent case concerned
the validity of a provision in a Council Regulation on aircraft noise standards.[144]
The High Court referred questions on the validity of the Regulation on March 23,
2000. This followed a similar reference on January 31, 2000 from the High Court
of Justice of England and Wales, Queen's Bench Division.[145] The cases were then
joined for hearing. The applicants argued that Article 2(2) of the Regulation
infringed the duty to state reasons under Article 253 (ex Article 190) EC, the
general principle of proportionality, the principle of equality and non-
discrimination, and the World Trade Organisation Technical Barriers to Trade
(TBT) Agreement. At issue was the prohibition of the registration and operation
of aeroplanes which had been fitted with "hush-kits" to bring their noise
emissions in line with relevant international standards. In its judgment the Court
held that the Regulation was valid, rejecting all of the applicant's arguments.
Nonetheless, the case is significant in that it demonstrates the receptiveness of the
national courts to arguments as to the validity of Community law, and the
willingness to take the *Foto-frost* obligation seriously.

2.(4) CONCLUSION

Judicial review proceedings take on different characteristics when issues of
Community law arise. Accordingly, it is of great concern to delimit just which
situations give rise to such a Community dimension. While certain cases are
clear, the scope of Community law is neither static nor certain. Thus, the issue
of determining the scope of Community law is likely to be the subject of some
controversy in the future.

---

[142] [1996] E.C.R. I–569.
[143] Case C–122/00 *Omega Air Ltd v. Irish Aviation Authority* March 12, 2002.
[144] Article 2(2) of Council Regulation (EC) No 925/1999 on the registration and operation
within the Community of certain types of civil subsonic jet aeroplanes which have been
modified and recertificated as meeting the standards of volume I, Part II, Chapter 3 of Annex
16 to the Convention on International Civil Aviation, third edition (July 1993) [1999] O.J.
L115/1 and L120/47.
[145] C–27/00.

Other issues of concern emerge. First, such reviews are characterised by the application of dual, if not triple standards (national, Community and ECHR) in terms of the grounds of review which may be invoked. This requires no small degree of finesse on the part of counsel and judges in dealing with such cases. In each case, the different strands of protection must be disentangled, in order to accord the appropriate degree of protection. *Duff* illustrates the benefits of attention to national and Community standards. However, in other cases, where national authorities are not afforded any discretion, national standards will not apply. Here the national authority is truly the "agent" of the Community. The only standard indisputably applicable is that embodied by the Community general principles, national standards set aside by Article 29.4.7 of the Constitution and/or the Community doctrine of supremacy. However, the Strasbourg decision in *Bosphorus* will elucidate the question as to whether ECHR standards have a role in such cases, notwithstanding the narrow scope for national manoeuvre.

Secondly, the standard of review to be exercised in such cases warrants careful attention to ensure that deferential standards do not degenerate from deference to disobedience. While Community law does not demand exacting standards of review in all cases, where substantive issues of Community law are concerned, such issues must be justiciable. The characterisation of determinations as purely factual may obscure the existence of important issues of Community law.

Thirdly, while the general principles of Community law are pervasive, their determinacy should not be overstated. The *Meagher* analysis is based on the false premise that they dictate certain policy outcomes. This appears to be a misapprehension which undermines the domestic separation of powers, and thereby national parliamentary scrutiny of Community implementation measures.

Finally, in raising Community issues in national judicial review proceedings, lawyers and judges must be alert to the possibility of references on validity. Such references are obligatory where there are real doubts as to the validity of the Community measure, and the role of the national judge is consequently reduced.

The role of the State has changed in the context of European integration. The national executive may undertake many different roles as a result of Community law. It may act as a dual Community/national authority subject to two sets of administrative laws. It may, alternatively, be a pure "agent" of Community law, devoid of policy role. Administrative bodies may claim to make factual determination, which in fact mask determinations as to the applicability of Community law. Most controversially, the national executive may be usurping national legislative functions under the guise of implementation of Community measures. It is for the courts to ensure that the complexities of Community law and the multiplicity of standards which govern the legality of these actions do not undermine the rule of law and the efficacy of national judicial review procedures.

BIBLIOGRAPHY

Afilalo, "How Far Francovich? Effective Judicial Protection and Associational Standing to Litigate Diffuse Interests in the European Union" Harvard Jean Monnet Center Working Paper, 1/98.

Boyron, "General Principles of Law and National Courts: Applying a *Jus Commune*" (1998) *ELRev* 171–178.

de Witte, "The past and future of the European Court of Justice in the protection of human rights", Alston, (ed), *EU and Human Rights*, (Oxford University Press, 1999), 859–897.

Delaney, *Judicial Review of Administrative Action*, (Round Hall Sweet & Maxwell, Dublin, 2001), 8–13.

Dillon, "The Mirage of EC Environmental Federalism in a Reluctant Member State Jurisdiction" (1999) *NYU Envtl LJ* 1.

Hogan & Morgan, *Administrative Law in Ireland*, (3rd ed., Round Hall Sweet & Maxwell, 1998), pp.643–644.

Hogan & Whelan, *Ireland and the European Union: Constitutional and Statutory Texts and Commentary*, (Sweet & Maxwell, 1995)

Hogan & Schuster, "Ireland" in Schwarze (ed.), *Administrative Law under European Influence,* (Nomos Verlagsgesellschaft, 1996)

Kumm, "Who is the Final Arbiter of Constitutionality in Europe?: Three Conceptions of the Relationship Between the German Federal Constitutional Court and the European Court of Justice" (1999) *CMLRev* 36 (1999) 351–386.

Lawson, "Confusion and Conflict? Diverging Interpretations of the European Convention on Human Rights in Strasbourg and Luxembourg" in Lawson, Rick & De Bloijs (eds) *The Dynamics of the Protection of Human Rights in Europe: Essays in Honour of Henry G. Schermers* (1994)

Lenaerts, "Fundamental Rights in the European Union" (2000) *ELRev* 575, 592.

MacEochaidh, "The application of the Environmental Impact Assessment Directive in Ireland" (2000) I.J.E.L. 4–22.

O'Keeffe, (ed.) *Judicial Review in European Union Law*, (Kluwer Law International, 2000)

O'Neill, "The Protection of Fundamental Rights in Scotland as a General Principle of Community Law – The Case of *Booker Aquaculture*" (2000) *European Human Rights Law Review* 18-32;

Schwarze, (ed.), *Administrative Law under European Influence,* (Sweet & Maxwell/Nomos, 1996).

Schwarze, *European Administrative Law*, (Sweet & Maxwell, 1992);

Szyszczak, "Judicial Review of Public Acts" (1998) *E.L.Rev* 89.

Tridimas, *General Principles of EC Law*, (OUP, 1999).

Usher, *General Principles of EC Law,* (Longman, 1998).

Ward, *Judicial Review and the Rights of Private Parties in EC Law,* (OUP, 2000).

Weiler, "The Transformation of Europe", (1991) 100 *Yale Law Journal* 2403 or updated in Weiler, J.H.H, *The Constitution of Europe*, (Cambridge University Press, 1999).

3. JUDICIAL REFORM UNDER THE TREATY OF NICE

LIZ HEFFERNAN*

3.(1) INTRODUCTION

In December 2000, the European heads of government, gathered in Nice, took several momentous steps in the constitutional development of the European Union. This article describes and assesses one significant substantive aspect of the Treaty of Nice,[1] namely, the proposed changes to the structure and operation of the Community Courts.[2]

The Treaty is the culmination of the Intergovernmental Conference (IGC) convened in February 2000 to tackle the so-called "Amsterdam leftovers", those issues of institutional reform left unresolved by the Treaty of Amsterdam. The central focus of IGC 2000, and of the publicity surrounding its negotiations, was reform of the political institutions, notably the Commission and the Council, in preparation for enlargement. Reform of the Community courts was a less conspicuous, but ultimately no less important, item on the agenda. In the case of the judicial branch, the new provisions are also inspired by an urgent need to remedy overburdened dockets and the attendant inefficiencies in the administration of justice. In Luxembourg, the problem of docket control is by no means new. For several years the European Court of Justice (ECJ) has been waging a losing battle to keep pace with the organic growth of Community litigation. The Court of First Instance (CFI), created in 1989, has played its part in alleviating caseload pressures. Nevertheless, the benefit of an additional Community forum has been offset by several factors,

* LL.B (Dub), LL.M. (Dalhousie), LL.M & J.S.D. (Chicago), B.L. Lecturer-in-law, Faculty of law, University College Dublin. The views expressed are purely personal and all errors remain the responsibility of the author.
1 Treaty of Nice Amending the Treaty on the European Union, the Treaties Establishing the European Communities and Certain Related Acts, Nice, February 26, 2001 [2001] O.J. C80/1.
2 See Heffernan, "The Treaty of Nice: Arming the Courts to Defend a European Bill of Rights?" (2002) 65 *Law and Contemp. Probs.* 189. Dashwood & Johnson (eds.), *The Future of the Judicial System of the European Union* (2001); De Búrca & Weiler (eds.), *The European Court of Justice* (2001); Johnson, "Judicial Reform and the Treaty of Nice" (2001) 38 C.M.L.R. 499; Dryberg, "What Should the Court of Justice be Doing?" (2001) 26 E.L.R. 291; Heffernan, "The Treaty of Nice and Reform of the Community Courts" (2001) 6 Bar Rev. 474; Rasmussen, "Remedying the Crumbling EC Judicial System" (2000) 37 C.M.L.R. 1071; Turner & Muñoz, "Revisiting the Judicial Architecture of the European Union" (1999–2000) 19 Y.E.L. 1; Costello, "Preliminary Reference Procedure and the 2000 Intergovernmental Conference" (1999) 21 D.U.L.J. 40.

such as the Kirchberg's unique multilingualism, the exclusivity of the Court's jurisdiction over requests for preliminary rulings, a steady rise in the number of appeals to the ECJ from decisions of the CFI and the challenging extensions of judicial jurisdiction introduced by the Treaties of Maastricht and Amsterdam. These days the CFI, no less than the ECJ, is working at the limits of its capacity; both courts are afflicted with burgeoning caseloads and the manifold side-effects of congestion.

From the point of view of the legal practitioner, an increase in the length of proceedings is the most telling symptom of the malaise. The duration of direct actions before the ECJ has been on the rise since 1996, a temporary decline following the creation of the CFI having run its course, and currently stands just shy of two years. The average length of proceedings before the CFI is over two years and an appeal to the ECJ an additional 19 months. The length of preliminary reference proceedings – on average over 21 months – is an even more serious indictment of the current system since the time and expense of the preliminary reference sojourn in Luxembourg must be added to the proceedings before the referring national court.[3] For the private litigant, for whom the national court is the natural point of access to the Community legal system, this state of affairs is clearly unsatisfactory.

3.(2) THE ROAD TO NICE

There are several drawbacks to the intergovernmental conference as a vehicle for reform of the judicial branch. As its title suggests, the process is akin to international treaty-making. Participation is limited to the Member States and issues are tabled and ultimately decided through barter and compromise among the national delegations. The mood is "make or break": the participants must broker a deal within a designated time-frame or live with the *status quo*. The proceedings are less open and transparent than national parliamentary proceedings and lack the democratic credentials associated with the amendment of national constitutions. The intergovernmental conference is, quintessentially, a political thicket.[4]

IGC 2000 followed a tradition among the Member States of prioritising reform of the political institutions over reform of the courts. Notwithstanding the extent of the caseload crisis, judicial reform was not tackled at Amsterdam nor included in the initial agenda of IGC 2000. Eventually, it was added to the miscellany of secondary items tackled at the Conference, but only after the

---

[3] These figures are drawn from the official statistics in relation to judicial activity at the ECJ and the CFI for 2000. See *http://www.curia.eu.int/ en/pei/rapan.htm*

[4] The current Convention on the Future of Europe, combined with the various national fora on Europe, suggest a more open and democratic preface to IGC 2004.

judiciary publicised the issue, both officially[5] and extra-judicially,[6] and the President of the Court, Judge Rodriguez Iglesias, took the unprecedented step of airing his concerns in the press.[7] Throughout the Conference, the future of the Community courts was overshadowed by controversy surrounding the fate of the Commission and Council. It is fair to say that, given the sum of tasks to be completed, the Conference was neither able nor disposed to give reform of the judicial system the attention it deserved.[8]

The sources to which the Conference referred in deciding the future of the Community courts were also limited. Reforming the judicial system had been the subject of low-key debate in academic and practising circles for several years[9] but debate at IGC 2000 focused principally on the submissions of the Community Courts,[10] the Commission[11] and individual Member States.[12] The European Bar was also represented in the guise of a report by the Council of the Bars and Law Societies of the European Union (CCBE) which shed some welcome light on the perspective of the litigant and practitioner.[13] Overall, the Conference did not approach reform from a *tabula rasa* but rather considered only somewhat conservative ideas drawn from conventional sources.

---

[5] Court of Justice and Court of First Instance, *The Future of the Judicial System of the European Union* (*Proposals and Reflections* (1999) (hereinafter *Courts' Discussion Paper*).

[6] See, *e.g.* Cooke, "European Judicial Architecture: Back to the Drawing Board" (1999) 5 Bar Rev. 14.

[7] Statement of the President of the ECJ , *The EC Court of Justice and Institutional Reform of the European Union* (April 2000).

[8] See Yataganas, *The Treaty of Nice: The Sharing of Power and the Institutional Balance in the European Union – A Continental Perspective* (Harvard Law School Jean Monnet Working Paper No. 1/01), http:///www.jeanmonnetprogram.org/papers/papers01.html (noting that reform of the courts was one of the less controversial chapters in the negotiations and that agreement was reached relatively quickly).

[9] See generally, Arnull, "Judicial Architecture or Judicial Folly? The Challenge Facing the European Union" (1999) 24 E.L.R. 516; Heffernan, "A Discretionary Jurisdiction for the European Court of Justice?" (1999) 34 Irish Jurist (n.s.) 148; British Institute of International and Comparative Law, *The Role and Future of the European Court of Justice* (1996); van Gerven, "The Role and Structure of the European Judiciary Now and in the Future" (1996) 21 E.L.R. 211; Scorey, "A New Model for the Communities' Judicial Architecture in the New Union" (1996) 21 E.L.R. 224; Jacques & Weiler, On the Road to European Union – A New Judicial Architecture: An Agenda for the Intergovernmental Conference (1996) 27 C.M.L.R. 224.

[10] See *Courts' Discussion Paper,* above n. 5; *Contribution by the Court of Justice and the Court of First Instance to the Intergovernmental Conference* (2000).

[11] See, *e.g.* Commission, *Report by the Working Party on the Future of the European Communities' Court System* (2000) (hereinafter *Due Report*); *Intergovernmental Conference: Commission Presents Additional Contribution on Reform of the Community Courts,* IP/00/213 (March 1, 2000).

[12] See, *e.g. IGC 2000: Contribution from the French Delegation on Reform of the Judicial System of the European Union,* CONFER 4726/00 (March 27, 2000).

[13] *Contribution from the CCBE for the Intergovernmental Conference,* CONFER/VAR 3966 (May 18, 2000).

Certain official reports proved particularly influential in shaping the reforms ultimately adopted, as well as those rejected, at Nice. The ECJ and the CFI published their views on the dilemma in a paper on the future of the judicial system in May 1999.[14] The Courts' paper was cast as a springboard for debate; the tone was reflective rather than directive, the Courts discussing the pros and cons of various reforms without endorsing any one, much less presenting a vision of where they see themselves 10 or 20 years down the line. The Commission took up the reins by setting up an independent working party under the chairmanship of former president of the ECJ, Ole Due. The *Due Report*, published in January 2000, contained a more comprehensive and rigorous analysis but, ultimately, settled for a relatively conservative approach to reform.[15] Finally, the Friends of the Presidency Group, consisting of legal experts from the Member States and Community institutions, was more intimately involved in IGC 2000, monitoring the negotiations, submitting draft texts and hammering out compromise formulae.[16]

3.(3) THE REFORMS

An eclectic range of judicial reforms was mooted in advance of IGC 2000. Proposals ranged from modest tinkering with current practice and procedure to radical ideas for restructuring the system. Several minor but important changes have been introduced since then, such as empowering the ECJ to issue practice directions[17] and to dispense with oral hearings in certain cases[18] and extending the circumstances in which it may respond to requests for preliminary rulings by reasoned order.[19] Similar steps have been taken to expedite proceedings before the CFI.

The following were among the broader issues canvassed at IGC 2000: limiting the number of judges on the ECJ and CFI; giving both courts the power to amend their Rules of Procedure; making the CFI the principal forum for direct actions; establishing specialised courts or tribunals; and introducing

---

[14] See *Courts' Discussion Paper*, above n. 5.
[15] See *Due Report*, above n. 11.
[16] See, *e.g.* Friends of the Presidency Group (Court of Justice and Court of First Instance), *IGC 2000: Proceedings and Amendments to be made with regard to the Court of Justice and the Court of First Instance*, CONFER 4747/00 (31 May 2000); Friends of the Presidency Group (Court of Justice and Court of First Instance), *IGC 2000: Interim Report on Amendments to be Made to the Treaties with regard to the Court of Justice and the Court of First Instance*, CONFER 4747/00 (March 2000).
[17] Rules of Procedure (hereinafter Rules), art. 125a. These practice directions relate in particular to the submission of pleadings and the preparation and conduct of oral argument.
[18] *ibid.*, arts. 44a & 104(4). The parties now bear the burden of justifying oral argument.
[19] *ibid.*, art. 104(3). The ECJ may respond by way of reasoned order where the question referred is identical to a question on which the Court has already ruled, or where the answer may be clearly deduced from existing case law or admits of no reasonable doubt.

a mechanism to filter appeals within the Community court system. Understandably, the bulk of attention was devoted to the preliminary ruling procedure, the very heart of the problem. Suggested reforms included limiting the referral powers of the national courts, giving the ECJ a discretionary jurisdiction over requests for preliminary rulings, conferring a preliminary rulings jurisdiction on the CFI, and establishing specialised preliminary rulings courts.

A dramatic overhaul of the judicial system was rejected virtually from the outset. In all likelihood, the decision to eschew radical reform was influenced by the cautious tenor of the *Courts' Discussion Paper* and the *Due Report*. The reticence of the Conference to grasp the proverbial nettle is also explained by the procedural labyrinth of reform methodology. At issue for the Conference was not only the nature and extent of reform but also the means and timing. Should the Conference redesign the system or maintain the current structure? Should it adopt any one or a combination of various proposed changes? Should the Conference decide these issues or delegate decision-making to the Council? And should these decisions be taken now or postponed until the next intergovernmental conference? Given the backdrop to IGC 2000, coupled with the Member States' propensity to "wait and see," it is not altogether surprising that the Conference chose the least adventurous answers to these questions. At the end of the day, the Conference opted to renovate rather than redesign the judicial architecture and, at the same time, to make the system more adaptable to change in the future. Thus, it adopted some proposals, rejected others, left to the Council the resolution of many of the details, and declared the debate on-going.

3.(3)(a) Flexibility

The role and operation of the Community courts is set out in the EC Treaty, the Statute of the Court of Justice (which is contained in a separate protocol to the Treaty) and the Rules of Procedure. The division of labour among the three reflects a certain hierarchy, not unlike regulation of the Irish courts under the Constitution, legislation and court rules. The European judicial code, however, is considerably more rigid. Many of the details surrounding the day-to-day operation of the Community courts, which could safely be housed in the Rules, are set out in the two primary sources and can be revised only through the cumbersome process of treaty amendment. Amendment of the Rules is more straightforward, but only in relative terms; changes in the Rules require the unanimous approval of the Council.

The Treaty of Nice re-organises these legal instruments in a sensible bid to rationalise the judicial code. In the first place, certain provisions will be transferred from the Statute to the Rules and vice versa, to ensure a proper hierarchy among the various provisions. By virtue of the second, and more important development, the method of amending the Statute and the Rules will be modified to facilitate future changes to the judicial code. The Council will be empowered to amend all parts of the Statute (except for Title I which deals with the appointment and replacement of judges and Advocates General) which will enable the Community to make substantial changes to the judicial system without recourse to treaty amendment.

The Conference was less generous with respect to the Rules: the Council will continue to have the final say over amendments, although its approval will be based on qualified majority vote rather than unanimity. The failure to confer the Community courts with autonomy over their Rules – a power that other courts, such as the European Court of Human Rights or the United States Supreme Court take for granted – is a setback, inspired by an overabundance of caution.[20] To an extent, the Courts have themselves to blame, having endorsed the "qualified majority vote option" as a fallback position.[21] The underlying premise, namely, that the Member States have reason to fear relinquishing control over the Rules, is difficult to defend, particularly since the Treaty of Nice also provides for the transfer from the Rules to the Statute of certain matters of special concern to the Member States.[22] Our lament is not that the Council is likely to stand in the way of change (particularly when acting by qualified majority), but that Council approval is precisely the kind of bureaucratic obstacle that the system can do without. Given the eclecticism of Community jurisdiction, it is in the Rules that flexibility is needed most.

Finally, it is worth noting that these changes to the judicial code are more than a housekeeping exercise. The "flexibility" promised by the Treaty of Nice is also a shorthand for the Conference's reform philosophy which eschewed a major overhaul of the system in favour of on-going, piecemeal reform. The changes crafted at Nice are not offered as an end in themselves but rather as a first, but by no means insubstantial, step in the process of reform. Some provisions will have immediate effect, others will be defined only in practice and others still have been left aside for another day.

3.(3)(b) Composition of the courts

3.(3)(b)(i) The Court of Justice

One possible and often-touted solution to the growing caseload of the Community courts is the appointment of additional judges. Extending the bench, however, is a deceptively thorny issue. Too many judges could lead to a judicial circus, undermining confidence in the administration of justice,

---

[20] Some delegations were in favour of the change (or, at least, did not come out against it). See, *e.g. Contribution from the Dutch Government – An Agenda for Internal Reforms in the European Union*, CONFER 4720/00 (March 6, 2000); *Information Note from the Italian Delegation, 2000 IGC: Italy's Position*, CONFER 4717/00 (March 3, 2000). However, the majority of the delegations expressed considerable reservations about giving the Courts the power to amend their rules. See Friends of the Presidency Interim Report, above n. 16, p.3.

[21] See *Courts' Discussion Paper*, above n. 5, p.14.

[22] Such as the provisions guaranteeing equality in the use of national languages before the Community courts.

particularly at the ECJ. As the Court warned, at the last enlargement of the Union, an increase in its current membership of 15[23] could transform the plenary session from a collegiate court to a deliberative assembly, while extensive recourse to decision-making by chambers could pose a threat to the consistency of Community law.[24] Of course, the problem is not merely one of numbers. The composition of the ECJ is defined by an unwritten nationality requirement: one judge per Member State has always been the convention, subject to the need for an uneven number of judges for purposes of decision.[25] While the practice ensures a measure of familiarity within the Community judiciary with the various national legal cultures and languages, it also necessitates an increase in the size of the bench with each new accession. With the prospect of enlargement to a Union of 20 or even 30 Member States, the possibility of abandoning the nationality requirement, in favour, for example, of a system of rotational appointments, had been mooted. Not surprisingly, however, it is a convention that the Member States are anxious to retain.

The issue of national representation in Community government is uniquely delicate and dominated negotiations on reform of each of the Community institutions under discussion at IGC 2000. In deciding the future size of the Commission, the Conference settled on a compromise solution: maintain the practice of one commissioner per Member State but restructure the institution so as to limit decision-making by the whole. The Conference applied the same model to the Community courts. The new version of Article 221 entrenches the principle that the ECJ shall consist of "one judge per Member State," but tempers its effect by providing that the Court shall sit in chambers and, only exceptionally, in plenary session. Thus, as between the seemingly irreconcilable demands of operational efficacy and national representation, IGC 2000 came down squarely on the side of the Member States.[26]

It is doubtful that the Conference was wise to maintain and, indeed, entrench the nationality requirement at the ECJ. Putting aside the propriety of this model for the Commission, what makes sense for a political institution does not necessarily hold true for a court. The administration of justice has its own special concerns, such as the quality and impartiality of judicial adjudication, which place a higher premium on size than national interest. The benefit of a full panoply of nationalities must be balanced against the cost in terms of functional capacity and jurisprudential integrity.

---

[23] EC Treaty, Art. 223 (ex Art. 167) stipulates that the ECJ shall consist of 15 judges, suitably qualified. The judges choose a president from among their number for a three-year term.

[24] *Report of the Court of Justice on Certain Aspects of the Application of the Treaty on European Union* (May 1995), p.16.

[25] For example, prior to the accession of Austria, Finland and Sweden in 1995, an additional judge from one of the five larger Member States was appointed to ensure a bench of 13 members.

[26] All but a couple of the delegations were unwilling to relinquish the nationality requirement. See Friends of the Presidency Interim Report, above n. 16, p.10.

As a practical matter, the significance of one judge per Member State may be more symbolic than real. When the ECJ sits in chambers, which it increasingly does, the participation of a judge from a particular jurisdiction is not guaranteed. Nor should it matter whether a particular Member State has judicial representation on a case; the judges should be (and should be seen to be) objective and impartial. Moreover, the national expertise that a judge brings to the ECJ, though beneficial, is hardly decisive. The ECJ has repeatedly stressed that it is not in the business of deciding national law – the preliminary reference procedure is premised on a neat distinction between national and Community law and competence. Judicial appointments aside, there are other means to enhance institutional familiarity with the various national systems, for example, through the role of support staff, particularly in the field of legal research. It is probable, from the perspective of the private litigant and of the public at large, that the issue of language, conducting legal proceedings and publishing judgments in the various Community languages, is more important than national representation on the Court itself.

These sentiments neither negate the importance of symbolism in the Community context nor belittle diversity as a virtue in the judicial scheme. Whatever its size, the membership of the Court should reflect the diversity of the Community, in nationality as well as other terms, to the utmost degree practicable. It cannot be gainsaid that, the *current* Court benefits from absolute national representation, both in terms of its internal workings and its external stature. The issue, however, is whether a future court, servicing a Union of 20 or 30 Member States, can afford the luxury of automatic and absolute national representation. The system of judicial appointments, however devised, must preserve equality of representation as among the Member States but it must do so in a manner that respects other virtues on which the integrity of the ECJ rests, such as collective deliberation, even-handed adjudication and a reasoned jurisprudence.

At the very least, the Conference could have settled on a compromise: including the Advocates General in the distribution of judicial posts at the ECJ. Currently, Advocates General are appointed under a distinct process which is conditioned in turn by national representation. Five of the nine Advocates General are nominated by the five largest Member States, while the remainder are drawn from the other Member States on a rotational basis.[27] The role and stature of the office is such that the periodic substitution of an Advocate General for a judge should not be a bitter pill for the Member States to swallow.[28] It would certainly make a difference to the numbers: the current

---

[27] The five Advocates General from the largest Member States are appointed for a renewable six-year term whereas the other posts are tenable for one term only.

[28] Advocates General are generally regarded as "members" of the Court, even though they lack ultimate decision-making authority. See Jacobs, "Advocates General and Judges in the European Court of Justice: Some Personal Reflections" in *Judicial Review in European Union*

arrangement (15 judges and nine Advocates General) could accommodate a membership of 23 Member States and, in all likelihood, the number of Advocates General will increase at some point in the future. However pragmatic, this idea never got off the ground at IGC 2000. For the larger Member States, it would involve forsaking a double entitlement – to both a judge and an Advocate General – in favour of just one or the other. For most of the smaller Member States, any diminution in the current level of national representation would raise the spectre of marginalisation within the Community, whether real or imagined. Against this backdrop, it comes as no surprise that the Member States, convened as IGC 2000, opted to endorse the *status quo*.

To allay concerns over the ECJ's functional cohesion, the Conference established a new structure, designed to accommodate a uniquely large and potentially unwieldy bench.[29] Currently, the ECJ sits as a grand plenum of 15 judges, as a petit plenum of nine or 11 judges, or as a chamber of five or three judges. Adjudication in petit plenum and chambers has increased in tandem with the workload and is fast becoming the norm. Grand plenum is reserved only for the most exceptional cases.[30] Under the new arrangement, the ECJ will sit in chambers of three and five judges, in a new grand chamber of 11 and in plenary session.[31] This is not a tremendous leap from the current structure, but it involves two important modifications.

In the first place, the grand chamber will serve as the storm centre in the new arrangement, handling cases currently heard in petit and grand plenum. Whereas privileged parties, a Member State or Community institution, will no longer have automatic access to the full court, they will be entitled to have their cases heard by the grand chamber. If the real judicial power is wielded in the grand chamber, we can expect that its composition will prove controversial. The Conference sensed as much and whereas under the current practice the petit plenum is constituted on an informal, *ad hoc* basis, the membership of the grand chamber will be imprinted in the Statute. Presided over by the President of the Court, it will comprise the presidents of the chambers of five judges (there are currently two such chambers) and other judges appointed under conditions laid down in the Rules, and it will function with a quorum of nine.[32] Both the President of the Court and the presidents of the five-judge chambers will hold their offices for three-year renewable terms

---

Law: Liber Americorum in Honour of Lord Slynn of Hadley (O'Keefe and Bavasso ed., vol. I, 2000), 17, p.18.

[29] The new structure is set out in the new Statute and, so located, can be amended only by a unanimous vote of the Council. As a result, the Court will no longer determine its own structure, although obviously the judges will determine how cases are assigned among the Court's various formations.

[30] A Member State or Community institution that is a party to proceedings enjoys the right to a plenary hearing. See EC Treaty, Arts. 221 & 223 (ex Arts. 165 & 167); Rules, art. 95(1).

[31] New version of the Statute, art. 16.

[32] *ibid.*, at arts. 16 & 17.

and, aside from their tenure on the grand chamber, will carry out important tasks within their respective spheres of influence. Thus, there is a danger that the new arrangement will create a sense of judicial hierarchy at the ECJ.[33]

The second significant development is that the plenary session will become very much the exception. The new version of the Statute provides that the ECJ will sit as a "full court" in certain specified proceedings or where, after hearing the views of the Advocate General, the Court considers that a case is "of exceptional importance."[34] Precisely how the full Court will function is an open question. A packed plenary session is curiously at odds with the ECJ's valued tradition of collegiate decision-making. At the same time, adjudication of these exceptional cases by a number less than the full complement may raise doubts about the unity of the bench and the equality of national representation. Looking at the overall structure, a more serious concern is whether the Court, sitting in its various satellite formations, will be able to maintain the jurisprudential integrity that is central to its constitutional mandate.

3.(3)(b)(ii) The Court of First Instance

The structure of the CFI is far less controversial. The Conference recognised that increasing the CFI's membership is a less risky proposition, not least because any threat to the consistency of Community law can be tackled on appeal by the ECJ. Thus, the new Article 224 provides that the CFI shall comprise "at least one judge per Member State." Given the CFI's expanded role under the Treaty of Nice, a larger bench will be essential.[35] Apparently, the Council has given the nod to an increase of six judges on the CFI, although a system for rotating the additional appointments among the Member States has yet to be settled.[36] Provision is also made for the CFI to sit in various formations, in accordance with its Rules of Procedure: in chambers of three and five judges, in a grand chamber, as a full court and as a single judge.[37]

For now, practice at the CFI is likely to continue much as before; over time, the CFI will grow within its current structure, no doubt continuing the trend in favour of adjudication by chambers or a single judge. Clearly, an increase in the CFI's labour and responsibility warrants a corresponding increase in finance and administrative resources. A more fundamental question, however, is how the CFI should structure and equip itself to meet the demands of its extended mandate. Thus, the time is ripe for a thorough review of its operational capacity and working practices.

---

[33] See comments of Mr. Justice Nial Fennelly, *Treaty of Nice: Reform of the Community Courts*, pp.7–8, Conference at the Irish Centre for European Law, February 2001.

[34] New version of the Statute at art. 16.

[35] This seems to have been the popular view among the delegations at IGC 2000. See Friends of the Presidency Interim Report, above n. 16, p.11.

[36] See Commission, *Memorandum to the Members of the Commission Summary of the Treaty of Nice* Brussels, Jan. 18, 2001 SEC (2001) 99, p.5.

[37] New version of the Statute, art. 50.

One possible reform is the creation of specialised chambers at the CFI; the judges at the CFI would remain generalists but would be assigned to specialist panels periodically. Specialised chambers could prove useful if confined to discrete fields which tend to dominate the CFI's docket, such as staff cases or, potentially, trademark cases.[38] Community causes of action, however, are not premised on clear subject-matter distinctions and it would be vital to ensure that specialisation did not presage strict substantive categorisation and a corresponding transformation of the CFI from a court of general jurisdiction to a mere collection of specialised tribunals.

Another interesting idea is a shift of emphasis in favour of settlement.[39] The small but increasing number of cases settled prior to decision at the CFI hint at the potentially beneficial role that mediation could play in proceedings before the CFI. In this regard, the prospective judicial panel for staff cases could provide fertile ground for experimentation.

3.(3)(b)(iii) Advocates General

The Conference resisted calls to reduce or even eliminate the role of the Advocate General at the ECJ, and sensibly so.[40] The Advocate General's opinion can, and generally does, exert a beneficial influence on deliberation at the Court and on the accessibility of its jurisprudence. However, occasionally, it can be redundant, for example, where proceedings are uncontested or relatively straightforward. In such instances, resources are needlessly expended and proceedings unjustifiably lengthened. The Treaty of Nice remedies this state of affairs by introducing an element of discretion. Under the new version of Article 223, the Advocate General will issue an opinion only on cases which "require his involvement." Whether the involvement of an Advocate General is required will be a matter for the Court, rather than the Advocate General, and will turn on whether the case raises some new point of law. Relieved of the duty to opine purely as a matter of form, the Advocates General should be free to concentrate on the more complex or testing cases, where their contribution is needed most.

Finally, under the new version of Article 224, the Council may, at some future time, make provision in the Statute for the CFI to be assisted by Advocates General. The CFI has rarely availed of its existing power to appoint one of its own to perform the function *ad hoc* in a particular case. Given the

---

[38] See *Due Report*, above n. 11, p.49.

[39] See generally Schonberg, "Coping with Judicial Over-Load: The Role of Mediation and Settlement in Community Court Litigation" (2001) 38 C.M.L.R. 333; Meij, "Guest Editorial: Architects or Judges? Some Comments in Relation to the Current Debate" (2000) 37 C.M.L.R. 1039, p.1042 (lamenting that recent developments in the field of mediation and alternative dispute resolution have escaped the reform debate).

[40] The number of Advocates General will remain unchanged and may even be increased by unanimous vote of the Council at the request of the Court.

CFI's essential trial function, the formal appointment of Advocates General seems neither necessary nor desirable.

3.(3)(c) Direct actions

3.(3)(c)(i) Extending the jurisdiction of the CFI

The jurisdiction of the CFI over direct actions has gradually increased over the years. Initially, the CFI was conferred with jurisdiction over limited categories of direct actions brought by natural or legal persons, principally in relation to staff and anti-dumping cases.[41] The jurisdiction was subsequently extended to cover all actions brought by natural or legal persons. Thus, at the current time, the CFI hears direct actions brought by private parties (individuals or corporations), and the Court actions instituted by privileged parties (Member States or Community institutions).[42]

The new version of Article 225 states that the CFI shall have jurisdiction over most classes of direct action, "with the exception of those assigned to a judicial panel and those reserved in the Statute for the Court of Justice." Although it falls short of declaring the CFI the first or primary judicial forum for all direct actions, Article 225 embodies an important change in emphasis: trial and adjudication by the CFI will become the rule rather than the exception. This is a natural and desirable development. As the legal system matures, it is appropriate that the CFI and the ECJ pursue their respective primary vocations, the former as a general trial court and the latter as an appellate supreme court.

What does this reform mean in practical terms? The Treaty of Nice changes nothing in itself; the details will be thrashed out in the Council and implemented by way of amendment to the Statute. Thus, this is one of the important reforms sketched only in principle by the Treaty. In a declaration attached to the Treaty, the Conference calls upon the ECJ and the Commission to consider the division of competence between the two courts and to tender proposals when the Treaty enters into force.[43] A meaningful improvement in working conditions at the ECJ will require a marked decrease in its responsibilities over direct actions. Hopefully, the ECJ and the Commission will propose as much.

When the CFI's jurisdiction is broadened, the change will affect its personal, as opposed to subject matter, jurisdiction. In other words, the CFI will continue to hear the same categories of cases but its competence will

---

[41] See EC Treaty, Art. 225 (ex Art.168a); Council Decision 88/591 establishing a Court of First Instance of the European Communities [1988] O.J. L319/1.

[42] EC Treaty, Art. 220 (ex Art.164) and 225a (ex Art.168).

[43] See Declaration on Article 225 of the Treaty Establishing the European Community, [2001] O.J. C80/79. The issue is not addressed in any detail in the reports of the Friends of the Presidency, above n. 16. The ECJ has taken a first step with the publication of a working

extend to at least some of the suits involving privileged parties, which are currently heard by the ECJ. How much of this extended jurisdiction, *i.e.* direct actions involving privileged parties, will be left to the ECJ is unclear.

3.(3)(c)(ii) Defining the ECJ's residual jurisdiction

The Nice reforms nudge the Community Courts in the direction of a conventional judicial hierarchy (comprising the ECJ, the CFI and judicial panels) involving a division of trial and appellate functions. These labels are not entirely helpful, however, given that the bulk of the ECJ's docket derives from the *sui generis* preliminary reference procedure.[44] Moreover, post-Nice, the ECJ will continue to exercise an unconventionally sizeable original or first instance jurisdiction, comprising most, if not all, preliminary references as well as enforcement actions,[45] advisory opinions[46] and other miscellaneous proceedings. In the case of direct actions (actions for judicial review of Community acts[47] and omissions[48] and actions for compensation),[49] relinquishing original jurisdiction is a simpler and less controversial step. There is no good reason why the CFI should not become the first judicial forum for direct actions. Any doubts about its ability to hear and determine proceedings for judicial review have been assuaged by its proven record and there remains the safeguard of appeals to the ECJ on points of law.[50] The time is ripe for the privileged parties to relinquish automatic access to the ECJ in exchange for a more robust judicial system[51] in which appellate proceedings are enhanced by the existence of a record below.

It has been suggested that that the ECJ should retain original jurisdiction over "important" direct actions.[52] However, defining jurisdiction *a priori* using a benchmark as elusive as "importance" seems a hopeless quest. For example, by virtually any yardstick, proceedings for annulment of Community legislation are "important", particularly where the legislation applies generally throughout the Community. These proceedings are sufficiently ubiquitous, however, that it would be false economy to entrust them to the ECJ alone. In theory we might conjure a division of labour between the ECJ and the CFI

---

document on the re-allocation of jurisdiction over direct actions. See http://www.curia.eu.int/en/txts/intergov/sn_4716.htm.

[44] EC Treaty, Art. 234 (ex Art. 177).
[45] EC Treaty, Art. 226–228 (ex Art. 169–171).
[46] EC Treaty, Art. 300(6) (ex Art. 228(6).
[47] EC Treaty, Art. 230 (ex Art. 173).
[48] EC Treaty, Art. 232 (ex Art. 175).
[49] EC Treaty, Arts. 235, 238 & 288 (ex Arts. 178, 181 & 215)
[50] EC Treaty, Art. 225a (ex Art. 168).
[51] For a different view, see Contribution from the French Delegation, above n. 12, p.12, which defended the current division of proceedings between the ECJ and the CFI on grounds of simplicity and clarity.
[52] See *Due Report*, above n. 11, p.25.

based on the normative value of the various Community acts but the Community's legislative structure is not patterned on a categorical normative distinction. Nor does the shorthand reference to general and specific legislation capture the distinction; normative issues surface across the board, before both the ECJ and the CFI.

The current regime invokes an alternative indicator of importance, namely, the identity of the parties: privileged applicants institute proceedings in the ECJ and private applicants in the CFI. Party labels provide a convenient means of assigning cases but, standing alone, can prove a poor barometer of the need for direct access to the ECJ. Litigation involving the Member States and Community institutions often raises serious constitutional questions, but not routinely so and, conversely, those same questions may surface before the CFI. A further vagary of the current division is the possibility of simultaneous challenges, in the CFI and the ECJ, at the behest of private and privileged litigants, respectively.

Direct access to the ECJ, if permitted at all, should be limited to cases of manifest urgency where, in the words of the Due Report, "a rapid judgment is essential to avoid serious problems in the proper functioning of the Community institutions."[53] The examples cited include actions for annulment of acts adopting the Community budget, acts suspending Member State rights, and acts authorising closer co-operation among certain Member States. Allowing direct access to the ECJ in these cases makes procedural sense, although it may be difficult to compile *a priori* an exhaustive list of similar, exceptional cases. As an alternative or, indeed, additional safeguard, the CFI might be afforded a catch-all discretion to decline jurisdiction in favour of the ECJ in any particular case.

3.(3)(c)(iii) Appeals

The Treaty of Nice is conspicuously silent on the subject of appeals from the CFI's decisions relating to direct actions,[54] so it can be assumed that the current system, whereby the parties and privileged interveners are automatically entitled to appeal on points of law, will continue unchanged. Presumably, the declaration attached to the Treaty concerning the division of competence between the two Courts will be read as an invitation for the ECJ and the Commission to include recommendations for limiting appeals.

One promising idea, sadly overlooked at IGC 2000, is the introduction of a discretionary jurisdiction for the ECJ, along the lines of the U.S. Supreme Court's *certiorari* jurisdiction.[55] A European *certiorari* could target all

---

[53] *ibid.*

[54] Notwithstanding considerable debate on the issue at IGC 2000. See *Friends of the Presidency Interim Report*, above n. 16 , p.9.

[55] 28 U.S.C. secs. 1254(1) & 1257; Sup. Ct. Rule 10. For an earlier and more cautious view, see Heffernan, above n. 9.

decisions of the CFI, whether in the context of direct actions, preliminary rulings or appeals from judicial panels. It would enable the ECJ to hear any case of its choosing while, at the same time, prioritising its agenda and maximising the use of its time and resources. The prospect of an enhanced appellate jurisdiction underscores the need for some method of case selection. From a pragmatic standpoint, a screening mechanism would ensure that the burden of the ECJ's original jurisdiction does not resurface in appellate form.

The Community should also consider limiting the right of privileged parties to lodge appeals. Currently, any Member State or Community institution may appeal a decision of the CFI, even if they are not party to the proceedings. In the case of the Commission, its function as guardian of the EC and EU Treaties[56] justifies the role. While it is appropriate that the Member States and other institutions retain the right to intervene in proceedings before the CFI and the ECJ, it is questionable whether they should enjoy the right to appeal a decision not so appealed by the parties.

3.(3)(d) Judicial panels

The most innovative change to the current system is the introduction of a new form of judicial institution, the specialised judicial panel. Under a new treaty provision, Article 225a, the Council "may create judicial panels to hear and determine at first instance certain classes of action or proceeding brought in specific areas." The judicial panels will be attached to the CFI and their jurisdiction and *modus operandi* determined at a later date by Council decision.

3.(3)(d)(i) Context

The concept of specialised judicial panels was inspired in part by the burden of staff cases which has dogged case management in Luxembourg over the years. In a Declaration attached to the Treaty of Nice, the Member States called on the Council to set up a judicial panel for staff cases as soon as possible.[57] The field of Community employment is particularly amenable to specialised institutions and procedures. Composed of lawyers and assessors, the proposed panel will function as an administrative court although its powers may extend to conciliation.[58] Another likely candidate is trademark cases, currently adjudicated by the Alicante Boards of Appeals established under the Community Trademark Regulation.[59] Looking to the future, judicial panels

---

[56] See EC Treaty, Art. 211 (ex Art. 155).
[57] Declaration on Article 225A, [2001] O.J. C80/79.
[58] See *Courts' Discussion Paper*, above n. 5, p.16.
[59] See Council Regulation 40/94 on the Community Trademark [1994] O.J. L11/1. Applications for registration of marks are filed with the Office for Harmonisation in the Internal Market (OHIM) in Alicante. Currently, the decisions of the OHIM may be appealed to the OHIM

may complement the creation of independent Community agencies in scientific and technical fields such as air and maritime safety and food safety.

Specialisation within the judicial system is an attractive development and one familiar to continental lawyers. However, it should not be given free rein. Most cases are not amenable to simple categorisation and it may be naïve to assume that the factors that lend staff and intellectual property cases to specialised treatment apply to other, wide-ranging areas of Community law.[60]

3.(3)(d)(ii) Appeals

Judicial panels will be a welcome complement to the extended role of the CFI over direct actions and hold the promise of significant caseload relief in areas that are a particular drain on judicial resources. The efficacy of this reform, however, will depend in large measure on appellate procedures. Article 225a states that "decisions given by judicial panels may be subject to a right of appeal on points of law only, or, when provided for in the decision establishing the panel, a right of appeal also on matters of fact, before the Court of First Instance." This wording is somewhat ambiguous; it is not clear whether the Council, in establishing a panel, may opt to limit appeals altogether, for example, through a filter or leave to appeal mechanism.

Further uncertainty surrounds the possibility of subsequent review by the ECJ. The new version of Article 225(2) provides that decisions by the CFI on appeal from judicial panels may "exceptionally" be subject to review by the Court "where there is a serious risk of the unity or consistency of Community law being affected." The assessment of a serious risk to the unity or consistency of Community law is made by the First Advocate General, who may propose that the ECJ review the CFI's decision. Thus, under the new regime, the First Advocate General will have a decisive gate-keeping role; cases will not reach the ECJ without his or her say-so. Where the First Advocate General does make a proposal, the ultimate decision in favour or against review lies with the ECJ.[61]

The same procedure will apply to review of the CFI's decisions in response to preliminary references from national courts. Preliminary references, of

---

Board of Appeals and from there to the CFI and on to the Court of Justice. Affording the OHIM Board of Appeals the status of a judicial panel would be a logical step. Its decisions could be appealed to the CFI and, in turn, only exceptionally, to the ECJ. The possibility of creating a judicial panel for cases relating to the Community patent has also been mooted.

[60] The *Due Report* canvassed the possibility of specialised regimes for other fields, such as private international law, judicial co-operation in civil matters, and competition. While the Working Party might be faulted for embracing specialisation with undue haste, the discussion provides a useful insight into the possible direction of future policy. See *Due Report*, above n. 11, pp.29–35.

[61] See new version of the Statute, Art. 62.

course, are subject to their own special conditions, distinct from a system of appeals. There, the intervention of the First Advocate General is in keeping with the practice of leaving the decision to seek Community review out of the hands of the parties. In contrast, the gate-keeping role of the First Advocate General departs from the principle of party autonomy that will guide proceedings before judicial panels and the CFI and places a uniquely judicial function in the hands of an official without ultimate judicial decision-making authority. It is somewhat incongruous that appellate options should end at the CFI in the case of a complex intellectual property dispute, for example, but extend to the ECJ in any other commercial case. Notwithstanding these anomalies, the limitation will have the welcome benefit of forestalling lengthy appellate proceedings.

An alternative solution would be to accommodate appeals from decisions of judicial panels within a general filtering system – a European *certiorari* – which would enable the ECJ to decide which cases to review. In such a scheme, it would be possible to side-step the CFI altogether and provide for a single appellate route directly to the ECJ. Since the judicial panels will be "attached" to the CFI and, presumably, will operate under the CFI's general supervision, it will be economical to supervise the decisions of judicial panels in the same way as decisions of the CFI itself. In both instances, a filtering mechanism would be an attractive option: appeals would be filed at the ECJ, which would be free to accept or decline them. Where the ECJ declined jurisdiction, the decision below, whether of the CFI or of a judicial panel, would be deemed final. In contrast, the regime projected by the Treaty of Nice involves three potential tiers of review – by a judicial panel, the CFI and, ultimately, the ECJ. At the very least, these lengthy proceedings should be reserved for truly exceptional cases.

3.(3)(e) Preliminary rulings

Appropriately enough, the preliminary reference procedure dominated negotiations on judicial reform at IGC 2000. The strategic importance of the procedure can scarcely be overstated. In terms of caseload, preliminary references occupy half of the ECJ's docket and, on average, proceedings take over 21 months to complete.[62] Even within this protracted time-frame, the ECJ is in danger of ruling with undue dispatch, placing in jeopardy the quality of judicial discourse, the integrity of the institution and, ultimately, the rule of law within the Community. Yet, if preliminary rulings are the key to reform, the results of IGC 2000 are disappointing; given the range and depth of the various proposals mooted in advance of the Conference, the modesty of the projected changes is striking.

---

[62] See Official Statistics on Judicial Activity at the Court of Justice for 2000, above n. 3.

3.(3)(e)(i) Transferring jurisdiction to the CFI

The significant step taken at Nice was to remove the exclusivity of the ECJ's jurisdiction. Under the new Article 225(3), the CFI "shall have jurisdiction to hear and determine questions referred for a preliminary ruling under Article 234, in specific areas laid down by the Statute." The envisaged role for the CFI marks a profound shift in traditional thinking which associates preliminary rulings with the ECJ's uniquely constitutional function. The Court itself had previously opposed the move, principally on the ground that it would threaten its special relationship with the national courts.[63]

It is too early to say whether the Treaty of Nice will lead to any demonstrable change in practice. It creates no more than a potential jurisdiction for the CFI; actual reform will follow later, if at all, in the form of an amendment to the Statute, which will require a qualified majority vote in the Council. In the meantime, the issue should be included in the proposals on the division of competence between the Community courts which the Treaty solicits from the ECJ and the Commission. In short, the future of the preliminary reference procedure remains very much on the drawing board.

3.(3)(e)(ii) Defining the CFI's jurisdiction

Assuming the CFI is conferred with *de facto* competence to deliver preliminary rulings, there is every reason to believe that its contribution will be limited, at least initially. For one thing, there are limits to the CFI's functional capacity. Its overburdened docket will expand with additional responsibilities over direct actions and appeals from judicial panels. The CFI could not assume the burden of a substantial preliminary reference jurisdiction without a significant increase in its judges and resources. Moreover, the larger the CFI becomes, the more pressing the question of the consistency of its judgments. Because preliminary references are procedurally distinct from appeals, legislating for appellate review, which safeguards against the vagaries of adjudication by chambers or a single judge, is precarious. This environment is hardly likely to inspire the ECJ, and ultimately the Council, to delegate measurable control over preliminary rulings.

Even if the ECJ were willing, and the CFI truly able, to share responsibility for preliminary rulings, serious questions remain. Staking out a distinct jurisdiction for the CFI is a testing puzzle. Article 235(3) speaks of the CFI's jurisdiction in terms of "specific areas laid down in the Statute," which suggests a substantive definition.[64] The specific areas might include the more

---

[63] See Courts' *Discussion Paper*, above n. 5, pp.25–26 (noting its previous objections but suggesting that the idea should not be dismissed out of hand).

[64] See Meij, above n. 39 (arguing, in advance of the Treaty of Nice, that "*a priori* regulatory definition of determined areas of jurisdiction (blocs de competence) designated for transfer is inevitable," and suggesting the field of intellectual property as a start).

technical fields, such as competition, that the CFI routinely tackles under the rubric of direct actions. They might also extend to the specialised fields that will comprise its appellate jurisdiction over judicial panels. For example, since the CFI hears appeals on the subject of trademark registration from the Alicante Boards of Appeals, it might exercise a corresponding jurisdiction over preliminary references concerning trademark infringement.[65]

Drawing jurisdictional boundaries through a system of subject matter categorisation may prove a double-edged sword. Certain practical considerations demonstrate the need to weigh the benefits of simplicity against the risk of arbitrary outcomes. In the first place, it would be difficult to devise a clear delineation of competence over hybrid requests, involving two or more subject areas. Secondly, subject matter categorisation could subvert the natural judicial hierarchy. The bulk of preliminary references are relatively mundane and could safely be tackled by the CFI. Yet, an issue of primary importance ideally destined for the ECJ may lurk in a case of any stripe or hue. The nub of the challenge, therefore, is to devise an effective and efficient means of delegating the more routine requests for preliminary rulings to the CFI while retaining the defining controversies of the day for the ECJ. The difficulty is that notwithstanding certain objective criteria, the identity of the parties, the subject matter of the proceedings, a threat to the consistency of Community law, *etc.*, there is no uniform understanding of what renders a case important. This is the premise on which the United States Supreme Court's *certiorari* jurisdiction rests: if the importance of the case is inherently subjective, it should be assessed by the ECJ on a case-by-case basis.

A possible solution is to identify the cases of primary importance *a priori*, at the time of filing, and assign them directly to the ECJ. An all-embracing formula might be devised, encapsulating the stated principle that cases of primary importance should go to the ECJ and cases of secondary importance to the CFI. Judge John Cooke has offered an interesting suggestion, grounded in Article 234's distinction between references emanating from lower national courts and those from national courts of last resort: give the CFI jurisdiction over the former and the ECJ jurisdiction over the latter.[66] Some such structural allocation may be as close as we can get to a workable formula of general application. The supposition that national courts of last resort are more likely to generate the more "important" cases, though hardly watertight, seems instinctively sound. The downside, however, would be an inevitable increase in the length and cost of proceedings in certain cases. Suppose, for example, that a novel and challenging issue of Community law is raised in proceedings before the High Court in Dublin. Having determined that a preliminary ruling is necessary, the High Court judge refers the case to the CFI and, in due

---

[65] A suggestion made by the Commission's Working Party. See *Due Report*, above n. 11, p.32.
[66] Cooke, above n. 6, p.18.

course, decides the case with the benefit of the CFI's ruling. The losing party subsequently appeals to the Supreme Court which concludes, in turn, that the case must be referred to the ECJ.[67] The timing and expense of two preliminary references during the course of a single case scarcely bears contemplating. The possibility of a single preliminary reference to the CFI, copperfastened with an immediate right of appeal to the ECJ, would be only marginally more palatable.

The introduction of a centralised system for the allocation of preliminary references might prove a more pragmatic and effective solution. Under such a system, all requests for preliminary rulings would be filed at the ECJ and subjected to an expedited screening process. The ECJ would allocate the requests on a case-by-case basis, retaining for itself the cases it considers of primary importance and referring all others to the CFI.[68] Unlike the United States Supreme Court's *certiorari* jurisdiction, the system would not operate as a discretionary filter. The mandatory character of the preliminary reference jurisdiction would remain unchanged and, consequently, any preliminary reference that crossed the current admissibility threshold would lead to a ruling, whether from the ECJ or the CFI.

Admittedly, there are drawbacks to this approach. *A priori* allocation might increase the margin of error. The importance of a case may be difficult to gauge from the face of the national court reference and may emerge only though its denouement before the ECJ or the national court. A more pressing concern is the timeframe for the putative screening process. Speed and efficiency would be essential but not at the expense of a judicial, as opposed to purely administrative, allocation of preliminary references. At the end of the day, the additional cost in terms of time would have to be weighed against the overall savings of a more efficient system. In particular, if the burden of preliminary references were shared with the CFI, the ECJ could issue its substantive rulings with greater dispatch. Above all, an allocation system would rule out a two-tiered review of preliminary references in Luxembourg – the ECJ reviewing the decisions of the CFI in response to national court requests.

3.(3)(e)(iii) Supervision by the Court

Regardless of how cases reach the CFI or, indeed, how many cases, it will be important to determine the circumstances in which they progress to the ECJ. The issue of supervising the CFI's jurisdiction over preliminary references is

---

[67] Recall that EC Treaty, Art. 234 (ex Art. 177) obliges a national court of last resort to seek a ruling from the ECJ on a point of Community law that is central to the resolution of national proceedings.

[68] See Costello, above n. 2, p.53 (defending *ad hoc* allocation against the objection that it offends the principle of *juge legal* or *gesetzlicher richter* whereby the judge in a particular case must be pre-ordained in advance by law).

framed by competing concerns: the need to preserve a role for the ECJ versus the need to reduce the length of proceedings. The Treaty of Nice confronts the issue in two ways.

First, under the new version of Article 225, the CFI may refer a case to the ECJ for a ruling where the CFI considers that the case requires "a decision of principle likely to affect the unity or consistency of Community law."[69] This preview mechanism is reminiscent of the proposal for a system of allocating preliminary references, just discussed, with two important distinctions. The preview mechanism is intended as an exceptional safeguard rather than a routine allocation procedure. In addition, the screening function will be conducted by the CFI rather than the ECJ.

Secondly, in exceptional circumstances, "where there is a serious risk of the unity or consistency of Community law being affected," a decision of the CFI in response to a preliminary reference may be reviewed by the ECJ, under the same conditions as a decision of the CFI in response to an appeal from a judicial panel. The assessment that such a risk exists will be made by the First Advocate General within a month of the CFI's decision; within a further month, the ECJ will determine whether or not the decision will be reviewed.[70] Thus, here also, the parties lack standing to challenge the CFI's ruling before the ECJ.[71] In a declaration attached to the Treaty of Nice, the Conference expressed the view that where the ECJ reviews a CFI decision in response to a preliminary reference, it should act under an emergency procedure.[72]

These preview and review mechanisms share similar flaws. The initial decision whether the ECJ should decide a case is essentially subjective[73] and it is made by an entity other than the ECJ itself. It is highly unusual in modern legal systems that a court should lack control over its own jurisdiction and, in this instance, that the jurisdictional gatekeeper should be a subordinate court or an officer that lacks ultimate judicial decision-making authority.[74] At the risk of overstating the point, leaving the decision in the hands of the CFI and the First Advocate General could in its own way threaten the uniformity, consistency and, indeed, objectivity of Community law. A further and more serious concern is that referral to the ECJ will become routine rather than exceptional and will increase the length and cost of proceedings. It will be

---

[69] This provision was influenced, in particular, by a proposal from the Dutch Government, above n. 20, p.15.

[70] See new version of the Statute, art. 62.

[71] A change recommended by the CCBE. See Contribution from the CCBE, above n. 13, p.9.

[72] See Declaration on Article 225, [2001] O.J. C80/79.

[73] The First Advocate General, at least, will have the benefit of the CFI's decision on which to base her assessment of a serious risk to the unity or consistency of Community law.

[74] Indeed, there is an inherent contradiction between the Conference's willingness to attribute this authority to the First Advocate General and its refusal to count Advocates General in the judicial tally for the composition of the Court.

important to ensure that the participation of the CFI does not simply add an additional tier of review, all the more so since the preliminary reference procedure effectively suspends national court proceedings.

The headaches do not necessarily end there. The finality of the CFI's decision will be crucial, and not merely as a matter of form. To hypothesise, where the CFI has delivered a preliminary ruling in response to a request from a lower national court, will it be possible for a national supreme court to appeal effectively the CFI's ruling by seeking a preliminary reference from the ECJ itself? The spectre of two distinct preliminary references within the same proceeding is equally apposite in this context. Thus, the success of the procedure will turn in no small measure on the CFI's ability to exercise a firm and decisive hand in responding to national court requests.

3.(3)(e)(iv) The national courts

Regrettably, the Treaty of Nice makes no attempt to address the problem at source, namely by reducing the volume of requests for preliminary rulings emanating from the national courts. Notwithstanding the many and varied proposals of the *Due Report* and others, the Conference decided against altering the mechanics of the preliminary reference procedure. Thus, the role of the national courts and the terms and conditions under which cases are currently referred will remain unchanged.[75] Retention of the *status quo* will assuage the concerns of many, anxious to preserve automatic access to the Community courts but it will not lead to any significant reduction in the length and cost of proceedings. For the time being at least, we can assume that preliminary references will continue to be an enormous drain on resources at the ECJ.

3.(4) CONCLUDING REMARKS

The Treaty of Nice does not alter the essential structure of the judicial system, comprising the ECJ, the CFI and the national courts. It does, however, presage two related, structural developments: increased responsibility for the CFI and the creation of specialised judicial panels. Both initiatives are welcome. Indeed, the shift in emphasis in favour of the CFI is one of the Treaty's most significant and attractive features. Potentially, the CFI will become the primary forum for direct actions, a secondary forum for preliminary references and an appellate forum for decisions from judicial panels. The CFI will no longer be simply "attached" to the ECJ;[76] rather, ensuring that the law is observed will

---

[75] See Meij, above n. 39, p.1043 (noting that the national courts were not associated with the reform negotiations in any way).

[76] In the words of the current version of EC Treaty, Art. 220 (ex Art. 164).

be the task of both courts, each within its own jurisdiction. At the same time, the Treaty incorporates certain safeguards to ensure that the ECJ has the final say on the validity and interpretation of Community law. Potentially, the enhanced role for the CFI and the creation of judicial panels should strengthen the judicial system and enable the ECJ to concentrate on its fundamental constitutional tasks.

One effect of the new regime is that there will be no other species of Community court, for the time being at least. In contrast to the U.S. system, to choose just one federal or quasi-federal example, there will be no Community trial courts located in the Member States nor any intermediary Community courts, whether defined by territorial or subject matter jurisdiction.[77] On this score, the Conference acted wisely. The conditions that led the U.S. Congress to establish federal district courts and, subsequently, courts of appeals, generally do not apply to the Community today. Moreover, there are persuasive grounds *against* limiting the national courts' Community tasks. The various Community courts would function using different languages and in cultures more diverse than those that span the federal districts in the United States. The system would be duplicative and could threaten the stature of the national court as the doorway through which individuals secure access to the Community system. In the United States, mixed cases routinely appear on both sides of the haphazard line that divides state and federal jurisdiction. Yet whereas federal adjudication of state questions can be controversial, a corresponding jurisdiction for the Community courts over national law would be an unthinkable affront to a still jealously guarded sovereignty. Even the ECJ, which has the power to condemn and penalise an errant Member State, lacks the authority to review national legislation or overturn national judgments. Thus, the most that a lower Community court would do is perform the functions currently entrusted to the CFI but with a greater geographical, but not necessarily ideological, proximity to the populace.

If the CFI needs structural support, the specialised judicial panels created by the Treaty of Nice are a superior model. Their specialised mandate may be used to target areas of Community practice that are particularly labour-intensive or that otherwise warrant special treatment. Attached to the CFI, the judicial panels can be incorporated within the existing system and, given their limited mandate and structural location, they are less likely to stray from the direction of the CFI and ECJ. These considerations do not alter the conclusion that the use of judicial panels should be reserved for a limited number of select areas that are conducive to specialisation. Certainly, the CFI should guard against a gradual dismantling of its jurisdiction through the expedient of judicial panels.

---

[77] See *Courts' Discussion Paper*, above n. 5, 26–27; Jacques and Weiler, above n. 9.

The problem with the Treaty of Nice is not the emphasis on the CFI, nor the addition of judicial panels *per se*. Rather the Conference's legacy turns on the questionable assumption that modifying the role of the CFI will cure the ills of the entire system. Thus, quantitative change at the CFI is designed to produce a qualitative change at the ECJ. If the centre of gravity, at least in terms of caseload, is moved to the CFI, the ECJ will be in a better position to pursue its constitutional mandate, or so the thinking goes. In effect, the ECJ will carry out the same essential functions but, it is hoped, in a more select fashion.

The promise will hold true, if at all, only if two conditions are met: the transfer of jurisdiction from the ECJ to the CFI must be real and substantial; and the CFI must be provided with adequate budgetary and administrative resources to equip it for the task. The fulfilment of either condition does not seem fanciful when applied to direct actions. The Council could make the CFI the *de facto* first judicial forum for direct actions and, presumably, marshal the necessary resources. Direct actions, however, account for far less of the judicial workload than preliminary references[78] and the gains for the ECJ must be counterbalanced against a projected increase in appeals.[79]

The fallacy of the Conference's reform strategy is revealed in its treatment of preliminary references. The Conference seised on the CFI as the key to reducing the length of Community law proceedings[80] in national courts by speeding up the preliminary reference procedure in Luxembourg. Yet, it is questionable whether the CFI has the capacity and resources to shoulder this burden effectively, given the totality of its responsibilities. The net result is no meaningful relief for the ECJ from the strain of preliminary references. The Conference made no effort to attack the problem at source, namely, by taking steps to stem the flow of preliminary references from the national courts. Consequently, whatever the division of labour in Luxembourg, the national courts will continue to request countless preliminary rulings. Nor did the Conference offer a framework for the potential sharing of the preliminary reference burden between the Community courts.

This fundamental deficiency in the Treaty of Nice underscores a continuing need to discuss alternative reform measures post-Nice. If the central objective is to render the legal system more efficient and to equip the ECJ to perform as a supreme court, as the reformists (including the Courts and the Commission's Working Group) contend, the Treaty falls short of the mark. The Nice reforms will undoubtedly improve the system but not to the extent necessary to remedy the workload crisis, much less prepare the courts for enlargement. Moreover,

---

[78] For example, of the 503 cases filed at the Court in 2000, 197 were direct actions as opposed to 224 preliminary references. See Official Statistics on Judicial Activity at the Court of Justice for 2000, above n. 3.

[79] *ibid.*, appeals accounted for 79 of the 503 cases filed at the Court in 2000.

[80] Of course, they are not Community law proceedings in the strict sense but rather Community law questions that arise during the course of national proceedings.

assuming that the Member States ultimately copperfasten the Charter of Fundamental Rights with judicial protection, the implications for the workload of the Community courts will be enormous.[81]

Several factors account for the Conference's conservatism: the limitations surrounding an intergovernmental conference, both practical and political; the caution of the contributors to the debate, including the Courts themselves; and the complexity of the preliminary reference procedure. The Treaty of Nice is also symptomatic of certain flaws in the underlying debate about judicial reform. Notwithstanding the strong language in which the crisis is commonly cast, there is an overriding tendency to underestimate the extent of the problem.[82] Thus, the typical discussion opens with a doomsday scenario and a call for radical action but hesitates at the brink and settles on a compromise solution. For all the talk, and the invocation of architectural analogies, at the end of the day, few are willing to countenance radical reform.

Yet, the crisis remains. There is consensus that the courts are working at the limits of their capacity in servicing the Community of 15 Member States at the present stage of European integration. The courts are not just stretched: they are so extended that the system can no longer be considered efficient or, more alarmingly, effective.[83] Even if the Community remained static, both in terms of membership and competence, the judicial system would be ill-equipped to handle the growth in Community litigation that will arise in the ordinary way. Thus, far-reaching reform would be an imperative even if the path of European integration were set in stone. The reality, of course, is that the Community's future is an open book: the membership will almost certainly increase by one-quarter in the next five years and could double, not at some unforeseen distant time, but within 30 years at the latest. With each enlargement, the Community will grow, not only in size, but also in diversity and in complexity, linguistically and culturally, with some states integrating more closely than others. At the same time, and notwithstanding the current climate of subsidiarity, we can anticipate that the Community's substantive competence will continue to encroach gradually on the national domain.

Today, a national court must stay proceedings for almost two years to facilitate a preliminary ruling from the ECJ. What can we expect in the future? Imagine the European Union 20 years hence, with a membership of 25 states, combining a population of several hundred million, sharing an internal market, a single currency, common policies in fields as diverse as foreign policy and crime, and a full-blown commitment to the protection of fundamental

---

[81] [2000] O.J. C364/1. On human rights and the EU see below Kingston Chap.12; Editorial Comments, "The EU Charter of Fundamental Rights Still under Discussion" (2001) 38 C.M.L.Rev. 1. The status of the Charter is tabled for discussion at IGC 2004. See Declaration on the Future of the Union [2001] O.J. C80/85.

[82] For an exception to this generalisation, see Rasmussen, above n. 2.

[83] An assessment contained in the Courts' own Discussion Paper, above n. 5.

Community rights. Now imagine the needs of that European society in terms of the administration of justice. Finally, imagine the current judicial system striving to meet those needs. This prospective reality encapsulates the challenge of reform.

The Community's response in the guise of the Nice reforms is not altogether unreasonable. Instead of meeting the challenge in one fell swoop, the Conference opted to start down the road to reform and, at the same time, give the system the necessary flexibility for the remainder of the journey. Thus, the Treaty of Nice is intended to mark the commencement or, more accurately, the continuation, rather than the culmination, of the reform process. As noted, several of its provisions lay the groundwork for future developments without necessarily committing the courts to their adoption. The increased flexibility in the rules governing the judicial system should be a boon to its evolution in so far as it will allow for gradual modifications in tune with developing needs. However, there are risks to "wait and see" as a reform philosophy. The crisis in the courts is too entrenched to permit a gradual, low-level recovery. More importantly, flexibility must be balanced against other core values in the legal system, such as legal certainty. The Community must ensure that reform does not become so piecemeal and protracted as to undermine the integrity of the rule of law. Constant, spasmodic change may also jeopardise the transparency and accessibility to which the system aspires. Flexibility is a poor substitute for a lasting design of the judicial system. This is perhaps the greatest indictment of IGC 2000: it leaves no roadmap but only a general sense of the direction in which the courts are headed.

The reform debate has obscured two important facts. First, the transfer of jurisdiction to the CFI must be accompanied by a transfer of real decision-making authority. In other words, there must be a sense that the CFI's decisions are final as a general rule and, only occasionally, subject to appellate review. The Conference has laid at least some of the groundwork for this decisive shift but it remains to be seen whether the various actors – the Council in amending the Statute and Rules and the Courts in applying its *imprimatur* – will implement it in practice. Secondly, some decentralisation of judicial responsibility is inevitable and even desirable.[84] Meeting the demands of a fully enlarged Community will prove a Herculean task for the ECJ and the CFI alone, even with the aid of judicial panels. The Community may create additional Community courts in time but that could prove a mixed blessing, for

---

[84] The proposed overhaul of the competition rules (in Regulation Implementing Articles 81 and 82 of the Treaty COM (2000) 582 final September 27,2000) which will involve a fundamental re-organisation of existing responsibilities between the Commission, national competition authorities and the national courts, points the way. See Ehlermann, "The Modernization of EC Antitrust Policy: A Legal and Cultural Revolution" (2000) 37 C.M.L.Rev. 537; and also see below Lucey, chap. 4. However the decentralisation of the competition regime may increase even further the workload of the Community Courts.

the reasons discussed above. Marshalling the assistance of the national courts, which serve as a species of Community court, would be a more sensible alternative. Whereas creating a lower tier of Community courts could duplicate the Community law functions of the national court, delegating responsibility directly to the national courts, thereby enhancing their Community law credentials, seems a more logical advance. The steps that the Community might take to achieve this goal are beyond the scope of the present discussion but there is ample scope to develop promising ideas for reform, including proposals that draw on comparative experience.

In summary, the Treaty of Nice signals an important step in the evolution of the Community's judicial system. Taken collectively, the reforms should go some way towards alleviating current pressures and preparing for future challenges. It is difficult, however, to predict the impact of many of the projected reforms; the devil will be in the details, many of which have yet to be decided. The starting point is clarification of the division of competence between the ECJ and the CFI. Similarly, the promised reductions in the length of proceedings will depend in large measure on how the ECJ's appellate jurisdiction is defined. Legal issues aside, the success of the reforms is linked to the provision of adequate financial and administrative resources, especially at the CFI. Ultimately, the Nice reforms, standing alone, are too modest to guarantee effective, lasting solutions to the present crisis, much less to equip the courts for future challenges. The pressure for further reform must be maintained.

BIBLIOGRAPHY

Arnull, "Judicial Architecture or Judicial Folly? The Challenge Facing the European Union" (1999) 24 *Eur.L.R.* 516.

British Institute of International and Comparative Law, *The Role and Future of the European Court of Justice* (1996).

Commission, *Report by the Working Party on the Future of the European Communities' Court System* (2000).

Cooke, "European Judicial Architecture: Back to the Drawing Board" (1999) 5 *Bar Rev.* 14 (1999).

Costello, "Preliminary Reference Procedure and the 2000 Intergovernmental Conference" (1999) 21 *D.U.L.J.* 40.

Court of Justice and Court of First Instance, *The Future of the Judicial System of the European Union (Proposals and Reflections)* (1999).

Dashwood & Johnson eds, *The Future of the Judicial System of the European Union* (2001).

De Burca & Weiler, eds., *The European Court of Justice* (2001).

Dryberg, "What Should the Court of Justice be Doing?" (2001) 26 *Eur.L.Rev.* 291.

Jacques & Weiler, On the Road to European Union – A New Judicial Architecture: An Agenda for the Intergovernmental Conference (1996) 27 *C.M.L.Rev.* 224.

Johnson, "Judicial Reform and the Treaty of Nice" (2001) 38 *C.M.L.Rev.* 499

Heffernan, "A Discretionary Jurisdiction for the European Court of Justice?" (1999) 34 *Irish Jurist (n.s.)* 148.

Heffernan, "The Treaty of Nice and Reform of the Community Courts" (2001) 6 *Bar Rev.* 474.

Heffernan, "The Treaty of Nice: Arming the Courts to Defend a European Bill of Rights?" (2002) 65 *Law & Contemp. Probs.* 189.

Rasmussen, "Remedying the Crumbling EC Judicial System" (2000) 37 *C.M.L.Rev.* 1071.

Turner & Munoz, "Revisiting the Judicial Architecture of the European Union" (1999-2000) 19 *Y.E.L.* 1.

Van Gerven, "The Role and Structure of the European Judiciary Now and in the Future" (1996) 21 *Eur.L.Rev.* 211.

4. APPLICATION OF EUROPEAN COMMUNITY COMPETITION LAW – SOME IMPLICATIONS OF BUNREACHT NA HÉIREANN

MARY CATHERINE LUCEY*

4.(1) INTRODUCTION

The Proposal for a Council Regulation on the Implementation of Rules on Competition[1] (hereinafter the Proposal) advances radical reforms for the *application* of European Community (EC) competition law.[2]

Of course, the substantive rules on competition contained in Articles 81 and 82 of the EC Treaty are not altered by the Proposal. Article 82 prohibits the abuse of a dominant position. Article 81(1) prohibits anti-competitive arrangements between undertakings and Article 81(2) provides that such prohibited arrangements are void. Under Article 81(3) some arrangements prohibited by Article 81(1) may be exempted. Pursuant to Regulation 17/62,[3] exemptions are granted exclusively by the European Commission and, in general, individual[4] exemptions can be granted only following *ex ante* notifications[5] of the

---

* Mary Catherine Lucey B.C.L., LL.M, B.L., Lecturer-in-Law, Faculty of Law, University College Dublin. I am grateful to my colleagues, Professor J.P. Casey and Mr John O'Dowd, for their comments on an earlier draft. Any errors remain the responsibility of the author.

[1] Proposal for a Council Regulation on the Implementation of Rules on Competition laid down in Articles 81 and 82 of the Treaty and amending Regulations (EEC) No. 1017/68, (EEC) No 2988/74, (EEC) No. 4056/86 and (EEC) No. 3975/87). "Regulation Implementing Articles 81 and 82 of the Treaty" COM (2000) 582 final September 27, 2000. At the time of writing the Proposal is under consideration within the European Council and the final version of the text has not been agreed.

[2] The Proposal succeeds the extensive review of EC Competition rules contained in the White Paper on *Modernisation of the Rules Implementing Articles 81 and 82 of the EC Treaty* adopted on April 28,1999. The reforms in the White Paper were described as representing "not only a legal but also a 'cultural' revolution." Ehlermann & Atanasiu, "Introduction" in *European Competition Law Annual 2000: The Modernisation of EC Antitrust Policy* (Hart Publishing, 2001), p.xvii.

[3] First Reg. implementing Articles 85 and 86 of the Treaty [1962] O.J. 13/204; Reg. as last amended by Reg. (EC) No 1216/1999 [1999] O.J. L148/5.

[4] Two types of exemptions (category and individual) are envisaged by Art. 81(3). Arrangements satisfying the terms of block exemptions (which are issued exclusively by the Commission) need not be notified in order to benefit from an exemption.

[5] Reg. 17/62 Art. 9. Under Art. 4 of Reg. 17/62 certain specified arrangements do not need advance notification.

arrangement to the European Commission. According to the jurisprudence of the European Court of Justice (ECJ), Article 81(1), Article 81(2) and Article 82 are directly effective, which is in stark contrast to Article 81(3).[6]

Innovative rules of implementation are set out in the Proposal whereby Article 81(3) would become directly applicable.[7] This would entail abolishing the notification system and assessing the compatibility of arrangements with Article 81 on an *ex post* basis or *exception légale*.[8] Under Article 5 of the Proposal the competition authorities of the Member States "shall have the power in individual cases to apply the prohibition in Article 81(1) of the Treaty where the conditions of Article 81(3) are not fulfilled, and the prohibition in Article 82." Their role is further detailed in the same Article:

> "For this purpose, acting on their own initiative or on a complaint, they may take any decision requiring that an infringement be brought to an end, adopting interim measures, accepting commitments or imposing fines, periodic penalty payments or any other penalty provided for in their national law. Where on the basis of the information in their possession the conditions for prohibition are not met they may likewise decide that there are no grounds for action on their part."

Therefore, it is proposed that Article 81 *in its entirety* and Article 82 be applied by national competition authorities (and national courts).[9]

Notwithstanding the proposed devolution, the European Commission would continue to perform a significant role in the enforcement and the development of competition policy. Under the Proposal it could intervene in proceedings before national courts and it could take over proceedings initiated by a national competition authority or authorities. It would also have the competence to take infringement decisions and issue declaratory decisions; to order remedies including those of a structural nature; to accept commitments; and to impose fines. In cases of urgency it could order interim measures. It would have power to issue Block Exemption Regulations, notices and guidelines. Its powers of investigation would be extended to include inspections of private homes, following judicial authorisation. The extent of the European Commission's competence has prompted some cynical and sceptical remarks concerning the

---

[6] Case 127/73 BRT v. SABAM [1974] E.C.R. 51; Case 234/89 *Delimitis v. Henniger Brau* [1991] E.C.R. I– 935.

[7] Whether this is compatible with the Treaty or whether the Treaty needs to be amended to achieve this result has been debated. Mestmaecker, "The Modernisation of EC Antitrust Policy: Constitutional Challenge or Administrative Convenience?", and Marenco, "Does a Legal Exception System require an Amendment of the Treaty?" in *European Competition Law Annual 2000: The Modernisation of EC Antitrust Policy* (Ehlermann & Atanasiu eds., Hart Publishing, 2001).

[8] Art. 1 provides: " Agreements, decisions and concerted practices caught by Article 81(1) of the Treaty which do not satisfy the conditions of Article. 81(3), shall be prohibited, no prior decision to that effect being required".

[9] Art. 6: "National courts before which the prohibition in Article 81(1) of the Treaty is invoked shall also have jurisdiction to apply Article 81(3)".

motivation of the Commission.[10] Irrespective of the motives[11] it is indisputable that the Proposal is predicated on the national competition authorities (and national courts) performing a major role in the application of EC competition law.

This chapter explores the implications of Bunreacht na hÉireann (the Irish Constitution) for the Irish competition authority charged with applying Articles 81 and 82.

4.(2) APPLYING EUROPEAN COMMUNITY COMPETITION LAW IN IRELAND

4.(2)(a) Duty to apply effectively

Article 36 of the Proposal provides that: "The Member States shall designate the competition authorities responsible for the application of Articles 81 and 82 and shall take the measures necessary to empower those authorities to apply those Articles before (unspecified date)." The effect of Article 36 combined with Article 5 of the Proposal is to impose a duty on Member States that EC competition law be applied by national competition authorities.

The Commission considers that the duty to apply EC competition law includes a duty to apply it effectively.

> "If they find that there is an infringement of Article 81 as a whole, or of Article 82, the competition authorities of the Member States are to take *effective* action against the conduct in question, acting in accordance with the proposed Regulation and applicable national procedural rules. Paragraph 3 lists the contents of the decisions they may take in that respect. While the proposed regulation does not foresee harmonisation of national sanctions, general

---

[10] "In reality [they] are maintaining the monopoly, even perhaps strengthening it under a different label. The only effect intended may be to get rid of the workload but not of any responsibility". The President of the German Federal Cartel Office in his evidence to the House of Lords Select Committee on European Union Fourth Report Part 2, para. 44. "The true Community blueprint is still 'hierarchical' institutional architecture with the Commission at superior level responsible for cases with 'political, legal or economic significance' and NCAs [national competition authorities] as auxiliary organs for cases without such importance." Kingston, "A 'New Division of Responsibilities' in the Proposed Regulation to Modernise the Rules Implementing Articles 81 and 82 EC ? A Warning Call", Eur. Competition L. Rev. 2001, 22(8), 340 at p.344. In contrast: "The primary objective of the reform is clearly to improve the efficiency of EC law enforcement, and not to reduce the workload of the Commission. Schaub "Panel Discussion" in *European Competition Law Annual 2000: The Modernisation of EC Antitrust Policy,* above n. 2, p.39.

[11] The Commission's motives were described as having "shifted from pure administrative concerns (disposing of the excessive workload), via constitutional objectives (bringing enforcement of EC antitrust in line with the subsidiarity principle) to, now, enhancing the protection of competition (increasing effectiveness)." Wesseling, "The Draft Regulation Modernising the Competition Rules: The Commission is Married to one Idea" E.L. Rev. 2001, 26(4), 357, p.362.

principles of Community law require that such sanctions ensure *effective* enforcement".[12]

Recital 6 of the Proposal provides: "in order to ensure that the Community competition rules are applied effectively, the competition authorities of the Member States must be associated more closely with their application. To this end, they must be empowered to apply Community law." At time of writing it is uncertain whether the finally agreed text of Article 36 will *expressly* impose an obligation of effectiveness. Following negotiations, one version of Article 36 was redrafted to state in paragraph 2 " the Member States shall designate the authority or authorities referred to in paragraph 1 in such a way that the provisions of this Regulation are effectively complied with."[13] However a later document contains a version of Article 36 without a reference to effectiveness.[14]

In any event there is a duty on Member States and national authorities, stemming *inter alia* from Article 10 of the EC Treaty,[15] to ensure that EC law is applied *effectively*. Specifically in the context of competition law it has been described as a "general duty of all national authorities, whatever their responsibilities and powers, not to do anything which would have the result of making Community competition rules ineffective."[16] Another basis for this duty has been identified,[17] namely an ECJ judgment[18] that national arrangements as a whole must be sufficiently effective to enable national authorities to apply EC law correctly and effectively.

---

[12] P.16 of the Explanatory Memorandum accompanying the proposed Regulation (emphasis added). The reference to 'paragraph 3' is puzzling since Article 5 of the Proposal does not contain such a paragraph.

[13] Document 8383/02 Report from the Presidency to the Permanent Representatives Committee/Council dated 21 May 2002.

[14] Document 11791/02 Report from the Competition Working Party to Permanent Representatives Committee dated 9 September 2002.

[15] "Article 10 does not create duties alone, by itself, but only together with some other identified rule of Community law or some principle or objective of Community policy which is to be facilitated, or at least, not jeopardised . . . Article 10 therefore does not create any wholly new duties, unrelated to those which are already binding on Member States or to which they have agreed as Community objectives or policies. (It may of course, like any other general rule, give rise to specific unforeseen consequences of already existing duties, or of objectives or policies already agreed.)" Temple Lang, "The Duties of Co-operation of National Authorities and Courts under Article 10 EC: Two More Reflections" E.L. Rev. 2001 26(1) 84; Temple Lang, "The Duties of National Authorities under Community Constitutional Law" (1998) 23 (2)E.L. Rev. 109; Temple Lang "Community Constitutional Law: Article 5 EEC Treaty" 27 C.M.L.Rev. 645 (1990); Finlay and Hyland " The Duties of Co-Operation of National Authorities and Courts and the Community Institutions under Article 10 EC" *Irish Journal of European Law* 2000 267; See above Keville Chap.1.

[16] Temple Lang, Foreword to Power, *Competition Law and Practice* (Butterworths, 2001). "I believe that there is also a duty under Community law on all Member States to provide reasonably efficient public authorities where the Member State has a duty to administer Community law". Temple Lang "The Duties of National Authorities under Community Constitutional Law" E.L.Rev 1998, 23(2) 109, p.120.

[17] Wesseling, *The Modernisation of EC Antitrust Law* (Hart, Oxford, 2000), p.196.

[18] Case C–8/88 *Germany v. Commission* [1990] E.C.R. I–2321 ECJ.

4.(2)(a)(i) Competition Authority

The Competition Authority is the obvious starting point in any discussion regarding the requirement that competition law be applied effectively in Ireland. This administrative body was established under the Competition Act 1991. However, it does not play the leading role in making determinations/ adjudications in relation to the domestic equivalents of Articles 81 and 82. Its role is to investigate breaches and to initiate court proceedings. Its competence in applying EC competition law has traditionally been negligible. The Minister for Enterprise and Employment (and not the Competition Authority) is designated by section 3 of the EC (Rules on Competition) Regulations 1993 as the competent authority for the purpose of Regulation 17/62.[19] Prior to the Competition Act 2002 the Competition Authority was not expressly empowered to apply Articles 81 or 82.[20] Section 14(2) of that Act, which came into effect on July 1st 2002, grants it the right to initiate civil actions for breaches of Articles 81 and 82 which may result in a Court ordering an injunction or a declaration but not damages.[21] A further innovation of the 2002 Act is its provision that breaches of Articles 81 and 82 are criminal offences.[22] Under Section 8(9) the Competition Authority may initiate proceedings for summary offences – the penalties for summary convictions are a maximum fine of €3000 and/or six months' imprisonment.[23] Only the Director of Public Prosecutions may bring proceedings for indictable offences. Penalties for convictions on indictment are potentially severe fines (a maximum of either €4,000,000 or 10% of the turnover) and/or a maximum of five years' imprisonment.[24]

The crucial question is whether the mechanisms under the Competition Act 2002 suffice for the *effective* application of European Community competition law. While the Member States are not required to copy the model of the European Commission, that integrated or unitary model can act as a touchstone. Under Regulation 17/62 the European Commmission has considerable powers to investigate alleged infringements and make orders which are binding on undertakings, including an order to bring the infringement to

---

[19] See Breen " Co-operation and the Future Role of the Competent Authority – an Irish Perspective [1997] *Irish Competition Law Reports* 2; The Competition and Merger Review Group recommended that amendment be made to replace the Minister with the Competition Authority(p65).

[20] S.14(2) of the Competition Act 2002 gives the Competition Authority a right of action in respect of conduct prohibited by Articles 81 and 82. As regards powers of enforcement s.31 allows it to summon witnesses, examine them on oath and require the production of documents. Powers of entry and search, exercisable by "authorised officers", are contained in s.45.

[21] Competition Act 2002. Under s. 14 (1): aggrieved person has *locus standi* to initiate proceedings and may be awarded damages including exemplary damages.

[22] ss. 6 and 7.

[23] s. 8(1)(a).

[24] The five-year term is significant because it makes available the arrest and detention provisions of the Criminal Justice Act 1984.

an end (so-called "cease and desist" order) and fines.[25] In contrast, the Competition Authority does not have competence, in individual cases, to issue any orders consequent upon a finding that an infringement of Article 81 or 82 has occurred. Clearly its powers fall far short of those permitted by the Proposal and *a fortiori* of those exercisable by the European Commission.

The reason why wide ranging powers could not be conferred on the Competition Authority is to be found in Article 34 of Bunreacht na hÉireann which reserves the administration of justice to the courts. It provides that:

> "Justice shall be administered in courts established by law by judges appointed in the manner provided by this Constitution and, save in such special and limited cases as may be prescribed by law, shall be administered in public."

The exception to Article 34, contained in Article 37 of Bunreacht na hEireann, only permits the exercise of "limited" judicial power. It states that:

> "Nothing in this Constitution shall operate to invalidate the exercise of limited functions and powers of a judicial nature, in matters other than criminal matters, by any person or body of persons duly authorised by law to exercise such functions and powers notwithstanding that such person or such body of persons is not a judge or a court appointed or established as such under this Constitution."

4.(2)(b) Article 29.4.7 of Bunreacht na hÉireann

The restrictions of Article 34 can be obviated if recourse to Article 29.4.7 of Bunreacht na hÉireann is possible. Article 29.4.7 provides:

> "No provision of this Constitution invalidates laws enacted, acts done or measures adopted by the State which are necessitated by the obligations of membership of the European Union or of the Communities, or prevents laws enacted, acts done or measures adopted by the European Union or by the Communities or by institutions thereof, or by bodies competent under the Treaties establishing the Communities from having the force of law in the State."

Essentially this Article bestows immunity from constitutional challenge if the measure is *necessitated*. In *Lawlor v. Minister for Agriculture* Murphy J. stated that this term:

> "could not be limited in its construction to laws, acts or measures all of which are required in all of their parts to be enacted, done or adopted by the obligations of membership of the Community. It seems to me that the word

---

[25] Regulation 17/62 confers extensive powers on the European Commssion. Art. 3 provides "Where the Commission, upon application or upon its own initiative, finds that there is an infringementof Article 81 or Article 82 of the Treaty, it may by decision require the undertakings or associations of undertakings concerned to bring such infringement to an end.".Art. 15(2) states that: " the Commission may by decision impose on undertakings . . . fines of from 1,000 to 1 million (ECU) , or a sum in excess thereof but not exceeding 10% of the turnover in the preceding business year."

necessitated in this context must extend to and include acts or measures which are consequent upon membership of the Community and in general fulfilment of the obligations of such membership and even where there may be a choice or degree of discretion vested in the State as to the particular manner in which it would meet the general spirit of its obligations of membership."[26]

This passage has been criticised for employing the phrase "consequent upon" on the basis that the Oireachtas expressly rejected this phrase and chose the term "necessitated" in its stead.[27] More recently, however, Carroll J. remarked that

"Murphy J. used the word 'consequent' in relation to Article 29.4.3 but the word was used in conjunction with the 'general fulfilment of the obligations of membership.' He was not seeking to interpret 'necessitated by' as being the equivalent of 'consequent on', which of course it is not".[28]

Indisputably some limits must exist to the scope of the concept. Murphy J. stated in *Greene v. Minister for Agriculture*: "Undoubtedly membership of the Communities required Ireland to implement a scheme complying with directive 75/268 but it does not follow that *any and every scheme drafted in pursuance of that directive and meeting its purpose* is necessarily required by our membership of the Communities."[29] He further stated:

"I have no doubt but that laws enacted, acts done and measures adopted by the State are necessitated...by the obligations of membership of the Communities even where the particular actions of the State involve a measure of choice selection or discretion. . . . On the other hand there must be a point at which the discretion exercised by the State or the national authority is so far reaching or so detached from the result to be achieved by the Directive that it cannot be said to have been 'necessitated' by it".[30]

In *Meagher v. Minister for Agriculture*[31] challenge was made to measures implementing EC Council Directives[32] which proscribed administering particular hormones to animals for fattening. The Directives were implemented by minis-terial regulations[33] pursuant to section 3 of the European Communities Act 1972.[34]

---

[26] [1990] 1 I.R. 356, at 377. Also cited in *Greene v. Minister for Agriculture* [1990] 2 I.R. 17, 25.

[27] The Third Amendment of the Constitution Bill 1971, 258 Dail Debates at Col. 402. See Hogan and Whelan, *Ireland and the European Union; Constitutional and Statutory Texts and Commentary* Sweet and Maxwell 1995, p.71.

[28] *Maher v. Minister for Agriculture, Food and Rural Development* [2001] 2 I.R. 139, 147.

[29] [1990] 2 I.R. 17 p.24 (emphasis added).

[30] *ibid.* p.25.

[31] [1994] 1 I.R. 329. For a critique of the judgment see above Costello, para. 2(2)(c).

[32] Including 85/358/EEC. For further details see above Costello, chap 2, n.92.

[33] European Communities (Control of Oestrogenic, Androgenic, Gestagenic and Thyrostatic Substances) Regulations 1988 and the European Communities (Control of Veterinary Medicinal Products and their Residues) Regulations 1990.

[34] s.3(1) European Communities Act 1973. A Minister of State may make regulations for enabling s.2 of the Act to have full effect. (2) Regulations under this section may contain such incidental,

The Supreme Court held that the power in Section 3 was "necessitated"[35] and thus could not be challenged as an unconstitutional delegation of the legislative power granted exclusively to the Oireachtas.[36] As Travers remarks:"The Court avoided developing a conceptual interpretation of what is or is not "necessitated" by the obligations of Community membership, but rather accepted the practicality argument advanced by the State."[37]

The implementing ministerial Regulations (i) created the offence of possession of the particular substances; (ii) extended the time-limit for instituting criminal proceedings;[38] and (iii) authorised District Judges/Peace Commissioners to issue a search warrant if there were reasonable grounds for suspicion of possession.[39] Regarding the deadline and search warrant, Blayney J. held that the Minister had "such power provided that it was necessary for the purpose of giving effect to the directives."[40] One of the Directives expressly required Member States to ensure that on-the-spot random controls (including taking samples) were made.[41] The Court found that the necessary investigations could not be carried out without the power to enable a compulsory search to be made of farms where animals were kept. Noting that no objection was made to the *creation* of offences by the Regulations, Blayney J. stated:

> "It is accordingly accepted by counsel for the applicant that this was required for the implementation of the relevant directives. And it must follow logically that the implementation required in addition that the offences could be *effectively* prosecuted. So the regulations had to be in a form to enable this to be done and if it was necessary for this purpose to allow a period of two years the Minister clearly had power to allow such a period."[42]

Thus, notwithstanding the absence of an express mention in the Directives, these powers were legitimately included in the implementing measure because they were necessary to secure their *effective* operation. On this basis, it could

---

supplementary and consequential provisions as appear to the Minister making the regulations to be necessary for the purposes of the Regulations (including provisions for the repealing, amending or applying, with or without modification, other law, exclusive of this Act).

[35] Finlay C.J. [1994] 1 I.R. 329, p.352" The power of regulation making contained in section 3 is *prima facie* a power which is part of the necessary machinery of the State which became a duty of the state upon joining the Community and therefore necessitated by that membership."

[36] Art. 15.2.1.provides: "The sole and exclusive power of making laws for the State is hereby vested in the Oireachtas: no other legislative authority has power to make laws for the state."

[37] Travers 1995 E.L. Rev. 20(1) 103, at 106.

[38] The six-month period under s.10(4) of the Petty Session (Ireland) Act 1851 was extended to two years by both Article 32 para. 8 of the 1988 Regulations and art. 11 para. 4 of the 1990 Regulations.

[39] Art. 16 of the 1988 Regulations.

[40] [1994] 1 I.R. 329, 356.

[41] 85/358/EEC Arts. 1, 3, 5and 6. In particular, Art. 6(2): "The competent authorities shall then ensure that (a) an investigation is made at the farm of origin to determine the reason for the presence of hormone residues".

[42] [1990] 1 I.R. 329, 358 (emphasis added).

be argued that the Competition Authority's powers to adjudicate and issue "cease and desist" orders (and perhaps to impose financial penalties) are "necessary" in practice to achieve the obligation to apply Articles 81 and 82 effectively notwithstanding the absence of a reference to these powers expressed in mandatory language in the Proposal. This proposition derives further support from a teleological interpretation of Article 36 which obliges Member States to empower national authorities to apply Articles 81 and 82.[43]

4.(2)(c) Discretion

When the Regulation was initially proposed, the 'competition authorities' cited in Articles 5 and 36 of the Proposal were understood to be the same bodies. However, it appears that clarifications have been made to their definition which may amend Article 36.[44] The possibility that the eventual text will allow Member States to designate courts to act as national competition authorities must be considered. Amendments to the Proposal redrafted Article 36 to provide "(1) The Member States shall designate the competition authorities responsible for the application of Articles 81 and 82 of the Treaty, and shall take the measures necessary to empower those authorities to apply those Articles before ***. The authorities designated may include courts."[45] It is important to emphasise that at the time of writing the final version has not been agreed so it is possible that further amendments may be made.

If the above cited version of Article 36 endures it would provide a discretion as to whether an administrative body or judicial body performs the tasks of the national competition authority. Some of the implications of such a discretion are examined below.

4.(2)(c)(i) Necessitated

A direct consequence of a discretion in chosing the type of body to act as the national competition authority in Ireland would be to foreclose recourse to

---

[43] Article 36 of the Proposal provides "The Member States shall designate the competition authorities responsible for the application of Articles 81 and 82 of the Treaty, and shall take the measures necessary to empower those authorities to apply those Articles before ***". The symbol *** indicates that the date has yet to be specified.

[44] Document 13563/01 Progress Report from the Presidency to COREPER dated 2 November 2001 in footnote 105 to Article 36 states "IRL,FIN note that the definition of national competition authorities as referred to in Articles 5,6,11 and 15 will be of crucial importance. COM will examine use of term" "competition authority" throughout the Regulation, with a view to improving clarity of terminology." It is important to note that that the time of writing this document was only partially acessible to the public.

[45] The symbol *** indicates that the date has yet to be specified. Presidency Report to Permanent Representatives Committee/Council 8383/02 dated 21 May 2002 p61.Similar text appears in the Report from the Competition Working Group to Permanent Representatives Committee Document 11791/02 dated 09 September 2002 p 54. It is stressed that these documents are only partially accessible to the public

Article 29.4.7.[46] This conclusion is based on the assumption that the existence of a discretion implies that there is no *obligation* on Ireland to designate an administrative body (such as the Competition Authority) as the national competition authority and to equip it with powers which may be "judicial". To decide whether a measure is "necessitated", a comparative approach surveying the Regulation's implementation in other Member States might be taken. In *Greene v. Minister for Agriculture*, Murphy J., having noted the permissive language of the Directive,[47] remarked that the fact that some Member States "have and others have not introduced such restrictive conditions demonstrates that such conditions are not required by membership of the Communities."[48] While it is impossible to predict the approaches which other Member States will adopt pursuant to the eventual Regulation it is noteworthy that a survey revealed that not all national competition authorities have the power to penalise.[49]

4.(2)(c)(ii) Court

At first glance, designating a court to be the Irish competition authority appears to be a solution to the strictures of Article 34.[50] However, the application of EC competition law by the European Commission, the European Court of First Instance and the European Court of Justice has always been grounded on a division between administrative and judicial bodies. The Proposal was initially constructed on the basis that separate and different functions would be performed by national competition authorities and national courts. Although not expressly stated in the Proposal that dichotomy between administrative and judicial coincides with the distinction between public and private enforcement. Article 6 is expressly dedicated to national courts and can be seen as the private law counterpart to public law enforcement under Article 5.

The Proposal is founded on the establishment of a consultative and informative network (horizontally) among the Member States' competition authorities and (vertically) with the Commission. Article 11 bears the heading

---

46   This observation was made by Michael Collins S.C. at a conference in Dublin in December 2001: An analogous point has been made in the context of Directives -"The constitutional rule under the Third Amendment to the Constitution is clear: if the Irish authorities have a discretion as to how to implement a directive it must be implemented in manner consistent with the Constitution, unless it cannot be so implemented." Temple Lang, "Constitutional Aspects of Irish Membership of the EEC"(1972) 9 C.M.L.Rev. 167, pp.175–6.

47   EC Dir. 75/269.Art. 6 (2) of the Directive expressly allowed Member States to introduce "additional or restrictive conditions".

48   [1990] 2 I.R. 17, 25.

49   Jones, "Regulation 17: The Impact of the Current Application of Articles 81 and 82 by National Competition Authorities on the European Commission's Proposals for Reform" Eur. Competition L.Rev . 2001, 22(10) ,405; Temple Lang, "General Report" at FIDE Congress: Application of Community Competition Law on Enterprises by National Courts and National Authorities.

50   This is on the assumption that the eventual Regulation will permit such an outcome.

of "Co-operation between the Commission and the Competition Authorities of the Member States." The national authorities' functions are predicated on a duty in that Article of close co-operation with the Commission and include: (i) informing the Commission at the outset of proceedings to apply Article 81 or 82; (ii) consulting the Commission in advance of making a decision requiring that an infringement be ended; accepting commitments or withdrawing a block exemption: to this end the Commission must be provided with a summary of the case and copies of the most important documents;[51] (iii) being relieved of competence to apply Articles 81/82 if the Commission initiates proceedings to adopt a decision. To impose such restrictions on judicial proceedings is not as practicable (or desirable) as imposing them on an entirely administrative procedure. In contrast Article 15 (entitled "Co-operation with National Courts") imposes relatively lighter burden of cooperation with the European Commission. In particular national courts *may* ask the Commission for information and shall send the Commission' copies of any judgments applying Articles 81 or 82 within one month of the date on which the judgment is delivered. Another illustration of the dichotomy occurs in the same Article. Where "questions concerning the application of Article 81 or 82 of the Treaty arise" in national courts the Commission

> "may have itself represented by competition authorities of Member States. Acting on their own initiative, competition authorities of Member States may likewise submit written or oral observations to the national courts of their Member States. To this end the Commission and the competition authorities of the Member States may request the national courts to transmit to them any documents necessary."

Moreover, some of the functions ascribed by the Proposal to the national competition authorities could not be carried out by Irish courts as currently constituted. In particular Irish courts would have difficulties in carrying out investigations as provided for under Article 21 of the Proposal. This includes conducting investigations on behalf of the Commission and/or a competition authority from another Member State. Further difficulty would arise under Article 20 which provides the national competition authority with a right to be consulted in the context of an undertaking being required to submit to inspections ordered by the Commission.[52]

---

[51] Article 11(4) of the Proposal provides "where competition authorities of Member States intend to adopt a decision under Article 81 or 82 of the Treaty requiring that an infringement be brought to an end, accepting commitments or withdrawing the benefit of a block exemption regulation they shall first consult the Commission. For that purpose, thay shall no later than one month before adopting the decision provide the Commission with a summary of the case and with copies of the most important documents drawn up in the course of their own proceedings. At the Commission's request, they shall provide it with a copy of any other document relating to the case."

[52] It provides that the "Commission shall take such decision after consulting the competition authority of the Member State in whose territory the inspection is to be conducted". It further

In fact, Article 34 of Bunreacht na hÉireann itself could constitute an obstacle to a court applying competition law. If the functions involved in applying (as opposed to enforcing) competition law amount to "the administration of justice", then Article 34.1 requires that justice be administered in public, save in exceptional circumstances. It is undesirable that investigations (an essential part of applying competition law) be conducted in public in light of the commercial sensitivity of otherwise confidential information. Conversely, if these activities do not amount to the administration of justice, it raises the question, beyond the scope of this chapter, of whether the doctrine of separation of powers precludes a court from engaging in non-judicial matters.[53]

It is clear that, for many reasons, an Irish court could not carry out *all* the functions of the national competition authority in applying EC Competition law. Thus, because the possibility of recourse to Article 29.4.7 is uncertain and no court could operate as the national competition authority it is imperative to explore the extent of what is prohibited by Bunreacht na hÉireann's Article 34 and what is permitted by its Article 37.

4.(3) RESTRICTIONS ON THE POWERS OF ADMINISTRATIVE BODIES

The interaction between Articles 34 and 37 is crucial when examining the permissible powers of the Competition Authority. The question can be reduced to whether:

> "[T]he congeries of the powers and functions conferred on the tribunal or any particular power or function is such as to involve the pronouncement of decisions, the making of orders, and the doing of acts, which on the true intendment of the Constitution are reserved to judges as being properly part of the administration of justice and not of the limited character validated by Article 37."[54]

4.(3)(a) "Judicial power"or "administration of justice"

Although the constitutional rule is clear that judicial power, unless limited, cannot be exercised by persons other than judges, difficulties prevail in formulating a comprehensive definition of "judicial power". A pessimistic, albeit prescient, note was sounded by Kingsmill Moore J.: "From none of the pronouncements as to the nature of judicial power which have been quoted can a definition at once exhaustive and precise be extracted, and probably no such definition can be framed."[55] Many attempts at a definition are "by way of

---

provides that officials of the competition authority shall "actively assist the officials of the Commission".

[53] See further Casey, *Constitutional Law in Ireland* (3rd ed., 2000), p.271. Morgan, *"The Separation of Powers in the Irish Constitution"* (1997) RoundHall Sweet & Maxwell. See *O'Donoghue v. Ireland* [2000] 2 I.R. 168.

[54] *Re Solicitors Act 1954, per* Kingsmill Moore J. [1960] I.R. 239, 264.

[55] In *Re Solicitors Act 1954* [1960] I.R. 239, 271 per Kingsmill Moore J.

description rather than by precise formula."[56] Several constitutive elements of judicial power, in a civil context,[57] were first elucidated by Kennedy C.J. in *Lynham v. Butler (No 2)*[58] as follows:

> "[T]he judicial power is exercised in determining in a final manner, by definitive adjudication according to law, rights or obligations in dispute between citizen and citizen, or between citizens and the State, or between any parties whoever they be and in binding the parties by such determination which will be enforced if necessary with the Authority of the State. Its characteristic public good in its civil aspect is finality and authority, the decisive ending of disputes and quarrels, and the avoidance of private methods of violence in asserting or resisting claims alleged or denied. It follows from its nature as I have described it that the exercise of the Judicial Power, which is coercive and must frequently act against the will of one of the parties to enforce its decisions adverse to that party, requires of necessity that the Judicial Department of Government have compulsive authority over persons as, for instance, it must have authority to compel appearance of a party before it, to compel attendance of witnesses, to order the execution of its judgements against persons and property."[59]

Four essential elements of the power were adumbrated in *The State (Shanahan) v. The Attorney General* as:

> "(1) the right to decide as between parties disputed issues of law or fact, either of a civil or criminal nature or both; (2) the right by such decision to determine what are the legal rights of the parties as to the matters in dispute; (3) the right, by calling in aid the executive power of the State, to compel the attendance of the necessary parties and witnesses; and (4) the right to give effect to and enforce such decision, again by calling in aid the executive power of the State."[60]

The enumerated list approach is also to be found in *Mc Donald v. Bord na gCon (No. 2)*.[61] The Supreme Court (Walsh J.)[62] accepted the characteristic features identified by the High Court (Kenny J.) as:

---

[56] *Blascaod Mor Teoranta v. Commissioner of Public Works in Ireland* High Court, Feb. 27,1998 [1998] IEHC 38, para. 231 echoing the dicta of Kennedy C.J. in *Lynham v. Butler (No 2)*. As Professor Gwynn Morgan states: "The conceptual approach . . . consists of scrutinising the types of function which have been traditionally vested in courts and attempting to abstract from it the more significant and distinctive of these features. The resultant model is then compared with the function which is being characterised to see whether it shares sufficient of these characteristics to a sufficient degree . . . Elsewhere, however, the inherent subjective nature and artificiality of this method have been emphasised". *The Separation of Powers in the Irish Constitution* (Dublin, 1997) p.41 (footnotes omitted).

[57] *In casu* the Land Commissioners.

[58] [1933] I.R. 74, *per* Kennedy C.J.

[59] *ibid.*, at 99. Cited in *John Keady v. Commissioner of An Garda Siochana* [1992] 2 I.R. 197.

[60] [1964] I.R. 239, 247, per Davitt P who modestly prefaced the above cited remarks with: "I have certainly no intention of rushing in where so many eminent jurists have feared to tread, and attempting a definition of judicial power; but it does seem to me that there can be gleaned from the authorities certain essential elements of that power."

[61] [1965] I.R. 217, 230 per Kenny J.

[62] *Mc Donald v. Bord na gCon* [1965] I.R. 235, 244. Other cases in which it was expressly adopted include *Goodman International v. Hamilton (No 1)* [1992] 2 I.R. 542, 589 *per* Finlay C.J.

1. A dispute or controversy as to the existence of legal rights or a violation of the law;

2. The determination or ascertainment of the rights of parties or the imposition of liabilities or the infliction of a penalty;

3. The final determination (subject to appeal) of legal rights or liabilities or the imposition of penalties;

4. The enforcement of those rights or liabilities or the imposition of a penalty by the Court or by the executive power of the State which is called in by the Court to enforce its judgment;

5. The making of an order by the Court which as a matter of history is an order characteristic of Courts in this country.

A proemial question is how many of the *McDonald* characteristics need to be satisfied before an activity can be classed as judicial? In *Goodman International v. Hamilton (No. 1)* no difficulty of classification arose because the Tribunal of Inquiry fulfilled none of the "fundamental conditions or characteristics of the administration of justice[63] as laid down in *McDonald*, with the possible exception of the first."[64] The Supreme Court in *Mc Donald v. Bord na gCon (No. 2)*,[65] reversing the decision of Kenny J., held that the Board or the Club "do not exercise powers of a judicial nature as they would only satisfy one of the tests referred to [by Kenny J.]".[66] Referring to this statement McCarthy J. remarked in *Keady v. An Garda Siochana*[67] that it "would appear to require that to qualify as being the administration of justice, each of the five *McDonald* tests must be satisfied". Arguably that statement of the Supreme Court in *McDonald* could be interpreted as meaning that an inadequate number were satisfied in the particular instance without necessarily requiring that all five criteria must be present. In *State (Plunkett and Ponderwood Society Limited) v. The Registrar of Friendly Societies* the Supreme Court held that the statutory[68] power of the Registrar to appoint an inspector to investigate and report to him on the affairs of a society was not judicial and *obiter* stated that it "seems clear that for an activity to qualify as being an administration of justice each of the five McDonald tests must be satisfied."[69] It is salutary to observe that in *Mc Donald v. Bord na gCon* the

---

63 It appears from the judgment of Finlay C.J. in *Goodman International v. Hamilton (No. 1)* 1992 2 I.R. 542 that the terms "administration of justice" and "judicial power" are interchangeable.

64 [1992] 2 I.R. 542, 589 *per* Finlay C.J. It was established under the Tribunals of Inquiry Acts 1921–79.

65 [1965] I.R. 217, 230 *per* Kenny J.

66 *ibid.* p.244.

67 [1992] 2 I.R. 197.

68 Industrial and Provident Societies (Amendment) Act 1978, s. 13 (1).

69 *State (Plunkett) v. Registrar of Friendly Societies (No. 1)* [1998] 4 I.R. 1, 5 *per* O'Flaherty J.

High Court found that the Board's power, to make an exclusion order under section 47 of the Greyhound Industry Act 1958, possessed "all the characteristics . . . of the administration of justice"[70] but the Supreme Court held that it possessed only one of them. This reveals that the outcome of applying the criteria can be unpredictable.

Simply to enquire whether the application of competition law, in every case, accords with the *McDonald* characteristics may be too blunt a question. A basic but significant observation is that competition law infringements occur in different situations which dictate that competition law be applied in the pursuit of diverse motives. In some cases those adversely affected by an infringement, *e.g.* a price-fixing cartel, may be a general class such as consumers. On occasion the injured may be an actual or potential rival undertaking, *e.g.* where a dominant firm engages in predatory pricing to drive a rival from the market. Sometimes there is a specifically identifiable complainant/plaintiff. In some cases the plaintiff is a participant in the illegal conduct, *e.g.* is seeking to withdraw from a contract.[71] Competition law can be applied, usually by a court, to determine as between private parties' rights and duties, and in other cases the enforcement authority acts as a "plaintiff" in pursuing a public interest.

Leaving aside the issue of whether all five of the *McDonald* criteria need to be satisfied, it is "possible to isolate two essential ingredients from these [*McDonald*] characteristics and they are that there has to be a *contest* between the parties together with the infliction of some form of *liability* or *penalty* on one of the parties."[72] Thus, for the application of competition law to be proscribed by Article 34.1, *at least* the twin elements of a contest and a liability/penalty must be present.[73]

4.(3)(a)(i) Contest

The requisite "contest" would patently exist if the authority adjudicated "adversarially" between two (or more) opposing parties, *e.g.* where private parties contest facts and/or law with contradictory assertions before the authority. Such adjudication *inter partes* would involve exercising judicial discretion. In *Kennedy v. Hearne* the absence of a controversy, about whether tax had been paid, in which the Collector General decided "in favour of one contender against the other" was a crucial finding and the Court held that "the Collector General in issuing the certificate did so on the basis that the tax

---

[70] [1965] I.R. 217 at 231.

[71] For example Case 161/84 *Pronuptia de Paris GmbH v. Pronuptia de Paris Irmgard Schillgallis* [1986]E.C.R. 353. An interesting aspect was judicially considered recently in C 453/99 *Courage v. Bernard Crehan* [2001] ECR 1 6297 namely whether a participant in an illegal agreement could recover damages.

[72] *Keady v. Commissioner of An Garda Siochana* [1992] 2 I.R. 197, at 212 *per* O'Flaherty J. [emphasis added].

[73] For a discussion of how the fifth criteria as described may be misleading see Casey, *Constitutional Law in Ireland* (3rd ed., 2000), p.260.

remained unpaid but did not make a judicial determination of that fact."[74] The European Commission does not apply competition law in a triangular model. It investigates alleged infringements and rather than adjudicating between adversaries it establishes whether an infringement occurred. Thus it is feasible for the public law enforcement of EC competition law to take place in the absence of a "contest" between private parties and without a determination in the form of a judgment in *favour* of any party.

4.(3)(a)(ii) Liability/penalty

An inherent element of the administration of justice is the power to make a binding determination or order.[75] Therefore, the nature of any determination or order in the specific context of applying competition law needs to be considered. It is submitted that competence to issue a "cease and desist" order is the very minimum which is required for the application of competition law. More punitive measures are framed in terms of financial penalties such as fines. In deciding whether an order imposes a liability it may be useful to refer to some determinations made under taxation law.[76]

In *Kennedy v. Hearne* it was held that a:

> "determination or a decision by the Collector General that the tax had not been paid could not and did not impose a liability on the taxpayer nor affect any of his rights. What was capable of imposing a liability or affecting rights was the fact of default in payments of levied tax…It was urged on behalf of the plaintiff that the notice to the sheriff and the consequential action of the sheriff, while admittedly a nullity, created embarrassment and imposed problems on the plaintiff. That is true but it is not to be equated with the imposition or affecting of a right".[77]

In *State (Calcul International Limited) and Solatrex (International) Limited v. Appeal Commissioners* the Court noted as regards the power of Appeal Commissioners to decide whether the determination by the tax inspector should be raised:

> "Such orders obviously imposed liabilities upon the taxpayer concerned but they do not deprive him of anything nor limit his freedom of action. They declare his liability for tax upon the basis of the facts as found by them. Having declared his liability they have no power to enforce their decision."[78]

Account however should be taken of the differences between the nature of competition and taxation law. The mathematical computation of a tax debt is

---

[74] *Kennedy v. Hearne* [1988] I.R. 481, 489.
[75] Expressed in the *McDonald* characteristics 2–5.
[76] See further *Orange v. Revenue Commissioners* [1995] 1 I.R. 517; *Deighan v. Hearne* [1990] 1 I.R. 499.
[77] *Kennedy v. Hearne* [1988] I.R. 481, 489.
[78] Unreported, High Court, Dec. 18, 1996 *per* Barron J.

more formulaic (and less discretionary) than calculating a financial sanction for an infringement of competition law. There is judicial authority that: " the exercise of the power to impose penalties is admittedly an exercise of the judicial power."[79] On the other hand a "cease and desist" order arguably falls within the category of "embarrassment and inconvenience" rather than of liability/ penalty.

Importantly, the Proposal *prima facie* does not *require* that the national competition authority be empowered to take decisions which impose liability. Article 5 states: "[T]hey *may* take any decision requiring that an infringement be brought to an end, adopting interim measures, accepting commitments or imposing fines, periodic penalty payments or any other penalty provided for in their national law."

Thus, literally interpreted, the obligation in Article 5 of the Proposal (which is to apply Articles 81 and 82) could be satisfied without granting the competition authority powers to impose a liability or penalty. If EC competition law can be applied in the sense of investigating to establish a breach, the competition authority may act without exercising "judicial power" as proscribed by Article 34. However, its operation would be confined to primarily an investigative role. It could exercise functions analogous to those of the Registrar of Friendly Societies in pointing to possible derelictions of duties and responsibilities and giving the applicants an opportunity to respond which is compatible with Article 34.1.[80] Another approach, also within Article 34, would be to constitute the authority as an Inquiry.[81]

While competence to issue "cease and desist orders" may be permissible, Article 34.1, most likely, precludes an administrative body from imposing fines in a manner identical to that of the Commission. Thus, EC competition law would be applied in Ireland in a restricted and less effective manner. This outcome may be technically in compliance with the proposed Regulation but may result in EC competition law being applied in Ireland in a manner which is inconsistent with its application in other Member States.

4.(3)(b) Article 37 of Bunreacht na hÉireann

Article 37 provides an exception to Article 34. It provides that:

> "Nothing in this Constitution shall operate to invalidate the exercise of limited
> functions and powers of a judicial nature, in matters other than criminal

---

[79] *Re Solicitors Act 1954*, [1960] IR 239 *per* Kingsmill Moore J. at 270. Also see *Lynham v. Butler (No 2)* [1933] I.R. 74, Kennedy C.J.

[80] *State (Plunkett) v. Registrar of Friendly Societies (No. 1)* [1998] 4 I.R. 1, 5; Industrial and Provident Societies (Amendment) Act 1978.

[81] For example, under the Tribunals of Inquiry Acts 1921–1979 which was considered in *Goodman International v. Hamilton (No. 1)* 1992 2 I.R. 542 and similarly, *Garda Siochana (Discipline) Regulations* giving power to the Garda Commissioner to dismiss members considered in *John Keady v. Commissioner of An Garda Siochána* [1992] 2 I.R. 197.

matters, by any person or body of persons duly authorised by law to exercise such functions and powers notwithstanding that such person or such body of persons is not a judge or a court appointed or established as such under this Constitution."

As recognised in *Madden v. The Land Commission*: "Experience has shown that modern government cannot be carried on without many regulatory bodies and those bodies cannot function effectively under a rigid separation of powers."[82] Depending on its nature and extent, judicial power may be exercised by a body other than a judge. The following test was articulated in *Re Solicitors Act 1954*: "If the exercise of the assigned powers and functions is calculated ordinarily to affect in the most profound and far reaching way the lives, liberties, fortunes or reputations of those against whom they are exercised they cannot properly be described as limited."[83]

This test is a substantive one in that it is the powers and functions "which are in their *own nature* to be "limited", not the ambit of their exercise. Nor is the test of limitation to be sought in the number of powers and functions which are exercised."[84] It has been interpreted as meaning the "foreseeable effects".[85]

Thus, the powers of the competition authority, in their own nature, to administer justice would have to be limited in their foreseeable effect on the addressee undertaking(s). Since it is possible for competition law to be applied other than by resolving a contest between parties, attention must be paid to the type of orders. Clearly the "cease and desist" type is the most limited order in its effect.[86] The more challenging question is whether a financial sanction can be so regarded. To impose a fine on an undertaking, and not on any individual person such as a director, is quite unlike professional disbarment which was described as "a sanction of such severity that in its consequences it may be more serious than a term of imprisonment."[87] Furthermore, a fine could be "limited" in the sense of being a liquidated amount. Admittedly it would be preferable to have flexibility in calculating a fine so that it is in proportion to the gravity of the infringement rather than a fixed sum. Fines imposed by the European Commission for breaches of Articles 81 and 82 are subject to a

---

[82] "Article 37 had no counterpart in the Constitution of Saorstát Éireann and in my view introduction of it to the Constitution is to be attributed to a realisation of the needs of modern government." McMahon J., unreported, May 22, 1980 at 8–9.

[83] [1960] I.R. 239, 264 *per* Kingsmill Moore J. The power of the Disciplinary Committee of the Incorporated Law Society to strike solicitors off the rolls was held to exceed the scope of "limited". This test was applied by Kenny J. in *Mc Donald v. Bord na gCon* [1965] I.R. 220, 233, who held that powers conferred were not limited.

[84] *ibid.*, at 263 (emphasis added).

[85] *James Madden v. Ireland and the Attorney General, The Land Commission*, Mc Mahon J. unreported May 22, 1980 at 8.

[86] That is assuming that it imposes a liability or penalty as proscribed by Art. 34 in the first event.

[87] *In re Solicitors Act* [1960] I.R. 239, 274.

maximum limit set either in absolute terms or as a percentage of the undertaking's turnover.[88] In *State (Calcul International Limited) and Solatrex (International) v. Appeal Commissioners* Barron J.[89] stated:

> "The payment of customs due to your value added tax is related proportionately to the relevant tax table income. Such payments cannot have far-reaching effects on the fortune of the taxpayer . . . since in each case the liability is relative being proportionate to either his income or his turnover as the case may be".

However, account should be taken of a subsequent High Court remark in relation to this comment: "It may well be that the revenue cases may best be regarded as a special category as far as the question of administration of justice is concerned."[90]

There is other authority that an administrative body may impose a financial onus on a party. In *Madden v. The Land Commission* the function of the Land Commission (or on appeal the appeal tribunal)[91] was held to be sanctioned by Article 37. "It is not the power to dispossess the owner which is in question here but the power to ascertain the fair market value of the land expropriated and on that basis to fix the price paid to the owner."[92] However, calculating the "fair market value" of land could be a more mechanical exercise than to calculate a fine proportionate to the severity of an infringement of competition law. Elsewhere the High Court has stated that: "there is authority for the proposition that the assessment of compensation is a limited function and that this role can be carried out by experts acting in a judicious manner."[93]

---

[88] Art. 15(2) of Regulation17/62 " the Commission may by decision impose on undertakings . . . fines of from 1,000 to 1 million (ECU) , or a sum in excess thereof but not exceeding 10% of the turnover in the preceding business year . . . " Guidelines for the imposition of fines are contained in [1998] O.J. C 9/3.

[89] Unreported, High Court, Dec. 18, 1996.

[90] *Blascaod Mor Teoranta v. Commissioner of Public Works in Ireland* High Court, Feb. 27. 1998. [1998] I.E.H.C. 38 para. 242. Kelly, *The Irish Constitution* (Hogan and Whyte eds., 3rd ed., 1994), p 569 states that the reasoning in *The State(Calcul and Solarex)* seems very questionable.

[91] s.5 of the Land Act 1950 gives the owner a right to have a price fixed at an amount equal to the market value.

[92] McMahon J., unreported, May 22, 1980.

[93] *Blascaod Mór Teoranta v. Commissioner of Public Works in Ireland per* Budd J. [1998] IEHC 38, at para. 253. The High Court examined the Commissioner's role in assessing compensation in the context of compulsory acquisition (Acquisition of Lands (Assessment of Compensation) Act 1919) and held that the five *McDonald* criteria were satisfied as follows: "(1) The property arbitrator has jurisdiction over any question of disputed compensation and so has power to determine disputes about entitlement to compensation as well as to amounts awarded. His jurisdiction is not confined to the question of quantum.(2)The property arbitrator decides whether the landowner is entitled to compensation and the award imposes a liability on the acquiring authority to pay the award.(3)The property arbitrator's award is final and binding on the parties...and there is no appeal from his award.(4)An award may be enforced in the same manner as a judgment or order by leave of a Court without the Court considering the merits of the dispute leading to the award.(5)The making of an Order which as a matter of history is an Order characteristic of the Courts."

However, the opportunity for a competition authority to award compensation may be of limited usefulness. In particular, in the absence of an adversarial dispute between opposing parties there is no party in whose favour an award of compensation could be made.

Mention of compensation raises the issue of the *purpose* of a sanction and is allied to the nature of proceedings for the breach of competition law. The type of liability is pivotal because the exception provided by Article 37 of Bunreacht na hÉireann is expressly ruled out if the matter is criminal. Furthermore, as the Competition and Merger Review Group noted in advance of the Proposal, Article 29.4.7 would likely not be available to immunise criminal powers from constitutional challenge.[94]

4.(3)(b)(i) Criminal

While the imposition by national competition authorities of fines and periodic penalty payments is expressly *permitted*, but not required, by the Proposal, it does not elaborate on their detailed operation. In contrast, the European Commission's power to impose substantial[95] fines, including periodic penalties[96] under Regulation 17/62 (and in identical terms Article 22(5) of the Proposal) is expressly described as not being of a criminal law nature. Nevertheless, Advocate General Darmon has opined that certain decisions of the Commission were "manifestly of a penal nature".[97] The ECJ has also recognised the punitive and deterrent purpose of fines.[98] Furthermore, a fine of five per cent of annual turnover under French competition law was held to be a "criminal charge" by the European Commission of Human Rights.[99]

---

[94] "It seems unlikely that it could be regarded as a necessary consequence of membership of the Community, no matter what powers are given to the Competition Authority to apply Articles 81 and 82 that the Competition Authority could necessarily have the power to convict persons of criminal offences since there is no concept of criminal offence under Community law (notwithstanding the penal nature of the fines which the Commission can impose which may require that procedures be adopted which give the sort of safeguards that one sometimes only finds in criminal law)" *Competition and Merger Review Group Report* para. 3.5.20 p.48.

[95] Art. 15(2) of Regulation 17/62 " the Commission may by decision impose on undertakings . . . fines of from 1,000 to 1 million (ECU) , or a sum in excess thereof but not exceeding 10% of the turnover in the preceding business year."

[96] Reg. 17/62. The fining power is not limited to established infringements of Articles 81 and/or 82 but is also available for failing to accurately supply information requested or for failure to discharge an obligation contained in an exemption.

[97] Cases 89, 104, 114, 116–117, 125–129/85 *Ahlström Oy v. Commission* [1993] E.C.R. I–1307. Similarly Case T 7/89 *Hercules v. Commission* AG Vesterdorf [1991] E.C.R. II 1711.

[98] C100&103 /80 *Musique Diffusion Francaise v. Commission* [1983] E.C.R. 1825 and Case 49/69 *BASF v. Commission* [1972] E.C.R. 713.

[99] *Societe Stenuit v. France* (1992) 14 E.H.R.R. 509. In Case C–185/95P *Baustahlgewebe v. Commission* Advocate–General Leger "it cannot be disputed-and the Commission does not dispute that in light of the caselaw of the European Court of Human Rights and the opinions of the European Commission of Human Rights, the present case involves a criminal charge" [1998] E.C.R. I–8417. It is beyond the scope of this Chapter to examine the implications of

This raises the question of whether under Irish law the power to impose a fine must be seen as criminal?

> "A criminal matter within the meaning of Article 37 can be construed as a procedure associated with the prosecution of a person for a crime . . . The essential ingredient of a criminal matter must be its association with the determination of a question as to whether a crime against the State or against the public has been committed."[100]

In *McLoughlin v. Tuite* the Supreme Court, considering whether the fiscal penalties in the Income Tax Act 1967 were criminal rather than civil ones recoverable as a liquidated sum, held that payment "of a sum of money . . . which is an involuntary payment and which is not related to any form of compensation or reparation necessary to the state but is rather a deterrent or a sanction"[101] by a party is not inevitably indicative of a crime in the context of Article 38.[102]

Courts examine the scheme and purpose of the Act to discern whether the legislature intended to create a civil or criminal penalty. To this end indicia of crimes have been identified from textual and contextual factors. Assessing section 186 of the Customs Consolidation Act 1867, Kingsmill Moore J. identified three criminal indicia the most relevant of which for this chapter is:

> "[T]he sanction is punitive, and not merely a matter of fiscal reparation, for the penalty is £100 or three times the duty paid value of the goods and failure to pay, even where the offender has not the means, involves imprisonment."[103]

In the same case a more expansive list of indicia was expressed in the judgment of Lavery J.[104] These were considered later in *McLoughlin v. Tuite*.[105]

---

the Human Rights Convention for procedures and the rights of defence such as the right against self incrimination.

[100] *The State (Murray) v. Mc Rann* [1976] I.R. 133 approved in *Keady v. Garda Commissioner* [1992] 2 I.R. 197 *per* O' Flaherty J.

[101] *McLoughlin v. Tuite* [1989] I.R. 82, 90.

[102] Article 38.1 states "No person shall be tried on any criminal charge save in due course of law"

[103] *Melling v. O'Mathghamhna* [1962] I.R. 1, 25, *per* Kingsmill Moore J. The other indicia cited are "'(i) they are offences against the community at large and not against an individual . . . (iii) they require *mens rea* for the act must be done 'knowingly' and 'with intent to evade the prohibition or restriction. '*Mens rea* is not an invariable ingredient of a criminal offence, and even in a civil action of a debt for a penalty it may be necessary to show that there was *mens rea* where the act complained of is an offence 'in the nature of a crime' . . . but where *mens rea* is made an element of an offence it is generally an indication of criminality".

[104] *ibid.*, at 9.

[105] "It is of significance, *though not a determining factor*, that a consideration of the statutory provisions . . . do not disclose any single one of the matters indicated by the learned judge in that case [Lavery J. in *Melling v. Mathghamhna*] as *indicia* of a criminal charge. No question of the detention or bringing into custody of a person who fails to make a return arises. There is no concept of nor provision for a charge in any way appropriate to or similar to the charge of a criminal offence. No right to search the person detained or to examine papers found

Greater importance may be attached to the descriptions in the text such as "offence" or "conviction" rather than the amount of the penalty.[106]

The Proposal does not regulate the effect, within the national systems, of decisions adopted by national competition authorities. Neither does it attempt to harmonise any of the national procedures, institutions or penalties. Indeed this has been voiced as a criticism by those concerned by the prospect of inconsistent application of EC competition law.[107] Because Article 5 of the Proposal is silent as regards any criminal indicia, and does not contain any words indicative of a crime, it would not prevent Irish implementing laws being drafted to provide for non-criminal financial sanctions to be imposed by an administrative body.

It is clear that if the competition authority is to stay within the combined terms of Articles 34 and 37 of Bunreacht na hÉireann it could be granted only limited powers to apply EC competition law. The possibilities for it to determine that an infringement occurred and, consequently, directly to impose sanctions are curtailed. The possibilities of administrative bodies making financial awards against corporate bodies have not been extensively tested under Article 37 which makes it impossible to state with certainty that even the essential power to make a "cease and desist" type of order would be within the terms of Article 37. The application of competition law by an Irish administrative body is thereby restricted to an investigation which relies on subsequent court proceedings for any eventual effect.

4.(4) NEW MODELS

To ensure the effective application of EC competition law, either increased powers must be given to the Competition Authority (or other administrative body) and/or efficient interaction between it and the courts must be institutionalised.

---

upon him arises by reason of his failure. He can never be brought in custody before any court in connection with the matter and no question of bail arises. Most importantly of all, he is never, by reason of the imposition on him of a penalty under this section, in any risk of being imprisoned for default of payment." [1989] I.R. 82 (emphasis added). In the High Court judgment in *Mc Loughlin*, Carroll J. expressly averted to the continuation of the liability after death as another of the indicia. [1986] I.L.R.M. 304 at 311. Also see *Downes v. DPP* [1987] I.R. 139 Barr J.

106 "A sum of £800 today or more particularly £500 in 1926 would represent a very substantial penalty for the offences in question . . . But it seems to me that the *crucial factors* in the present case are the presence of the words "an offence" and "on summary conviction." *DPP v. Boyle* [1994] 2 I.R. 221, at 226 (emphasis added). Also *Downes v. DPP* [1987] I.R. 139, 142 *per* Barr J.

107 Mavroidis and Neven "The White Paper: A Whiter Shade of Pale of Interests, and Interests"in "*European Competition Law Annual 2000: The Modernisation of EC Antitrust Policy* Ehlermann & Atanasiu,eds (Hart Publishing, 2001), p.207

Granting the Competition Authority competence to make orders imposing liability/penalties and simply providing for an appeal to court from the decision would be inadequate.[108] Of course, if the Competition Authority was granted combined investigative and adjudicatory functions, due regard would have to be given to the principles of constitutional justice, namely, *nemo iudex in causa sua* and *audi alteram partem*. Assuming that immunity under Article 29.4.7 is unavailable, the scope of Article 37 is pivotal: namely can the power of an administrative body to impose penalties, in any circumstances, be regarded as "limited"?

Limiting the effect of a power to penalise could be achieved by providing for fixed amount penalties which eliminate any discretion to be exercised.[109] While this is most viable regarding procedural breaches it may be possible regarding substantive breaches. It has been suggested that fines to correct public law wrongs against the Community be fixed and imposed by the European Commission with a percentage going to the relevant investigating authority.[110] The amount recoverable by the Irish administrative authority, under such an arrangement, could be fixed in Irish legislation as a specified percentage which would preclude the exercise of any discretion.

Another part of the solution may lie in drawing a distinction between substantive breaches and procedural (technical) infringements of competition law. Procedural infringements could include malfeasance other than a breach of Article 81 or 82, *e.g.* undertakings refusing to cooperate with an investigation or supplying incorrect information. The effect of a measure taken by the Competition Authority in the second scenario could be of relatively limited effect. An interesting approach is taken in the Company Law Enforcement Act 2001. Under Section 66 the Registrar of Companies can deliver a notice to a company stating that it has failed to deliver, file or make a return or document required under the Companies Acts. The recipient can remedy the default and make a payment of the prescribed amount and thereby avoid prosecution.[111] It may be possible to specify that failure to perform certain procedural events would trigger similar action by the Competition Authority.

To allocate the adjudicatory and penalising functions between the Competition Authority and the courts while ensuring the effective application

---

[108] "[T]he existence of an appeal to the Courts cannot restore constitutionality to a tribunal whose decisions if unappealed, amount to an administration of justice". *In Re Solicitors Act 1954* [1960] I.R. 239, 275.

[109] See *McLoughlin v. Tuite* [1989] I.R. 82.

[110] By a delegate at the Freiburg Competition Law Conference on November 9 and 10, 2000 as reported in Jones "Regulation 17: The Impact of the Current Application of Articles 81 and 82 by National Competition Authorities on the European Commission's Proposals for Reform" Eur. Competition L.Rev. 2001, 22(10) 405, at p.406. From a European Community perspective this has the attraction of resolving problems of extra-territorial effect and eliminating discrepancies in national competition authorities' procedures.

[111] See above Doherty para 5(6) on the possibility of "financial payment obligations" and "on the spot" fines, under the Communications Regulation Act 2002.

of competition law requires legislative creativity. If the final version of Article 36 of the Proposal allows courts to be designated as national competition authorities that would permit interaction between the administrative and judicial bodies for the *public enforcement* of EC Competition law in Member States, such as Ireland, which do not have the integrated enforcement system.[112] Pursuant to the Competition Act 2002 investigations of civil and criminal infringements of Articles 81 and 82 may be carried out by the Competition Authority which may initiate civil and minor criminal proceedings and only courts may determine a breach and decide on a penalty.[113] Defining the concept of 'national competition authority' so that some functions can be ascribed to an administrative body and others to a judicial body will impose restrictions and obligations on a court adjudicating, in a public enforcement capacity, on infringements. This outcome raises difficulties in an Irish context. Perhaps the greatest concerns in this regard stem from the fact that under the Competition Act 2002 infringements of Articles 81 and 82 may be criminal offences. Article 11(6) of the Proposal provides "The initiation by the Commission of proceedings for the adoption of a decision under this Regulation shall relieve the competition authorities of the Member States of their competence to apply Articles 81 and 82 of the Treaty." Ousting of jurisdiction for an Irish court hearing a criminal case raises serious questions about, *inter alia*, due process. The potentially criminal nature of infringements is also relevant for exchanges of information among the competition authorities under Article 12 of the Proposal. In particular there is a limitation in Article 12 (b) to the extent that only financial penalties may be imposed when applying EC Competition law on the basis of the exchanged information. At the very least this complicates prosecutions in Ireland if the penalty of imprisonment available under the 2002 Act must be ruled out where evidence comes from information exchanges.

Another relevant consideration is that particular duties are imposed by EC law on courts which may exceed those imposed on administrative bodies. As Dr Temple Lang points out: "National courts have a duty to raise questions of Community law (not just competition law) on their own initiative (Peterbroek . . .)" and "National courts are obliged by Article 10 EC Treaty to give effective remedies to protect Community law rights even if this means disregarding a rule of national law and providing a remedy which did not previously exist under national law (Borelli and Simmenthal)."[114]

Thus the allocation of the national competition authority's competence in Ireland between administrative and judicial instititions is not without difficulty.

---

112 This term describes the European Community model of the Commission.
113 See above para 4(2)(a)(i).
114 Temple Lang, Foreword to Power, *Competition Law and Practice* (Butterworths, 2001) references omitted. See above Keville, para 1(1)(c).

It is submitted that innovative legislation providing for interaction between administrative and judicial may need to be drafted in Ireland.

The Competition and Merger Review Group, subsequent to the White Paper but in advance of the Proposal, recommended that the Competition Authority be empowered to apply "any rules of Community law which form part of Community competition law insofar as such rules, as a matter of Community law, may be applied by a national authority."[115]

Specifically it recommended that:

> "Consideration be given to constituting the Competition Authority as an adjudicatory body to hear and adjudicate upon complaints [of domestic law] and/or Articles 81 and 82 within constitutional limits. In that context and with a view to ensuring that breaches of national and Community law can be dealt with in a common procedure and having regard to the constitutional limitations in entrusting an adjudicatory function in respect of national law to the Competition Authority consideration should be given to the replacement of criminal sanctions whereby the Competition Authority would recommend fines which would be finally determined by a court. In that context the function of the enforcement of competition law should be entrusted to a Director of Competition law enforcement who would be entirely independent of the Competition Authority. Consideration should be given to an alternative method of confining the adjudicatory function of the Competition Authority to ascertaining the facts, to be embodied in a report to be transmitted to the High Court which would then decide upon the issue of whether any breach of the legislation had occurred and the consequences thereof."[116]

It should be noted that the position of Director of Competition law enforcement, created under the Competition (Amendment) Act 1996, was not continued in the Competition Act 2002. Difficulties may arise with the proposition that the Competition Authority ascertain facts and send them in a report to the court, if the veracity of the facts was contested. In *K v. An Bord Altranais*[117] the applicant sought an order directing that contested issues of fact which arose in a hearing before the Fitness to Practice Committee should be tried by the High Court on oral evidence. The High Court denied the application but the Supreme Court allowed the appeal. The Supreme Court noted that the issue was not "as to whether certain agreed events or conduct constituted unprofessional conduct or not, but rather the straightforward question as to whether the events as alleged by the witnesses occurred or not".[118] It is possible that particular facts of the case, which entail serious personal consequences for professional misconduct, may have dictated the approach. Nonetheless, it is noteworthy that the Supreme Court concluded:

---

[115] Competition and Merger Review Group Report para. 3.4.5 p.38.
[116] Competition and Merger Review Group Report para. 3.5.29 p.51.
[117] [1990] 2 I.R. 396. I am grateful to John O' Dowd for drawing my attention to this case.
[118] [1990] 2 I.R p.402. It is clear that this finding will not apply to every case involving professional disciplinary procedures. " . . . there are a great number of cases . . . in which the

"[W]here the whole question as to whether the applicant is a fit person to remain as a registered nurse depends on the truth or falsity of evidence as to her conduct and not on any question of standards or rules or principles of professional conduct, it seems to me essential that the High Court must reach its own conclusion as to the truth or falsity of those allegations. In order for it to do so, it must, it seems to me, hear the witnesses, for not on any other basis could it safely reach any such conclusion. Were the matter now to be tried on affidavit . . . and the High Court to be bound by the findings of fact made by the Fitness to Practice Committee, then the effective decision with regard to the erasure of the applicant's name from the register would necessarily have been made by that Committee.The High Court would, in the particular facts of this case, if it confined itself to affidavit evidence, be merely endorsing the procedures of that Committee and, of necessity, accepting its findings of the facts."[119]

Another means of enhancing the role of the Competition Authority would be to empower it to accept binding promises (e.g to amend conduct) from undertakings which admit to being in breach of competition law. Failure to respect the promises could be actionable in the courts.[120] Another possibility is for the Competition Authority to set a deadline within which an infringement is to be remedied and failure to so do could be punishable by a fine imposed by the courts. Inspiration for more radical amendment could be drawn from the Employment/Labour Law field. The Employment Appeals Tribunal, Labour Court, the Equality Authority and the Director of Equality Investigations enjoy significant powers, including the power to order payment of monies.[121]

---

issues are not direct issues of fact but rather are questions of propriety, professional conduct, professional standards and the consequences of undisputed facts. In all those cases no necessity may arise in any proceedings . . . for any oral evidence in the High Court" p.404.

[119] *ibid.*, p.403.

[120] This approach is analogous to the power in the Proposal given to the European Commission to accept "undertakings" and to the mechanism in the Competition Act 2002 (ss20 and 26)for the Competition Authority to accept commitments in the context of negotiations for merger approval.

[121] Employment Equality Act 1998, s.62 allows the Equality Authority to serve a non-discrimination notice on a person who, *inter alia*, has discriminated or has failed to comply with an equality clause or equal remuneration term. The notice *inter alia* "requires the person on whom it is served not to commit the act or omission constituting the discrimination or contravention, or where appropriate to comply with the equality clause or equal remuneration term" and " specify, in the case of discrimination, what steps the Authority requires to be taken by the person on whom it is served in order not to commit the discrimination". A person served with a non-discrimination notice may appeal to the Labour Court which can either confirm the notice or allow the appeal (s.63). Failure to comply with a non-discrimination notice is an offence under s.65. Pursuant to s.82 (1) the Director of Equality Investigations in a decision may order redress in the following forms (*inter alia*) (a) an order for compensation in the form of...arrears of remuneration...(b) an order for equal remuneration...(c) an order for compensation for the effects of acts of discrimination . . . (d) an order for equal treatment and (e) an order that a person or persons specified in the order take a course of action which is so specified: Financial limits are specified in s.84(4) "the maximum amount which may be ordered by the Director of Equality Investigations or the Labour Court . . . by way of compensation . . . in any case where the complainant was in

However, the constitutionality of some of these institutions' powers may not be free from doubt.[122]

4.(5) IMPLEMENTATION OF REGULATIONS IN IRISH LAW

If the Competition Act 2002 is inadequate *vis à vis* Ireland's duties under the eventual Regulation, consideration must be given as to how the reforms may be effected in Irish law. It is significant that they will be contained in a Regulation. A Regulation is expressly prescribed by Article 249 (ex Article 189) as being "binding in its entirety and directly applicable in all Member States." Regulations, unlike Directives, do not usually require legislation for their implementation[123] and, in fact, implementing measures are undesirable.[124] However, some Regulations may either require or permit Member States to adopt rules as, for example, in the recent judgment in *Maher v. Minister for Agriculture, Food and Rural Development.*[125] This case provides guidance regarding the reception into the Irish legal system of EC Regulations which expressly allow a discretion to the Member States regarding the attainment of

---

receipt of remuneration . . . shall be an amount equal to either 104 times either (a) the amount of that remuneration determined on a weekly basis, or (b) where it is greater, the amount determined on a weekly basis which the complainant would have received at that date but for the act of the discrimination or victimisation in question, and in any other case shall be £10,000.". Interest may be ordered at the rate applicable under the Courts Act 1981.The decision of the Director may be appealed to the Labour Court. Under s.91, the Circuit Court may order a person bound by a final decision of the Director or a final determination of the Labour Court to comply with the decision/determination. Pursuant to the Equal Status Act 2000, s.27 (1) "(a)Director may make an order for compensation for the effects of discrimination or (b) an order that a person . . . specified in the order take a course of action which is so specified. (2) the maximum amount which may be ordered by the Director by way of compensation under subsection (1)(a) shall be the maximum amount that could be awarded by the District Court in civil cases in contract." Decision of the Director may be appealed to the Circuit Court (s.28).

122 See Casey, *Constitutional Law in Ireland* (3rd ed., 2000), p.265 where the Employment Appeals Tribunal and the Labour Court are treated under the heading of "unresolved questions". Also Kelly, *The Irish Constitution* (Hogan and Whyte eds., 3rd ed.,1994), p.564 contains the heading "Functions of the Employment Appeals Tribunal Constitutionally Suspect?"

123 "The direct application of a Regulation means that its entry into force and its application in favour of or against those subject to it are independent of any measure of reception into national law. By virtue of the obligations arising from the Treaty and assumed on ratification, Member States are under a duty not to obstruct the direct applicability inherent in Regulations and other rules of Community law. Strict compliance with this obligation is an indispensable condition of simultaneous and uniform application of Community Regulations throughout the Community."; Case 34/73 *Variola v. Amministrazione delle Finanze* [1973] E.C.R. 981, 990; also Case 94/77 *Zerbone v. Amminstrazione delle Finanze dello Stato* [1978] E.C.R. 99, para. 23.

124 "Member States must not adopt . . . a measure by which the Community nature of a legal rule and the consequences which arise from it are obscured" Case 94/77 *Zerbone v. Amminstrazione delle Finanze dello Stato* [1978] E.C.R. 99, at para. 26.

125 [2001] 2 I.R. 139. For a critique of the judgment see above Costello, para 2(2)(c).

a mandatory goal.[126] The Supreme Court cited *Eridania v. Minister of Agriculture and Forestry* in which the ECJ stated that:

> "The fact that a Regulation is directly applicable does not prevent the provisions of that Regulation from empowering a community institution or a Member State to take implementing measures. In the latter case the detailed rules for the exercise of that power are governed by the public law of the Member State in question; however, the direct applicability of the measure empowering the Member States to take the national measures in question will mean that the national courts may ascertain whether such national measures are in accordance with the content of the community regulation."[127]

The law was thus summarised in *Maher* by Fennelly J

> "Member States, acting within the framework of Community regulations, exercise powers or discretion which are conferred on them for the furtherance of the objectives of the scheme in question. Community law does not require any particular form of implementation. That is a matter for the legal system of the Member State concerned, except that the implementation must not have the effect of impeding the *effectiveness* of Community law."[128]

Depending on the particular circumstances, three types of measures are potentially available for the implementation of EC measures, namely: Acts of the Oireachtas; Ministerial Regulations in the form of Statutory Instruments (S.I.s);[129] and administrative measures. Keane C.J. in *Maher*, having ascertained that the implementation of the Regulation by legislation was clearly necessitated[130] by the obligations of membership, considered the mode of its implementation by posing the question:

> "[W]hether, given that the making of detailed rules in legislative form, to at least that extent, was necessitated by the obligations of membership, their being made in the form of SI 2000 other than by an Act was in conflict with the exclusive legislative role of the Oireachtas under Article 15.1 and was not necessitated by the obligations of membership."[131]

---

[126] As described by Keane C.J. "[T]he EC Regulations required the Member States to adopt detailed rules as to the transfer of quotas with land and it also required the authorisation of temporary transfers. . . . However in three areas it was left to the Member States to decide whether they elected to pursue specified courses of action" [2001] 2 I.R. 139, 183.

[127] Para. 34.

[128] [2001] 2 I.R. 139, 251 (emphasis added). It is outside the scope of this chapter (with its focus on the implications of Bunreacht na hÉireann) to examine the implications of the EC duty that EC law be applied uniformly so as to avoid unequal treatment of producers and traders.

[129] European Communities Act 1972, s. 3.

[130] Art. 7.1 expressly required the making of detailed rules by the member States as to the transfer of quotas with a holding in the case of its sale, lease or transfer by inheritance to purchasers" (paras. 89–90).

[131] Para. 91.

Delegated legislation, according to *CityView Press v. An Comhairle Oiliúna*,[132] is only permitted if it does not exceed the principles and policies of the "parent" Act. This was applied in the European context as follows:

> "Regulations, being part of domestic law of the State, may be treated as instruments setting out the policies and principles for subordinate legislation. If the principles and policies are set out in Community regulations then there may be no role for the national parliament to determine principles and policies. If the principles and policies are established in law in the State, albeit in Community regulations rather than domestic legislation, then it is open to the Minister to make the required and technically detailed statutory instruments."[133]

The possibility that a court may act as the national authority gives Ireland some discretion as to which bodies it designates as "national competition authorities". The existence in the eventual Regulation of a discretion will not, in itself, rule out the option of a Statutory Instrument.

> "[I]f the principles and policies are to be found in the European regulations then it is open to the Minister to proceed by way of statutory instrument. If there are choices to be made within a scheme then these choices may not be policy decisions. The exercise of a choice governed fully by a structure established in a policy document (such as a European regulation) is not the determination of a policy."[134]

Clearly whether any changes to Irish law may be made in the form of a Statutory Instrument rather than an Act depends on the substance of the eventual Regulation:

At present it is premature to speculate on how the eventual Regulation may be implemented. Also it is possible that to identify the pertinent policies and principles account may be taken not just of the Regulation alone. Fennelly J. in *Maher* considered the particular nature, needs and position of the Common Agricultural Policy. He noted that:

> "[T]his recital and the general scheme of the milk quota regime demonstrate that the State is acting as a delegate of the Community in making the choice to separate land and milk quota. As is shown by the case law, the fact that Community regulations authorise the Member States to exercise discretion does not take action of the latter kind outside the scope of the Community regime. *Member States' discretionary action is circumscribed by the objectives*

---

[132] [1980] I.R. 381. A more recent case is the majority decision of *Laurentiu v. Minister for Justice* [2000] I.L.R.M. 1. For discussion on the application of the test see above Costello para 2(2)(c).

[133] Para. 169 *per* Denham in *Maher.* Similarly *per* Keane C. J.: "In each case it is necessary to look to the Directive or Regulation and, it maybe, the Treaties in order to reach a conclusion as to whether the statutory instrument does no more than fill in the details of the policies and principles contained in the EC or EU legislation" para. 99.

[134] Para. 174, *per* Denham in *Maher.*

of the scheme authorising it. The milk quota is itself a creature entirely of Community law".[135]

Thus, the position of competition law as one of the foundations of the Treaty and other principles of EC law may be relevant in circumscribing the discretion available to Ireland in implementing the Regulation.

4.(6) CONCLUSION

The extensive changes proposed by the European Commission for the application and enforcement of EC competition law are significant for every Member State. In the case of Ireland the challenges presented to the legal system are of a constitutional magnitude. If the Competition Act 2002 is inadequate for the purposes of the eventual Regulation additional implementing measures will need to be drafted. New legislation would present an opportunity to re-draw the existing relationships between administrative bodies and the courts and specifically to test the boundaries of Article 37 of Bunreacht na hÉireann.

---

[135] *ibid.*, p.257 (emphasis added).

BIBLIOGRAPHY

Casey, *Constitutional Law in Ireland* (3rd ed., 2000).

Ehlermann & Atanasiu, *European Competition Law Annual 2000: The Modernisation of EC Antitrust Policy* (Hart Publishing, 2001).

Finlay and Hyland, "The Duties of Co-Operation of National Authorities and Courts and the Community Institutions under Article 10 EC" *Irish Journal of European Law* 2000, 267.

Hogan and Whelan, *Ireland and the European Union; Constitutional and Statutory Texts and Commentary* (Sweet and Maxwell 1995).

Morgan, *The Separation of Powers in the Irish Constitution* (Round Hall Sweet & Maxwell, 1997).

Power, *Competition Law and Practice* (Butterworths, 2001).

Temple Lang, "The Duties of Co-operation of National Authorities and Courts under Article 10 EC: Two More Reflections" E.L. Rev. 2001 26(1) 84.

Temple Lang, "The Duties of National Authorities under Community Constitutional Law" (1998) 23 (2)E.L. Rev. 109.

Temple Lang "Community Constitutional Law: Article 5 EEC Treaty" 27 C.M.L.Rev. 645 (1990).

Wesseling, *The Modernisation of EC Antitrust Law* (Hart, Oxford, 2000).

5. EC TELECOMMUNICATIONS LAW IN IRELAND

BARRY DOHERTY*

5.(1) INTRODUCTION

This chapter examines how European Community (EC)[1] telecommunications law applies in Ireland. As will be seen, the original Irish law has been changed greatly by EC Directives. Those Directives in turn are in the process of being modified, and new legislation has recently been adopted in Ireland as well. For these reasons, the topic is divided as follows:

5.(2) Original Irish law
5.(3) The first wave of EC Directives 1988–98
5.(4) Irish legislation based on the new Directives
5.(5) The new EC legislation
5.(6) The Communications Regulation Act 2002

It does not aim to be an exhaustive guide to either the EC Directives or the Irish law (these can be found elsewhere)[2] but instead attempts to provide an overview of the issues involved.

---

* LLB. (Dub.), LL.M. (Bruges), Ph.D. (Dub.), Barrister-at-Law. Senior Legal Adviser, Office of the Director of Telecommunications Regulation. The views expressed are purely personal.
[1] This text uses the term "EC" throughout to describe Community law. This may seem old-fashioned to those who use the more recent term "EU" but strictly speaking the European Union does not deal with telecommunications matters. These are governed by the European Community Treaty (in particular Arts. 95 and 86), not the Treaty on European Union. The term "telecommunications" itself may become a quaint anachronism: as discussed below, the new Directives use the term "electronic communications." It remains to be seen how popular this term will become.
[2] The background to the Irish legislation can be found in Hall, *The Electronic Age*, (Oak Tree Press, Dublin, 1993). Unfortunately, this only goes up to 1993. On EC telecommunications law, the history and policy behind the Directives (especially the interplay between liberalisation and harmonisation Directives) is found in Larouche, *Competition Law and Regulation in European Telecommunications*, (Hart, Oxford and Portland (Oregon), 2000), hereafter called "Larouche." This work is quite academic in focus; for a text more aimed at practitioners, see Garzaniti, *Telecommunications, Broadcasting and the Internet: EC Competition Law and Regulation* (Sweet & Maxwell, London, 2000). In a series of chapters by different authors, *Telecommunications Law* (Walden and Angel eds., Blackstone, London, 2001) goes into detail on the U.K. situation. Some passages discuss general technological issues (*e.g.* interconnection) and there is a specific chapter on EC law. Finally, the World Bank has published an interesting handbook describing policy approaches in developed countries generally: it is available at *http://www.infodev.org/projects/314regulationhandbook/*

5.(2) ORIGINAL IRISH LAW

The story of what is now called "telecommunications" can be traced back to
the nineteenth century, perhaps with the invention of the telegraph (1844) or
the telephone (1875). Each country in Europe began regulating these new
media, but in general the new technology was rapidly brought under the
control of the State.[3] In the United Kingdom, this was done by section 4 of the
Telegraph Act 1869[4] which vested the statutory monopoly in the Postmaster
General and later in a Minister.[5] In a development which shows how technology can outstrip the law, it was later held that the telephone (although
invented after the 1869 Act) came within the legal definition of "telegraph"
and, hence, infringed the monopoly.[6] For a period there was competition
between telephone networks run by private operators and a network set up by
the Post Office until the Telephone Transfer Act 1911 merged the existing
networks into a single publicly-owned one.[7]

On independence, the newly-established Irish Free State inherited this
model of state-owned telecommunications which was not seriously questioned
until the 1980s. A similarly important role for the Minister is to be found in the
Wireless Telegraphy Act 1926 which made it illegal to use or possess "apparatus
for wireless telegraphy" without a licence from the same Minister. Surprising
though it may seem, these venerable pieces of legislation are still with us
today: today's telecommunications operators require licences under the 1926
Act if they wish to use radio waves, and their right to operate networks is
defined in law as an exception to the Minister's monopoly under the Telegraph
Act 1869.

This system was largely unchanged until the 1980s, and meant that the
Department of Posts and Telegraphs was both operator and regulator. It had a
monopoly on providing telecommunications services (and on building
networks, etc., for them) and also decided on matters which are now left to the
regulator, such as price increases, technical standards, etc. The Department
was also the only postal operator.

The Postal and Telecommunications Services Act 1983 made some
organisational changes. It created two companies (An Post and Telecom
Éireann) and granted them both a monopoly in their respective fields. Under
sections 16–19 of the Act the companies were still controlled by the Minister,
who continued to act as regulator.

---

[3] See generally Hall, *The Electronic Age*, above n.2, chap 8, on the early legislation.

[4] 32 & 33 Vict. c. 73.

[5] At present, the powers described refer to the Minister for Communications, Marine and
Natural Resources. Since the title of the relevant Minister has changed over the years (from
1997 to 2002 it was Minister for Public Enterprise), this text will use the term "the Minister"
for simplicity.

[6] *AG v. Edison Telephone Co. of London* (1880) 6 QBD 244.

[7] See generally Hall, above n.2, pp.99–105.

Today, the situation of both companies is strikingly different. An Post is still controlled by the Minister and has a legal monopoly on certain services. Telecom Éireann (renamed eircom) is now in private hands and has lost all its former monopoly rights. Both are now subject to regulation by the Office of the Director of Telecommunications Regulation rather than the Minister.

These changes were all caused by EC directives, discussed in the next section.

5.(3) FIRST WAVE OF EC DIRECTIVES

By the 1970s, the telephone had "developed from a service restricted mainly to business and emergency use to a feature present in two out of every three households in the European Community."[8] In all EC countries, telephone services (and the sale of telecommunications equipment) were in the hands of monopolies which aimed to provide telephone services to as many subscribers as possible. In order to do this, rental and connection charges were kept low (and to compensate, call charges kept high). Equally, the price of local calls was subsidised by higher prices for long-distance and international calls.[9] Overall, many European telecommunications monopolies only offered a mediocre service for a high price.[10]

5.(3)(a) Background to the Directives

In the 1980s two factors combined to challenge this state of affairs, namely a political consensus in favour of market forces and renewed activism by the European Commission.

5.(3)(a)(i) Market forces – free trade and liberalisation

One writer identifies 1979 as a turning point; at a meeting hosted by the European Commission in Dublin that year, it was agreed that Europe was lagging behind in the market for "teleinformatics" compared to Japan and the United States. Although the steps proposed by the Commission were modest, without this industrial policy focus perhaps nothing would have been done.[11] (When the story of European attitudes to the Internet comes to be written, the Lisbon summit of March 2000 may prove to be a similar turning point). In addition, this industrial policy focus might explain why the first steps were towards

---

[8] Ungerer and Costello, *Telecommunications in Europe*, (Office for Official Publications of the EC, Luxembourg, 1990) p.25.

[9] *ibid.*, p.30.

[10] See Larouche, above n.2, pp.1–3.

[11] Ramsey in *Proceedings of the Fordham Corporate Law Institute* 1995 (Hawk, ed., Simon Bender & Sons, New York 1996) p.561, 562.

liberalising equipment – creating markets for existing manufacturers, not new markets for new entrants. In particular, the EC came under pressure from the United States to open up markets for American firms.[12]

The European governments of the day, often from the right of the political spectrum, agreed that free trade required barriers to be abolished. At EC level it was the era of the Single European Act and a political consensus that a single European market could be created by reducing legal barriers. At national level this was an era of experiments with privatisation: in the United Kingdom the Thatcher government privatised large sectors of the economy, including the state-owned British Telecommunications (BT). BT was privatised in 1984, and a second operator, Mercury, was allowed to compete with it. Privatisation was seen as a means of improving performance and raising capital for new investments. In addition, the growth of digitisation meant that the unregulated computer market was bound to collide with the highly regulated telecommunications market.[13]

5.(3)(a)(ii) Commission activism

For many years, competition law had *de facto* not applied to the telecommunications sector. One author, Thomas J. Ramsay, identifies three obstacles to activism by the Commission:

> "(i) the economic and political clout of PTTs,[14] their associated labor unions and 'national champion' equipment suppliers; (ii) the lack of pan-European providers of telecommunications services; and (iii) the relative inefficiency of the Community's institutions in carrying out objectives of the Treaty of Rome. In sum, few in Brussels at that time were prepared to declare war – or even have a skirmish – with Europe's PTTs."[15]

From the 1980s, the political consensus in favour of free trade made it possible to propose changes which might have been resisted in a different political climate. The case law of the European Court of Justice (ECJ) had also given heart to those who argued that competition law could be used to tackle public monopolies. In a case involving BT, the ECJ held that telecommunications services, even if they were provided by a State-owned body, did not *per se* fall outside the ordinary competition laws.[16]

In a 1987 Green Paper, the Commission stressed the role of competition law in opening telecommunications markets.[17] It rejected the view that monopolies

---

12   Grewlich (1999) 36 C.M.L.Rev. 937, 944–45.
13   *ibid.*
14   The term "PTT" in the jargon of the time meant a publicly-owned telecommunications monopoly, which usually also provided postal services.
15   Ramsey above n.11, p.563.
16   Case 41/83, *Italy v. Commission* [1985] ECR 873, [1985] 2 C.M.L.R. 368, para. 18.
17   COM(87) 290 final, p.121. See also Council Resolution of June 30, 1988, O.J. 1988 C257/1. The Green Paper itself built on a Commission "action plan" for the telecommunications sector, COM(84)277.

were necessary in telecommunications to achieve economies of scale, and argued that such monopolies should have to allow access to outsiders. Similarly, technical advances meant that more frequencies were available and "spectrum management" should no longer be an obstacle to entry.[18]

It is arguable that an Irish Commissioner, Peter Sutherland, was the first to see the potential of ex Article 90(3), now Article 86(3), which allows the Commission to adopt directives in the field of competition without the Council or Parliament having the last say, as is the case for all other legislation.[19] During his term of office in charge of competition, the Commission used this power to liberalise the market for selling telephone handsets and other equipment. Although it may seem strange now, the rule in most Member States used to be that only the telephone monopoly could sell handsets.

In 1988, the Commission took the unprecedented step of abolishing this monopoly by a Directive.[20] Despite initial resistance and a court challenge,[21] this succeeded, and over the next decade a series of Commission Directives abolished all other "exclusive rights" to provide services and infrastructure.[22]

5.(3)(a)(iii) Parallel legislation 1988–98

From 1988 to 1998, there was an unprecedented explosion of legislation along two parallel lines.

First, the Commission continued to enact Directives based on Article 86 (ex Article 90) abolishing exclusive rights. However, it was not enough to abolish rules and leave nothing in their place: for new entrants to be able to offer services, there had to be specific rules on how operators should behave, *e.g.* data protection, numbering, consumer rights, etc. In addition, the consensus was that new entrants would need access to the networks of the incumbents on regulated terms, at least for a transitional period.

This was addressed in the second strand of Directives, adopted under the internal market provisions of the Treaty Article 95, (originally Article 100a). These provided for free trade by laying down uniform standards. For the sake of simplicity, these two types of legislation will be called "liberalisation" and "harmonisation" Directives. Although the two aims led to similar rules, the legal basis for each is distinct. It is to be noted that liberalisation Directives under Article 86 were adopted by the Commission alone, while harmonisation Directives were adopted by the Council (and, after the Maastricht Treaty, by the Council and Parliament).[23]

---

18 Hall, above n.2, p.196.
19 Middlemas, *Orchestrating Europe* (Fontana, London, 1995), p.586; Grant, *Delors: Inside the House that Jacques Built* (Nicholas Brealy, London 1994), p.161.
20 Commission Directive 88/301 [1988] O.J. L131/73 (corrigendum [1988] O.J. L317/59).
21 Case C–202/88 *France v. Commission* [1991] ECR I–1223, [1992] 5 C.M.L.R. 552.
22 Commission Directive 90/388, [1990] O.J. L192/10 , successively extended to cover all services and infrastructure by Commission Directives 94/46, 95/51, 96/2, 96/19 and 1999/64.
23 For more on the comparisons between liberalisation and harmonisation Directives, see Larouche, above n.2, especially pp.60–91.

The legislation will be examined in detail below. In summary, the liberalisation Directives of 1988 and 1990 were the beginning of a radical change in the European telecommunications landscape. In 1988 the Commission first liberalised the sale of handsets and other "terminals"; a decade later, all services had been liberalised. In parallel, the Council agreed a package of harmonisation Directives providing the detailed rules for the new liberalised environment. For most Member States, the telecommunications market has been fully liberalised since January 1, 1998 (December 1, 1998 in Ireland).

5.(3)(b) Outline of liberalisation Directives

As noted above, a 1988 Directive of the European Commission abolished exclusive rights to provide "telecommunications terminals" (the definition of which included telephones, fax machines, etc.). The Directive survived a challenge by France in the ECJ save for two aspects. As well as "exclusive rights" the text had also abolished "special rights" but the Court held that it had not given adequate reasons. The Court also struck down one Article which provided that subscribers could terminate contracts for the supply of telecommunications equipment.[24] Despite this setback, the judgment vindicated the Commission's legal analysis of its powers under competition law.[25]

The result was that telecommunications equipment from any Member State could be used in any other Member State provided that it was technically compatible. The Directive further provided that the decision on compatibility was to be taken by an independent body and not by the telecommunications operators which had traditionally sold equipment.

Although it had demonstrated its legal right to abolish monopolies unilaterally, the Commission sought to build a consensus with the Council for future legislation. The next Directives came in 1990 and liberalised services: the Commission and Council adopted legislation the same day which was designed to work together. The Commission's liberalisation Directive 90/388[26] opened the market for telecommunications services to competition, while leaving the incumbent telecommunications operators with monopoly rights on voice telephony, which accounted for most of their incomes.[27] The Council's harmonisation Directive 90/387[28] defined the principles and technical rules for providing services and connecting to the telecommunications network. The details are discussed in the next section.

---

24 Case C–202/88 *France v. Commission* [1991] ECR I–1223, [1992] 5 C.M.L.R. 552
25 See Larouche, above n.2, pp.45–82 for a further analysis of the judgment.
26 Commission Directive 90/388, [1990] O.J. L192/10 (services).
27 Taylor, "Art. 90 and Telecommunications Monopolies" [1994] 6 E.C.L.R. 322, 323.
28 Council Directive 90/387, [1990] O.J. L192/1 (open network provision) (corrigendum in [1993] O.J. L85/28).

Despite its attempts to build a consensus with the Council, the Commission's Directive on telecommunications services (90/388) was challenged before the ECJ by a number of Member States.[29] Like the 1988 Directive on terminal equipment (88/301), the services Directive was partly annulled for failing to identify why it was necessary to abolish "special rights" and for interfering in private contracts. However, the Member States in question failed in their challenge to the rest of the Directive. Thereafter, the political consensus was that liberalisation was inevitable. Directive 90/388 had deliberately not liberalised "voice telephony."[30] However, during 1992, the debate shifted from whether voice telephony would be liberalised to when this would happen. The date of January 1, 1998 was mooted for liberalisation, subject to derogations.[31] In 1993 the European Parliament and the Council both expressed support for further liberalisation.[32]

5.(3)(b)(i) Infrastructure

Neither Directive 88/301[33] nor Directive 90/388[34] challenged the fact that the public telecommunications network was still operated by a single monopoly. However, the competition analysis underlying Directive 90/388 was in part that dominant undertakings with a monopoly over infrastructure could not be allowed leverage this monopoly into a further monopoly over services.[35] As a result, Directive 90/388 liberalised services but stopped short of requiring any change to the monopolies regarding infrastructure, save for a provision requiring the incumbents to provide leased lines.

If more competition was to be introduced, it was clear that infrastructure would continue to be a trump card in the hands of the incumbents. As long as the incumbents retained a monopoly on all infrastructure, this continued to give them an advantage in providing services. The next step was Directive 95/51[36] which sought to free the most obvious source of alternative infrastructure, namely cable television. Although cable networks were far from ideal for telecommunications purposes, they did provide a network which reached as far as individual homes and could (with some investment) be upgraded to carry voice or data signals.

---

[29] Case C–271/90, *Spain and others v. Commission*, [1992] ECR I–5859. Larouche above n.2, pp.54–60 gives his view of the policy positions of the Member States at the time.

[30] The Directive gave a legal definition of voice telephony but in essence it means conversation over a telephone line in the ordinary way.

[31] Commission communication of October 21, 1992 to the Council and the European Parliament on the review of the situation in telecommunications, SEC(92)1048.

[32] Parliament resolution A–3–0113/93 of April 20, 1993, [1993] O.J. C150/42. Council resolution of July 22, 1993, [1993] O.J. C213/1.

[33] Commission Directive 88/301/EEC of May 16, 1988 on competition in the markets in telecommunications terminal equipment, [1988] O.J. L131/73 (corrigendum [1988] O.J. L317/59).

[34] [1990] O.J. L192/10.

[35] Recitals 29–31 to the Directive.

[36] [1995] O.J. L256/49.

5.(3)(b)(ii) Mobile

The early 1990s saw a number of technological breakthroughs in mobile telephone technology. Mobile phones began to be produced at prices which made them affordable for small businesses and then consumers, while the handsets became more manageable than the earlier versions, which were only truly "mobile" if installed in a vehicle. As mobile phone networks developed (thanks to agreement on a common technical standard called GSM which was adopted by all EC countries) there suddenly appeared a telephone network separate to the fixed one. Moreover, many countries awarded more than one mobile licence so that for the first time there was competition at the consumer level for a telecommunications service. In 1996, the Commission adopted Directive 96/2[37] which brought mobile telephony into the general system of Directive 90/388 and required competition for licences.

5.(3)(b)(iii) Full competition

Two months later, the Commission adopted Directive 96/19[38] ("full competition") which abolished the last remaining restrictions on providing services and infrastructure. These restrictions were to be lifted by July 1, 1996, except that for voice telephony the restrictions could remain in place until January 1, 1998. Extensions were possible for Member States with less developed networks (as there had been in Directive 96/2) and also "very small networks", a criterion devised with Luxembourg in mind. Five such derogations were granted: to Ireland, Spain, Portugal, Greece and Luxembourg. Ireland was granted a derogation allowing it to postpone liberalisation in the following fields: voice telephony and the provision of public networks (until January 1, 2000), direct interconnection of mobile networks with foreign networks (until January 1, 1999) and restrictions on providing liberalised services on networks provided by the operator itself or by third parties (July 1, 1997).[39] The derogation was subject to certain conditions concerning the timetable for liberalisation and the management of Telecom Éireann, the Irish incumbent, during the interval. (In the event, the Irish government decided unilaterally to liberalise more rapidly than required so that all restrictions were lifted by December 1, 1998). The other countries granted derogations liberalised somewhat later, with Greece keeping a monopoly on voice telephony until the end of 2000.

5.(3)(c) Harmonisation Directives

As noted above, Directive 90/387 of the Council was adopted on the same day as Commission Directive 90/388. While the Commission Directive abolished

---

[37] [1996] O.J. L20/59.
[38] [1996] O.J. L74/13.
[39] Commission Decision 97/114 of November 27, 1996, [1997] O.J. L41/ 8.

barriers, the Council Directive put in place positive rules aimed at promoting the internal market and creating a truly European-wide telecommunications network. This Directive was to provide the blueprint for legislation over the next decade. The heart of the Directive was the idea of "open network provision" or "ONP" which meant that all operators (including new entrants) were to have access on regulated terms to the networks of other operators.

5.(3)(c)(i) Outline of harmonisation Directives

The 1990 Directive was updated by further measures during the 1990s. It is beyond the scope of this text to attempt more than a sketch of the Directives as they exist today.[40] The three most important Directives, still in force today, were adopted on the eve of full liberalisation in 1998. They cover:

- licensing – licences are to be awarded fairly and there are strict limits on the conditions which Member States can require (Directive 97/13);[41]

- universal service– market forces are not allowed to prevail if this means basic services become unaffordable; there is a definition of what users are entitled to and rules for funding if the market does not deliver (Directive 98/10);[42] and

- interconnection – all operators can get interconnection with each other, and those with "significant market" power have to offer non-discriminatory access and cost-oriented prices (Directive 97/33).[43]

The licensing Directive 97/13[44] filled in principles already set out in the Commission's liberalisation Directives. Licences could no longer be awarded at the whim of a Minister or a regulator: instead, any procedures put in place had to be transparent, objective, proportional and non-discriminatory. There is a presumption against limits on the numbers of licences, although these can be limited where the service in question uses a scarce resource such as radio frequencies or numbers. The Directive also lays down time limits for awarding licences (which can be extended if a tender procedure is used). The annex to the Directive defines in some detail the type of conditions which can be attached to licences.

The universal service Directive[45] aims to define a minimum set of consumer rights which should be available to all customers. The aim was to ensure that competition did not lead operators to "cherry-pick" profitable customers or

---

[40] See Garzaniti, *Telecommunications, Broadcasting and the Internet: EC Competition Law and Regulation* Sweet & Maxwell, London 2000 pp.11–62 and chap. 8, "European Union Telecommunications Law" in Telecommunications Law (Walden and Angel ed., Blackstone, London, 2001) pp.279–313.

[41] [1997] O.J. L117/15.

[42] Directive 98/10/EC on voice telephony and universal service [1998] O.J. L101/24.

[43] Directive 97/33, [1997] O.J. L199/ 32.

[44] [1997] O.J. L117/15.

[45] Directive 98/10/EC on voice telephony and universal service [1998] O.J. L101/24.

regions and leave less profitable ones unserved (or served at an exorbitant price). The Directive provides that operators can be designated as "universal service operators" and required to provide services on a cost-oriented basis to users. If the cost of providing a universal service is a "net burden" on an operator (taking account of the direct and indirect benefits it gains from providing the service, according to a calculation method set out in annex III to the interconnection Directive)[46] there is provision for certain compensation mechanisms. The Directive also provides for procedures for resolving complaints by users.

The interconnection Directive[47] provides that operators have a right to connect their networks and equipment to the networks of other operators. Without such a rule, customers of different operators might not be able to call each other. This is especially useful to new entrants, who can gain access to the networks of incumbent operator such as eircom on regulated terms. The interconnection Directive distinguishes between the obligations of small operators and those with "significant market power." This concept is at the heart of all the current telecommunications Directives, and deserves some explanation.

5.(3)(c)(ii) Significant market power

"Significant market power" (SMP) measures the market power of an operator to establish whether it should be subject to additional duties such as price control or non-discrimination. The Directives address the operator's power on four markets, all defined in advance.[48] The Directives require national regulators to consider the following factors in deciding on SMP: "the organization's ability to influence market conditions, its turnover relative to the size of the market, its control of the means of access to end-users, its access to financial resources and its experience in providing products and services in the market."[49]

The Directives set the threshold for SMP at about 25 per cent market share, although it is possible to have SMP below that figure or possibly not have SMP with a market share above 25 per cent.[50] While market share is not the only criterion in competition law, it is still important. There is a presumption of dominance for a market share of 50%[51] but this is not necessarily conclusive.

---

[46] Directive 97/33, [1997] O.J. L199/32.
[47] *ibid.*
[48] These are fixed public telephony networks/services; mobile public telephony networks/ services; leased lines, and the national market for interconnection. The first three markets are explicitly identified in Annex I to Directive 97/33 on interconnection; the fourth is mentioned in Art. 7(2) of the Directive.
[49] Art. 4(3) of Directive 97/33 on interconnection.
[50] *ibid.*
[51] Case C–82/86 *Akzo v. Commission* [1991] ECR I–3359 [1993] 5 C.M.L.R. 215, para. 60.

The difference between SMP and dominance is vividly illustrated by a recent judgment which held that Eircell (now Vodafone) did not have a dominant position on the market which the High Court considered relevant, although it has been designated as having SMP.[52]

At first sight, SMP might sound as if it is simply a weaker form of the notion of dominance. However, on closer examination, the two concepts are quite different in scope and (more subtly) in effect.[53]

The telecommunications Directives impose special obligations on an SMP operator in order to change its behaviour *ex ante*. It can therefore be required to do things such as publish prices and lodge documents with the national regulatory authority without any suggestion that it has breached the law. Although the competition rules imply some obligations on a dominant undertaking, they are most often used *ex post facto* to punish behaviour which has already happened. As a result, the case law applying competition principles is most clear on defining what a dominant undertaking is *not* allowed to do (rather than any positive duty it may have).

The duties of an SMP operator are found in three different Directives covering leased lines, interconnection and universal service. At the risk of over-simplifying, they boil down to half a dozen main obligations:

1. An SMP operator has a general duty to offer its services and cannot refuse to sell to a willing purchaser (unless there are objective technical reasons);[54]

2. An SMP operator may not discriminate in the terms on which it sells its products, so if it sells a particular product to one customer it must sell the same to any other at the same price. In particular, the SMP operator must offer products to third parties on exactly the same terms as it offers them to its own subsidiaries or even different parts of its own company, *e.g.* if there is a wholesale arm dealing with other operators and a retail arm dealing with the public, the retail arm is not to be advantaged;[55]

3. An SMP operator may not bundle two products together, *i.e.* force customers to buy product A if they want an unrelated product B;[56]

---

[52] *Meridian Communications Ltd v. Eircell Ltd* (1999 No. 5306 P), High Court, O'Higgins J., judgment of April 5, 2001. In an earlier judgment of October 4, 2000 in the same case, the court held that there was no proof of joint dominance between Eircell and Esat Digifone.

[53] For further discussion on this topic, see Doherty, "Competition Law and Sector-specific Regulation" (2001) 7 *Computer and Telecommunications Law Review* 225.

[54] Directive 97/33 on interconnection, [1977] O.J. L 199/32; Arts. 4(2) and 7(4); Directive 92/44 on leased lines, [1992] O.J. L165/27 (as amended by Directive 97/51, [1997] O.J. L 295/23) Art. 7; Directive 98/10/EC on voice telephony and universal service [1998] O.J. L101/24, Art. 15(1). In this passage, these will be called the interconnection, leased lines and voice Directives respectively.

[55] Interconnection Directive, Art. 6(a); leased lines Directive Art. 8(2).

[56] Interconnection Directive, Art. 7(4) – if the operator has SMP in fixed markets.

4. An SMP operator is subject to price regulation. Its prices must be transparent and cost-oriented;[57]

5. To reinforce this, it must submit its accounts to independent scrutiny, but also keep its accounts in such a way as to show the activities of separate parts of its business as if they were free-standing entities;[58]

6. The SMP operator must provide certain information to the national regulatory authority (NRA);[59]

7. The SMP operator is subject to quality rules.[60]

5.(4) IRISH LAW IMPLEMENTING THE EC RULES

The survey of Irish law in part 5.(2) showed that under the Postal and Telecommunications Services Act 1983 Telecom Éireann had a monopoly on all telecommunications services and infrastructure. More precisely, this was defined as an exclusive right to transmit and receive messages up to a connection point in the subscriber's premises.[61] Interestingly, the 1983 Act set out arguments for the privilege, and explicitly stated that "a viable national telecommunications system involves subsidisation of some loss-making services by profit-making services."[62]

Under the 1983 Act the Government still controlled Telecom Éireann but the Minister's role was redefined to cover regulatory functions. Section 89 of the 1983 Act also provided for the possibility that rival operators could obtain licences but the process required them to apply in the first instance to Telecom Éireann itself for a licence. If Telecom Éireann refused a competitor's application for a licence, there was a right of appeal to the Minister.[63] Alternatively, section 111 provided that competitors could apply directly to the Minister, who could also license applicants after consulting Telecom Éireann.

Viewed from today's perspective, the role of Telecom Éireann in the licensing process seems strange and even unfair. Even if it was only consulted by the Minister, it could still be accused of having an unfair influence on the entry of competitors.[64]

---

[57] Leased lines Directive Art. 10(1); interconnection Directive, Art. 7(2) – this does not apply to mobile operators unless they have SMP in the interconnection market.
[58] Interconnection Directive, Arts. 7(5) and 8(2); leased lines Directive Art. 10(2).
[59] Interconnection Directive, Arts. 6(c) and 7(3); leased lines Directive Art. 11(2).
[60] Voice Directive, Arts. 12(1) and 13(1).
[61] Postal and Telecommunications Services Act 1983, s. 87.
[62] *ibid.*, s. 87(2)(c).
[63] *ibid.*, s. 89.
[64] Cf. Flynn, "Locating the Missing Link: Postal Communication Monopolies in Ireland and EC Law" (1992) 10 I.L.T. (n.s.) 247, at p.249 on a similar provision in the postal provisions of the 1983 Act.

5.(4)(a) Impact of the Directives

The Irish rules have been modified dramatically in the light of EC directives. As noted above, Directive 88/301 abolished exclusive rights to provide telecommunications terminals, *i.e.* telephones, fax machines, etc. The Postal and Telecommunications Services Act 1983 provided that the Telecom Éireann monopoly only extended to the connection point, leaving the subscriber free to install any type of telephone or fax machine, etc., provided that it was technically compatible with the network. Despite this, in practice Telecom Éireann apparently kept a monopoly on providing subscribers with their first telephone. The Commission commenced proceedings against Ireland on this topic in 1990[65] but dropped them after the Irish rules were changed.[66]

The 1990 Directives (90/387 and 90/388) liberalising services were implemented by means of a statutory instrument under the European Communities Act 1972.[67] This has been the technique for virtually all legislation implementing telecommunications Directives since. These statutory instruments generally add little to the text of the Directives, although there are times when more detailed implementing rules might have been welcome.

For example, Article 3 of the Open Network Provision (ONP) Directive[68] provided that service providers were to be given access to the public network on conditions which are objective, non-discriminatory and published. Instead of elaborating these concepts, the statutory instrument implementing the 1990 Directives in Ireland[69] simply stated that "the Company [*i.e.* Telecom Éireann] shall comply with Article 3."[70]

Later directives have been implemented by further statutory instruments as set out (in rough chronological order) in the following table.[71] The most important statutory instruments are in bold.

---

[65] O.J. 1990 C232/26.
[66] Frances Murphy in *Butterworths Competition Law*, (1993 looseleaf), p.IX/29.
[67] European Communities (Telecommunications Services) Regulations 1992, S.I. 45 of 1992.
[68] Directive 90/387, O.J. 1990 L192/1.
[69] European Communities (Telecommunications Services) Regulations 1992, S.I. 45 of 1992.
[70] Art. 4(1)(a) of S.I. 45 of 1992.
[71] The table is based on the former Department of Public Enterprise website http://www.irlgov.ie/tec/communications/comlegislation/#Secondary

Topic	Directive(s)	Corresponding Irish Law
Terminal and radio equipment (including technical standards)	88/301; 91/263 [repealed]; 93/97 [repealed]; 99/5	S.I. 73 of 1997 [since revoked]; S.I. 22 of 19⬛ part replaced by **S.I. 240 of 2001**[72]
Freedom to provide telecommunications services and infrastructure	90/387, amended by (inter alia) 97/51; 90/388 amended by (inter alia) 96/19	**S.I. 45 of 1992**; S.I. 338 of 1997; S.I. 286 of ⬛ S.I. 180 of 1998; **S.I. 70 of 1999**[73]
Leased lines	92/44 amended by 97/51	S.I. 328 of 1994; now **S.I. 109 of 1998**[74]
Satellite	94/46	S.I. 372 of 1997
TV standards and conditional access	95/47; 98/84	S.I. 262 of 1998 and S.I. 357 of 2000.
Licensing (including mobile)	97/13 and 96/2	S.I. 123 of 1996; now **S.I. 96 of 1998**,[75] as am⬛ by S.I. 286 of 1998 and S.I. 70 of 2000
Interconnection	97/33	**S.I. 15 of 1998**[76] as amended by S.I.s 69 and 249 of 2000
Voice telephony and universal service	98/10 (replacing 95/62)	S.I. 445 of 1997 replaced by **S.I. 71 of 1999**[7⬛]
Data protection	97/66	S.I. 192 of 2002[78]
Number portability	98/61	S.I. 249 of 1999

The piecemeal approach to implementing the Directives means that Ireland does not have a telecommunications code or even a comprehensive Act which governs the whole sector but instead a collection of legislation written over 130 years[79] and scattered in several dozen different texts. Moreover, even the more recent texts have been amended quite extensively. This has a number of

---

[72] European Communities (Radio Equipment and Telecommunications Terminal Equipment Access) Regulations 2001, S.I. No. 240 of 2001.

[73] European Communities (Voice Telephony and Universal Service) Regulations 1999, S.I. No. 71 of 1999.

[74] European Communities (Leased Lines) Regulations 1998, S. I. No. 109 of 1998.

[75] European Communities (Telecommunications Licences) Regulations 1998, S.I. 96 of 1998.

[76] European Communities (Interconnection in Telecommunications) Regulations 1998, S.I. 15 of 1998.

[77] European Communities (Voice Telephony and Universal Service) Regulations 1999, S.I. No. 71 of 1999.

[78] European Communities (Data Protection and Privacy in Telecommunications Terminal Equipment Access) Regulations 2002, S.I. No. 192 of 2002.

[79] The Telegraph Act 1869 was last amended in 1999 by the European Communities (Telecommunications Infrastructure) (Amendment) Regulations 1999, S.I. 70 of 1999.

disadvantages: if a particular provision is off the beaten track it can require some research to establish whether it is still in force. Moreover, when it is necessary to compare pieces of legislation written at different times, there are variations in terminology which can lead to confusion.

In implementing the Directives, procedural and institutional matters were only addressed on a case-by-case basis. Where the Directive required a national authority to have certain powers, these were usually given to the Minister.

5.(4)(b) Creation of the ODTR

By the mid 1990s, a number of new entrants had taken up the limited liberalisation offered in 1992 to compete with Telecom Éireann. As a result, the Government considered that it was no longer appropriate for the Minister to control one operator (Telecom Éireann) while on the other hand deciding on the terms of entry for its rivals. Moreover, a political consensus had emerged at European level that there would be full liberalisation by 1998 (subject to derogations such as the one ultimately given to Ireland).

The result was the Telecommunications (Miscellaneous Provisions) Act 1996. The Act set up a new body called the Office of the Director of Telecommunications Regulation (ODTR), which has been in place since mid-1997. The Director was granted most of the powers previously exercised by the Minister although in some matters she is required to obtain the consent of the Minister, *e.g.* for regulations under the Wireless Telegraphy Act 1926 – fees for these telecommunications licences also require the consent of the Minister for Finance. Section 7 of the 1996 Act provides for a more scientific basis for price control than had obtained previously: the price of certain services was to be linked to changes in the consumer price index using a "CPI – X" formula. Section 6 of the 1996 Act provided that the Director's office was to be funded by a levy on telecommunications operators – this distinguishes it from other bodies such as the Competition Authority which depend on the Minister for Finance for resources.

As well as taking over the Minister's functions existing in 1996, the Director was given new functions as and when new Directives were adopted. Thus, the Director was given the power to issue telecommunications licences under Directive 97/13 and monitor breaches of them. In case of breach the Director's options are somewhat limited: she can take a summary prosecution but this is slow and the fine is capped at €1900 – not a very powerful deterrent if the operator stands to gain financially from the breach. Alternatively, she can remove the operator's licence (a drastic step which would hurt customers as much as the operator concerned, especially if it has universal service obligations) or else impose what Article 9(4) of the licensing Directive calls "specific measures." These are not further explained in the Irish implementing regulations but other countries apparently interpret the term to mean a power to impose fines. The Director also has functions to adjudicate on complaints by operators (following on from Directive 97/33) and consumers (Directive 98/10). Finally, although it does not concern telecommunications, the Director was given the function of regulating postal services in 2000.[80]

The 1996 Act also made the necessary legislative changes to allow part of Telecom Éireann to be sold to strategic partners (in the event, the state-owned Swedish and Dutch telecommunications operators Telia and KPN took a stake). To complete the story, Telecom Éireann was later renamed as eircom, floated on the stock exchange in 1999 and bought by a private consortium in late 2001.

The ODTR was set up in mid-1997 at a time when it was expected that full competition would not come until the end of 1999 (the date provided for by the Commission decision granting a derogation to Ireland under Directive 96/19).[81] However, in May 1998 the Government decided that it would liberalise within six months. As a result, the telecommunications market in Ireland has been liberalised since December 1, 1998.

At the time of writing, the Irish market has 89 licensed operators of whom 39 are active. New entrants account for 21% of the fixed market.[82] After the last review of SMP in June 2002 there are three SMP operators.[83] eircom has SMP in the public fixed telephony services market and the leased lines market. Two mobile operators were designated as having SMP: Eircell (now called Vodafone) and Digifone (now called O2).

The latter are two of the three mobile operators: the third is Meteor which only launched in 2001 despite having come first in a tender procedure in 1998. The reason was that an unsuccessful bidder in the same tender, Orange, challenged the outcome before the courts – at the time, the relevant rules meant that the Director's decision was automatically suspended. Although Orange succeeded in its arguments before the High Court, the Supreme Court unanimously reversed this decision and upheld the procedures followed by the ODTR in that case.[84]

---

[80] European Communities (Postal Services) Regulations 2000, S.I. 310 of 2000.

[81] Commission Decision 97/114 of November 27, 1996, [1997] O.J. L41/ 8.

[82] For a fuller view of the market, see the Quarterly Reviews published every three months by the ODTR. The latest edition (document ODTR 02/76, September 5, 2002) is published at http://odtr-web/docs/odtr0276a.doc.

[83] Significant Market Power in the Irish Telecommunications Sector – Decision Notice D8/02 (document ODTR 02/53, June 21, 2002), available at http://odtr-web/docs/odtr0253.doc

[84] *Orange Telecommunications Ltd. v. Director of Telecommunications Regulation* High Court, (Macken J.) March 18 and October 4, 1999; Supreme Court, May 18, 2000. Reported at [2000] 4 IR 136 (HC) and 159 (SC) ; [1999] 2 ILRM 81 (HC). The texts are available on the Internet at the following locations: http://www.bailii.org/ie/cases/IEHC/1999/254.html (HC, March 18, 1999); http://www.bailii.org/ie/cases/IEHC/1999/132.html (HC, October 4, 1999); http://www.bailii.org/ie/cases/IESC/2000/22.html (SC)

5.(4)(c) The Orange case

As this is the leading reported case involving the ODTR it is worth considering briefly. The judgments cast some interesting light on administrative law principles but only examined the EC Directives (and Irish regulations implementing them) to determine the scope of the appeal and the extent of the ODTR's duty to give reasons. Moreover, the Irish regulations in question (S.I. 123 of 1996) have since been replaced (by S.I. 96 of 1998). For this reason there is no need to examine the judgments in detail. Suffice it to say that the Court found it difficult to decide whether the relevant provisions provided for an appeal on the merits or the more limited grounds of appeal typical of judicial review proceedings. In March 1999, Macken J. in the High Court held that the relevant subsection was:

> "drafted in such terms as to provide for a review type appeal, perhaps slightly wider than judicial review simpliciter, as known in this jurisdiction, and by which the reasonableness of the Director's decision is ascertained by reference only to the materials which she had before her, and none other, so as to permit the Court to decide if her decision should be confirmed."[85]

The High Court, therefore, decided to hear oral evidence. In October 1999, Macken J. decided that the Director's decision was flawed by a series of errors.[86] On appeal, the Supreme Court held that Macken J. had applied an incorrect standard of review. In the words of Keane C.J.:

> "In short, the appeal provided for under this legislation was not intended to take the form of a re-examination from the beginning of the merits of the decision appealed from, culminating, it may be, in the substitution by the High Court of its adjudication for that of the Director. It is accepted that, at the other end of the spectrum, the High Court is not solely confined to the issues which might arise if the decision of the Director was being challenged by way of judicial review. In the case of this legislation at least, an applicant will succeed in having the decision appealed from set aside where it establishes to the High Court as a matter of probability that, taking the adjudicative process as a whole, the decision reached was vitiated by a serious and significant error or a series of such errors. In arriving at a conclusion on that issue, the High Court will necessarily have regard to the degree of expertise and specialised knowledge available to the Director."[87]

Keane C.J. returned to the question of the expert knowledge later in his judgment:

---

[85] [2001] 4 I.R. 136, at 157; [1999] 2 I.L.R.M. 81, at 102; HC, Macken J., at p.320 of the typescript judgment; para. 70 of the version at http://www.bailii.org/ie/cases/IEHC/1999/132.html.

[86] http://www.bailii.org/ie/cases/IEHC/1999/254.html.

[87] [2001] 4 I.R. 159, at 184–185, (pp. 118–119 of the typescript judgment).

"I have already emphasised the importance in a case such as this of the High Court recognising that the Oireachtas has entrusted the impugned decision to a body with a particular level of expertise and specialised knowledge or which, at the least, has the capacity, which the court has not, to draw on such specialised knowledge, as the Director did in this case by retaining the services of AMI [a firm of consultants]. I have no doubt that wholly insufficient weight was given to that aspect of the case both in the judgment under appeal and in the submissions addressed to this court on behalf of Orange."[88]

In deciding that it could hear evidence, the High Court had included material which was inadmissible:

"The evidence on this issue before the Court was wider than it should have been. But the fact that more evidence was before the Court than there should have been does not justify a finding that even more inadmissible evidence should have been admitted. This is emphasised by the substantial difference between the cases pleaded and as submitted at the hearing and on appeal. The latter arose from a trawling through the documents which were discovered. As a result Orange in the main lost sight of the rules of the competition, the breach, if any, of which should have been the sole basis of complaint."[89]

Moreover, the High Court was also mistaken on interpreting some rules of administrative law. As regards the duty to give reasons in particular, the ODTR had given Orange an explanation of the weak points in its bid. Orange sought more detailed reasons and in particular a comparison between its bid and that of Meteor. The High Court held that the Director had failed in her duty to give reasons, but the Supreme Court held that the information given was sufficient.

Keane C.J. again upheld the procedures adopted by the ODTR:

"[I]t must not be forgotten, although it frequently was in the course of argument, that there was in fact no obligation whatever in law on the Director to adopt the particular procedure she did. There was nothing to stop her adopting a procedure which, at the end of the day, would have left the unsuccessful applicant in a far greater state of uncertainty than was the plaintiff as to why it had failed to secure the licence. It may be that any particular procedure might, depending on its nature, be challenged on the ground that it failed to meet the criteria laid down by the Commission that the procedure should be open, non-discriminatory and transparent. Not merely did the use of the comparative bidding procedure meet those requirements: it did so in a manner which, as the evidence made plain in the High Court met even higher standards of openness, lack of discrimination and transparency."[90]

---

88 *ibid.*, at 190–191, (p. 128 of the typescript judgment).
89 *ibid.*, at 240 *per* Barron J. (p. 68 of the typescript judgment says "Orange" instead of "the plaintiff"). Keane C.J. agreed at 190 (p.127 of the typescript judgment).
90 *ibid.*, at 191, (p. 128 of the typescript judgment).

Since the Orange case some of the Irish regulations have been altered to provide that a court challenge does not automatically suspend the Director's decision[91] although not all the regulations have been amended to reflect this. Not all the regulations defining the Director's powers specify the rules for court challenges, and even where procedures are specified they vary considerably from regulation to regulation. The Communications Regulation Act 2002, described in 5.(6), might have been an opportunity to create a uniform procedure in these matters but did not address the topic.

5.(5) THE NEW PACKAGE OF DIRECTIVES

As noted above, the current Directives were adopted in 1997 and 1998. Some had included a mechanism by which the Commission would review their implementation after a number of years.[92] The Commission also took the view that some of the directives needed to be adapted or even repealed once full liberalisation was established.

5.(5)(a) The 1999 Review

The result was a Commission policy document, generally called the *1999 Review*. This set out a vision for the future of the telecommunications sector, and the media/broadcasting sectors which increasingly overlap with telecommunications.[93]

One spur to action was the growing phenomenon of "convergence" – once a picture or a sound is reduced to ones and zeros in a computer memory, it becomes easier to adapt that item for transmission by a variety of methods. As a result, the same picture or text can be transmitted by e-mail or by fax or by a mobile phone; the same sound can be sent down a telephone line or a computer connection. A radio station can put its broadcasts on the Internet and they can be heard on the other side of the planet by somebody sitting at a computer. This new technology makes it very hard to apply traditional legal criteria – is an Irish radio station "broadcasting" in Australia if its output can be heard there ? Is a group of electrons travelling down a telephone line to be classified as "voice" or "data" for some regulatory purpose ?

The first principle the Commission enunciated was that of "technological neutrality" – the rules should no longer make legal consequences flow from

---

[91] European Communities (Interconnection in Telecommunications) (Amendment) Regulations 2000, S.I. 69 of 2000 and European Communities (Telecommunications Licences) (Amendment) Regulations 2000, SI 70 of 2000.

[92] Commission communication *Towards a new framework for Electronic Communications infrastructure and associated services* COM (1999) 539, November 10, 1999. For the text, see http://europa.eu.int/ISPO/infosoc/telecompolicy/review99/review99en.pdf

technological categories which could be circumvented or made obsolete. The second was an assumption that the market would require less regulation once competition developed. As competition increased, the Commission proposed to abandon some elements of sector-specific regulation which were no longer necessary, and leave more to competition law.

> "The existing legislative framework was primarily designed to manage the transition to competition and was therefore focused on the creation of a competitive market and the rights of new entrants. The new policy framework will seek to reinforce competition in all market segments, particularly at local level. It should be designed to cater for new, dynamic and largely unpredictable markets with many more players than today. In line with the results of the debate on convergence, the Commission foresees a light regulatory approach for new service markets, while ensuring that dominant players do not abuse their market power. Regulation implemented as a proxy for competition will be reduced as markets become more competitive. Regulation will therefore be progressively limited to areas where policy objectives cannot be achieved by competition only."[94]

The proposal was therefore to simplify the existing sector-specific Directives (reducing the number of Directives from 26 to six).[95] The Commission proposed drafts in July 2000.[96] There were five Directives: (i) access and interconnection to networks[97]; (ii) data protection[98]; (iii) licensing[99]; (iv) universal service and users' rights; and (v) an overall Directive setting out the common regulatory framework.[100] In addition, there was a draft regulation on unbundling the local loop and a draft decision on how radio frequencies should be allocated.[101]

5.(5)(b) The new legislation

All of the above texts have now been adopted although the Data Protection Directive has fallen behind the others. The Regulation on local loop unbundling was adopted in December 2000 and came into force immediately. The spectrum decision and four of the five Directives, *i.e.* all but the Data Protection Directive, were agreed in late 2001 and early 2002 and formally

---

[93] See Larouche,above n.2, pp.441–445 on the *1999 Review*.
[94] 1999 *Review*, p.iv.
[95] *ibid.*, p.vi.
[96] The proposals were published in [2000] O.J. C365E. They can be seen at the following web sites: http//europa.eu.int/ISPO/infosoc/telecompolicy/review99/Welcome.html; http://www.europa.eu.int/comm/information_society/policy/framework/index_en.htm
[97] COM (2000) 384 final, July 12, 2000.
[98] COM (2000) 385 final, July 12, 2000.
[99] COM (2000) 386 final, July 12, 2000.
[100] COM (2000) 393 final, 12 July 2000.
[101] COM (2000) 407 final, 12 July 2000.

published in the Official Journal on April 24, 2002.[102] The date of publication is important, and had been eagerly awaited, as it triggers a 15-month period for implementing the Directives. This means that national implementing measures are to come into force by July 24, 2003. Ordinarily, Member States can make the necessary adjustments and bring them into effect at any time during the implementation period. In this case, however, the Directives specify that the new rules are to be applied "from" July 25, 2003. The logic appears to be that the new regime is a package with burdens and benefits for operators, and it might cause difficulties if parts of the package came into force before others. The spectrum decision needed no implementation and is legally binding now that it has been published.

The details of the new legislation are described below. The impact of the Directives on the current Irish rules will depend on how they are implemented: whether by primary legislation or by further regulations under the European Communities Act. These are policy choices for the Minister, as is the question of what powers to give to what body, *e.g.* the universal service Directive provides for certain functions to do with consumer complaints which could be given either to the ODTR or to the Director of Consumer Affairs.

5.(5)(b)(i) LLU (Local Loop Unbundling) Regulation

The Regulation on unbundling the local loop was adopted in less than six months and was adopted at the end of 2000[103] (in the Commission's original plans, this was to have been a Directive: changing it to a Regulation saved time by avoiding the need for transposition into national law). This aimed to grant a long-standing wish of new entrants by requiring fixed operators with significant market power (in the case of Ireland, this means eircom) to offer access on regulated terms to the "local loop".

The logic behind this is explained in ODTR decision notice D8/01 of April 30, 2001:

> "The 'local loop' is the copper pair connecting an individual telephone subscriber to the nearest point of interconnection with the main telephone network at the local exchange. This "last mile" of network is accepted to be the most difficult for new entrants to replicate. "Local Loop Unbundling" implies that the network owner is required to provide access to this copper pair, so that new entrants can offer their services across the local loop. This allows new entrants to provide a full range of services directly to the customer. In particular, new entrants can offer the new range of broadband services (such as

---

102 The texts are in [2002] O.J. L 108, available at http://europa.eu.int/eur-lex/en/archive/2002/l_10820020424en.html.

103 Regulation 2887/2000 on unbundled access to the local loop, [2000] O.J. L 336 /4. The text is available at http://europa.eu.int/eur-lex/pri/en/oj/dat/ 2000/ l_336/ l_336 20001 230en 00040008.pdf

high-speed Internet access) even if the incumbent operator has not chosen to offer such services. As a result, Local Loop Unbundling has the potential to increase significantly the range of competitive services available to businesses and consumers."[104]

At the time of writing negotiations were continuing between eircom and interested operators on the details of local loop unbundling. In its decision D8/01 the ODTR set interim prices for LLU; this was challenged by eircom but has since been replaced by a new price, and the litigation has been settled.

5.(5)(b)(ii) Framework Directive

One Directive sets out principles and procedures common to all the Directives in the new package.[105] This "framework" Directive (2002/21) is the one which most clearly shows the difference between the old and the new regimes.

The first point of difference is that the new texts no longer speak of "telecommunications" but of "electronic communications." The difference in terminology is to reflect an important difference in scope – the new Directives cover domains which were previously excluded such as the world of broadcasting.[106] This reflects the issue of "convergence" above. The Directive extends the telecommunications rules to networks carrying any kind of "signals" but says that "the type of information conveyed" is irrelevant. However, the new rules do exclude some "broadcasting" activities. The definition of "electronic communications service" in Article 2 (c) excludes:

> "services providing, or exercising editorial control over, content transmitted using electronic communications networks and services; it does not include Information Society services, as defined in Article 1 of Directive 98/34/EC, which do not consist wholly or mainly in the conveyance of signals on electronic communications networks".

Next, there are major changes to the concept of Significant Market Power. To decide which operators have SMP, the Directives no longer define markets in advance in legislation. Instead, national regulators are to define markets on a case-by-case basis using much the same criteria as in competition law and subject to supervision by the Commission. The threshold for SMP is now defined in Article 14 and Annex II as very similar to the competition law concept of dominance.

The *1999 Review* had suggested that sector-specific rules should be rolled back as competition strengthens, with the ultimate aim of controlling market

---

[104] http://odtr-web/docs/odtr0127R.doc
[105] Framework Directive (2002/21/EC) [2002] O.J. L108/33.
[106] This paper focuses on telecommunications. For an examination of the effect of the 1999 Review on the broadcasting sector, see Libertus, *International Journal of Communications Law and Policy*, Issue 6, Winter 2000/01. http://www.ijclp.org/6_2001/ijclp_webdoc _ 10_6 _2001.html

power via competition law.[107] The Commission also suggested that the threshold of market power required to trigger SMP obligations should be raised. Under the current rules, the threshold for SMP is 25 per cent market share with some scope for deviation.[108] While market share is not the only criterion in competition law, it is still important. There is a presumption of dominance for a market share of 50 per cent[109] but this is not necessarily conclusive.

The present Directives provide that SMP status automatically brings certain obligations, such as non-discrimination, cost orientation, etc. Under the new framework Directive these would not be applied automatically but on a case-by-case basis, allowing the regulator to impose only those conditions which are necessary.[110]

Another feature of the new regime is that national regulators will be subject to much more control by the European Commission. Previously, national regulatory authorities (NRAs) had to inform the Commission of certain decisions, *e.g.* SMP designations, but the Commission took no part in them. The Commission's original proposal in July 2000 was that it would have a power of veto over important decisions of the NRAs. Although supported by the European Parliament, this was less welcome to the Council.

The issues involved were complex and even within the Council or Parliament different shades of opinion were put forward. At the risk of over-simplifying, the Commission and Parliament were concerned that the single market would be jeopardised if the same Directives were interpreted differently from one Member State to another – an example often raised was the different methods used to award third generation "3G" mobile telephone licences, which were subject to auctions in some countries and "beauty contests" in others.[111] The Council, on the other hand, took the view that Directives always imply different national implementing measures (and the relevant rules did not lay down any single method of awarding 3G licences). For the Council, any serious obstacle to the single market could be dealt with without a wide-reaching power of veto by the Commission.

For several months the relevant provision (Article 6) was subject to intense discussions as texts and counter-texts flew back and forth. Article 6 became extremely elaborate as it defined procedures and variants covering several pages in some drafts. In the final compromise, hammered out in December 2001, these difficult issues were split off into a separate Article 7. Article 6 now contains a general consultation duty while Article 7 provides that NRAs

---

[107] *1999 Review*, p.49.
[108] Art. 4(3) of Directive 97/33 on interconnection.
[109] Case C–82/86 *Akzo v. Commission* [1991] ECR I–3359 [1993] 5 C.M.L.R. 215 para. 60.
[110] See Art. 16(4) of the Framework Directive. The same principle is reflected in the specific provisions of the other Directives.
[111] A "beauty contest" is the informal term for a selection on the basis of comparing bids for quality.

must co-operate in general, and specifically consult the Commission and other NRAs before adopting certain decisions. The question of defining markets and deciding on SMP obligations was identified as especially sensitive: in these cases, Article 7(3) provides that if a draft decision would affect trade between Member States, the Commission and the other NRAS must be given a month to comment. Under Article 7(4) if the Commission considers that the draft measure "would create a barrier to the single European market" or if it has "serious doubts as to its compatibility with Community law" the Commission can block the NRA's decision for up to two months and require the NRA to abandon or modify its proposed decision.

As mentioned above, the new regime requires NRAs to apply a more complex market definition procedure than in the past. As a result, Article 15(2) provided that the Commission was to publish guidelines on market analysis and SMP at the same time as the framework Directive came into force.

5.(5)(b)(iii) Authorisations Directive

This Directive, 2002/20,[112] is not dramatically different from the previous licensing Directive, 97/33. The most important difference, reflected in the title, is that, in principle, most operators will no longer need individual licences for their activities and will be able to operate under a system of simplified "authorisations." The operator does not need a decision from the NRA to begin operations – it need only notify its details (Article 3). It is only if the operator requires the use of radio frequencies (spectrum) or the use of numbers that it requires a specific approval – Articles 5 to 7 contain a number of rules designed to ensure that this is speedy and simple.

Directive 97/33 had contained similar principles, but the new authorisations Directive goes much further in specifying (in the annex) the type of conditions which can be inserted into authorisations and in defining what information operators can be required to provide (Article 11). For example, authorisations may not repeat obligations which already exist under other areas of law. The Directive also makes some changes to matters such as fees and enforcement, etc., but the impact of this on the Irish system will depend on how the Directives are implemented.

5.(5)(b)(iv) Access and Interconnection Directive

Again, this Directive[113] is similar to the interconnection Directive (97/33) which it replaces. It allows operators to have access to the networks of others; however, its scope extends to the new concept of "electronic communications networks" so that it may cover networks previously excluded from the interconnection rules, *e.g.* those used for broadcasting. The Directive also

---

[112] Authorisations Directive (2002/20/EC) [2002] O.J. L108/21.
[113] Access and Interconnection Directive (2002/19/EC) [2002] O.J. L108/7.

specifically includes rules imported from the broadcasting world such as "conditional access" (Article 6 and annex I) and widescreen TV formats (Article 4(2)).

Articles 9–13 provide that SMP operators can be subject to obligations such as non-discrimination, cost orientation, etc. In keeping with the new approach, obligations are not to be imposed automatically on SMP operators but only to the extent that they are justified by the "nature of the problem identified" (Article 8(4)). Under Article 7 any special obligations are to be reviewed periodically to see if they are still needed but Article 7(1) provides that existing SMP obligations remain in place until reviewed .

5.(5)(b)(v) Universal service Directive

This Directive[114] provides that certain services are to be available to all users at an affordable price regardless of location (Article 3). The services are access to the public telephone network and publicly available services, directories and directory enquiries and public payphones. The European Parliament had wanted to add other topics such as mobile phones but this was not adopted. Article 7 provides for special measures for disabled users. Article 8 provides that one or more undertakings can be designated to provide the universal service, and under Article 9 the universal service operator(s) can be subject to measures such as special tariffs or price caps. Like Directive 98/10 the Directive provides that operators can be compensated if the universal service obligation is an "unfair burden" (Article 13).

As in the other Directives, SMP operators can be subject to special rules, including price control (Article 17). Again, any special obligations are to be reviewed periodically to see if they are still needed but existing SMP obligations remain in place until reviewed (Articles 16–19). The Directive also contains consumer protection rules: users have the right to a contract giving certain details (Article 20) and information on prices and services generally (Article 21 and annex II). There are also rules on quality of service (Article 22). In case consumers have disputes with operators, Member States must provide "transparent, simple and inexpensive out-of-court procedures" (Article 34).

5.(5)(b)(vi) Spectrum decision

This decision[115] provides for procedures at EC level to co-ordinate the use of radio spectrum. Although there is co-ordination at international level in bodies such as the International Telecommunications Union, the Community had not previously been involved in these matters to a great extent. As the subject matter is technical and the new rules are largely procedural, it is enough to say

---

[114] Universal Service Directive (2002/22/EC) [2002] O.J. L108/51.
[115] Spectrum Decision (766/2002/EC) [2002] O.J. L108/1.

that the European Commission will play a greater role in deciding how spectrum is to be used.

5.(5)(b)(vii) Data Protection Directive

This text fell behind the rest of the package but was adopted a few months after the others.[116] The text aims to update the rules in Directive 97/66 (which applies specifically to the telecommunications sector) in order to deal with such issues as unwanted e-mails ("spamming"), "cookies" (which track sites visited by Internet users, often without them knowing) and similar questions. As in all data protection legislation, there is a balance to be struck between the wishes of industry to harvest data for marketing purposes and the concerns of those who do not want information stored about them. One particular issue is whether unsolicited commercial messages (ranging from e-mails to faxes) can be sent to recipients who have not given their prior consent. There has also been a debate about civil liberties and the powers of law enforcement agencies.

5.(6) COMMUNICATIONS REGULATION ACT 2002

This Act came into force on April 27, 2002 (though, as discussed below, some of its provisions require a Ministerial order before they take effect). New legislation in the telecommunications sector had been under consideration for some time. In March 2001 the Cabinet had agreed Heads of a Bill for new legislation[117] but by the time the Communications Regulation Bill was initiated in the Seanad in February 2002[118] the text was much shorter than the text agreed by Cabinet the previous year.

The reason may have been a shortage of parliamentary time: the Oireachtas considered a very large volume of legislation before the general election was called in April 2002. From the outset the Minister for Public Enterprise indicated that some topics which might have been included in the Bill would be considered in transposing the new Directives. For example, in addressing the Seanad on March 21, she said that appeals would be examined in the transposition process:

> "Regarding appeals against decisions made by the proposed Commission, the advice of the Office of the Parliamentary Counsel to the Government was that there were legal policy difficulties involved in the insertion into the Bill of a

---

[116] Directive 2002/58, was adopted in July 2002 and is to be implemented by October 2003. Text in [2002] O.J. L201/37.

[117] The text as of March 2001 is available at http://www. irlgov.ie /tec/ communcations /comlegislation/schemeregbill2001.html

[118] Bill No. 11 of 2002 initiated on February 27, 2002. Text available at http://www.irlgov.ie/ bills28/bills/2002/1102/b1102s.pdf.

single procedure for appeals against regulatory decisions. Related appeals processes are set out in various pieces of primary and secondary legislation. As many of these decision-making powers will be revised in the transposition of the new directives into Irish law by means of regulations to be made under the European Communities Acts, the transposition will provide the opportunity to put in place a consistent and appropriate appeals process."

However, during the parliamentary debates the Minister did agree to some changes including new enforcement provisions. The Bill was debated in March and April; it was passed by both Houses on April 19 and signed by the President on April 27. The text is available on the Oireachtas web site.[119]

In outline, the Act has three aspects:

1. It makes organisational changes to the ODTR;

2. It consolidates some provisions on enforcement;

3. It imposes new rules for road works.

The Act replaces the ODTR with a "Commission for Communications Regulation" of minimum 1 and maximum 3 members. Under section 15(5) the present Director is automatically a member of the new Commission and under section 15(2) any other members are to be appointed under a competition run by the Civil Service Commission.

Part 2 of the Act addresses organisational rules (pensions, conflicts of interests, term of office, etc., as well as more general matters such as the functions and objectives of the Commission (sections 10 and 12), ministerial directions (13) and answerability to the Oireachtas (34). The overall theme is that the Regulator is given more explicit policy aims (copied from the EC Directives) but there are also greater controls by the Department of Finance over staffing issues. Section 13 allows the Minister to give policy directions to the Regulator: the text requires that these directions must be published and there must be public consultation on them.

Part 3 deals with enforcement. On this point, the text proposed in March 2001 proposed two novel additions to the regulator's existing remedies of summary prosecution or civil actions. First, the regulator was to have had a power to take prosecutions on indictment (a power currently reserved to the DPP). Secondly, there was also a novel provision by which the regulator could impose "financial payment obligations" as a price for not continuing with a criminal or civil action (much as "fines" imposed for motoring offences where the motorist can avoid prosecution by paying a defined amount). The text originally introduced to the Seanad dropped these, but during the debate the Minister proposed an amendment to section 44 restoring the "financial payment obligations." The text copied the powers of the Director of Corporate

---

[119] http://www.irlgov.ie/bills28/acts/2002/a2002.pdf

Enforcement under section 109 of the Companies Act 2001 but limited the "fines" to €1000.

Part 5 of the Act is an updated version of the Infrastructure Bill first mooted in 1999.[120] It aims to regulate road works by network operators and gives the new regulator a role in disputes between local authorities and operators.

Sections 53 to 56 deal with relations between operators and local authorities. The basic rule is that operators need permission from the appropriate road authority (which is usually the county council) before digging roads to lay networks, etc. Road authorities can charge network operators for any costs incurred. The only role for the regulator in these sections is that if a road authority wants to oblige an operator to lay extra ducts it must consult the regulator (section 53(9)). Some aspects of these procedures are to be subject to guidelines from the Department of the Environment. Section 57 deals with relations between operators and replaces regulation 12 of the Interconnection regulations which had covered similar topics.[121] Operators can ask to use the infrastructure of another operator; if they start negotiations they are to serve notice on the regulator under section 57(2). The regulator can decide to intervene in the negotiations. The Act requires the regulator to draw up procedures under section 57(6) – section 57(8) provides that the procedures must provide for public consultation. The decision itself must take into account criteria set out in section 57(9).

The President signed the Bill into law on April 27, 2002. Under section 52(3), Part 5 of the legislation (on road works) comes into force immediately with the Director assuming the functions of the future Commission. However, the rest of the legislation requires a ministerial order to bring it into force (section 4).[122] Section 44 will also require the Minister to adopt regulations prescribing the form of the "on-the-spot fines" that the new Regulator can impose – see the definition of "prescribed" in section 2. At the time of writing, no date had been set for bringing the rest of the legislation into force (and establishing the new Commission).

5.(7) CONCLUSIONS

The chief influence on Irish telecommunications law in the last twenty years has been successive EC Directives. The present situation is in a state of flux: the legislative package adopted in February 2002 will mean considerable

---

[120] The text was introduced in the Seanad in March 1999 but never progressed beyond initial stages. For the text see http://www.irlgov.ie/bills28/bills/1999/1299/b1299.pdf.

[121] European Communities (Interconnection in Telecommunications) Regulations, 1998, S.I. No. 15 of 1998.

[122] It has been suggested that s.45 (increase of penalties) also came into force on the date of entry of the Act.

changes to the present law and licensing regime. This might be an opportunity to simplify some of the present rules which are scattered in a number of statutory instruments – the debate on the Communications Regulation Act suggested that the Directives would be implemented by new regulations under the European Communities Acts which would also address general issues such as appeals, etc. If the current law is consolidated and simplified, this can only help operators and regulators.

BIBLIOGRAPHY

Doherty, *Competition Law and Sector-specific Regulation* (2001) 7 Computer and Telecommunications Law Review 225.

Garzaniti, *Telecommunications, Broadcasting and the Internet: EC Competition Law and Regulation* (Sweet & Maxwell, London, 2000).

Grant, *Delors: Inside the House that Jacques Built* (Nicholas Brealy, London, 1994) p. 161.

Hall, *The Electronic Age* (Oak Tree Press, Dublin, 1993).

Larouche, *Competition Law and Regulation in European Telecommunications*, (Hart, Oxford and Portland (Oregon), 2000).

Middlemas, *Orchestrating Europe* (Fontana, London, 1995) p. 586.

Ungerer and Costello, *Telecommunications in Europe* (Office for Official Publications of the EC, Luxembourg, 1990).

Walden and Angel, (ed) *Telecommunications Law* (Blackstone, London, 2001).

6. ENVIRONMENTAL LAW: INTEGRATED CONTROL OF POLLUTION?

ALAN DOYLE*

6.(1) Introduction and background

Environmental law in the European Union is based on Article 2 of the EC Treaty which sets out that the objective of the European Community (EC) is to secure harmonious, balanced and sustainable development and, after a list of other economic objectives, a high level of protection and improvement of the quality of the environment. This sets out the fundamental tension between economic development and environmental protection, and conceptualises economic development as a positive force subject to restriction by the negative principle of environmental protection. This conception results from the fact that economic theory is well developed, whereas understanding of the environment is in its infancy: the European Union was set up initially as an economic community; concern for the environment was only introduced at a later stage.

Article 174 of the EC Treaty (ex Article 130r) sets out the objectives and goals of European environmental law. It is based on theories and principles of international environmental law and policy. The objectives of EC environmental law are: to preserve, protect and improve the quality of the environment; protect human health; and ensure prudent and rational utilisation of natural resources. EC law should be based on a number of principles: a high level of protection, precautionary and preventive action, rectification at source, and the polluter pays principle. Policy should be based on data, environmental conditions, and a balancing of costs and benefits. These objectives and principles, which originate in international law, should be implemented through European legislation and through a European international environmental policy.

6.(1)(a) Techniques of environmental law

There are several recognised techniques used internationally in environmental law. These include the setting of standards for environmental quality, processes or emissions; licensing; the adoption of plans and programmes; penalties and

---

* LL.M. (Bruges). Solicitor (Partner in the firm of Barry Doyle and Co.) All errors remain the responsibility of the author.

liabilities; and economic incentives or disincentives, such as taxes, emission charges, loans and grants.[1]

EC Directives create a range of environmental quality standards which are given effect through plans and licences. The Directives lay down emission standards for inclusion in licences. They deal with waste, air and water as distinct areas of concern. Each Directive usually covers a single area of environmental concern. There are some measures which straddle these sectors, and there are limited efforts to integrate consideration of effects on different areas. In some cases a framework Directive is followed by subordinate implementing Directives (known as "Daughter Directives"). States must nominate competent authorities to apply and implement the Directives. Directives require designation of sensitive sites and early consideration of potential effects, as well as public participation and access to information held by administrative bodies.

In environmental law, it is not possible to compartmentalise any one area, although the Directives generally attempt to do so and make little provision for the overlap of different Directives. The uncoordinated nature of EC environmental legislation is its greatest weakness, and makes it difficult for a Member State to implement it properly. Terminology is not used consistently from one Directive to another. The relationship between Directives is often poorly thought out. This is particularly the case in the interplay between integrated pollution prevention and control (IPPC), waste, environmental impact assessment (EIA) and habitats.

6.(1)(b) The Irish regulatory framework

Irish environmental law is derived almost exclusively from EC Directives and can be boiled down to four main Acts: the Local Government (Water Pollution) Act 1977 (amended by the Local Government (Water Pollution) (Amendment) Act 1990; the Air Pollution Act 1987; the Environmental Protection Agency Act 1992 (EPA Act) setting up a licensing system known as Integrated Pollution Control (IPC); and the Waste Management Act 1996 (amended by the Waste Management (Amendment) Act 2001 (WMAA)). Since 1992 Irish law has distinguished between environmental law, which deals with the emission of pollutants, and planning law.[2] Each Act gives effect to the Directives in its area, except the EPA Act which pre-dated the corresponding Directive. Some defects in the Irish system spring from the non-integrated nature of EC legislation; other problems are entirely our own.

A characteristic of Irish implementing legislation is that it implements substantive requirements, but does not mention the objectives of the Directive, so that these are not given legal effect. This may amount to defective

---

[1] See Commission *Community Guidelines on State Aids for Environmental Protection* O.J. C3/73: February 3, 2001.

[2] Planning and Development Act 2000.

implementation because there is no provision of national law which sets out the purpose of the legislation, and which could be used to interpret the implementing legislation. Competent authorities are, however, bound by the obligation which lies on all organs of the State (legislative, administrative and judicial) to give effect to Community law[3] and to interpret Irish law in light of the object and purpose of a Directive. Although a competent authority cannot rely on this obligation in order to impose additional obligations on individuals, since this would amount to horizontal direct effect.[4] EC law can be used to interpret national obligations, but only national law can impose the basic obligations. Another limitation is that a competent authority can only give effect to a Directive in so far as it is competent. If national law makes an authority competent in respect of an aspect of a Directive, it cannot expand its competence to remedy a defect in respect of an area where a different authority is competent.

It may be rather unfair on the competent authority to require it to take upon itself the task of determining the objective of EC law in order to give effect to it: but an authority which failed to have regard to the objectives of a Directive in reaching a decision on any of its functions under the Acts would be failing to take account of relevant considerations. Its decision would therefore be *ultra vires* under Irish judicial review rules, and would be liable to be struck down by the High Court.

6.(2) Water Legislation

EC water legislation comprises a series of water quality Directives, a Directive controlling industrial emissions (supplemented by a series of daughter Directives dealing with emissions of specific substances), and a new framework Directive gradually replacing the existing measures. The Irish implementing legislation consists of the Local Government (Water Pollution) Acts 1977–90 and a series of implementing Regulations which deal with water quality standards and emission standards. The framework Directive has not yet been implemented.

6.(2)(a) Framework Directive

Directive 2000/60/EC[5] is the new framework Directive as a result of which many existing Directives will be replaced over the coming years. Most of the existing Directives continue in force for the time being and some will be

---

[3] Case 103/88 *Fratelli Costanza* [1989] ECR 1839. See also Case 14/83 *Von Colson and Kamann v. Land Nordrhein-Westfalen*, [1984] ECR 1891); Case C–106/89 *Marleasing SA v. La Comercial Internacional de Alimentacion SA* [1990] ECR I–4135); Case C–168/95 Arcaro [1996] ECR I–4705.

[4] Case C–168/95 Arcaro [1996] ECR I–4705

[5] O.J. L327/1 December 22, 2000, establishing a framework for Community action in the field of water policy.

subsumed into the new order. The objectives of the Directive are: to stop deterioration of, and improve, aquatic ecosystems; to achieve long-term water resource sustainability; to reduce emissions of dangerous substances; to reduce pollution; and to protect drinking water supplies.

Quality levels are set for different types of water,[6] and existing water quality must be maintained (particularly where quality is high), then improved to "good" quality (that is, only slightly modified from its natural state) by December 2015. Member States must prevent or limit the input of pollutants to groundwater, ensure that the standstill provision is respected, and protect, enhance and restore all surface and groundwater. Slightly lower standards are set for heavily polluted waters. There are limited exceptions to deadlines and standards, to be interpreted strictly, and states must classify waters as polluted in advance to avail themselves of the exceptions. The core obligations of Article 4 should form a body of substantive rules which individuals can rely on as against the state and against the competent authorities, and which the competent authorities must take into account in the exercise of their functions. Relationship to other water Directives is defined.

Implementation measures should be based on individual river basins, with a competent authority responsible for each basin or group of basins.[7] Member States must collect data for each river basin, adopt a "Programme of Measures" to give effect to the framework Directive, and adopt a river basin management plan for each basin.[8] The idea of incorporating planning and enforcement measures into a single programme sits uneasily with Irish law where choosing what measures should be available is a matter for legislation, while planning and implementation is a matter for competent authorities.

Member States must implement charges for drinking water, structured so as to constitute an incentive to reduce consumption by 2010. Given the attitude of the Irish electorate to all forms of service charges, this should prove interesting.

There must be proportionate, effective and dissuasive penalties for breach of the national implementing regulations. The deadline for implementation of the framework Directive is December 22, 2003. Ireland has not yet implemented it.

6.(2)(b) Control of industrial emissions

Directive 76/464 is the principal Directive dealing with industrial pollution. Under the framework Directive, it will continue in force with some amendments until December 22, 2013. Directive 76/464 is implemented in Ireland

---

[6] Article 2 and 4.

[7] Article 3. This principle already applies in Ireland to fisheries boards which have concurrent responsibility for water pollution (along with the Environmental Protection Agency and local authorities which do not operate on the basis of river basins) under the Fisheries Consolidation Act 1959 as amended.

[8] Articles 5, 11 and 13.

primarily by the Local Government (Water Pollution) Acts 1977–90, but also to an extent by the EPA Act.

The Directive applies to fresh water and to sea waters within national jurisdiction.[9] Polluting substances are divided into two lists:[10] List I contains the most polluting substances for most of which emission limits have been set in implementing Directives; and List II contains less polluting substances as well as those List I substances for which specific emission limits have not yet been set. Pollution by List I substances must be eliminated, and pollution by List II substances must be reduced. All discharges of List I substances must be subject to a licensing regime and licences must fulfil certain requirements.[11] Member States must establish programmes to deal with discharges of List II substances and discharges should be subject to a licensing regime aimed to achieve standards set in the programme. Programmes and licences should be used to give effect to water quality standards in other Directives and to cover pollution by all the listed substances and classes of substance. In time, the framework Directive will replace Directive 76/464 in dealing with these substances.

Implementing measures must not increase pollution of waters to which it does not apply; and must "on no account" lead, either "directly or indirectly", to an increase in pollution to waters to which the Directive does apply.[12] This is an important standstill provision: it is effectively a "no new pollution" rule.[13] These provisions constitute a useful obligation which a court would be bound to apply in interpreting Irish law under its duty to give effect to EC law. Member States may take more stringent measures.[14]

6.(2)(c) Implementing Directives and Regulations

A series of implementing Directives adopted under Directive 76/464 set specific emission limits for List I substances.[15] Directive 86/280, for instance,

---

[9] Article 1. Originally it applied to groundwater as well as surface water; but there is now a separate groundwater Directive.

[10] Article 2.

[11] Articles 3, 5 and 6.

[12] Articles 8 and 9.

[13] It does not say there can be no new emissions, but it does say there can be no extra pollution.

[14] Article 10.

[15] Council Directive 82/176/EEC O.J. L81/29 March 27, 1982 on limit values and quality objectives for mercury discharges by the chloralkali electrolysis industry; Council Directive 83/513/EEC O.J. L 291/1 October 24, 1983, on limit values and quality objectives for cadmium discharges; Council Directive 84/156/EEC O.J. L74/49, March 17, 1984, on limit values and quality objectives for mercury discharges by sectors other than the chlor-alkali electrolysis industry; Council Directive 84/491/EEC O.J. L 274/11, October 17, 1984, on limit values and quality objectives for discharges of hexachlorocyclohexane; and Council Directive 86/280/EEC O.J. L 181/16, July 4, 1986, on limit values and quality objectives for discharges of certain dangerous substances included in List I of the Annex to Directive 76/464/EEC O.J. L 181/16 as amended by Council Directive 88/347/EEC O.J. L158/35, June 25, 1988, and Council Directive 90/415/EEC O.J. L219/49, August 14, 1990.

sets out emission limits, water quality standards and time limits for compliance for a range of substances. It lays down limits and standards which must be included in a licence, and which must be met if a licence is to be granted; and it requires that Member States draw up programmes of measures to eliminate pollution by unlicensable emissions. The implementing measures must not lead to increased pollution of air or soil; this is an early attempt at integrated pollution control, to which the IPPC Directive now contributes. A series of Regulations, adopted under the Water Pollution Acts, establishes implementing rules for the various EC Directives. The implementing regulations tend to share one common flaw: whereas the Directives lay down a minimum quality standard which must not be breached, and a target standard of which there can be no new breach, and with which existing polluted areas must endeavour to comply as soon as possible, the Irish regulations lay down only the minimum standard. There is therefore nothing to prevent Irish waters deteriorating to such a stage that they breach the target standard, contrary to the provisions of the Directives.

Directives on water quality deal with the quality of waters for bathing, shellfish and freshwater fish.[16] Such Directives are relevant to the control of emissions because licences must ensure that water will meet the required quality standards. Therefore a licence must be drafted in such a way as to prevent any emission which would, on its own or together with other emissions, be liable to cause a breach of a quality standard.

6.(2)(d) Water pollution Acts

The Local Government (Water Pollution) Acts 1977–90 implement the substantive provisions of Directive 76/464.[17] Discharge of polluting matter to waters is forbidden, unless it is licensed.[18] Polluting matter is anything which is injurious to fish or liable to render waters harmful or detrimental to public health or to domestic, commercial, industrial, agricultural or recreational uses. The phrase "liable to" indicates that it should not be necessary to show that the harm or detriment has actually happened.

There are two licensing regimes under the Water Pollution Acts: one for discharges of trade effluent to waters under Section 4, the other for discharges of trade effluent to sewers under Section 16. Emissions without a licence or in breach of a licence are prohibited and are an offence. "Trade" includes agriculture which is interesting: in theory it should mean that any outflow from a

---

[16] Council Directive 76/160/EEC O.J. L31/1 February 5, 1976 concerning the quality of bathing water;(,5.2.1976) Council Directive 78/659/EEC O.J. L222, August 14, 1978, on the quality of fresh waters needing protection in order to support fish life; 14.8.1978) Council Directive 79/923/EEC O.J. L281/47, November 10, 1979, on the quality required of shellfish waters.

[17] See discussion above about non-implementation of Directive objectives.

[18] Section 3.

farming activity is licensable but in practice only piggeries and poultry farms are regulated – and then under the EPA Act.

A licence is granted by a local authority (*e.g.* County Council). The procedure for both types of licence is broadly similar. There is a right of appeal to An Bord Pleanála (the Board): any person can appeal a decision on a Section 4 application; only the applicant or landowner can appeal on a Section 16 application.[19] On an appeal, the Board issues a direction to the local authority, and the authority then issues the final decision to the applicant.[20]

When application for a licence is made to it, a local authority (or the Board on appeal) can refuse, grant, or grant subject to conditions. In considering the application, the authority must have regard to any water quality management plan, and it cannot grant a licence which will cause a breach of a water quality standard, hence the standards in water quality Directives must be incorporated into a licence.

Conditions in a licence can deal with the nature of emissions, monitoring, accident prevention and costs. Conditions are mandatory and must be complied with. A licensee must commence using the licence within three years, otherwise it will lapse; but once the licensee commences in time and continues to use the licence, it cannot be revoked, although it can be reviewed. There is a question mark over whether a permanent licence complies with EC law. A review can take place after three years, or can occur sooner if the licensee consents, where the local authority reasonably believes the discharge is likely to be injurious to public health or to render the waters in question unfit for use, new information has come to light, or new standards have been adopted.

A local authority is exempt from the need to obtain a licence, so that sewer outflows are not licensable; but they are subject to an Urban Waste Water Treatment Directive and implementing regulations.[21]

6.(2)(e) Water quality management plans

The 1977 Act also provides for water quality management plans. A local authority may make a plan, and must do so if directed by the Minister. There is no general obligation to make a plan. The procedure is laid down in implementing

---

[19] Presumably this is because, once the effluent is discharged to a sewer, it is removed from public concern, and should – at least in theory – be properly handled by the local authority.

[20] In the pre-1992 scheme of environmental law, pollution law and planning law were closely parallel, and the Board heard appeals from the local authority in relation to both the planning and environmental aspects of any operation, creating a reasonably integrated system. Since the adoption of the EPA Act, the two systems of law have diverged. Sections 4 to 8 and 16 to 20 elaborate on the licensing regime, and procedural rules are laid down in the various Local Government (Water Pollution) Regulations 1978–99, most notably those of 1978 and 1992.

[21] Council Directive 91/271/EEC O.J. L135/40, May 30, 1991 concerning urban waste water treatment implemented by Environment Protection Agency Act 1992 (Urban Waste Water Treatment) Regulations 1994, S.I. 419/1994 and Environmental Protection Agency Act 1992 (Urban Waste Water Treatment) (Amendment) Regulations 1999, S.I. No. 208/1999.

regulations under the Act. It seems that few local authorities have made plans, and such plans as may be in existence are not easily accessible.

6.(2)(f) Agricultural pollution

Other measures in the 1990 Act allow the local authority to regulate and control agricultural activities through bye-laws, and to require any person who puts natural or artificial fertiliser on land to draw up a nutrient management plan to monitor and reduce the impact of fertilisers, a matter now covered by the agricultural nitrates Directive.[22] The Environmental Protection Agency, in its recent report on river quality,[23] has noted a continuing decline in the standard of surface waters in Ireland, much of it due to excessive use of fertilisers. Implementing measures are essentially advisory rather than mandatory, and effective measures are urgently required in order to comply with the Directive's objectives.

6.(2)(g) Drinking water

Directives regulate both the input and the output of drinking water systems. Quality of drinking water supplied to consumers is dealt with in Directive 98/83/EC[24] implemented in Ireland by the European Communities (Drinking Water) Regulations 2000 which are not due to come into force until January 1, 2004.[25]

Quality of water from which drinking water supplies may be extracted is governed by Directive 75/440,[26] one of the earliest pieces of EC environmental

---

[22] Council Directive 91/676/EEC , O.J. L375/1, December 31, 1991 concerning the protection of waters against pollution caused by nitrates from agricultural sources. "Eutrophication" of waters, due to run-off of fertilisers and slurries arises where farmers spread more fertiliser than crops require, is one of the greatest pollution problems in the State. The excess fertiliser cannot be absorbed and is washed off into streams and groundwater where it is used as food by micro-organisms which feed on it, increasing their rate of growth. They very quickly use up all the oxygen in the water, and cause the death of other plants and animals which depend on the oxygen for survival. State efforts to convince farmers that over-use of fertiliser is just throwing money away – since the plants cannot use the fertiliser – and is bad for the environment, have had negligible success, and the level of pollution from this source continues to rise. It is contributed to by the spreading of slurry from piggeries, which is not regarded as waste disposal if it is for the benefit of land, but which often involves excess spreading with the same effects as the excess use of any fertiliser.

[23] *Interim Report on the Biological Survey of River Quality – Results of 2000 Investigations and Ireland's Environment – A Millennium Report.*

[24] Directive 98/83/EC O.J. L330/32, December 5, 1998 on the quality of water intended for human consumption.

[25] S.I. No. 439 of 2000.

[26] O.J. L194/26 July 25, 1975. Since writing this the ECJ has held, on the basis of an EPA Report on water quality that Irish group water schemes fail to comply with Directives 80/778/EEC, the existing drinking water directive which is replaced by Directive 98/83/EC. (*Commission v. Ireland*, Case C–316/00 Judgment of 14 November 2002).

legislation. For the three categories of acceptable water, a table sets out the amount of various substances which water classified as A1, A2 or A3 may contain. (Water which is below A3 quality cannot normally be used as drinking water.) Two types of value are set, an imperative ("I") value which must be met and a guide ("G") value which must be aimed for.[27]

6.(2)(h) Groundwater

Protection of groundwater is effected under Council Directive 80/68/EEC[28] until 2013 when the provisions required by the framework Directive should be completed, and when the framework Directive will operate to repeal the existing groundwater Directive.

Directive 80/68 is closely modelled on Directive 76/464 and its objective is to prevent pollution of groundwater by polluting substances named in two lists which are essentially the same as the lists in Directive 76/464. Discharge of List I substances is prohibited and any disposal which might indirectly cause a discharge to groundwater must be investigated and either prohibited or allowed subject to conditions which will prevent the discharge – effectively through licensing procedures, particularly waste licences. Similar investigation and authorisation requirements apply to List II substances; but emissions are not forbidden, just limited so as not to cause pollution. Authorisation may only be granted for a limited period, and must be reviewed at least every four years. Authorisation cannot be granted if the licensee will be unable to comply with the conditions; and if the licensee does not comply with the conditions, the competent authority must take steps to ensure that the conditions are complied with, if necessary by withdrawing the licence.[29]

The application of measures taken pursuant to the Directive must not lead to pollution of groundwater.

6.(3) AIR POLLUTION

Air pollution is a broad topic which covers everything from emissions from a single car, to the ozone layer and global warming. Directives address the environmental problems posed by emissions. They attempt to control particular industrial sectors or polluting substances and products. They set

---

[27] The Directive is implemented by the European Communities (Quality of Water Intended for Human Consumption) Regulations 1988, S.I. 81/1988, which lay down limit values but no guide values.

[28] Council Directive 80/68/EEC O.J. L 20/43, January 26, 1980, on the protection of groundwater against pollution caused by certain dangerous substances.

[29] The Groundwater Directive has not been specifically implemented apart from the Protection of Groundwater Regulations 1999, S.I. 41/1999, which cover licensing of local authorities, although licensing in general is covered by the Water Pollution Acts. The real problem in

standards for emissions and environmental quality. As a rule, the implementation of the various obligations falls to the designated competent authorities.

EC air pollution legislation can be divided into three main categories: global issues, air quality controls, and regulation of diffuse sources.

6.(3)(a) Climate change: global warming

Global issues are essentially global warming and the ozone hole. The framework for global warming legislation is the United Nations Environment Programme's Convention on Global Warming, and the Kyoto Protocol adopted under it. The Convention is a perfect example of an application of the precautionary principle (in Article 174 EC Treaty), being based on reasonable apprehension of environmental damage, rather than established facts. It has foundered on United States intransigence and European lip-service. Ireland played the "developing country" card at Kyoto and secured a 10% *increase* in emissions over 1990 levels by 2005 as its contribution to the reduction. Because the Protocol has not actually come into force, Ireland has done little to comply, and, in fact exceeded in 2000 its negotiated ceiling. The major sources of greenhouse gases in the State are cows and cars: draconian legislation will be required to reduce their number or impact. Ireland's obligations exist in international law only and are not enforceable before the Irish courts.

6.(3)(b) Ozone depletion

The other big issue at global level has been the hole in the ozone layer. Various manufactured chemicals, particularly chlorofluorocarbons (CFCs), break down ozone in the upper atmosphere causing a hole in the ozone layer above the poles. This allows harmful ultraviolet light to enter, increasing the global risk of skin cancers and necessitating a global solution. Accordingly, a Convention on Ozone Depleting Substances was adopted at Vienna which laid out a framework for action, with specific goals agreed in a subsequent Protocol concluded at Montreal, and hence known as the Montreal Protocol. The specific goals were progressively increased, and implemented in the European Union by a series of Regulations, culminating in Council Regulation (EEC) No 3952/92[30] which prohibits the manufacture, placing on the market and importation into the Union of ozone depleting substances. The measure is contained in a Regulation because it concerns trade policy, an area of exclusive EC competence, so a directly applicable act was required. From the practical

---

Ireland is with unlicensed, accidental discharges. These are covered by the Water Pollution Acts, but their application is limited: there is a growing problem with pollution of groundwater.

[30] Council Regulation (EEC) No. 3952/92 O.J. L405/41, December 31, 1992, amending Regulation (EEC) No. 594/91 in order to speed up the phasing our of substances that deplete the ozone layer.

point of view it is interesting because it appears to be successful: it was reported in 2001 that the ozone hole over Antarctica was not as big as the previous year. Although this may be a result of weather conditions for the year, it provides some hope that environmental action can actually work, and that environmental law can have some useful effect.

6.(3)(c) Long range transboundary air pollution

Air pollution problems are overwhelmingly international in nature: emission of pollutants in one country can cause pollution hundreds of kilometres away. The UN Convention on Long Range Trans-Boundary Air Pollution, adopted by the Council of Ministers,[31] gives an international dimension to European air pollution policy. Its objectives are to limit and, as far as possible, eliminate pollution; it requires states to co-operate and consult with one another and to develop best policies and strategies, including air quality management systems and control systems to this end. European policy is related to these objectives. EC legislation gives effect to these provisions.

6.(3)(d) Ambient Air Directive

The principal EC air quality measure is the ambient air quality Directive.[32] Like the water framework Directive, this is a Directive under which a series of daughter Directives is being adopted. The objective is to set air quality objectives, assess air quality, maintain the quality of air where it is already good and improve it where it is not. Limit values for sulphur dioxide, nitrogen dioxide, nitrous oxides, lead and particulates are set in Directive 99/30/EC.[33] Limit values for carbon monoxide and benzene are set in Directive 2000/69.[34] Other limit values have still to be set. The new limits are to be phased in gradually, replacing limits set under earlier Directives.

The Directives set a "limit value" for a pollutant and a "margin of tolerance". Over time, the margin of tolerance is reduced to zero. Emissions must meet the limit value plus margin of tolerance threshold, and should be reduced to reach the limit value. Once they reach the limit value, they must not exceed it again, even if the margin of tolerance has not expired. The Directives also set an "alert threshold" which is the level at which even short-term exposure will cause damage to human health. Whenever the alert threshold is breached, the

---

[31] Council Decision 81/462/EEC O.J. L171/11, June 27, 1981, on the conclusion of the Convention on long-range transboundary air pollution.

[32] Council Directive 96/62/EC O.J. L 296/55 September 27, 1996 on ambient air quality assessment and management.

[33] Council Directive 1999/30/EC O.J. L163/41, June 29, 1999 relating to limit values for sulphur dioxide, nitrogen dioxide and oxides of nitrogen, particulate matter and lead in ambient air OJ L163/41 29.06.1999, purportedly amended by Commission Decision 2001/744/EC O.J. L 278/35, October 23, 2001.

[34] Council and Parliament Directive 2000/69/EC O.J. L 313/12 relating to limit values for benzene and carbon monoxide in ambient air. OJ L 313/12, December 13, 2000.

public must be informed immediately so that they can take precautions.[35] The Environmental Protection Agency can comply with this obligation by relying on Section 67 of the 1992 Act.

Competent authorities are responsible for carrying out the obligations in the Directive. In Ireland, the competent authority is the Environmental Protection Agency[36] but the Regulations do not give the Agency the powers necessary to give effect to the Directive in full.[37] Indeed they only cover the first stage of the procedure, namely establishing basic data.[38] In other respects the Agency can only give effect to the Directive by using its existing powers, and these are not sufficient to give effect to all obligations.

Competent authorities must monitor air quality and ensure that the limit values in the daughter Directives are met,[39] and must draw up action plans for breaches or potential breaches. The Agency has power to carry out monitoring or to require others to do it.[40] It can prepare the required action plans;[41] but it has no power to make those plans legally binding,[42] and further legislative action will be required for this.

Plans to deal with potential breaches of air quality standards must not displace air pollution to water or land.[43] Measures designed to achieve ambient air standards must take account of EC health and safety legislation. Emissions must have no significant effect on the environment of other Member States.

The ambient air Directive and its implementing Directives will gradually replace the series of Directives dealing with individual pollutants. The new Directives essentially take up where the old left off, setting tighter standards, and requiring Member States to do more to comply.

6.(3)(e) Directive 84/360: Industrial Emissions

Council Directive 84/360/EEC on the combating of air pollution from industrial plants[44] sets down a requirement that certain industrial activities can only be carried on subject to a licence. The Integrated Pollution Prevention and Control Directive,[45] which traverses much of the same ground, unites consideration of

---

[35] Article 10.

[36] So designated by the Environmental Protection Agency Act 1992 (Ambient Air Quality Assessment and Management) Regulations 1999, S.I. No. 33/1999.

[37] It may be intended that there will be further Directives, but this is not evident from the Regulations.

[38] Article 5, Directive 96/62.

[39] Article 7.

[40] S. 65 of the 1992 Act.

[41] ss. 75 and 76 of the 1992 Act.

[42] In particular it cannot prohibit car traffic in an area –one of the potential requirements of the Directive.

[43] This is a link to the objectives of the Integrated Pollution Prevention and Control Directive.

[44] O.J. L 188/20, July 16, 1984.

[45] See below para 6(4).

air, water and waste but fails to ensure that it applies to all of the same activities, because it employs a different list of licensable activities. The definition of pollution in these two Directives and the ambient air Directive are also slightly different.

6.(3)(f) Air Pollution Act

The Air Pollution Act was adopted in 1987 to give effect to Directive 84/360 and to allow for the implementation of air quality standards. It has been amended, principally by the EPA Act.

Part V authorises the making of statutory instruments specifying air quality standards and emission limit values and regulating the quality of fuels.[46] It also authorises the Minister to issue guidelines on air pollution. Some of the Minister's functions are now exercised by the Environmental Protection Agency under the EPA Act.[47]

Local authorities have the power to make Air Quality Management Plans, but are under no obligation to do so unless the Minister so directs. The public may make submissions on a draft plan. A plan should include such measures as the authority considers appropriate. This apparently unfettered discretion is not in fact absolute: a local authority would have to include measures to achieve the objectives of EC air quality Directives. Failure to address an applicable Directive would amount to a failure to take account of relevant considerations, and would render the plan liable to judicial review. An authority which failed to make a plan when a Directive required that a programme of measures be drawn up would be in breach of its obligations as a competent authority and might be compelled to adopt a plan.[48]

An area may be designated as a Special Control Area. The objective of designation is to deal with areas where there are particular air pollution problems. The Special Control Area procedure has been used to resolve a problem of air pollution from coal burning in Dublin and other urban areas.

A licensing regime for listed types of industrial plant gives effect to Council Directive 84/360, but is not as significant as it once was, since most licensable industrial plants now need an Integrated Pollution Control (IPC) licence instead. The licensing procedure follows the same model as the procedure under the Water Pollution Acts: the application is to the local authority with a right of appeal to An Bord Pleanála. An air pollution licence is a means to require an industrial plant to conduct its activities in such a way as to respect

---

[46] *e.g.* European Parliament and Council Directive 94/63/EC O.J. L365/24, December 31, 1994, on the control of volatile organic compound (VOC) emissions resulting from the storage of petrol and its distribution from terminals to service stations implemented by Air Pollution Act 1987 (Petroleum Vapour Emissions) Regulations 1997, S.I. 375/1997.

[47] ss. 50–53.

[48] ss. 47–50.

air quality standards and atmospheric emission standards, and not to cause air pollution. Provisions for review of the licence every three years, or more frequently in certain circumstances, are also present.

Part II contains provisions for controlling pollution by individuals. The Minister can make regulations prohibiting any emission or any substance which may cause pollution, or any emission of smoke.[49] The occupier of premises must not cause or permit any emission which causes a nuisance. Where the premises is not a private dwelling, the occupier must use the Best Practicable Means available.[50] There is provision for injunctions, civil liability for damage, and criminal liability for breach of any section of the Act.

6.(4) THE ENVIRONMENTAL PROTECTION AGENCY AND INTEGRATED POLLUTION CONTROL

The Environmental Protection Agency (the Agency) was set up under the Environmental Protection Agency Act 1992 (the EPA Act) which also established a system of Integrated Pollution Control (IPC) licensing for large industrial or agri-industrial activities, previously introduced in England in 1990. The idea was subsequently taken up at EC level in Council Directive 96/61/EC on Integrated Pollution Prevention and Control (IPPC).[51] The concept is that, where an activity needs different licences for its emissions to air or water, or for disposal of its waste, it may be tempted to maximise the emissions to the least tightly-controlled environmental medium, but that this will not occur if there is only one licence for all media.

Since the IPPC Directive postdates the EPA Act, the Act cannot be regarded as the implementing legislation and Ireland still has not adopted implementing legislation.[52] However, the EPA Act can, and indeed must, be interpreted in order to give effect to the IPPC Directive and to Article 174EC on which it is based.[53] Because the Directive is very similar to the Irish provisions, the application of the rule is relatively easy, though there may be some difficulties.

The IPPC Directive applies in addition to other EC measures on air, water and waste.[54]

---

[49]   s. 23.
[50]   s. 24.
[51]   O.J. L 257/26, October 10, 1996.
[52]   The deadline was October 30,1999.
[53]   See above, nn. 3 and 4.
[54]   Article 8 and Preamble; other measures include Council Directive 85/337 on Environmental Impact Assessment, and the Habitats Directive 92/43, as well as Directives 76/464 on water pollution and Council Directive 84/360 on discharges to the atmosphere from industrial plants.

6.(4)(a) Obligation to hold a licence

New and existing installations cannot be operated without a permit[55] and there is an extended deadline for existing installations. The EPA Act has already introduced licensing for all new and most existing installations.[56] The lists of installations covered by the Directive (in the Annex) and the Act (in the Schedule) are not identical; the Act may be insufficient in relation to some activities, particularly in the agricultural and food sectors. If the Irish legislation is inadequate, the Agency could probably give a broad interpretation to the obligation to hold a licence; but it could not go beyond the meaning of the words in the Schedule as a result of the rule in *Arcaro*.[57] The problem can only be fully rectified by further legislation. If an unlicensable activity for which the Directive requires a licence were causing pollution, and an effective licence would eliminate the pollution, Ireland could possibly find itself responsible in damages under the *Francovich*[58] line of authority.

Thresholds are set by reference to capacity: in practice, capacity is a notoriously elastic concept, varying according to a wide number of factors, such as the length of the working day, or the size of a pig, for instance.

6.(4)(b) The Agency as licensing authority

The Licensing Regime applied to new and existing activities is the same. Under section 83 of the EPA Act, where application is made to the Agency, it may grant a licence, with or without conditions, or may refuse a licence. The Agency is thereby constituted as the competent authority for the purposes of giving effect to the permit system required by the IPPC Directive. The Agency must have regard to relevant air quality, water quality and waste management plans, to any special control area under the Air Pollution Act 1987, to any noise regulations, and to any other matters relating to environmental pollution which it considers necessary. The Agency must also have regard to any environmental impact statement submitted, and to any further information from the applicant and any comments or submissions from the public or other Member States relating to it. The Agency is thereby made the competent authority responsible for carrying out an environmental impact assessment (EIA) for the purposes of Council Directive 85/337EEC[59] in relation to matters within its jurisdiction.

The Agency cannot grant a licence unless it is satisfied that emissions to air and water, and waste disposal or recovery, will comply with any relevant

---

[55] Articles 4 and 5.
[56] s. 82 plus Environmental Protection Agency (Licensing) Regulations 1994–95 and Environmental Protection Agency (Established Activities) Orders 1995–99.
[57] Case C–168/95 Arcaro [1996] ECR I–4705.
[58] Cases C–6/90 and C–9/90 [1991] ECR I–5357. For the possibility of damages for breach of EC law see above Keville para 1(3).
[59] See below para 6(6) on Environmental Impact Assessment.

environmental quality standards and emission limits, whether relating to air, water, waste, noise, or otherwise. To reinforce this, the Agency cannot grant a licence unless it is satisfied that the emissions from the activity will not cause significant environmental pollution. In exercising its jurisdiction, the Agency must have regard to the requirements of Articles 3, 9 and 10 of the IPPC Directive (and the context of Article 174EC) which include requirements for the elimination, control and monitoring of emissions, prevention of pollution and protection of environmental media, reduction of waste and improvement of energy efficiency. Finally, the Agency must be satisfied that the Best Available Technology Not Entailing Excessive Cost (BATNEEC) will be used.

The requirement that the Agency must consider factors relating to areas covered by other Directives is how the Act achieves integrated control by concentrating decision-making powers in the hands of one authority. The only place where an overlap (between environmental pollution and planning issues, particularly with reference to Environmental Impact Assessment (EIA)) remains, is the area which has caused most difficulty. The fact that the Agency only carries out part of the EIA, the remainder being carried out as part of the planning process, has caused a substantial amount of litigation but very few decisions.[60]

The Agency may decide to grant a licence, refuse one, or grant subject to conditions. There is a general power to impose conditions, which must be exercised in order to give effect to the Directive, and to include the sorts of conditions which the Directive requires. Where a licence is granted, operation must commence within three years. If it does not, or if it ceases for three years, the licence will lapse.

In considering whether to grant a licence, the Agency has to decide whether conditions can deal with any risk. One key requirement is the obligation to consider potential accidents. It is a truism to say that accidents will happen, or that if something can go wrong, it will. Risk analysis generally divides risk into two components: likelihood and severity. There may be a large risk of a small accident, or a small risk of a catastrophic accident. Some places may be more sensitive than others to the same risk, for instance an explosives factory in a residential area, or a piggery beside a river. In any assessment of risk, at a certain stage in the assessment the risk becomes so great as to be unjustifiable. At this point, even though the activity, if carried on in accordance with conditions, would not cause environmental pollution, a licence should be refused because there is an unacceptable risk of environmental pollution. This fundamentally alters the nature of the assessment which the Agency has to carry out under section 83.

There is a divergence between the Directive and the Act as to the standard of technology required to prevent pollution. The Act requires BATNEEC while

---

[60] See further below para. 6(6).

the Directive requires the use of BAT (best available technology). BAT is a higher standard, although the requirement that it be available means it cannot set an impossibly high standard. BATNNEC can be brought into line with BAT by refusing to hold that a cost is excessive once the technology is available.

6.(4)(c) The licence procedure

The licence application must contain detailed information about the proposed activity.[61] The list of contents is broadly in line with Article 6 of the Directive, except that it does not require the application to specify the technology which will be used to limit and prevent emissions and does not require a technical summary. The Agency can use its power to request further information to require these things.[62] Where the proposed activity is of a class subject to environmental impact assessment, the application must include an environmental impact statement (EIS).[63]

The Agency assesses the validity of the licence application, and may request further information or notices, or reject the application. The procedure before the Agency goes through two stages which may be called the "proposed determination" (where it considers the application and submissions, and indicates its proposed determination) and the "objection" (where anyone who is dissatisfied with the proposed determination may submit grounds of objection, and the Agency will consider these in a procedure which may include an oral hearing). When this procedure was introduced there was speculation that it might be unconstitutional because it made the Agency the judge in an appeal against its own decision, thereby breaching rules of natural and constitutional justice. In fact, the proposed determination is not a decision, merely a stage in the process, and the opportunity to object at this stage, before a final decision, enhances the rights of an objector. The validity of the procedure now appears to be generally accepted.

6.(4)(d) Review of licences

The Directive requires Member States to ensure that licences are periodically reviewed.[64] A review must take place in certain circumstances. The Agency can review a licence after three years without further justification or sooner if environmental conditions or new laws require.[65] On a review the Agency has no power to refuse the licence. This appears to accord with the IPPC

---

[61] Article 10, Environmental Protection Agency (Licensing) Regulations 1994, S.I. 85/1994.
[62] The Supreme Court held in *Ni Eili v. Environmental Protection Agency* S.C. unrep 30. 07. 99 that the applicant did not need to provide design details of the proposed technology, since the exact design could not be finalised until the emission limits were set; but the Directive requires inclusion of details of the technology, if not the precise design.
[63] Articles 12–13, Environmental Protection Agency (Licensing) Regulations 1994 S.I. 85/1994.
[64] Article 13.
[65] s. 88, EPA Act.

Directive,[66] but may not comply with Directives 76/464 or 84/360 if they require that a licence can only be granted for a limited period.[67]

6.(4)(e) Modification of installations

Where the operator of an activity proposes to carry out any reconstruction, or to modify the activity, where this would materially change or increase the emissions, the Agency must be informed,[68] and it may decide to review the licence. The Directive goes further and requires that a review *must* be carried out where a substantial change is proposed.[69]

6.(4)(f) Relationship to other legislation

Article 8 of the Directive requires that the licensing procedure, and the actual conditions imposed, must be fully co-ordinated where more than one competent authority is involved in the licensing decisions. Section 98 of the EPA Act deals with the relationship of IPC to other procedures, and has been amended by section 34 of the Planning and Development Act 2000. Where an application is made for planning permission for a plant which will be used for an activity, a planning authority or An Bord Pleanála may request the Agency's views on the proposed plant. Permission may be refused on the basis that it will cause environmental pollution, but cannot be granted with conditions intended to control pollution. This provision may only be workable if the planning decision is taken in the light of the prevention principle: whether the risk of environmental pollution is acceptable, having regard to the risk of breach of conditions by a putatively licensed activity, in the light of proper planning and sustainable development of the area, given that conditions can always ensure that pollution will not occur – so long as they are complied with. The difficulty is that they will, for whatever reason, not always be complied with. The practical application of the new section 98 will cause substantial difficulty.

The earlier section 98 was even more difficult to apply and is still applicable to many applications made before the Planning and Development Act came into force.[70]

---

[66] Article 13.

[67] It may have been felt that this was necessary to protect a licensee's proprietary interest in a licence, but if so this appears to be misconceived. There seems to be no insuperable obstacle, as a matter of Irish constitutional law, to the grant of a licence for a number of years only: a licence to emit matter to the environment is a concession from the State, not some property right, because it is not one of the normal uses of property.

[68] s. 92.

[69] Article 12.

[70] It attempted to draw a rigid distinction between environmental pollution and planning, and the State conceded in the case of *O'Connell v. Environmental Protection Agency* unreported, High Court, April 25, 2002, Butler J., to which it was a notice party, that s. 98 was contrary to the requirements of the Environmental Impact Assessment Directive.

6.(4)(g) **Monitoring and enforcement**

The IPPC Directive requires that licensed activities should be monitored, and that the monitoring results should be communicated quickly to the competent authority which should ensure that the licence conditions are complied with. The Agency lays down monitoring requirements in IPC licences and prosecutes for breach of conditions under Section 84(2) of the Act. Whilst the fines imposable on summary prosecution are minuscule for the large activities licensed under the EPA Act, experience has been that the prospect of a trip to court concentrates the mind of the defendant, and generally results in the carrying out of works required to prevent future pollution. Some sectors have proven problematic, particularly pig and poultry installations, and the large agro-food industry.

The Agency is also responsible for enforcing the requirement to hold a licence (under section 83) and section 8 which makes it an offence to breach any provision of the Act.

6.(5) WASTE

The basic EC measure relating to waste is the Waste Framework Directive of 1975, the text of which was effectively completely replaced in 1991.[71] The Irish implementing legislation is the Waste Management Act 1996, and amending Act of 2001, and various regulations adopted under those Acts.

6.(5)(a) **Obligation to minimise waste production**

The Framework Directive requires states to take measures, first, to minimise production of waste through promoting clean technologies, efficient use of energy, products which cause less waste – and less harmful waste – in their lifetime and in their ultimate disposal, and techniques for safe disposal of hazardous waste; and secondly, to promote maximum recovery of waste through recycling, re-use, reclamation, and use of waste to produce energy.

Part III of the Act gives the Minister for the Environment power to make regulations covering reduction and recovery but, though some measures have been adopted in relation to packaging and plastic bags (see below), none of these has had much effect, and the State has done little to give concrete effect to this primary objective of the Directive.

---

[71] Council Directive 75/442/EEC O.J. L194/39, July 25, 1975 on waste and Council Directive 91/156/EEC O.J. L78/32, March 26, 1991 amending Directive 75/442/EEC on waste.

6.(5)(b) Disposal and recovery of waste

The Directive applies to disposal and recovery of waste. Waste is difficult to define, and the European Court of Justice (ECJ) has not managed to fashion a useful EC definition. It is felt that the essence of waste is that it is something which is got rid of or abandoned. Material stored in the open for a long time has been held to constitute waste.[72] Disposal is defined by reference to a list of disposal operations in Annex III; recovery by reference to a list of recovery operations in Annex IV[73] and the Act copies this list. The essential difference between disposal and recovery is that disposal activities involve getting rid of something permanently or abandoning it, whereas recovery activities involve getting rid of something to someone who will put all or part of it to some use.

6.(5)(c) Control of pollution by waste

Member States must ensure that waste is recovered or disposed of without endangering human health, without using processes or methods which could harm the environment, without causing a nuisance through noise or odours, and without adversely affecting the countryside or places of special interest. They must also prohibit the abandonment, dumping or uncontrolled disposal of waste.[74] This is transposed into Irish law by section 32 of the Act which requires that a person must not hold, transport, recover or dispose of waste in a manner which causes or is likely to cause environmental pollution, defined in accordance with the Directive.

6.(5)(d) Plans

Member States must establish an integrated and adequate network of disposal installations, taking account of BATNEEC, and aiming for self-sufficiency in waste disposal. States must adopt waste management plans to promote waste minimisation, recovery and recycling,[75] to ensure that waste is disposed of

---

[72] Recently, Advocate General Jacobs advised the ECJ to hold that granite blocks which were perfectly usable, but which had been left in an abandoned quarry for a considerable time, pending sale, were waste:Case C–9/00 *Palin Granit Oy v. Lounais-Suomen Ymparistokeskus*, opinion of January 17, 2002. Previously, the Court has held that products do not escape from the definition of waste just because they have a commercial value: wood chips which can be sold as fuel are still waste if they are a residue from another process: joined Cases C–418/97 and C–419/97 *ARCO Chemie Nederland Ltd And Minister van Volkshuisvesting, Ruimtelijke Ordening en Milieubeheer* judgment of June 19, 2000. In Case C–304/94 *Euro Tombesi and AdiNo. Tombesi* judgment of June 25, 1997 the Court held that processing waste to deactivate it, tipping in hollows and embankments, and incineration all constituted disposal or recovery of waste, even if the material used was classified as a reusable residue.

[73] The Commission has purported to amend Annexes III and IV in Commission Decision 96/350/EC adapting Annexes IIA and IIB to Council Directive 75/442/EEC O.J. L135/32, June 6, 1996, on waste, but it may be doubted whether a Decision can amend a Directive.

[74] Article 4.

[75] Referring back to Article 3.

without causing environmental pollution,[76] and to create a self-sufficient network of disposal installations.[77] Plans should identify what waste exists and the best way to deal with it, who can deal with it, the costs, and the rationalisation of collection and disposal systems. Under the Act the Agency has drawn up a national hazardous waste management plan, and each local authority should have drawn up a waste management plan (but most have not, as the issue is politically contentious). In an attempt to remedy this breach of the Directive, the 2001 Act authorises City and County Managers to adopt waste management plans where the councillors have failed to do so.

Local authority functions include collecting domestic waste, and providing disposal and recovery facilities in its functional area, as well as enforcement. In carrying out its functions, the authority will be bound by its plan when adopted. A question has been raised in the courts as to whether an authority can act without a plan, and a decision may be given on this shortly. The interaction between the authority as planner and as provider of services raises interesting competition law questions.

6.(5)(e) Licensing

Member States must take steps to ensure that any person who holds waste has it handled by a licensed or registered[78] waste collector,[79] or that they transfer it to a person licensed to carry out disposal or recovery activities.[80] A disposal licence must address certain specified issues. Directive 99/31[81] lays down further requirements which must be included in licences for landfill sites, while Directive 2000/76/EC on waste incineration[82] lays down requirements which must be included in incineration licences.

Waste collectors must have a local authority permit under Section 34 of the Act. Section 39 covers static facilities and prohibits the carrying on of a disposal or recovery activity without a licence. The Agency is the licensing authority. The licensing procedure is fundamentally the same as for IPC licensing, with a two-stage procedure and provision for submissions by the public and for an oral hearing. The Waste Management (Permit) Regulations 1998[83] purport to exempt certain disposal and recovery activities from waste licensing, and to make them subject to a local authority permit or to registration. Although the Directive allows this, the Regulations are based on an amendment of the Waste Management Act which is suspected of being

---

[76] Referring back to Article 4.
[77] Referring back to Article 5.
[78] Article 12.
[79] Article 8.
[80] Articles 9 and 10.
[81] O.J. L182/1, July 16, 1999.
[82] O.J. L 332/91, December 28, 2000.
[83] S.I. No. 165/1998.

invalid,[84] and the Regulations themselves exceed the scope allowed by the Directive. Anything done under them is therefore liable to be quashed.

An interesting innovation in waste licensing is that a licence can only be granted to a fit person or a local authority. An applicant must satisfy the Agency that it has no criminal record under the Act, is solvent, and has the necessary technical expertise in order to be considered 'fit'.

6.(5)(f) Consideration and determination of a licence application

The Agency must have regard to any relevant environmental plan, any environmental quality standard or emission standard, any environmental impact statement and any submissions on it, any other matters which it considers necessary, and any other matters which are prescribed. In the last two headings would come all requirements of EC waste Directives, implemented and unimplemented, for instance the Landfill Directive and the Waste Incineration Directive. It cannot grant a licence unless satisfied that the activity will not breach any environmental standard, will not cause environmental pollution, and will use BATNEEC. In addition, any applicant other than a local authority must have satisfied the Agency that it is a fit person, and must satisfy the Agency that it fulfils financial requirements in Section 53.

Licences may be granted, with or without conditions, or may be refused. There is a list of mandatory and optional conditions. Any person may challenge the validity of the Agency's decision on a licence application, provided the grounds are substantial and the application is by way of judicial review within two months of the decision.

6.(5)(g) Hazardous waste and waste transport

Council Directive 91/689/EEC on hazardous waste[85] combines the requirements of the framework Directive with the EC's "cradle to grave" system for monitoring the production and disposal of hazardous waste throughout the EU. A series of Directives and implementing Regulations covers the transport of waste, but will not be addressed here.

6.(5)(h) Packaging and packaging waste

Part III of the Waste Management Act provides a blueprint for action to reduce waste production through programmes of measures for individuals and public

---

[84] European Communities (Amendment of Waste Management Act 1996) Regulations 1998, S.I. No. 166/1998. The Regulations appear to exceed the discretion of the State outlined in *Meagher v. Minister for Agriculture* [1994] I.R. 329. For further discussion of *Meagher* see above, Costello, para. 2(2)(c) and Lucey, para. 4(2)(b).

[85] O.J. L377/20, December 31, 1991, and see Commission Decision 2000/532/EC O.J. L226/3, September 6, 2000, replacing Decision 94/3/EC establishing a list of wastes pursuant to Article 1(a) of Council Directive 75/442/EEC on waste and Council Decision 94/904/EC

bodies, and to increase recycling through waste collection and recovery systems. Apart from the Packaging Waste Regulations mentioned below, this Part appears to have been forgotten: indeed, the shopping bag Regulations are based on a new section[86] even though a power to adopt them already existed in Part III.

The Waste Management (Packaging) Regulations 1997–98[87] which give effect to the Packaging and Packaging Waste Directive[88] provide that producers of packaging must take certain steps for waste recovery. Major producers must accept packaging back free of charge, provide facilities for it, arrange for its recovery or recycling, collect it from the person to whom it is supplied if asked to do so, and display prominent notices saying that packaging will be accepted back. Packaging includes packaging of final products for consumers. Packaging is supplied when a product in the package is supplied to an end consumer, as well as when it is supplied to someone who uses it to package something. In effect, practically every major retailer in Ireland is a major supplier of packaging and obliged to take it back from customers unless they are a member of an approved scheme. Whilst there are some approved schemes they do not apply in all areas, and producers and local authorities may be in breach of the Regulations.

The Waste Management (Farm Plastics) Regulations 1997[89] use a similar format, but with a deposit and refund scheme, to attempt to control plastics used on farms, particularly for the storage of silage and other fodder.

6.(6) Environmental Impact Assessment

There are two Environmental Impact Assessment Directives (EIA Directives).[90] EIA is a gateway control: before a project can go ahead, it must be assessed to determine what effects it is likely to have on the environment so that a licence or planning permission can take steps to prevent those effects and protect the environment. Ireland gives effect to the Directives through the Planning and Development Act 2000, through IPC and waste licensing, and through the European Communities (Environmental Impact Assessment) Regulations, 1989–99 (EIA Regulations). For matters within their respective jurisdictions

---

establishing a list of hazardous waste pursuant to Article 1(4) of Council Directive 91/689/EEC on hazardous waste.

[86] s. 72 inserted into the 1996 Act by the 2001 amending Act.

[87] S.I.s 242 of 1997 and 392 of 1998.

[88] European Parliament and Council Directive 94/62/EC O.J. L365/10, December 31, 1994 on packaging and packaging waste.

[89] S.I. No. 315/1997.

[90] Council Directive 85/337/EEC O.J. L175/40, July 5, 1985, on the assessment of the effects of certain public and private projects on the environment and Council Directive 97/11/EC (O.J. L73/5, March 14, 1997) amending it.

the Agency on the one hand and the local authorities and An Bord Pleanála on the other must carry out assessments.

The EIA Directives apply to industrial, mining, energy, agri-industrial, infrastructure and waste projects listed in Annex I. Less significant activities in the same broad classes are included in Annex II and must be subject to assessment where Member States decide. All projects must be assessed if, by virtue of their nature, size or location, they are likely to have significant effects on the environment. The two Annexes are implemented in the latest EIA Regulations.[91]

In the EIA procedure a developer must submit a description of the project, its likely effects and their remedies, the alternatives, the data necessary to assess the issues, and a non-technical summary. The public, relevant public bodies, and other Member States have the opportunity to comment. The information which the developer submits is known in Irish law as the Environmental Impact Statement, or EIS. The competent authority must take all submissions into consideration and make a decision. The decision and the reasons for the decision must be communicated to the public and to the interested States and bodies. The entire procedure is the EIA. The EIA must identify, describe and assess in a suitable manner the likely impact of the project on the environment, including human beings, fauna, flora, soil, air, water, climate, landscape, material assets and cultural heritage, and the inter-action between these things; but it is not a written document. The competent authority does not have to publish its assessment, only its decision and the reasons for it. Irish administrative law says that the reasons for a decision are sufficient if the decision, along with the stated reasons, and any conditions, read in the context of the entire file, would enable a reasonably competent person to understand how the decision was arrived at.[92] It might be desirable to have a written document called an EIA, but the Irish law requirements for IPC and waste licensing come nearer this goal because there is an inspector's report to the Agency which contains an analysis of the issues and the public can comment on it in the course of an objection.

The EIA Directives say EIA can be incorporated into existing consent procedures or into new procedures; and the IPPC Directive says there may be an integrated procedure to comply with the requirements of the EIA and IPPC Directives. By implication, EIA does not have to be integrated into IPPC. In Irish law, EIA is incorporated into planning, IPC and waste licence applications, and a division of responsibility is set out.

---

[91]   Parts I and II of the First Schedule of the European Communities (Environmental Impact Assessment) (Amendment) Regulations 1999, S.I. No. 93 of 1999.

[92]   *O'Keeffe v. An Bord Pleanála* [1993] I.R. 39 and *Ni Eili v. Environmental Protection Agency* S.C. unrep 30. 07.99. On judicial review and the EIA Directive in Ireland see above Costello para 2(2)(d)(ii).

Where a development is below the threshold size for EIA, the planning authority or An Bord Pleanála can, and under EC law must, start an EIA where the project is likely to have significant effects on the environment. Where IPC or waste licence applications are made to the Agency, an EIA is only required if it has been required in the planning process. The Agency has no formal power to start an EIA if the planning authorities have decided not to. However, it can require the developer to submit further information and comply with the Directive requirements in that way.

This division has caused problems and has been amended.[93] Now the planning authority or An Bord Pleanála can decide to refuse (but not impose conditions) if they feel that the development would, notwithstanding the grant of a licence with appropriate conditions, be unacceptable on environmental grounds, having regard to the proper planning and sustainable development of the area.[94] The authority or the Board may ask the Agency for its opinion. This provision will itself be difficult to apply. The Agency should probably express a view on two questions: would it expect to be able to grant a licence and impose conditions which would prevent environmental pollution; and would this development be a good idea in this area, having regard to the environmental issues? On the planning side, the authorities should probably ask if the Agency believes it can grant a licence to control emissions, and whether, having regard to the risk of accidents and all the issues raised in the EIA taken as a whole, this development would be a good idea in this place and would accord with the proper planning and sustainable development of the area. Although application of this provision will be difficult, only experience will tell if it is workable.

6.(6)(a) Thresholds

Where thresholds are set so high as to exclude EIA for an entire class of development, the State has exceeded its discretion in implementing the Directive.[95] The 1999 EIA Regulations set thresholds for some Annex II

---

[93] Up to the time of writing the Agency has been responsible for environmental pollution issues and the planning authorities have been responsible for everything except environmental pollution, and have been specifically prohibited from taking environmental pollution into consideration at all. Several applicants had sought to argue at various times that this was an improper implementation because it meant there was a risk that things would not be properly considered by either licensing or planning authorities. The applicants had always failed on some other ground. In *O'Connell v. Environmental Protection Agency*, Butler J., April 25, 2002, the point was raised that neither the Agency nor An Bord Pleanála could have considered the interaction between different factors as required by the Directive, and the State conceded that this was so, but supported the Agency's argument that the particular development in question was not subject to a mandatory EIA requirement, and that only An Bord Pleanála (which was not before the court) could consider whether to require an EIS from the developer.

[94] *O'Connell v. Environmental Protection Agency*, s.98 of the EPA Act or s.54 of the Waste Management Act.

[95] Case C–72/95 *Kraaijveld v. Gedepudfeerde Staten van Zuid-Holland* [1996] ECR I–5403.

activities which are practically the same as for Annex I activities and apparently conflict with this rule.

The ECJ has condemned the State for defective implementation in exempting certain forestry and peat extraction projects from planning permission unless they were of such a size as to require EIA, with the result that sub-threshold projects were not assessed to see if they were nonetheless likely to have significant effects on the environment, and there was no way to control them if they were.[96] This exceeded the State's discretion in implementing the Directive. It is said that the Commission believes that the thresholds for peat extraction activities are still too high.

The Commission is in the course of a complaint to the effect that the Irish implementing law never requires the competent authority to carry out an assessment. Although technically true, the Commission's complaint is groundless: a competent authority must consider information which is validly before it under the rules of natural justice; if it failed to do so, its decision would be struck down by the courts. A mere recital that "the authority shall consider" would add nothing. Reliance on a fundamental common law rule should not constitute a non-implementation of a Directive.

6.(6)(b) EIA, IPPC and waste

The thresholds in the EIA and IPPC Directives are structured differently, with different classes of activity covered. Where the Directives overlap, in the area of large polluting activities, little effort has been made to ensure that the terminology is the same.[97] This non-integrated approach reveals again the intellectual incoherence of EC environmental law. Both Directives cover significant polluting activities, yet no attempt has been made to use common definitions or terms, nor to integrate the procedures where they overlap. It is actually possible that EC law itself prevents Member States from properly implementing environmental Directives.

The EIA Directives require that certain waste disposal activities should be subject to assessment. In the first Directive, 85/337/EEC, the term "disposal" is used. In 1985 disposal was not distinguished from recovery, so it could apply to recovery activities. In the second Directive, 97/11/EC, the term "disposal" is used in a manner which can only refer to the updated Waste Framework Directive, thereby almost casually excluding EIA for recovery activities. Meanwhile, the IPPC Directive very clearly includes installations for the disposal or recovery of hazardous waste where capacity exceeds 10

---

[96] Case C–392/96, *Commission v. Ireland*. [1997] ECR I–5901.

[97] One outstanding example is energy-generating installations, which are subject to IPPC on the basis of their thermal output, and to EIA on the basis of their thermal input. A reading of some other language versions of the Directives shows that this is a purely linguistic aberration: what is really meant is the amount of energy used in the process, the gross energy burnt rather than the useful energy obtained.

tonnes per day, eliminating an exemption for such activities under Article 11 of the Waste Framework Directive and requiring them to have a more onerous IPPC licence.

One severe difficulty with EIA, IPPC and Waste is the attempt to define the link between them: under Article 6(2) of the IPPC Directive, information "supplied in the context of an EIA" may be "included in or attached to" the licence application. Article 9(2) of the IPPC Directive is similar, and the recitals state that the Directive is to apply without prejudice to the EIA Directive. The EIA Directives on the other hand refer to IPPC only once, at Article 2a, where it is provided that Member States may provide a single procedure for EIA and IPPC. So although IPPC is supposed to be an integrated procedure, it is an integrated procedure alongside other procedures. And although EIA is about assessing the impact of a project on the environment, which is exactly what a competent authority must do before it can decide whether to grant a licence, there is no requirement that the EIA must be the licensing application, or must form part of it. Coupled with the disparity of the thresholds, this is intellectual disjunction on a grand scale.

The installations listed in the Annex to the IPPC Directive are similar to, but not the same as, those listed in Directive 84/360 on industrial air emissions so that there is an overlap. However, one can only tell from a case-by-case analysis whether a particular activity is subject to one Directive or both or neither. It is regrettable that the EC did not see fit to use the same terminology in both Directives. It might be thought that integrated control should be integrated.

The level of incoherence between the EC's various environmental measures, even those intended to provide an integrated approach, makes it miraculous that Member States can implement them at all.

6.(7) PROTECTION OF SENSITIVE AREAS

Two Directives provide for protection of specific sensitive areas: the Habitats Directive and the Birds Directive.

6.(7)(a) Habitats

Under the Habitats Directive Member States must designate a network of sensitive habitats containing priority species of plants or animals. A list must be drawn up and submitted to the Commission which then has to draw up a EC list of habitats designated for protection. Member States must then designate those sites as special areas of conservation (SAC). It is not clear how much discretion Member States have in relation to designating sites as candidates: the Directive appears to give full discretion to the States to choose, and then to take that discretion away by requiring, in respect of species that range over a wide area, that all areas suitable for them should be designated. The French text does not clarify the matter. The Commission has power to request that the Member State designate a site which it believes to be essential for the survival of a species. This would indicate that, unless the Commission so believes, it cannot complain about the exclusion of a site. Nonetheless, it might be argued that every rural part of Ireland should be designated in an attempt to protect the corncrake.

Member States must take appropriate steps to ensure that there is no deterioration of designated habitats in a SAC. They must conduct an "appropriate assessment" of any project likely to have significant effects on the environment. The assessment will identify what effects the project will actually have. A SAC is almost a sterilisation order for an area: States can only allow developments which would have a significant effect on a SAC for imperative reasons of public interest, including economic and social reasons. This is a slippery provision which will have to be interpreted very restrictively if it is not to deprive the Directive of all useful effect. Already Germany has sought a derogation in order to extend a runway into a marsh so that large jets could land to be painted. It is hard to see what imperative reason could justify this: generally an aircraft painting facility can go anywhere there is an airport runway, and it is inconceivable that the social objective of providing employment in a poor area could not be fulfilled in some way other than painting aeroplanes. Being an exception, the provision should be interpreted restrictively and it should be necessary to establish that the project is imperative because there is no alternative and it is essential.

States also have to encourage the retention of river banks and hedgerows as habitats and migratory routes. This would appear to require that there should be no building alongside rivers, that bridge piers should be set far enough from the bank to leave a route by which animals can pass from one side to the other, and that the Irish farming practice of ripping out hedgerows should be stopped and reversed.

The Habitats Directive is implemented in Ireland by Habitats Regulations[98] under which the Minister for Arts, Heritage, Culture, Gaeltacht and the Islands must draw up a candidate list and submit it to the Commission. The Minister must then designate SACs in accordance with the final European list.

A planning authority or An Bord Pleanála, on a planning application, or the Agency, on an IPC or waste licence application, must take account of the SAC and must conduct an "appropriate assessment". The same applies to a local authority or An Bord Pleanála on an air pollution licence application or an application for a licence to discharge polluting matter to waters or to a sewer. There are similar requirements for local authorities carrying out exempted development, roads development or development requiring an EIA. For roads

---

[98]   European Communities (Natural Habitats) Regulations 1997, S.I. No. 94/1997.

and EIA, these obligations will be affected by the transfer of approval powers to An Bord Pleanála under the Planning and Development Act 2000. Similar requirements also apply to state authorities.

In carrying out an appropriate assessment, where an EIA is required it may be regarded as an appropriate assessment; otherwise it is left up to the competent authority to determine what is appropriate. A permission or licence or authorisation must not be granted unless the competent authority is satisfied that the proposed project will not adversely affect the habitat in question. This is probably the strongest prohibition on development ever imposed in Ireland.

For every other use of land for which permission is not required but which is nonetheless likely to have a significant effect on a SAC, Dúchas has the power to apply to court for an injunction to restrain the use, and the court may make an order to that effect, and may make such further order as it deems appropriate. The Regulations require the payment of compensation to any landowner whose land has been designated as a SAC.

6.(7)(b) Birds

The Birds Directive applies to wild birds and requires Member States to take measures to maintain their populations at a level dictated by ecological, cultural and scientific requirements, but having regard to economic development requirements, and to maintain a sufficient diversity of habitats to support sustainable populations of all birds. To do this, Member States must designate bird sanctuaries, particularly for migratory birds and protected birds, and avoid significant pollution or deterioration of habitats or disturbance. The ECJ has held that this obligation requires States to designate all such sites. It is possible to make a similar argument for designation of habitats as SACs, although it is unclear whether such an argument would find favour with the Court.

The fact that a site is designated as a bird sanctuary restricts the development which can take place on it, because development cannot be allowed which would disturb, pollute or cause a deterioration of environmental quality. This is a relevant factor which must be taken into account in a licensing or planning application. An impact on a bird sanctuary would be relevant to the determination of whether to require an EIA and would have to be taken into consideration in the assessment itself. Bird sanctuaries must be designated as SACs by Member States and by the Commission and are effectively subsumed into the protection of habitats.

6.(8) Monitoring and Enforcing Irish Implementing Measures

There are several features relating to enforcement which the various Irish Acts share.

6.(8)(a) Public involvement

The right of the public to become involved and to make submissions and appeals is one of the key features of Irish environmental and planning law and is increasingly found in Directives, as it is believed that public scrutiny improves decision-making, enforcement and monitoring. Unfortunately, much public comment is more colourful than useful.

Each of the Irish Acts requires the keeping of a register of licences. In recent Acts the requirements are more elaborate. The Access to Information on the Environment Regulations[99] and Freedom of Information Act ensure that information which is not on a register is also available.

6.(8)(b) Criminal enforcement

The Acts confer various monitoring and detection powers on the competent authorities which may be used to gather information on which to base enforcement action. Contravention of the requirements of the various Acts is an offence which the competent authority may prosecute summarily. There is also a power to prosecute on indictment which can be exercised by the Director of Public Prosecutions.

It is an offence to cause or permit polluting matter to enter waters; to cause or permit trade effluent or sewage to enter waters without a licence; to cause or permit an emission to air from a premises in such a manner as to constitute a nuisance; to hold, transport, dispose of or recover waste in a manner which causes or is likely to cause environmental pollution; to transfer waste to an unauthorised person, or to carry on any activity, licensable under any of the Acts, without a licence or in contravention of a licence.

Offences under the Water Pollution Acts are offences of strict liability, *i.e.* it is not necessary to prove intention.[100] Offences under the Air Pollution Act, EPA Act and Waste Management Act are also presumed not to require proof of intention; the logic of the Water Pollution Acts seems equally applicable.

---

[99]   Council Directive 90/313/EEC O.J. L158/56, June 23, 1990 on the freedom of access to information on the environment implemented by European Communities Act 1972 (Access to Information On The Environment) Regulations 1998, S.I. 125/1998.

[100] *Shannon Regional Fisheries Board v. Cavan County Council* [1996] 3 I.R. 267 approving *Maguire v. Shannon Regional Fisheries Board* [1994] 3 I.R. 580 and *Alphacell v. Woodword* [1972] A.C. 824. This is justified on the basis that environmental offences are "not criminal in the real sense" but merely "prohibited under penalty". From an environmental point of view, it is possible to welcome the policy which makes it easier to secure the conviction of an offender through strict liability, whilst regretting the implication that causing pollution which may poison an entire town water supply is in some way less criminal than stealing a purse. Surely, one might argue, the effectiveness of EC environmental law requires that national criminal law should apply the same stigma of conviction to corporate cowboys as it does to petty criminals.

It is a defence to some offences to show that the defendant took all reasonable care, or used the Best Practicable Means to avoid pollution, or that the emission was in accordance with a licence or did not breach an emission limit value or a special control area order.

6.(8)(c) Civil remedies

Injunctive relief is available under the Air and Water Pollution Acts for emissions or discharges which create a risk of pollution, or which are made contrary to or without a licence where one is required. Injunctive relief is available under the Waste Management Act, but only where waste is being held, disposed of or recovered in a manner which causes or is likely to cause environmental pollution. There is no remedy for not having or breaching a licence, a significant omission. There is no injunctive relief in respect of an IPC licence either, except in so far as the other Acts provide one: another serious gap in the available enforcement measures.

6.(8)(d) Civil liability

There is civil liability for damage caused by air pollution or discharges of polluting matter to waters under the Water and Air Pollution Acts. There is no such statutory liability for pollution caused by waste. For all types of pollution, it may be possible to establish civil liability at common law on the basis of negligence, nuisance, or the rule in *Rylands v. Fletcher*.[101] Normally the most difficult part of an environmental case is establishing causation, and the statutory remedies may not go any further than the existing tort remedies in this respect.

6.(9) CONCLUSION

EC environmental law provides a vast array of obligations and procedures, all aimed at improving or maintaining environmental quality. This range of measures is let down by the failure to integrate the different areas in anything more than name, and the practice of leaving this crucial obligation to Member States to implement as best they can in the face of a host of confusing and sometimes contradictory measures. At the national level, procedures are generally good, but they are too lax in some areas, and their implementation can be patchy. In addition, the current enforcement measures are not as comprehensive as they should be to ensure the effectiveness of EC legislation.

---

[101] (1868) L.R. 3 H.L. 330,(1866) L.R. 1 Ex 265. See McMahon and Binchy, *Irish Law of Torts*, (2nd ed., 1990) pp.480–491.

7. THE EUROPEANISATION OF CONTRACT LAW

PAUL ANTHONY Mc DERMOTT*

7.(1) INTRODUCTION[1]

The Europeanisation of contract law is said to be desirable because the European Union (EU) is primarily an economic community. One of the EU's essential purposes is to ensure the free flow of goods, persons, services and capital. The more freely these items flow between Member States, the richer and better off everyone will be, or at least that is the theory. Contract law constitutes the principal body of law that regulates cross-border transactions. Thus, the argument goes, it should be made easier both to conclude contracts and to quantify contract risks. Lando has summarised this approach succinctly:

> "Anyone doing business abroad knows that some of his contracts with foreign partners will be governed by a foreign law. The unknown laws of the foreign countries is one of his risks. They are often difficult for him and his local lawyer to get to know and understand. They make him feel insecure, and may keep him away from foreign markets. This is an impediment to world trade. In Europe the existing variety of contract laws is a non-tarrif barrier to the inter-union trade. It is the aim of the Union to do away with restrictions of trade within the Communities, and therefore the differences of law which restrict trade should be abolished."[2]

Of course, not everyone agrees that the harmonisation of European contract law is a good thing. There are those who argue that each national legal system should possess its own distinctive legal culture and identity.[3] Others focus on

---

* B.C.L., LL.M (Cantab), Ph.D, Barrister-at-law. Lecturer-in-Law, University College Dublin. Any errors remain the responsibility of the author.

[1] See generally Clark, "Irish Contract Law Reform and the European Commission's Agenda" (2002) 7 Bar Rev. 126; Lando, "Some Features of the Law of Contract in the Third Millennium" 40 *Scandinavian Studies in Law* 343, pp.345–346; Basedow, "A Common Contract Law for the Common Market" (1996) 33 C.M.L.R. 1169, Lando & Beale ed., *Principles of European Contract Law Parts I and II* (Kluwer Law International, 2000); *Kötz European Contract Law, Vol. 1* (trans. Tony Weir Clarendon Press, Oxford, 1997); *European Contract Code – Preliminary Draft* (Universita Di Pavia, 2001). An interesting discussion of this topic is also to be found in Furmston ed., *Law of Contract* (Butterworths, 1999), paras 1.125 – 1.141.

[2] Lando "Some Features of the Law of Contract in the Third Millennium" 40 *Scandinavian Studies in Law* 343, pp.345–346.

[3] See, *e.g.* Legrand "Against a European Civil Code" (1997) 60 M.L.R. 44 and Hobhouse,

the problematic nature of ever succeeding in such a grand project.[4] Some criticisms are born of self-interest. For example, the English Bar has warned that what it views as the European Commission's apparent desire to form a harmonised contract law contains extremely dangerous business implications.[5] This concern stems from the fact that the English legal system has achieved a disproportionate share of the global legal services market. English law effectively acts as an invisible export worth some £800 million sterling a year. This impressive figure reflects the large number of international contracts that use English law as their governing law even in cases where neither party has any obvious connection with the country. Ireland attracts far less international litigation and thus has less to lose from any harmonisation of contract law.

Some Europeanisation of contract law has already occurred in the form of the uniform choice of law rules of the Rome Convention. However, the extent to which the Convention can provide harmonisation is dependent on the willingness of national courts to give it a uniform interpretation and in this respect it has been observed that the courts "have cast covetous eyes on what they consider to be the just and equitable outcome of the case."[6] In addition, the large number of Directives in the field of consumer protection has led to some convergence between national systems of contract law. As Lord Denning once famously observed, EC law "is like an incoming tide. It flows into the estuaries and up the rivers. It cannot be held back."[7]

This essay begins by briefly surveying the extent to which EC law has already impacted on domestic contract law. Recent case law of the European Court of Justice (ECJ) interpreting the legislation will be referred to where relevant. Next, the potential impact of the European Convention on Human Rights (ECHR) on domestic contract law will be analysed. Consideration will then be given to the European Commission Communication on European Contract Law[8] which was published in July 2001. Finally, an attempt will be made to summarise the current state of play in the Europeanisation of contract law.

"International Conventions and Commercial Law: The Pursuit of Uniformity" (1990) 106 L.Q.R. 530.

[4] See, *e.g.* Teubner "Legal Irritants: Good Faith in British Law or How Unifying Law Ends Up in New Divergences" (1998) 61 M.L.R. 11.

[5] See "Barristers object to proposals by Brussels to reform contract law" *Financial Times*, October 30, 2001.

[6] Lando, "Some Features of the Law of Contract in the Third Millennium" 40 *Scandinavian Studies in Law* 343, p.351.

[7] *HP Bulmer v. J Bollinger SA* [1974] 2 All E.R. 1226, 1231.

[8] *Communication From the Commission to the Council and the European Parliament on European Contract Law* COM (2001) 398 Final.

7.(2) EC LEGISLATION

7.(2)(a) Introduction

A large volume of EC legislation now affects Irish contract law, predominantly, though not exclusively, in the context of consumer rights.[9] This is usually done in the form of Directives. These measures are transposed into domestic law by means of a statute or, more usually, by means of a statutory instrument. In interpreting such national legislation, its origin as an EC measure must be borne in mind so that effect is given to the parent Directive. In *Marleasing SA v. LA Commercial*[10] the ECJ stated:

> "[T]he member-states' obligation arising from a Directive to achieve the result envisaged by the Directive and their duty under Article 5 EEC to take all appropriate measures, whether general or particular, to ensure the fulfilment of that obligation, is binding on all the authorities of member-states including, for matters within their jurisdiction, the courts. It follows that, in applying national law, whether the provisions in question were adopted before or after the Directive, the national court called upon to interpret it is required to do so, as far as possible, in the light of the wording and the purpose of the Directive in order to achieve the result pursued by the latter and thereby comply with the third paragraph of Article 189 EEC."[11]

There are two principal concerns behind these Directives: the first is the completion of the internal market; the second is the protection of consumer rights. Irish contract law is familiar with the latter purpose (for example, one only has to think of cases on contracts of adhesion such as *McCord v. ESB*) [12] and thus has little difficulty in incorporating it into its existing rules. However, the first purpose is less familiar to domestic courts. The constant stream of Directives has provided domestic law reform with an impetus that would otherwise be missing. Clark has pointed out that "without the need to transpose EU Directives as a counterweight to the virtual apathy that exists in Leinster House to reform of lawyers' law, such as the law of contract, the scope of our commercial law statute book does not bear thinking about."[13]

Although these Directives have provided some Europeanisation of contract law, they have been described as providing only a "fragmentary harmonisation".[14]

---

[9] For the rights of the Irish consumer, see below Ní Shuilleabháin, chap. 8. Directives have also been passed in areas which have broader concerns than the protection of consumers, but which also impact on contract law. Examples include the Commercial Agents Directive (86/653/EEC; [1986] O.J. L382/17) and the E–Commerce Directive (2000/31/EC; [2000] O.J. L171/1). For a detailed discussion of the E-Commerce Directive see below Cahill, chap. 9.

[10] [1992] 1 C.M.L.R. 305.

[11] [1992] 1 C.M.L.R. 305 at pp.322–323.

[12] [1980] I.L.R.M. 153.

[13] "Irish Contract Law Reform and the European Commission's Agenda" (2002) 7 Bar Rev 126, p.129.

[14] Lando "Some Features of the Law of Contract in the Third Millennium" 40 *Scandinavian Studies in Law* 343, p.346.

The increasing volume of piece-meal EU regulation brings its own problems, since it means that conflicts between Directives are more inevitable. For example, in *Georg Heininger v. Bayerische Hypo- und Vereinsbank AG*[15] the ECJ rejected a claim by the German Government that parts of the Directive on Contracts Negotiated Away from Business Premises[16] were limited by the Consumer Credit Directive.[17] The Court held that neither the preamble to nor the provisions of the Consumer Credit Directive contained anything to show that the Community legislature intended, in adopting it, to limit the scope of the Doorstep-Selling Directive in order to exclude secured credit agreements from the specific protection provided by that Directive. These potential problems have been recognised by the Commission which has stated that:

> "In the area of contract law the European legislator has taken a 'piecemeal' approach to harmonisation. This approach combined with unforeseen market developments, could lead to inconsistencies in the application of EC law. For example, under certain circumstances it is possible to apply both the doorstep selling Directive and the Timeshare Directive. Both Directives give the consumer a right of withdrawal; however the time period during which the consumer can exercise this right is different."[18]

The use of abstract terms in EC parent law can also cause problems for implementing and applying it in a uniform way.[19] Abstract terms may represent a legal concept for which there are different rules in each national body of law. The Commission has observed that, among the lacunas in EC Directives concerning contract law, there is an absence of any reference to the formation of a contract and the sanctions that will apply in case of the non-adherence to obligations concerning pre-contractual information.[20] Clark has pointed out that the piecemeal nature of the Directives makes identifying an *acquis communautaire* far from easy since "it is difficult to disentangle "core" values from the "penumbra""[21] and thus "Community legislation cannot be said to represent a coherent and consistent set of norms."[22]

---

[15] Unreported, December 13, 2001, Case C–481/99.
[16] Directive 87/102; as amended by Directive 90/88/EEC.
[17] Directive 85/577; [1985] O.J. L372/31.
[18] *Communication From the Commission to the Council and the European Parliament on European Contract Law* COM (2001) 398 Final, para. 35.
[19] *ibid.*, para. 36.
[20] *ibid.*,Annex 1, para. 1.
[21] Clark, "Irish Contract Law Reform and the European Commission's Agenda" (2002) 7 Bar Rev 216, p.217.
[22] *ibid.*

7.(2)(b) The Unfair Contract Terms Directive

The Unfair Contract Terms Directive 93/13/EEC[23] has the potential to have the greatest effect on domestic contract law. The Directive has been transposed into Irish law by virtue of the European Communities (Unfair Terms in Consumer Contracts) Regulations 1995.[24] The Regulations apply to all consumer contracts concluded after December 31, 1994[25] so long as the contract is between a consumer and the seller of goods or supplier of services and the sale or supply is related to the seller or supplier's business. As a result of the Directive, the concept of good faith has been firmly planted into Irish contract law. The Regulations are not limited to assessing the fairness of exclusion or limiting clauses and extend to all contractual terms save those which are individually negotiated.[26] The Regulations are restricted to contracts between "consumers"[27] and "a seller of goods or supplier of services" and apply a general test of unfairness. They contain a grey list of terms which may be unfair. There is no black list of automatically ineffective terms. Under the Regulations, the Director of Consumer Affairs may apply to the High Court for an order prohibiting the use of any term in contracts concluded by sellers or suppliers adjudged by the Court to be an unfair term. There may be cases where a term falls within the scope of both the "fair and reasonable" test of the Sale of Goods and Supply of Services Act 1980 and the European Communities (Unfair Terms in Consumer Contracts) Regulations 1995. It is not clear how the two pieces of legislation interact and this is a matter which remains to be teased out by the courts. In the first major Irish case to consider the Regulations, fifteen sample terms in building contracts were declared to be unfair by Kearns J. in the High Court.[28] There are many more standard form contracts imposed on Irish consumers that would be unlikely to survive scrutiny against the Regulations.

---

[23] [1993] O.J. L095/29. For an analysis of the Directive see: Dean (1993) 56 M.L.R. 581; Collins, "Good Faith in European Contract Law" (1994) O.J.L.S 229; Brandt and Ulmer, "The Community Directive on Unfair Terms in Consumer Contracts" (1991) C.M.L Rev 647. For a discussion of how the Directive applies to public services see Whitehouse, "Unfair Contract Terms, Public Services and the Construction of a European Conception of Contract" (2000) 116 L.Q.R. 95. The Directive was considered in the English case of *Director General of Fair Trading v. First National Bank Plc* [2002] 1 All E.R. 97, [2001] 2 All E.R. (Comm) 1000. For a general discussion of the Directive see McDermott, *Contract Law* (Butterworths, 2001) para. 11.135 et seq.

[24] S.I. No. 27 of 1995.

[25] UTCC 1995, regulation 1(2).

[26] Regulation 3(1) provides that: "Subject to the provisions of Schedule 1, these Regulations apply to any term in a contract concluded between a seller of goods or supplier of services and a consumer which has not been individually negotiated."

[27] In *Cape Snc v. Idealservice Srl*, unreported, November 22, 2001, ECJ joined cases C–541/99 and C–542/99, the ECJ held that the term "consumer" in the Directive must be interpreted as referring solely to natural persons.

[28] *In the Matter of an Application pursuant to regulation 8(1) of the European Communities (Unfair Terms in Consumer Contracts) Regulations 1995*, unreported, High Court, December

7.(2)(c) The Misleading Advertising Directive

The Misleading Advertising Directive[29] was adopted in September 1984 and implemented into Irish law by the European Communities (Misleading Advertising) Regulations 1988.[30] The Directive has since been amended so as to broaden the scope of regulation to include comparative advertising.[31] The Director of Consumer Affairs, on a request being made to him or her in that behalf or on his or her own initiative, may request any person engaging or proposing to engage in any advertising which is misleading advertising to discontinue or refrain from such advertising.[32] Where the Director has made such a request and it has not been complied with, the Director may apply to the High Court for an order prohibiting the further publication of the misleading advertising.[33] The Directive was recently considered by the ECJ in *Toshiba Europe GmbH v. Katun Germany GmbH*.[34] Toshiba Europe distributed photocopiers and spare parts made by the Toshiba Corporation in Japan. Katun sold spare parts which could be used for Toshiba photocopiers. Each Toshiba product had a product number in order to identify it. Toshiba complained about the fact that in Katun catalogues the Toshiba product number appeared alongside the Katun product number. The question arose as to whether the use of the product numbers in this way amounted to comparative advertising. The Court noted that specification of the product numbers of the equipment manufacturer alongside a competing supplier's product numbers enables the public to identify precisely the products of the equipment manufacturer to which that supplier's products correspond. However, such an indication constituted a positive statement that the two products have equivalent technical features. Thus, it amounted to comparative advertising. The Court went on to hold that the use of the product numbers of an equipment manufacturer in the catalogue of a competing supplier enables the supplier to take unfair advantage of the reputation attached to those marks only where the effect of the reference to them is to create, in the mind of the persons at whom the advertising is directed, an association between the manufacturer and the supplier: in other words, where such persons associate the reputation of the manufacturer's products with the products of the competing supplier. In order for a national court to determine whether this condition is satisfied, account should be taken of the overall presentation of the impugned advertising and the type of persons

---

5, 2001. For an analysis of the case see Dorgan, "Safe as Houses?" (2002) *Gazette* 12 (Jan/Feb) and Breslin, "What Makes a Term in a Standard Contract Unfair?" (2002) 7 *Bar Review* 131.

29   Council Directive 84/450; [1984] O.J. L250/17.
30   S.I. No. 134 of 1988. For a case on the Regulations see *Dunnes Stores v. Mandate* [1996] 1 I.R. 55.
31   Council Directive 97/55; [1997] O.J. L290/18.
32   European Communities (Misleading Advertising) Regulations 1988, Regulation 3.
33   *ibid.*, Regulation 4(2).
34   nyr, October 25, 2001, Case C–112/99.

for whom the advertising is intended. Here, the persons at whom the Katun catalogue was aimed were specialist traders who were much less likely than final consumers to associate the reputation of the equipment manufacturer's products with those of the competing supplier. The ECJ observed that in the present case Katun would have difficulty in comparing its products with those of Toshiba if it did not refer to the latter's product numbers. Furthermore, a clear distinction had been made in the Katun catalogue between Katun and Toshiba Europe and it did not appear to give a false impression concerning the origin of Katun's products.

7.(2)(d) The Directive on Contracts Negotiated Away from Business Premises

The Directive on Contracts Negotiated Away from Business Premises was first proposed in 1977 and amended in 1978.[35] It was transposed into national law by the EC (Cancellation of Contracts Negotiated Away from Business Premises) Regulations 1989.[36] The Regulations contain special provisions to protect consumers against certain types of "high pressure" sales techniques. The trader must provide written notice of a 7-day cooling-off period in the case of contracts negotiated away from business premises. The Regulations do not require the contract itself to be in writing but do require the trader to supply the consumer with a notice in a form specified in the Regulations informing the consumer of his right to cancel. The consumer must also be supplied with a notice of cancellation in a prescribed form. In *Georg Heininger v. Bayerische Hypo-und Verenisbank AG*[37] the ECJ held that a secured credit agreement did fall within the scope of the Directive. Whilst the secured credit agreement in question was linked to a right relating to immovable property (which is expressly excluded from the Directive), in that the loan must be secured by a charge on immovable property, that feature was not sufficient for the agreement to fall outside the Directive. This judgment is an example of the principle that derogations from Community rules for the protection of consumers must be interpreted strictly. The Court noted that the Directive provided that there should be a minimum period of seven days prescribed for cancellation of the contract by the consumer, calculated from the date when the consumer received a notice concerning his right of cancellation. In addition, the ECJ ruled that German legislation which provided for a long-stop period of one year within which to cancel a contract, even where one had never been given the required notice of one's rights, was a breach of the Directive. If a credit institution wanted legal certainty as to the

---

[35] Directive 85/577; [1985] O.J. L372/31.
[36] S.I. 224 of 1989. The Regulations came into operation on November 1, 1989.
[37] nyr, December 13, 2001, Case C–481/99.

status of a particular contract it could easily achieve this by giving the consumer the appropriate notice.

7.(2)(e) The Distance Selling Directive

The Distance Selling Directive[38] seeks to regulate the sale of products to consumers when the contract is concluded at a distance. Examples of such contracts include direct marketing, telesales and internet sales. The Directive was transposed into national law by the European Communities (Protection of Consumers in Respect of Contracts Made by Means of Distance Communication) Regulations, 2001.[39] Key provisions deal with the information which a consumer must be given before entering into a contract, subsequent written confirmation of that information, and a cooling-off period in which the consumer may cancel the contract. Importantly, it is not possible for a consumer to waive the rights conferred on him or her under the Regulations.[40] A consumer is defined as "a natural person who, as regards a distance contract, is acting for purposes which are outside that person's trade, business or profession."[41] The Regulations apply to contracts for goods or services (other than financial services) to be supplied to a consumer where the contract is made exclusively by means of distance communication, *i.e.* without the simultaneous physical presence of the supplier and the consumer. A non-exhaustive list of means of distance communication is given in the first Schedule to the Regulations.

7.(2)(f) The Product Liability Directive

The Product Liability Directive[42] does not affect any of the rights available under contractual liability. Traditionally contract law deals with non-dangerous defects, *i.e.* defects in quality, whereas tort deals with dangerous defects. However, in recent years the line has become blurred. In the case of non-dangerous defects it will often be more advantageous for a consumer to rely on a contractual remedy such as the implied terms under the Sale of Goods and Supply of Services Act 1980. The Product Liability Directive has been transposed into national law by the Liability for Defective Products Act 1991. Under the Act the producer is liable in damages in tort for damage caused wholly or partly by a defect in his product.[43] The onus is on the injured person concerned to prove the damage, the defect and the causal relationship between

---

[38] Directive 97/7; [1985] O.J. L144/19. See McMahon, "Contracts Negotiated Away From Business Premises and the 1997 Distance Selling Directive" (1999) I.L.T.R. 139.
[39] S.I. No. 207/2001.
[40] Regulation 18.
[41] Regulation 2(1).
[42] Council Directive 83/374; [1985] O.J. L210/29
[43] s.2(1).

the defect and damage.[44] Once this is done, strict liability is imposed on the producer unless he can establish one of the following defences.

7.(2)(g) The Directive on Consumer Guarantees

The Directive on Certain Aspects of the Sale of Consumer Goods and Associated Guarantees[45] was enacted on May 25, 1999 and was supposed to have been transposed into Irish law by January 1, 2002.[46] The Directive deals with the contractual liability of the seller for defective movable consumer products and provides the consumer with a two-year minimum guarantee period for goods bought anywhere in the European Union. Unlike the Sale of Goods and Supply of Services Act 1980 the Directive is limited to the sale of consumer goods. A consumer is defined in the Directive as "any natural person who . . . is acting for purposes which are not related to his trade, business or profession."[47]

7.(2)(h) The Timeshare Directive

The Timeshare Directive[48] was transposed into Irish law by European Communities (Contracts For Time Sharing of Immovable Property – Protection of Purchasers) Regulations, 1997.[49] The Regulations provide that consumers may withdraw from the contract within a 10 day cooling-off period or, in the absence/non-provision of certain information, within 3 months. The Regulations also provide that those seeking information on timeshare properties must be supplied with a brochure giving a description of the property, details on the vendor, location of property, its current status, (*e.g.* under completion), associated services and facilities, the price and right to cancellation. The contract must include the foregoing and other specified information, *e.g.* the right or otherwise of resale or exchange for another property. Under the Regulations the vendor is prohibited from seeking deposits. A contract to which the Regulations apply must be in writing and must include at least the terms referred to in the Annex to the Regulations.

---

[44] s.4.
[45] Directive 99/44/EC [1999] O.J. L171/12. For a discussion of the Directive see below Ní Shúilleabháin, chap.8; Walley, "The Directive on Certain Aspects of the Sale of Consumer Goods and Associated Guarantees – Implications for Irish Consumer Sales Law" (2000) I.L.T. 23, and White "The EC Directive on Certain Aspects of the Sale of Consumer Goods and Associated Guarantees: One Step Forward, Two Steps Back?" (2000) 7 C.L.P. 3.
[46] Article 11(1).
[47] Article 1(2)(a).
[48] Directive 94/47/EC; [1994] O.J. L280/83.
[49] S.I. No. 204 of 1997 as amended by The European Communities (Contracts For Time Sharing of Immovable Property – Protection of Purchasers)(Amendment) Regulations 1997; S.I. No. 144 of 2000. The Regulations came into operation on May 14, 1977.

7.(2)(i) The Package Holidays Directive[50]

The Directive on Package Travel, Package Holidays and Package Tours[51] was transposed into Irish law by the Package Holidays and Travel Trade Act 1995. The Act sets out minimum standards for brochure content, pre-contractual disclosure, provision of information as well as obligations to be met before the package commences, a number of essential terms, a booking transfer right and restrictions on the right to vary prices. The contract must be in writing.[52] A person who organises package holidays may not make a brochure available to a possible consumer unless it indicates in a legible, comprehensible and accurate manner the price and adequate information about the following matters:[53]

7.(3) THE EUROPEAN CONVENTION ON HUMAN RIGHTS

7.(3)(a) Introduction

At the time of writing, proposals to give the European Convention on Human Rights[54] some sort of status in Irish domestic law are still being considered by the Oireachtas. In the United Kingdom, the Human Rights Act 1998 came into force on the October 2, 2000. The aim of the 1998 Act is to give "further effect" in domestic law to the rights and freedoms guaranteed under the Convention. Already this has had an impact in some contract cases. The current status of the Convention in Ireland is that it is not part of domestic law and so cannot be directly relied upon by litigants.[55] However, the Convention may be relied upon in domestic proceedings in a number of ways. In *Brennan*

---

50   See generally Buttimore, *Holiday Law in Ireland* (Blackhall, 1999).
51   Council Directive 90/314/EEC of June 13, 1990[1990] O.J. 158/59
52   s.15.
53   s.10.
54   For a discussion of the relationship between the ECHR and the EU see below, Kingston, para. 12(4).
55   This was established in *Re Ó Laighléis* [1960] I.R. 93 at 125 where Maguire C.J. stated:
     "The Oireachtas has not determined that the Convention of Human Rights and Fundamental Freedoms is to be part of the domestic law of the State, and accordingly this Court cannot give effect to the Convention if it be contrary to domestic law or purports to grant rights or obligations additional to those of domestic law."
     See also *Norris v. The Attorney General* [1984] I.R. 36 at 67 where O'Higgins C.J. said: "Neither the Convention on Human Rights nor the decision of the European Court of Human Rights in *Dudgeon v. United Kingdom* is in any way relevant to the question which we have to consider in this case." Similarly in *O'B v. S* [1984] I.R. 316 at 338 Walsh J. stated that a case of the E.Ct.H.R. to which he had been referred "can have no bearing on the question of whether any provision of the Act of 1965 is invalid having regard to the provisions of the Constitution." See generally Lester, "The Challenge of Bangalore: Making Human Rights A Practical Reality" [1999] E.H.R.L.R. 273; Hunt, *Using Human Rights Law in English Courts* (1997); Hogan, "The Belfast Agreement and the Future Incorporation of the European Convention on Human Rights in the Republic of Ireland" (1999) 4 *Bar Review* 205.

v. Governor of Portlaoise Prison[56] Budd J. held that although the ECHR was not binding in this jurisdiction the court could look to it "as being an influential guideline with regard to matters of public policy."[57] Secondly, there is authority for the view that international human rights treaties can be used as a guide to statutory interpretation. For example, in *O'Domhnaill v. Merrick*[58] McCarthy J. said that in appropriate cases a statute can be construed "if possible, so as to conform to international law, when the nature of that international law is established."[59] Thirdly, it is also possible for international treaties to give rise to a legitimate expectation in domestic law that the State will abide by their terms.[60] So far Irish jurisprudence has limited this to occasions where a Minister has written a letter expressly stating that procedures found in an international treaty will be observed by the State.[61] Courts in Australia and New Zealand have gone further and held that the mere signing of an international human rights treaty can give rise to a legitimate expectation that its procedures will be taken into account.[62]

7.(3)(b) Applying the Convention to private disputes

The extent to which one can rely on the ECHR in the context of private contract law disputes remains to be teased out. There will be less difficulty where one of the contracting parties is complaining about legislation that affects his or her rights or remedies. A full discussion of this issue is beyond the scope of this article. A lot will depend on the wording of any future legislation giving effect to the Convention in domestic law. English courts which have had to grapple with the applicability of the Human Rights Act

---

[56] [1999] 1 I.L.R.M. 190.

[57] *ibid.*, at 210.

[58] [1984] I.R. 151.

[59] *ibid.*,at 166. In England see *R v. Radio Authority* [1997] 2 All E.R. 561.

[60] It is important to note that the doctrine of legitimate expectation can only give rise to procedural and not substantive rights in this context. In other words, so long as the relevant Minister or authority takes the international treaty into account in reaching his decision, he can still find against the applicant.

[61] See *Fakih v. Minister for Justice* [1993] I.L.R.M. 274 and *Gutrani v. Minister for Justice* [1993] 2 I.R. 427. (Although, in the latter case McCarthy J. preferred not to use the phrase "legitimate expectation", it is difficult to know how else to describe the effect of his judgment).

[62] See respectively, *Minister for Immigration and Ethnic Affairs v. Teoh* (1995) 183 C.L.R. 273 and *Tavita v. Minister for Immigration* [1994] 2 N.Z.L.R. 257. In the latter case Cooke P. stated at p.266:
"A failure to give practical effect to international instruments to which New Zealand is a party may attract criticism. Legitimate criticism could extend to the New Zealand Courts if they were to accept the argument that, because a domestic statute giving discretionary powers in general terms does not mention international human rights norms or obligations, the executive is necessarily free to ignore them."

1998 to contract law cases, have generally applied it, albeit with occasional concerns. For example, in *Shanshal v. Al-Kishtaini*[63] Mummery L.J. stated:

> "I must make it clear that this judgment must not be understood as endorsing the proposition that the claimant had a right under s.6(1) of the 1998 Act to invoke the Convention right retrospectively in respect of private law issues arising between one citizen and another. No such proposition was developed in argument. The research which the court has conducted does not disclose any decision on the 1998 Act which holds that s.6(1) can be retrospectively applied by an appellate court to remove a common law defence of illegality raised by one private individual against another in private law proceedings based on a contractual or restitutionary claim, which were tried before the 1998 Act was brought into effect."[64]

7.(3)(c) Illegality and the Convention

Irish courts are placed in a difficult position when a litigant seeks to enforce an agreement which has been either made or performed in a manner that breaches a rule of substantive law or has an effect which is regarded as being contrary to public policy. To permit the contract to be sued on might be to diminish the law or the public policy interest infringed. On the other hand, if the breach is a trivial one and there is no apparent harm to the public policy interest, it might be thought oppressive to strike down the entire agreement. The common law has grappled with this problem over a number of years, without ever developing any conclusive rules. What has emerged has been a series of general principles. Sometimes these principles can operate in a manner that appears harsh and inflexible. The question that arises is whether, when they operate unfairly, such principles are compatible with the Convention. This has been considered in two recent English cases.

In *Shanshal v. Al-Kishtaini*[65] the claimant had repaid money which had been loaned to him by the defendant. In fact the claimant had overpaid the defendant because of exchange rate fluctuations and now sought to recover the overpayment. Under the Control of Gold, Securities, Payments and Credits (Republic of Iraq) Directions 1990, no order requiring payment or the parting with gold or securities given by or on behalf of any person normally resident in Iraq on August 4, 1990 or at any later time, was to be carried out except with the permission of the Treasury.[66] These Directions had been made in implementation of the United Nations sanctions against Iraq, as contained in resolutions adopted by the Security Council in 1990 following the invasion and occupation of Kuwait by Iraq. The defendant had been resident in Iraq at

---

[63] [2001] 2 All E.R. (Comm) 601.
[64] *ibid.*, at 613.
[65] [2001] 2 All E.R. (Comm) 601.
[66] The Directions were made pursuant to the Emergency Laws (Re-enactments and Repeals) Act 1964.

the time of the coming into force of the Directions on August 4, 1990. He argued that the claimant's repayment to him was an illegal act and that the claimant was therefore precluded from obtaining any recovery of over-payment.

The Court of Appeal (Mummery, Rix L.J.J. and Holman J.) held that, when properly interpreted, the Directions of 1990 did indeed cover the impugned transaction. It followed that the claim for the repayment was based on an illegal act, namely the contravention of the Directions, and the claimant was accordingly prevented from recovering under the contract. In reaching this conclusion it was irrelevant whether or not the claimant had intended to break the law or was unaware that he was doing so. The claimant argued that a bar to recovery on grounds of illegality would amount to a deprivation of his right to possession of the money claimed which would be incompatible with Article 1 of the First Protocol to the European Convention on Human Rights.[67] Article 1 provides:

> "Every natural or legal person is entitled to the peaceful enjoyment of his possessions. No one shall be deprived of his possessions except in the public interest and subject to the conditions provided for by law and by the general principles of international law.
>
> The preceding provisions shall not, however, in any way impair the right of a State to enforce such laws as it deems necessary to control the use of property in accordance with the general interest or to secure the payment of taxes or other contributions or penalties."

The Court of Appeal concluded that the case fell squarely within the public interest exception to Article 1 and that the illegality defence was therefore not incompatible with the Convention right. Mummery L.J. observed that the public interest element in the case exhibited two striking features:

i) The Directions embodied a very high public interest originating in the resolutions of the Security Council of the United Nations in an international emergency. If public interest of this degree did not fall within the exception in Article 1, it would be difficult to conceive of any other matters which would fall within it.

---

[67] Counsel for the Claimant relied on *Sporrong and Lonnroth v. Sweden* (1982) 5 E.H.R.R. 35. That was a case concerned with compulsory acquisition or "expropriation permits" as they were called. The applicants were complaining of the uncompensated effect of such permits which had been in force for periods of up to 23 years, and which had caused planning blight and had prohibited the owners of the land affected from building on it. In the end the permits were cancelled, no expropriation took place, and the redevelopment planned by the local authority never went ahead. The European Court of Human Rights held by a narrow margin that there had been a breach of Art 1. It held that there had been no deprivation of the applicants' possessions within the meaning of the second sentence of the first paragraph, but an interference with their peaceful enjoyment under the first sentence. It also held that the second paragraph was not invoked.

ii) The prohibition in the Directions was not an absolute one. It only operated in cases in which the requisite permission had not been sought and obtained. It was open to the claimant, and to any one else in a similar situation, to obtain advance clearance from the Treasury, so that he could find out precisely where he stood before entering into and carrying out a potentially illegal transaction. It was for the Treasury, acting through the Bank of England, and not for the claimant himself to judge whether it was an appropriate case for the grant of permission. The public interest in effective official control of the specified transactions would not be properly served by allowing a person and his advisers to decide for themselves whether Treasury permission was required. The proper course was to apply to the Bank of England to exercise its discretion to grant permission for the proposed transaction. That precaution had been available to the claimant in the present case but had not been taken.

Mummery L.J. rejected a claim that the English courts should have applied a test of proportionality to the transaction:

> "In those circumstances I fail to see how compatibility with the Convention right in art. 1 of the First Protocol requires the national court to apply a principle of proportionality, so as first to divine, and then to exercise, a discretion to relieve the claimant from the consequences of his own illegal act. In such a case it does not offend the principle of proportionality invoked by the claimant to apply to its full extent the high public policy applicable to this case, so as to prevent the enforcement of his claim. No decision of the European Court of Human Rights was cited to demonstrate that this result was inconsistent with the Convention. The arguments of counsel were confined to points on the scope of the Convention right in art. 1 of the First Protocol."[68]

Holman J., concurring, concluded that the present case revealed a proportionate response that struck a fair balance between the demands of the general interest of the community and the requirements of the protection of the individual's fundamental rights. Rix L.J. also concluded that a fair balance had been struck:

> "[T]he facts of this case are in my judgment compelling. On the one hand, the public interest here invoked is very strong. It reflects the resolutions of the Security Council of the United Nations in response to the invasion by Iraq of Kuwait. Those resolutions were binding on all members of the United Nations . . . On the other hand, the claimant had it in his own hands to make representations to the Bank of England to the effect that, as the defendant had ceased at the relevant time to be a resident of Iraq, he should be permitted to make the payment requested. The evidence is that the Bank of England was quite ready to give permission where an Iraqi resident ceased to be resident in Iraq. Because the statutory control was linked to a system whereby permission could

---

[68] [2001] 2 All E.R. (Comm) 601, 612–613.

be sought in advance, not only was it possible for someone in the position of the claimant to know where he stood before he committed himself to any course of action, but the public interest entrusted to the Treasury, and through the Treasury to the Bank of England, could be interpreted in a flexible way which was able, to some degree at any rate, to meet the practicalities and justice of particular situations. In the present case, the evidence showed that the claimant was aware of and understood the Directions and their prohibitions, was familiar with the practice of consulting the Bank of England and did so in transacting his own affairs, but omitted to do so in the case of the relevant payment at the defendant's request in part at any rate because he considered it to be relatively too small to be of much concern."[69]

A passing reference to the Convention was made in *Hall v. Woolston*[70] where it was held that an employee was entitled to recover compensation under the Sex Discrimination Act 1975 notwithstanding the fact that her contract of employment was tainted with illegality. Peter Gibson L.J. stated that:

> "the correct approach of the tribunal in a sex discrimination case should be to consider whether the applicant's claim arises out of or is so clearly connected or inextricably bound up or linked with the illegal conduct of the applicant that the court could not permit the applicant to recover compensation without appearing to condone that conduct."

On the facts of the case the applicant had not actively participated in the illegality. No benefit was shown to have been received by her from her employer's failure to deduct tax and national insurance contributions and to account for the same to the revenue. Her "acquiescence" in her employer's conduct, which was the highest that her involvement in the illegality could be put, simply reflected the reality that she could not compel her employer to change its conduct. That acquiescence was in no way causally linked with her sex discrimination claim. In reaching this conclusion, the Court noted that both the construction of the Act and the identification or development of the relevant common law principles, were influenced by Council Directive 76/207 and Article 6 of the ECHR. Mance L.J. stated:

> "The draftsmen of the Convention are unlikely to have set out to confer protection in respect of – indeed are probably unlikely even to have contemplated – employment, vocational training or working conditions the essence of which was illegal, for example employment, training or working conditions as part of a hit-squad or by a company known to have been established to carry

---

[69] *ibid.*, at 620.
[70] [2001] I.C.R. 99, [2000] I.R. 578. The English Court of Appeal held that sex discrimination which is unlawful under the Sex Discrimination Act 1975 is a statutory tort, to which the tortious measure of damages is applicable. Thus, the case is not strictly speaking an authority for contract law. However, the Court took the opportunity to conduct a useful review of the case law on illegal employment contracts.

out bank robberies or to launder stolen money. It would seem improbable, therefore, that a national court called upon to shape its national law as far as possible 'in the light of the wording and purpose of the Directive in order to achieve the result pursued by the latter' would be expected to afford a remedy even for sex discrimination in such a context. But any limitation of this nature in the protection in respect of sex discrimination afforded by the Directive must be derived from the wording and purpose of the Directive. It cannot be determined by any rule of domestic public policy, especially one which is not a principle of justice and may operate indiscriminately. I have in mind in this respect of course Lord Goff of Chieveley's description of the English doctrine of illegality in *Tinsley v. Milligan* [1994] 1 AC 340, 355 B–C".[71]

7.(3)(d) The incorporation of contractual terms

An oral or written contract may not be complete in itself. There may be further terms contained in other documents. Where this occurs, it is said that the other documents have been incorporated into the contract. If a term has not been properly incorporated into a contract, it may not be relied on as a contractual term. The court must be satisfied that the document relied on as containing a particular term is a part of the contract. It must have been intended as a contractual document and not, for example, as a mere acknowledgement of payment. Sometimes the courts place convenience above justice in a particular case. Thus, it is for everybody's convenience that they can board a bus or a train without having to be first handed a manual containing all the conditions of carriage. The idea that such conditions are incorporated into the contract because the passenger could stop the bus and demand a copy of them is little more than a fiction. The question arises as to whether the artificial common law rules of incorporation are consistent with the Convention.

It should be noted first that the European Communities (Unfair Terms in Consumer Contracts) Regulations, 1995[72] contains in its list of terms that may be regarded as unfair a term "irrevocably binding the consumer to terms with which he had no real opportunity of becoming acquainted before the conclusion of the contract."[73] The common law requirement of notice would seem to satisfy this concept. However, it is less certain whether some of the old transport cases, where an artificial view of notice was taken for the purposes of convenience, would survive scrutiny under the Regulations.

It is a basic rule of incorporation that signature of the contract, in the absence of fraud or misrepresentation, will incorporate all the clauses contained therein. To date no direct attack has been made in this jurisdiction on this rule. There is an element of artificiality that may be present in incorporating contract terms based solely on signature and this may be relevant

---

[71] *ibid.*, at 118.
[72] S.I. No. 27 of 1995.
[73] *ibid.*, 3rd Schedule, term (i).

if the fairness test under the European Communities (Unfair Terms in Consumer Contracts) Regulations, 1995[74] is in question. It has been suggested that in such a situation "the consent and knowledge of the relevant party should be judged objectively but without the artificiality which may be present in the rules as to incorporation."[75]

The Convention was cited in the recent English case of *Cigna v. Intercaser*,[76] where the question arose as to whether a reinsurance contract had incorporated within its terms the contents of another contract known as the "I" contract. The dispute arose because the "I" contract contained an arbitration clause. The High Court held that the arbitration clause had not been incorporated into the reinsurance contract. This was because an agreement to arbitrate disputes was to be regarded as personal to the parties to the agreement and collateral to the main obligations under the contract. In addition, the parties had not properly identified the document whose terms were to be incorporated: there was no "I" contract in existence when the reinsurance contract was entered into. What is of interest is that the party arguing that the arbitration clause was not incorporated bolstered its arguments by relying on Article 6 of the ECHR. In reaching the conclusion that the clause was not so incorporated, Morison J. did not advert to the Convention.

7.(3)(e) Non-compliance with mandatory requirements of consumer law

Non-compliance with the often highly detailed requirements of consumer law can have catastrophic consequences for a trader. For example, a technical breach of a mandatory notice requirement can mean that the customer is free to walk away from the contract notwithstanding the fact that the breach has not caused any prejudice to him or her. The compatibility of such an outcome with the Convention was considered by the English Court of Appeal in *Wilson v. First County Trust*.[77] The claimant signed a loan agreement with the defendant pawnbroker and pledged her car as security. The agreement was a regulated agreement for the purposes of the Consumer Credit Act 1974. This Act set out conditions which had to be satisfied if a regulated agreement was to be treated as properly executed. In particular, both parties to the transaction had to sign a document which included a term stating "the amount of the credit".[78] An improperly-executed regulated agreement was enforceable against the creditor only on the order of the court. Section 127(d) of the 1974 Act provided that the court could not make such an order unless the conditions had been satisfied. Thus, the court had no power to make such an order in cases where the debtor

---

[74] S.I. No. 27 of 1995.
[75] Furmston, *The Law of Contract* (1999), para. 3.11.
[76] [2002] 1 All E.R. (Comm) 235.
[77] [2001] 3 All E.R. 229.
[78] This requirement came from para. 2 of Sched. 6 of the Consumer Credit (Agreements) Regulations 1983.

had not signed a document containing all the prescribed terms, even though the omission of a prescribed term had caused no prejudice to anyone. In such cases, the security taken for the loan would also prima facie be rendered unenforceable by the terms of the Act. In the present case the claimant's agreement with the pawnbroker stated the amount of the loan to be £2,500. However, this sum in fact contained £250 which was stated to be a document fee. The question arose as to whether this meant that "the amount of the credit" had been misstated.

The Court of Appeal held that "the amount of the credit" had been misstated and that accordingly the agreement was not a properly executed regulated agreement. The Court further held that the agreement was unenforceable against the claimant and that, at least prima facie, the pawnbroker could not rely on the security. In those circumstances the Court indicated that it was considering making a declaration that section 127(3) was incompatible with the right to a fair hearing under Article 6 of the Convention and the prohibition against depriving a person of his possessions under Article 1 of the First Protocol to the Convention. The case was adjourned for further hearing after notice had been given to the Crown.

After further hearing, the Court held that where there was no loan agreement signed by the debtor which contained all of the prescribed terms, section 127(3) affected the creditor's ability to enforce the agreement but did not prevent the creditor from acquiring contractual rights under the agreement. Accordingly, the creditor had property rights guaranteed by Article 1 of the First Protocol to the Convention. This finding also potentially engaged Article 6 of the Convention. Although the policy aims of requiring a written document setting out of the terms of the agreement were legitimate, the exclusion of a judicial remedy in section 127(3) preventing the court from doing what was just in cases where there was no such document was disproportionate to the policy aims. In all the circumstances, section 127(3) infringed the rights guaranteed by Article 6 of the Convention and Article 1 of the First Protocol. Since it was not possible to read and give effect to section 127(3) in a way which was compatible with the Convention, it was appropriate for the court to make a declaration that it was incompatible with the Convention. Sir Andrew Morritt V.C. explained that:

> "It is the restrictions on enforcement which engage article 6(1) of the Convention. The guarantee, in relation to the determination of a party's civil rights, of a fair and public hearing by an independent and impartial tribunal is of no substance if the outcome is determined by a statutory inhibition which not only prevents the court from doing what is just in the circumstances, but does so (a) in the context of a legislative scheme which gives the court a discretion to do what is just in other, very similar, circumstances and (b) for reasons which (if they exist at all) are wholly opaque. If there is some legitimate aim in pursuit of which the guarantee enshrined in article 6(1) needs to be wholly or partially curtailed, then it is necessary to ask whether the

statutory inhibition is proportionate to that aim. Is there a proper balance between ends and means?"[79]

Morritt V.C. observed that the policy aims of the legislation were clear enough. Regulated agreements ought to be made with an appropriate degree of formality; that requires that the terms of the agreement should be set out in a document which is signed by the debtor; the document should contain information relevant to the transaction; and, where those requirements are not met, the agreement is not to be enforced against the debtor except through the court. It could not be suggested that those were not legitimate objectives of social policy. Nor could it be suggested that judicial control pursuant to the Act was not a legitimate means of pursuing those objectives. However, he concluded that the Act was a disproportionate response to the legitimate policy aims it purported to fulfil:

> "But section 127(3) of the Act goes beyond that. The policy aim, reflected in that section, is to ensure that particular attention is paid to the inclusion in the document to be signed by the debtor of certain terms which will, or may, be prescribed by the Secretary of State in the future. Again, it cannot be suggested that that is not a legitimate policy objective. But it does not follow that the means by which that policy aim is to be achieved, under the provisions of section 127(3) of the Act are also legitimate. The means will not be legitimate if guaranteed Convention rights are infringed to an extent which is dispropor-tionate to the policy aim. That, in our view, is the effect of the inflexible prohibition – imposed by section 127(3) of the Act – against the making of an enforcement order in a case where the document signed by the debtor does not include the prescribed terms. There is no reason that we can identify – and, as we have said, no reason has been advanced – why an inflexible prohibition is necessary in order to achieve the legitimate policy aim. There is no reason why that aim should not be achieved through judicial control; by empowering the court to do what is just in the circumstances of the particular case."[80]

---

[79] [2001] 3 All E.R. 229, 240. The principle was expressed in the majority judgment in the European Court of Human Rights in *Osman v. United Kingdom* (1998) 29 E.H.R.R. 245, 315 para. 147:

> "However, [the right of access to a court under article 6(1) of the Convention] is not absolute, but may be subject to limitations; these are permitted by implication since the right of access by its very nature calls for regulation by the state. In this respect, the contracting states enjoy a certain margin of appreciation, although the final decision as to the observance of the Convention's requirements rests with the court. It must be satisfied that the limitations applied do not restrict or reduce the access left to the individual in such a way or to such an extent that the very essence of the right is impaired. Furthermore, a limitation will not be compatible with article 6(1) if it does not pursue a legitimate aim and if there is not a reasonable relationship of proportionality between the means employed and the aim sought to be achieved."

[80] [2001] 3 All E.R. 229, 244–245.

7.(4) THE LANDO COMMISSION

The Lando Commission commenced its work on the Principles of European Contract Law in the mid-1970s. In 1995 the Commission published Volume 1 of this work. This comprised of some 59 articles which covered the areas of General Provisions, Terms and Performance of the Contract, Non-Performance and Remedies in General, and Particular Remedies for Non-Performance. Volume 2 of the work covers other areas of contract law. The Commission views these principles as having both immediate and longer-term objectives and has stated that: "They are available for immediate use by parties making contracts, by courts and arbitrators in deciding contract disputes and by legislators in drafting contract rules whether at the European or the national level. Their longer-term objective is to help bring about the harmonisation of general contract law within the European Community."[81]

Thus, it would be open to Irish contracting parties to include a clause in their contract to the effect that it is to be governed by the Principles of European Contract Law. It is of interest to note that the Table of Cases at the end of the combined volumes lists 28 Irish contract law cases.[82]

7.(5) THE COMMISSION'S COMMUNICATION

In July 2001 the European Commission published its Communication on European Contract Law.[83] Commissioner David Byrne, responsible for Health and Consumer Protection, introduced the Communication by stating that:

> "Up to now we have successfully used an approach of harmonising specific contracts or marketing techniques where a particular need for harmonisation was identified. I think the time might have come to change the approach in order to ensure that business as well as consumers are able to take full advantage of the Internal Market. That is why we are launching this broad consultation exercise. The upcoming practical introduction of the euro and the surge of e-commerce make this discussion even more urgent as they will facilitate price comparison and the conclusion of cross-border contracts."[84]

The Communication set out four options for discussion:

(a) *Let market forces decide*: This option would permit market forces to deal with any problems that may exist. In many cases the market creates problems

---

[81] Lando & Beale, ed. *Principles of European Contract Law: Parts I and II* p.xxiv. See also *European Contract Code – Preliminary Draft* (Universita Di Pavia, 2001).

[82] Lando & Beale ed., *Principles of European Contract Law: Parts I and II* pp.494–495.

[83] *Communication From the Commission to the Council and the European Parliament on European Contract Law* COM (2001) 398 Final.

[84] Press release, July 13, 2001, Brussels.

of public concern, but it also develops its own solutions. As a result of competitive behaviour, many of the problems created by the market may be solved automatically by the pressure exercised by the interest groups involved, *e.g.* consumers, NGOs, enterprises. Public authorities can enhance this coincidence of self-interest and public interest. Different incentives by Member States and trade associations, *e.g.* offering assistance and advice on cross-border transactions, can efficiently channel the market in a specific direction, *e.g.* speeding up the use of new technologies or encouraging new types of commercial practices.

(b) *Creating guidelines*: This option would seek to identify the elements common to most national contract law rules and to use them as guidelines for national legislators, national courts and arbitrators and contractual parties. Once those common principles or guidelines were established and agreed upon by all interested parties in the Member States, broad dissemination would be encouraged. This would ensure coherent and uniform application of the common principles or guidelines. These common principles or guidelines would only be applied on a voluntary basis. If this were done continuously by a sufficiently large number of legal practitioners as well as EC and national legislators, it would hopefully bring about greater convergence in the area of European contract law.

(c) *Improving existing legislation*: This option would review and amend all relevant legislation with a view to its simplification and to improving its quality. The Lisbon European Council has already asked the Commission, the Council and the Member States "to set out by 2001 a strategy for further co-ordinated action to simplify the regulatory environment".[85] The Commission has stated its intention to build on action already undertaken on consolidating, codifying and recasting existing instruments centred on transparency and clarity.[86] The quality of drafting could also be reviewed and presentation and terminology could become more coherent. Efforts could also be made to simplify and clarify the content of existing legislation. Finally, the Commission could evaluate the effects of Community legislation and will amend existing acts if necessary. Where appropriate, Directives could be subject to simplification of their provisions.

(d) Creating a new legal instrument: This option would focus on the creation of a new legal instrument at Community level. This could, for example, be an optional model chosen by the contractual parties or a safety net of fallback provisions in case parties have not foreseen a solution for an eventual problem in the contract. It could consist of a Directive, a Regulation or a Recommendation.

---

[85] Communication, para. 57.
[86] *ibid.*, para. 58.

Essentially, the purpose of the Communication is to stimulate debate rather than to dictate policy (although Clark has observed that the title of the document itself suggests some kind of expansionist agenda on the part of the Commission),[87] and it concludes by stating that:

> "The purpose of this Communication is to initiate an open, wide-ranging and detailed debate with the participation of the institutions of the European Community as well as of the general public, including businesses, consumer associations, academics and legal practitioners. In the light of the feedback received, the Commission will, within its right of initiative, decide on further measures."[88]

7.(6) CONCLUSION

The key question is whether 15 states (or even more in an enlarged Union) can ever agree on a unified contract law. Much is often made of the divergence between the common law of the United Kingdom and Ireland and the civil codes of the continent. However, less is written about the common factors between the different legal systems. Until comparatively recently, Roman law was still taught in Irish universities. A study conducted by Schlesinger disclosed that despite the fact that different courts used different techniques for the solution of contractual problems, there was some similarity in the ultimate resolution of the problems.[89] Lando has written of the common ideology that exists among European judges and among European academics.[90] For example, the different national judges of the ECJ somehow manage to reach a consensus on cases more often than not, even though applying different techniques. Books such as Kötz, *European Contract Law*[91] have shown the remarkable extent to which common principles of European contract law can be identified. Education will be key to any such enterprise and before a European contract law can become a reality, "lawyers need to be educated in the private law of Europe as a whole, not just the law of their own country."[92] It will not be an easy task. In the words of Lando:

> "To introduce a new contract law in Europe will admittedly cost sweat, tears, and money. And many lawyers will hate to see all that which they themselves

---

[87] Clark, "Irish Contract Law Reform and the European Commission's Agenda" (2002) 7 Bar Rev. 126, p.216.

[88] Communication, para. 71.

[89] Schlesinger, *Formation of Contracts, A Study of the Common Core of the Legal Systems* I–II (1968).

[90] Lando, "Some Features of the Law of Contract in the Third Millennium" 40 *Scandinavian Studies in Law* 343, pp.356–358.

[91] *Vol 1* (trans. Tony Weir, Clarendon Press, Oxford, 1997).

[92] *ibid.*, page vi.

have learned and practised disappear and to have to learn a new contract law. They will no longer be able to 'sell their legal secrets' as *Thibaut* said.

No doubt the emotional wish to preserve the peculiar character of each national law will prove to be a serious political obstacle to unification, but it is one which must be overcome if the European Union is to function satisfactorily. Contract and commercial law are not folklore. And who today in Paris mourns for '*Les costumes de Paris*' or in Prussia for '*Das allgemeine Landrecht für die preussichen Staaten*'?"[93]

Some convergence in contract law is inevitable. For example, spontaneous convergence in contract law can be expected as cross-border trade develops.[94] The real question is the extent to which such natural processes should be facilitated and accelerated. Clark has argued that there is not sufficient evidence to support the two central propositions that in his opinion are implicitly asserted by the Commission's Communication, namely:[95]

(a) that the common market is being impeded by national contract laws; and

(b) that there is sufficient common ground between Member States to justify the creation of a model contract code that could pass either the subsidiarity or proportionality tests.

Given the very different approaches adopted by common law and civil law systems to some areas of contract, it is certainly difficult to see how the development of a common contract law could be a realistic goal in the immediate future. For example, many civil law systems recognise a concept of good faith in negotiating and impose liability in certain circumstances for simply breaking off negotiations. On the other hand, the Irish common law generally does not recognise any such concept and in particular does not recognise what is known as a contract to contract. It may therefore be better to permit a European contract law to grow organically over time. The current system of a Directive on a particular area which is implemented nationally by legislation or a statutory instrument has worked extremely effectively. It has filled some glaring gaps in such areas as consumer protection without altering the fundamental principles that underlie Irish contract law. A continuation of this system in areas where national divergence is causing a particular problem in cross-border trade would seem to be the obvious way forward. This creeping harmonisation will not be to everyone's liking; it will seem too timid, too slow, too uncertain. However, in defence of prudence, it can be argued that the incoming tide of European law needs to be properly channelled if it is not to wash away too much national practice and custom.

---

[93] Lando, "Some Features of the Law of Contract in the Third Millennium" 40 *Scandinavian Studies in Law* 343, 358–359.

[94] Furmston, ed., *Law of Contract*, para. 1.126.

[95] Clark, "Irish Contract Law Reform and the European Commission's Agenda" (2002) 7 Bar Rev. 126, p.129.

BIBLIOGRAPHY

Basedow, "A Common Contract Law for the Common Market" (1996) 33 CMLR 1169.

Clark, "Irish Contract Law Reform and the European Commission's Agenda" (2002) 7 Bar Rev 126.

Kötz, *European Contract Law, Vol 1* (trans. Tony Weir, Clarendon Press, Oxford 1997).

Furmston (ed.), *Law of Contract* (Butterworths, 1999).

Lando, "Some Features of the Law of Contract in the Third Millennium" 40 Scandinavian Studies in Law 343.

Lando & Beale (ed.), *Principles of European Contract Law, Parts I and II* (Kluwer Law International, 2000).

Schlesinger, *Formation of Contracts, A Study of the Common Core of the Legal Systems* I–II (1968).

8. DIRECTIVE 1999/44 ON CERTAIN ASPECTS OF THE SALE OF CONSUMER GOODS AND ASSOCIATED GUARANTEES: IMPROVING THE RIGHTS OF THE IRISH CONSUMER?

MÁIRE NÍ SHÚILLEABHÁIN*

8.(1) INTRODUCTION

8.(1)(a) "Consumer" and "mercantile" buyers

The common law did not draw a distinction between consumer sales on the one hand and mercantile sales between two businesses on the other. Consequently, when the common law rules of sale were codified by the Sale of Goods Act 1893, the business buyer and the consumer buyer were treated in the same way. In amending the 1893 Act, however, the Sale of Goods and Supply of Services Act 1980 did confer extra protection on the consumer. New remedies of repair and replacement were made available to the consumer buyer of defective goods.[1] The implied terms as to quality were reinforced by the automatic avoidance of exclusion clauses in consumer contracts.[2] In so distinguishing between consumer and mercantile sales, the 1980 Act reflected the emerging consumer-protection ethos of European Community (EC) law which has since spawned a series of measures intended to cater for the particular needs of the consumer buyer.[3] One of the latest in this long line is

---

* B.C.L., LL.M (NUI), B.C.L. (Oxon.), M.L.E. (Hannover), Barrister-at-Law. The author would like to thank Professor Robert Clark for his comments on an earlier draft of this chapter. However, any errors remain the responsibility of the author.
[1] s.53(2) of the Sale of Goods Act 1893, as inserted by s.21 of the Sale of Goods and Supply of Services Act 1980.
[2] s.55(4) of the Sale of Goods Act 1893, as inserted by s.22 of the 1980 Act.
[3] Council Directive 93/13/EEC on unfair terms in consumer contracts [1993] O.J. L95/29, as implemented by S.I. No. 27 of 1995, European Communities (Unfair Terms in Consumer Contracts) Regulations 1995, as amended by S.I. No. 307 of 2000, European Communities (Unfair Terms in Consumer Contracts) (Amendment) Regulations 2000. Council Directive 85/374/EEC on the approximation of the laws, regulations and administrative provisions of the Member States of the European Communities concerning liability for defective products [1985] O.J. L210/29, as implemented by the Liability for Defective Products Act 1991. Amended by Directive 1999/34/EC of the European Parliament and the Council [1999] O.J. L141/20, as implemented by S.I. No. 401 of 2000; European Communities (Liability for Defective Products) Regulations 2000. Council Directive 92/59/EEC on General Product Safety [1992] O.J. L228/24, as implemented by S.I. No. 197 of 1997, European Communities

Directive 1999/44/EC on certain aspects of the sale of consumer goods and associated guarantees (hereafter the "consumer goods" Directive).[4]

8.(1)(b) The consumer goods Directive in outline

This Directive marks the first attempt on the part of the EC to legislate on the relationship between buyer and seller in a general way and it traverses much of the same territory as the Acts of 1893 and 1980. In parallel with sections 13 to 15 of the 1893 Act (as inserted by section 10 of the 1980 Act) it imposes an obligation on sellers not to supply defective goods, and prescribes a scheme of remedies for the benefit of the consumer buyer of defective goods. As the title

---

(General Product Safety) Regulations 1997. Council Directive 84/450/EEC relating to the approximation of the laws, regulations and administrative provisions of the Member States concerning misleading advertising [1984] O.J. L250/17, as implemented by S.I. No. 134 of 1988, European Communities (Misleading Advertising) Regulations 1988. Council Directive 85/577/EEC to protect the consumer in respect of contracts negotiated away from business premises [1985] O.J. L372/31, as implemented by S.I. No. 224 of 1989, European Communities (Cancellation of Contracts Negotiated Away from Business Premises) Regulations 1989. Directive 97/7/EC of the European Parliament and of the Council on the protection of consumers in respect of distance contracts [1997] O.J. L144/19, as implemented by S.I. No. 207 of 2001, European Communities (Protection of Consumers in Respect of Contracts Made by Means of Distance Communication) Regulations 2001. Directive 98/27/EC of the European Parliament and of the Council on injunctions for the protection of consumers' interests [1998] O.J. L166/51, as implemented by S.I. 449 of 2001, European Communities (Protection of Consumers' Collective Interests) Regulations 2001. Directive 98/6/EC of the European Parliament and of the Council on consumer protection in the indication of prices of products offered to consumers [1998] O.J. L80/27, as implemented by S.I. No. 422 of 2001, European Communities (Requirements to Indicate Product Prices) Regulations 2001. Council Directive 90/314/EEC on package travel, package holidays and package tours [1990] O.J. L158/99, as implemented by the Package Holidays and Travel Trade Act 1995. Council Directive 87/102/EEC for the approximation of the laws, regulations and administrative provisions of the Member States concerning consumer credit [1987] O.J. L042/48, as amended by Council Directive 90/88/EEC [1990] O.J. L61/14, as implemented by the Consumer Credit Act 1995. Amended by Council Directive 98/7/EC [1998] O.J. L101/17, as implemented by S.I. No. 294 of 2000, European Communities (Consumer Credit) Regulations 2000. Directive 94/47/EC of the European Parliament and of the Council on the protection of purchasers in respect of certain aspects of contracts relating to the purchase of the right to use immovable properties on a timeshare basis [1994] O.J. L280/83, as implemented by S.I. No. 204 of 1997, European Communities (Contracts for Time Sharing of Immovable Property – Protection of Purchasers) Regulations 1997. For an outline of these measures, see above McDermott para. 7(2).

4 [1999] O.J. L171/12. See generally Shears, Zollers, Hurd "Consumer law" [2000] JBL 262; Twigg-Flesner, Bradgate, "The EC Directive on certain aspects of the sale of consumer goods and associated guarantees – all talk and no do?" [2000] 2 Web JCLI www.spade3.ncl.ac.uk/2000/issue2/flesner2; U.K. Department of Trade and Industry *Consultation Papers (I and II)* available on www.dti.gov.uk; Oughton and Lowry *Consumer law* (2nd ed., Blackstone Press, 2000); Atiyah, Adams and MacQueen, *The Sale of Goods* (10th ed., Longman, 2001); Bradgate, *Commercial law* (3rd ed., Butterworths, 2000); and for two other Irish perspectives, Bird, "Directive 99/44/EC on certain aspects of the sale of consumer goods and associated guarantees: its impact on existing Irish sale of goods law" (2001) 9 *European Review of Private Law* 279; White "The EC Directive on certain aspects of consumer sale and associated guarantees: one step forward, two steps back?" (2000) *Commercial Law Practitioner* (January) 3.

suggests, the Directive is also concerned with the regulation of manufacturers' guarantees and to that extent it also concerns itself with the relationship between buyer and manufacturer.

8.(1)(c) The objectives of the consumer goods Directive

Article 153 EC commits the EC to the achievement of a higher level of consumer protection. However, it is clear from its Preamble that the consumer goods Directive is also concerned with the more fundamental Treaty principle of achieving market integration. Recitals (2) to (5) express the view that disparate levels of consumer protection had engendered a consumer reluctance to purchase goods in other Member States. The Directive purports to tackle this reluctance and to dismantle the resultant market barriers by "the creation of a common set of minimum rules of consumer law".[5]

8.(2) THE RELATIONSHIP BETWEEN BUYER AND SELLER

8.(2)(a) The contracts of sale affected by the consumer goods Directive

The Directive applies to contracts whereby a "consumer" is buying "consumer goods" from a "seller". "Consumer" is defined as "any natural person who . . . is acting for purposes which are not related to his trade, business or profession".[6] "Seller" is defined as any "natural or legal person who . . . sells consumer goods in the course of his trade, business or profession".[7] "Consumer goods" are defined as "any tangible movable item".[8]

Section 3 of the 1980 Act sets a narrower definition of "consumer goods". The goods in question must be "of a type ordinarily supplied for private use or consumption". So the individual who is purchasing, for his private purposes, an item ordinarily purchased for business purposes (for example an office desk or a filing cabinet) would appear to be protected by the Directive but would not qualify as a consumer buyer under the 1980 Act.

In other respects, however, the concept of consumer sale may be broader under the 1980 Act. In terms of defining the "consumer buyer", section 3 simply excludes a person who buys "in the course of a business".[9] There is no

---

[5] Recital 5.
[6] Article 1(2)(a).
[7] Article 1(2)(c).
[8] Article 1(2)(b). The only "consumer goods" excluded from the scope of the Directive are:
  "– goods sold by way of execution or otherwise by authority of law,
    – water and gas where they are not put up for sale in a limited volume or set quantity,
    – electricity".
[9] s. 3 of the 1980 Act provides as follows:
  "(1) In the Act of 1893 and this Act, a party to a contract is said to deal as consumer in relation to another party if—

requirement that the consumer be a natural person and in the UK case of *R & B Customs Brokers v. UDT Ltd*,[10] a company qualified as a consumer and an exclusion clause was therefore ruled inoperative under the UK equivalent to section 55(4) of the 1893 Act.[11] Further, it seems that Article 1(2)(a)'s exclusion of purchases "related" to the buyer's business is more far-reaching than section 3 which only excludes purchases "in the course of a business". For example, the Court of Appeal in *R & B* concluded that a purchase by a company of a car for the use of one of its directors was not "in the course of a business" because the transaction was incidental to the company's business and was not of a kind carried out regularly. It seems, however, that the court would not have been able to conclude that the company was acting for purposes "not related" to its business.

In the end, however, the definition of "consumer sale" is not such a critical matter under the sale of goods legislation. All buyers, consumer and mercantile alike, are entitled to rely on the implied terms of sections 13 to 15.[12] It is true that there is an absolute ban on the exclusion of these implied terms in the context of a consumer sale. However, even in the context of a mercantile sale an exclusion clause will only be effective if it is "fair and reasonable".[13] In relation to remedies, the buyer who does not qualify as a consumer is still entitled to the remedies of rejection and/or damages.

      (a) he neither makes the contract in the course of a business nor holds himself out as doing so, and

      (b) the other party does make the contract in the course of a business, and

      (c) the goods or services supplied under or in pursuance of the contract are of a type ordinarily supplied for private use or consumption.

   (2) On—

      (a) a sale by competitive tender, or

      (b) a sale by auction—

         (i) of goods of a type, or

         (ii) by or on behalf of a person of a class defined by the Minister by order,

      the buyer is not in any circumstances to be regarded as dealing as consumer.

   (3) Subject to this, it is for those claiming that a party does not deal as consumer to show that he does not."

[10]   [1988] 1 WLR 321.

[11]   As inserted by s.22 of the 1980 Act. The equivalent provision to s. 55(4) was s.6 of the Unfair Contract Terms Act 1977. S.12 of that Act defined "dealing as a consumer" in terms similar to s.3 of the 1980 Act. The subsequent decision of the Court of Appeal in *Stevenson v. Rogers* [1999] 1 All E.R. 613, may, however, cast some doubt on the authority of the *R&B* Case

[12]   s.14 is preceded by the requirement "where the seller sells goods in the course of a business". Thus, s.14 may not be relied upon in relation to a private sale. Ss.13 and 15 are, however, applicable even in the context of a private sale.

[13]   s.55(4) of the 1893 Act, as inserted by s.22 of the 1980 Act. "Fair and reasonable" is defined in the Schedule to the 1980 Act.

8.(2)(b)   Substantive rights conferred by the Directive

8.(2)(b)(i)   The rule of "conformity"

Article 2 of the Directive sets the basic requirement of "conformity with the contract of sale". This concept of "conformity" requires that the goods be fit for their usual purposes, be fit for any particular purpose indicated by the buyer and that they conform to any description or sample given by the seller. Thus, in general terms this requirement of "conformity" covers the same ground as sections 13 to 15 of the Sale of Goods Act 1893.

8.(2)(b)(ii)   Fitness for purpose

Article 2(2) of the Directive stipulates as follows:

> "Consumer goods are presumed to be in conformity with the contract if they . . .
> (b) are fit for any particular purpose for which the consumer requires them and which he has made known to the seller at the time of conclusion of the contract and which the seller has accepted;
> (c) are fit for the purposes for which goods of the same type are normally used;
> (d) show the quality and performance which are normal in goods of the same type and which the consumer can reasonably expect, given the nature of the goods . . . ".

In substance these requirements are very similar to those set by subsections (2), (3) and (4) of section 14 of the 1893 Act.[14] There is, however, one potential difference in that the Directive requires that goods be fit for the purposes for which they are *normally used* whereas section 14 requires that they be fit for the purposes for which they are *commonly bought*. In reference to section 14 of the U.K. Act of 1979 which requires goods to be fit for the purposes for which they are "commonly supplied", Shears *et al* argue that "used" gives the Directive broader scope.[15] The example is given of a screwdriver which would frequently be used to open pots of paint but would be

---

14   "(2) Where the seller sells goods in the course of a business there is an implied condition that the goods supplied under the contract are of merchantable quality . . .
 (3)   Goods are of merchantable quality if they are as fit for the purpose or purposes for which goods of that kind are commonly bought and as durable as it is reasonable to expect having regard to any description applied to them, the price (if relevant) and all the other relevant circumstances, and any reference in this Act to unmerchantable goods shall be construed accordingly.
 (4)   Where the seller sells goods in the course of a business and the buyer, expressly or by implication, makes known to the seller any particular purpose for which the goods are being bought, there is an implied condition that the goods supplied under the contract are reasonably fit for that purpose, whether or not that is a purpose for which such goods are commonly supplied . . . ".

15   Shears, Zollers and Hurd "Consumer law" [2000] JBL 262, 272. However, it seems that this argument must apply with less force in the Irish context where the word "bought" is used. As Shears *et al* point out, the use of "supplied" is particularly oriented to the seller.

bought for other purposes. If the screwdriver buckles in the course of such a use there would be a remedy under the Directive but none under the sale of goods legislation. Bradgate and Twigg-Flesner[16] suggest that "normally" may be wider than "commonly". A use may be rare or uncommon, but not abnormal and in such circumstances it would fall within the Directive but outside the existing sale of goods legislation.

The Directive also goes further in specifically providing in Article 2(5) that goods will be considered not to be in conformity "if the product, intended to be installed by the consumer, is installed by the consumer and the incorrect installation is due to a shortcoming in the installation instructions". There is no equivalent provision in the sale of goods legislation. However, there is English authority to the effect that goods are considered to be unmerchantable when they are accompanied by incorrect user instructions.[17] In the end, therefore, the specific provision in the Directive may leave the consumer with less protection as regards defective instructions – in singling out installation instructions in this way, it is implied that instructions in general are not covered by the fitness for purpose rule set down by the Directive.

8.(2)(b)(iii) Exceptions to the fitness for purpose requirement

As regards exceptions, there may be further subtle differences between the Directive and the existing sale of goods legislation. Article 2(3) of the Directive provides for a general defence for the seller as regards obvious defects: "There shall be deemed not to be a lack of conformity for the purposes of this Article if, at the time the contract was concluded, the consumer was aware, or could not reasonably be unaware of, the lack of conformity . . . ".

Under the 1893 Act, the seller can only escape the general fitness for purpose requirement in two situations; either the buyer examined the goods and the defect is one which ought to have been revealed by that examination, or the seller must have specifically drawn the defect to the buyer's attention.[18] So the general implied condition of merchantability will still apply even as regards obvious defects if the buyer did not examine the goods. In relation to fitness for a particular purpose, the seller has a defence under the Act "where the circumstances show that the buyer does not rely, or that it is unreasonable

---

[16] Twigg-Flesner and Bradgate "The EC Directive on certain aspects of the sale of consumer goods and associated guarantees – all talk and no do?" [2000] 2 Web JCLI *www.spade3. ncl.ac.uk/2000/issue2/flesner2*

[17] *Wormell v. RHM Agriculture (East) Ltd* [1986] 1 All E.R. 769; see Miller, Harvey and Parry *Consumer and trading law* (Oxford, 1998) pp.110–112.

[18] s.14(2) of the 1893 Act as inserted by s.10 of the 1980 Act, provides that the implied condition of merchantability does not apply:

"(a) as regards defects specifically drawn to the buyer's attention before the contract is made, or

(b) if the buyer examines the goods before the contract is made, as regards defects which that examination ought to have revealed."

for him to rely, on the seller's skill or judgement."[19] Under the Directive the seller may avail of the general defence of Article 2(3).

8.(2)(b)(iv) Correspondence with description/sample.

In terms of correspondence with description and sample, Article 2(2)(a) requires that the goods "comply with the description given by the seller and possess the qualities of the goods which the seller has held out to the consumer as a sample or model". This provision is substantially similar to the provisions of sections 13[20] and 15[21] of the 1893 Act. However, the Directive goes on in Article 2(2)(d) to require that "conformity" be assessed "taking into account any public statements on the specific characteristics of the goods made about them by the seller, the producer or his representative, particularly in advertising or on labelling."

This provision is subsequently qualified in Article 2(4) as regards statements which were subsequently corrected and statements of which the seller or buyer could have had no knowledge.[22] Nonetheless, these provisions appear to afford the consumer more extensive protection than the sale of goods legislation as regards statements made in advertising. Whilst there is a lack of authority on the point, the general view appears to be that statements made at

---

[19] s.14(4) of the 1893 Act, as inserted by s.10 of the 1980 Act.

[20] s.13 1893 Act (as inserted by s.10 1980 Act) provides:

" (1) Where there is a contract for the sale of goods by description, there is an implied condition that the goods shall correspond with the description; and if the sale be by sample as well as by description, it is not sufficient that the bulk of the goods corresponds with the sample if the goods do not also correspond with the description.

(2) A sale of goods shall not be prevented from being a sale by description by reason only that, being exposed for sale, they are selected by the buyer.

(3) A reference to goods on a label or other descriptive matter accompanying goods exposed for sale may constitute or form part of a description."

[21] s.15 of the 1893 Act (as inserted by s.10 of the 1980 Act) provides:

"A contract of sale is a contract for sale by sample where there is a term in the contract, express or implied, to that effect.

(2) In the case of a contract for sale by sample—

(a) There is an implied condition that the bulk shall correspond with the sample in quality:

(b) There is an implied condition that the buyer shall have a reasonable opportunity of comparing the bulk with the sample:

(c) There is an implied condition that the goods shall be free from any defect, rendering them unmerchantable, which would not be apparent on reasonable examination of the sample."

[22] Article 2(4):"The seller shall not be bound by public statements, as referred to in paragraph 2(d) if he:

– shows that he was not, and could not reasonably have been, aware of the statement in question,

– shows that by the time of the conclusion of the contract the statement had been corrected

– shows that the decision to buy the consumer goods could not have been influenced by the statement."

a completely different time are not actionable as descriptions under the sale of goods legislation. Section 13(3) lends some support to this view; it provides that "a label or other descriptive matter *accompanying goods* exposed for sale may constitute or form part of a description." [Emphasis added].

8.(2)(c) Remedies

8.(2)(c)(i) General remedial scheme of the consumer goods Directive

Under the Directive the primary remedy conferred on the consumer buyer of defective goods is the right to have the goods replaced or repaired by the seller without charge. Article 3(2) provides: "In the first place the consumer may require the seller to repair the goods or he may require the seller to replace them, in either case free of charge, unless this is impossible or dispro-portionate."

The consumer is only entitled to reject the goods and reclaim his purchase monies if the seller fails within a reasonable time to replace or repair the goods or if replacement or repair is not possible. This is apparent from Article 3(5):

> "The consumer may require an appropriate reduction of the price or have the contract rescinded:
> – if the consumer is entitled to neither repair nor replacement, or
> – if the seller has not completed the remedy within a reasonable time, or
> – if the seller has not completed the remedy without significant inconvenience to the consumer."

8.(2)(c)(ii) General remedial scheme of the sale of goods legislation

Under the Sale of Goods legislation the remedial framework is very different.[23] It is clearly envisaged that rejection of the goods will be a primary remedy. The rights conferred by sections 13 to 15 are described as implied conditions

---

[23] The principal provisions are ss. 11, 34, 35, 51 and 53 of the 1893 Act:
S.11 of the 1893 Act (as inserted by s.10 1980 Act) provides:
"(1) Where a contract of sale is subject to any condition to be fulfilled by the seller, the buyer may waive the condition, or may elect to treat the breach of such condition as a breach of warranty, and not as a ground for treating the contract as repudiated.
(2) Whether a stipulation in a contract of sale is a condition, the breach of which may give rise to a right to treat the contract as repudiated, or a warranty, the breach of which may give rise to a claim for damages but not to a right to reject the goods and treat the contract as repudiated, depends in each case on the construction of the contract. A stipulation may be a condition, though called a warranty in the contract.
(3) Where a contract of sale is not severable, and the buyer has accepted the goods, or part thereof, the breach of any condition to be fulfilled by the seller can only be treated as a breach of warranty, and not as a ground for rejecting the goods and treating the contract as repudiated, unless there be a term of the contract, express or implied, to that effect.
(4) Nothing in this section shall affect the case of any condition or warranty, fulfilment of which is excused by law by reason of impossibility or otherwise."

and section 11(2) provides that a breach of condition gives rise to a right to treat the contract as repudiated. The buyer who opts to reject the goods and treat the contract as repudiated may also claim damages for any consequential loss under section 51. Alternatively, pursuant to sections 11(1) and 53(1), the buyer may elect to retain the goods, thereby treating the breach of condition as a breach of warranty, and claim damages for any loss resulting from the seller's breach of duty. However, pursuant to section 11(3), the breach of condition may be automatically relegated to a mere breach of warranty where the buyer has "accepted" the goods. Under sections 34 and 35, the buyer is deemed to have accepted the goods where he has had an opportunity to examine them, and either he has intimated to the seller that he has accepted them, he has acted in a manner inconsistent with the seller's ownership or he has retained them without good and sufficient reason.

In general, business buyers and consumers are treated in the same way as regards remedies; however, section 53(2) confers a special right to repair or replacement on the consumer buyer:

> "Where –
> (a) the buyer deals as a consumer and there is a breach of a condition by the seller which, but for this subsection, the buyer would be compelled to treat as a breach of warranty, and
> (b) the buyer, promptly upon discovering the breach, makes a request to the seller that he either remedy the breach or replace any goods which are not in conformity with the condition,

---

S.34 of the 1893 Act (as inserted by s.20 1980 Act) provides:

"(1) Where goods are delivered to the buyer, which he has not previously examined, he is not deemed to have accepted them unless and until he has had a reasonable opportunity of examining them for the purpose of ascertaining whether they are in conformity with the contract. . . ."

S.35 of the 1893 Act (as inserted by s.20 1980 Act) provides:

"The buyer is deemed to have accepted the goods when he intimates to the seller that he has accepted them, or, subject to section 34 of this Act, when the goods have been delivered to him and he does any act in relation to them which is inconsistent with the ownership of the seller or when, without good and sufficient reason, he retains the goods without intimating to the seller that he has rejected them."

S.51 of the 1893 Act entitles the buyer to an award of damages for non-delivery:

"(1) Where the seller wrongfully neglects or refuses to deliver the goods to the buyer, the buyer may maintain an action against the seller for damages for non-delivery.

(2) The measure of damages is the estimated loss directly and naturally resulting, in the ordinary course of events, from the seller's breach of contract . . . ".

S.53(1) of the 1893 Act (as inserted by s.21 of the 1980 Act) provides:

"[W]here there is a breach of warranty by the seller, or where the buyer elects, or is compelled, to treat any breach of a condition on the part of the seller as a breach of warranty, the buyer is not by reason only of such breach of warranty entitled to reject the goods, but he may—

(a) set up against the seller the breach of warranty in diminution or extinction of the price, or

(b) maintain an action against the seller for damages for the breach of warranty."

then, if the seller refuses to comply with the request or fails to do so within a reasonable time, the buyer is entitled:

   (i) to reject the goods and repudiate the contract, or
   (ii) to have the defect constituting the breach remedied elsewhere and to maintain an action against the seller for the cost thereby incurred by him."

Section 53(2) thus entitles the consumer who has "accepted" the goods and who would otherwise be limited to a remedy in damages, to insist on repair or replacement, and if the seller fails to provide such a remedy the right to reject is revived.

8.(2)(c)(iii) *Extra protection conferred by the consumer goods Directive*

In general terms section 53(2) and Article 3(2) are similar: both entitle the consumer buyer to request repair or replacement of defective goods. There are, however, some significant differences and in some respects the remedy conferred by the Directive is more generous. Firstly, Article 5(1) of the Directive provides that the Article 3(2) remedy is available in respect of all defects which manifest themselves within two years from the time of delivery. Article 5(3) of the Directive further provides that any lack of conformity which becomes apparent within 6 months of delivery of the goods shall be presumed to have existed at the time of delivery. These provisions afford considerable latitude to the dilatory buyer. Under the sale of goods legislation, by contrast, the buyer is under much greater pressure not to delay. Whilst in theory the right to repair or replacement is available for a period of six years (the relevant statutory limitation period),[24] section 53(2) limits its availability to the buyer who acts with promptness and section 53(3) provides that the onus of proving that the buyer acted with promptness lies on him. The Directive imposes no such requirement; however, Article 5(2) permits Member States to make the remedy subject to the buyer notifying the seller within two months of his having detected the non-conformity.

In terms of additional protection under the Directive, Recital 10[25] makes it clear that it is the buyer rather than the seller who gets to decide whether the remedy is to be repair or replacement. By contrast, the language of section 53(2) suggests that the buyer's remedy is limited to requesting either repair or replacement, leaving it to the seller to decide which remedy is to be provided. Whilst the sale of goods legislation is silent on the point, the Directive specifically provides that the seller must cover all costs incurred in providing

---

[24] s.11(1)(a) of the Statute of Limitations 1957 prescribes a limitation period of six years for an action in contract.

[25] Recital 10: "Whereas, in the case of non-conformity of the goods with the contract, consumers should be entitled to have the goods restored to conformity with the contract free of charge, *choosing* either repair or replacement, or failing this, to have the price reduced or the contract rescinded." [Emphasis added].

the repair/replacement remedy including postal costs. Further, the Directive sets the extra requirement that the remedy be provided without significant inconvenience to the buyer. The Directive does not elaborate on the meaning of this requirement. However, it seems that it might have a particular application where the goods are unwieldy – the buyer is relieved of the burden of transporting them to the seller's premises but rather the seller is obliged to collect them.

8.(2)(c)(iv) Extra protection conferred by the sale of goods legislation

If section 52(3) is less generous to the consumer in the above ways, in other respects it is more generous than the Directive. Under the Directive, the seller is relieved of the obligation to replace or repair where that would be impossible or disproportionate. "Disproportionate" is defined as follows:

> "A remedy shall be deemed to be disproportionate if it imposes costs on the seller which, in comparison with the alternative remedy, are unreasonable taking into account:
> – the value the goods would have if there were no lack of conformity,
> – the significance of the lack of conformity, and
> – whether the alternative remedy could be completed without significant inconvenience to the consumer."

Where the seller avails of one of these defences, he must provide an alternative remedy, either by refunding the price or allowing a price reduction. It is not clear from the Directive whether the choice of remedy lies with buyer or seller at this stage. If the seller availing of such a defence is entitled to insist that the buyer accept a reduction of price instead, then the Directive seems to be very much narrower than section 53(2). The seller has no defence of disproportionality or impossibility under section 53(2) and it is clear that he cannot insist that the buyer accept a reduction in price instead. If he fails to repair or replace, the buyer is automatically entitled to reject the goods or have them repaired elsewhere at the seller"s expense. The Directive does not permit of the latter option at all. Further, whilst it is clear that the Directive does confer a right to reject where the seller fails to repair or replace and there is no defence of disproportionality or impossibility, this is subject to two further exceptions. In the first instance, Recital 15 provides that Member States may provide that any reimbursement to the consumer may be reduced to take account of the use the consumer has had of the goods since they were delivered to him. And secondly, Article 3(6) provides that "[t]he consumer is not entitled to have the contract rescinded if the lack of conformity is minor."

Under the sale of goods legislation the buyer who is entitled to reject is entitled to a total refund regardless of the extent of use (although of course the extent of use will be relevant to the issue of whether the goods really were defective and to the question of acceptance under section 35). Further, there is no general defence in respect of minor defects. In the U.K., such a defence has been introduced, although it is not applicable in the context of consumer sales.[26] However, it does seem from the leading English authorities (which precede the amendment) that where a defect is minor there may be no breach of the section 14 implied condition of fitness for purpose at all. For example, in *Bartlett v. Sidney Marcus,*[27] Lord Denning ruled that an article (in this case a second-hand car) was fit for its purpose in terms of section 14 even if it was not in perfect condition, if it was in usable condition. In the subsequent case of *Rogers v. Parish (Scarborough) Ltd,*[28] whilst the Court of Appeal indicated that mere "driveability" was not enough where the sale was of an expensive, top-of-the-range car, it was again accepted that a minor defect would not necessarily put the seller in breach of his section 14 duties.

It seems, however, from the decision of the House of Lords in *Arcos v. Ronaasen,*[29] that failure to correspond to description will be actionable under section 13 even if it is minor and does not affect the suitability of the good for the buyer's intended use. In this case a buyer, who had agreed to buy staves which were half of an inch thick, was entitled to reject where the staves delivered were almost all of a width between half of an inch and five-eighths of an inch thick, even though they were still suitable for his stated purpose of making cement barrels.

8.(2)(c)(v) Conclusion

It seems that the remedial scheme proposed by the Directive is less advantageous to the consumer than the existing regime under Irish law. Under the existing sale of goods legislation, the consumer has a whole range of options as long as he is willing to act quickly. He may reject the goods and reclaim his purchase monies; he may retain the goods and seek damages; he may request repair or replacement by the seller;[30] and if the seller is not forthcoming, he can have the goods repaired elsewhere at the seller's expense. Whether rational or not, the buyer of defective goods will frequently feel mistrustful of the relevant brand or source in general and for such a buyer the immediate right to a refund as a primary remedy is vital. Under the scheme of the Directive there is no such right and the seller is entitled to insist on replacing or repairing the goods.

---

[26] The new s.15A(1), inserted into the U.K. Act of 1979 by s.4(2) of the Sale and Supply of Goods Act 1994, provides as follows:
   "Where in the case of a contract of sale–
      (a) the buyer would, apart from this subsection, have the right to reject goods by reason of a breach on the part of the seller of a term implied by section 13, 14 or 15 above, but
      (b) the breach is so slight that it would be unreasonable for him to reject them,
   then, if the buyer does not deal as a consumer, the breach is not to be treated as a breach of condition but may be treated as a breach of warranty."

[27] [1965] 2 All E.R. 753.

[28] [1987] 2 All E.R. 232.

[29] [1933] A.C. 470.

[30] Under the U.K. Act of 1979 there is no right to repair or replacement, so Article 3(2) has a more significant impact on existing U.K. law, than on existing Irish law.

Further, the Directive's provision of ill-defined defences for sellers has the practical effect of significantly undermining the consumer's rights. Such provisions make it much easier for the seller to persuade the less-informed consumer to abandon what would otherwise have been a valid claim. Moreover, even where a consumer is properly appraised of his rights, he is far less likely to pursue a remedy where he cannot be certain of success. Under the existing sale of goods legislation, the position is much clearer. Whilst there is an element of uncertainty in the rules on deemed acceptance, even then the consumer can be assured that he is entitled to insist on repair or replacement and an automatic refund if the seller fails or refuses to repair or replace. It is really only in the case of the buyer who delays that the scheme of remedies envisaged by the Directive may be more advantageous.

8.(3) REGULATION OF OTHER RELATIONSHIPS: BUYER AND MANUFACTURER, RECIPIENT AND SUPPLIER OF SERVICES

8.(3)(a) Manufacturers' warranties

8.(3)(a)(i) General

As has been indicated earlier, the consumer goods Directive also regulates the provision of manufacturers' warranties or "guarantees" as they are described in the Directive. "Guarantee" is defined in Article 1(2)(e) as "any undertaking by a seller or producer to the consumer, given without extra charge, to reimburse the price paid or to replace, repair or handle consumer goods in any way if they do not meet the specifications set out in the guarantee statement or in the relevant advertising". At common law there was a lot of uncertainty as to the effect of manufacturers' warranties. They were thought to be potentially unenforceable because of the absence of a contractual relationship between manufacturer and buyer.[31] In other words the doctrine of privity of contract was thought to undermine the enforceability of such guarantees. Article 6 of the Directive confirms that manufacturers' guarantees are legally binding and in England this is thought to be one of the principal benefits of the consumer goods Directive, that it clarifies this point.

8.(3)(a)(ii) Existing regulation of the "guarantee" in Ireland under the 1980 Act

In Ireland, the position had already been clarified by sections 15 to 19 of the Sale of Goods and Supply of Services Act 1980 and in fact these existing provisions on guarantees are generally more extensive and confer more

---

[31] See Benjamin's *Sale of Goods* (5th ed., Sweet & Maxwell, 1997), pp.696–697; Bradgate, *Commercial Law* (3rd ed., Butterworths, 2000) p.353; Atiyah, Adams and MacQueen, *The Sale of Goods* (10th ed., Longman, 2001), pp.287–290.

protection than does the Directive. "Guarantee" is defined in section 15 as meaning "any document, notice or other written statement, howsoever described, supplied by a manufacturer or other supplier, other than a retailer, in connection with the supply of any goods and indicating that the manufacturer or other supplier will service, repair or otherwise deal with the goods following purchase." Section 15 appears to embrace a narrower concept of guarantee than the Directive in so far as the latter specifically envisages (in Article 1(2)(e) and Article 6(1)) the enforceability of statements made in advertising as part of the guarantee. Section 15's requirement of a written statement supplied in connection with goods certainly excludes reliance on any oral assurance given in advertising and probably also written assurances unless copies are supplied with the goods.

The section 15 definition would also suggest that the Act is of a narrower scope than the Directive in that retailers' guarantees are excluded. However, section 17(3) provides that these "undertakings" are similarly governed by sections 16, 18 and 19. And, finally, the section 15 definition indicates a broader definition of guarantee than the Directive in so far as there is no exclusion of guarantees for which the consumer had to pay an extra charge. The extended, insurance-style warranties which are frequently provided by retailers in relation to expensive goods, *e.g.* computers, are covered by the 1980 Act but not by the Directive.

8.(3)(a)(iii) Requirements as to content under the 1980 Act

Sections 16 and 18 of the 1980 Act stipulate certain content requirements for manufacturers' warranties. Pursuant to section 16, they must be clearly legible and must state the name and address of the manufacturer and the duration of the guarantee. They must specify the precise nature of the manufacturer's undertaking (what he is promising to do), and must indicate how the buyer should go about bringing a claim and any charges which he or she will be expected to bear, for example in relation to carriage. A manufacturer who issues guarantees which are in breach of these requirements commits an offence. Section 18 renders void any provisions in a guarantee which tend to delimit the buyer's statutory rights or to impose extra burdens on the buyer, or to give the guarantor sole authority to decide whether goods are defective.

8.(3)(a)(iv) Enforcement under the 1980 Act

Sections 17 and 19 deal with enforcement. Section 17 provides that the seller is also liable under the manufacturer's guarantee, unless he either provided his own "undertaking" or specifically excluded such liability at the time of delivery. So, in general, the Act gives the buyer the option of enforcing the guarantee against the seller rather than the manufacturer if he so wishes. In addition, under section 19 (which confirms that manufacturers' guarantees are enforceable) persons other than the original buyer who acquire title to the goods during the currency of the guarantee are entitled to enforce it against the manufacturer.

8.(3)(a)(v) Limited regulation under the consumer sales Directive

In general, the scheme of the Directive is similar to that set down by the 1980 Act. Like the 1980 Act, it does not require the provision of a manufacturer's warranty but simply regulates the contents of such warranties where they are voluntarily provided. Furthermore, like the 1980 Act it confirms that these warranties are enforceable.

The Directive regulates guarantees in Article 6 which provides as follows:

> "1. A guarantee shall be legally binding on the offeror under the conditions laid down in the guarantee statement and the associated advertising.
> 2. The guarantee shall:
>   – state that the consumer has legal rights under applicable national legis-lation governing the sale of consumer goods and make clear that those rights are not affected by the guarantee,
>   – set out in plain intelligible language the contents of the guarantee and the essential particulars necessary for making claims under the guarantee, notably the duration and territorial scope of the guarantee as well as the name and address of the guarantor.
> 3. On request by the consumer, the guarantee shall be made available in writing or feature in another durable medium available and accessible to him.
> 4. Within its own territory, the Member State in which the consumer goods are marketed may, in accordance with the rules of the Treaty, provide that the guarantee be drafted in one or more languages which it shall determine from among the official languages of the Community.
> 5. Should a guarantee infringe the requirements of paragraphs 2, 3 or 4, the validity of this guarantee shall in no way be affected and the consumer can still rely on the guarantee and require that it be honoured."

In terms of enforcement the Directive does not go nearly as far as the Act. The manufacturer's guarantee is enforceable only as against the manufacturer and there is no extension of rights to a third party acquiring title through the initial buyer.

As regards mandatory contents, the Directive's requirements are generally the same as those imposed by the 1980 Act. It does go further in requiring the guarantor to state the territorial scope of the guarantee and perhaps, more significantly, in requiring the guarantee to specifically state that the consumer has statutory rights which are not affected by the guarantee. It is perhaps a shortcoming of the 1980 Act that such a statement is not included as a necessary term under section 17. Section 18 does render void any statement which purports to limit statutory rights, but the consumer may not be aware of that and may abandon his or her rights in reliance on an ineffective clause in the guarantee. It does, however, seem that section 11(4) of the 1980 Act has the effect of requiring guarantors to include such a statement:

"It shall be an offence for a person in the course of a business to furnish to a buyer goods bearing, or goods in a container bearing, or any document including, any statement, irrespective of its legal effect, which sets out, limits or describes rights conferred on a buyer or liabilities to the buyer in relation to goods acquired by him or any statement likely to be taken as such a statement, unless that statement is accompanied by a clear and conspicuous declaration that the contractual rights which the buyer enjoys by virtue of sections 12, 13, 14 and 15 of the Act of 1893 are in no way prejudiced by the relevant statement."

8.(3)(b) Regulation of the relationship between the supplier and recipient of services

8.(3)(b)(i) Contracts for labour and materials

Article 1(4) of the Directive provides that "[c]ontracts for the supply of consumer goods to be manufactured or produced shall also be deemed contracts of sale for the purpose of this Directive." Under the existing sale of goods regime such contracts may be regarded as "contracts for labour and materials" (a species of services contract) rather than as contracts of sale of goods. If a contract is found to be for labour and materials then it falls to be governed by the provisions of Part IV of the 1980 Act on the "supply of services" rather than by the generality of the 1893 Act, as amended. The courts have, however, experienced great difficulty in determining the appropriate boundary-line between these two species of contracts. As Goode describes it:

"English courts have wobbled uncertainly from one test to another, first adopting the criterion of relative importance of the labour and the materials, then shifting position to hold that any transaction under which the work results in the production of an article that can be said to be the subject of a sale is a contract of sale, and finally reverting to a modified form of the original test, namely whether the substance of the contract is the exercise of skill and labour, in which the provision of materials is subsidiary, or whether it is the supply of a finished product by way of sale."[32]

8.(3)(b)(ii) Contracts of work and labour

The Directive also presupposes that some contracts of work and labour can be classed as contracts for the sale of goods. This is apparent from Article 2(3) which provides a defence for sellers where "the lack of conformity has its origins in materials supplied by the consumer." This is in contrast to the existing practice under the sale of goods legislation whereby such contracts are classed as being for services and fall to be considered under Part IV of the 1980 Act.

---

[32] Goode, *Commercial law* (2nd ed., 1995) p.203.

8.(3)(b)(iii) Installation services

The Directive trespasses further into what is traditionally regarded as the "supply of services" domain in Article 2(5):

> "Any lack of conformity resulting from incorrect installation of the consumer goods shall be deemed to be equivalent to lack of conformity of the goods if installation forms part of the contract of sale of goods and the goods were installed by the seller or under his responsibility."

8.(3)(b)(iv) Regulation of services under Part IV of the 1980 Act

In so far as the recipients of such services must rely on Part IV of the 1980 Act, they enjoy a far lower level of protection than those entitled to benefit from the statutory regime of protection for buyers. Section 39 sets down the terms implied in favour of the recipients of services:

> "Subject to section 40, in every contract for the supply of a service where the supplier is acting in the course of a business, the following terms are implied—
> (a) that the supplier has the necessary skill to render the service,
> (b) that he will supply the service with due skill, care and diligence,
> (c) that, where materials are used, they will be sound and reasonably fit for the purpose for which they are required, and
> (d) that, where goods are supplied under the contract, they will be of merchantable quality within the meaning of section 14 (3) of the Act of 1893 (inserted by section 10 of this Act)."

The first two implied terms, (a) and (b), relating to the rendering of the service with due skill and care, add very little to the duties already imposed under the law of negligence. This "duty of care" standard is very different to the "strict liability for latent defects" standard imposed by section 14 in respect of goods. Furthermore, section 39 describes the duties imposed as "terms", not as "conditions", and pursuant to section 40, all of the implied terms imposed by section 39 may be excluded even where the recipient is a consumer, provided the exclusion clause is "fair and reasonable" and has been specifically brought to the consumer's attention. Having said that, section 39 does provide that where goods are supplied under a services contract, there is an implied term that they will be of merchantable quality within the meaning of section 14(3).

8.(3)(b)(v) Implications for recipients of services caught by the Directive

It is clear that those recipients of services who are caught by the Directive will derive significant benefit from that inclusion. For the first time they will be entitled to rely on an implied term as to correspondence with description. The consumer party to a contract for labour and materials will for the first time be able to insist on repair or replacement. The same will be true for the consumer party to those contracts of work and labour covered by the Directive, provided the defect does not spring from the materials supplied by the consumer. Where there has been defective installation by the supplier, the consumer may insist on repair or replacement and may even be able to repudiate the entire contract. And it will be no defence for the seller to show that he exercised reasonable care. Furthermore, it will not be possible for the recipient of such a service to contract out of his entitlements under the Directive. Article 7(1) provides that: "Any contractual terms or agreements concluded with the seller before the lack of conformity is brought to the seller's attention which directly or indirectly waive or restrict the rights resulting from this Directive shall, as provided for by national law, not be binding on the consumer."

Article 7 has very little significance for the buyer protected as such under the sale of goods legislation. He is already extensively protected against exclusion clauses under section 55(4). It is, however, of importance for the recipient of services who may be bound by an exclusion clause pursuant to section 40 of the 1980 Act. Finally, the specific inclusion of these recipients of services under the Directive creates some level of certainty for those who were previously left stranded in the grey area between goods and services, unsure as to whether they could benefit from the superior buyers' regime, or whether they could only have recourse to the protection conferred by part IV of the 1980 Act.

8.(4) CONCLUSIONS

The consumer goods Directive does add a little to the armoury of the Irish consumer buyer. However, in so far as it does go a little further than the existing sale of goods regime, the advantage of any extra protection is offset by the confusion and uncertainty which the Directive will generate. Whilst Article 9(2) makes it clear that Member States are entitled to adopt or maintain in force more stringent provisions, the fact that the Directive does go further in certain respects means that there will have to be implementing legislation. Further, it seems that this must take the form of either a separate stand-alone set of regulations to which the consumer may have recourse as an alternative to the existing sale of goods legislation, or else a complete overhaul of the existing sale of goods legislation.

The first of those two options is attractive in that it facilitates speedy transposition and permits a wording closely based on the Directive's own wording so that there can be no question of having failed to properly implement the Directive. On the other hand, this approach will make the law very complex, and complexity is particularly undesirable in the arena of consumer protection where the amount of money at stake does not generally warrant recourse to detailed legal advice.

The latter option, of amending and consolidating the existing sale of goods legislation so as to accommodate the additional protections of the Directive within the existing regime, is attractive in so far as it would make the law clearer and more accessible. Additionally, apart from the need to transpose this Directive, the sale of goods legislation is thought to be generally in need of amendment and reform.[33] As against this approach, it must be said that it will be very difficult to accommodate the additional features of the Directive without significantly altering the existing framework. The Directive and the sale of goods legislation are very different in terms of their first principles and foundational divisions. And, of course, if a new sale of goods code is devised using different language, then the benefit of existing case-law would be lost and at least in the short-term, the law would revert to a state of uncertainty.

In terms of the general effects of the Directive, the move towards further differentiation of consumer and mercantile buyers is to be welcomed. The needs of the consumer buyer are very different to those of the mercantile buyer. He generally suffers a much greater inequality of bargaining position vis-à-vis the seller, than does the mercantile buyer. In general the seller will be far more concerned about the repeat custom of a mercantile buyer and will be more inclined to bow to his wishes and to provide an effective remedy. The consumer buyer is less knowledgeable about the law and less skilled in nego-tiation; the mercantile buyer, by contrast, will very often have had the benefit of specific legal advice in relation to the transaction. And finally in the context of consumer sales, very often the cost of litigation will be grossly dispro-portionate to the cost of the goods, and will not be resorted to for that reason.

The Directive's capacity to achieve its aim of encouraging cross-border shopping by consumers is more doubtful. This justification for the Directive presupposes a consumer who is aware not only of the level of consumer-protection in his own country, but also of that in other Member States. Even if it were realistic to expect consumers to be so informed, the Directive only sets a minimum standard of protection. It allows Member States to retain their higher standards, with the result that market barriers will remain as between states opting for the Directive standard and those retaining higher standards. Furthermore, this justification of market integration presupposes that the consumer who buys abroad will be willing to make a return trip for the purposes of seeking a remedy in respect of a defective product. The only alternative (unless the seller has a presence in the buyer's home state) is to post the defective good to the seller, in which case the buyer is very much reliant on the seller's goodwill and efficiency. It seems likely that most buyers would probably prefer to retain their defective good rather than run the risk of being left with nothing at all. It is probably only the exceptional buyer who lives on the border of two Member States or who travels back and forth regularly who will be able to seek a remedy from the seller.

---

[33] For example, there is a general consensus that the formality requirements of s.4 of the 1893 Act and the market overt exception to the *nemo dat* rule (s.22) are anachronisms. The question of when property passes in quasi-specific goods is another question which is ripe for reform.

BIBLIOGRAPHY

Atiyah, Adams & MacQueen, *The Sale of Goods* (10th ed., Longman, 2001).

Benjamin's *Sale of Goods* (5th ed., Sweet & Maxwell, 1997).

Bird "Directive 99/44/EC on certain aspects of the sale of consumer goods and associated guarantees: its impact on existing Irish sale of goods law" (2001) 9 European Review of Private Law 279.

Bradgate, Com*mercial Law* (3rd ed., Butterworths, 2000).

Bridge, *The Sale of Goods* (OUP, Oxford, 1997).

Goode, *Commercial law* (2nd ed., Penguin, 1995).

Miller, Harvey & Parry, *Consumer and trading law* (OUP, Oxford, 1998).

Oughton and Lowry, Consumer law (2nd ed., Blackstone Press, 2000).

Shears, Zollers & Hurd, *Consumer law* [2000] JBL 262.

Twigg-Flesner and Bradgate "The EC Directive on certain aspects of the sale of consumer goods and associated guarantees – all talk and no do?" [2000] 2 Web JCLI (www.spade3.ncl.ac.uk/2000/issue2/flesner2).

U.K. Department of Trade and Industry Consultation Papers (I and II) available on www.dti.gov.uk.

White, "The EC Directive on certain aspects of consumer sale and associated guarantees: one step forward, two steps back?" (2000) *Commercial Law Practitioner* (January) 3.

9. SCOPE AND GENERAL PRINCIPLES OF THE ELECTRONIC COMMERCE DIRECTIVE

DERMOT CAHILL*

9.(1) INTRODUCTION

Directive 2000/31 of the European Parliament & Council on Certain Legal Aspects of Information Society Services, in particular Electronic Commerce, in the Internal Market[1] (hereinafter "the Directive") was adopted on June 8, 2000.[2] This chapter will outline the main principles underlying the Directive, as well as give some consideration to limitations on the scope of the Directive.

---

* Dermot Cahill, B.C.L., LL.M (NUI), DAELS (Bruges), Solicitor, Lecturer in European Union and Corporate Finance Law, Faculty of Law, University College Dublin.

[1] This chapter was the subject of an earlier paper delivered by the author at the *Electronic Commerce in the European Community* conference in June 2001, jointly organised by the Academy of European Law, Trier & the Irish Centre for European Law. My thanks to Joe Kelly, Partner, A&L Goodbody; TP Kennedy, Law Society; and Mark Hyland, Research Fellow, The Interdisciplinary Centre for Law and IT, Leuven University, for their comments on earlier drafts of this paper. All errors and opinions contained herein are the author's alone.

[2] O.J. L 178/1, published on June 17, 2000 and to be implemented in all Member States by January 17, 2002. The Directive was to be implemented in all Member States by January 2002, yet its transposition history in Ireland has been both bizarrely early and late at the same time! In the normal course of events, one expects the State to transpose a Directive into national law some time *after* the Directive's adoption at Community level. However, in the case of the Directive in issue, the State, in its zeal to portray Ireland as an E–Commerce-friendly jurisdiction, hastily enacted the so-called *Electronic Commerce Act 2000* (shortly *before* the Directive was published), and then commenced the Act shortly after the Directive had been published (by way of S.I. 293 of 2000 on September 20, 2000). However, the difficulty with this was that while certain of the 2000 Act's provisions are harmonious with some of the Directive's objectives, the 2000 Act in no way can be said to be a measure which implements *the bulk* of the Directive's provisions, because the 2000 Act (despite its title) would appear to be more concerned with implementing the Electronic Signatures Directive 1999/93 of December 13, 1999 on a Community Framework for Electronic Signatures than the Directive itself. Therefore, at the time of writing, Ireland (as well as several other Member States) is late in properly transposing the Directive into national law. Therefore, as the Electronic Commerce Act 2000 is more concerned with implementing the Electronic Signatures Directive than the Directive itself, it is not proposed to enter into detailed consideration of the 2000 Act, as the Signatures Directive is not the focus of this chapter, though reference will be made to those relevant aspects of the 2000 Act that concern the (E–Commerce) Directive itself.

At the outset, it should be emphasised that the Directive is very much a work in progress. According to its own terms[3] it will have to be reviewed by 2003 as it is recognised that in this very dynamic area, legal frameworks have to be reviewed periodically in order to keep pace with technological development as well as future challenges thrown up by the provision of electronic services in the internal market and beyond.

Essentially, what the Directive seeks to do is harmonise the law to a minimum extent in order to remove legal obstacles to the proper functioning of the common market in the area of Information Society Services. In essence, it was perceived that the development of a functioning internal market in such services, and the attractiveness of European Union (EU) Member States as a location for the provision of such services, would be hampered by (a) legal uncertainty as to which national rules apply to such services and their providers, and (b) diverging legal criteria that might have to be satisfied by service providers operating under divergent national laws.

Therefore, what the Directive seeks to achieve is to eliminate such obstacles by co-ordinating certain national laws and clarifying certain key concepts at Community level, while at the same time making it clear that the measures provided for in the Directive are the minimum necessary for the proper functioning of the internal market.

The Directive seeks to achieve these objectives by:

1. providing a definition for "Information Society Services";

2. requiring Member States to change their laws to allow electronic contracts to be enforceable and effective under national law, and makes it clear that it is building on existing Community laws, particularly those that protect consumer interests and public health;

3. providing that the law that shall apply to service providers is the law of their State of *establishment*. This is achieved by the enunciation of a *home State supervision principle* in Article 3 (whereby each Member State will be responsible for supervising Information Society services providers which are *established* in their own States) while at the same time the Directive states that it does not seek to interfere with existing European Community (EC) national legislation regarding consumer protection (Article 1(4)). Furthermore, the Directive states that it does not develop new rules of private international law[4];

---

[3] Art. 21.1.

[4] Art.1(4). This whole area is not without controversy. See Moerel, "The Country of Origin Principle in the E-Commerce Directive: The Expected "One Stop Shop?" *Computer & Telecommunications Law Review*, Issue 7, 2001, p.189; Long, "European Rules for Financial Services Providers" E.B.L., April 2000, p.6; Fenn, "Review of recent EU Legislative Developments" E.B.L. February 2000. New rules on jurisdiction and choice of law have been formulated recently. At jurisdictional level, the 1968 Brussels Convention on Jurisdiction & Enforcement of Judgments was superceded by the "Brussels Regulation", (on March 1, 2002),

4. providing that Member States cannot require service providers based in other Member States to require prior authorisation before they can supply services into the States, yet permits States to control supply of services if based on protection of certain interests;

5. providing limited exemption from liability for intermediary service providers in certain instances;

6. requiring a certain minimum level of transparency in commercial communications;

7. encouraging the development of online dispute settlement;

8. requiring Member States to ensure that their court systems provide effective and proportionate legal remedies for infringements.

9.(1)(a) Information Society Services

The term "Information Society Services" is not defined in the Directive itself. Instead, the Directive[5] adopts the definition given in Directive 98/34 on the Provision of Information in the Field of Technical Standards & Regulations and of Rules for Information Society Services[6] (as amended and renamed by Directive 98/48).[7] Essentially, something is an Information Society Service if *it is a service, normally provided for remuneration, at a distance, by electronic means, at the individual request of the recipient of the services.*[8]

9.(1)(b) Recital 18

Before looking more closely at the several ingredients of this definition which require further elaboration, it is first useful to note that paragraph 18 of the Recitals to the Directive provides that Information Society Services span a wide range of economic activities which take place on-line, in particular the on-line selling of goods. Information Society Services are not confined merely to services which give rise to on-line contracting, but also includes (in so far as they represent an economic activity) services which are not remunerated by

---

namely Regulation 44/2001 on Jurisdiction and Enforcement of Judgments 2001 O.J. L12/1. The Brussels Regulation provides that a consumer is free to sue in their home State, where an undertaking directs activities at the consumer from outside the State. However, this apparently conflicts with the E-Commerce Directive (Art.3) which can be interpreted to mean that the consumer should have to institute suit in the jurisdiction where the service provider is established. Therefore, the assertion in the Directive (Art.1(4)) that it is not affecting existing rules of private international law is a cause of some confusion. Until this dilemma is resolved, this issue of where suit is to be instituted will be unclear.

[5] Art. 2.
[6] O.J. L 204 21.7.1998 p.37.
[7] O.J. L 217 5.8.1998 p.18.
[8] Art. 1 of Directive 98/34 as inserted by Art. 1 of Directive 98/48.

those who receive them, such as services offering on-line information or commercial communications, or those providing search tools for allowing search and retrieval of data.[9] Also included in the definition are services which consist of the transmission of information *via* a communication equipment network, or services providing access to a communication network, or in hosting information provided by a recipient of the service.

Commercial communication by electronic mail is an Information Society Service. However, paragraph 18 excludes electronic mail used to conclude transactions entered into by natural persons acting outside their trade, business or profession for the conclusion of contracts.[10] It also declares that activities such as the delivery of goods as such, or the provision of services off-line are not Information Society Services.

Having got a flavour of what Information Society Services might encompass, at this point a closer look at the criteria used in the definition of Information Society Services is instructive.

9.(1)(c) The legal definition

9.(1)(c)(i) At a distance

First, the requirement that the service is provided "at a distance" means that the parties cannot be physically present in the same place at the same time. An illustrative list[11] of services not regarded as those that are provided "at a distance" (even though they involve the use of electronic devices) includes:

– medical examinations where the patient is physically present (though presumably this will not cover diagnostic services conducted from a remote location, *i.e.* doctor and patient not in physical proximity to each other);

– consultation of an electronic catalogue in a shop where the customer is in the shop (so even though the goods may be stored elsewhere, nevertheless, the customer and supplier are regarded as not being "at a distance" from each other);

– reservation of airline tickets at a travel agency where the customer is physically present;

– electronic games played by a customer in a video arcade.

9.(1)(c)(ii) Electronic means

The term "electronic means" means that the service is sent initially and also received at its destination by means of electronic equipment for the processing

---

[9] Recital para. 18.
[10] And also states that "the contractual relationship between an employer and employee is not an Information Society Service."
[11] Annex V of Dir. 98/34 O.J. (1998) L204/37 as inserted by Dir. 98/48 O.J. (1998) L217/18.

and storage of data. Transmission must be entirely by wire, radio, optical or electromagnetic means. An illustrative list[12] of services that are not regarded as being provided by electronic means is provided and is based on the rationale that they do not involve the processing and storage of data. The illustrative list includes the following services (even though they may involve the use of electronic devices):

– ATM or ticket dispensing machines;

– Devices which control entry and exit to car parks or road networks;

– Off-line services,[13] to include distribution of CD roms or software on diskettes;

– Services which are not provided via electronic processing /inventory systems, such as: voice telephony services; telex/fax services; services provided via either of the foregoing; telephone/fax consultation with a doctor or lawyer; telephone/fax direct marketing.

9.(1)(c)(iii) At the individual request of the recipient

Another requirement is that services be supplied "at the individual request of the recipient". This is defined further to mean that the service must be provided through the transmission of data on individual request. Consequently, "point to multi-point" transmission is not capable of satisfying this "individual request" requirement. What this means is that where a particular service, though it may be provided by electronic means, is in fact not individually requested, it will fall outside the definition of an Information Society Service. An illustrative list[14] is provided to include examples of excluded services such as television broadcast services within the meaning of Directive 89/552 (including near-video on–demand services);[15] radio broadcast services; and televised teletext.

9.(2) PRINCIPLE OF HOME STATE SUPERVISION COMBINED WITH PROHIBITION ON PRIOR AUTHORISATION

9.(2)(a) A different approach

As the internal market programme has developed since the late 1980s, different approaches have been taken at different times and in different sectors

---

[12] Annex V of Dir. 98/34 as inserted by Dir. 98/48.

[13] According to para. 18 of the Recitals, Information Society Services span a wide range of economic activities which take place *on-line*; however, the provision of services off-line are not Information Society Services.

[14] Annex V of Dir. 98/34 as inserted by Dir. 98/48.

[15] By contrast, video on-demand services are Information Society Services because they are provided on individual request, *i.e.* on a point-to-point basis: see Recital para.18.

to facilitate inter-State market penetration while at the same time ensuring that adequate regulatory supervision of economic actors was respected. The Directive uses an amalgam of some of these approaches to create a regime whereby the principle of home state supervision is employed in order to prevent duplication of regulation (and the maintenance of regulatory barriers to inter-State penetration). However, what is perhaps controversial in this instance is that, in the past, in areas such as the Banking Directives, Directives laid down technical requirements to be satisfied, specifying them in some detail, and leaving it to the home State to supervise adherence to these Community criteria. Other Member States (host States) were required to permit the home State-approved entity to operate within their jurisdiction once notified of its intention to do so. Although the operator would have to adhere to any local non-discriminatory requirements of an objective nature dedicated to the protection of the general good, crucially, fresh authorisation to operate in the host State was not permitted. In this way, host States would have to give mutual recognition to such entities authorised to operate in the home State.

However, what is different about the E-Commerce Directive is that while it utilises the home State supervision principle to the extent that it provides that each Member State must supervise the setting up of an Information Society Services provider,[16] it does not elaborate a set of common EU-wide technical criteria that such operators must adhere to in all Member States.

What this means is that each Member State is obliged to ensure that the Information Society Services provided by a service provider established on its territory comply with the national provisions applicable in that Member State which govern the taking up and pursuit of an Information Society Service within that territory.[17] The national provisions in question are known as the *co-ordinated field*.[18]

This raises several issues. For example, what does the co-ordinated field mean? Can a Member State prevent an Information Society Service provider based in another Member State from providing services into the State unless it complies with the State's co-ordinated field? Has the State any freedom to restrict the provision of Information Society Services under the Directive? And finally, how does one decide which Member State the Information Society Service provider is based in? These matters will now be addressed.

9.(3) What does the co-ordinated field mean?

The "co-ordinated field" is the set of requirements laid down by each Member State's legal system which is applicable to Information Society Services or

---

[16] An Information Society Services provider is any natural or legal person providing an Information Society Service: Art. 2(b).

[17] Art. 3(1).

[18] Art. 2(h).

providers of same. What this means is that each Member State will have various requirements, which service providers based there have to comply with in order to take up and pursue the activity of an Information Society Services provider, such as qualifications, authorisations, behaviour, quality and content of service requirements, requirements concerning service provider liability, etc. The E-Commerce Directive does not provide an exhaustive list of what kind of requirements can fall within the co-ordinated field, so the foregoing list (which appears in Article 2(h) of the Directive) is indicative of what we might call prudential rules designed to ensure that those who intend to operate as Information Society Service providers meet certain professional and prudential standards.

9.(3)(a) Matters that fall outside the co-ordinated field

Importantly, it is also provided that while the co-ordinated field concerns requirements relating to on-line activities, *i.e.* on-line information, shopping, advertising or contracting,[19] it expressly does *not*[20] include requirements such as those:

– applicable to goods as such;

– applicable to the delivery of goods; or

– applicable to services not provided by electronic means.

In essence, this means that Member State rules concerning matters such as:[21]

– safety standards;

– labelling obligations;

– liability for goods; and

– requirements relating to delivery/transport of goods,

must be respected by foreign Information Society Service providers based in other Member States who wish to supply such goods into the Member State.

9.(3)(b) Matters excluded from the co-ordinated field

There are certain matters that cannot fall within the co-ordinated field.[22] These are set out in the Annex to the Directive. Basically these items are not permitted to fall within the co-ordinated field rubric for a variety of reasons ranging from a lack of Community harmonisation or approximation of

---

[19]   Recital para. 21.
[20]   Art. 2(h)(ii).
[21]   Recital para. 21.
[22]   Art. 3.3.

national laws, to difficulties presented by the existing EC jurisprudence. While the Directive's Annex can be consulted by the reader for a complete list of items which fall outside the co-ordinated field rubric, some of the more significant are listed below:

- copyright, neighbouring rights, rights referred to in Directives 87/54 (on the legal protection of topographies of semiconductor products), and 96/9 (on the legal protection of databases), and industrial property rights;

- emission of electronic money by institutions in respect of which Member States have applied one of the derogations provided for in Art 8(1) of Directive 2000/46 (on the pursuit and supervision of the business of electronic money institutions);

- the freedom of parties to choose applicable law for their contract;

- contractual obligations concerning consumer contracts;

- formal validity of contracts creating or transferring rights in real estate;

- the permissibility of unsolicited commercial communications by electronic mail.

In essence, an Information Society Service provider cannot utilise the home State principle in order to "clear the bar" on the above issues. Instead they will have to comply with the relevant EC/Member State regimes in place at the time, pending harmonisation occurring in these areas.

9.(3)(c) Can a Member State prevent an Information Society Service provider based in another Member State from providing services into the State unless it complies with the State's own *co-ordinated field*?

.A Member State cannot, in the ordinary course of events, restrict the freedom of an Information Society Services provider based in another Member State from providing services into the State. Essentially, provided the Information Society Services provider will have satisfied the requirements of the co-ordinated field in their own home Member State jurisdiction, they cannot be required to further satisfy the possibly different co-ordinated field requirements in another Member State into which the services provider wishes to provide services. Article 3.2 is quite clear on this point.

There are two categories of exception to this prohibition. The first, activities that fall outside the Article 3.2 prohibition simply because of currently inconsistent national regimes and other legal obstacles, has already been considered above. The second, based chiefly on protection of the public considerations, will be considered below at para. 9(4). However, before considering the public policy exception, it is first appropriate to briefly mention the principle prohibiting prior authorisation.

9.(3)(c)(i) Principle prohibiting prior authorisation

The important point to note at this juncture is that the emphasis on home State supervision of an Information Society Service provider (Article 3.1) and the prohibition on Member States restricting the freedom of an Information Society Service provider based in another Member State from providing Information Society Services in other Member States, is bolstered by a further principle, the principle prohibiting prior authorisation.

This principle, found in Article 4.1 of the Directive, provides that Member States shall ensure that the taking up and pursuit of the activity of an Information Society Service provider may not be made subject to prior authorisation or any other requirement having equivalent effect. Therefore, the Directive makes it quite clear that Member States are not to attempt to use the requirements of domestic regulatory regimes, *i.e.*, the local co-ordinated field requirements, to stymie the provision of an Information Society Service into their territories by service providers established in another Member State(s)[23] who (presumably) comply with co-ordinated field rules applicable in their home State(s).[24]

9.(4) HAS THE MEMBER STATE ANY FREEDOM TO RESTRICT THE PROVISION OF INFORMATION SOCIETY SERVICES UNDER THE DIRECTIVE?

As has been noted, although the Directive provides that as a basic premise a Member State does not have the right to restrict the provision of Information Society Services, there are two categories of exception. A Member State may restrict the provision of an Information Society Service by a service provider based in another Member State. This has already been considered (at para. 9.3 above). We shall now consider the second.

---

[23] Unless of course the scenario outlined in Recital para. 57 applies, that is, a Member State retains the right to take measures against a service provider established in another Member State where that provider directs most of its activity towards the first State if the choice of establishment was made with a view to evading the legislation that would have applied to the service provider had it been established in the first State.

[24] Though note that Art. 4.2 qualifies this Art. 4.1 prohibition expressly by providing that the prohibition in Art. 4.1 is without prejudice to authorisation schemes which are not specifically and exclusively targeted at Information Society Services providers, or which are covered by Dir. 97/13 on a common framework for general authorisations and individual licences in the field of telecommunications services. Recital para. 28 of the Directive provides further examples, such as postal services covered by Dir. 97/67 on common rules for development of the internal market in postal services which involve physical delivery of printed electronic mail messages.

9.(4)(a) Public policy

Article 3.4 provides several grounds, all based on *public policy*, on which Member States may take measures to derogate. In other words, notwithstanding Article 3.2's prohibition (that Member States may not rely on a *co-ordinated field reason* to restrict an Information Society Services provider located in another Member State from providing services), a Member State may nevertheless so restrict on public policy grounds.

In order to derogate compatibly with the Directive, the restricting Member State must be genuinely relying on one of the grounds of derogation, and comply with notification requirements.

9.(4)(a)(i) Grounds of derogation

The grounds of derogation are:

– public policy, in particular the prevention, detection and prosecution of crime, including the protection of minors, as well as tackling incitement to hatred on grounds of sex, race, religion or nationality, or violation of individual dignity;

– protection of public health;

– public security, national security and defence;

– protection of consumers, including investors.

The Directive requires that reliance on one of the foregoing grounds of derogation be "necessary";[25] that the threat posed be either an actual one or one that presents a "serious and grave" risk;[26] and furthermore that the measures adopted by the concerned state be "proportionate".[27] It is reasonable to conclude that where a Member State does intend to rely on this derogation mechanism in order to restrict an Information Society Service, the European Court of Justice (ECJ)(and indeed the national courts) will construe the grounds of derogation strictly against the State. In EC jurisprudence, derogations from free movement are typically strictly construed in order to prevent States from making excessive use of derogation grounds, or making disproportionate or discriminatory responses to "threats" emanating from activities of traders in other Member State territories, *i.e.*, the response of the State must not be disproportionate to the threat. A perusal of freedom of services/establishment ECJ case law will readily bear this out and it is not proposed to go over this well-worn terrain here.[28]

---

[25] Art. 3(a)(i).

[26] Art. 3(a)(ii).

[27] Art. 3(a)(iii).

[28] *e.g.* Case 205/84 *Commission v. Germany* [1986] E.C.R. 3755; Case C–180/89 *Commission v. Italy* [1991] E.C.R. I–709; Case 33/72 *Van Binsbergen v. B.M.M.* [1974] E.C.R. 1299; Case 279/80 *Criminal Proceedings against Webb* [1981] E.C.R. 3305.

9.(4)(a)(ii) Obligation to request other Member State to act /unilateral action

Before a Member State can rely on derogation grounds, it must first ask the other Member State to take measures, and can only act if any such measures (if taken) prove inadequate. Should this be the case, the Directive further obliges the concerned State to notify both the Commission and the other Member State of its intention to take measures itself. This obligation to notify the other Member State first does not prevent the concerned State from taking preliminary measures in the courts or proceeding with a preliminary criminal investigation, but it does oblige the concerned State to try and get the other Member State to bring the Information Society Services provider into line. This reflects the principle of co-operation that is evident in various provisions of the Directive.

Notwithstanding the foregoing, the Directive further provides that a Member State can short-circuit this procedure by, in cases of "urgency", taking measures itself without first approaching the other State. In this event, the concerned State must notify the measures it has adopted to the Commission and the other state within the "shortest possible time" and indicate the reasons for such urgent action.[29] The Commission is obliged to examine the notified measures within the "shortest possible time" and can ask the State to refrain from adopting/continuing such measures or to bring them to an end.[30]

9.(5) HOW DOES ONE DECIDE IN WHICH MEMBER STATE THE INFORMATION SERVICE PROVIDER IS BASED, OR TO USE THE PROPER TERM, "ESTABLISHED"?

This is an important question, because under the Article 3.1 home State supervision principle, each Member State is obliged to ensure that the Information Society Services provided by a service provider established on its territory comply with the *national provisions* applicable in that Member State, *i.e.*, the co-ordinated field, which governs the taking up and pursuit of an Information Society Service within that territory.

9.(5)(a) "Established service provider"

The Directive[31] defines the "established service provider" as being a service provider who effectively pursues an economic activity using a fixed establishment for an indefinite period. What is interesting about this definition is that it explicitly provides that "the presence and use of the technical means and

---

[29] Art. 4(5).
[30] Art. 4(6).
[31] Art. 2(c).

technologies required to provide the service do not, in themselves, constitute an establishment of the provider." In other words, the place of establishment of an Information Society Services provider is not where its servers or technology supporting its website is located, or even the place where its website is located.[32] It is quite clear from the Directive that the place of establishment is the place where the services provider carries on its economic activities for an indefinite period from a fixed place of business. This can be constituted by the place where the services provider is incorporated (its seat).[33] In the event that a services provider has several places of establishment, it will be necessary to establish which place of establishment is most closely associated with the particular Information Society Service in issue. The Directive acknowledges that this may not be an easy matter to determine, and so, as guidance the Recitals declare that it is the place where the service provider has the centre of its activities relating to the particular Information Society Service.[34]

Once a service provider is deemed to be established in a Member State, then that Member State is obliged by Article 3 of the Directive to ensure that any Information Society Services sourced at that place of establishment come under its supervision in accordance with the Article 3.1 home State supervision principle and the co-ordinated field requirements of that State. The Recitals exhort the Member State to take into account, in its supervision duties, not only the protection of its own citizens, but also all EU citizens.

While the provisions of the Directive which are relevant in this regard, *i.e.*, Articles 3 and 4, are silent on this issue, paragraph 22 of the Recitals does further provide that: "in order to effectively guarantee freedom to provide services and legal certainty for suppliers and recipients of services, such information society services should in principle be subject to the law of the Member State in which the service provider is established." While this is all very well in the present context, it is also suggested that there is a further more contentious context to this statement, *i.e.*, the intention that Information Society Services should only be subject to the law of the State of origin of the services, and that this may lead to displacement of the rules of private international law on choice.

In this writer's view, until this issue is resolved confusion will result (particularly in view of Article 1 of the Directive which states, *inter alia*, that the Directive does not establish any new rules of private international law) as the Directive, if given the wider interpretation set out above, will clearly be in conflict with the Brussels Regulation.[35]

---

[32] Preamble para. 19 specifically so states.

[33] *ibid.*

[34] *ibid.*

[35] The Brussels Convention is now reformulated in the form of the "Brussels Regulation", namely Regulation 44/2001 on Jurisdiction and Enforcement of Judgments (2001) O.J. L12/1. The Brussels Regulation provides that a consumer is free to sue in their home State, where an undertaking directs activities at the consumer from outside the State. However,

9.(6) PRINCIPLE OF TRANSPARENCY

The Directive seeks to strike a balance by requiring that certain information be furnished by service providers to service recipients. Several illustrations of this now follow.

9.(6)(a) General information to be provided

While Community law may require certain information to be supplied to recipients of services pursuant to various Directives, the Directive itself requires, at a minimum,[36] certain information to be made available by a service provider of Information Society Services to both recipients and competent authorities on a "directly and permanently accessible basis". The minimum requirements are:

– service provider name;

– geographic address where the service provider is established;

– service provider email address;

– trade register details (where applicable);

– supervisory authority contact details (where applicable);

– VAT number;

– Prices, where indicated, must be expressly inclusive or exclusive of taxes and delivery costs.

9.(6)(b) "Regulated Professions"

For Information Society Services providers who are also members of "regulated professions"[37] there are further requirements, namely that they must provide details of:

– professional title and Member State where title was obtained;

– professional body with which service provider is registered;

– reference to applicable professional rules and means of access to them.

---

while admittedly the matter is far from clear, this may potentially conflict with the E–Commerce Directive which can be interpreted to mean that the consumer should have to institute suit in the jurisdiction where the service provider is established: see further n.4 and accompanying text in the Introduction above.

[36] Art. 5.1.

[37] Within meaning of Art 1(d) of Dir. 89/48 (on a general system for recognition of higher education diplomas awarded upon completion of professional education and three-year

9.(7) COMMERCIAL COMMUNICATIONS

The Directive defines "commercial communications" as being any form of communication designed to promote, directly or indirectly, the goods, services or image of a company, organisation or person pursuing a commercial, industrial or craft activity or exercising a regulated profession.[38]

The Directive requires that where Information Society Services providers either provide communications which constitute an Information Society Service or which are part of such, then apart from any other EC law information or transparency requirements,[39] the Directive itself requires certain information to be divulged at a minimum:[40]

- It must be clear that the communication is a commercial communication;

- The identity of the natural or legal person on whose behalf the communication is made must be stated;

- Promotional offers or promotional games or competitions must be clearly identifiable as such.

9.(7)(a) Regulated professions & commercial communications

So far as regulated professions are concerned, the Directive makes special provision in order to remove barriers to the development of cross-border Information Society Services provided by members of regulated professions.[41] Member States must ensure that where commercial communications form part of Information Society Services provided by members of a regulated profession, then the professional rules of that profession must be complied with, in particular, rules pertaining to the dignity of the profession, its independence, and rules pertaining to professional secrecy, and fairness towards clients and other members of that profession. The Directive exhorts the Member States and Commission to encourage the professional bodies to establish codes of conduct at Community level in order to determine the types

---

training period) or 1(f) of Dir. 92/51 (on a second general system for the recognition of professional education and training (supplementing Dir 89/48)).

[38] Art. 2(f). The following are excluded from the definition: (i) information allowing direct access to the company, organisation or person, *e.g.*, domain name or email address; (ii) communication about the goods, services or image of the company, organisation or person, where compiled in an independent manner.

[39] Such as those in Dir. 97/7 (on the protection of consumers in respect of distance contracts) and Dir. 98/43 (on the approximation of laws of the Member States relating to advertising and sponsorship of tobacco products)(as mentioned in Recital para. 29).

[40] Art. 6.

[41] Art. 8(4) provides that the Directive shall apply in addition to Directives which concern access to, and exercise of, regulated professions' activities.

of information that can be given. The Commission is given the power to draw up Community initiatives should it be necessary to do so.[42]

9.(7)(b) Unsolicited commercial communications

Article 7.1 provides that, in addition to other EC Law regimes which inhibit unsolicited communications,[43] Member States which permit receipt of unsolicited commercial communications must ensure that such services provided by a service provider established in the State's territory shall be clearly and unambiguously identifiable as such as soon as received by the recipient. Where a Member State does permit unsolicited commercial communications by email, the Directive provides that Member States shall take measures to ensure that service providers engaging in such activity consult regularly, and respect opt-out registers used by natural persons.

It is significant to note that the Directive does not regulate the issue of consumer consent to unsolicited communication *per se*. This is significant because in permitting unsolicited commercial communication to fall outside the Article 3.1 and 3.2 home State/co-ordinated field principle,[44] the Member States can effectively continue to set their own requirements in this area, rather than having to adhere to a harmonised or common principled approach.

9.(8) AMENDMENT OF MEMBER STATE LAW TO FACILITATE CONTRACTS CONCLUDED BY ELECTRONIC MEANS

Article 9 obliges Member States to ensure that their legal systems allow electronic conclusion of contracts. What is the extent of this obligation? It appears that it is confined to the removal of legal obstacles in the Member States' legal systems, but not practical obstacles[45] to the conclusion of contracts by electronic means. So far as legal obstacles are concerned, the Directive requires their systematic removal from national legislation,[46] and stipulates that national legal requirements cannot either deprive electronically concluded contracts of effectiveness nor create obstacles for their use.[47]

---

[42] Art. 8(3).
[43] *i.e.* other EC legislation such as Dirs. 97/7 (on consumer protection in distance contracts) and 97/66 (processing of personal data and protection of privacy in the telecommunications sector which restricts unsolicited telephone calls and faxes) which have addressed the question of consent.
[44] Art. 3.3 which, via the Annex, provides that unsolicited commercial communications by email fall outside the home State/Co-ordinated Field mechanism. According to Recital para. 30, this issue of recipient consent is already dealt with in Dirs. 97/7 and 97/66.
[45] Recitals para. 37.
[46] Recitals para. 34.
[47] Art. 9(1).

It appears that of particular concern are national rules on the form a contract may take, and the Recitals[48] to the Directive require Member States to pay particular attention to this area when removing obstacles.[49]

9.(8)(a) Excluded contracts

Article 9.2 provides a number of situations where Member States have a discretion to exclude certain or all contracts in a number of areas from the requirement that electronic conclusion of contracts be capable and effective and valid under national law:

– Contracts that create or transfer rights in real estate, except for rental rights;[50]

– Contracts requiring by law the involvement of the courts, public authorities or professions exercising public authority;

– Contracts of suretyship granted, and on collateral securities furnished, by persons acting outside their trade, business or profession;

– Contracts governed by family law or succession.[51]

Member States are required to indicate to the Commission those categories that they have chosen to exclude from the regime.[52]

---

[48] Recitals para. 34.

[49] In this regard, s.9 of the Electronic Commerce 2000 Act provides that information (including information incorporated by reference) shall not be denied legal effect, validity or enforceability solely on the grounds that it is wholly or partly in electronic form, whether as an electronic communication or otherwise; s.19 provides that: (1) An electronic contract shall not be denied legal effect, validity or enforceability solely on the grounds that it is wholly or partly in electronic form, or has been concluded wholly or partly by way of an electronic communication; (2) In the formation of a contract, an offer, acceptance of an offer or any related communication (including any subsequent amendment, cancellation or revocation of the offer or acceptance of the offer) may, unless otherwise agreed between the parties, be communicated by means of an electronic communication.

[50] For a very interesting critique of how s.10 of the Electronic Commerce Act 2000 conflicts with the apparent intention underlying the potential for Member States to exclude contracts concerning real estate, except rental rights, see Brennan, "Trouble down the Line", *Law Society Gazette*, June 2001, pp.18–25 – effectively, it would appear that contracts for the sale of land were permitted by the Directive to be excluded (if Member States so wished) in order that consumers be protected from the hazard of entering into binding contracts for the purchase of land without adequate protection. According to that author, this risk has been aggravated by the choice of words used in s.10, which it is argued, may permit the conclusion of very onerous contracts by electronic mail to the detriment of consumers.

[51] Section 10(1)(a) of the Electronic Commerce Act 2000 is consistent with this requirement in so far as it excludes wills, trusts and enduring powers of attorney from the scope of the 2000 Act.

[52] In the case of contracts requiring, by law, the involvement of the courts, public authorities or professions exercising public authority, Member States are required to justify to the Commission every 5 years why they consider it necessary to continue such exclusion (Art. 9.3); s. 10 permits the Minister for Public Enterprise to bring any sector excluded by s. 10 into the electronic realm if technology has advanced to such an extent and adequate procedures have developed and the public interest so warrants.

9.(8)(b) Obligation to provide information prior to contract

It is important to note that the Directive does not harmonise Member States' laws on the issue of when a contract has come into effect. However, what the Directive does is require the Information Society Services provider, prior to the order being placed by the service recipient, to provide certain minimum information[53] (in addition to information required by other EC legislation), on matters such as:

– the different technical steps to follow in order to conclude the contract;

– whether the contract will be filed by the service provider or not, and whether it will be accessible;

– the technical means for identifying and correcting input errors prior to the placing of the order;

– the languages offered for the conclusion of the contract.[54]

However, dramatically, Article 10.4 provides, *inter alia*, that contracts concluded exclusively by exchange of electronic mail or equivalent communication are excluded from the above minimum information obligation. This may pose a great danger to consumers as typically the vendor of a product or service will load the contract in their favour and there is a danger that the consumer may have contracted unwittingly.

It is further provided that contract terms and general conditions provided to the recipient must be available in a form that allow their storage and reproduction by the recipient.[55] Member States must also ensure that where service providers subscribe to a code of conduct, the service provider provides the recipient with information on how these codes may be consulted electronically.[56]

9.(8)(c) Placing of the order

Member States must ensure that where the service recipient places their order through technological means, that (a) the service provider has to acknowledge the receipt of the order by electronic means, and (b) the order and acknowledgment are deemed to be received when the parties to whom they are addressed are able to access them.[57] Similarly, the service provider must make an effective and accessible technical means of correcting errors available to the service recipient prior to the placing of the order.[58] Contracts concluded

---

[53] Though this may be waived by service recipients who are not "consumers".
[54] Art. 10.1.
[55] Art. 10.3.
[56] Art. 10.2 – this obligation may be waived where the service recipient is not a consumer.
[57] Parties who are not consumers can agree to opt out of these requirements.
[58] Parties who are not consumers can agree to opt out of these requirements.

exclusively via email or equivalent communication are excluded from all of
the foregoing regime, apart from requirement (b).[59]

9.(9) LIABILITY OF INTERMEDIARY SERVICE PROVIDERS

The Directive provides[60] that where a service provider is "conduiting", *i.e.*
providing access to a communication network, or where an Information
Society Service is provided over a communications network where such
service consists of the transmission of information provided by a recipient of
a service, then the service provider will not be liable for the information
transmitted provided the service provider does not select or modify the
information or have anything to do with selecting the recipient of the
transmission or its initiation. In other words, where the service provider is
merely providing the technical means to make the transmission possible, and
does not have anything active to do with the content of the transmission, then
liability cannot arise merely on account of the service provider being a passive
transmitter of the information. Similarly, with "caching", meaning the
automatic, intermediate and temporary storage of information, the service
provider is not liable on account of mere caching.[61]

Of course, liability does not arise for mere "conduiting" or mere "caching"
under the Directive's definition of those terms, but this does not preclude
Member State courts or administrative authorities from granting injunctions to
require the termination or prevention of infringements.[62] Where an Information
Society Service is provided which consists of a service provider storing information provided by a service recipient ("hosting"), service provider liability
cannot arise merely on account of such hosting provided the service provider does
not have actual knowledge of illegal activity or information, and upon becoming
so aware, acts quickly to remove or disable access to the information.

The Directive is similar to the U.S. legislation in this area[63] in that it
employs similar concepts and terminology (hosting, caching, conduiting, etc.),
though it does not, unlike the U.S. legislation, refer to exemption from liability
where service providers are linking to material in infringement of copyright.[64]

---

[59] Art. 11.3.
[60] Art. 12.
[61] Art. 13, though in the case of caching, the conditions required to be satisfied in order for the
exemption to apply are more onerous than in the case of conduiting: see further Art. 13.
[62] Arts. 12.3 and 13.2 respectively.
[63] The Digital Millenium Copyright Act 1998 Pub. L. No. 105–304, 1132 Stat. 2860 (1998).
[64] While the proposed Copyright Directive will provide service providers with some degree of
protection from copyright owners, Yakobson, "Copyright Liability of Online Service
Providers" (2000) Ent.L.R. 144 points out at p.150 that the Electronic Commerce Directive
immunity from liability provisions are deficient and that it would be would be appropriate to
extend service providers immunity from liability to this area, *i.e.* protection against copyright

9.(9)(a) Hyperlinks /notice and take-down

The Directive does not cater for the issue of whether there should be exemption of service provider liability *vis-à-vis* hyperlinks, or develop notice and take-down procedures. It is envisaged that such matters will be dealt with in future Directives.[65]

This has been criticised as being "an urgent matter to focus on for it leaves the new legislation bare of effective instructions for a unified and standard approach to [copy]right owners' concerns."[66] However, notwithstanding that the Directive has covered some of the issues concerning liability of service providers (as described immediately above, *i.e.*, caching, hosting and conduiting), paragraph 40 of the Recitals declares that the Directive's liability provisions should not preclude the development and technical operation by different interested parties of technical systems of protection and identification and of technical surveillance instruments made possible by digital technology within the limits laid down by Directives 95/46 (on the protection of individuals with regard to the processing of personal data and its free movement) and 97/66 (concerning the processing of personal data and the protection of privacy in the telecommunications sector).

9.(10) No general obligation on service providers to monitor information

While Member States shall not impose a general obligation on service providers to monitor the information they transmit or store, nor a general obligation to seek facts or circumstances indicating illegal activity, nevertheless the Directive does permit Member States to establish rules under which service providers must promptly inform the relevant authorities of alleged illegal activities undertaken, or reported, by recipients of services.[67]

9.(11) Codes of conduct

Member States and the Commission are to encourage trade, consumer and professional associations to draw up codes of conduct at Community level

---

infringement, in a manner similar to that in the U.S. legislation, the DMCA 1998. That author also proposes a similar exemption for educational institutions which provide online services and are exposed to liability due to infringing conduct of third parties who have access to their facilities.

[65] Art. 21.
[66] Yakobson, above n.64, at p.151 proposes that either the Directive be amended to cater for this concern, or alternatively, that codes of conduct be drawn up, and following their successful use, be incorporated into future EC legislation.
[67] Art. 15.

designed to contribute to the proper implementation of the Directive.[68] This, however, is a voluntary regime. They are also to encourage the involvement of consumer associations in this process.[69] While this is all very exhortatory, more concrete obligation is provided for in the case of associations representing the visually impaired and disabled – the Directive provides that they "should be consulted" to take account of "their specific need" "where appropriate".[70]

On the whole, the code of conduct regime is not a mandatory one as the Directive's language does not envisage the adoption of codes as a mandatory obligation, though there is nothing to prevent Member States so imposing. However, what is proposed is that codes be drawn up by the interested parties (as mentioned above), and that draft codes of conduct, whether at national or EC level, be voluntarily transmitted to the Commission.[71] The codes must be accessible electronically and those who draw up codes of conduct must give their assessment of the application of their codes to the Member States and the Commission. The aspiration to draw up codes of conduct is not confined to any particular area, though specific mention is made of the need to draw up codes of conduct regarding the protection of minors and human dignity.[72]

9.(12) ALTERNATIVE DISPUTE RESOLUTION

The Directive obliges Member States to ensure that national law does not inhibit the use of out-of-court dispute resolution methods where a dispute arises between an Information Society Service provider and a service recipient. Also, Member States are to ensure that nothing in national law will inhibit the use of electronic means of effecting alternative dispute resolution.

9.(13) COURT ACTIONS

Recognising that damage caused in connection with Information Society Services is characterised by both rapidity and geographical extent,[73] Member States are to ensure that rapid remedies are available for the adoption of measures designed to terminate alleged infringements, and are to explore the need for access to judicial procedures by electronic means.[74] The Directive also brings itself within the regime set out in Directive 98/27 which provides

---

[68] This echoes the approach taken at EU level, namely, the *Action Plan on Promoting Safer Use of the Internet* (Council Decision 276/1999 O.J. (1999) L. 33).
[69] Art. 16.2.
[70] Art. 16.2.
[71] Art. 16.1(b).
[72] Art. 16.1(e).
[73] Recitals para. 52.
[74] Art 18.

for injunctions to be sought where the collective interests of consumers are under threat.

In exhorting the Member States to provide effective judicial remedies, the Directive operates without prejudice to remedies that may already exist under national law. Article 20 of the Directive leaves the Member States free to determine what sanctions shall apply under national legislation adopted to implement the Directive. While the Directive does not require criminal sanctions to be provided under national law, though Member States are permitted to adopt such course if they so wish,[75] the Directive does require sanctions to be "effective, proportionate and dissuasive." Traditionally, in its case law on remedies for breach of EC obligations, Member States have been brought to book by the ECJ where the principles of effectiveness and proportionality have not been respected by the Member States when providing remedies. While it is not proposed to cover such case law here,[76] suffice it to say that there is no reason why the ECJ's traditional approach would be modified if faced with a Member State remedy that was not effective, or one which violated the principle of proportionality under EC law.

9.(14) Regimes which the Directive professes not to affect

The Directive's application to Information Society Services is stated in the Preamble to be without prejudice to existing EC laws in areas such as consumer protection and public health legislation.[77] National laws which implement such EC laws are similarly unaffected provided they do not restrict the freedom to provide Information Society Services.[78]

Usefully, the Recitals set out a large (though non-exhaustive) number of Directives whose regimes are not prejudiced by the enactment of the Directive, including:

Council Directive 93/13 Unfair Contract Terms in Consumer Contracts; Parliament & Council Directive 97/7 on Consumer Protection in Distance Selling Contracts; Council Directive 84/450 on Misleading Advertising;

---

[75] Recitals para. 52.

[76] *e.g.* Case 14/83 *Von Colson & Kamann v. L.N.F.* [1984] ECR 1891; Case 80/86 *Criminal Proceedings against Kolpinghuis Nijmegin* BV [1987] ECR 3969; Case 106/89 *Marleasing SA v. La Comercial Internationale de Alimentacion SA* [1990] ECR I–4135. For a detailed discussion on effectiveness see above Keville, chap.1.

[77] Article 1.3 and Recital para 11. On the rights of the Irish consumer see above Ní Shúilleabháin, chap. 8.

[78] Art 1.3; s. 15 of the Electronic Commerce Act 2000 provides that all electronic contracts within the Member States shall be subject to all existing consumer law and the role of the Director of Consumer Affairs in such legislation shall apply equally to consumer transactions, whether conducted electronically or non-electronically.

Council Directive 87/102 on Approximation of Member State Consumer Credit Laws; Council Directive 93/22 on Investment Services in the Securities Field; Council Directive 90/314 on Package Holidays; Council Directive 85/374 on Liability for Defective Products; Parliament & Council Directive 98/43 on Approximation of Laws relating to advertising and sponsorship of tobacco products.[79]

9.(14)(a) Private international law

Article 1.4 provides that the Directive does not establish additional rules on private international law, nor does it deal with the jurisdiction of the courts. However, as noted earlier, in the Introduction (and also footnote 4), pending clarification, there may be potential for conflict between the Directive and the private international law Brussels Regulation regime on the appropriate forum for suit. This matter awaits clear resolution.

9.(15) EXCLUDED FIELDS (ARTICLE 1)

The Directive also refers to several areas in which it cannot apply:

(a) Taxation: the Recitals to the Directive[80] state that the Directive does not aim to establish rules on fiscal obligations nor does it pre-empt the drawing up of Community instruments concerning fiscal aspects of electronic commerce. It is also made clear that VAT issues arising out of the provision of Information Society Services is not a concern of the Directive, and may be dealt with by other separate instruments.

(b) Processing of Personal Data within the ambit of Directives 95/46 (on the protection of individuals with regard to the processing of personal data and its free movement) and 97/66 (concerning the processing of personal data and protection of privacy in the telecommunications sector): questions relating to Information Society Services that are already covered by Directives 95/46 and 97/66 fall outside the scope of the Directive. The Recitals[81] provide that these two Directives (the former which concerns the protection of individuals with regard to the processing of personal data and its free movement, and the latter which concerns the processing of personal data and protection of privacy in telecommunications) establish an EC legal framework, and so the Directive should not intrude on such areas. In support of this delineation, the Recitals continue by providing that when Member States go about implementing the Directive, they should ensure that in its application it respects the

---

[79] For a description of many of these Directives see above McDermott, para 7(2).
[80] Paras. 12 & 13.
[81] Para. 14.

principles of the aforementioned two regimes, in particular ensuring that the prohibition on interception or surveillance by third parties, by means of any kind, of communications whose confidentiality is guaranteed in accordance with Directive 97/66,[82] is respected except where legally authorised.

(c) Issues arising out of the application of cartel law.

(d) Information Society Services which consist of:

   – the activities of notaries or equivalent professions to the extent that they involve a direct and specific connection with the exercise of official authority;
   – the representation of a client and defence of a client's interests before the courts;
   – gambling activities which involve wagering a stake with monetary value in games of chance, including lotteries and betting transactions; however, promotional competitions or games whose purpose is to encourage the sale of goods and where payments (if they arise) serve only to acquire the promoted goods or service, are not within this excluded field.[83]

(e) Measures taken at EC level (or national level in respect of EC law obligations) which seek to promote cultural or linguistic diversity, or pluralism.

Finally, although not mentioned as such in the Directive, service providers established in Third Countries are discussed in Recital 58. It provides that they fall outside the scope of the Directive, but that the EC's aim is to develop rules that are harmonious with international rules.

9.(16) CO-OPERATION

Member States are obliged to co-operate with each other.[84] For this purpose, they are to appoint "contact points" in order to liaise with other Member States and the Commission. Furthermore, these contact points must be accessible electronically by both service providers and service recipients, and be in a position to give general information on contractual rights and obligations as well as on the complaint and redress mechanisms available in the event of disputes.

---

[82] Para. 15.
[83] Para. 16
[84] Art. 19.

9.(17) THE FUTURE

It is clear from the Directive that it is only a starting point in the area of harmonisation of Member State laws. Article 21 obliges the Commission, on or before July 17, 2003 to submit to the European Parliament, the Council and the Economic and Social Committee a report on the application of the Directive, as well as a proposal for adapting it to legal, technical and economic developments in the field of Information Society Services.

In particular, issues that are yet to be resolved include the liability of:

– providers of hyperlinks and location tool services;

– notice and take-down procedures of illegal or contentious content;[85]

– attribution of liability following take-down of content.

Also to be considered are:

– whether additional conditions require to be provided for service provider liability regarding mere conduiting or caching;[86]

– whether the regime on unsolicited commercial communications requires incorporation into the internal market regime.[87]

Finally, the domestic implementation of the Directive in Ireland, while partially effected by the Electronic Commerce Act 2000, awaits the adoption of Ministerial Regulations. At the time of writing these are overdue.

---

[85] Recital para. 40 provides that the Directive should provide the basis for the "development of rapid and reliable procedures for removing and disabling access to illegal information" and it is envisaged that such development would take place on a voluntary basis.

[86] Arts 12 and 13.

[87] Art. 7.

BIBLIOGRAPHY

Brennan, "Trouble down the Line", *Law Society Gazette*, June 2001, 18.

Coleman, "The Irish Electronic Commerce Bill", *Commercial Law Practitioner*, 2000, 139.

Davies, "Electronic Commerce – Practical Implications of Internet Legislation", *Communications Law*, vol 3, no. 3, 1998, 82.

De Foestraets, "E-Commerce – a new European Legal Framework", *International Business Lawyer*, October 2000, 389.

Fenn, "Review of recent EU Legislative Developments", EBL February 2000, 4.

Goodger, "Legal Issues of E-Commerce: Some Current Practical Issues", *IT Law Today*, October 2000, 7.

Long, "European Rules for Financial Services Providers" EBL April 2000, 6

Mullany, "Legal Aspects of Electronic Contracts in Ireland", *E-Journal*, December 2000, 10.

Yakobson, "Copyright Liability of Online Service Providers" (2000) Ent.L.R. 144.

10. FREE MOVEMENT OF GOODS

JAMES McDERMOTT*

10.(1) INTRODUCTION

One of the foundation stones of the Single Market is provided by Article 28 (ex. Article 30) of the EC Treaty, which prohibits Member States from using quantitative restrictions to impede the free flow of goods within the European Community (EC). It is, therefore, aimed at eliminating non-fiscal barriers to trade and states that: "Quantitative restrictions on imports and all measures having equivalent effect shall be prohibited between Member States."[1]

It is obvious that a quota system, which prohibits imports above a certain level, will impede trade between Member States. The concept of a measure having equivalent effect to a quantitative restriction (MEQR) is one which has been utilised by the European Court of Justice (ECJ) in numerous cases to prohibit various schemes which would distort natural trade patterns. The best statement of the scope of Article 28 was provided in the *Dassonville* decision when the ECJ stated that it will forbid as a MEQR: "All trading rules enacted by Member States which are capable of hindering, directly or indirectly, actually or potentially, intra-Community trade."[2]

The ECJ has made it clear that it is the effect of the trading rule rather than its actual form that is of crucial importance in establishing that a MEQR is present which is likely to impede market integration. There are a great variety of cases in which it has examined trading rules which have the effect of discriminating between domestic and imported goods. This chapter will consider how the ECJ has dealt with one major kind of discrimination, namely where Member States have actively sought to promote domestically-produced goods at the expense of goods produced in other Member States. It will look in particular at three types of activity, namely state-supported campaigns to promote domestic goods, rules on origin-marking of goods and public procurement procedures.

---

* James Mc Dermott B.C.L., LL.M., Barrister-at-law. Tutor in the Law Faculty, University College Dublin. Any errors remain the responsibility of the author.
[1] In addition, Art. 29 (ex. Art.34) prohibits quantitative restrictions on exports.
[2] [1974] E.C.R. 837, 852.

10.(2) STATE-FUNDED PROMOTIONS

The most blatant example of State promotion of domestic produce occurs when the State actively seeks to directly or indirectly promote the purchase of domestically-produced goods. In *Commission v. Ireland (Buy Irish)*[3] the ECJ examined the legality of a "Buy Irish" campaign which had been launched by the Irish Government in the hope that it would create an additional ten thousand fulltime jobs in Ireland by encouraging Irish consumers and manufacturers to buy Irish rather than imported goods. At the launch of the scheme, the then Minister for Industry, Commerce and Energy stated that the aim of the campaign was to achieve "a switch from imports to Irish products equivalent to 3% of total consumer spending".[4]

The campaign had several different strands to it. First, a "Guaranteed Irish" symbol was created which could be attached to products made in Ireland. This would encourage Irish consumers to look for and purchase products bearing this symbol, which they knew had been produced domestically. Secondly, a limited company known as the Irish Goods Council was established to run the campaign. This Council had its management committee appointed by the Minister and was financed by subsidies received from both the State and the private sector. The Council would organise publicity campaigns and print literature in favour of Irish products and would make exhibition facilities under its control available exclusively to domestic producers. Thirdly, a "shoplink" service was established which provided information to consumers free of charge on what Irish goods were available and where they could be obtained.

An infringement action was initiated by the European Commission under Article 226 (ex Art.169) seeking a declaration that by organising a campaign to promote the sale and purchase of Irish products in its territory, Ireland had failed to fulfil its obligations under the EC Treaty. The Irish Government attempted to defend the validity of the "Buy Irish" campaign on several grounds. First, they argued that it did not come within the ambit of Article 28 as it was not a campaign of the Irish State but merely one being organised by a private company. The ECJ accepted that the prohibition in Article 28 is limited to the actions of public authorities. However, as the Irish Government was active in providing a significant part of the funding for the Irish Goods Council, as well as appointing its board members and defining the aims and outlines of the campaigns that it ran, there was enough state involvement to bring it within the ambit of Article 28.

Secondly, the Irish government argued that for a measure to be caught within the definition of an MEQR, it must involve binding provisions issued by a public authority. The "Buy Irish" campaign was not binding in that it

---

[3] Case 249/81 [1982] E.C.R. 4005.
[4] *ibid.* 4007.

merely encouraged consumers to purchase domestically-produced goods, it did not force them to do so. The ECJ, however, preferred to give a much broader definition to an MEQR and held that it could catch state actions which were of persuasive rather than binding effect. What was important was the fact that the campaign reflected the Irish Government's "considered intention to substitute domestic products for imported products on the Irish market and thereby to check the flow of imports from other Member States."[5]

The third justification put forward by the Irish Government was based on statistics which showed that the "Buy Irish" campaign had not been successful. Trade figures showed that the percentage of imports sold in Ireland had risen during the period of the campaign. In other words, the attempt to boost the sales of domestic products had been a failure. Not surprisingly this argument was also rejected by the Court who pointed out that the *Dassonville* formula prohibits all schemes capable of hindering trade, regardless of their actual effect. The statistics produced by the Irish Government were not able to rule out the possibility that the level of imports into Ireland would have been even higher were it not for the effects of their campaign.

The issue of state promotion of domestic produce was considered again by the ECJ in the *Apple and Pear Development Council*[6] case. This Council was set up under a United Kingdom statutory instrument[7] and had its members appointed by the Minister of Agriculture, Fisheries and Food. It had a range of functions to promote and carry out research into the apple and pear industry. Its activities were financed by a levy paid by the growers of these products. The principle activities of the Council financed by the levy were advertising, promotion and publicity and included both television and press advertising and in-store merchandising and promotional material. Such advertising promoted varieties grown in England and Wales such as Cox and Bramley apples and Conference pears and included slogans such as "polish up your English". The Council instituted civil proceedings for unpaid annual levies against three growers who counter-claimed for all sums they had previously paid to the Council to be returned on the basis that the scheme discriminated against imported fruit in breach of Article 28.

The matter was referred to the ECJ for a preliminary ruling under Article 234 (ex. Art.177), which, referring to *Commission v. Ireland*, made it quite clear that the freedom of public authorities to promote the consumption of domestic produce was severely limited:

> "As the Court held in its judgement in *Commission v. Ireland* a publicity campaign to promote the sale and purchase of domestic products may, in certain circumstances, fall within the prohibition contained in Article 30 [now

---

[5] *ibid.*, at 4022.
[6] Apple and Pear Development Council v. K.J. Lewis Ltd [1983] E.C.R. 4083.
[7] Apple and Pear Development Council Order of May 6, 1980 (S.I. 1980 No. 623).

Art. 28] of the Treaty, if the campaign is supported by the public authorities. In fact a body such as the Development Council, which is set up by the government of a Member State and is financed by a charge imposed on growers, cannot under Community law enjoy the same freedom as regards the methods of advertising used as that enjoyed by producers themselves or producers' associations of a voluntary character.

In particular such a body is under a duty not to engage in any advertising intended to discourage the purchase of products of other Member States or to disparage those products in the eyes of consumers. Nor must it advise consumers to purchase domestic products solely by reasons of their national origin."[8]

However, the Court made it clear that it was legitimate to promote a product by referring to its qualities even where the qualities in question were characteristic of national production. It stated: "On the other hand, Article 30 [now Art. 28] does not prevent such a body from drawing attention, in its publicity, to the specific qualities of fruit grown in the Member State in question or from organizing campaigns to promote the sale of certain varieties, mentioning their particular properties, even if those varieties are typical of national production."[9]

The Commission attempted to derive some general principles from these cases by issuing guidelines[10] in which they gave examples of promotional actions which clearly infringe Article 28 and others which are not open to objection under Article 28. The guidelines make it clear that when developing a campaign which refers to both the qualities of the product and also its origin, greater prominence should be given to the former rather than the latter:

"Identification of the producing country by word or symbol may be made by providing that a reasonable balance between references, on the one hand to the qualities and varieties of the product and, on the other hand, its national origin is kept. The references to national origin should be subsidiary to the main message put over to consumers by the campaign and not constitute the principal reason why consumers are being advised to buy the product."[11]

10.(3) ORIGIN MARKING

Article 28 also prohibits other state practices to promote the consumption of domestic goods. Member States have on occasion attempted to promote domestic goods by insisting that all goods clearly display their place of origin. Although such rules on their face apply equally to all goods (be they domestic or imported) they provide the consumer with the necessary information to discriminate in favour of domestically-produced goods.

---

8 [1982] E.C.R. 4005, 4119–4120.
9 *ibid.*, 4120.
10 Commission Guidelines for Member States' Involvement in Promotion of Agricultural and Fisheries Products, Article 30 Aspects (1986) O.J. C 272/3.
11 *ibid.*, at para. 2.3.1.

In *Commission v. United Kingdom*[12] the Court of Justice looked at the legitimacy of U.K. legislation[13] which prohibited the sale of certain goods[14] imported from other Member States unless they were marked with or accompanied by an indication of origin. The U.K. Government attempted to defend its legislation on two main grounds: first, the requirement of origin marking applied equally to all goods, and secondly, such information was a necessary part of consumer protection as consumers regard the origin of the goods which they buy as an indicator of their quality.

The Court rejected both these arguments and concluded that the legislation constituted an MEQR and was therefore prohibited by Article 28 of the Treaty. It had no doubt about the true purpose of origin-marking stating that: "[I]t has to be recognised that the purpose of indications of origin or origin-marking is to enable consumers to distinguish between domestic and imported products and that this enables them to assert any prejudices which they may have against foreign products."[15]

The argument that consumers regard information on the origin of goods as an indicator of quality was also rejected by the ECJ which pointed out that:

> "[I]f the national origin of goods brings certain qualities to the minds of consumers, it is in the manufacturers' interests to indicate it themselves on the goods or on their packaging and it is not necessary to compel them to do so. In that case, the protection of consumers is sufficiently guaranteed by rules which enable the use of false indications of origin to be prohibited. Such rules are not called into question by the EEC Treaty."[16]

It is clear, therefore, that mandatory origin-marking of goods will breach Article 28 in the vast majority of cases and will only be acceptable in very limited circumstances:

> "Member State legislation which contains rules on origin-marking will normally only be acceptable if the origin implies a certain quality in the goods, that they were made from certain materials or by a particular form of manufacturing, or where the origin is indicative of a special place in the folklore or tradition of the region in question."[17]

There is, however, nothing stopping manufacturers themselves deciding to attach indicators of origin if they believe that they can boost sales by so doing. In addition, Member States clearly have the right to take action to prevent false or inaccurate indicators of origin being placed on products.

---

[12] Case 207/83 [1985] E.C.R. 1201.
[13] Trade Descriptions (Origin Marking) (Miscellaneous Goods) Order 1981.
[14] Clothing and textile goods; domestic electrical appliances; footwear and cutlery.
[15] [1985] E.C.R. 1201 at 1211.
[16] *ibid.*, at 1212.
[17] Case 12/74 *Commission v. Germany* [1975] E.C.R. 181 and Case 113/80 *Commission v. Ireland (Irish Souvenirs)* [1981] E.C.R. 1625.

In *Commission v. Ireland (Irish Souvenirs)*[18] the ECJ considered the legality of Irish legislation[19] which it was alleged discriminated against imports. It required imported items of jewellery which possessed characteristics suggesting that they were souvenirs of Ireland (for example by being designed in the shape of a shamrock or wolfhound) to bear an indication of origin or use the word "foreign" or other words to clearly indicate that they were manufactured outside Ireland. Similar souvenirs produced in Ireland were not affected by the legislation.

The ECJ concluded that the legislation did infringe Article 28 as they imposed an extra burden on imports and thereby reduced their sales opportunities. The Irish Government had attempted to defend their legislation on the basis that it was aimed at consumer protection. As the legislation was on its face discriminatory against imports the defences available to the Irish Government were limited to those expressly outlined in Article 30 (ex. Art. 36) which do not include consumer protection. More general defences concerning the protection of economic interests are only available where the national measure which one is attempting to defend is equally applicable to both domestic and imported goods.

10.(5) Public Procurement

Another area in which the ECJ will prohibit discrimination in favour of domestic producers is in the area of public procurement. Preference should not be given to domestic tenders.

In *Commission v. Ireland (Dundalk Water Supply)*[20] the ECJ examined a possible violation of Article 28 by a local authority. The case concerned the fairness of the tendering process for the supply of water conducted by Dundalk Council. The specifications for the tender included a clause stipulating that the asbestos cement pipes to be used must be certified as complying with a national technical standard[21] which had been drafted by the Institute for Industrial Research and Standards. The awarding authority made it clear to prospective bidders that a tender which proposed to use Spanish pipes would not be acceptable despite the fact that these pipes did comply with international standards[22] and were suitable for the project.

The ECJ ruled that Ireland was guilty of breaching Article 28. The challenged clause prevented companies producing pipes equivalent to the Irish

---

[18] Case 113/80 [1981] E.C.R. 1625.
[19] Merchandise Marks (Restriction on Sale of Imported Jewellery) Order 1971 and the Merchandise Marks (Restriction on Importation of Jewellery) Order 1971.
[20] Case 45/87 [1988] E.C.R. 4929.
[21] Irish Standard Specification 188: 1975.
[22] In particular, with I.S.O. 160:1980 of the International Organisation for Standardization.

standard from entering the tendering process. The inclusion of this clause had the effect of restricting the supply of suitable pipes to Irish manufacturers alone.[23] By the simple measure of incorporating into the notice in question the words "or equivalent"[24] after the reference to the Irish standard, the Irish authorities could have verified compliance with the technical conditions necessary for the successful completion of the project without from the outset restricting the contract to those tenders proposing to utilise Irish materials. Whilst it may be acceptable to reject foreign-made pipes in individual cases where such pipes did not meet the requirements of the project, a blanket ban not related to quality was unacceptable.

In *Du Pont*[25] the ECJ gave a preliminary ruling concerning the validity of Italian rules under which a percentage of public supply contracts were reserved to undertakings located in the economically deprived South of Italy. The Court held that Article 28 of the Treaty prohibited national rules which reserved to undertakings established in particular regions of the national territory a proportion of public supply contracts. It was clear from the terms of the scheme that those undertakings who would lose out on the possibility of obtaining these contracts included not only non-Italian undertakings but also Italian undertakings not located in the southern part of the country. However, this was not enough to save the scheme as it was quite clear that all the undertakings which were going to gain under the scheme were Italian. The fact that the measure did not benefit all domestic producers but only some of them did not exempt it from the prohibition in Article 28. The Court stated that:

> "It must be emphasized in the first place that, although not all the products of the Member State in question benefit by comparison with products from abroad, the fact remains that all the products benefiting by the preferential system are domestic products; secondly, the fact that the restrictive effect exercised by a State measure on imports does not benefit all domestic products but only some cannot exempt the measure in question from the prohibition set out in Article 30 [now article 28]."[26]

In *Campus Oil*[27] the High Court was considering the legitimacy of Irish rules[28] which required the importers of petroleum products to purchase, at a price fixed by the Minister for Industry and Energy, a certain proportion of their requirements from a State-owned company which operated a refinery in Ireland. The scheme was challenged by an importer before the Irish courts

---

[23] Documents before the Court showed that only one company had been certified by the Institute of Industrial Research and Standards to I.S. 188:1975 and that undertaking was located in Ireland.

[24] As provided for by Directive 71/305; Case C–21/88 *DuPont de Nemours Italiana Spa v. Unita Sanitaria Locale No. 2 Di Carrara.*

[25] Case C–21/88 *DuPont de Nemours Italiana SpA v. Unità Sanitaria Locale No.2 di Carrara* [1990] E.C.R. I–889.

[26] *ibid.*, at 920.

[27] Case 72/83 *Campus Oil Limited v. Minister for Industry and Energy* [1984] E.C.R. 2727.

[28] Fuels (Control of Supplies) Order 1982.

who made a preliminary reference under Article 234. The ECJ found a clear breach of Article 28. In attempting to defend this breach the Irish Government sought to rely on the public security derogation. Without the guaranteed trade that this scheme ensured, there was a grave danger that the Whitegate Refinery (which was the only refinery in Ireland) would no longer be economically viable.

The Court did accept that the aim of ensuring a minimum supply of petroleum products at all time transcended purely economic interests and was, thus, capable of constituting an objective covered by the concept of public security in Article 30 of the Treaty. Concern about energy supplies could impinge upon national security, as energy supplies are vital for the very existence of the state. However, to rely successfully on Article 30 the Irish Government would have to show that the refinery would not be able to find purchasers for its output in a fully competitive market. In addition, the Court held that the amount of petroleum that an importer was obliged to buy should be no higher than necessary to keep the refinery in business.

The ECJ will look at the actual effect of the domestic practice and not merely its legal form when deciding whether a Member State has favoured domestic products over competing imports. This was made clear in *Commission v. France*.[29] That case concerned a French law which provided that all postal franking machines intended to be used in France must be approved. The law had previously discriminated against foreign machines in a blatant manner but had been changed as a result of intervention by the Commission. However, despite this revision a U.K. manufacturer alleged that, over a period of several years, they had been unable to obtain the necessary approval of the French postal authorities for their franking machines despite having obtained such approval in several other countries. The ECJ made it quite clear that a systematically unfavourable attitude towards imported machines was not acceptable and would not be allowed to hide behind a law which on its face did not discriminate:

> "The fact that a law or regulation such as that requiring prior approval for the marketing of postal franking machines conforms in formal terms to Article 30 [now Art. 28] of the EEC Treaty is not sufficient to discharge a Member State of its obligations under that provision. Under the cloak of a general provision permitting the approval of machines imported from other Member States, the administration might very well adopt a systematically unfavourable attitude towards imported machines, either by allowing considerable delay in replying to applications for approval or in carrying out the examination procedure, or by refusing approval on the grounds of various alleged technical faults for which no detailed explanations are given or which prove to be inadequate.

---

[29] Case 21/84 [1985] E.C.R. 1356.

The prohibition on measures having an effect equivalent to quantitative restrictions would lose much of its useful effect if it did not cover protectionist or discriminatory practices of that type."[30]

The Court went on to make it clear that for a practice to be caught in this manner under Article 28 then it would have to be shown that it was of general rather than sporadic application:

"It must however be noted that for an administrative practice to constitute a measure prohibited under Article 30 [now Art. 28] that practice must show a certain degree of consistency and generality. That generality must be assessed differently according to whether the market concerned is one in which there are numerous traders or whether it is a market, such as that in postal franking machines, on which only a few undertakings are active. In the latter case, a national administration's treatment of a single undertaking may constitute a measure incompatible with Article 30 [now Art. 28]."[31]

As Weatherill and Beaumount have observed:[32]

"Although it might prove difficult in practice to draw the demarcation between an isolated act that is not caught by Article 28 (ex. Article 30) and an established practice that is, the logic of this decision conforms to the Court's fundamental Dassonville formula. It is the effect of the legislation rather than its form that governs the legal response, and the French practices clearly exerted a restrictive effect on imported goods."

10.(6) CONCLUSION

The ECJ has adopted a strict approach towards attempts by Member States to discriminate in favour of their domestic products. Whilst the motives behind such discrimination may be understandable, if permitted it would undermine the attempts to create a single market. The strict approach has also been a necessary response to the often ingenious methods that Member States have engaged in to give their own products an advantage. The jurisprudence is relatively well settled at this stage but is likely to come under pressure again once new Member States are admitted to an enlarged EU.

---

[30] *ibid.*, at1364.
[31] *ibid.*, at 1364–65.
[32] Weatherill and Beaumont, EU Law (3rd ed.), p.511.

11. TRANSFER OF UNDERTAKINGS

CATHY MAGUIRE*

11.(1) INTRODUCTION

Directive 2001/23[1] provides for the protection of employees when the business in which they are employed changes hands. It provides for the automatic transfer of the employment relationship, together with concomitant rights and obligations; it protects employees from dismissal by reason of the transfer and it requires the transferor and the transferee to inform and consult with the employees affected by the transfer.

This chapter considers the manner in which the Irish legislature has sought to transpose the law in this area, and the manner in which Irish tribunals and courts have applied that law. It will be seen that the two are not always *ad idem*, and that it has been for the tribunals and courts to cure the apparent reluctance of the legislature to provide for the full protection of employees in this regard.[2]

11.(2) LEGISLATIVE HISTORY

The protections now contained in Directive 23/2001 were introduced by Directive 77/187 and subsequently amended by Directive 98/50. Directive 2001/23 is a consolidating Directive; it repealed and replaced Directive 77/187 as amended by Directive 98/50, without prejudice to the deadlines for transposition set out in those Directives.[3] Directive 77/187 was transposed into Irish law by the European Communities (Safeguarding of Employee Rights on a Transfer of Undertakings) Regulations 1980 (S.I. No. 306 of 1980), hereafter referred to as "the Regulations" and "S.I. No. 306 of 1980" interchangeably. While the Regulations have been

---

* Barrister-at-law. Any errors remain the responsibility of the author.
[1] Directive 2001/23 on the approximation of the laws of the Member States relating to the safeguarding of employees' rights in the event of transfers of undertakings, businesses or parts of undertakings or businesses.
[2] This chapter does not attempt to summarise the case law of the European Court of Justice (ECJ), or indeed the case law of Irish courts and tribunals. See Barnard, *EC Employment Law* (2000), chap. 7 for the former and McMullen, "Transfer of Undertakings – Perspectives from Britain and Ireland" (2000) *Irish Jurist* 83 for the latter.
[3] Directive 2001/23, Article 12.

amended with regard to the obligation to inform and consult,[4] so as to properly implement the requirements of Directive 77/187, the changes effected by Directive 98/50 have not yet been transposed into Irish law, in breach of the deadline of July 17, 2001.

The Regulations faithfully reproduced Directive 77/187. However, their major deficiency was that while they imposed obligations on employers and conferred rights on employees as required by that Directive, they did not provide for a civil remedy for breach of those obligations and rights; rather they provided only for criminal sanctions. Further, any offence was to be prosecuted by the Minister.

This failure to provide for a civil remedy was surprising, given that, when the Regulations were promulgated, there already existed an extensive statutory system for the vindication of employees' rights which might have been amended to provide a civil remedy for breach of the Regulations. In particular, the system provided by the Unfair Dismissals Act 1977 was ideally suited to providing vindication for employees dismissed in breach of the Regulations, yet was not amended in this regard.

It therefore appeared that employees were without any civil remedy for breach of their rights until the High Court clarified matters in *Mythen v. Employment Appeals Tribunal.*[5] Mr Mythen's employer was a limited liability company, Joseph Downes and Sons Limited. A debenture holder appointed a receiver over the assets of the company. The receiver negotiated the sale of a portion of the assets to another limited liability company, Buttercrust Limited. On the date of the sale, Mr Mythen's employment was terminated by reason of redundancy and he was subsequently paid his statutory redundancy and minimum notice payments. Buttercrust Limited re-employed a number of the employees who had been employed by Joseph Downes and Sons Limited in the portion of the business where Mr Mythen had worked. Mr Mythen referred a claim to the Employment Appeals Tribunal under the Unfair Dismissals Act 1977, naming both Joseph Downes and Sons Limited and Buttercrust Limited as respondents. When the matter came before the Tribunal, it declined to apply S.I. No. 306 of 1980:

> "In considering this case, the Tribunal notes that but for E.E.C. Directive No. 77/187 and consequent S.I. No. 306 of 1980, the position would have been quite clear. It could be stated clearly that the claimant's position terminated when Joseph Downes and Sons Limited ceased to carry on business and the claimant received redundancy payment and received a minimum notice award from the Tribunal. But for S.I. No. 306 of 1980 it could not be claimed that the claimant was an employee of Buttercrust Limited. The Tribunal has considered if the regulations have changed the position. The Tribunal considers Regulation 5 to be the relevant provision in this case. This appears to constitute

---

4   S.I. No. 487 of 2000.
5   [1990] 1 I.R. 98.

a fundamental change, if not overturning, of the common law provision in relation to who a new employer shall or shall not employ. However, it makes no express amendment of statute law. No reference is made in the regulations to the Employment Appeals Tribunal or to the Redundancy Payments Acts 1967 to 1979; the Minimum Notice and Terms of Employment Act 1973; the Unfair Dismissals Act 1977, or the Maternity (Protection of Employees) Act 1982. The Tribunal can only have expressed, not implied, powers. Accordingly, the claims fail."

Mr Mythen applied to the High Court by way of judicial review. Counsel on his behalf argued that the determination was bad on its face. While the determination recognised the overriding nature of the Directive and S.I. No. 306 of 1980, it failed to recognise that these instruments altered existing contracts of employment and created new employment relationships which the Tribunal had jurisdiction to, and was required to, consider. Barrington J. did not comment on this submission, but held that the Tribunal had erred in refusing to entertain Mr Mythen's claim.

Mythen, delivered in 1990, opened the way for the civil enforcement of the right not to be dismissed through the Unfair Dismissals Act 1977. In 1993, however, the legislature enacted a provision which seemed to qualify this advance. Section 15 of the Unfair Dismissals (Amendment) Act 1993 amends the Minimum Notice and Terms of Employment Act 1973 in the following terms:

> "Where the whole or part of a trade, business or undertaking was or is transferred to another person either before or after the passing of this Act, the service of an employee before the transfer in the trade, business or undertaking or the part thereof so transferred –
> (a) shall be reckoned as part of the service of the employee with the transferee, and
> (b) the transfer shall not operate to break the continuity of the service of the employee
> unless the employee received and retained redundancy payment from the transferor at the time of and by reason of the transfer."

This provision is difficult to reconcile with S.I. No. 306 of 1980 which, so far as is relevant, is in the following terms:

> "5.(1) The transfer of an undertaking, business or part of a business shall not in itself constitute grounds for dismissal by the transferor or the transferee and a dismissal, the grounds for which are such a transfer, by a transferor, or a transferee is hereby prohibited. However nothing in this Regulation shall be construed as prohibiting dismissals for economic, technical or organisational reasons entailing changes in the workforce."

Again, it has fallen to Irish courts and tribunals to interpret the legislation in such a manner that employees receive the protection to which they are entitled. If section 15 is to be interpreted in a manner which does not conflict with the Regulations, it may apply only in respect of dismissals which do not offend against the Regulations. In other words, an employee's continuity of employment will only be broken if he or she receives and retains a redundancy payment consequent on dismissal for economic, technical or organisational reasons.

The Employment Appeals Tribunal adopted this approach in the case of *Brett v. Niall Collins Limited.*[6] A receiver was appointed to Niall Collins Limited. He contracted to sell the premises, equipment and good will of the company to Oyster Investments Limited. The receiver purported to dismiss the staff on the grounds of redundancy prior to the transfer. Following the transfer a number of employees were re-employed by reason of the skills that they possessed. The employees who had not been re-employed initiated a claim under the Unfair Dismissals Acts 1977–1993. The respondents relied upon the terms of the Unfair Dismissals (Amendment) Act 1993, section 15.

The Tribunal held that the purported dismissals were motivated by the fact that the undertaking was saleable without the statutory liabilities that the workforce attracted. The decision to dismiss was taken in the interest of selling the business and not in the best interest of running the business after the transfer. Therefore, the receiver could not rely on the exception allowing for dismissal due to economic, technical or organisational reasons as set out in S.I. No. 306 of 1980, regulation 5(1). The Tribunal concluded that the dismissals were null and void and of no effect. A redundancy payment requires a dismissal; since there was no dismissal, the payment made by the receiver was not a redundancy payment. On this reasoning, section 15 of the Unfair Dismissals (Amendment) Act 1993 did not apply.

The courts continued to have regard to the Regulations in exercising their general jurisdiction. In *Maybury v. Pump Services and Eldea Limited*[7] the plaintiff sought an interim Order restraining a transfer of undertaking on the grounds that the defendants, the transferor and transferee, had failed to discharge the obligation to inform and consult. The High Court granted the interim Order sought. The matter was subsequently settled. In *Hyland Shipping Agencies v. Weir,*[8] the plaintiffs claimed that there had been a transfer of undertakings. They sought interlocutory injunctive relief restraining their dismissal until the trial of the action. Flood J. accepted that the High Court had jurisdiction to rule on the application of the Directive to the facts of the case, and accepted that it had jurisdiction to grant the relief sought. However, he ruled against the plaintiffs on the balance of convenience.

Notwithstanding these judicial developments, the European Commission took the view that Ireland had failed to provide an effective remedy for breach

---

[6] [1995] E.L.R. 65.
[7] Unreported, High Court, Blayney J., May 2, 1990. See Byrne, *Transfer of Undertakings* (1999), pp.272–273.
[8] Unreported, High Court, Flood J., February 2, 1996. See Byrne, *Transfer of Undertakings* (1999), pp.273–275.

of the obligation to inform and consult and delivered a reasoned opinion on the point. The result was S.I. No. 487 of 2000, which defines the term "representatives" and provides a civil remedy for the breach of the obligation to inform and consult. Employees may now apply to a Rights Commissioner for a decision requiring an employer to comply with the obligation to inform and consult and may also seek modest compensation for any failure in that regard.[9] Given that there is now an express remedy for breach of this right, it is probable that the Irish Courts will decline to exercise their jurisdiction in this regard.[10]

The latest chapter in the legislative history is the failure to implement Directive 98/50 and, latterly, Directive 23/2001. July 17, 2000, the deadline for transposition of Directive 98/50 (preserved by Directive 23/2001) has now passed. Yet again, it will fall to Irish courts and tribunals to cure this omission, so far as possible, through their interpretation of the Regulations as amended by S.I. No. 487 of 2000.

11.(3) SCOPE

The Regulations apply upon the transfer of an undertaking, business or part of a business.[11] Directive 2001/23 is more expansive, specifying that it applies to the transfer of an undertaking, business or part of a business to another employer as a result of a legal transfer or merger.[12] The term "undertaking" is not defined either by Directive 2001/23 or the Regulations. However, the Directive makes it clear that the term is intended to encompass a wide variety of entities:

> "[T]here is a transfer within the meaning of this Directive where there is a transfer of an economic entity which retains its identity, meaning an organised grouping of resources which has the objective of pursuing an economic activity, whether or not that activity is central or ancillary."[13]

In determining whether a transfer of undertakings has occurred, a variety of factors are relevant:

> "[I]t is necessary to determine whether what has been sold is an economic entity which is still in existence and this will be apparent from the fact that its operation is actually being continued or has been taken over by the new employer, with the same or similar economic activities.

---

[9] S.I. No. 487 of 2000, regulation 5(2). It is noteworthy that, where the undertaking transfers after the contravention to which the complaint relates occurred, redress lies against the transferee rather than the transferor. It may be argued that this allows the transferor to ignore his obligations with impunity.

[10] As did the UK High Court in *Betts v. Brintel Helicopters Ltd* [1996] IR.L.R. 45.

[11] This is apparent from the express words of regulations 5 and 6, and seems to apply by implication to regulations 3, 4, 7 and 8.

[12] Directive 2001/23, Article 1.

[13] *ibid.*

To decide whether these conditions are fulfilled it is necessary to take account of all the factual circumstances of the transaction in question. These include the type of undertaking or business in question, the transfer or otherwise of the circle of customers and the degree of similarity between activities before and after the transfer and the duration of any interruption in those activities. It should be made clear however, that each of these factors is only a part of the overall assessment which is required and therefore they cannot be examined independently of each other."[14]

The factors to be taken into account are as follows:

- the type of undertaking or business;

- whether or not tangible assets such as buildings and movable property are transferred;

- the value of intangible assets at the time of transfer;

- whether or not the majority of the employees are taken over by the new employer;

- whether or not the customers are transferred;

- the degree of similarity between the activities carried on before and after the transfer;

- the period, if any for which those activities were suspended.

All of these factors are taken into account; no single factor is of itself conclusive evidence of a transfer of undertakings. While it appeared initially that the resumption of an identical activity was determinative of a transfer of undertakings,[15] it became clear that this was not so. Thus, in Case C–13/95 *Süzen v. Zehnacker Gebäudereinigung GmbH Krankenhausservice*[16] where a contract transferred such that the transferee was carrying out the same activity as the transferor, but no assets and no employees transferred, the European Court of Justice (ECJ) held that a transfer of undertakings had not taken place.

Indeed, even if all of these factors are present, but there is no transfer of a stable economic entity, no transfer of undertakings will have occurred. Thus in Case C–209/91 *Rygaard*[16a] where a builder transferred certain assets and certain workers to another employer for the purpose of completing a single works contract, the ECJ held that a transfer of undertakings had not occurred.

In Ireland, the Employment Appeals Tribunal has applied the test laid down by the ECJ. In *Cannon v. Noonan Cleaning Company Ltd*[17] a cleaning contract was transferred from one cleaning company to another. Neither assets nor

---

[14] Case 24/85 *JMA Spijkers v. Gebroeders Benedik Abbatoir CV* [1986] E.C.R. 1119.

[15] Case C–392/92 *Schmidt v. Spar und Leihkasse* [1994] E.C.R. I–1311.

[16] [1997] E.C.R. I–1259.

[16a] *Ledernes Hovedorganisaton (Acting on behalf of Rygaard) v. Dansk Arbejdsgiverforening (Acting on behalf of Strø Mølle Amstik A/s).*

[17] [1998] E.L.R 153. See also *Shiels v. Noonan* UD 461/97 and *Bruton v. Knights Cleaning Service Ltd* UD 803/97 to similar effect.

employees passed with the transfer. The Tribunal applied the test laid down in Süzen and concluded that a transfer of undertakings had not taken place. It remarked, however, on the unfortunate situation arising from the application of Süzen:

> "There is no doubt that in a service undertaking the workforce and its expertise constitute a major aspect of the undertaking but it is difficult to understand how where an employer refuses to take on the workers of the previous contractor he can escape the rigours of the Directive while a contractor who takes on a major part of the workforce, perhaps out of magnanimity, will be caught by it. It would seem that the Directive, in the former instance, has not addressed the mischief in the law that it was intended to do."

Power v. St Paul's Nursing Home[18] provides a contrast to the circumstances arising in *Cannon*. The first respondent had employed several cleaners, including the claimants. It decided to contract out the cleaning service, and awarded the contract to the second respondent. It transferred cleaning equipment and other minor assets at the same time. The employees were dismissed by the first respondent on the grounds of redundancy, but were informed that the second respondent would have no objection to employing them under new contracts of employment and the claimants were interviewed for such employment. However, the second respondent made it clear to the claimants that there would be no continuity of employment and that there would be some changes in working hours. The claimants claimed that they had been unfairly dismissed. The Employment Appeals Tribunal determined that a transfer of undertakings had taken place and that the claimants had been unfairly dismissed, and awarded compensation.

11.(3)(a) Insolvency

Directive 2000/23 and national legislation implementing the Directive do not apply to transfers of undertakings arising upon an insolvency. This exception was not explicit in Directive 77/187. However, the ECJ made it clear that Directive 77/187 did not apply to such transfers. The rules relating to insolvency have precedence.

This exception first became apparent in Case 135/83 *Abels v. Bedrijfsverniging voor de Metaalindustrie en de Electrotechnische Industrie.*[19] The exception was confirmed by subsequent case law to apply only in the context of insolvency proceedings instituted with a view to liquidating the transferor's assets under the supervision of a competent judicial authority. In brief, the exception applies to insolvency rather than pre-insolvency situations.

This distinction has proven somewhat difficult to apply to the various systems in place in the Member States. It seems clear, however, that in the

---

[18] [1998] E.L.R 212.
[19] [1985] E.C.R. 469.

Irish context the Regulations do not apply to a transfer following a court liquidation but do apply to a transfer following voluntary liquidation or the appointment of a receiver or an examiner.[20]

The High Court considered this exception in the case of *Mythen* which, as noted above, concerned a transfer of undertakings following the appointment of a receiver by a debenture holder. The Court quoted at length from *Abels* and indicated strongly that the Regulations applied to a transfer following the appointment of a receiver by a debenture holder.[21]

This exception is now explicit. It was incorporated into Directive 98/50 and is now contained in Directive 2001/23 and is expressed in the following terms at Article 5:

> "Unless Member States provide otherwise, Articles 3 and 4 shall not apply to any transfer of an undertaking, business or part of an undertaking or business where the transferor is the subject of bankruptcy proceedings or any analogous insolvency proceedings which have been instituted with a view to the liquidation of the assets of the transferor and are under the supervision of a competent public authority (which may be an insolvency practitioner authorised by a competent public authority)."

Member States may provide that this exception will not apply. If they so provide, they may also provide that certain employee debts will not transfer and/or that alterations to the employees' contracts of employment may be agreed between the transferee or transferor and the employee representatives. Ireland has failed to transpose either Directive 2000/23 or its predecessor Directive 98/50. Therefore the general exception applies.

11.(4) EFFECT

11.(4)(a) Preservation of employment

The principal protection provided by the Regulations is that the contract of employment is preserved and transfers from the transferor to the transferee. All rights and liabilities arising from the contract of employment or from the employment relationship existing on the date of transfer are transferred. Continuity of employment is preserved and all of the employees' rights are preserved and protected.[22]

Thus, immediately following the transfer of undertakings, the transferee will be the employer of all the employees in the business. The transferor's

---

[20] See *Blaney v. Vanguard Plastics Ireland Limited (in voluntary liquidation)* U.D. 271/2000.
[21] [1990] 1 I.R. 98 at 108.
[22] S.I. No. 306 of 1980, regulation 3. Note, however, the exception with regard to pensions provided by regulation 4(2) and discussed below.

rights and obligations in respect of the employees will thereby pass to the transferee regardless of any refusal on his part to fulfil his obligations.[23]

The Employment Appeals Tribunal has not always been scrupulous in applying this aspect of the Regulations. In *Keenan v. Professional Contract Services Ltd*[24] the transferee required employees to complete forms indicating their interest in transferring employment. Certain of the employees did not do so and another did not complete the form properly. The transferee ultimately offered alternative employment which was not acceptable to them. While the Tribunal held that there had been an unfair dismissal, it held that the claimants had contributed to their dismissal by failing to inform the transferee that they wished to transfer and reduced the compensation awarded to the claimants as a consequence. This seems to offend against the terms of the Regulations which provide for the automatic transfer of employment upon a transfer of undertakings.

11.(4)(b) Employees dismissed prior to transfer

In the normal course of events, only those employees employed at the time of transfer will obtain the benefit of the Regulations. However, if employees are dismissed shortly before the transfer and by reason of the transfer, they are to be regarded as employed at the time of transfer and may make a claim against the transferor or the transferee or against both of them.[25] Even if the employees accept redundancy payments from the transferor, the best view is that this will not prevent them from claiming unfair dismissal against the transferee.[26] Note, however, that a transferor may lawfully dismiss employees for "organisational, economic or technical reasons entailing changes in the workforce", a concept discussed below.[27]

---

[23] Case C–305/94 *Rotstart de Hertaing v. J Benoidt SA in liquidation* [1996] E.C.R. I–5927. See also *Gray v. Irish Society for Prevention of Cruelty to Animals* [1995] E.L.R. 225 which demonstrates that an employer is not entitled to require the transferring employees to apply and undergo an interview for their own jobs.

[24] U.D. 454/98.

[25] S.I. No. 306 of 1980, Article 5(1). See also Case C–319/94 *Jules Dethier Equipement SA v. Dassy and Sovram SPRL* [1998] E.C.R. I–1061 and *Bannon v. Employment Appeals Tribunal* [1993] 1 I.R. 500.

[26] *Mythen v. Employment Appeals Tribunal* [1990] E.L.R. 1 at 11. The best view is also that the employees' continuity of employment is preserved even if they accept a redundancy payment. The Minimum Notice and Terms of Employment Act 1973, Schedule I, paragraph 7 (as amended by the Unfair Dismissals Act 1993, section 15) provides that on a transfer of undertakings, employees' continuity of employment is preserved unless they have accepted a redundancy payment from the vendor at the time of transfer and by reason of the transfer. However, this provision is commonly accepted as being contrary to Directive 77/187 and therefore void: Byrne, *Transfer of Undertakings* (1999) at p.318. In practice, this provision is not applied by the Employment Appeals Tribunal: *Brett v. Niall Collins (in Receivership)* [1995] E.L.R. 69.

[27] S.I. No. 306 of 1980, regulation 5(1).

11.(4)(c) Employees dismissed following the transfer

All of the employees of the business will become the transferee's employees
on the transfer of the business. If the transferee does not treat them as such, or
dismisses them by reason of the transfer, they may claim unfair dismissal
under the Unfair Dismissals Acts 1977–2001, if they come within the terms of
the Acts.[28]

However, the Regulations permit dismissals for "economic, technical or
organisational reasons entailing changes in the workforce".[29] In Ireland, this
defence has been equated with the defence of redundancy. Thus, if a transferee
acknowledges that employees will transfer, and if a redundancy situation
thereby arises, he may fairly dismiss employees for redundancy. It is essential,
however, that a genuine redundancy situation exist, and that the dismissed
employees be fairly selected for redundancy. This obliges the transferee to
consider his pool of employees and make an assessment with regard to that
entire group. It may be that, applying a fair selection criterion, the transferee
may be required to select some of its pre-existing work force for redundancy
prior to those employees acquired by reason of the transfer.

A redundancy situation exists in the following circumstances:[30]

  (i) the employer has ceased to carry out his business or intends to cease to
      carry out his business for the purposes for which the employee is employed
      or the employer has ceased, or intends to cease, to carry on that business in
      the place where the employee was so employed;

 (ii) the requirements of that business for employees to carry out work of a
      particular kind in the place where the employee was employed have ceased
      or diminished or are expected to do so;

(iii) the employer has decided to carry on the business with fewer or no
      employees, whether by requiring the employee's work to be done by other
      employees or otherwise;

 (iv) the employer has decided that the employee's work should be done in a
      different manner for which the employee is not sufficiently qualified or
      trained; or

  (v) the employer has decided that the employee's work should be done by a
      person who is also capable of doing other work for which the employee is
      not sufficiently qualified or trained.

---

[28] S.I. No. 306 of 1980, regulation 5(1)l; *Gray v. Irish Society for the Prevention of Cruelty to
      Animals* [1994] E.L.R. 225.
[29] S.I. No. 306 of 1980, regulation 5(1).
[30] Redundancy Payments Act 1967, s. 7(2), as amended.

Dismissal on the grounds of redundancy will normally be fair unless:[31]

(a) the redundancy situation is not genuine (*i.e.* it is given as a false excuse for the dismissal);

(b) the employee was selected for redundancy in contravention of an agreed redundancy procedure or one established by custom and practice and there was no special reason justifying departure from the procedure;

(c) the employee was unfairly selected for dismissal. If the employee was selected for a reason which would not justify dismissal or for any of the reasons set out below, the selection will be unfair:

- the trade union membership or activity of the employee;
- the religious or political opinions of the employee;
- the employee's involvement as a party or witness in a civil case against the employer;
- the fact that the employee has made, proposed or threatened to make a statement in a criminal case against the employer, or if the employee was or is likely to be a witness in a criminal case against the employer;
- the race, colour or sexual orientation of the employee;
- the age of the employee;
- the employee's membership of the travelling community;
- the exercise or proposed exercise by the employee of the right to parental leave or force majeure leave under the Parental Leave Act 1998 or carer's leave under and in accordance with the Carer's Leave Act 2001;
- the employee's pregnancy, giving birth, breastfeeding or any connected matters;
- the exercise or proposed exercise by the employee of rights under the Maternity Protection Act 1994;
- the exercise or proposed exercise by the employee of the right to leave under the Adoptive Leave Act 1995.
- the exercise or proposed exercise by the employee of rights under the Minimum Wage Act 2000, or the opposition by the employee of an act which is unlawful under that Act, or the acquisition by the employee of rights under that Act.

It should be noted that, since continuity of employment is preserved, the transferee may be obliged to pay large sums of money in discharge of employees' statutory redundancy entitlement; the entitlement will be calculated by reference to their entire continuous and computable period of service.

---

[31] Unfair Dismissals Act 1977, s. 6.

11.(4)(d) Alteration of terms or conditions of employment

S.I. No. 306 of 1980 provides that the rights and obligations of the transferor arising from a contract of employment or employment relationship existing on the date of transfer shall be transferred to the transferee.

This matter came before the ECJ in Case C–209/91 *Rask and Christensen v. ISS Kantinenservice.*[32] The transferee changed the date of payment of the employee's salary from the last Thursday in the month to the last day in the month. The transferee also changed the composition of the payment, although the total pay was unchanged. The Court held that the Directive prohibited the variation of the terms of the contract of employment, notwithstanding that total pay remained unchanged. However, the Court made it clear that the Directive does not preclude an amendment to the employment relationship, in so far as national law allows such a change other than through the transfer of an undertaking.

The Employment Appeals Tribunal has applied a less exacting standard in this regard. The claimant in *O'Donovan v. Ryanair Ltd*[33] was employed by the first respondent until March 20, 1995 when his employment transferred to the second respondent by way of a transfer of undertakings. He had enjoyed travel concessions during his employment with the first respondent. However, these were removed following the transfer. In addition, the method whereby his remuneration was calculated was changed without consultation. The claimant resigned his employment on April 5, 1995. He then claimed that he had been constructively dismissed. The first respondent gave evidence that the travel concessions were not considered to be part of normal pay and that it was within the power of the first respondent to vary or withdraw them at any stage. The second respondent gave evidence that the claimant was in fact at a financial advantage under the new pay calculation methods introduced by the second respondent.

Section 1 of the Unfair Dismissal Act 1977 defines constructive dismissal in the following terms:

> "The termination by the employee of his contract of employment with his employer, whether prior notice of the termination was or was not given to the employer, in circumstances in which, because of the conduct of the employer, the employee was or would have been entitled, or it was or would have been reasonable for the employee, to terminate the contract of employment without giving prior notice of termination to the employer."

The Tribunal determined as follows:

> "In the opinion of the Tribunal the claimant has not proved a constructive dismissal in this case. From the evidence before it the Tribunal is satisfied that

---

[32] [1992] E.C.R. I–5755.
[33] [1997] E.L.R. 63.

the claimant did not and would not have suffered any reduction in his pay. Moreover it is the view of the Tribunal on balance, that the claimant would have enjoyed an increase in pay under the new calculation arrangements with his employer."

With respect, the fact that the claimant would have enjoyed an increase in pay should not of itself have been determinative of the issue. The Tribunal did not consider the key questions, *i.e.* whether the claimant was entitled to travel concessions as a term of his contract of employment, and whether the breach of that obligation constituted a fundamental breach of contract. If each of these questions had been answered in the affirmative, then the claimant would have been entitled to treat himself as constructively dismissed regardless of the increase in pay.

11.(4)(e) Employees who choose not to transfer

Employees are not required to transfer employment upon a transfer of undertakings; they may elect to remain in employment with the transferor. However, it is likely that the employee will be dismissed on the grounds of redundancy, given that the transferor no longer owns the undertaking in which he was employed. Is such an employee entitled to a redundancy payment? It appears so. The Redundancy Payments Act 1967, section 9(3), provides that an employee shall not be taken to be dismissed within the meaning of the Act where he is re-engaged by another employer immediately upon the termination of his employment, and the re-engagement takes place with the consent of the employee and both of the employers. Clearly an employee who objects to a transfer of employment cannot be considered to be "re-engaged" by the transferee and the sub-section has no application. Accordingly, the employee will be entitled to a redundancy payment in the ordinary way.

11.(4)(f) Pension

A transferee is not required to offer pension benefits to the transferring employee, even if the right to those benefits formed part of the contract of employment or employment relationship prior to transfer.[34] However, the transferee must ensure that pension and associated rights are protected, *i.e.* adequately funded. This responsibility applies to the rights of employees engaged at the time of transfer and persons no longer employed at the time of transfer. The transferee should assess the adequacy of the pension funding. If there is a short-fall or inadequate coverage, the transferee should ensure that the transferor brings the funding up to the necessary level. If the transferor fails to do so, responsibility will rest with the transferee.

---

[34] S.I. No. 306 of 1980, regulation 4(2).

11.(4)(g) Collective agreements

Collective agreements survive a transfer of undertakings and the transferee must continue to observe the agreement until the date of termination or expiry of the agreement or the entry into force or application of another collective agreement.[35]

11.(4)(h) Employers' liability

The transferee acquires all rights and obligations of the transferor arising out of the contract of employment or employment relationship existing on the date of transfer. This will include liability in respect of all causes of action so arising whether at common law or under statute. This will include, for example, liability in tort in respect of employee accidents and liability under the Employment Equality Act 1998 for sexual harassment or breach of an equal pay clause.

The transferee should seek a comprehensive indemnity in respect of such liabilities. The indemnity should cover those causes of action arising before the date of transfer. It should also take account of those causes of action arising both before and after the date of transfer, *e.g.* ongoing sexual harassment; repetitive strain injury. If the transferor is a limited liability company, and if it did not have employer's liability insurance, any indemnity may be of limited value. In these circumstances, it may be prudent to seek an indemnity from the company together with an indemnity from a natural person, *e.g.* a director of the company.

11.(5) INFORMATION AND CONSULTATION

The Regulations provide[36] that the transferor and the transferee must inform the representatives of their respective employees affected by the transfer of:

– the reasons for the transfer;

– the legal, economic and social implications of the transfer for the employees; and

– the measures (if any) envisaged in relation to the employees.

The transferor must so inform the employee representatives in good time before the transfer is carried out. The transferee must so inform the employee representatives in good time, and in any event before the employees are directly

---

[35] *ibid.*, regulation 4(1).
[36] *ibid.*, regulation 7(1).

affected by the transfer as regards their conditions of work and employment. The transferor and the transferee are under a duty to take reasonable care to ensure that statements made to employees in the context of a transfer of undertakings are true.[37]

If the transferor or the transferee envisage measures in relation to their respective employees, they must consult the representatives of the employees in good time on such measures with a view to seeking an agreement.[38]

The term "representatives" is defined as follows:[39]

- a trade union, staff association or excepted body with which it has been the practice of the employees' employer to conduct collective bargaining negotiations; or

- in the absence of such a trade union, staff association or excepted body, a person or persons chosen (under an arrangement put in place by the employer) by such employees from among their number to represent them in negotiations with the employer.

If there are no representatives of the employees, the transferor or transferee, as appropriate, must give each employee in the undertaking the requisite information in writing in good time before the transfer is carried out and post notices containing that information in a prominent place in the workplace.[40]

The High Court considered these requirements in *In the Matter of Irish Life Assurance Limited.*[41] The Court was called upon to sanction a transfer of business from one insurance company to another under the Assurance Companies Act 1909. Employees of the transferor raised certain objections to the transfer. In discharging its jurisdiction under the 1909 Act, the Court considered the degree to which the transferor had complied with S.I. No. 306 of 1980 as amended by S.I. No. 487 of 2000.

Kearns J. wrote as follows:

> "Finally, I turn to the complaints of Irish Life employees, contained both in the Affidavits placed before the Court and in concerns expressed in Court both by Counsel on behalf of those employees who were represented and by individual employees who spoke themselves.
>
> Before doing so, it is only appropriate to say that the extent to which employee concerns can affect the exercise of the Court's discretion in an application of this nature is necessarily limited. The statutory framework for the transfer of assurance business requires only consultation with policyholders,

---

[37] *Hagan v. ICI Chemicals and Polymers Limited* [2002] I.R.L.R. 192, approved in *King v. Aer Lingus plc* unreported, High Court, Kearns J., October 8, 2002.

[38] *ibid.*, regulation 7(2).

[39] *ibid.*, regulation 2, as amended by S.I. No. 487 of 2000.

[40] *ibid.*, regulation 7(3).

[41] Unreported, High Court, Kearns J., February 27, 2002.

although on the hearing of the petition, the Court may hear the Directors and "other persons whom it considers entitled to be heard". The protection afforded to employees under the European Communities (Safeguarding of Employees Rights on Transfer of Undertakings) Regulations, 1980 provides for a separate regime for infoming representatives of employees affected by a transfer of the matters set out at Article 7 of the Regulations. To that extent, the Court must obviously have regard to the Regulations because a substantial or egregious breach of the obligations therein contained would inevitably influence the Court in the exercise of its discretion. The essential requirements are for the giving of information to unions and staff about the reasons for the transfer, the implications of same for employees and the measures envisaged in relation to employees in good time before the transfer is carried out. It is not a requirement of the Regulations that negotiations of the working conditions of each and every employee who is affected by the transfer take place and be resolved to that employee's satisfaction before the obligation under the Regulations is discharged. Still less can this Court be the adjudicator or arbitrator of ongoing grievances or disputes between management and staff arising from likely changes to work conditions in the context of a transfer. The Regulations themselves expressly envisage that economic, technical and organisational aspects of transfers may entail changes in the workplace, up to and including dismissals and do not prohibit dismissals thus arising. As the historical analysis shows, the role of the Court in applications of this nature derives more from the fact that policyholders had in the past suffered significantly through the absence of effective regulation. It is unfortunately the case, as pointed out by Mr Gallagher, that one aspect of the transfer of a business is that employees, or some of them, are affected to a greater or lesser degree. It seems to me, however, that the Court, if otherwise satisfied to approve a scheme, should only withhold its approval if there has been a substantial or egregious breach of the Transfer of Undertakings Regulations, or if satisfied that the disruption to the employees of an undertaking is so severe in its implication as to cast in doubt the conclusions of the independent actuary."

The Court then summarised the submissions made by the aggrieved employees and stated as follows:

"I am satisfied that, broadly speaking, Irish Life has complied with the requirements of the Regulations. To put it another way, no substantial or egregious breach of those Regulations has been established on the material placed before the Court which would justify the Court in holding that Irish Life had disregarded its obligations under those Regulations.

It may be, though I am not making any positive finding to this effect, that certain employees who were absent from work on sick leave received only at a late stage the detailed information which was available to active employees through their unions and place of work at all material times. Even if some lapses of this nature did occur, and I stress I am making no positive findings to that effect, they related to a small number of employees only and could not by any stretch of the imagination be regarded as constituting a significant breach of a transferor's obligations under the Transfer of Undertaking Regulations, such as would warrant this court in withholding its approval for the proposed

Scheme. Still less do these complaints and objections go to the conclusions expressed by the independent actuary in his report, nor do they affect his conclusions in any way."

Kearns J. expressed his conclusion in the following terms:

"While it is only natural to feel a measure of sympathy for employees whose association as home service representatives with Irish Life extends back over many years in what might be described as a traditional role as collectors, at the end of the day my decision and conclusion must be that no sufficient objection has been made out in this case. I would stress, as has been pointed out several times during the hearing before this Court, that all legal rights and entitlements of the affected employees are preserved in the context of the proposed transfer and I have already referred to the different rights available to employees under the Transfer of Undertaking Regulations as amended.

I will therefore sanction the arrangements set out in the Scheme for the proposed transfer in accordance with section 13 of the Assurance Companies Act, 1909."

As may be seen from the passages quoted above, *In the Matter of Irish Life Assurance Ltd* did not concern the exercise of jurisdiction under S.I. No. 306 of 1980 as amended. Rather it concerned the exercise of jurisdiction under the Companies Act 1909 and a "substantial or egregious" breach of S.I. No. 306 of 1980 was relevant to the exercise of that jurisdiction. It seems clear therefore that the standard set by the Court was less exacting than that which the Rights Commissioner will set in exercising jurisdiction under S.I. No. 306 of 1980.

However, it appears to this writer that the Rights Commissioner might adopt an approach similar to that adopted by Kearns J., particularly that set out in the second passage quoted above.

BIBLIOGRAPHY

Barnard, *EC Employment Law* (Oxford, 2000).
Byrne, *Transfer of Undertakings* (Blackhall Publishing, 1999).
McMullen, "Transfer of Undertakings – Perspectives from Britain and Ireland" (2000) *Irish Jurist* 83.

12. HUMAN RIGHTS AND THE EUROPEAN UNION – AN EVOLVING SYSTEM

JAMES KINGSTON*

12.(1) INTRODUCTION

Towards the end of the Second World War and in its immediate aftermath, attempts were made to prevent future global conflicts and to protect human rights at the international level through the adoption of the United Nations Charter in 1945 and the Universal Declaration of Human Rights in 1948. In Europe, where the two World Wars had originated, the establishment of the Council of Europe in 1949 and the adoption under the auspices of that organisation of the European Convention for the Protection of Human Rights and Fundamental Freedoms (European Convention on Human Rights, or ECHR) in 1950 represented a regional attempt to achieve those aims. Ambitious plans for the setting up of a European Political Community, which would have incorporated the substantive provisions of the ECHR, were however abandoned in 1953 and instead the European Coal and Steel Community (ECSC) of 1950 (now defunct) was supplemented by the European Economic Community (EEC) and the European Atomic Energy Community (EAEC) in 1957. None of the Treaties setting up the Communities made any reference to fundamental rights, although, as is outlined below, some specific and limited provisions relating to what might be termed fundamental rights were included. The decision of the founding fathers of the European Communities to eschew a "big bang" approach to European integration in favour of pragmatic and incremental progress has meant that the development of a human rights framework for the Communities/Union has likewise proceeded in a piecemeal fashion.[1] In this regard it may be noted that while the individual is the central

---

* LL.B., LL.M., Barrister-at-Law; Deputy Legal Adviser, Department of Foreign Affairs. The views of the author are of an exclusively personal nature and do not necessarily reflect those of the Minister for Foreign Affairs or the Department of Foreign Affairs. All errors remain the responsibility of the author.

[1] Perhaps the most comprehensive analysis of the EU and human rights is (the appropriately titled) Alston (ed), *The EU and Human Rights* (1999) which draws on *Leading by Example: A Human Rights Agenda for the European Union in the Year 2000* launched in 1998 by a *Comité des Sages* consisting of Judge Antonio Cassese, Catherine Lalumière MEP, Professor Peter Leuprecht and High Commissioner Mary Robinson. See also in the last ten or so years *inter alia*: Craig and de Búrca, *EU Law: Text, Cases and Materials* (3rd ed., 2002) Chap. 7;

focus of many domestic constitutions and human rights treaties, Community law, at least initially, took cognisance of individuals only in their capacity as workers or other economic agents.

This chapter will look at the genesis and development of human rights competences within the European Union (EU).[2] The chapter looks first at how human rights norms have been developed by the Court of Justice of the European Communities (ECJ). Secondly, it looks at how the other institutions of the Union and the Member States have contributed to the development of a human rights framework through the adoption of non-binding Bills of Rights and the inclusion of particular fundamental rights provisions in the EU treaties. Thirdly, it examines the relationship between the EU and the ECHR. Finally, it outlines briefly the prospects for future human rights developments within the EU in the Treaty expected to emerge from the negotiations of the Inter-Governmental Conference (IGC) of 2004. Two of the concerns most commonly expressed about the Union and human rights are that to date it has neither a legally binding, judicially reviewable Bill of Rights, nor is it a party to any universal or regional human rights treaties. These issues, which are dealt with throughout this chapter, are the subjects of on-going debate, including in the framework of the Convention on the Future of Europe, which has been set up in advance of the IGC in 2004.

12.(2) DEVELOPMENT OF FUNDAMENTAL RIGHTS JURISPRUDENCE BY THE COURT OF JUSTICE

12.(2)(a) Initial moves to police the acts of the Institutions

The ECJ has been one of the most active agents of European integration from the earliest days of the Communities. As far back as 1964 the Court established the well-known principle of the supremacy of Community law

---

Lenaerts and de Smijter, "A 'Bill of Rights' for the European Union" (2001) 28 CMLR 273; de Búrca, "The Drafting of the European Union Charter of Fundamental Rights" (2001) 26 ELR 126; Jacobs, "Human Rights in the European Union: the Role of the Court of Justice" (2001) 26 ELR 331; Eicke, "The European Charter of Fundamental Rights – Unique Opportunity or Unwelcome Distraction" [2000] EHRLR 280; Lenaerts, "Fundamental Rights in the European Union" (2000) 25 ELR 575; von Bogdandy, "The European Union as a Human Rights Organisation?" (2000) 37 CMLR 1307; Weiler, *The Constitution of Europe* (1999), Chap. 3; Betten and Grief, *EU Law and Human Rights* (1998); Twomey, "The European Union: Three Pillars Without a Human Rights Foundation" in *Legal Issues of the Maastricht Treaty* (O'Keeffe and Twomey ed., 1996); Weiler and Lockhart, "'Taking Rights Seriously' Seriously" (1995) 32 CMLR 51 and 579; de Búrca, "Fundamental Rights and the Reach of Community Law" (1993) 13 OJLS 283; Coppel and O'Neill, "Taking Rights Seriously" (1992) 29 CMLR 669; Phelan, "The Right to Life of the Unborn v Promotion of Trade in Services" (1992) 55 MLR 670.

2   The term "human rights" is used in this chapter to describe rights protected by international treaties and adhering to all individuals by virtue of their humanity, although some rights, such

over domestic law.[3] The enunciation of such a doctrine was hardly a surprise, given the well-established principle that at the international level international law prevails over domestic law,[4] but two years previously, the Court had broken new ground in the landmark case of *van Gend en Loos v. Nederlandse Administratie der Belastingen*,[5] by ruling that Community law gave rights to individuals that the Member States were obliged to give effect to at domestic level.

Initially, the ECJ had been reluctant to have regard to principles of fundamental rights when interpreting Community law.[6] However, in response to indications from the German and Italian constitutional courts that they were not prepared to accept the doctrine of the supremacy of Community law where individual rights protection was concerned (because of the lack of such protection at Community level), it began to use the discourse of fundamental rights. It has been argued that this use of fundamental rights was motivated, at least partly, by the desire to protect the integrity of the Community legal order rather than because of a desire to protect the rights of individuals as such.[7] The landmark case in which the ECJ first stated that fundamental rights formed part of the general principles of Community law was *Stauder v. Ulm*,[8] where it ruled that a Community scheme providing cheap butter to certain people as part of their social welfare entitlements had to be interpreted in a manner consistent with the fundamental rights enshrined in the general principles of Community law. In a later case the ECJ emphasised that the fundamental rights provisions of the Member States did not themselves form part of Community law or "trump" its provisions; rather domestic constitutions could be looked to as a source of inspiration by the Court in identifying the

---

as the right to enter or work in a country or to exercise voting rights there, may adhere to individuals only *vis-à-vis* their state of nationality; the term fundamental rights, however, is used to describe rights protected by national constitutions which may apply in certain instances to a more restricted class of persons, such as nationals of a particular country. However, the terms are sometimes used interchangeably and in the EU context "fundamental rights" may include both rights granted irrespective of nationality, such as the right to equal pay, and rights granted only to Union citizens, such as the right to vote in local and European Parliament elections.

3   Case 6/64, *Costa v. ENEL* [1964] ECR 585.
4   The Court's assertion of the supremacy of EC law over domestic law reflects the general rule of international law that a state cannot plead its domestic law as justification for its failure to comply with an international obligation: see, *e.g.* Article 27 of the Vienna Convention on the Law of Treaties 1969, which in turn reflects customary international law in this instance. For an analysis of the conflict between the national courts and the Court of Justice with regard to supremacy in the field of fundamental rights, see, *e.g.* Rasmussen, *On Law And Policy in the European Court of Justice* (1986), p.393 *et seq;* Phelan, *Revolt or Revolution?* (1997).
5   Case 26/62 [1963] ECR 1.
6   See, *e.g.* Case 1/58, *Stork v. High Authority* [1959] ECR 17, where the Court rejected a complaint that a decision of the ECSC High Authority was invalid on the basis that it infringed principles of German fundamental rights law.
7   For a discussion of this issue, see Coppell and O'Neill, "Taking Rights Seriously" and Weiler and Lockhart, "'Taking Rights Seriously' Seriously", *op.cit.*
8   Case 29/69 [1969] ECR 419.

fundamental rights that formed part of the general principles of Community law.[9]

While the early cases referred solely to principles derived from national constitutional law, with the accession of France to the ECHR in 1974 all Community Member States were parties thereto. Almost immediately, the ECJ began to refer to "international treaties for the protection of human rights on which the Member States have collaborated or of which they are signatories" as a source from which Community fundamental rights could be derived and in this regard referred specifically to the ECHR.[10] Indeed, in *Rutili v. Minister for the Interior*[11] the ECJ made reference to the Fourth Protocol to the ECHR, notwithstanding the fact that not all Member States were party to it, in interpreting the validity of French public policy restrictions on the freedom of movement of Community nationals. In many later cases, such as *Johnston v. RUC*,[12] the ECJ emphasised the "special significance" of the ECHR as a source of inspiration for it in determining the scope of the fundamental rights protected by the Communities. Since 1996, in its decision in *P v. S and Cornwall County Council*,[13] the ECJ has referred not only to the ECHR itself, but also to the case law of the European Court of Human Rights, in determining the content of the fundamental rights protected by Community law.

The special position of the ECHR and the jurisprudence of its organs as identified by the ECJ is reflected, as is illustrated below, in the significance afforded to it in political and legislative responses and initiatives on human rights, but other international human rights treaties, such as the European Social Charter (ESC) of 1961, the International Covenant on Civil and Political Rights (ICCPR) and various conventions of the International Labour Organisation (ILO) have also been cited in the jurisprudence of the ECJ.[14] It is important to bear in mind, however, that, as has already been mentioned, the constitutional provisions of the Member States on fundamental rights are not, as such, part of Community law. They form rather a source of inspiration from which the ECJ can identify the general principles of Community law relating to fundamental rights. Nor are the provisions of international human rights treaties to which the Member States are party themselves part of Community law, but, as a reflection of the Member States' views on human rights, they too

---

[9] Case 11/70, *International Handelsgesellschaft v. Einfuhr und Vorratstelle fuer Getreide und Futtermittel* [1970] ECR 1125. For the scope of application of general principles of Community law see above Costello para 2(2)(a).

[10] See Case 4/73, *Nold No. 2* [1974] ECR 491.

[11] Case 36/75 [1975] ECR 1219.

[12] Case 222/84 [1986] ECR 165.

[13] Case C–13/94 [1996] ECR I–2143.

[14] See, *e.g.* Case 43/75, *Defrenne v. Sabena No. 3* [1976] ECR 455 (ESC and ILO Convention No. 111 concerning Discrimination in respect of Employment and Occupation); Case 6/75, *Horst v. Bundesknappschaft* [1975] ECR 823 (ILO Convention No. 48 on the Maintenance of Migrants' Pension Rights); Case C–249/96, *Grant v. South West Trains Limited* [1998] ECR I–621 (ICCPR).

provide a source of inspiration for the ECJ in developing its own fundamental rights jurisprudence.

It is clear that when reviewing acts of the institutions the ECJ will be prepared to interpret them in light of fundamental rights principles and, if necessary, it will strike them down if such an interpretation is not possible. However, the ECJ has no power to strike down provisions of primary Community law should they contravene international human rights treaties or Member State constitutions. Furthermore, it is important to note that while the ECJ is prepared to look to Strasbourg for inspiration, it has held that the Community does not have the competence to accede to the ECHR, on the basis that the "entry of the Community into a distinct international institutional system as well as the integration of all the provisions of the Convention into the Community legal order", with "fundamental institutional implications for the Community and for the Member States" does not fall within the existing functions or objectives of the Community.[15]

12.(2)(b) ECJ surveillance of the activities of the Member States

The first cases concerning fundamental rights dealt with by the ECJ concerned acts of the institutions. Later cases involved acts of the Member States but the ECJ has been careful to limit the scope of its fundamental rights competence in this regard. When the Member States are acting effectively as agents of the Community, the ECJ is prepared to review and strike down their acts if they conflict with fundamental rights principles.[16] For example, in the context of the common fisheries policy, the ECJ has struck down a U.K. statutory instrument that purported to penalise certain acts that were not offences at the time that they were committed on the basis that retroactive criminal laws contravene fundamental rights.[17] In a subsequent case the ECJ has stated clearly that as the Community institutions must act in accordance with principles of fundamental rights in their actions, so too must Member States acting in the implementation of Community rules, in so far as those rules give them a choice as to how to implement the Community rule in question.[18] The ECJ has also held that outside of "agency" cases, it requires that the acts of the Member States be examined for conformity with fundamental rights standards whenever they are applying exceptions provided for by Community law. That this is the case was made clear in the context of free movement of persons as far back as the ECJ's decision in *Rutili*. This line of reasoning has been upheld in more recent cases, such as the so-called *ERT* case, where the ECJ held that limitations on the freedom to provide services, in this case broadcast media,

---

[15] Opinion 2/94, *Accession by the Community to the ECHR* [1996] ECR I–1759, at paras 34 and 35.
[16] See above, Costello, para. 2(2)(a)(i).
[17] Case 63/83, *R v. Kirk* [1984] ECR 2689: the Court drew inspiration from Article 7 of the ECHR that prohibits such laws.
[18] Case 5/88, *Wachauf v. Germany* [1989] ECR 2609.

had to be interpreted in light of the right to freedom of expression guaranteed by Article 10 of the ECHR.[19] Even more clearly, where Community law does not provide for a relevant exception, national laws will be struck down where they contravene Community rules inspired by fundamental rights.[20]

However, it is clear that the ECJ will only review acts of the Member States for compatibility with the ECHR when those acts fall within the scope of Community law. In *Cinéthètheque v. Fédération Nationale des Cinémas Français* the ECJ held that while it had the duty to ensure observance of fundamental rights "in the field of Community law", it had no power to examine the compatibility with the ECHR of national legislation falling "within the jurisdiction of the national legislator".[21] In a subsequent case the ECJ, while referring to its judgment in *Cinéthètheque*, slightly reformulated the test, perhaps extending somewhat its own jurisdiction, holding that it had no power to examine legislation "lying outside the scope of Community law".[22] At one point it appeared that the ECJ might take a very extensive view of what fell within the scope of Community law: in *Konstantinidis v. Stadt Altensteig* Advocate General Jacobs argued that any Community national exercising the right of free movement within the Community was entitled to be treated in accordance with a common European code of fundamental values, in particular those laid down in the ECHR.[23] In this instance the Advocate General opined that Article 8 of the ECHR, on the right to respect for private life, was at issue. However, the ECJ declined to follow this reasoning in that case and relied solely on Community rules on freedom of establishment. The ECJ has made known its unwillingness to follow the reasoning of Advocate General Jacobs in a number of subsequent cases, even where no specific Community rule could be referred to.[24] In the Irish context, the ECJ refusal to rule on the compatibility with Community rules on freedom to provide services of a constitutional ban on the supply of information concerning the identity and location of clinics providing abortion facilities in other Member States, on the basis that providers of the information had no link with the providers of the facilities,[25] shows the reluctance of the ECJ to trespass on areas felt by the Member States to be exclusively a matter of domestic concern.[26]

---

[19] Case C–260/89, *Elliniki Radiophonia Tileorassi AE v. Dimotiki Etairia Pliroforissis and Sotirios Kouvelas* [1991] ECR I–2925.

[20] *Johnston v. Chief Constable of the Royal Ulster Constabulary, op cit.*

[21] Cases 60 and 61/84 [1985] ECR 2605, at para. 26.

[22] Case 12/86, *Demirel v. Stadt Schwaebisch Gmuend* [1987] ECR 3719, at para. 28.

[23] Case C–168/91 [1993] ECR I–1191.

[24] See, *e.g.* Case C–299/95, *Kremzow v. Austria* [1997] ECR I–2629, where the Court refused to accept a preliminary reference regarding the right to compensation for unlawful detention.

[25] Case C–159/90, *SPUC Limited v. Grogan* [1991] ECR I–4685.

[26] In this regard, while the Irish courts generally have been prepared to accept the supremacy of Community law in Ireland, remarks by McCarthy and Walsh J.J. in the Supreme Court, in the

12.(2)(c) Limitations of the ECJ's approach

From the foregoing it can be seen that, whatever its initial motivation, the ECJ has been to the forefront of moves to integrate human rights concerns into the European Union's framework of action. The fact that the Treaties contain little in the way of guidance has left the ECJ free to identify fundamental rights in a way that is familiar to Irish lawyers brought up on the Supreme Court's doctrine of un-enumerated rights. However, perhaps mindful of Member States' concern at any attempts to encroach upon their freedom to determine fundamental aspects of their domestic legal orders, it has proceeded carefully and taken pains to integrate a fundamental rights analysis into its interpretation of existing Community law and the obligations of the Member States thereunder, rather than to expand wholesale the scope of Community law. One of the more obvious difficulties with judge-made human rights is the inability of the judiciary to formulate a comprehensive set of rights, thus reducing transparency and hindering the individual bearer of those rights from identifying them and acting upon them. As is explained in the next section, the other institutions of the Union, with a degree of assistance from the Member States, have, over the years, gone some way towards remedying this deficit.

12.(3) BILLS OF RIGHTS AND TREATY PROVISIONS ON HUMAN RIGHTS

12.(3)(a) Pre-European Union developments

The Treaty establishing the European Economic Community in 1957 was the only one of the three Communities Treaties to contain provisions relating to what might be called fundamental rights. Discrimination on the basis of nationality was prohibited by Article 7 thereof.[27] Title III of the Treaty provided for free movement rights for workers, self-employed persons and those seeking to provide or avail of services. Both the general non-discrimination provision and the free movement rights were limited to nationals of the Member States and applied only to persons coming within the scope of the Treaty, *i.e.* economically active persons. Article 119 (now Article 141) provided for a right of employed men and women to equal pay for equal work

---

period after the High Court had referred the issue of the compatibility of the ban on abortion information with Community law but before the Court of Justice had delivered its opinion, indicate an unwillingness to subordinate the constitutional protection of fundamental rights to Community law: see *SPUC Limited v. Grogan* [1989] I.R. 753, discussed in Kingston, Whelan and Bacik, *Abortion and the Law* (1997), Chap. 5. Ultimately, the ban was found by the European Court of Human Rights to contravene Article 10 of the ECHR: see *Open Door Counselling v. Ireland* (1992) Series A No. 246 and it was modified following the enactment of the Fourteenth Amendment of the Constitution Act 1992 and the Regulation of Information (Services Outside the State for the Termination of Pregnancies) Act 1995.

[27] Article 7 of the EEC Treaty subsequently became Article 6 of the EC Treaty and is currently Article 12 thereof.

irrespective of whether they were Community nationals. These Treaty provisions were supplemented by secondary legislation. Furthermore, in 1976 the Act on European Parliament elections gave Member State nationals the right to elect directly Members of the European Parliament.

As has been explained above, it was the ECJ that initiated the development of a so-called fundamental rights doctrine within the Communities. At a political level, as far back as 1977 the European Parliament, the Council and the Commission responded to this initiative by adopting a Joint Declaration on Fundamental Rights.[28] The very short, non-binding Declaration noted the ECJ's recognition of fundamental rights and the fact that all Member States were party to the ECHR, and the institutions undertook to respect fundamental rights "as derived in particular from the constitutions of the Member States and the European Convention for the Protection of Human Rights and Fundamental Freedoms" in the exercise of their powers. The Member States subsequently responded by including in the (non-binding) preamble to the Single European Act a reference to fundamental rights, including those enshrined in the Constitutions of the Member States, the ECHR and the ESC, as one of the corner-stones of democracy on which the Communities are based. In 1989 the European Parliament adopted a Declaration of Fundamental Rights and Freedoms that referred to fundamental rights as deriving from the EC Treaties, the constitutional traditions common to the Member States, the ECHR and other international instruments.[29] Unlike the earlier Joint Declaration, this document, though also non-binding, contained a wide range of civil, cultural, economic, political and social rights and thus represents the first attempt to set out a comprehensive Bill of Rights for the Communities. While some of the rights listed, such as the right to dignity contained in Article 1, would appear to be human rights properly so-called, *i.e.* available to all individuals irrespective of nationality, Article 25 states that the Declaration is applicable only to the nationals of the Member States (and within the field of application of Community law). Also in 1989, eleven of the then twelve Member States (the U.K. being the exception) signed the Community Charter of the Fundamental Social Rights of Workers, which did not form part of the Treaty system and only had limited legal effect.[30]

12.(3)(b) The Maastricht and Amsterdam Treaties

In 1992, the Treaty on European Union for the first time in a substantive Treaty provision referred to the Convention: Article F(2) (now Article 6(2)) of the TEU provides that: "The Union shall respect fundamental rights, as guaranteed by the European Convention for the Protection of Human Rights and

---

[28] [1977] O.J. C 103/1.
[29] [1989] O.J. C 120/52.
[30] See Weatherill and Beaumont, *EU Law*, (3rd ed., 1999), p.751.

Fundamental Freedoms . . . and as they result from the constitutional traditions common to the Member States, as general principles of Community law."

The somewhat confusing reference to Community law might be taken to mean that only the first (Communities) pillar of the Union is based on fundamental rights, but the post-Amsterdam Treaty version of Article 6(1) (ex Article F(1)) makes it clear that the Union as a whole is based on fundamental rights.[31] While the Treaty on European Union made it clear in a primary legal document that the Union is based on fundamental rights, it did not go so far as to incorporate a comprehensive set of such rights in any of the Union Treaties. Accordingly, the individual, or at least the individual without a good grasp of international and comparative human rights law, was still not given a clear picture of what those rights might be. Furthermore, although post-Maastricht the newly formed Union consisted of three "pillars": the first and original (Communities) pillar, consisting of the EC, EAEC and ECSC Treaties; the second (Common Foreign and Security) pillar; and the third (Justice and Home Affairs) pillar, the ECJ's jurisdiction did not extend to the new pillars.

The Treaty on European Union did however introduce the concept of "Citizenship of the Union" for Member State nationals in Part Two of the EC Treaty and set out in that Part some of the rights of such citizens, based on existing and new Treaty provisions: these rights consisted of free movement and voting rights, consular protection rights, the right to petition the European Parliament and the right to apply to the European Ombudsman.[32] Building on the Community Charter of the Fundamental Social Rights of Workers, the same eleven Member States concluded in Maastricht an Agreement on Social Policy annexed to the Protocol on Social Policy, which in turn was annexed to the EC Treaty. Finally, a new Article 130u (now Article 177) was inserted into the EC Treaty, providing a specific competence for the Community in the field of development co-operation, paragraph 2 of which provides that such co-operation shall contribute to respect for human (rather than fundamental) rights.

The Amsterdam Treaty, as mentioned above, clarified that the Union as a whole was based on fundamental rights. Article 46 (ex Article L) further provides that the ECJ shall apply principles of fundamental rights when reviewing the acts of the Union's institutions, in so far as it has jurisdiction under the Treaties and extended that jurisdiction to a limited extent over the third, but not the second, pillar. This confirms an aspect of the ECJ jurisprudence mentioned above, but does not incorporate the Court's holding that it has jurisdiction over the actions of the Member States when they act

---

[31] Article 6(1) provides that: "The Union is founded on the principles of . . . human rights and fundamental freedoms . . . principles which are common to the Member States."

[32] These "rights" did not in fact amount to very much over and above what was already provided by Community law. For an analysis of Union citizenship see O'Leary, *The Evolving Concept of Union Citizenship* (1996); Kingston, "Citizenship of the European Union" in *Citizenship: The White Paper* (Gardner ed., 1997); O'Leary and Tillikainen ed., *Citizenship and Nationality Status in the New Europe* (1998).

within the scope of Community law (and now within the scope of the third pillar also). Article 49 (ex Article O) of the Treaty also provides an explicit requirement that only states that respect principles of fundamental rights as set out in Article 6(1) may join the Union. Article 7 (ex Article F.1) provides that Member States that seriously and persistently breach those fundamental rights principles may be subjected to sanctions. This provision appears to give a potentially very far-ranging fundamental rights jurisdiction to the Union as it could cover human rights violations, albeit only gross violations, committed by Member States even in fields normally regarded as coming within their exclusive jurisdiction.

The Amsterdam Treaty also supplemented the existing provisions of the Treaties dealing with fundamental rights issues in a number of ways. Existing provisions on equality between men and women were highlighted by an amendment of Article 2 of the EC Treaty to provide that the purposes of the Community include the promotion of equality and Article 3 provides for gender-proofing of the Community's activities.[33] Article 141 (ex Article 119) was amended to reflect ECJ jurisprudence to the effect that the entitlement to equal pay arises in the context of work of equal value as well as equal work. Further equality provisions include a new Article 13 in the EC Treaty providing a basis for legislative action to combat discrimination based on sex, racial or ethnic origin, religion or belief, disability, age or sexual orientation. Data protection rights were provided for in Article 286 of the EC Treaty. Declarations were made in respect of the Treaty on European Union on the status of churches and non-confessional bodies and on the death penalty and in respect of the EC Treaty on disability-proofing the Community's legislative actions in the sphere of the internal market. Finally, the provisions of the Protocol on Social Policy were incorporated into the main body of the EC Treaty.

However, the Member States in the IGC leading up to the conclusion of the Amsterdam Treaty refused to give the European Community, much less the European Union, a specific competence to accede to the ECHR or any other international human rights treaty of a similar nature; nor were they prepared to include a comprehensive Bill of Rights within the new Union's legal order, despite the attempts of certain Member States and Union institutions to include such measures.[34] The Member States were not prepared to countenance giving the Community or Union the competence to accede to the ECHR in the IGC leading up to the Nice Treaty either. Prior to the conclusion of that Treaty, the

---

[33] Article 3 provides that in its activities the Community shall "aim to eliminate inequalities, and to promote equality, between men and women", thus envisaging both positive and negative measures to ensure such equality. For discussion on recent developments in equality law see below, Kimber, Chap. 13.

[34] For an analysis of the negotiation and conclusion of the fundamental rights provisions of the Amsterdam Treaty see Kingston, "Fundamental Rights and Non-Discrimination in the Treaty of Amsterdam" in *Legal and Constitutional Implications of the Amsterdam Treaty* (IEA ed., 1997).

Member States had set up a "Convention" to draft a Charter of Fundamental Rights of the European Union. However, although the Convention had completed its draft, the Member States decided not to incorporate it within the Treaties at the December 2000 European Council. The Nice Treaty's only changes with regard to fundamental rights relate to the procedure set out in Article 7 of the Treaty on European Union. The procedure introduced by the Amsterdam Treaty is supplemented by the addition of a procedure that allows the Union to deal with a "clear risk" of a serious breach of fundamental rights by a Member State; furthermore, Article 46 of the Treaty on European Union is amended to give jurisdiction to the ECJ in respect of "purely procedural" aspects of Article 7.

12.(3)(c) The Charter of Fundamental Rights of the European Union

As has been mentioned, the Charter of Fundamental Rights of the European Union was drafted by a Convention. The Convention consisted of representatives of the Member State Governments, the national parliaments, the European Parliament and the European Commission.[35] The preamble to the Charter sets the scene by pointing to the necessity of strengthening the protection of fundamental rights by increasing their visibility in the Charter. Thus the Charter does not seek to identify new rights; rather it reaffirms existing rights. In this the Charter goes beyond the piece-meal identification of rights in the case law of the ECJ and the Treaties and updates the rights set out in the European Parliament's Declaration of 1989. Thus, notwithstanding the formally non-binding nature of the Charter, it provides the individual with a source of information as to his or her rights and gives impetus to the protection of those rights by the Court[36] and the other institutions of the Union.[37]

As has been set out above, the ECJ has confined itself to exercising a human rights jurisdiction only in areas where it already has jurisdiction; similarly the 1977 and 1989 declarations on fundamental rights relate only to areas falling within the scope of application of Community law. Article 51 of the Charter likewise provides that its provisions are addressed to the institutions and bodies of the Union and to the Member States, but only when

---

[35] On the Charter, see de Búrca, "The Drafting of the European Union Charter of Fundamental Rights", *op.cit.*; Jacobs, "Human Rights in the European Union: the Role of the Court of Justice", *op.cit.*; Eicke, "The European Charter of Fundamental Rights – Unique Opportunity or Unwelcome Distraction", *op.cit.*; Lenaerts, "Fundamental Rights in the European Union", *op.cit.* and Hayes, "Negotiating the EU Charter on Fundamental Rights", Long, "The EU Charter – The European Commission's Position", Whelan, "Competence Questions Raised by the EU Charter" and Costello, "The Legal Status of the Charter" all in *Fundamental Social Rights* (Costello ed., 2001).

[36] See, *e.g.* the Opinion of Advocate General Tissano in Case C–173/99, *BECTU*, unreported, February 8, 2001.

[37] See, *e.g.* the Commission's reference to the Charter in its proposal for a Directive on the right of citizens of the Union and their family members to move and reside freely within the territory of the Member States, COM(2001) 257 final at para. 2.4.

they are implementing Union law. Paragraph 2 of Article 51 further provides that the Charter does not establish any new power or task for the Community or the Union, or modify existing powers or tasks. Thus, in this regard, the Charter merely confirms the *status quo*.

The rights protected by the Charter cover aspects of international human rights of all complexions: civil, cultural, economic, political and social. The rights affirmed include those with an EU legal basis: the EU Treaties, the Community Charter on the Fundamental Social Rights of Workers and ECJ case law; the constitutional traditions common to the Member States and the international obligations common to them: in the latter context specific reference is made to the ECHR and the case law of the European Court of Human Rights and to the ESC and the Revised European Social Charter.[38] The Praesidium, in its explanation of the Charter,[39] states that references to the ECHR cover both the Convention and the Protocols to it. This, as has been explained above, reflects ECJ case law, and thus both the ECHR Protocols and the Council of Europe Social Charters provide a source of inspiration for Community fundamental rights notwithstanding that not all Member States are party thereto.

In light of the special place already given to the ECHR in Community law, it is hardly surprising that in formulating many of the civil and political rights, such as the right to freedom from torture (set out in Article 4), the Charter draws heavily on the equivalent ECHR provisions. The economic, social and cultural rights, such as the rights to health care (set out in Article 35), on the other hand, are drawn largely from existing provisions of the Treaties and the EC and Council of Europe Social Charters. In fact, the Charter illustrates the difficulty of dividing human rights into water-tight categories like "civil and political" and "economic, social and cultural"; for example, the right to freedom of assembly and association set out in Article 11 draws on both the ECHR and the ESC, while the right to education set out in Article 14 draws on the First Protocol to the ECHR and the Community Charter of the Fundamental Rights of Workers, as well as the constitutional traditions of the member States. As well as the ECHR and the ESC, other Council of Europe treaties drawn on include the Convention on Human Rights and Biomedicine (see Article 3) and the Convention for the Protection of Individuals with regard to Automatic Processing of Personal Data (see Article 8). Universal instruments, such as the Universal Declaration of Human Rights (see Article 1), the Refugee Convention (see Article 18), the Convention on the Rights of the

---

[38] The reference to ECHR case law reflects Court of Justice jurisprudence: interestingly, no reference is made to decisions of the European Committee of Social Rights made under the ESC. This may reflect the lack of weight given to the decisions of international human rights bodies without judicial status, such as the UN Human Rights Committee which operates under the ICCPR: see Fitzpatrick, "European Union Law and the Council of Europe Conventions" in Costello (ed.), *Fundamental Social Rights* (2001).

[39] Available at *http://db.consilium.eu.int/df/default.asp?lang=en*.

Child (see Article 24) and the Statute of the International Criminal Court (see Article 3) are also drawn on. As well as human rights properly so-called, other fundamental rights are included in the Charter, such as the right to environmental protection set out in Article 37, which has not yet received recognition at international level. Citizens' rights, *inter alios*, those contained in Part Two of the EC Treaty (set out in Chapter V) and other rights, such as consumer protection, set out in Article 38, which might be regarded as being of lesser importance than internationally recognised human rights, are also included in the Charter.

As has been mentioned, the Member States decided not to incorporate the Charter into the Nice Treaty, but instead it was "solemnly proclaimed" at the European Council summit in December 2000 by the European Parliament, the Council and the Commission. The legal status of the Charter is thus, like that of the 1977 and 1989 Declarations and the Community Charter of the Fundamental Rights of Workers, somewhat uncertain and not particularly high.[40] However, despite the uncertainty as to its legal status, the proclamation of the Charter has gone a considerable way towards addressing one of the two main issues arising in any discussion of the human rights structures of the Union, namely its lack of a comprehensive Bill of Rights. Furthermore, the Declaration on the Future of the European Union appended to the Nice Treaty called for a deeper and wider debate on the future of Europe, with a view to preparing for some sort of constitutional settlement of the medium term future of the Union at the 2004 IGC. This debate has commenced with the setting-up by the European Council of a Convention on the Future of Europe in December 2001, which is discussed briefly in the final section of this chapter.

12.4 THE STRUCTURAL RELATIONSHIP BETWEEN THE EUROPEAN UNION AND THE EUROPEAN CONVENTION ON HUMAN RIGHTS

As has been set out in the previous section, recent developments, *i.e.* the drafting and proclamation of the Charter of Fundamental Rights, have gone some way towards providing the Union with a Bill of Rights; however, the

---

[40] For an analysis of the legal status of the Charter see Costello, "The Legal Status of the EU Charter of Fundamental Rights" *op.cit*. Notwithstanding its lack of formal legal status, the Charter has been referred to on numerous occasions by the Court of First Instance (see, *e.g.* SA Case T–177/01, *Jégo-Quéré et Cie,* judgment of May 3, 2002, unreported) and various Advocates-General (see, *e.g.* Case C–173/99, *BECTU v. Secretary of State for Trade and Industry*, opinion of AG Tizzano of February 8, 2001, unreported and Case C 50/00P, *Union de Pequneos Agricultores v. Council*, opinion of AG Jacobs of March 21, 2002, unreported), although it has not yet been referred to in a judgment of the Court of Justice. The Court of Justice, perhaps pointedly, did not refer to the Charter in its findings on the latter case (judgment of July 25, 2002, unreported).

other perennial issue arising with regard to human rights and the European Union, the relationship between EU law and international legal instruments, of which the ECHR is the prime example,[41] has not been resolved by the Member States. It is also clear from Article 51(2) of the Charter that, even were it to become binding at a future date, it would not give rise to any additional competence on the part of the Union or the European Community enabling them to accede to the ECHR.[42] Accordingly, this matter has been left to the two European Courts – of Justice and of Human Rights – to deal with. For many years, the relationship between the two European Courts was one of comity, with the ECJ expressing a general willingness to ensure that Community protection of fundamental rights did not fall below ECHR standards and with the Court of Human Rights refraining from interference with the ECJ's policing of fundamental rights. Beyond this policy of non-interference, there is positive interaction between the two systems. As discussed above, the ECJ has a policy of looking both to the text of the ECHR and to the European Court of Human Rights's jurisprudence in its formulation of Community fundamental rights; furthermore, the traffic is not wholly one-way: in its recent judgment on the right of transsexual persons to marry under Article 12 of the ECHR, the Court of Human Rights overturned its previous case law with reference to the reformulation of the right to marry in Article 9 of the Charter of Fundamental Rights.[43] However, there are signs that the relationship between the two courts is coming under strain for a number of reasons.

---

[41] This section of the chapter focuses largely on the relationship between the Union and the ECHR and its organs rather than on the relationship between the Union and other regional human rights treaties, such as the ESC, or universal human rights treaties, such as the ICCPR and the International Covenant on Economic, Social and Cultural Rights. This is because the relationship between the EU and the ECHR is the one that has been most focused on in practice; it is hoped that the discussion of this relationship may also prove useful in any future consideration of the relationship between the EU and other human rights instruments and bodies. For further analysis of the relationship between the EU and the ECHR see, *inter alia*, Spielmann, "Human Rights Case Law in the Strasbourg and Luxembourg Courts: Conflicts, Inconsistencies and Complementarities" in *The EU and Human Rights* (Alston ed,, 2000), Chap. 23, p.770; Canor, *"Primus Inter Pares.* Who is the Ultimate Guardian of Fundamental Rights in Europe?" (2000) 25 ELR 3; Demetriou, "Using Human Rights Through European Community Law" [1999] EHRLR 484.

[42] It would be interesting to speculate whether the Union could, provided suitable amendments were made to the ECHR to permit accession by non-State entities, accede thereto. Arguably, the Union now has legal personality, particularly in light of its conclusion, pursuant to Article 24 TEU, of agreements with third states in its own name, *e.g.* the stabilisation agreement with FYROM. Such agreements are concluded by the Presidency in the name of the Union, rather than in the name of the Member States. According to Article 11, one of the objectives of the Union's common foreign and security policy is consolidation and development of human rights and fundamental freedoms.

[43] See *Goodwin v. UK*, judgment of July 11, 2002, unreported, at para. 100: "[t]he Court would also note that Article 9 of the recently adopted Charter of Fundamental Rights of the European Union departs, no doubt deliberately, from the wording of Article 12 of the

First, notwithstanding the ECJ's willingness to have regard to the ECHR and the jurisprudence of the Convention organs, there are instances where its case law appears to be in conflict with that of the Court of Human Rights. For example, the ECJ has held that Article 8 of the ECHR (to which Article 7 of the Charter corresponds) on respect for private and family life, home and correspondence does not apply to legal persons,[44] whereas the Court of Human Rights has held that legal persons are entitled to the protection of that provision.[45] No case has arisen, however, where the ECJ has deliberately challenged ECHR case law,[46] but future differences of interpretation are likely to arise. Much as one might like, on an intellectual level, to see a "perfect fit" between the rights protected by the Convention and those protected by the Union, it could be argued that a certain amount of divergence could be accommodated and that such divergence would have been accommodated within the old relationship of comity between the two European Courts. However, while it is clear that neither the Community nor the Union as such can be brought before the European Court of Human Rights,[47] the continuance of the long-standing *modus operandi* whereby the Strasbourg organs declined to review the acts of the EU Member States when they are acting within the scope of their EU obligations has been weakened in recent times.

The old European Commission and Court of Human Rights declared inadmissible a number of challenges to such actions on the basis that the Convention does not prohibit States from transferring powers to international organisations such as the European Community; nonetheless, such a transfer of powers does not necessarily exclude the responsibility of States under the Convention with regard to the transferred powers. However, if within that organisation fundamental rights receive protection equivalent to that provided

---

Convention in removing the reference to men and women". The Court's reliance on Article 9 is made notwithstanding the explanatory note thereto, which provides that: "[t]he wording of this Article has been modernised to cover cases in which national legislation recognises arrangements other than marriage for founding a family. This Article neither prohibits nor imposes the granting of the status of marriage to unions between people of the same sex. The right is thus similar to that afforded by the ECHR, but its scope may be wider when national legislation so provides."

44 See Joined Cases 46/87 and 227/88, *Hoechst AG v. Commission* [1989] ECR 2859.
45 See *Chappell v. UK* (1989) Series A, No 152; *Niemietz v. Germany* (1992) Series A, No 251–B.
46 In this regard, the view of Dean Spielmann that "the Luxembourg Court would not adopt conflicting solutions to the problems at stake if there were the relevant case law from Strasbourg" is probably correct: see "Human Rights Case Law in the Strasbourg and Luxembourg Courts: Conflicts, Inconsistencies and Complementarities", *op.cit*. See also Case C94/00 *Roquette Frères SA v. Directeur général de la concurrence, de la consommation et de la répression des fraudes* unreported judgment of October 22, 2002 in which the ECJ held (at para. 29) that the jurisprudence of the European Court of Human Rights subsequent to *Hoechst* had to be taken into account when determining the scope of the right to privacy afforded to legal persons by EC Law.
47 See Application 8030/77, *CFDT v. European Communities* (1978) 13 DR.

by the Convention, the Strasbourg organs would not exercise jurisdiction.[48] Recent developments suggest that the new European Court of Human Rights may be prepared to take a more proactive approach: in *Matthews v. U.K.*[49] the European Court of Human Rights held that the Act Concerning the Election of Representatives of the European Parliament by Direct Universal Suffrage of 1976 – a piece of primary Community law – contravened the rights of the applicant, a resident of Gibraltar, under Article 3 of Protocol No. 1 to the ECHR, in that it denied to her the right to vote in European Parliament elections. One of the significant factors that led the Court of Human Rights to rule on the merits of this case was the lack of jurisdiction of the ECJ with regard to the Act. Nonetheless, it is hard to see how the ECJ could have interpreted the Act in such a way as to afford Ms Matthews the right to vote had its provisions been contained in the EC Treaty itself and yet the Court of Human Rights might still have felt impelled to assert its jurisdiction. Furthermore, the decision of the Strasbourg Court to declare admissible a case against Ireland where the Irish Government had acted in implementation of EC sanctions against Yugoslavia in the manner required of it by the ECJ, which had determined that the sanctions were not incompatible with Community fundamental rights,[50] may indicate a new willingness on behalf of the European Court of Human Rights to review the acts of the Member States even where they are in effect acting as agents of the Community and the ECJ has jurisdiction over their actions.

12.(5) THE FUTURE OF DEVELOPMENT OF A HUMAN RIGHTS FRAMEWORK FOR THE EUROPEAN UNION

This chapter has sought to examine the development of a human rights framework within the European Union. As has been outlined, such a framework has been developed incrementally and in a somewhat piece-meal fashion, reflecting the rather sporadic process of integration in the European Communities/Union. The initial Communities Treaties adopted in the 1950s reflected a desire on the

---

[48] See, *e.g.* Application 13258/87, *M and Co v. Germany* (1990) 64 DR.

[49] (1999) 28 EHRR 361. For an analysis of this case see: Doherty and Reid, "Voting Rights for the European Parliament: Whose Responsibility?" [1999] EHRLR 420.

[50] Application 45036/98, *Bosphorus Airways v. Ireland*, decision of September 13, 2001, unreported (the author was the agent of the Irish Government in this case). For the Court of Justice judgment in this case see Case C–84/95, *Bosphorus Hava Yollari ve Ticaret AS v. Minister for Transport, Energy and Communications* [1986] ECR I–3953. For analyses of the case see Canor, "Can Two Walk Together Except They Be Agreed?" (1998) 35 CMLR 137 and above, Costello, para 2(2)(b)(iii). A decision of the Court of Human Rights is still awaited on the admissibility of a claim by a German company against all fifteen Member States of the Union claiming that the failure of the Community courts to suspend a decision of the European Commission deprived it of the right to a fair trial guaranteed by Article 6(1) of the Convention: Application 56672/00, *DSR–Senator Lines GmBH v. Member States of the*

part of the founders to ensure peace by inter-locking the economies of the main continental Western European protagonists of the Second World War. In 1992 the European Union was established, reflecting a desire for further integration in non-economic spheres, with European Political Co-operation, first given a Treaty basis in the Single European Act, being expanded into the more formal Common Foreign and Security Policy and with the introduction of the Justice and Home Affairs pillar. The desire to move beyond purely economic concerns was also reflected in the dropping of the word "Economic" from the title of the E(E)C Treaty, in the introduction of the concept of a Union citizenship, albeit of a limited nature, and further limited references to fundamental rights. However, the Member States were not prepared to countenance integration in the new pillars to the same extent as in the first pillar. In particular, they were reluctant to give the Union a legal personality, to permit the ECJ to exercise jurisdiction, to allow the Commission or Parliament a significant role in the law-making process or to formulate a Bill of Rights making the rights of the individual the prime concern of the Union.

The Treaty on European Union was the last of the Treaties with a name reflecting an overall theme, or significant shift in European integration – the Treaties of Amsterdam and Nice are simply entitled treaties "amending the Treaty on European Union, the Treaties establishing the European Communities and certain related Acts". This lack of desire for major change was reflected in the human rights field by a continuing reluctance to formulate a legally binding Bill of Rights or to countenance the Communities or Union acceding to international human rights treaties, such as the ECHR. However the decision of the December 2001 European Council to set up a Convention on the Future of Europe, with a membership similar to that of the Convention that drafted the Charter of Fundamental Rights,[51] and a Forum that is supposed to allow participation of civil society in the debate on the Union's future,[52] appears to reflect a view amongst the Member States that a shift in the relationship between the Union and its citizens is required to allow for further development along clearly-defined lines and to ease the process of further enlargement. This is reflected in the reference in the Laaken Declaration adopted at the December 2001 summit to the possibility of developing a Constitution for the Union.

One aspect of a Constitution adhering to the liberal democratic ideals set out in Article 6(1) of the EU Treaty might be a Bill of Rights. The Charter of Fundamental Rights obviously provides a comprehensive set of rights that

---

European Union. Interestingly, the European Commission was permitted to make submissions to the Court of Human Rights in this case. This case has recently been referred to the grand Chamber of the Court for a decision.

[51] The Convention's web-site is located at *http://european-convention.eu.int/.*

[52] The Forum's web-site is located at *http://europa eu.int/futurum/forum convention/index _en.htm.*

could at least provide a basis from which a final list of rights could be drawn up. If the Bill were to be legally binding, the question of its status would also have to be considered and it is most likely that, if it is to be regarded as a constitutional document, it would have to be placed high, if not at the apex, of the hierarchy of norms constituting the Union's legal order. If a Bill of Rights is to be given legal status, then the next issue to consider would be whether the ECJ should be given the jurisdiction to review acts of the institutions and the Member States for conformity with the Bill. As has already been outlined, the ECJ does not have any jurisdiction over the Common Foreign and Security pillar of the Union and it remains to be seen whether the Member States will be prepared to extend the jurisdiction of the Court in this field. Another issue that falls to be considered is whether the Bill of Rights should apply solely to the institutions and to the Member States only where they act within the scope of Community, or Union, law. As has been mentioned above, Article 7 of the EU Treaty appears to allow for a potentially wide exercise of subject-matter jurisdiction by the Union in situations where a Member State seriously and persistently breaches fundamental rights. However, it appears unlikely that the Member States would countenance permitting the Union, and the ECJ in particular, to exercise jurisdiction across the range of their activities and so any Bill of Rights will probably contain a clause equivalent to Article 51 of the Charter.

The Convention on the Future of Europe set up a Working Group on Fundamental Rights, which issued its Final Report to the Convention Plenary on October 22, 2002. One of the two main issues it concentrated on was the modalities and consequences of possible incorporation of the Charter into the Treaties. While stressing that this is a political question for the Convention Plenary, all members of the Group either supported strongly an incorporation of the Charter into the EU treaties framework in a form that would make it legally binding and give it constitutional status or did not rule out giving favourable consideration to such incorporation. The issue of incorporating the Charter has also been flagged in the Preliminary draft Constitutional Treaty presented to the Plenary of the Convention by its Praesidium on October 28, 2002 as an issue to be considered (see Article 6 of the draft).

Another important issue that falls to be considered is the extent to which individuals have the right of access to the ECJ in respect of an alleged violation of their rights arising in a field where the Court has jurisdiction: at present individuals may indirectly gain access to the ECJ via a preliminary reference made by a domestic court thereto pursuant to Article 234 (ex Article 177) of the EC Treaty. Preliminary references may be made by domestic courts in areas falling within the third pillar pursuant to Article 35 of the EU Treaty, but only where the Member State in question has made a declaration permitting them to do so. Individuals may not directly access the ECJ with regard to third pillar matters. Article 230 (ex Article 173) of the EC Treaty permits individuals to bring direct actions of the acts of the institutions, but not against acts of the Member States acting within the scope of Community law. Challenges to the acts of the institutions may be brought on grounds of lack of competence, infringement of an essential procedural requirement, infringement of the Treaty or of any rule of law relating to its application, or misuse of powers. However, an individual may only bring an action in respect of decisions addressed directly to him or her or in respect of other decisions or regulations that are of direct and individual concern to that individual. Article 232 permits individuals to challenge a failure to act on the part of the institutions. The relatively restricted access to the ECJ afforded to individuals claiming breaches of their fundamental rights may need to be addressed in the context of a new Bill of Rights, particularly in light of the rights to a fair trial and to an effective remedy set out in Articles 6(1) and 13 of the ECHR respectively and reiterated in Article 47 of the Charter of Fundamental Rights.[53]

Another issue to be considered is the relationship of the EU and in particular any Bill of Rights with the ECHR (and other human rights treaties). The Charter, being formally non-binding, obviously cannot resolve the manner in which the Union should interact with the ECHR, but does it point the way to a future resolution? Article 53 of the Charter provides that nothing in it "shall be interpreted as restricting or adversely affecting human rights and fundamental freedoms" as recognised *inter alia* by the ECHR, but this would not appear to cover a situation where there is a direct clash between a Treaty provision and the ECHR or where the balance between individual rights struck in the latter context differs from those struck in the Union's legal order.[54] Accession by the Community, or the Union, to the ECHR might be seen as a solution, but it should be noted that even were the Community or the Union to accede, the Union Treaties could still take precedence over the ECHR in cases of direct conflict. Having regard to international agreements in general, the ECJ has determined that while international agreements are superior to secondary EC law and national law, they are subordinate to the Treaties themselves.[55] Thus it would appear that if one wished to ensure that the ECHR

---

[53] Recently, with specific reference to Article 47 (on the right to an effective remedy) of the Charter of Fundamental Rights, both the Court of First Instance (see *Jégo-Quéré et Cie SA, op.cit.*) and Advocate General Jacobs (see *Union de Pequenos Agricultores v. Council, op.cit.*) indicated a willingness to broaden the definition of "individual concern", however, the Court of Justice in the latter case has foreclosed the possibility of a judicial resolution of this issue. It has been raised in the course of the deliberations of the Convention on the Future of Europe's Working Group on Fundamental Rights as a matter of concern, but the Group's final report does not make any concrete recommendations, on the ground that the issue of the right of individuals to access the Court of Justice arises in a wide range of areas, not just those coming within its mandate.

[54] In this regard see the convincing analysis of Liisberg, *Does the EU Charter of Fundamental Rights Threaten the Supremacy of Community Law?*, Harvard Jean Monnet Working Paper 04/01, available at *http://www.jeanmonnetprogram.org/papers.*

[55] See, *e.g.* Case C–12/95, *Germany v. Council* [1998] ECR I–973. For a good analysis on the relationship between EU and international law see Lenaerts and de Smijter, "The European Union as an Actor under International Law" [1999–2000] *Yearbook of International Law* 95.

– representing the wider Europe – were to take precedence over the narrower Europe of the Union, accession would have to take place pursuant to a Treaty amendment specifically giving it precedence, along the lines of Article 29.4.7 of the Irish Constitution. The Working Group on Fundamental Rights of the Convention on the Future of Europe dealt with this question as the second main issue in its deliberations and in its Final Report of October 22, 2002. Again, while this is a political question for the Plenary, all members of the Group supported strongly or were ready to give favourable consideration to the creation of a legal basis enabling the Union to accede to the ECHR.[56]

The Convention and Forum on the Future of Europe, along with the Irish National Forum on Europe, provide an opportunity to improve the quality of the debate on the future of the European Union, including a future framework for human rights protection in the EU. It is to be hoped that any human rights measures included in a future Treaty arising out of the 2004 IGC are underpinned by broad and informed popular support.

---

[56] The Convention's Working Group on Legal Personality, in its Final Report of October 1, 2002, stated that it had reached a very broad consensus (with one member against) in favour of a treaty provision explicitly conferring legal personality on the Union and recommended that it should be a single legal personality, replacing the existing personalities. This broad consensus was maintained in the subsequent meeting of the Plenary on the issue and Article 4 of the Praesidium's Preliminary draft Treaty provides for explicit recognition of the Union's personality.

13. RECENT DEVELOPMENTS IN EC EQUALITY LAW

CLÍONA J. M. KIMBER*

13.(1) INTRODUCTION

European Community (EC) law has come a long way from the tentative inclusion of the principle of equal pay in the Treaty of Rome signed in 1957. With the adoption of the sex equality Directives as well as the progressive jurisprudence developed by the European Court of Justice (ECJ), a comprehensive sex equality code has now been built up at EC level. Nevertheless, there is still ongoing litigation in the area of sex equality law which is endeavouring to fill the gaps and to answer many outstanding questions. Thus, sex equality law is still developing, particularly with regard to the thorny issue of positive discrimination. However, by far the greatest changes have been brought in by the Treaty of Amsterdam and the new Article 13 of the EC Treaty. This Article extended the mandate of the EC social policy beyond sex equality law to a wide range of other forms of discrimination. The European Commission has not been slow to act. Already two new Directives, the so-called Article 13 Directives, have been adopted: the first, the Race Directive, is designed to prohibit discrimination on grounds of race and ethnicity; the second, the Framework Directive, extends the equal treatment principle to religion or belief, disability, age and sexual orientation. These Directives are due to be implemented by the Member States by 2003.[1]

The adoption of these legal instruments is a welcome development for disadvantaged minorities in the European Union (EU). Nevertheless, the coming into force of these measures will brings with it a certain amount of confusion and upheaval. With the adoption of the Race and Ethnicity Directive in 2000, the prohibition of race discrimination moves to the top of the hierarchy of rights in EC law. The rights of those discriminated against because of their race or ethnic origin are far greater and extend to a larger number of areas than those of other disadvantaged groups, including women. A clear hierarchy of equalities now exists, with sex equality having been displaced by racial equality from a position of historical dominance in EC

---

* Barrister-at-Law, LL.B, LL.M, M.A. All errors remain the responsibility of the author.
[1] July 19, 2003 for the Race and Ethnicity Directive; December 2, 2003 for the Framework Directive.

anti-discrimination law.[2] In the legal systems of many Member States, including Ireland, due to the influence of EC law, sex equality still benefits from greater legal protection, and for many Member States, the protections afforded to minorities by the new Directives will be entirely new in their legal systems.

The purpose of this chapter is to discuss these recent developments in EC equality law. It will be divided into two parts. In the first part (13.(2)). I will consider the significant developments in the jurisprudence of the ECJ. In the second part (13.(3)). I will examine the adoption of the new Directives and the amendment of the existing Equal Treatment Directive. In doing so, I will come to some conclusions about the overall direction of EC equality law as a whole, and make some suggestions for the future.

13.(2) RECENT DECISIONS OF THE EUROPEAN COURT OF JUSTICE

Following more than 20 years answering the questions of Member States with regard to the meaning of the EC legal instruments on sex discrimination, it is surprising that the ECJ is still required to rule on the interpretation of these instruments. Nevertheless, it is still the case that very many questions are still referred by national courts to the ECJ on a variety of matters. In some instances, the ECJ is merely filling in the gaps in what is already a comprehensive jurisprudence in a given area. Issues relating to pregnancy discrimination, pensions and equal pay fall into this category. In other areas, the ECJ is still sailing into new waters and developing a jurisprudence. The best example of the latter is the litigation surrounding the legality of positive measures. The combination of both types of case law leads to a dynamic and interesting field of consideration.

13.(2)(a) Pregnancy and dismissal

The case law of the ECJ was quite clear that discrimination on grounds of pregnancy was direct discrimination[3] contrary to the Equal Treatment Directive.[4] It also ruled in *Webb v. EMO*,[5] that Article 10 of the Pregnancy Directive protected women from dismissal from the beginning of their pregnancy to the end of the maternity leave. However, after this decision it was not clear whether this protection extended to women on temporary contracts

---

[2] Waddington and Bell, "More Equal than Others: Distinguishing European Equality Directives" C.M.L.Rev. [2001] 587.

[3] Case C–177/88 *Dekker v. Stichtung Vormingscentrum Voor Jong Volwassenen (VJV) Plus* [1990] ECR I–3941.

[4] For a discussion of Community law on pregnancy discrimination, see Bolger and Kimber, *Sex Discrimination Law* (2000).

[5] Case C–32/93 [1994] ECR I–3567.

who were recruited to cover another employee on maternity leave. This gap has now finally been filled by *Tele Danmark*.[6]

In June 1995, Ms Brandt-Nielsen was recruited by Tele Danmark for a period of six months from July 1, 1995, to work in its customer service department for mobile telephones. In August 1995, Ms Brandt-Nielsen informed Tele Danmark that she was pregnant and expected to give birth in early November. Shortly afterwards, on August 23, 1995, she was dismissed with effect from September 30, on the ground that she had not informed Tele Danmark that she was pregnant when she was recruited. Tele Danmark argued that the prohibition under EC law of dismissing a pregnant worker did not apply to a worker, recruited on a temporary basis, who, despite knowing that she was pregnant when the contract of employment was concluded, failed to inform the employer of this, and because of her right to maternity leave was unable, for a substantial part of the duration of that contract, to perform the work for which she had been recruited. It argued that it was not Ms Brandt-Nielsen's pregnancy which was the determining fact of her dismissal but the fact that she would be unable to perform a substantial part of the contract. Ms Brandt-Nielsen and the European Commission submitted, on the other hand, that neither the Equal Treatment Directives 76/207 nor the Pregnancy Directive 92/85 nor the case law of the Court made a distinction according to whether the contract under which the worker has been recruited is for a fixed or an indefinite period.

In rejecting the arguments of Tele Danmark the Court ruled that:

> "Since the dismissal of a worker on account of pregnancy constitutes direct discrimination on grounds of sex, whatever the nature and extent of the economic loss incurred by the employer as a result of her absence because of pregnancy, whether the contract of employment was concluded for a fixed or an indefinite period has no bearing on the discriminatory character of the dismissal. In either case the employee's inability to perform her contract of employment is due to pregnancy."[7]

Due to pregnancy, an employee was unable to work during a substantial part of the term of a fixed contract under which she was recruited. However, the nature of the contract *i.e.* fixed term, did not affect the prohibition on dismissing her on the ground of pregnancy. The Court also found that it was irrelevant that Ms Brandt-Nielsen had not informed her employer that she was pregnant at the time of her recruitment.

This case provides clarity that was absent after *Webb v. EMO*. It copperfastens the strong support that EC law gives to women during the period of pregnancy and maternity leave and provides protection for temporary workers.

---

[6] Case C–109/00 *Tele Danmark A/S v. Handels– og Kontorfunktionærernes Forbund i Danmark (HK)*, [2001] ECR I-6993.

[7] *ibid.*, para. 31.

It is also interesting to note that another judgment highly protective of pregnant women, *Jiménez Melgar v. Ayuntamiento de Los Barrios*[8] was handed down the same day. Taken together, *Tele Danmark* and *Melgar* are indications of the extent to which the ECJ expects employers to safeguard womens' employment rights during this crucial time.

Ms Jiménez Melgar had been employed as a home and mother's help by the Local Municipality on a succession of fixed-term part-time contracts which generally lasted three months. After she informed her employer about her pregnancy, her existing contract was terminated even though it had only been in being for one month. She took the view that this dismissal was discriminatory.

In coming to its decision, the ECJ referred to its decision in *Tele-Danmark* and reaffirmed that the prohibition of discrimination laid down in Article 10 of Directive 92/85 applies to both employment contracts for an indefinite period and fixed-term contracts. Applying this to the circumstances of Ms Jiménez Melgar's complaint, the Court ruled that although non-renewal of such a contract, when it comes to an end as stipulated, cannot be regarded as a dismissal prohibited by that provision, where non-renewal of a fixed-term contract is motivated by the worker's state of pregnancy it constitutes direct discrimination on grounds of sex, contrary to Article 2(1) and 3(1) of Directive 76/207.[9]

These decisions taken together answer the questions left open by *Webb*, and make it clear that a dismissal on grounds of pregnancy which takes place during a fixed-term contract, even of short duration, is discrimination on grounds of sex, contrary to the Pregnancy Directive. In *Melgar*, the ECJ is perhaps going even one step further by ruling that non-renewal of a series of fixed-term contracts, which is motivated by pregnancy, is also discrimination on grounds of sex. This is in line with Irish law on unfair dismissals which provides that under certain circumstances non-renewal of a series of fixed-term contracts could amount to unfair dismissal.[10]

13.(2)(b) Pensions

It is now many years since Senator Mary Robinson challenged the rules regarding the provision of pensions for Senators in Ireland, that allowed widows but not widowers to claim state pensions on the death of their spouse. Nevertheless, the issue of the provision of pensions on an equal basis to male and female employees still causes difficulty. *Mouflin* and *Menauer* are two recent cases in which the ECJ has once more been required to rule on equality and pensions.[11]

---

[8]   Case C–438/99, [2001] ECR I 6915.
[9]   *ibid.*, paras 45–47.
[10] See s. 2(2) of the Unfair Dismissal Act 1977 as amended by the Unfair Dismissals (Amendment) Act 1993.
[11] For a more detailed discussion of EC law and pensions equality, see Bolger and Kimber, above n.4, chap. 6.

The case of *Mouflin v. Recteur de l'académie de Reims*[12] concerned the rules of the French retirement scheme for civil servants which provided that female civil servants whose husbands suffered from a disability or incurable illness making it impossible for them to undertake any form of employment were entitled to a retirement pension with immediate effect, but did not give the same entitlement to male civil servants in the same situation. Mr Mouflin, a school-teacher and civil servant sought to be allowed to claim his retirement pension rights with immediate effect so as to be able to care for his wife who was suffering from an incurable illness. This application was denied on the basis that the right to retire to care for an invalid spouse was reserved exclusively to female civil servants. The ECJ had little difficulty in ruling that such a difference in treatment infringed the then Article 119 (renumbered Art. 141) of the EC Treaty.

A similar issue had in fact arisen in the case of *Menauer*,[13] in which judgment was given two months earlier. The difference in *Menauer*, however, was that the discriminatory criteria were contained in the rules of a private company to which the employer had contracted out the pensions' provision.

Mr Menauer's late wife had been employed by Barmer Ersatzkasse and had been a member of her employer's associated Pensions Fund throughout the time of her employment. This Fund was managed by a private institution independent of the employer and the employer paid contributions into it for its employees. Under the provisions of the Fund, a widower's pension could only be paid to a husband on the death of a wife where the deceased was the main breadwinner in the family. Mr Menauer brought an action against the employer and the Fund claiming that this additional requirement was discriminatory and therefore invalid. Under German labour law the employer remained liable to provide the pension to which the employee was entitled, even where a Fund's rules contravened the prohibition on discrimination. The employer must make good the shortfall itself by providing the benefits concerned, and cannot avoid that obligation. The central question, therefore, was whether a private Fund itself, even in circumstances where an employer was required to remedy any lack of equal treatment, could have discriminatory rules with regard to the provision of survivors' pensions.

In a detailed judgment, the ECJ held that the rules of an independent fund must also conform to the equal treatment principle. Referring to its earlier jurisprudence in *Barber* and *Coloroll Pension Trustees*,[14] it stated that:

> "[T]he applicability of Article 119 of the Treaty to an occupational pension scheme is not thwarted by the fact that the scheme has been set up in the form of a trust and is administered by trustees who are technically independent of the

---

[12] Case C–206/00, December 13, 2001 (nyr).
[13] Case C–379–99 *Pensionskasse für die Angestellten der Barmer Ersatzkasse VVaG v. Hans Menauer*, (2001) ECR I–7275.
[14] See *Barber*, paras. 28 and 29, and *Coloroll Pension Trustees*, para. 20).

employer, since Article 119 also applies to consideration received indirectly
from the employer.

It follows from the foregoing that if the persons who are entrusted with
administering an occupational pension scheme are required to pay benefits
which constitute pay within the meaning of Article 119 of the Treaty, they are
bound to comply with the principle of equal treatment laid down in that
provision, whatever the legal form of those persons or the manner in which
they are responsible for administering that pension scheme."[15]

It emphasised that the effectiveness of the Treaty Article would be considerably diminished and the legal protection required to ensure real equality
would be seriously impaired if an employee or an employee's dependants
could rely on that provision only as against the employer, and not as against
those who are expressly charged with performing the employer's obligations.[16]
Thus the Court reinforced its earlier finding in *Barber* that a private institution
to which an employer has contracted out its pensions' provision, is also subject
to Article 141 (ex Art. 119).

13.(2)(c) Part-time workers and selection for dismissal

In contrast with the forthright stance taken by the ECJ in relation to
discrimination resulting from pregnancy and in relation to equality and
pensions, the ECJ has stopped short of a strong enforcement of the equal
treatment principle in other areas and allowed Member States significant room
for manoeuvre in formulating their employment policies. *Kachelmann*,[17] a case
in which the issue raised was whether the selection for dismissal of part-time
workers as compared with full-time workers was discriminatory treatment
contrary to the Equal Treatment Directive 76/207, is an example of this trend.

Ms Kachelmann was employed by Bankhaus on a part-time basis as a
qualified banker. Owing to a reduction in the Bank's activities, there was a
downsizing of staff and Ms Kachelmann was dismissed on economic grounds.
The basis on which full-time workers were selected for dismissal was more
favourable than that on which part-time workers were selected in that social
criteria were to be taken into account in selecting full-time workers for
dismissal but were not considered for part-time workers. Ms Kachelmann
argued that such a distinction was indirect discrimination on grounds of sex.

In coming to its decision, the ECJ reaffirmed its earlier ruling in
Jorgensen[18] that where national rules, although worded in neutral terms, work
to the disadvantage of a much higher percentage of women than men, they
discriminate indirectly against women, unless that difference in treatment is
justified by objective factors unrelated to any discrimination on grounds of sex.

---

[15] *Menauer* at paras. 20 and 23.
[16] *ibid.*, at para. 29.
[17] Case C–322/98 *Kachelmann v. Bankhaus Hermann Lampe* [2000] ECR I–7505.
[18] Case C–226/96 *Jorgensen v. Foreningen af Speciallaeger* [2000] ECR 1–2447.

On this basis, the Court found that the lack of comparability of full-time and part-time workers under the German legal provisions was indirectly discriminatory on grounds of sex. However, it went on to find that the difference in treatment was objectively justified as it had been based on considerations unrelated to the sex of the workers. The Court stated expressly that social policy was a matter for the Member States, which enjoyed a reasonable margin of discretion as regards the nature of social protection measures and the detailed arrangements for their implementation. In its reasoning, it was mindful of the fact that it was a matter for national legislatures to find a fair balance in employment law between the various interests concerned.

The extent to which the ECJ was willing to stand back and allow Member States to determine their own rules for deciding on dismissals even though they are *prima facie* discriminatory, is particularly surprising given that the Court had earlier noted that: "the number of workers employed full-time in Germany, and probably throughout the Community, is significantly higher in all sectors than the number of part-time workers. It follows that, where jobs are being cut, part-time workers are in general put at a greater disadvantage because they have less chance of finding another comparable job."[19]

It is surprising that while recognising the disadvantage from which part-time workers suffer, the Court was unwilling to assist them. While it is certainly true that the disputed criteria in *Kachelmann* was a consideration unrelated to sex, it was nevertheless a criterion that operated to the disadvantage of a substantially higher percentage of women than men. It is difficult to see therefore, how such a consideration could somehow justify itself. Ultimately, it is clear that notwithstanding its pronouncements that discrimination against part-time workers is indirect discrimination, the Court is willing to leave the Member States quite a wide margin of discretion in dealing with difficult issues of employment law such as the redundancy of workers.

13.(2)(d) Equal pay

The recent case law of the ECJ shows that it is still occupied with the question of the justification of unequal levels of pay between men and women. Although the Equal Pay Directive has been in place since 1975, there is still a significant pay gap between men and women in the EU. While there are many factors contributing to the continuance of such a difference, a robust examination by the ECJ of attempts to justify differential levels of pay can only assist in narrowing the gap. Such a stance was taken by the ECJ in *Brunnhofer*,[20] a case in which an Austrian Bank sought to justify unequal pay on the basis of the greater efficiency of a male employee.

---

[19] *ibid.*, para. 27.
[20] Case C–281/99 *Susanna Brunnhofer v. Bank der österreichischen Postsparkasse AG*, [2001] ECR I–4961.

Ms Brunnhofer, who was employed by the Bank, complained that she had suffered discrimination based on sex, contrary to the principle of equal pay, on the ground that she received a monthly salary lower than that paid to a male colleague. The difference in salary between the two employees arose from the fact that, under his employment contract, Ms Brunnhofer's male colleague received an individual supplement the monthly amount of which was higher than the supplement which Ms Brunnhofer received under her contract with the Bank. The level of the supplements were fixed at the time at which the employees commenced their employment with the bank and before the bank had had an opportunity to assess their work effectiveness. Both employees were classified in the same job category.

The central issue for the Court's consideration was whether a difference between a woman's and a man's pay for the same work or work of equal value is capable of being objectively justified, *inter alia*, by factors which are known only after the employees have taken up their duties and which can be assessed only while the employment contract is being performed, such as a difference in the individual work capacity of the employees concerned or in the effectiveness of an employee's work in relation to that of a colleague.[21] Unsurprisingly, the Court ruled that such *ex post facto* justifications were not permissible. It stated that excluding work paid at piece rates, with regard to work paid at time rates:

> "circumstances linked to the person of the employee which cannot be determined objectively at the time of that person's appointment but come to light only during the actual performance of the employee's activities, such as personal capacity or the effectiveness or quality of the work actually done by the employee, cannot be relied upon by the employer to justify the fixing, right from the start of the employment relationship, of pay different from that paid to a colleague of the other sex performing identical or comparable work."[22]

The ECJ noted that there was nothing to stop individual work capacity being taken into account in career development and, hence, on the subsequent posting and salary of the persons concerned, even though at the beginning they might have performed the same work.

Brunnhofer is one of a long line of cases in which the ECJ has undertaken a rigorous examination of the objective justification of equal pay and is to be welcomed on that basis.[23]

---

[21] The Court was also asked to consider whether such a difference is capable of being objectively justified by circumstances not taken into consideration under the collective agreement applicable to the employees concerned. It ruled, at para. 68, that such factors could be taken into account, in so far as they constituted objectively justified reasons unrelated to any discrimination based on sex and in conformity with the principle of proportionality.

[22] *Brunnhofer*, para. 76.

[23] See, *e.g.* Case C–243/95 *Hill and Stapleton v. Revenue Commissioners* [1998] 3 C.M.L.R. 81 and Case C–184/89 *Nimz* [1991] ECR I–297.

13.(2)(e) Positive discrimination

As was noted earlier, in contrast with its rulings on equal pay, pregnancy discrimination and discrimination against part-time workers, the issue of positive discrimination is a relatively new one for the ECJ. Although Articles 2(3) and 2(4) of the Equal Treatment Directive of 1976 did allow for the taking of "positive measures" as they are called in EC law, in furtherance of sex equality, the first time that Article 2(4) was fully analysed by the ECJ was in the mid 1990s.[24] While positive measures would appear to have been legally permissible, it seems likely that such measures were not politically acceptable until the 1990s and so were put in place at Member State level. Once adopted, positive measures then became a source of dispute at national level, which has resulted in the referral of a spate of questions to the ECJ for preliminary rulings. The legal legitimacy of positive measures was reinforced by the placing in the Treaty, following the Treaty of Amsterdam, of a provision permitting positive measures. Article 141(4) EC (amending Article 119).

At present, therefore, there are three legal bases in EC law for the taking of positive measures. The first is contained in Article 2(4) of the Equal Treatment Directive, and provides that the equal treatment principle: "shall be without prejudice to measures to promote equal opportunity for men and women, in particular by removing existing inequalities which affect women's opportunities in the areas referred to in [relation to access to employment, promotion, vocational training and working conditions]." The second is in Article 2(3) of the Equal Treatment Directive: "[T]his Directive shall be without prejudice to provisions concerning the protection of women, particularly as regards pregnancy and maternity." Article 141(4) of the EC Treaty contains the third permission, as it allows Member States to: "maintain [. . .] or adopt [. . .] measures providing for specific advantages in order to make it easier for the under-represented sex to pursue a vocational activity or to prevent or compensate for disadvantages in professional careers".

On looking at the decisions of the ECJ on positive measures, it is fair to say that the ECJ is feeling its way on this issue. Its first decision *Kalanke*,[25] in which it struck down a positive measure adopted by the German civil service in Bremen on the basis that it gave an unconditional priority to women applicants for promotion, it attracted a flood of criticism from academic and practising lawyers as well as from the Commission. In its next decision, *Marschall*,[26] it took a completely different approach and held that positive measures adopted by another German state were permissible under Article 2(4) of the Equal Treatment Directive. It ruled that positive measures could not be justified by Article 2(1) and 2(4) of the Equal Treatment Directive if they

---

[24] Case C–450/93 *Kalanke v. Freie Hansestadt Bremen* [1995] ECR I–3051.
[25] *ibid.*
[26] Case C–409/95 *Marschall (Hellmut) v. Land Nordrhein Westfalen* [1997] ECR I–6363.

result in an automatic preference being given to candidates for a post. However, the Equal Treatment Directive did not preclude a rule of national law under which a candidate belonging to the under-represented sex was granted preference over a competitor of the opposite sex, provided that the candidates possessed equivalent or substantially equivalent merits, and where the candidatures are subjected to an objective assessment which took account of the specific personal situations of all the candidates. On this basis the measures adopted in *Marschall* were permissible. In truth, there was little difference between the measures adopted in *Kalanke* and in *Marschall*. In subsequent cases the ECJ appeared to follow its reasoning in *Marschall*,[27] but more recent developments have shown a change of approach and, in particular, the making of distinctions between measures designed to compensate for past discrimination and those designed to promote equal opportunities in the future. It has also tended to make distinctions between the types of positive measures that are permitted by the three legal provisions set out above.

13.(2)(e)(i) Positive action as a remedy for present or future discrimination?

In *Griesmar*[28] the central issue was whether a provision of French law, which gave female civil servants who had raised children a service credit which was applied in calculation of the pension paid at the end of their career, infringed the equal treatment principle. Mr Griesmar, a French *magistrat* and father of three children, was granted a pension upon his retirement from the French civil service. For the calculation of that pension, account was taken of the years of service actually completed by Mr Griesmar. However, no account was taken of the service credit provided for under national legislation to which female civil servants were entitled in respect of each of their children. Mr Griesmar argued that this difference in treatment was contrary to Article 141 (ex Art. 119) of the Treaty and to the objectives of both the occupational social security Directive,[29] and the occupational social security Directive.[30]

The ECJ considered whether the preferential treatment accorded to women was contrary to Article 141 (ex Art. 119). In coming to a decision, the ECJ first considered whether male and female workers were in comparable situations, *i.e.* whether the situations of a male civil servant and a female civil servant who are respectively the father and mother of children are comparable. The Court drew a distinction between the situations of women in the period

---

[27] Case C–158/97 *Badeck v. Landesanwalt beim Staatsgerichthof des Landes Hessen* (1999) ECR I–1875. For a discussion of *Badeck, Kalanke and Marschall* and other early cases see Bolger and Kimber, above n.4 at 384–394.

[28] Case C–366/99 *Joseph Griesmar v. Ministre de l'Économie, des Finances et de l'Industrie, Ministre de la Fonction publique, de la Réforme de l'État et de la Décentralisation* (2001) ECR I–9383.

[29] Council Directive 86/378 of July 24, 1986 [1986] O.J. L283/27 as amended by Dir. 96/97.

[30] Council Directive 79/7 of December 19, 1978 [1979] O.J. L6/24.

following pregnancy and childbirth, and the situation of women in their capacity as parents. Relying on settled case law, including *Hoffmann* and *Commission v. France*,[31] it stated that:

> "While the Court has ruled that maternity leave granted to a woman on expiry of the statutory protective period falls within the scope of Article 2(3) of [the Equal Treatment] Directive 76/207, it has also held that measures designed to protect women in their capacity as parents, which is a capacity which both male and female workers may have, cannot find justification in that provision of Directive 76/207."[32]

Article 2(3) provides that "this Directive shall be without prejudice to provisions concerning the protection of women, particularly as regards pregnancy and maternity". Thus, the ECJ was stating that the only special or positive measures in favour of women which can be justified by the Equal Treatment Directive are those which directly relate to the situation of women in the period following pregnancy and childbirth. The Court reasoned that the credit offered by the French civil service was not designed to offset the occupational disadvantages which arise for female workers as a result of being absent from work during the period following childbirth, but to offset the occupational disadvantages which arise for female workers as a result of having brought up children. Any difference in treatment could not therefore be justified by the Equal Treatment Directive. The Court did not consider whether the service credit could be justified by Article 2(4) of the Directive.

Having held that the difference in treatment could not be justified by the Equal Treatment Directive, the question arose as to whether it was permissible under what is now Article 141(4). The French Government argued that the greater frequency of the use of parental leave by women, which affects their pension rights, and the duration of the careers of female civil servants, which is on average two years shorter than that of male civil servants, justified the provision of the service credit. It stated that even though the statistics do not establish a direct link between the benefit of parental leave and length of career, it can hardly be doubted that the bringing-up of children is an important factor, perhaps the most important factor, in explaining the shorter duration of the careers of female civil servants at the date of their retirement. The credit was, thus, designed to offset, for the benefit of women, the disadvantages, in so far as the rate and basis of calculation of retirement pensions were concerned, ensuing from a break in career for the purpose of bringing up children.

The Court did not accept these arguments. It ruled that the credit was not a measure which contributed to helping women conduct their professional life on an equal footing with men, and it was only such measures which were

---

[31] Case 184/83 *Hofmann v. Barmer Ersatzkasse* [1984] ECR 3047, Case 312/86 *Commission v. France* [1988] ECR 6315.

[32] *Griesmar* at para. 44.

permitted by Article 141(1): "The measure is limited to granting female civil servants who are mothers a service credit at the date of their retirement, without providing a remedy for the problems which they may encounter in the course of their professional career."[33]

In essence, therefore, the ECJ is applying a very strict interpretation of Article 141(4) so that a measure must be very specifically directed at contributing in the present or in the future to helping women conduct their professional life on an equal footing with men before it is permitted under that Article. This might be termed a positive measure with future effect. It seems that the ECJ is taking the view that a measure which merely compensates women afterwards for the difficulties that they have encountered will not be justifiable. This interpretation seems strange given that Article 141(4) expressly allows for the provision of specific advantages for the under-represented sex to "compensate for disadvantages in their professional careers". The service credit, in that it compensated women for any disadvantage suffered by virtue of bringing up children, would seem to fall full square within this exception. This is in contrast with the case of *Schnorbus*, discussed below, in which a measure designed to compensate men for time spent doing military service, was held not to infringe the equal treatment principle.

The Court also stated that the credit infringed the principle of equal pay in as much as it excluded male civil servants who were able to prove that they assumed the task of bringing up their children from entitlement to the credit in the calculation of retirement pensions. It is submitted that this additional reasoning for rejecting the service credit is fairer and more acceptable. If men have assumed the task of bringing up children, and suffer disadvantage as a result, it would only seem just that they too should be compensated for such disadvantage. To fail to do this is to fall into the trap of assuming that the responsibility for child-rearing is always performed by women, and can lead to the danger of adopting or maintaining measures that reinforce this stereotypical role.[34]

13.(2)(e)(ii) Requirement of proportionality for positive action?

A contrasting result can be seen in *Lommers v. Minister van Landbouw, Natuurbeheer en Visserij*.[35] At issue was the legality of a scheme set up by a Minister to tackle extensive under-representation of women within his Ministry. In the context of a proven insufficiency of proper, affordable care facilities, a limited number of subsidised nursery places made available by the Ministry to its staff was reserved for female officials alone whilst male officials could have access to them only in cases of emergency. Mr Lommers

---

[33] *ibid.*, at para. 65.

[34] For a discussion of the role of EC law in reinforcing traditional roles of motherhood see McGlynn, "Ideologies of Motherhood in European Community Sex Equality Law" (2000) 6 *European Law Review* p.31.

[35] Case C–476/99 *Lommers* of March 19, 2002 nyr.

was an official at the Netherlands Ministry of Agriculture. His wife was employed elsewhere. On seeking to reserve a nursery place, his request was rejected on the ground that children of male officials could be given places in the nursery facilities in question only in cases of emergency. Mr Lommers complained that this policy was contrary to the equal treatment principle in EC law. The Minister for Agriculture argued that the policy reflected the Ministry's determination to tackle the under-representation of women in the Ministry, and that on that basis it was justified under Article 2(4) of the Equal Treatment Directive.

The ECJ found that since the scheme was designed to assist women in the pursuit of their careers and to eliminate the causes of women's reduced opportunities for access to employment, in principle it could fall within Article 2(4). However, the Court went on to question whether the policy as presently formulated was proportional: did it remain within the limits of what was appropriate and necessary in order to achieve the aim in view? To decide this question, the Court considered on the one hand submissions before it that a measure such as the policy in question whose purported aim is to abolish a *de facto* inequality might nevertheless also help to perpetuate a traditional division of roles between men and women, and on the other hand recognised the acknowledged difficulty faced by female officials at the Ministry of Agriculture in finding nursery places. It also found relevant the fact that male officials were not totally excluded, but could be granted a nursery place in an emergency. In light of these considerations it concluded that the scheme was permissible and proportional if it did not exclude male officials who take care of children by themselves.

The decision in *Lommers* was handed down by the ECJ after its judgment in *Griesmar*; indeed the Court referred to *Griesmar* in the course of its reasoning. If the Court in *Griesmar* was saying that Article 141(4) only permits positive measures with future effects, in *Lommers* it did not comment either positively or negatively on this interpretation of Article 141(4). Rather it chose to confine its enquiry to whether the measure was permissible under Article 2(4) of the Equal Treatment Directive. In interpreting this provision, it added a requirement of proportionality to any measure which wishes to be permissible under Article 2(4).

It would seem also that the Court was reinforcing the individualistic nature of EC sex equality law in general and positive measures in particular, rather than seeing them as a tool whose effects should be considered across society as a whole. It was argued that Mr Lommers' wife might have difficulty in pursuing her career because if no nursery place were made available for their children, she would be forced to undertake their care. The Court took the view, however, that this was not relevant as: "[The Equal Treatment] provision cannot therefore be construed as requiring an employer who adopts a measure to tackle under-representation of women amongst his own staff to take account of considerations related to the maintenance in employment of women not belonging to that staff."[36]

Ultimately, therefore, the measure in question was permitted where it benefited the employees in one workplace, even though it did not benefit women in society as a whole. This interpretation of the measures permitted by Article 2(4) is one which prevents a consideration of the position of women in the EU in general, and allows positive measures which merely displaces a problem from one employer to another.

13.(2)(e)(iii) Positive action measures favouring men

The case of *Schnorbus v. Land Hessen*[37] is another recent decision handed down by the ECJ concerning the legality of positive action. It is an unusual case in a number of respects. First, the positive discrimination in question favoured men rather than women. Secondly, none of the three legal bases for positive measures were relied upon by the ECJ in its ruling that the measure was permissible. Rather the ECJ simply took the view that the measure in question was not discriminatory because it was objectively justifiable.

In October 1997 Ms Schnorbus applied for admission to the practical legal training course which is a mandatory stage in the training of lawyers in Germany. Her application was rejected twice, in relation to two consecutive admission dates, on the basis that since too many applications had been received, it had been necessary to make a selection in accordance with the applicable national regulations. These regulations favoured applicants who had completed compulsory military service. Ms Schnorbus objected on the grounds that the selection procedure discriminated against women because of the preference accorded to applicants who had completed compulsory military or civilian service, which can be done only by men.

The ECJ considered the matter and held that the national provisions at issue were indirectly discriminatory on grounds of sex, but were objectively justifiable. In a decision which did not do much to explain its reasoning it held that:

> "[A] measure giving priority to persons who have completed compulsory military or civilian service is evidence of indirect discrimination in favour of men, who alone are subject by law to such an obligation. However, it is clear that the provision at issue, which takes account of the delay experienced in the progress of their education by applicants who have been required to do military or civilian service, is objective in nature and prompted solely by the desire to counterbalance to some extent the effects of that delay. In such circumstances, the provision at issue cannot be regarded as contrary to the principle of equal treatment for men and women. Furthermore, as the Commission points out, the advantage conferred on the persons concerned, whose enjoyment of priority

---

[36] *ibid.*, para. 49.
[37] Case C–79/99 *Julia Schnorbus v. Land Hessen,* [2000] ECR I–10997.

may operate to the detriment of other applicants only for a maximum of 12 months, does not seem disproportionate, since the delay they have suffered on account of the activities referred to is at least equal to that period."[38]

The ECJ did not address the question put by the Court in Frankfurt, namely whether the preference was unjustified because it automatically gave preference to men. The ECJ had earlier declared in its decisions in *Badeck*[39] and *Abrahamsson*[40] that the existence of an automatic preference meant that positive discrimination could not be justified. Nor did the ECJ address another important question raised at the national level, that is whether Article 2(4) of the Equal Treatment Directive is confined solely to measures which are in *favour* of women, or whether it also permits measures which favour men. This is surprising given that on the face of it, Article 2(4) would only appear to permit positive measures which have as their aim the removal of existing inequalities which affect women's opportunities in employment. In *Schnorbus*, the Court seems to have simply sidestepped its earlier view on positive measures as well as the legal provisions. It is submitted that if it had in fact applied the relevant legal provisions, or followed its reasoning in *Marschall*, *Badeck* and *Abrahamsson*, that the automatic preference given to males who had undergone military service would not have been permissible, either because it was not flexible enough (the *Marschall* test), or because the legal provisions only permit measures to assist women or the underrepresented sex. The decision in *Schnorbus* can therefore be said to be seriously flawed.

In summary, the three cases discussed above add new layers to the developing jurisprudence on positive measures. *Griesmar* seems to be authority for two propositions. First, that Article 2(3) of the Equal Treatment Directive can only justify measures directly related to pregnancy and maternity and not to parenthood. Secondly, that Article 141(4) can only justify measures designed to assist women in the future, and not to compensate them for past wrongs. *Lommers*, where the Court was interpreting Article 2(4), adds a proportionality requirement to positive measures, and limits the consideration of the permissibility of such measures to their effects on employees of a single employer, rather than the effects of a given positive measure on the EU as a whole. Finally, in *Schnorbus*, the ECJ seems to be saying that positive measures may have been permitted all along by the principle of equal treatment, without the need for an express permission in either the Equal Treatment Directive or the EC Treaty. It is also interesting to note that while in *Griesmar* the Court was not willing to accept a measure which compensated women for a past disadvantage which resulted from caring for children, it had no difficulty whatsoever in compensating men for any past disadvantage

---

[38] *ibid.*, paras. 43–46.
[39] Case C–158/97 *Badeck v. Landesanwalt beim Staatsgerichtshof des Landes Hessen* [1999] ECR I–1875.
[40] Case C–407/98 *Abrahamsson & Andersen v. Fogelgvist* [2000] ECR I–5539.

arising from completing military service. It remains to be seen whether future decisions of the ECJ will affirm the approaches taken recently, or plough a different furrow.

13.(3) DIRECTIVES ON EQUALITY

13.(3)(a) The Article 13 Directives[41]

The two new Directives providing for equal treatment in relation to sex, race, religion, disability, age and sexual orientation are the direct result of the inclusion of a new Article 13 in the EC Treaty following the adoption of the Treaty of Amsterdam in 1999. Article 13 provides a new competence for the EC to "take appropriate action to combat discrimination based on sex, racial or ethnic origin, religion or belief, disability, age or sexual orientation." The inclusion of such a general non-discrimination Article was a highly controversial element of the Intergovernmental Conference which concluded in Amsterdam. There was strong opposition from both the British and Dutch governments and there were doubts that the Article would in fact make its way into the Treaty.[42] Once it was included, the forces which had pressed for its inclusion turned their attention to its concretisation in Directives. To this end there was much behind-the-scenes campaigning and lobbying by NGOs, the Commission and some national government representatives.[43] It is fair to say that the new Article 13 Directives, build on the experience gained in combating gender discrimination at EC level, and broaden the scope of EC law from sex discrimination. The first sex equality Directive, the Equal Treatment Directive, was adopted in 1976, over 25 years ago. In the intervening years much more was learnt about fighting discrimination, and about the effectiveness of the legal instruments charged with this task. Much of this experience was channelled into the new Article 13 Directives.

13.(3)(a)(i) The scope of application of the Directives

The scope of application of the new Directives is related to the competence permitted by Article 13. The Race and Ethnicity Directive applies to discrimination based on racial or ethnic origin, while the Framework Directive on Employment applies to discrimination on the grounds of religion or belief, disability, age or sexual orientation. What is significant about the new

---

[41] Council Directive 2000/43 of June 29, 2000 implementing the principle of equal treatment between persons irrespective of racial or ethnic origin [2000] O.J. L180/22.

[42] See Waddington, "The New Equality Directives: Mixed Blessings" in *The Article 13 Directives* (forthcoming)

[43] Davies, "Article 13 EC: The European Commission's Anti-Discrimination Proposals" 29 [2000] *Industrial Law Journal* 79.

Directives is that there is no further definition of these terms. Thus, it is unclear what is meant by racial or ethnic origin, or by disability, religion or belief. This ambiguity is certain to give rise to much litigation before the ECJ as the Member States struggle to decide who exactly is covered by the new Directives. This uncertainty is given an added twist by the fact that following the implementation of the Race Directive, the category of race and ethnicity equality enjoys the highest level of protection in EC law compared with all other disadvantaged groups, including women. The distinction between the level of protection granted on the one hand to those of a particular race or ethnic origin, compared with the protection of other disadvantaged groups on the other hand, will place great pressure on discrimination law in the EU. Many litigants seek to argue that the discrimination they experience comes under the heading of race discrimination rather than discrimination on grounds of religion, (the latter not covered by the Race Directive as is the former) or discrimination on grounds of nationality, which is not prohibited at all.[44] The only aspect of the personal scope of either of the Directives which is clear is that the Race Directive does not apply to discrimination on the grounds of nationality or to any treatment which arises from the legal status of third country nationals and stateless persons.[45] This has been much criticised.[46]

A further ambiguity is apparent in the material scope of both Article 13 Directives. In contrast with the Framework Directive, and the Sex Equality Directives, which broadly speaking are applicable to employment-related discrimination, the Race Directive also applies to discrimination outside the field of employment, *i.e.* discrimination in regard to social protection (including social security and healthcare), social advantages, education and the provision of goods and services.[47] However, at present it is uncertain what is meant by "social protection" or "social advantages". Even if these terms are interpreted narrowly, it is clear that the Race Directive will apply to a much broader range of activities than the existing Sex Equality Directives, or its

---

[44] In the U.K., in the case of *CRE v. Dutton* [1989] Q.B. 783. the Court of Appeal concluded that "gypsies", as opposed to travellers such as new age travellers, were an ethnic group on the basis that they were a wandering race of Hindu origin; they had a long shared history, common geographical origin, their own customs, language, folk tales and music. A similar test might be adopted by the E.C.J.

[45] Article 3(2) of the Directive.

[46] Bell, "Meeting the Challenge? A Comparison between the EU Racal Equality Directive and the Starting Line" in *The Starting Line and the Incorporation of the Racial Equality Directive in the National Laws of the EU Member States and Accession States* (Chopin and Niessen ed., Commission for Racial Equality and Migration Policy Group). See also Bell, *EU Anti-Discrimination Policy: From Equal Opportunities Between Women and Men to Combating Racism.* (European Parliament Working Document, 1998), pp.20–22.

[47] There is a vital and important difference between what is meant in the Race and Ethnicity Directive by the term "goods and services", and what this term means under Irish law. Irish law does not confine the provision of goods and services to those provided for money, while the Directive does.

companion Framework Directive. This is just one of the reasons why the Race
Directive is now top of the tree in terms of equality legislation. As Waddington
and Bell write: "in one step . . . victims of race discrimination have achieved
the greatest level of protection available under Community law, far exceeding
that offered under the long-standing sex discrimination provisions and the
other newly recognised grounds."[48]

Having said that, the Framework Directive does apply to self-employment
and occupation, as well as to "membership of and involvement in an organisation of workers or employers, or any organisation whose members engage in
a particular profession, including the benefits provided for by such
organisations",[49] which the sex equality Equal Treatment Directive does not.

The additional areas of application both in terms of material scope and
personal scope of the new Article 13 Directives will extend the ambit of non-
discrimination law into entirely new spheres, and will result in the creation of
substantial new responsibilities in the private realm.[50]

13.(3)(a)(ii) The meaning of discrimination

The departure from the established definition of indirect discrimination in the
Sex Equality Directives is also a significant feature of the new Article 13
Directives, which prohibit both direct and indirect discrimination. While direct
discrimination is defined in a similar manner[51] to the definition in the Equal
Treatment Directive,[52] the definition of indirect discrimination which was
developed by the ECJ in the context of sex equality law[53] has been
emphatically rejected.[54] In relation to the sex equality Directives, indirect
discrimination is defined as taking place where an apparently neutral
provision, criterion or practice operates to: "disadvantage[s] a *substantially
higher proportion* of one sex than another unless that provision, criterion or
practice is appropriate and necessary and can be justified by objective factors
unrelated to sex".[55] (emphasis added) However, in the new Race Directive it is
defined as follows:

---

[48] Waddington and Bell, "More Equal than Others: Distinguishing European Equality
      Directives" 2000 C.M.L.Rev at pp.588–589.
[49] Article 3(1)(d).
[50] Or the imposition of "substantial burdens" depending on the point of view.
[51] Framework Directive, Race and Ethnicity Directive, Article 2(1) defines direct discrimination
      as occurring "where one person is treated less favourably than another is, has been or would
      be treated in a comparable situation".
[52] Article 2(1) of that Directive provides that "the principle of equal treatment shall mean that
      there shall be no discrimination whatsoever on grounds of sex either directly, or indirectly by
      reference in particular to marital or family status."
[53] See Case 96/80 *Jenkins v. Kingsgate (Clothing Production) Ltd* [1981] E.C.R. 9111 and Case
      170/84 *Bilka Kaufhaus v. Weber von Hartz* [1986] E.C.R. 1607.
[54] This was codified in the Burden of Proof Directive in 1997. Directive 97/80/EC on the
      Burden of Proof in Sex Discrimination [1997] O.J. L14/6.
[55] Burden of Proof Directive, Article 2(2).

"Indirect discrimination shall be taken to occur where an apparently neutral provision, criterion or practice *would put persons of a racial or ethnic origin at a particular disadvantage* compared with other persons, unless that provision, criterion or practice is objectively justified by a legitimate aim and the means of achieving that aim are appropriate and necessary."[56] (emphasis added)

The definition in the Framework Directive is worded in similar terms.

It might be said that in adopting this new definition of indirect discrimination, the EC is learning from past experience. The sex equality test is seriously flawed as it focuses on whether a criterion or practice causes disadvantage to a *substantially higher proportion* of one sex than another. This has led to a necessity to find statistical evidence that a particular condition has a disproportionate impact on one sex. The requisite statistical and numerical calculations have plagued sex discrimination law and have been a significant barrier to achieving redress for individual litigants.[57] The new definition in the Article 13 Directives does not require that a substantially higher proportion of one group than another be disadvantaged. Instead it only requires proof that a requirement would put persons of a racial or ethnic origin at a particular disadvantage compared with other persons.[58] Thus, there should no longer be a need to demonstrate statistically that indirect discrimination has occurred. The rejection of this test is one of the major successes of the new Directives. This is a major step forward, as statistical evidence may simply not be available in relation to discrimination on the new grounds. It is disappointing, however, that the proposed amendment of the Equal Treatment Directive, which is currently wending its way through the EU institutions, does not take the opportunity to adopt a similar definition of indirect discrimination in relation to sex equality law. It is not clear why this opportunity has not been taken.[59]

---

[56] Above n.41, at Art.2(b).

[57] Bell, "Article 13 EC: The European Commission's Anti-discrimination Proposals." 29 (2000) *Industrial Law Journal* 79 at 82. For a discussion of the difficulties this has caused in Ireland see Bolger and Kimber above n.4, pp.12–13.

[58] It is heavily influenced by the principle established by the ECJ in Case 237/94 *O'Flynn v. Adjudication Officer* [1996] E.C.R. I–2671 on nationality discrimination. In that case the complainant, a migrant worker, was refused a funeral grant because such grants were only made available if the funeral took place in the United Kingdom. The Court ruled that: "[U]nless objectively justified and proportionate to its aim, a provision of national law must be regarded as indirectly discriminatory if it is intrinsically liable to affect migrant workers more than national workers and if there is a consequent risk that it will place the former at a particular disadvantage. It is not necessary in this respect to find that the provision in questions does not in practice affect a substantially higher proportion of migrant workers. It is sufficient that it is liable to have such an effect.

[59] The European Women's Lobby (EWL) in its comments on the Commission's proposals to amend the Equal Treatment Directive has called for a move away from the "substantially higher proportion" test to one which is line with the Article 13 Directive. See the Comments of the EWL of November 22, 2000.

13.(3)(a)(iii) Harassment

The new Directives have also taken the opportunity to define "harassment". The inclusion of such an express prohibition on harassment can also be seen as a lesson learnt from the sex discrimination legislation as the sex equality Directives had been silent on the subject of sexual harassment. This did not mean, however, that sexual harassment was not prohibited by EC law; it was accepted that it was contrary in principle to the Equal Treatment Directive. In any event, one of the proposed amendments to the Equal Treatment Directive is the inclusion of an express prohibition on sexual harassment.[60]

The definition of harassment in the Race Directive is quite broad and provides that: "harassment shall be deemed to be discrimination when an unwanted conduct related to racial or ethnic origin takes place with the purpose or effect of violating the dignity of a person and of creating an intimidating, hostile, degrading humiliating or offensive environment."[61]

The definition in the Framework Directive is almost identical. Harassment on any of the protected grounds is prohibited in both of the new Directives. The Directives further provide that the concept of harassment may be defined in accordance with the national laws and practice of the Member States. It is interesting to note, however, that the definition of harassment is not limited in any way by a requirement of reasonableness or objectivity. In fact, by incorporating conduct that has either the *purpose* of violating the dignity of a person or the *effect* of violating such dignity, there is a very clear subjective element in the definition. Thus, a person could say that certain conduct has had the effect of violating their dignity, and who else, other than that person can properly say whether or not that is so? Such a completely subjective definition of harassment is at variance with the general principles governing proof of sexual harassment.

13.(3)(a)(iv) Positive action

Unsurprisingly, given the extensive mandate in the EC Treaty for positive action in relation to sex equality, the new Directives both permit positive action in certain circumstances. The Race Directive provides that: "with a view to ensuring full equality in practice, the principle of equal treatment shall not prevent any Member State from maintaining or adopting specific measures to prevent or compensate for disadvantages linked to racial or ethnic origin."[62]

Article 7 of the Framework Directive contains a similar provision. There would appear to be a difference, however, between the positive action permitted by the Race and Framework Directives and that permitted in relation

---

[60] For a more detailed discussion of sexual harassment and Community law, see Bolger and Kimber, above n.4., pp.258–261.
[61] Article 2(3) of the Race Directive.
[62] Article 5.

to sex equality law. The new Directives seem to focus on positive action as compensation for, or prevention of, past wrongs and do not include the additional mandate in relation to sex equality of allowing positive measures which would benefit a minority in the future. Article 141(4) in particular, allows a Member State to maintain or adopt "measures providing for specific advantages in order to make it easier for the underrepresented sex to pursue a vocational activity".[63] The Framework Directive does seem to provide for this future element in relation to people with disabilities as Article 7(2) provides that: "With regard to disabled persons, the principle of equal treatment shall be without prejudice to the right of Member States to . . . measures aimed at creating or maintaining provisions or facilities for safeguarding or promoting their integration into the working environment."

It remains to be seen whether these textual differences will result in certain types of positive measures including "future" measures being permitted in relation to sex equality and disability, and a lesser range of "past compensation only" measures being permitted with regard to the other grounds of discrimination. Some commentators doubt that such differences will have any significance in practice. However, in *Griesmar*, discussed above, it can be seen that the ECJ made a clear distinction between measures which merely compensated women afterwards for difficulties which they had suffered, and measures directed at assisting women to conduct their professional life on an equal footing with men and ruled that in fact only the latter "future" remedies were permitted by Article 141(4). It may continue to make such a distinction in future.

These differences aside, given that the definition of positive action in the new Article 13 Directives is very similar to the definition in Article 2(4) of the Equal Treatment Directive, it is highly likely that the general principles already developed by the ECJ[64] in the context of sex equality law, will be extended to the new grounds of discrimination.

13.(3)(a)(v) Exemptions

The new Article 13 Directives contain a number of exceptions to the equal treatment principle. A genuine and determining occupational requirement that is legitimate and proportionate is permitted.[65] Age discrimination is permitted

---

[63] This point is made by Waddington and Bell, above n.48, p.588. They question, however, whether this difference in wording will result in a significantly altered scope for positive action.

[64] See Case C–450/93 *Kalanke v. Frei Hansestadt Bremen* [1995] E.C.R. I–3069; Case C–409/97 *Marschall v. Land Nordrhein Westfalen* [1997] E.C.R. I–6363; Case C–158/97 *Badeck v. Landesanwalt beim Staatsgerichthof des Landes Hessen*, [1999] ECR I–1875; Case C–407/98 *Abrahamsson and Anderson v. Fogelqvist*, [2000] ECR I–5539. For a detailed discussion of positive action and these cases see Bolger and Kimber, above n.4, pp.384–394.

[65] Article 4 of the Race Directive provides, *e.g.*: "Member States may provide that a difference of treatment which is based on a characteristic related to racial or ethnic origin shall not

in certain circumstances, including where a discriminatory requirement is objectively and reasonably justified by a legitimate employment or labour market policy or vocational training objective, and also in relation to setting ages for retirement.[66] In addition, churches and other bodies with a religious ethos will be allowed to take the religion or belief of an individual into account in employing a person, where the nature or context of the position justifies it.[67] Finally, there is a specific exemption in relation to recruitment of police and teachers in Northern Ireland.[68]

It is interesting to note that the only exception permitted under the Race Directive is a genuine and determinate *occupational* requirement, even though the material scope of the Directive is a good deal broader than the employment field. Does this mean that outside the employment field, with regard to the provision of goods and services for example, no exceptions at all are permitted? It is also the case that the age discrimination exception is extremely wide, more so than any of the other exceptions. Thus, it is fair to say that age is one of the least protected of all the grounds. The religious ethos exception also has the potential to conflict with broader fundamental human rights, such as freedom of expression, and respect for private and family life.[69] Beyond such general remarks, it is difficult to engage in much deeper analysis, as the effect of the exemptions will depend on whether they are interpreted broadly or restrictively by the ECJ. If too wide an interpretation is made, the basic right to equal treatment itself will be weakened.

13.(3)(a)(vi) Disability discrimination

It has been said that one of the more controversial elements of the Framework Directive is that it contains a requirement of reasonable accommodation for people with disabilities.[70] Article 5 provides that:

> "In order to guarantee compliance with the principle of equal treatment in relation to persons with disabilities, reasonable accommodation shall be proved. This means that employers shall take appropriate measures, where needed in a particular case, to enable a person with a disability to have access to, participate in, or advance in employment, or to undergo training, unless such measures would impose a disproportionate burden on the employer."

---

constitute discrimination, where by reasons of the nature of the particular occupational activities concerned or of the context in which they are carried out, such a characteristic constitutes a genuine and determining occupational requirement, provided that the objective is legitimate and the requirement is proportionate."

66 Framework Directive, Article 6.
67 *ibid.*, Article 4(2).
68 *ibid.*, Article 15.
69 See Bolger, paper for Dublin Castle Conference on Discrimination on Grounds of Religion or Belief in the Framework Directive.
70 Waddington and Bell, *op.cit.*

The concept of reasonable accommodation is a common tool for dealing with disability and equality and is to be found in the legislation of most states who have adopted disability discrimination laws, including Ireland.[71] The question of what is a "disproportionate burden" is one which will give rise to much litigation and it is fair to say that the strength of the equal treatment provision in relation to disability will depend on this concept being interpreted restrictively.[72]

13.(3)(a)(vii) Other issues

One of the fundamental problems with the sex equality legislation of the EC is its reliance on the individual model of equality.[73] In requiring actual harm of a particular victim before an act of discrimination becomes justiciable, it mandates that the main enforcers of equality will be individual litigants. However, as one writer has recognised:

> "[W]hilst the right to enforce equality through individual legal proceedings remains a cornerstone of equal opportunities law, it must also be recognised that there are certain forms of discrimination which are not amenable to correction through individual complaint. In particular, structural or institutionalised discriminations usually operate through processes and procedures, not obvious to the individuals disadvantaged as a result."[74]

Such criticisms seem to have been taken on board in relation to the new Article 13 Directives, as two measures have been included which are designed to alleviate some of the difficulties caused by the need for individual litigation.

13.(3)(a)(vii)(1) Bodies for the promotion of equal treatment

Section 13 of the Race Directive requires Member States to designate a body or bodies for the promotion of equal treatment of all persons without discrimination on the grounds of racial or ethnic origin. The competences of these bodies shall include (i) the provision of independent assistance to victims of discrimination in pursuing complaints about discrimination (ii) conducting independent surveys concerning discrimination (iii) publishing independent reports and making recommendations on any issue relating to such discrimination. It does not appear to be necessary that such bodies are solely devoted to race discrimination, but can be part of other agencies at national

---

[71] Employment Equality Act 1998, s.16(3)(b). See Quinn, McDonagh and Kimber, *Disability Discrimination Law in the US, Australia and Canada; Jackson Disability Discrimination Law* (UK), Kimber, *Equality and Disability,* Part I, [2001] 6 *Bar Review* 494, Part II, [2001] 7 *Bar Review* 66.

[72] The test of "disproportionate burden" is in conflict with Irish law which requires an employer to engage in reasonable accommodation unless it would give rise to more than a nominal cost. Thus Irish law will have to be changed in order to implement the Directive.

[73] Bell, *European Parliament*, above n.46, p.27.

[74] *ibid.*

level charged with the defence of human rights or the safeguard of individuals rights.

This measure is unique to that Directive and does not appear in the Framework Directive. The proposals to amend the Equal Treatment Directive do provide for such a body in relation to sex equality law. It is unclear why discrimination on the remaining grounds covered by the Framework Directive, namely age, disability, religion or belief or sexual orientation, remain the poor relation and are not included in the remit of a body or bodies set up to promote equal treatment on the grounds of race or sex.

13.(3)(a)(vii)(2) Rules of standing

The second innovation which is contained in both of the new Directives is the requirement that Member States provide greater legal standing for NGOs wishing to bring what might be termed class actions. Article 7(2) of the Race Directive provides that Member States shall ensure that entities which have a legitimate interest in ensuring that the provisions of the Directive are complied with, may engage, either on behalf or in support of the complainant, in any procedure provided for the enforcement of Directive obligations. Article 9(2) of the Framework Directive is written in identical terms.[75] This measure will make it easier for victims of discrimination to bring proceedings to obtain legal redress for that discrimination

13.3.(b) New Developments and the Equal Treatment Directive

After a number of years' preparation, an EC Directive amending the 1976 Directive (76/207) on equal treatment for men and women as regards access to employment, vocational training, promotion and working conditions has now been adopted.[76] The text of the proposal for amendment was initially presented by the Commission on June 7, 2000.[77] Following a detailed consultation process and further amendments suggested by the European Parliament and by various lobby groups,[78] a joint Council of Ministers/European Parliament (EP)

---

[75] Whyt, Social Inclusion and the Legal System: Public Interest Law in Ireland (2001).

[76] Directive 2002/73/EC Amending Council Directive 76/207/EEC on the implementation of the principle of equal treatment for men and women as regards access to employment, vocational training and promotion, and working conditions.

[77] COM(2000)334 final.

[78] See Second Reading Opinion of European Parliament October 24, 2001 proposing 15 changes to the Commission text. For a discussion of the suggested changes see House of Lords Select Committee on European Scrutiny, 12th Report, Annex 3, January 16, 2002. The Commission accepted seven of the changes proposed by the European Parliament and rejected eight. See Commission Opinion on the European Parliament's amendments to the Council's common position regarding the draft Directive amending Council Directive 76/202 EC, (23013) 14492/01 COM (01) 689. The European Women's Lobby also made comments and suggested further amendments.

conciliation committee issued an agreed joint text of a draft Directive on April 18, 2002. The amending Directive was finally adopted on September 23, 2002 and contains some significant amendments to the Equal Treatment Directive.

Perhaps the most significant of the amendments is the inclusion of a new Article stating that harassment on the basis of sex as well as sexual harassment constitutes discrimination. For the first time the Directive will contain a definition of sexual harassment. Article 2 provides as follows: "Sexual harassment: where any form of unwanted verbal, non-verbal or physical conduct of a sexual nature occurs, with the purpose or effect of violating the dignity of a person, in particular when creating an intimidating, hostile, degrading, humiliating or offensive environment".

As discussed above, sexual harassment was hitherto not expressly prohibited by EC law, but it was accepted that it was in principle contrary to the Equal Treatment Directive.

The Directive also contains definitions of direct and indirect discrimination which are in line with those contained in the Race and Framework Directives.[79] This is an extremely important amendment. The original Equal Treatment Directive did not contain a definition of indirect discrimination on grounds of sex, and that developed by the ECJ focused on situations where a requirement disadvantaged a substantially higher proportion of members of one sex than the other. As discussed above, this text created great difficulties by making it necessary to find statistical evidence that a particular condition had a disproportionate impact on one sex over the other. The change from "substantially higher proportion" to "at a particular disadvantage" is to be welcomed.

Following the suggestions of the European Parliament, the amended Directive will also contain much stronger provisions in relation to enforcement of the principle of equal treatment.[80] Furthermore, as mentioned above, in line with the Race Directive, a new responsibility will be imposed on Member States to establish agencies with specified powers to promote equal opportunities.[81] The available remedies are also to be improved, as any upper limit imposed by Member States on compensation and reparation will be required to be removed.[82]

Finally, the amended Directive provides for employment safeguards for new parents of either sex who are seeking leave to look after infants. In particular,

---

[79] The European Women's Lobby in particular called for a move away from the "substantially higher proportion" test. Indirect discrimination is defined as occurring "where an apparently neutral provision, criterion or practice would put persons of one sex *at a particular disadvantage* compared with persons of the other sex, unless that provision, criterion or practice is objectively justified by a legitimate aim, and the means of achieving it are appropriate and necessary. (Article 2)(Emphasis added).

[80] New Article 6.

[81] New Article 8(a).

[82] New Article 2, and 6.

the new Article 2(7) will expressly protect the right of a woman who has given birth to return to her job, or to an equivalent post.

The amendments to the Directive also contain a number of soft-law measures designed to facilitate equal treatment of men and women in the workplace, but which do not appear to be legally binding. For example, the new Article 8(b) encourages the social partners to contribute to the implementation of the principle of equality of treatment by adopting collective agreements laying down anti-discrimination provisions.

Overall, the amendments to the Equal Treatment Directive are to be welcomed. Over 25 years have passed since the Directive was first adopted and there have been many developments in sex equality since that date. In particular, the litigation before the ECJ has exposed many deficiencies in the Directive which needed to be recited. The stronger provisions on enforcement in the Directive also reflect the greater understanding of the role of law, and its weaknesses, in combating sex discrimination. After 25 years it has become apparent that adequate machinery for enforcing equal treatment guarantees is at least as important as putting in place the substantive rights themselves. The new provisions in the Directive go some way to improving this situation. It is disappointing, however, that there were no amendments in relation to the thorny issue of positive discrimination. As can be seen from the earlier part of this paper, there is much litigation on this issue and the rulings of the ECJ have often been conflicting. More detailed provisions on positive measures in the amended Equal Treatment Diective would have been desirable to introduce some clarity to this tangled field of law.[83]

13.(4) CONCLUSIONS – THE FUTURE

Recent developments in equality law at EC level show a distinct trend towards the broadening rather than the deepening of the protection of minorities and women in the EU. The two new Directives which have been adopted have significantly expanded the range of application of EC equality law by extending the protection of the principles of equal treatment to a much wider range of people in the Union. The EC has also begun the process of amending the first generation equality Directives, those dealing with sex equality. These developments are very welcome and will lead to real changes in the lives of many ordinary Europeans.

However, although the new and amended Directives show that some important lessons have been learnt from the experience of the sex equality Directives, the improvements have been largely of style rather than substance.

---

[83] The European Women's Lobby in their comments on the Commission's proposals for amendments to the Equal Treatment Directive in fact called for a draft Directive on positive measures.

The new Directives are significantly better in terms of defining the central principles on which equal protection is placed, and have made explicit protections which were implicit, such as in relation to harassment. Nevertheless, there is little radical or innovative in terms of approaches taken by the new Article 13 Directives. The requirement that Member States establish bodies for the promotion of equal treatment and amend the rules on standing are perhaps the most radical steps. Strangely, however, the former requirement has been omitted in relation to the Framework Directive. Apart from these innovations, the Directives merely extend the protection formerly available to women to other disadvantaged groups in the EU. This is despite the fact that statistical evidence is showing that the sex equality Directives have not been as effective as was once hoped, and that women still suffer from significant discrimination in the world of work. It might have been better to consider why these Directives have not fully achieved their aims, to examine what new steps should be taken to increase the effectiveness of equality law and to incorporate such understandings into the new Article 13 Directives. It is to be hoped that the future developments in EC equality law will move in this direction.

14. THE FREE MOVEMENT OF PERSONS AND IRELAND

BERNARD RYAN*

> – *Goloshes, Julia! exclaimed her sister. Goodness me, don't you know what goloshes are? You wear them over your . . . over your boots, Gretta, isn't it?*
> – *Yes, said Mrs Conroy. Guttapercha things. We both have a pair now. Gabriel says everyone wears them on the continent.*
> – *O, on the continent, murmured Aunt Julia, nodding her head slowly.*

James Joyce, The Dead (1907)[1]

14.(1) INTRODUCTION

It is widely accepted that membership of what is now the European Union (EU) has contributed to the profound changes that have occurred in Irish[2] society over recent decades.[3] This chapter attempts to substantiate that general claim through an examination of EU law[4] relating to the free movement of persons in the Irish context. It begins with a summary of the main principles of EU law in the field. It goes on to consider the manner of the translation of those principles into Irish law, and their impact both upon Irish immigration law and rights of equal treatment in economic and social matters. The chapter then addresses other possible effects of EU rights of personal movement. It will be argued that the impact of EU principles on patterns of migration to and from Ireland has been at most modest; this continues to occur primarily to and from Britain. Instead, it will be suggested that the greater influence of these

---

* B.C.L. (NUI), Ph.D (European University Institute), Lecturer, Law School, University of Kent at Canterbury. I am grateful to Síofra O'Leary and Harm Schepel for their comments on the chapter in draft, although responsibility for any errors of fact or interpretation remain my own.

[1] Taken from *Dubliners* (Everyman ed., 1991), pp.205–6.
[2] The terms "Irish" and "Ireland" are used here to refer to the Irish State, and do not include Northern Ireland. The terms "British" and "Britain" refer to the United Kingdom.
[3] See for example Garvin, "The French Are on the Sea" and Halligan, "What Difference did it Make? Setting the Scene" in *Europe: The Irish Experience* (O'Donnell ed., 2000).
[4] The term "EU law" is preferred in this chapter. It should be appreciated, however, that the legal principles to which reference is made arise under the EC Treaty.

EU law principles has been on public policy in Ireland and Britain in relation to movement between the two states.

14.(2) EU RIGHTS OF PERSONAL MOVEMENT

A detailed analysis of the law relating to personal movement between EU Member States is not provided here as the subject has been comprehensively treated by others.[5] Instead, the main categories of rights of personal movement – deriving from the rules on the free movement of workers, freedom of establishment, the provision of services, vocational training, and EU citizenship – will be outlined, together with the exceptions to those rights, and the special position of non-EU nationals. A more detailed account of other points is also given where required in subsequent sections.

14.(2)(a) Free movement of workers

The conventional starting-point for the analysis of EU rights of personal movement is the provision made for the free movement of workers by Article 39 EC and secondary legislation. For these purposes, the test of a "worker" is a matter for EC rather than national law, and a "worker" is an EU national employed in a Member State other than their own.[6] It is clear that the notion of a "worker" includes part-time workers as long as their work is "genuine and effective".[7] The notion of "worker" may also include EU nationals who are looking for employment in another Member State, although in their case, it remains to be determined whether there are limits to their entitlements.[8] Those who are "workers" are entitled to take up employment in another Member State; to travel to and reside in that state; and, to unhindered access to its labour market.[9] Workers also have rights of equal treatment in other Member States by labour market authorities, by employers and in "social and tax advantages."[10] Workers are entitled to take certain family members with them, irrespective of their nationality: the worker's spouse, their descendants who are under 21 or dependent upon them, and their ascendants who are dependent upon

---

5   For example by Craig and de Búrca, *EU Law: Text, Cases and Materials* (3rd ed., 2002, chaps 17–19).
6   Case 66/85 *Lawrie-Blum v. Land Baden-Württemberg* [1986] E.C.R. 2121, [1987] 3 C.M.L.R. 389.
7   Case 53/81 *Levin v. Staatssecretaris van Justitie* [1982] E.C.R. 1035, [1982] 2 C.M.L.R. 454.
8   Compare Case C–85/96 *Martínez Sala v. Freistaat Bayern* [1998] E.C.R. I–2691, at para. 32 and Case C–292/89 *Antonissen* [1991] E.C.R. I–745, [1991] 2 C.M.L.R. 373 at paras. 12 and 13.
9   See Directive 68/360 O.J. Sp. Ed. L257/13 and Case C–415/93, *URBSFA v. Bosman* [1995] E.C.R. I–4921, [1996] 1 C.M.L.R. 645.
10 See Regulation 1612/68 [1968] O.J. L257/2, and, in particular, Art. 7(2) and Case C–281/98 *Angonese v. Cassa di Risparmio di Bolzano*, [2000] E.C.R. I–4139, [2000] 2 C.M.L.R. 1120.

them.[11] Finally, workers and their families may be entitled to continue to reside in another Member State after employment there where the worker is retired, incapacitated or subsequently takes up employment in another Member State.[12]

14.(2)(b) Freedom of establishment

Freedom of establishment is protected by Article 43 EC *et seq*. This principle permits EU nationals to move to other states in order to set up a business, and is of particular relevance to self-employed persons. In practice, the recognition of qualifications is frequently a pre-condition of establishment, and as a result, the Court of Justice (ECJ) and EU legislature have developed a set of principles designed to ensure respect for equivalent qualifications and experience.[13] Freedom of establishment requires equality of treatment by the second Member State in the rules governing the pursuit of occupational activities, but also in "the various general facilities which are of assistance in the pursuit of those activities."[14] Those who move to another Member State in exercise of the freedom of establishment have rights of entry and residence in the other state, and are entitled to take with them the same family members as workers (above).[15] They and their families are also entitled to continue their residence in the other Member State upon the cessation of their self-employed activity.[16]

14.(2)(c) Cross-border provision of services

The third source of rights of personal movement is the provision for the cross-border provision of services in Article 49 EC *et seq*. For these purposes, a "service" must be "normally provided for remuneration", with the result that many public services are excluded from the scope of the provisions.[17] The rules on the cross-border provision of services confer rights upon individuals based in one Member State to *provide* services in another whether they are EU nationals or the employees, irrespective of nationality, of an EU company.[18] As a result of legislative suggestion and ECJ case law, these rules also protect

---

[11] Art. 10 of Regulation 1612/68.
[12] Regulation 1251/70, [1970] O.J. L142/24.
[13] See in particular Case 340/89 *Vlassopoulou* [1991] E.C.R. 2357, [1993] C.M.L.R. 221, Directive 89/48, [1989] O.J. L19/16 (as amended) and Directive 92/5, [1992] O.J. L 209/25 (as amended).
[14] Case 63/86, *Commission v. Italy* [1988] E.C.R. 29, [1989] 2 C.M.L.R. 601, at para. 14.
[15] Directive 73/148 [1973] O.J. L172/14.
[16] Regulation 75/34, [1975] O.J. L14/10.
[17] Case 263/86 *Belgium v. Humbel* [1988] E.C.R. 5365, [1989] 1 C.M.L.R. 393, in relation to public education. Note, however, the Court's judgment in Case C–368/98 *Vanbraekel* [2001] E.C.R. I–5363 [2002] 2 C.M.L.R. 20, in which Art. 49 was applied to medical services without any indication that public health systems might be exempt.
[18] Case C–13/89 *Rush Portuguesa Ld v. Office National d'Immigration* [1990] E.C.R. I–1417, [1991] 2 C.M.L.R. 818 and Case C–43/93 *Vander Elst v. Office des Migrations Internationales* [1994] E.C.R. I–3803, [1995] 1 C.M.L.R. 513.

those who wish to *receive* services in or from another Member State, as this is considered the "necessary corollary" of the provision of services.[19] One effect of that extension is to give EU nationals, though probably not other EU residents,[20] a right to travel to other Member States. EU nationals who are service providers and recipients have a right of entry to other Member States, a right of residence for the duration of the service, and are entitled to take with them the same family members as workers.[21] They also have a right of equal treatment by other Member States in matters connected with the exercise of those rights of movement.[22]

14.(2)(d) Vocational training

The categories referred to so far may be the source of rights to education in other Member States, whether because of the rights of equal treatment of workers,[23] the self-employed and their families or because the education is provided for remuneration and is therefore classed as a "service". The ECJ has in addition developed an autonomous set of student rights based upon the EC Treaty provisions on vocational training (now Article 150 EC). As a result of the Court's case law, EU nationals have a right of equal treatment in access to vocational training in other Member States, including higher-level education.[24] Entry conditions and tuition fees must be equal, and students must be permitted to reside in the other Member State.[25] The position as regards access to social benefits is, however, less certain. Initially, the ECJ held that the right of equal treatment did not extend to state provision for student maintenance through grants and loans.[26] As a result, Member States were entitled to make a student's right of residence subject to conditions as to their capacity to maintain themselves and their families, and the possession of adequate health insurance.[27] That approach was then reiterated in Directive 93/96 on the right

---

[19] Cases 286/82 and 26/83 *Luisi and Carbone v. Ministero del Tesoro* [1984] E.C.R. 377, [1985] 3 C.M.L.R. 52, at para. 10. Earlier references to a right to receive services are to be found in Art. 1 of Directive 64/221 [1964] O.J. B56/850 and Art. 1 of Directive 73/148.

[20] It is not altogether clear why, if the right to receive services is a "corollary", non-EU residents of a Member State should lack the right to travel to another Member State in order to receive services there. The Court of Justice has however limited the right to travel to receive services to EU nationals: see Case C–45/93 *Commission v. Spain* [1994] E.C.R. I–911 at para. 10.

[21] See Art. 1 of Directive 73/148.

[22] See for example Case 186/87 *Cowan v. Le Trésor Public* [1989] E.C.R. 1985, [1990] 2 C.M.L.R. 613.

[23] See in particular the provision in Art. 12 of Regulation 1612/68 for the children of EU migrant workers.

[24] Case 24/86 *Blaizot v. University of Liège*, [1988] E.C.R. 379, [1989] 1 C.M.L.R. 57.

[25] Case 293/83 *Gravier v. City of Liège*, [1985] E.C.R. 593, [1985] 3 C.M.L.R. 1 and Case C–357/89 *Raulin* [1992] E.C.R. I–1027, [1994] 1 C.M.L.R. 227.

[26] Case 39/86 *Lair v. Universität Hannover*, Case 39/86 [1988] E.C.R. 3161, [1989] 3 C.M.L.R. 545 and *Brown v. Secretary of State for Scotland* [1988] E.C.R. 3205, [1099] 3 C.M.L.R. 403.

[27] *Raulin*, above n. 25, at para. 39.

of residence of students and their families – in this case, defined to mean the spouse and dependent children only.[28] Article 1 of Directive 93/96 provides that it is a precondition of a student's right of residence that the student "assures the relevant national authority, by means of a declaration or by such alternative means as the student may choose that are at least equivalent" that they have "sufficient resources to avoid becoming a burden on the social assistance system". However, the decision in *Grzelczyk* in 2001 suggests that EU law is more protective of EU migrant students than was previously thought. The Court of Justice held that an EU student who was initially able to meet the maintenance requirement, but whose circumstances changed, could claim equal treatment in social assistance by virtue of their status as an EU citizen (on which, see below). It also held that, because of amendments to Article 150 EC and the introduction of EU citizenship, the earlier case law denying migrant students equal treatment in relation to maintenance payments did not prevent reliance upon EU citizenship in this way. The only possible way out for Member States was to withdraw the residence permit of students who become dependent upon social assistance, but the Court emphasised that that could not be the automatic consequence of recourse to social assistance.[29]

14.(2)(e) European Union citizenship

There are finally some more general provisions on the personal movement of EU nationals to consider. The starting-point is Directives 90/364 and 90/365, which confer a right of residence upon persons of independent means and retired persons. This right of residence extends to family members, here defined as for workers, save for the exclusion of non-dependent descendants under 21. In each case, it is required that the EU national and family have sufficient resources to avoid having recourse to social assitance, and have adequate health insurance.[30]

The 1990 Directives must now be read in the light of the provisions on European Union citizenship inserted in the EC Treaty by the Maastricht Treaty. Article 18 EC provides that "every citizen of the Union shall have the right to move and reside freely within the territory of the Member States". In *Baumbast*, the Court of Justice concluded for the first time that Article 18 was directly effective. It also held that although the rights set out in Article 18 were "subject to the limitations and conditions laid down in the Treaty and by the measures adopted to give it effect", any such limitations had to respect the requirement of proportionality. In *Baumbast* the result was that a German national was entitled to reside in Britain even though they fell outside of Directive 90/364 because their

---

28 Directive 93/96 [1993] O.J. L317/ 59, re-enacting the provisions of Directive 90/366 [1990] L180/30, which had been annulled in Case C–295/90 *Parliament v. Council* [1992] E.C.R. I–4193 [1992] 3 C.M.L.R. 281.

29 Case C–184/99 *Grzelczyk* [2001] E.C.R. I–6193, [2002] 1 C.M.L.R. 543.

30 Directive 90/364, [1990] O.J. L 80/26 and Directive 90/365, [1990] O.J. L180/28.

medical insurance entitled them to treatment in Germany alone.[31] The implication of *Baumbast* is that other apparent exceptions to the rights of movement of EU citizens may also be found to be inoperable on the grounds that they are disporportionate limitations on the rights in Article 18 EC.

European Union citizens can also rely upon the combination of Article 12 EC – which prohibits discrimination on grounds of nationality within the "scope of application" of the EC Treaty – and Article 17 EC – which states that "citizens of the Union shall enjoy the rights conferred by this Treaty". In *Martínez Sala*, the combination of Articles 12 and 17 was found to require equal treatment in relation to social assistance of EU nationals lawfully resident in another Member State by virtue of *national law*.[32] It was that argument which was then extended in *Grzelczyk* to require the equal treatment of EU students, on the ground that they were exercising the right of residence contained in Article 18 EC. As we have seen, in *Grezelczyk* the limitations on the right of residence contained in Article 1 of Directive 93/96 neither prevented a claim of equal treatment nor permitted the automatic withdrawal of the right of residence itself. It remains to be seen if the requirement of equal treatment also applies to those exercising rights of residence under the two 1990 Directives or (post-*Baumbast*) under Article 18 EC. In any event, the *Baumbast* decision implies that, if Member States wish to withdraw a right of residence because social benefits have been claimed, they will have to respect the principle of proportionality."

14.(2)(f) Exceptions

These rights of personal movement are subject to a number of exceptions. Member State limitations to free movement rights may first be justified on grounds of "public policy", "public security or public health".[33] A Member State may only use the "public policy" and "public security" exceptions to refuse entry or residence to an individual where there is "a genuine and sufficiently serious threat to the requirements of public policy affecting one of the fundamental interests of society" and where "repressive . . . or other genuine and effective measures" are taken against the state's own nationals for the same conduct.[34] Individuals are also entitled to a number of procedural safeguards in cases where these grounds are being relied upon.[35] Secondly,

---

[31] Case C–413/99, *Baumbast and R v. Secretary of State for the Home Department*, judgment of September 17, 2002, paras 80–94.

[32] Case C–85/96 *Martínez Sala v. Freistaat Bayern.* above n.8.

[33] Arts. 39(3), 46 and 55 EC. A similar limitation applies to Directives 90/364, 90/365 and 93/96: see Art. 2(2) in each case.

[34] Case 30/77 *R v. Bouchereau* [1977] E.C.R. 1999, [1977] 2 C.M.L.R. 800, at para. 35 and Cases 115 and 116/81, *Adoui and Cornuaille* [1982] E.C.R. 1665, [1982] 3 C.M.L.R. 631, at para. 9. See too Arts. 2 and 3 of Directive 64/221.

[35] Arts. 6–9 of Directive 64/221.

where the national rule in question is generally applicable, a state may be able to argue that it is "justified by imperative requirements in the general interest".[36] It is well-established that EU nationals cannot plead these rights in "wholly internal" situations against their own state,[37] save that they can do so where they are returning having exercised free movement rights in another Member State[38] or where they use their home Member State as a base for economic activity elsewhere in the EU.[38a] The Court of Justice has held that the introduction of EU citizenship does not affect that conclusion, even if the result is that a Member State's own nationals suffer "reverse discrimination" by comparison with nationals of other Member States.[39] Finally, it should be noted that the rules on equal treatment do not fully apply to employment in the "public service", while those on the rights of establishment and the provision of services do not apply to "activities . . . connected . . . to the exercise of official authority".[40]

14.(2)(g) Non-EU nationals

The position of non-EU nationals, usually known as "third country nationals", may also be summarised.[40a] The general position is that they do not benefit from rights of personal movement, unless as the family members of EU nationals or the employees of service providers themselves exercising rights of movement. Some non-EU nationals do however benefit from protection under EU agreements with other states. The European Economic Area Agreement between the EU, Norway, Iceland and Liechtenstein permits movement by the nationals of the participating states for the purposes of employment, establishment and the cross-border provision of services; the same principle will eventually apply to Switzerland under the Agreement on the free movement of persons between it and the EU, which came into force on June 1, 2002.[41] The EU-Turkey Agreement confers a number of rights upon Turkish nationals who are "duly registered as belonging to the labour force of a Member State", including the right to free access to the labour market after

---

[36] Case C–55/94 *Gebhard* [1995] E.C.R. I–4165, at para. 37.

[37] Case 175/78 *R v. Saunders* [1979] E.C.R. 1129, [1979] 2 C.M.L.R. 216 and Cases 35 and 36/82 *Morson and Jhanjan v. Netherlands* [1982] E.C.R. 3723, [1983] 2 C.M.L.R. 221.

[38] Case C–370/90 *R. v. Immigration Appeal Tribunal and Singh, ex p. Secretary of State for the Home Department* [1992] E.C.R. I–4265, [1992] 3 C.M.L.R. 358.

[38a] Case C–60/00 *Carpenter v. Secretary of State for the Home Department*, judgment of July 1, 2002. For discussion of this judgment also see below Barrett para 15(4)(a).

[39] Case C–64/96 *Land Nordrhein-Westfalen v. Uecker and Case C–65/96 Jacquet v. Land Nordrhein-Westfalen* [1997] E.C.R. I–3171, [1997] 3 C.M.L.R. 963.

[40] Arts. 39(4), 45 and 55 EC. For reasons of space, the restrictive interpretation given these exceptions is not considered here.

[40a] For a detailed treatment of third country family members see below Barrett, chap.15.

[41] See Arts. 28, 31 and 36 of the Agreement on the European Economic Area [1994] O.J. L 1/3 and the Agreement between the European Community and the Swiss Confederation on the free movement of persons, [2002] O.J. L 114/6.

four years' employment, the right of family members to free access to the labour market after five years' residence, and a right of equal treatment in the legislation of the Member State.[42] The Europe Agreements with ten Central and Eastern European states meanwhile provide a right of establishment in the EU for nationals of these states, and for the equal treatment of workers from those states who are legally employed in the territory of a Member State.[43] Agreements with Morocco and Tunisia have provided for the equal treatment of workers from those states legally employed in an EU state.[44] Finally, there are EU rules which confer rights to travel between EU Member States upon persons who are not EU nationals. By virtue of Articles 19–21 of the Schengen Implementing Convention, which is now part of EC law, non-EU nationals legally in the EU typically have the right to travel within the Member States for up to three months.[45] Because Ireland is not automatically bound by the Schengen *acquis*, these provisions do not apply to entry into Ireland. It is, however, possible for these obligations to be extended to Ireland at a later date.[46]

14.(3) THE FREE MOVEMENT OF PERSONS IN IRISH LAW

The direct effect of EU rights of personal movement means that they may be relied upon against Irish public authorities. Nevertheless, Member States are obliged to ensure that: "legal rules [are] worded unequivocally so as to give persons concerned a clear and precise understanding of their rights and obligations."[47] It is therefore appropriate to consider the manner in which these

---

[42] These rights are in Arts. 6 and 7 of Decision 1/80 and Art. 3 of Decision 3/80 of the EEC-Turkey Association Council. The relevant provisions of these Decisions can be found in Guild, *Immigration Law in the European Community* (2001), pp.87–88. It has also been decided that, by virtue of Art. 41 of the 1970 Additional Protocol to the EU-Turkey Agreement, Member States are precluded from introducing new restrictions on the right of establishment of Turkish nationals: see Case C–37/98, *Savas* [2000] E.C.R. I–2927, [2000] 3 C.M.L.R. 729.

[43] The Europe Agreements have been concluded between the EU and Bulgaria, the Czech Republic, Estonia, Hungary, Latvia, Lithuania, Poland, Romania, Slovakia and Slovenia, and came into force between 1995 and 1999. For a detailed discussion of the immigration law aspects of these Agreements, see Guild, chap. 6. The scope of the provisions on the freedom of establishment was given a restrictive interpretation in the judgments in Case C–63/99 *Gloszczuk* [2001] E.C.R. I–6369 [2001] 3 C.M.L.R. 1035, Case C–235/99 *Kondova* [2001] E.C.R. I–6427 [2001] 3 C.M.L.R. 1077 and Case C–257/99 *Barkoci and Malik* [2001] E.C.R. I–6557 [2001] 3 C.M.L.R. 1124. The direct effect of the provision for the equal treatment of workers was confirmed in Case C–162/00, *Pokrzeptowicz-Meyer* [2002] E.C.R. I–1049; [2002] 2 C.M.L.R. 1.

[44] See Art. 64 of each of the Euro-Mediterranean Agreements with Tunisia [1998] O.J. L97/2 and Morocco [2000] O.J. L 70/2.

[45] Convention Implementing the Schengen Agreement (1990), published in [2000] O.J. L239/19, and Council Decision 1999/436 [1999] O.J. L176/17.

[46] See Art. 4 of the Protocol integrating the Schengen *acquis* into the framework of the European Union, [1997] O.J. C340/1, p.93.

[47] Case 143/83 *E.C. Commission v. Denmark* [1985] E.C.R. 427, para. 10.

rights have been made effective in Irish law and practice. For this purpose, the law relating to entry and residence may be distinguished from questions of access to economic activity and social provision.

14.(3)(a) Entry and residence

Implementation of EU rights of personal movement in Irish law requires that exceptions be made to the ordinary rules concerning entry and residence. The starting-point is that Irish immigration law treats all persons other than Irish and British nationals as "aliens".[48] The legal provisions relating to aliens then depend upon whether they seek to enter from Britain. Those who wish to enter Ireland other than from Britain must land at a designated port.[49] They must also obtain leave to land, which may be refused on various grounds, including that they are not in a position to support themselves and their accompanying dependants; that they wish to take up employment but do not have a valid work permit issued by the Minister for Enterprise, Trade and Employment; that they suffer from a disease or disability specified in the 1946 Order; that they have been convicted of an offence punishable by imprisonment for a maximum of one year; and that they are subject to a visa requirement but do not possess a valid visa.[50] By contrast, aliens who arrive from Britain do not ordinarily require leave to enter Ireland. If they are visa nationals, they are instead required to possess a visa. If they intend to take up employment or establish themselves in business, they are also required to register their presence within seven days and to obtain leave to remain within one month. In other cases, they must obtain leave to remain within three months. In addition, since 1997, immigration officers have had the power to selectively examine aliens entering from Britain, and to apply the same conditions to them as if they had arrived from elsewhere.[51] Irrespective of where they enter from, aliens who take up residence in the State are also required to register with the "registration officer" of their district, and to notify them of changes in their place of residence and of absences of more than a month.[52] In practice, this is the mechanism by which residence is controlled, in the absence of general provision in Irish law for the issuing of residence permits.[53]

---

[48] See Aliens Amendment (No. 2) Order 1999 (S.I. No. 24 of 1999), art. 3 and Aliens (Exemption) Order 1999 (S.I. No. 97 of 1999). Prior to 1999, the exception for British nationals referred to those *born* in the United Kingdom. For a discussion of the change, see Ryan "The Common Travel Area between Britain and Ireland" (2001) 64 *Modern Law Review* 855, 862.

[49] Art. 6 of the Aliens Order 1946 (S.R.& O. 1946 No. 395), as amended. The Immigration Act 1999, s. 2, provides that the 1946 Order (with the exception of its art. 13), and amendments to it prior to that Act, have the status of an Act of the Oireachtas.

[50] Art. 5 of the Aliens Order 1946 (S.R.& O. 1846 No. 395), as amended.

[51] See Aliens (Amendment) (No. 3) Order 1997 (S.I. No. 227 of 1997), amending art. 5(7) of the Aliens Order 1946.

[52] Art. 11 of the Aliens Order 1946.

[53] The introduction of a system of residence permits was, however, suggested by the Department

Special provision has been made in Irish law for EU rights of entry and residence in order to overcome the various restrictions which would otherwise apply to persons other than Irish and British nationals. The European Communities (Aliens) Regulations 1977[54] make provision for the right to enter Ireland of those who fall within one of the categories of economic activity recognised in EU law, *i.e.* those who are "coming to take up or pursue an activity as an employed person"; are established in the state or wish to become so; or are "coming to provide or receive a service". The 1977 Regulations also apply to those who have a right of residence in Ireland having ceased employment or self-employment there, and to the required family members. All of these persons are given the right to enter Ireland, provided they produce a valid identity card or passport, save where they are suffering from a specified disease or disability,[55] or their "personal conduct has been such that it would be contrary to public policy or would endanger public security" for them to be permitted to enter. The 1977 Regulations also provide for a right of residence.[56] Those covered by the Regulations may remain in the State for three months without applying for a residence permit. It is then stated that they "may" apply to the local registration officer for a residence permit or (for non-EU family members) a residence document. Application for a residence permit or document is not however stated to be compulsory, and neither does it appear to be an offence to fail to obtain these documents.[57] If that is the position, then it is consistent with the Court of Justice's view that residence documentation evidences, rather than constitutes, a right of residence.[58]

Provision for other categories of EU national is made by the European Communities (Right of Residence for Non-Economically Active Persons) Regulations 1997,[59] which implement the 1990 and 1993 Directives on the right of residence. The 1997 Regulations apply to EU nationals who are students, defined to mean those "enrolled in an educational establishment in the State for the principal purpose of following a vocational training course there"; those who have retired from employed or self-employed activity; and "other economically non-active persons." They also extend to certain of the

---

of Justice, Equality and Law Reform in 2001: see its *Public Consultation on Immigration Policy* (June 2001), pp.5 and 14.

[54] S.I. No. 393 of 1977.

[55] The diseases and disabilities specified in Schedule 2 of the 1977 Order are the same as those specified for aliens in general in Schedule 5 of the 1946 Order (as amended by the Aliens Amendment Order 1975, S.I. 1975 No. 128). These are: diseases subject to World Health Organisation Regulations; tuberculosis; syphilis; "other infectious or contagious diseases in respect of which special provisions are in operation"; drug addiction; and "profound mental disturbance" or "manifest psychotic disturbance".

[56] 1977 Regulations, reg. 5.

[57] The only offence set out in the 1977 Regulations is that of failure to comply with a requirement to leave the state: reg. 8.

[58] Case 48/75 *Royer* [1976] E.C.R. 497, [1976] 2 C.M.L.R. 619.

[59] S.I. No. 57 of 1997.

dependants of these individuals: in the case of students, the spouse and their children under 18; and, in the other cases, the spouse, the dependent children and grandchildren of the individual and spouse, and their ascendants who are dependent.

The 1997 Regulations confer a right of entry to the State upon the persons to whom they apply.[60] As in the 1977 Regulations, the only requirement is the production of a valid national identity card or passport, and the only exceptions are that the individual is suffering from a specified disease or disability, or that their "personal conduct" justifies their exclusion on public policy grounds. The reference in the 1997 Regulations to "other economically active persons" moreover implies that *all* EU nationals and their families, have a right of entry. By contrast, the 1990 and 1993 Directives themselves confer a right of entry only upon those eligible for a right of residence, *i.e.* those who can meet the requirements as regards adequate resources and possession of health insurance.[61] Under Irish law, those additional requirements appear relevant only to the issuing of residence documentation.

At the same time, it appears that the persons covered by the 1997 Regulations are *required* to apply to the local registration officer for a residence permit or (for non-EU family members) a residence document. This may be inferred from the statement that the persons covered by the Regulations who intend to take up residence in the State "shall" apply for one of these documents.[62] The impression of an obligation is, moreover, reinforced by the provision that a person who fails to comply with the 1997 Regulations, unlike the 1977 Regulations, is guilty of an offence and liable to be deported.[63] The 1997 Regulations therefore appear to reflect the view that possession of the relevant documents is constitutive of the right of residence under the 1990 and 1993 Directives. That is almost certainly incorrect in the case of students, since their right of residence derives from the Treaty provisions on equal treatment and vocational training.[64] It may also be thought doubtful in other cases, given that Article 18 EC provides for the right of residence of EU citizens in other Member States and that, as we have seen, the Court of Justice has insisted upon the evidential role of residence permits in other contexts.

The 1997 Regulations appear defective in three further respects. One difficulty is with their treatment of dependants. In the case of students, no provision is made for dependent children over 18, while in the other cases, no provision is made for dependent descendants other than children and grandchildren. In this, the 1997 Regulations are narrower than the Directives

---

[60] 1997 Regulations, reg. 4.
[61] See Art. 2(2) of each of Directive 90/364, Directive 90/365 and Directive 93/96.
[62] 1997 Regulations, regs. 6(1) and (2).
[63] 1997 Regulations, reg. 19.
[64] See in particular paras. 36 and 37 of the judgment in *Raulin*, above n. 25.

which they are intended to implement.[65] A second difficulty concerns the treatment of British nationals. The 1997 Regulations do not in general apply to British-born persons, save for a requirement that their non-EU family members acquire a residence permit if they intend to reside in Ireland.[66] The exemption of those born in Britain does, however, create the lacuna that their family members who are not EU nationals lack an explicit legal right to *enter* Ireland.[67] Thirdly, the decision in Baumbast (discussed in section 14(2)(e)), suggests that there may be EU nationals with a right of residence in Ireland who fall outside the 1990 Directives and therefore by extension the 1997 Regulations.

Finally, what provision is made in Irish law for other non-EU nationals who wish to exercise rights of entry and residence? The provisions of the EEA Agreement in relation to personal movement are covered by section 4 of the European Communities (Amendment) Act 1993, one effect of which is to require that the 1977 Regulations be construed to apply to non-EU EEA nationals. A similar provision has now been made for Switzerland by section 3 of the European Communities and Swiss Confederation Act 2001. No specific provision appears, however, to have been made in Irish law for rights of entry or residence in other cases, particularly of employees of cross-border service providers, or arising under the association agreement with Turkey and the Europe Agreements.

14.(3)(b) Economic and social rights

Irish immigration law ordinarily prohibits aliens from employment unless they have a work permit issued by the Minister for Enterprise, Trade and Employment.[68] The provision in EU law for EU nationals and certain others to engage in employment is not, however, made explicit within Irish immigration law. The apparent requirement to obtain a work permit seems inconsistent with the obligation on Member States not to impose conditions upon the taking up of employment by EU nationals which are not applicable to their own nationals.[69] The apparent requirement to obtain a work permit is likely to be especially problematic for non-EU nationals with a right to work in Ireland by virtue of EU law, whether as the family members of EU nationals,[70] the employees of cross-border service providers, or as Turkish nationals.

---

[65]　Compare the definition of "dependants" in Regulation 2(1) of the 1997 Regulations with Art. 1 of each of Directives 90/364, 90/365 and 93/96.

[66]　1997 Regulations, reg. 3(2).

[67]　It also seems desirable that the exemption of those *born* in Britain in the 1997 Regulations be brought into line with the exemption since 1999 of British *nationals* from Irish immigration law as a whole. For discussion see above n. 50.

[68]　Art. 4 of the Aliens Order 1946, as substituted by the Aliens (Amendment) (No. 2) Order 1999 (S.I. No. 24 of 1999).

[69]　Art. 3(1) of Regulation 1612/68.

[70]　Article 11 of Regulation 1612/68 provides that the spouse and children under 21 of dependant

By contrast, Irish law does not specifically prohibit aliens from engaging in business, unless this is made a condition of their entry to Ireland.[71] No attempt has been made to modify Irish immigration law to the benefit of persons with EU rights. In particular, if non-engagement in business were to be made a condition of entry, an individual would have to rely upon EU law alone in any attempt to avoid having the condition applied. Here too, the absence of explicit provision for these rights may be thought to have an especially harsh impact upon non-EU nationals, whether as the family members of EU nationals exercising rights under the 1990 and 1993 Directives or in reliance upon the provision for establishment in the Europe Agreements.

The requirement of equal treatment on grounds of nationality which derives from the rules on the free movement of persons is broadly respected in Irish law. This is partly the consequence of general legislation on equal treatment passed in recent years. The Employment Equality Act 1998 requires employers to accord equal treatment in all aspects of employment relationships, and includes "nationality" among the prohibited grounds of discrimination.[72] Similarly, the Equal Status Act 2000 prohibits discrimination in the provision of goods and services to the public, and again lists "nationality" among the prohibited grounds.[73] For present purposes, it is of particular significance that the definition of a "service" as "a service or facility which is available to the public generally or a section of the public" is taken to mean that public services are covered by the Act.[74]

Irish law also makes adequate provision for equal treatment in access to social provision. Basic medical care and the main non-contributory social benefits are open to anyone resident in the State, so that in theory no question of unequal treatment on grounds of nationality arises.[75] It may happen of course that these benefits are denied in practice to some EU residents who are not economically active. If so, that would seem contrary to the decision in *Martínez Sala* in the case of British nationals, who, as we have seen, are by definition lawfully in Ireland. The same might also be said of other EU nationals whose residence in Ireland is tolerated, even though they lack a

---

of an EU national who is employed *or* self-employed in another member state may themselves engage in employment there. Directive 90/364, 90/365 and 93/96 each permit the spouse and dependent children of an EU national exercising the rights of residence provided for by those directives to engage in employment of self-employment: see Article 2 in each case.

[71] See Art. 5(6) of the Aliens Order 1946, inserted by the Aliens (Amendment) Order 1975 (S.I. No. 128 of 1975).

[72] See the definition of "the ground of race" in the Employment Equality Act 1998, s.6(2)(h).

[73] See the definition of "the ground of race" in the Equal Status Act 2000, s.3(2)(h).

[74] Equal Status Act 2000, s. 2. For the interpretation that the Act applied to public services, see Minister for Justice, Equality and Law Reform, John O'Donoghue, *Seanad Debates*, vol. 162, col. 585–587, February 23, 2000. The Act does not however apply where the action in question is required by an enactment: s. 14(1).

[75] See Department of Justice, Equality and Law Reform, above, n. 55, p.7.

residence permit or have ceased to comply with the conditions for one. The effect of *Martínez Sala* is that Member States cannot pick and choose: EU nationals who are permitted to reside in the State must be accorded equal treatment.[76]

The right of equal access to vocational training and higher education is also generally respected in Ireland. University applicants from other EU states apply to third-level institutions through the same centralised application system as Irish residents (the Central Applications Office). Different institutions then take their own approaches to the conversion of British A-level results, and consider applicants from other states on an individual basis.[77] The requirement of equal treatment in vocational training was also the basis for the decision of Laffoy J. in the High Court in *Bloomer* in 1995 that law graduates from Queen's University Belfast were being unlawfully discriminated against in the rules on admission to training for the legal professions.[78] More recently, the guarantee of equality in higher education has been reinforced by the Equal Status Act 2000, which prohibits discrimination on grounds of nationality in educational establishments, including universities and other third-level institutions.[79]

Finally, reference may be made to the EU provision for the co-ordination of Member States' social security schemes applicable to workers, the self-employed and their families.[80] Because of the extent of migration to and from Britain, these are of great practical significance in Ireland. The EU system of co-ordination has, in particular, ensured payment by Britain for health care for those who retire in Ireland, as well as the payment of British pensions in Ireland. It has also enabled those moving between Britain and Ireland to aggregate periods of employment in the two states for the purposes of claims for unemployment benefit, and to "export" their benefits for a period of up to three months.[81]

---

[76] See O'Leary, "Putting Flesh on the Bones of European Union Citizenship" (1999) 24 *European Law Review* 68, at p.78.

[77] Information taken from Commission on the Points System, *Final Report and Recommendations* (1999), pp.74–76, available at http://www.gov.ie/educ/comm.htm.

[78] *Bloomer v. Incorporated Law Society of Ireland* [1995] 3 I.R. 14. Laffoy J. also quashed the exemption provisions in the Society's regulations, and that position was (with transitional arrangements) maintained by the Society thereafter. By contrast, the King's Inns has continued to exempt the holders of "approved law degrees" from its Diploma in Legal Studies, and includes law graduates from Queen's University Belfast in that category.

[79] Equal Status Act 2000, s. 7. Discrimination in relation to fees and the allocation of places in universities is, however, permitted between EU nationals and others: s.7(d)(i).

[80] The EC provisions have their origins in Regulation 1408/71 [1971] O.J. L149/2, and are consolidated in Regulation 118/97 [1997] O.J. L28/1.

[81] See Cousins "Regulation 1408/71 in Ireland – An Overview" and Mangan "Implementing Regulations 1408/71 and 574/72" in Collins ed., *Irish Social Security Law in a European Context* (2000).

14.(4) THE EFFECTS OF EU RIGHTS ON PERSONAL MOVEMENT

EU rules on personal movement may also have had other effects, beyond their impact on Irish law, upon Ireland and Irish citizens. In order to address this general question, evidence on patterns of migration is examined first, before considering some of the possible political consequences of the EU requirements.

14.(4)(a) Migration

The available material suggests that EU rights of personal movement have not significantly altered patterns of migration into and out of Ireland since the early 1970s. There has in particular been only a low level of migration between Ireland and the continental Member States. Thus, Eurostat estimates for 1997 show only 35,700 Irish citizens resident in the twelve continental Member States other than Austria. This corresponded to 0.9 per cent of the total of Irish citizens resident in the fourteen EU states other than Austria at that time.[82]

The level of migration from continental Member States to Ireland was, until recently, even less. This can be seen from the Appendix, which summarises census information on the place of birth of persons in Ireland from 1971 to 1996. It shows that the number of persons born in Belgium, Denmark, France, Germany, Italy and the Netherlands who were *present* in Ireland at the time of a census between 1971 and 1991 was extremely low – albeit increasing gradually from 4,946 (0.17 per cent) in 1971 to 14,859 (0.42 per cent) in 1991. More significantly, the 1996 census, which for the first time asked about *residence*, found only 19,232 residents (0.5 per cent of the resident population) who had been born in the continental Member States.[83] Migration from the continental Member States to Ireland has admittedly increased in recent years, and the official estimate is that *gross* immigration to Ireland by nationals of those states was 36,000 between 1996 and 2001.[84] Allowance must, however, be made for emigration from Ireland by nationals of those states over the same period, for which estimates have not been published. Even with these recent increases, therefore, it is likely that nationals of continental Member States make up at most 1 per cent of the Irish resident population.

The low level of migration between Ireland and continental Member States may be contrasted with that between Ireland and Britain. On the one hand, the most recent census results in Britain for 1991 found 627,400 persons who had been born in Ireland.[85] It is particularly significant that in the years 1987–1990,

---

[82] Eurostat, *Yearbook 2000*, pp.110–111. No data was supplied for Austria.
[83] Central Statistical Office, *Statistical Abstract 1998–1999* (1999), Table 2.22.
[84] Central Statistical Office, *Population and Migration Estimates April 2001*, Table 7.
[85] This total made up of 592,020 resident in Great Britain and 35,380 resident in Northern Ireland. See Office for Population Censuses and Surveys, *1991 Census: Report for Great*

the last occasion on which there was significant net migration from Ireland, Britain was the primary direction of emigration. In those four years, net migration from Ireland was estimated at 131,700, of which 73 per cent (96,400) was to Britain, 15 per cent (20,300) to the USA, but only 1 per cent (1,500) to other EU states.[86]

At the same time, the history of Irish migration to Britain has meant that there are significant numbers of British-born persons in Ireland. This too can be seen from the Appendix, which shows that 190,648 persons who are usually resident (or 5.3 per cent of the total) were recorded as British-born in 1996.[87] The 1996 figure was all the more striking because it was an increase on the number of British-born persons *present* in Ireland at the time of previous censuses. The number of British-born persons is likely to have increased in recent years, and it has been estimated that the net migration of all persons from Britain to Ireland between 1996 and 2001 was 55,000.[88] It can be seen, therefore, that notwithstanding an ebb and flow in response to prevailing economic conditions, migration between Britain and Ireland remains a significant phenomenon in both directions.

14.(4)(b) Public policy

It is not just migration into and out of Ireland which is far more likely to occur to and from Britain than to and from the continental Member States. The impact of EU law upon public policy too has mainly been confined to the British-Irish axis.[89] This general point can be illustrated by a number of examples: two concerning the legal status of Irish citizens in Britain, and two concerning the impact of free movement principles upon public policy in Ireland.

Britain: Part I, vol. 1, Table 7 and Department of Health and Social Services, *Northern Ireland Census 1991: Summary Report* (1992), Table 7. These figures were only slightly down on 1981, when 642,455 persons were recorded as born in Ireland.

[86] Author's calculation based on the Central Statistical Office estimates summarised in Courtney, "A Quantification of Irish Migration with Particular Emphasis on the 1980s and 1990s," in *The Irish Diaspora* (Bielenberg ed., 2000), Table 15.9. The shares of gross emigration for the same period were: Britain, 64 per cent (146,200); USA, 15 per cent (33,700); the rest of the EU, 6.5 per cent (14,900); and, the rest of the world, 15 per cent (33,200).

[87] This total was made up of 151,081 born in Great Britain and 39,567 born in Northern Ireland: see Central Statistical Office, above n. 85, Table 2.22.

[88] Central Statistical Office, above n. 86.

[89] Case 379/87 *Groener v. Minister for Education and City of Dublin Vocational Educational Committee* [1989] E.C.R. 3967 [1990] 1 C.M.L.R. 401 may be thought a counter-example, in that it concerned a Dutch national who was denied employment as an art teacher because of a lack of knowledge of the Irish language. The Court of Justice concluded that the public policy of promoting the Irish language meant that adequate knowledge of it was a "condition [ ] relating to linguistic knowledge required by reason of the nature of the post to be filled" which was in principle permitted by Art. 3(1) of Regulation 1612/68. While that was admittedly a questionable result, given the evidence before the Court that the teaching in

The legal position as regards the employment of Irish nationals in Northern Ireland is a first illustration of the general point. When Britain and Ireland joined the then EEC, the usual position under Northern Ireland's Safeguarding of Employment Act 1947 was that persons born outside that jurisdiction required a work permit in order to take up employment there.[90] The primary effect of that rule appears to have been to prevent the employment in Northern Ireland of persons born in Ireland. It was for that reason that the Northern Irish Cabinet considered the need to abandon the 1947 Act an undesirable consequence of British and Irish accession to the EEC when that was under consideration in the late 1960s.[91] While the post-1968 conflicts presumably curtailed migration to Northern Ireland, the EU rules on the free movement of persons changed the formal position as regards employment there. It seems likely, therefore, that the EU rules have made at least a modest contribution to the presumed "dilution" of the Irish border as a consequence of EU membership.[92]

The use of EU rules on the free movement of persons to challenge exclusion orders made under Britain's Prevention of Terrorism Acts is the other circumstance in which the status of Irish citizens in Britain has been in issue.[93] The first such challenge was in *Gallagher*, which concerned the exclusion from Britain as a whole of an Irish citizen employed in London. The main issue in the proceedings was whether the procedures leading to the exclusion decision were contrary to Directive 64/221. In argument before the Court of Justice, the British government accepted that, as there was no requirement upon Irish citizens resident in Britain to acquire a residence permit, they were entitled for the purposes of Directive 64/221 to be treated as if they had one. In the Court's judgment, it followed that Irish residents were entitled to the protection of Article 9(1) of the Directive. Accordingly, a decision to exclude could only be taken after a "competent authority" had delivered an opinion, having itself given the individual the opportunity to make

---

question would be "conducted essentially or indeed exclusively in the English language" (see para.15) – it meant that the policy on the Irish language in certain public employments was consistent with EU law. Neither is there evidence more generally that membership of the EU has influenced policy on this question, and even were it to do so, the main beneficiaries would almost certainly be those educated in Britain.

90 The consistency of the 1947 Act with the Government of Ireland Act 1920 was affirmed by the Northern Ireland Court of Appeal in *Duffy v. Ministry of Labour and National Insurance* [1962] N.I. 6. That case concerned a prosecution for employing an Irish citizen as a domestic servant.

91 See, for example, the report of the Northern Irish Cabinet's discussions in 1967 in "Open border after joining EEC feared by cabinet", *The Irish Times*, January 2, 1998.

92 On which, see Anderson and Bort, "Change and the Irish Border: An Introduction" in *The Irish Border: History, Politics, Culture* (Anderson and Bort ed., 1999).

93 These powers were first set out in the Prevention of Terrorism (Temporary Provisions) Act 194, ss. 3–6. They were contained most recently in the Prevention of Terrorism (Temporary Provisions) Act 1989, ss. 4, 5 and 7, which permitted exclusion from Great Britain, Northern Ireland or Britain as a whole.

representations.[94] As this had not occurred in Gallagher's case, the decision to exclude him was invalid.[95]

Two further challenges dealt with exclusion from Great Britain only. In *Adams* the applicant wished to travel from Northern Ireland to London in order to speak at a political meeting.[96] Because he was not thought to be engaged in economic activity, the main EC law issues concerned the provision in Article 18 EC for the right of EU citizens to "move . . . freely within the territory of the Member States". The English High Court referred questions to the Court of Justice both as to the direct effect of Article 18 EC, and as to its application to situations "wholly internal" to a single Member State. While no reference was made to the applicant's nationality in *Adams*, it appears that Irish citizenship was nevertheless in play. Otherwise, it would have been unnecessary for the High Court to have referred to the Court of Justice the further question whether, if Article 18 EC did not apply to "wholly internal" situations, this was indeed such a situation. In the event, the lifting in October 1994 of the exclusion order against Adams led to the withdrawal of the request for a preliminary ruling, notwithstanding the applicant's argument that it should have been maintained as the legislation that permitted exclusion orders remained in force.[97] The other case was *McQuillan*,[98] where it was explicitly argued that the applicant's dual British and Irish nationality meant that he could not be confined to a part of Britain; and, that the right to move throughout Britain derived both from the provisions on EU citizenship and from the rules on the free movement of workers. Despite these novel arguments, Sedley J. preferred to stay the proceedings pending the outcome of the *Adams* reference. By the time the *Adams* reference had been withdrawn, the exclusion order against McQuillan had also been lifted.[99]

The powers relating to exclusion lapsed in March 1998. It is nevertheless significant that a number of EU law issues remain unresolved which could re-surface in the event that similar powers of exclusion were re-instated. First, the essential question posed by *Adams* and *McQuillan* remains unanswered: can EU law prevent Britain from limiting Irish citizens to part of its territory? There is also doubt as to whether the British authorities were entitled to refuse

---

[94] Case C–175/94, *R. v. Secretary of State for the Home Department, ex parte Gallagher* [1995] E.C.R. I–4253, [1996] 1 C.M.L.R. 557.

[95] Gallagher's claim for damages under the principle of state liability was however rejected by the Court of Appeal, which reasoned that, had the correct procedure been followed, he would probably have been excluded anyway: see [1996] 2 C.M.L.R. 951.

[96] *R. v. Secretary of State for the Home Department, ex parte Adams* [1995] All E.R. (EC) 176. The preliminary ruling request was registered as Case C–229/94.

[97] *R. v. Secretary of State for the Home Department, ex parte Adams (no. 2)* [1995] 3 C.M.L.R. 476.

[98] *R. v. Secretary of State for the Home Department, ex parte McQuillan* [1995] 4 All E.R. 400.

[99] *The Guardian*, March 9, 1995.

in all cases to specify the reasons for an exclusion order.[100] This point was raised in both *Gallagher* and *Adams*, but on each occasion a reference to the Court of Justice was refused on the grounds that it was clear that a state was entitled not give reasons for an exclusion where that would be contrary to its security.[101] These unresolved questions concerning the legality of parts of the system of exclusion orders may be considered a modest contributory factor in their disappearance.

EU principles on the free movement of persons have also had important effects upon public policy in Ireland. The tension between EU law on the cross-border provision of services and Irish law on abortion is a familiar example. After a 1983 amendment gave protection to the right to life of the unborn in Article 40.3.3 of the Constitution, it had been held unconstitutional to provide information in Ireland in relation to facilities for abortion in Britain.[102] When proceedings were taken in *Grogan* against the officers of a number of students' unions for publicising that information, they argued that a restriction on its availability would be an impermissible interference with the cross-border provision of services.[103] In a preliminary ruling, the Court of Justice's answer was that, while the termination of pregnancy in accordance with national law in a Member State was indeed a "service" within the meaning of the EC Treaty, the students' unions could not rely upon the Treaty provisions, as their connection with the providers of abortions in other Member States was "too tenuous."[104] Although disposing of the particular case, the Court's judgment left open the possibility that Article 40.3.3 of the Constitution, as interpreted, might be found inconsistent with the EC Treaty provisions on the cross-border provision of services. That possibility was given support by the Opinion of Advocate-General Van Gerven in *Grogan*. Although he considered the restrictions on information acceptable, he suggested that there might be limits, deriving from the principle of proportionality or the requirement to respect fundamental rights, to the reach of Ireland's constitutional protection of the unborn. His opinion itself turned out to be too cautious, as the European Court of Human Rights found in October 1992 that the absolute nature of the Irish ban on the provision of information concerning abortion was contrary to the principle of freedom of expression in Article 10 of the

---

[100] See O'Leary, Note on *Gallagher* (1996) 33 C.M.L.Rev. 777, 788–789.

[101] In *R. v. Secretary of State for the Home Department, ex parte Gallagher* [1994] 3 C.M.L.R. 295, the Court of Appeal referred to Art. 6 of Directive 64/ 221 alone in support. Steyn L.J. reached a similar conclusion in the High Court in Adams [1995] All E.R. (EC) 176, at 189, but relied in addition upon Art. 296 (ex Art. 223) EC.

[102] *A.G. (at the relation of the Society for the Protection of the Unborn Child (Ireland)) v. Open Door Counselling and Dublin Wellwoman Centre* [1988] I.R. 593, [1988] 2 C.M.L.R. 443.

[103] *Society for the Protection of the Unborn Child (Ireland) v. Grogan* [1989] I.R. 753, [1990] 1 C.M.L.R. 689.

[104] Case C–159/90 *Society for the Protection of the Unborn Child (Ireland)) v. Grogan* [1991] E.C.R. I–4685, [1991] 3 C.M.L.R. 849.

European Convention on Human Rights (ECHR).[105] This raised the possibility that an absolute ban on such information was also contrary to EC law.[106]

A further invocation of EC law soon followed in *A.G. v. X*,[107] when the Attorney-General sought an injunction to prevent a pregnant fourteen-year-old from travelling to Britain in order to obtain an abortion. The Supreme Court refused the request because the risk of her suicide meant that there was a right to abortion under Irish law. Because of that outcome, the Supreme Court did not address the argument that X had a right to travel to Britain by virtue of the "services" provisions of the EC Treaty. That argument had, however, been considered and rejected by Costello J. in the High Court. His conclusion was that the granting of an injunction in order to advance the public policy of upholding the right to life of the unborn was a permissible derogation from the rules on the cross-border provision of services. But that conclusion seemed questionable, not least because a ban on travel was one of the examples of a disproportionate restriction on the supply of services suggested by Advocate-General Van Gerven in *Grogan*.[108]

The Government's initial response to the possibility of conflict between Article 40.3.3 and the cross-border supply of services was to seek to defend Irish constitutional law. It accordingly secured agreement to a Protocol to the Treaty on European Union, which was formally signed in February 1992, to the effect that "nothing in the Treaty on European Union or the Treaty establishing the European Communities . . . shall affect the application in Ireland of Article 40.3.3 of the Constitution of Ireland."[109] But the "public dismay and outrage"[110] generated by the *A.G. v. X* litigation led to a significant shift in the debate over abortion in Ireland.[111] The result was that attempts were instead made to give effect to rights to information and travel in Ireland. In May 1992, the Government secured a "declaration" of the Member States that "it was and is their intention that the Protocol shall not limit freedom to travel between Member States or . . . to obtain or make available in Ireland information relating to services lawfully available in other Member States."[112] That was followed by referenda in November 1992 which amended Article

---

[105] *Open Door Counselling and Dublin Well Woman Centre v. Ireland* (1993) 15 E.H.R.R. 244.
[106] This was the position if Member States were not entitled to override the fundamental rights set out in the ECHR in derogating from free movement principles. For a Court of Justice statement to that effect, see Case C–260/89 *Elliniki Radiophonia Tiléorassi* [1991] E.C.R. I–2925, at para. 43. On the general question, see de Búrca, "Fundamental Human Rights and the Reach of EC Law," (1993) 13 *Oxford Journal of Legal Studies* 283. For a discussion on human rights and the EU see above Kingston, chap.12.
[107] [1992] 1 I.R. 1, [1992] 2 C.M.L.R. 277.
[108] See para. 29 of the Opinion.
[109] The text of the Protocol is at [1992] O.J. C191/94.
[110] Murphy, "Maastricht: Implementation in Ireland" (1994) 19 *European Law Review* 94, at 95.
[111] See Girvin, "Moral Politics and the Irish Abortion Referendums, 1992" (1994) 47 *Parliamentary Affairs* 203
[112] [1992] O.J. C191/ 109.

40.3.3 so that the right to life of the unborn would not limit either "freedom to travel between the State and another state" or the "freedom to obtain or make available in the State, subject to such conditions as may be laid down by law, information relating to services lawfully available in another state."[113] Since 1992, a general right to abortion has effectively been recognised in Irish law, provided that the operation occurs in another jurisdiction.[114] It is significant too that the Government proposals contained in the Twenty-Fifth Amendment of the Constitution (Protection of Human Life in Pregnancy) Bill 2001, which were defeated in a referendum in March 2002, did not involve any attempt to modify the law on access to abortion in other states. It seems, therefore, that EU law on the free movement of services acted as a catalyst in the early 1990s for an enduring change in Irish attitudes and law on the question of access to abortion, while suggesting the most suitable path (recognition of rights to travel and information) for a compromise.

The common travel area is the other aspect of Irish public policy upon which EU rules concerning the free movement of persons may have had an impact. When the Member States agreed in the 1997 Treaty of Amsterdam to incorporate the Schengen *acquis* into the EU framework, special provision was made for Britain and Ireland, including a Protocol on the application of Article 14 (then 7a) EC to Britain and Ireland. Article 1 of that Protocol affirms the right of Britain to maintain immigration controls, including those whose purpose is to verify rights of entry under EU law. Article 2 of the Protocol then provides as follows:

> "The United Kingdom and Ireland may continue to make arrangements between themselves relating to the movement of persons between their territories ('the Common Travel Area'), while fully respecting the rights of persons referred to in Article 1 . . . of the Protocol. Accordingly, as long as they maintain such arrangements, the provisions of Article 1 of this Protocol shall apply to Ireland under the same terms and conditions as for the United Kingdom. Nothing in Article [14] of the Treaty establishing the European Community, in any other provision of that Treaty or of the Treaty on European Union or in any measure adopted under them, shall affect any such arrangement."

The legal implications of Article 2 are admittedly somewhat difficult to identify. The term "arrangements . . . relating to the movement of persons" is necessarily imprecise, given that the common travel area is not based upon an

---

[113] Legislation on the subject is contained in the Regulation of Information (Services Outside the State for Termination of Pregnancies) Act 1995, the constitutionality of which was approved by the Supreme Court: see [1995] 1 I.R. 1.

[114] Figures are published annually for the place of origin given by those who obtain an abortion in Britain. An examination of these figures since 1974 shows that the number of women giving an Irish address has increased year by year, with the exception of a period of fluctuation between 1984 and 1989. The most recently published total was 6391 for 2000: Office for National Statistics, *Abortion Statistics* (2001), Table 24a.

international agreement and the practices of which it is comprised are only partly in the public domain. It is also unclear what is to happen when there is a conflict between the "rights of the persons referred to in Article 1" and the common travel area arrangements, given that Article 2 appears in different places to give each priority over the other. More basically, it is uncertain what the possible conflicts between EC rights of personal movement and the common travel area are thought to be. It does not appear for example that Britain and Ireland would otherwise be bound to abolish immigration controls for nationals of other Member States.[115] Neither is there any authority that Britain and Ireland are precluded from giving preferential treatment to each other's nationals in relation to immigration controls. The only relevant comparison is between a state's treatment of *its own* nationals and those of other Member States – and the Court has accepted that in the field of immigration control, a Member State is entitled to distinguish between them.[116] If there is a conflict between EU law and the common travel area, it may instead be in situations where Britain and Ireland attempt to enforce one another's decisions as regards individuals. That was illustrated by *Kweder v. Minister for Justice*, which concerned a Syrian national who wished to join his British wife in Ireland, but who was refused entry because he had previously been deported from Britain. In the High Court, Geoghegan J. held that the maintenance of the common travel area was a legitimate public policy for Ireland, but that consideration had also to be given to whether an application for entry to Ireland was "a device in order to obtain entry into the United Kingdom." As that test had not been satisfied there, the refusal to issue an entry visa was quashed.[117] It is arguable that Article 2 of the Protocol might preclude a challenge such as that in *Kweder* in the future.

Despite these uncertainties as to the legal position, it is nevertheless significant that the Treaty of Amsterdam arrangements have contributed to the greater attention which has been paid to the common travel area in recent years in Ireland.[118] The need to account for Ireland's position under the Treaty led

---

[115] In particular, in Case C–378/97 *Wijsenbeek* [1999] E.C.R. I–6207, [2001] 2 C.M.L.R. 1403, paras. 40–43, the Court of Justice concluded that Member States were permitted to retain controls on frontiers. It reached this conclusion notwithstanding the provision in Art. 14 EC for "an area without internal frontiers" and that in Art. 18 EC for the rights of movement of EU citizens. In either case, it thought that an obligation to dispense with controls presupposed the harmonisation of immigration law by the Member States.

[116] See for example Case C–171/96 *Pereira Roque* [1998] E.C.R. I–4607, [1998] 3 C.M.L.R. 143, at para. 38.

[117] [1996] 1 I.R. 381. An entry visa was subsequently issued to the applicant. For further discussion of this case see below Barrett, para 15(2)(c).

[118] This has been reflected in the new interest in the subject by academic and legal commentators. In addition to Ryan, above n. 51, see Hogan, "The Common Travel Area and Community Law" in *The Free Movement of Workers within the European Union* (Hyland ed., 1999) and Meehan, *Free Movement between Ireland and the UK: From the "Common Travel Area" to the Common Travel Area* (2000).

both ministers and officials to public justification of the common travel area, on the basis that it facilitates personal movement to and from Ireland.[119] The common travel area has been under scrutiny anyway in recent years because of the changes to Irish law and practice that have followed from it, including new powers of detention of non-nationals, and the introduction of direct provision for asylum applicants.[120] This combination of European and domestic stimuli may yet lead to greater formalisation of the arrangements that make up the common travel area. For that, the Schengen system might itself provide a model, in particular, for a joint visa policy, or for the creation of legal rights for non-EU nationals who legally enter or reside in one state to travel to the other.

14.(5) Conclusion

This chapter has sought to outline the main effects of the EU rules on the free movement of persons in the Irish context. It has shown that EU law has had important implications for Irish immigration law and for the exercise of economic and social rights within the State. It has also shown that, while there have been some modest effects in encouraging migration between Ireland and the continental Member States, the traditional route to and from Britain has remained the most significant one. That pattern of migration has had its counterpart in the political sphere, where EU rights have called into question important aspects of public policy as regards personal movement between Britain and Ireland. In the examples outlined here, the result has been actual or potential improvement in the legal position of Irish nationals in Britain, and greater debate about the peculiarities of Irish public policy in relation to personal movement.

For some, the limits to Irish connections with continental Member States may be a matter of regret. Certainly, events do not appear to have lived up to the expectations of Jack Lynch, who was Taoiseach of the government which negotiated Irish entry to the then EEC. His optimistic prediction was that:

> "For some centuries past the outside influences have come mainly from one source. The wider range of stimuli which would result from close relations with continental Europe would correct any such imbalance and be of potential beneficial influence."[121]

---

[119] See the explanation of the Amsterdam negotiations on the common travel area given by Foreign Minister, David Andrews, *Dáil Debates* vol. 481, col. 1096, October 16, 1997, and by one of the Irish negotiators, Bobby McDonagh, in his *Original Sin in a Brave New World: An Account of the Negotiation of the Treaty of Amsterdam* (1998), pp.169–170.

[120] For a discussion of developments in recent years connected with the common travel area, see Ryan, above n. 51, pp.871–874.

[121] *Dáil Debates*, vol. 247, cols. 1650–1651, June 23, 1970.

Britain's proximity, a shared language, and the history of Irish migration perhaps made it inevitable that personal movement, with its many consequences, would continue to occur primarily along that route. Nevertheless, the EU rules on the free movement of persons may well have performed a useful service – not the Europeanisation of Irish society, but rather the subtle transformation of Ireland's relationship with its closest neighbour.

APPENDIX: IRISH POPULATION BY PLACE OF BIRTH 1971–1996

	1971	1981	1986	1991	1996
Ireland	2840952	3211020	3316643	3296994	3344919
Britain	110221	186965	177790	173851	190648
Germany	2066	3842	3853	5792	6343
France	701	1997	2460	4512	3593
Italy	1022	1350	1314 1	507	–
Netherlands	712	1710	1888	1985	–
Belgium	240	490	497	600	–
Denmark	205	410	366	463	–
Spain	–	–	1113	1801	–
Greece	–	109	124	197	–
Portugal	–	–	124	147	–
Luxembourg –	20	30	44	–	
Other EU	–	–	–	–	9296
USA	11145	16591	15350	14533	15619
Other	10984	19261	19089	23293	26125
Total	**2978248**	**3433405**	**3540643**	**3525719**	**3596543**
EU6	4946	9439	10378	14859	–

Source: Compiled from census information published by the Central Statistical Office. Note that the figures for 1971 to 1991 are for persons enumerated, *i.e.* those present on the date of the census. The figures, therefore, include visitors, and are likely to be higher than the number of Irish residents *born* in other states. The figures for 1996 are for persons usually resident. The "EU6" figure is the total for the six Member States other than Ireland and Britain for which information was provided throughout the 1971–1991 period.

BIBLIOGRAPHY

Curtin, Note on *Grogan* (1992) 29 *Common Market Law Review* 585.

Fries and Shaw, "Citizenship of the Union: First Steps in the European Court of Justice," (1998) 4 *European Public Law* 533.

Guild, *Immigration Law in the European Community* (2001, Kluwer).

Handoll, *Free Movement of Persons in the EU* (1995, Wiley).

Handoll, "State Definition and the Free Movement of Workers (with Special Reference to Linguistic Policy)" (1987) 9 *Dublin University Law Journal* 64.

Hyland (ed.), *The Free Movement of Workers within the European Union* (1999, Irish Centre for European Law).

Mancini, "The Free Movement of Workers in the Case-Law of the European Court of Justice," in D. Curtin and D. O'Keeffe (eds), *Constitutional Adjudication in European Community and National law* (1992, Butterworths).

Meehan, *Free Movement between Ireland and the UK: From the "Common Travel Area" to the Common Travel Area* (2000, Policy Institute).

O'Leary, "The Free Movement of Persons and Services," in P. Craig and G. de Búrca (eds), *The Evolution of EU Law* (1999, Oxford University Press).

O'Leary, "Putting Flesh on the Bones of European Citizenship," (1999) 24 *European Law Review* 68.

O'Leary, "The Court of Justice as a Reluctant Constitutional Adjudicator," (1992) 17 *European Law Review* 138.

O'Leary, Note on *Gallagher* (1996) 33 *Common Market Law Review* 777.

Reich, "Union Citizenship – Metaphor or Source of Rights?" (2001) 7 *European Law Journal* 4.

Ryan, "The Common Travel Area between Britain and Ireland" (2001) 64 *Modern Law Review* 855.

Watson, "Wandering Students: Their Rights under Community Law," in D. Curtin and D O'Keeffe (eds.), *Constitutional Adjudication in European Community and National Law* (1992).

Wilkinson, "Abortion, The Irish Constitution and the EEC," [1992] *Public Law* 20.

15. THE RIGHTS OF THIRD-COUNTRY FAMILY MEMBERS UNDER EUROPEAN COMMUNITY LAW

GAVIN BARRETT*

15.(1) INTRODUCTION: PRIMARY, DERIVATIVE AND NON-ADDRESSEES OF COMMUNITY LAW

Dedicating a chapter of this book to analysing the rights of a category of persons whose status for the purposes of European Community (EC) law may be described as that of "third-country family members" seems particularly justified at the present time, by virtue of, *inter alia,* the gradual but significant increase in the kinds of such persons on whom Community law sees fit to confer rights, as well as the growing extent of the rights which are now conferred on such persons, or seem likely to be conferred on them.

15.(1)(a) Market citizens – a taxonomy or spectrum

Persons who for any reason come within the scope of EC law have sometimes, albeit in language which by now has been overtaken to some considerable extent by the evolution of the European Union (EU), been referred to as "market citizens".[1] Within the broad church of "market citizenry", however, there are many identifiable sub-groups, and, therefore, it seems useful to have some kind of taxonomy or scheme of classification according to which various persons may be categorised according to how they are regarded by EC law. One way of approaching the matter is by describing individuals viewed

---

* Ph.D., Barrister, Lecturer-in-Law, University College Dublin. Some of the contents of this chapter were presented as a paper at the Irish Centre for European Law conference on the rights of third-country nationals in EC Law held in Trinity College Dublin on November 25, 2000. My thanks are due to Cathryn Costello, Director of the Irish Centre for European Law and Lecturer in Law in Trinity College Dublin for originally suggesting the topic and for calling my attention to some sources which have been drawn upon in parts of this chapter. Any errors or omissions remain the responsibility of the author.

[1] See Everson "The Legacy of the Market Citizen" in Shaw and More, *New Legal Dynamics of European Integration* (Clarendon, 1995). Note also More "The Principle of Equal Treatment: From Market Unifier to Fundamental Right" in Craig and de Búrca, *The Evolution of EU Law* (Oxford University Press, 1999). The same terminology is used by Baldus in his "Codification of Private Law in the European Community: Legal Basis, Subsidiarity and Other Questions" in Barrett and Bernardeau *Towards a European Civil Code* (Academy of European Law Trier, 2002).

through the prism of Community law as falling along different points of a spectrum.[2]

15.(1)(a)(i) Primary addressees of Community law

At one end of this spectrum there is that category of persons who may be described as relatively legally privileged by EC law, namely primary addressees of Community law. These may be broadly defined as individuals who, by virtue of their activities or status, are regarded as being of direct interest to Community law without reference to any connection they may have with any other specific individual. In so far a certain activity or status is required, their activities might have involved, *e.g.* exercising a right of free movement as a worker[3]; or as a student[4]; or freedom to provide, or (indeed receive) a service; or freedom of establishment.[5] They may have the status of retired persons[6] or merely that of persons not otherwise enjoying rights under Community law who have sufficient resources to avoid becoming a burden on the social assistance system.[7] Those enjoying what have been until very recently the somewhat limited rights conferred on citizens of the EU to date may also be regarded as falling within this category of addressees.[8]

---

[2] It should be borne in mind that this division necessarily involves a degree of simplification and that the complete picture looked at in more detail is somewhat more nuanced. See also paragraph 15(1)(b) below. For a discussion on the free movement of persons (in general) and Ireland see above Ryan, Chap.14.

[3] See in particular the provisions of Arts. 39 to 42 (ex 48 to 51) of the EC Treaty, Council Regulation (EEC) 1612/68 of October 15, 1968 on Freedom of Movement for Workers Within the Community [1968] O.J. Sp. Ed. L257/2 and Council Directive 68/360/EEC of October 15, 1968 on the Abolition of Restrictions on Movement and Residence Within the Community for Workers of Member States and their Families [1968] O.J. Sp. Ed. L257/13 at 485.

[4] See in particular Council Directive 93/96/EEC of October 29, 1993 on the Right of Residence for Students [1993] O.J. L317/59.

[5] See in particular Arts. 43 to 48 (ex 52 to 58) of the EC Treaty (concerning establishment), Arts. 49 to 55 (ex 59 to 66) of the EC Treaty (concerning services) and Council Directive 73/148/EEC of May 21, 1973 on the Abolition of Restrictions on Movement and Residence Within the Community for Nationals of Member States With Regard to Establishment and the Provision of Services [1973] O.J L172/14. In relation to freedom to receive a service, see in particular Cases 286/82 & 26/83 *Luisi and Carbone v. Ministero del Tesoro* [1984] E.C.R. 377.

[6] See in particular Council Directive 90/365/EEC of June 28, 1990 on the Right of Residence for Employees and Self-Employed Persons Who Have Ceased Their Occupational Activity [1990] O.J. L180/28. See in relation to that sub-category of retirees consisting of migrant workers who wish to remain in another Member State, having been employed in that State, Art. 39(3)(d) of the EC Treaty and Commission Regulation (EEC) 1251/70 of June 29, 1970 on the Right of Workers to Remain in the Territory of a Member State After Having Been Employed in that State [1970] O.J. Sp. Ed. L142/24 at 402.

[7] Council Directive 90/364/EEC of June 28, 1990 on the Right of Residence [1990] O.J. L180/26, Art. 1 provides, *inter alia*, that "Member States shall grant the right of residence to nationals of Member States who do not enjoy these rights under other provisions of Community law . . . provided that they . . . are covered by sickness insurance in respect of all risks in the host Member State and have sufficient resources to avoid becoming a burden on the social assistance system of the host Member State during their period of residence."

[8] See Arts. 17 to 22 (ex 8 to 8e) of the EC Treaty and see more generally O'Leary *The Evolving*

15.(1)(a)(ii) Derivative addressees of Community law

The second band of the spectrum is made up of individuals who may be described as derivative addressees of Community law.[9] These are individuals who benefit in some measure from Community law because of the relationship they enjoy with another person, *e.g.* their status as somebody's family member. Such persons may be said to enjoy "derived" rights, not necessarily because the rights they enjoy are conferred any less directly by the Community legal system, but rather because the interest which Community law has in conferring rights upon them derives from the relationship which these individuals enjoy with another person, whose benefit is the main interest of Community law.[10] In certain cases, the rights conferred on derivative addressees of Community law may be so extensive as to match, or even better, in significant respects, those of certain persons in the first "legally privileged" category,[11] although more often this will not be the case, and the rights conferred on the first "legally privileged" category will be more extensive than the derivative rights which are conferred on family members.

15.(1)(a)(iii) Non-addressees of Community law

The third band in our spectrum is made up of individuals who are, for most purposes,[12] non-addressees of Community law. This band is composed of that

---

Concept of European Citizenship (Kluwer, 1996). A useful bibliography relating to the topic of Community citizenship is to be found in Weiler *The Constitution of Europe* (Cambridge University Press, 1999), pp.356–357. In a series of cases beginning with the landmark decision in Case C–85/96 *Martínez Sala v. Freistaat Bayern* [1998] E.C.R. I–2691, what heretofore might have been regarded as the relatively empty vessel of EU citizenship has now begun to be judicially filled. It was recently observed that the Court does not derive new residence rights directly from the EC Treaty rules on Union citizenship, but rather refers to those rules as an additional argument to interpret other provisions. (A Castro Oliveira, "Workers and Other Persons: Step-By-Step From Movement to Citizenship – Case Law 1995–2001" (2002) 39 C.M.L.Rev. 77) See now however the judgment of the European Court of Justice in Case C–413/99 *Baumbast and R. v. Secretary of the State for the Home Department* (judgment of the Court of 17 September, 2002).

9   This language is not especially novel. Note that the Court of Justice itself has used the expression "derived rights", *e.g.* in Case 40/76 *Kermaschek v. Bundesanstalt für Arbeit* [1976] E.C.R. 1669 and Case C–243/91 *Belgian State v. Taghavi* [1992] E.C.R. I–4401. Note also that in his Opinion to the Court in Case C–413/99 *Bambaust and R. v. Secretary of State for the Home Department* (Opinion delivered 5 July, 2001), Advocate General Geelhoed referred to 'derivative' rights. (See para. 34 of his Opinion). Such rights are sometimes also termed "indirect" or "secondary" rights. See, *e.g.* the Opinion of Advocate General La Pergola in Case C–356/98 *Kaba v. Secretary of State for the Home Department* [2000] E.C.R. I– 2623 at paras. 34 and 36.

10 It would not be inaccurate to say that one of the advantages of many (but not all) primary beneficiaries of Community law is that they are capable of giving rise to rights on the part of secondary beneficiaries.

11 Compare the rights of a family member of a worker under Regulation 1612/68/EEC below and those enjoyed by a national of a Member State of the European Community who has not exercised a free movement right.

12 Rights such as the right to rely on adherence on the part of the Community to human rights standards are being left to one side here.

category of persons who, broadly speaking, are not covered by EC law, and whose rights in EU countries are thus largely or exclusively dictated by the domestic law of those States with no, or at least very little, input by Community law. As far as Community law is concerned, therefore, such persons are relatively legally unprivileged, although of course they may enjoy very extensive rights under the domestic law of a particular Member State. This band is, in fact, composed exclusively of third-country nationals, see below.

15.(1)(b) Movement within spectrum

Two further points should be added. First, it should be noted that there is often an element of fluidity both within and between the bands of our spectrum. Hence, for example, EU citizens, already defined as primary addressees of Community law, could improve their position within the category of primary addressees by, for example, exercising a Treaty free movement right, with all the benefits, in terms of attracting the application of provisions both of the Treaty and of secondary legislation, which doing this would entail for them. Secondly, the same person can be a derivative addressee for one purpose and a primary addressee for another purpose, and therefore be properly located in two or more positions of the spectrum. Hence, for example, a Community national who is a spouse of a migrant worker for the purposes of Article 39 will enjoy rights both as a primary addressee (for example, as a citizen of the Union) and as a derivative addressee (as the spouse of a worker).[13]

15.(1)(c) Third-country nationals

Third-country nationals may be found in all three bands of the spectrum although most of them find themselves in the third band. To date, Community law has had a pronounced tendency to bestow its favours only on those fortunate enough to have the nationality of a Member State. The Treaty establishing the European Community (the EC Treaty) does contain some – to date under-used – provisions authorising legislation regarding the status of the third-country nationals.[14] However, notwithstanding this, thanks to secondary

---

[13] Another variant is that an individual might enjoy rights both as the spouse of a migrant Community worker and as a worker in his or her own right, although in this situation the rights attaching to the status of being a migrant Community worker would include and surpass the rights which attach to being the spouse of a migrant Community worker.

[14] The Treaty establishing the European Community (the EC Treaty) does contain some – to date under-used – provisions: see the second indent of Art. 49 of the EC Treaty (in that Chapter of the Treaty dealing with free movement of services) which provides that "the Council may, acting by a qualified majority on a proposal from the Commission, extend the provisions of the Chapter to nationals of a third country who provide services and who are established within the Community." Note also Title IV of the EC Treaty (which deals with such matters as visas, asylum, immigration and other policies related to the free movement of persons), which contains several provisions authorising (and, indeed, requiring) Community legislation concerning third-country nationals.

legislation, agreements with third countries, and to some extent, judgments of the European Court of Justice (ECJ), certain categories of third-country nationals are firmly located in the first and second bands of the spectrum, even if they populate these bands in lesser numbers than they do the third band.

Thus, for example, the category of primary addressees of Community law is made up in large part of Community nationals, who by virtue of their activities, *e.g.* exercising some free movement right, have brought themselves directly within the scope of Community law. However, certain third-country nationals can also fall within this category too, such as, for example, nationals of (non-EU) European Economic Area States (EEA)[15] who exercise the free movement rights conferred upon them by virtue of the EEA Agreement, and nationals of a State with which the Community has concluded an association agreement.[16] Should the Community choose to adopt legislation dealing with the rights of third-country nationals regardless of their status as members of a family, then even nationals of non-EEA and non-association agreement States would properly be regarded as primary addressees of Community law within the chosen definition.[17]

Certain constituent members of the second band of our spectrum, *i.e.* the derivative addressees of Community law, are of most interest for the purposes of this chapter, however. Like the first band of addressees, the category of derivative addressees of Community law is made up both of Community nationals and third-country nationals. Derivative addressees of Community law do not constitute a homogenous group, since, for example, different rights will be conferred on individuals depending on the precise nature of the relationship they enjoy with the primary addressee of Community law, for example, depending on whose family member they are, and which member of the family they are.[18]

This chapter examines the rights of a sub-category of derivative addressees of Community law which is made up of persons who derive Community law rights from their status as somebody's family member, namely third-country family members.

---

[15] Namely Iceland, Norway or Liechtenstein.

[16] See below and see more generally Hailbronner, *Immigration and Asylum Law and Policy of the European Union* (Kluwer, 2000), p.220 *et seq*. See generally in relation to such agreements, Hartley, *The Foundations of European Community Law* (4th ed., Oxford University Press, 1998), chap. 6.

[17] Such legislation is specifically envisaged by the EC Treaty. See Treaty provisions cited at n.14 above and note the recent Proposal for a Council Directive Concerning the Status of Third-Country Nationals Who Are Long-Term Residents (COM (2001) 127 final).

[18] It should be pointed out that the respective rights of the spouse, children and grandparents of an individual may be very different under Community law. It should also be pointed out that Community nationals who come within this band will enjoy at the very least a prominent second position on the spectrum within the band of primary addressees of Community law since they will enjoy the rights conferred by the Treaty on EU citizens, whereas third-country nationals will not.

15.(2) ON WHICH THIRD-COUNTRY FAMILY MEMBERS DOES COMMUNITY LAW CONFER RIGHTS, WHY HAVE THEY BEEN SO FAVOURED AND WHAT ELSE SHOULD WE KNOW ABOUT THEM AS A CATEGORY OF INDIVIDUALS?

Several questions may be asked in relation to third-country family members who benefit under EC law. To whose family does one have to belong in order to qualify as a derivative beneficiary of Community law? What kind of family member must one be, *e.g.* a spouse, a son, a daughter, a cousin? Will being an unmarried partner suffice? Or a grandparent, for example? Once a third-country national brings him or herself within the band of derivative addressees of Community law, what kind of Community law rights will he or she enjoy?

The answers to these questions are in large part determined by the kind of third-country family member one is. There are a number of different categories of third-country nationals who enjoy rights under Community law by virtue of their status as a family member. Among them are:

(a) third-country family members of Community nationals who have exercised their right to move freely as workers under Article 39 (ex 48) TEC;

(b) third-country family members of Community nationals who have exercised their right of establishment under Article 43 (ex 52)TEC;

(c) third-country family members of Community nationals who have exercised their right to provide services under Article 49 (ex 59) TEC;

(d) third-country family members of Community nationals who come within Council Directive 90/364/EEC of June 28, 1990 on the Right of Residence[19]; Council Directive 90/365/EEC of June 28, 1990 on the Right of Residence for Employees and Self-Employed Persons Who Have Ceased Their Occupational Activity[20]; Council Directive 93/96/EEC of October 29, 1993 on the Right of Residence for Students[21]; Commission Regulation (EEC) 1251/70 of June 29, 1970 on the Right of Workers to Remain in the Territory of a Member State After Having Been Employed in that State[22]; or Council Directive 75/34/EEC of December 17, 1974 Concerning the Right of Nationals of a Member State to Remain in the Territory of Another Member State After Having Pursued Therein an Activity in a Self-Employed Capacity[23];

---

[19] [1990] O.J. L180/26.

[20] [1990] O.J. L180/28.

[21] [1993] O.J. L317/59. This Directive re-adopted the contents of Directive 90/366/EEC of June 28, 1990 on the Right of Residence for Students [1990] O.J. L180/30) after the ECJ annulled this last-mentioned Directive in Case C–295/90 *European Parliament v. Council of the European Communities* [1992] E.C.R. I –4193

[22] [1970] O.J. Sp. Ed. L142/24 at 402.

[23] [1975] O.J. L14/10.

(e) third-country family members of nationals of European Economic Area States which are not also Member States of the European Community,[24] which nationals have exercised any of the above rights; and

(f) third-country family members of nationals of non-EU States which have entered into Association Agreements under Article 310 TEC with the Community, *e.g.* the Europe Agreements and the EEC-Turkey Association Agreement.

Before looking at the rights of third-country family members who fall into the various categories set out above, and the rights which they enjoy, three observations may be made.

15.(2)(a) Why community law is concerned with third-country family members who fall into the various categories set out above

First, the question should be addressed of why Community law confers any rights at all on such family members. By way of answer it may be said that, at least originally, it was not solely for reasons of humanitarian concern.[25] Indeed, on the contrary, the main initial core reason seems to have stemmed from the economics of a common market.[26] A common market is an area in which there is free movement of the factors of production, *i.e.* those elements necessary to productive economic activity.[27] The goal of setting up a European common market was that of reproducing the freedom of a national market, where factors of production – often identified as goods, persons (as workers, service providers and as establishers of businesses), services and capital – would go to where the requirements of supply and demand dictated. People, however, as the Community has gradually discovered, are more resistant to free movement than other "factors of production". One important reality here is that without conferring rights on persons to bring close family members with them when they migrate, and further, conferring reasonably extensive rights on those family members, Community law provisions aimed at securing

---

[24] Namely Iceland, Norway or Liechtenstein.

[25] If it was, the question would arise of why an individual who is a family member of a primary addressee of Community law would be more deserving of humanitarian concern than any other third-country national. Perhaps one might argue that their lives might be particularly negatively affected by, *e.g.* separation from the primary beneficiary of Community law. This seems unconvincing as a rationale, however, since no matter how desperate the plight of other third-country nationals, Community law makes no such substantive provision for them.

[26] The element of concern for human betterment in setting up such a common market in the first place should not, of course, be ignored, and it should further be noted that such economic reasons may well have been supplemented by other non-economic concerns. See the concerns expressed for fundamental rights and the improvement of workers' living and working conditions and social advancement in the third "Whereas" clause in the preamble of Regulation (EEC) no. 1612/68 of the Council of October 15, 1968 on freedom of movement for workers within the Community.

[27] See Swann, *The Economics of the Common Market* (7th ed., Penguin, 1992), pp.11–12.

that free movement of economic actors which the Community needed in order to make the common market a reality were likely to be doomed to failure.[28] It is probably for this reason that, notwithstanding the absence of any mention in the Treaty of Rome itself of rights for family members of individuals exercising fundamental Community economic freedoms, Community secondary legislation has made extensive provision for the conferring of such rights. What is of interest for the purpose of this chapter is that such provisions have benefited third-country family members of economic actors.

15.(2)(b) The lack of special treatment for family members who are third-country nationals

The second observation which may be made is that, except in so far as concerns Category (f) of third-country family members, Community law does not manifest any general desire on the part of the legislator to single out family members who come from third countries for special treatment. Rather, the more normal situation is that Community law has, primarily for the reasons just outlined, provided for rights to be conferred on family members of the primary addressee of the Community interest, and it does not impose any particular requirements regarding the nationality of that family member. In a sense therefore, it is a case of third-country family members being welcomed into a kind of club rather than having a club specially created for them. It may be further noted that not alone does Community law not manifest any general desire on the part of the legislator to single out third-country family members for special treatment, it also tends to make no distinction between third-country family members according to their nationality. In other words, in none of the provisions dealing with the above listed categories of persons is a general stipulation laid down to the effect that the individual family member benefiting from Community law rights must be a national of any particular state. Thus, for example, a third-country family member of a worker who enjoys rights under a Europe Agreement may come from a country which has no such Agreement with the Community, and yet still enjoy the rights conferred on family members by the Agreement.

15.(2)(c) The double requirement on the primary addressee – nationality and status

Thirdly, it should be borne in mind that the mere fact of being a Community national (or a citizen of the European Union) has not as yet been deemed sufficient to confer Community law rights on one's third-country family

---

[28] An acknowledgment of this point is to be seen in the fifth "Whereas" clause in the preamble of Regulation (EEC) no. 1612/68 of the Council of October 15, 1968 on freedom of movement for workers within the Community.

members. Or, expressed from another perspective, the mere fact of being a third-country family member of a Community national/EU citizen will not (pending judicial or legislative development of the rights adhering to citizenship of the Union)[29] be sufficient to bring one within the scope of Community law. Rather, one must be a family member of an individual who is a primary addressee of Community by virtue of (i) his or her nationality and (ii) some activity or status other than merely that of being a Community national/EU citizen.

This point was illustrated starkly in *Morson and Jhanjan v. Netherlands.*[30] This case involved the right of family members to install themselves with a Community national who exercises free movement rights. It will be seen presently that this right of instalment (or right of family reunification) is one of the rights which is provided for under Community secondary legislation. But in this case, two Dutch nationals, both working in the Netherlands, were held to have had no right under Community law to bring their non-Community national (Surinamese) parents into the country. The reason for this was that it was held that the Dutch individuals were nationals working in their own Member State "who had never exercised the right to freedom of movement within the Community." Thus, condition (i) above had been met, but not condition (ii). As a result, the ECJ took the view that this was a totally internal situation, in other words, one which was of no concern to EC law.

A similar conclusion was reached in the subsequent joined cases of *Ücker and Jacquet.*[31] These cases concerned non-Community national spouses rather than parents. Mrs Ücker was Norwegian. Mrs. Jacquet was Russian. Both of them had married Community (German) nationals and come to live in Germany with their spouses. Neither of their husbands had worked outside the Member State at any material time. Both women obtained jobs with German universities which, however, refused to give them anything more than short-term contracts. They felt they were being unequally treated and sought to challenge this inequality under Community legislation protecting the families of workers. The answer of the ECJ was that Community legislation regarding freedom of movement of workers could not be applied to the situation of Mr. Ücker and Mr. Jacquet – workers who had never exercised the right to freedom of movement within the Community – and hence their third-country spouses could derive no benefit from Community law. Once again, therefore, this

---

[29] Regarding legislative development of such rights, see the Proposal for a European Parliament and Council Directive on the Right of Citizens of the Union and Their Family Members to Move and Reside Freely Within the Territory of the Member States COM (2001) 257 final.

[30] Cases 35 and 36/82 [1982] E.C.R. 3723. See also Case 147/87 *Zaoui v. Caisse régionale d'assurance maladie de l'Ile-de-France* [1987] E.C.R. 5511 and the list of cases cited by Hailbronner in *Immigration and Asylum Law and Policy of the European Union* (Kluwer Law International, 2000), p.179 at n. 169.

[31] Cases C–64/96 *Land Nordrhein-Westfalen v. Ücker* and C–65/96 *Jacquet v. Land Nordrhein-Westfalen* [1997] E.C.R. I 3171.

situation was regarded as a totally internal one and once again, the reason for this was that condition (ii) above had not been met. In other words, Mr. Ücker and Mr. Jacquet had not done something (such as exercising their Community free movement rights as workers) which would bring them within the category of primary addressees of EC law and their spouses within the category of derivative addressees.

The foregoing cases are to be contrasted with *R v. Immigration Appeal Tribunal and Surinder Singh ex parte Secretary of State for the Home Department*.[32] In this case, the Community national, Mrs. Singh, had exercised her free movement rights and was thus capable of conferring on her spouse the status of what is defined above as a derivative beneficiary of Community law. The facts of the case were that a British national married a third-country (Indian) national. Both worked for a number of years in Germany before returning to the United Kingdom. As far as the ECJ was concerned, this enabled Mr. Singh to assert the rights which were conferred by Community secondary legislation on the spouse of a worker. The view of the Court was that:

> "a national of a Member State might be deterred from leaving his country of origin in order to pursue an activity as an employed or self-employed person as envisaged by the Treaty in the territory of another Member State if, on returning to the Member State of which he is a national in order to pursue an activity there as an employed or self-employed person, the conditions of his entry and residence were not at least equivalent to those which he would enjoy under the Treaty or secondary law in the territory of another Member State.
>
> He would in particular be deterred from doing so if his spouse and children were not also permitted to enter and reside in the territory of his Member State of origin under conditions at least equivalent to those granted them by Community law in the territory of another Member State."[33]

It may be remarked that the reasoning of the Court at this point does not seem entirely satisfactory. It seems a rather curious argument to say, in effect, that an individual will be deterred from going to another Member State because the conditions of entry and residence in that other Member State are better than in the individual's own State.[34] However, one should not be over-critical of the judgment since it is true that the individual might well be deterred from going back to his or her own State, which would also arguably do damage to the notion of a common market involving free movement of workers and self-employed persons.

---

[32] Case 370/90 [1992] E.C.R. I– 4265.

[33] Paras. 19 and 20 of the Court's judgment.

[34] A more convincing argument can be made that a national of Member State A might be deterred from going to Member State B by any rule that the conditions of entry and residence in Member State A would be somehow thereby diminished.

In the wake of *Surinder Singh*, therefore, the obvious (if not always practical) solution in order to attract whatever protection Community law has to offer for third-country family members is for the Community national in the family to exercise free movement rights as a worker or self-employed person in another Member State of the EU before returning home, and asserting that he is now a primary beneficiary of Community law, and his non-Community national family members are now derivative addressees, and could invoke, *inter alia*, the right of instalment, or family reunification. According to one Department of Justice source, it is now a not infrequent occurrence that a United Kingdom resident couple, of which one partner is British and the other partner is a non-EC national who is facing potential expulsion from the United Kingdom, now travel to Ireland so that the U.K. national can exercise the right to work here and return home to the United Kingdom after some months.[35]

An attempt by the Irish authorities to prevent one such couple bringing themselves within the scope of Community law came unstuck in the case of *Wael Kweder v. Minister for Justice*.[36] In this case a Syrian national married to a British national was deported from the United Kingdom for working part-time in contravention of the conditions of his student visa. His wife exercised her EC law free movement rights by moving to Ireland and taking up employment as a cook in the Little Chef restaurant near Dublin Airport. Her husband then applied for a visa to be admitted to Ireland so that he could be reunited with his wife. In other words, he sought to exert his derivative right of instalment (or right of family reunification) as provided for under Community secondary legislation. His reliance on Community law was vindicated. Geoghegan J. quashed the decision of the Minister for Justice to refuse Mr. Kweder a visa, and observed that the existence of a United Kingdom deportation order against Mr. Kweder could not be relied upon by the Minister to justify the refusal of a visa for public policy reasons. Nor could the acknowledged intention of the Kweders to return to the United Kingdom in the long term, since it could well be that any such return would be lawful.[37]

Notwithstanding the assistance which Community law rendered to the Kweders in this case, it is submitted that the law in this area seems open to criticism in several respects. To begin with, it is lacking in clarity. Thus, for instance, the question of how long the Community national must remain in this jurisdiction before coming within the ambit of Community law is not precisely defined. Nor is there clarity as to the extent to which the rights of the non-Community national are dependent on the continued economic activity of the

---

[35] See Ingoldsby, "Free Movement – A Department of Justice Perspective" in Hyland *The Free Movement of Workers Within the European Union* (Irish Centre for European Law, 1999), p.26.

[36] [1996] 1 I.R. 381. Also see above Ryan para. 14(4)(b) for discussion of this case.

[37] Geoghegan J. noted that: "any such return would be in the context of a lawful entry into the United Kingdom by the applicant in accordance with legal advice which she and the applicant have received which would seem to be fully justified by the case law", *ibid.*, at 388.

Community spouse.[38] What if the Community national spouse, on returning to his or her own country, ceases to work? Furthermore, although it is admittedly the case that there must be some dividing line between situations in which Community law rights apply and those in which they do not, the present cross-border requirement, in the era of European Union citizenship and of an area of freedom, security and justice does seem to have a somewhat artificial air about it. If it is a requirement which, in any case, can be relatively easily met (subject only to the imposition of very considerable cost and inconvenience on persons to whom the rule applies) one is tempted to question the point in having the rule in the first place.[39]

No rights of third-country family members who fall into the various categories set out above are stipulated in the Treaties of Rome or Maastricht as amended. Hence, in order to determine what rights exist, recourse must be had to secondary legislation and to the jurisprudence of the ECJ.

15.(3) THIRD-COUNTRY FAMILY MEMBERS OF COMMUNITY NATIONALS WHO HAVE EXERCISED THEIR RIGHT TO MOVE FREELY AS WORKERS UNDER ARTICLE 39 (EX 48) TEC

15.(3)(a) Freedom of Movement for Workers Within the Community and Council Regulation 1612/68

By far the most important legislative instrument relating to the rights of family members of workers within the meaning of Article 39 (ex 48) of the EC Treaty is Council Regulation (EEC) 1612/68 of October 15, 1968 on Freedom of Movement for Workers Within the Community.[40] It is consequently a measure which must be looked at in some detail in this chapter. The provisions of this

---

[38]   See Watson "Free Movement of Workers: A One-way Ticket?" (1993) 22 I.L.J. 68; Craig and de Búrca, *EU La*w (2nd ed., Oxford University Press, 1998), p.707. The provisions of U.K. law dealing with this situation are to be found in para. 11 of the Opinion of Advocate General La Pergola in Case C–356/98 *Kaba v. Secretary of State for the Home Department* [2000] E.C.R. I–2623.

[39]   The Commission proposed the abolition of this requirement of a cross-border element, but negotiations on these proposals were discontinued. See COM(88)815 final and see generally Hailbronner, above n.16 , pp.181–182. An additional possible criticism (although admittedly this is an aspect of criticism which may be addressed at any situation in which so-called "reverse discrimination" is permitted) is that it may seem curiously anti-egalitarian for it to be acceptable in Community law that the position of third-country family members of a national of a Member State may be worse under that Member State's laws than that of a third-country family member of a national of *another* Member State.

[40]   [1968] O.J. Sp. Ed. L257/2. See for recent reform proposals, the Proposal for a European Parliament and Council Regulation amending Council Regulation (EEC) 1612/68 of October 15, 1968 on Freedom of Movement for Workers Within the Community. COM (1998) 394 Proposal submitted to Council and Parliament on October 14, 1998 [1998]O.J. C344/9.

instrument which are of primary relevance for present purposes[41] are Articles 10 to 12, which appear in the Regulation under the rubric "Workers' Families". It should be noted that it is specifically acknowledged by more than one provision under this rubric that the rights which it confers on family members apply regardless of the fact that such persons may be third-country nationals.[42] The Regulation has tended to be broadly construed in favour of workers and their families by the ECJ, which has stressed that free movement of workers under Regulation 1612/68 must be guaranteed in compliance with principles of liberty and dignity, and that this requires the best possible conditions for the integration of the Community worker's family in the society of the host Member State. Furthermore, Regulation 1612/68 is, according to the case-law of the Court, to be interpreted in the light of the requirement of respect for family life.[43]

15.(3)(a)(i) The impact on the rights of third-country family members of Articles 10 to 12 of Regulation 1612/68

Under Article 10, it is provided that the following persons shall, "*irrespective of their nationality*", have the right to install themselves with a worker who is a national of one Member State and who is employed in the territory of another Member State:

(A) his spouse and their descendants who are under the age of 21 years or are dependents;

(B) dependent relatives in the ascending line of the worker and his spouse.

The expression "their descendants" has been broadly interpreted by the Court as meaning both the descendants of the worker and of his or her spouse, rather than merely the children common to the migrant worker and of his or her spouse. This is an interpretation which favours children of third-country nationality, since it means that a step-child of a Community national migrant worker, neither of whose natural parents is a Community national, can benefit under Article 10.[44]

Member States are, however, required to "facilitate the admission" of any member of the family not coming within the above categories if these are dependent on the worker or living under his roof in the country from whence

---

[41] See Part I, Title III of the Regulation.

[42] See below concerning Arts. 10 and 11 of the Regulation.

[43] See generally Case C–413/99 *Baumbast and R. v. Secretary of the State for the Home Department* (judgment of the European Court of Justice of September 17, 2002) at paras 50 and 72.

[44] Case C–413/99 *Baumbast and R. v. Secretary of the State for the Home Department* (judgment of the European Court of Justice of September 17, 2002) at paras 57 and 63. A similar approach has been adopted as regards the scope of Article 12. (See para. 63 of *Baumbast* and see the discussion of Article 12 in the text *infra.*).

he comes.[45] However, a condition is imposed by Article 10 on the worker as regards benefiting either from this family right of instalment or from the imposition of an obligation on the Member State to facilitate admission of family members. Article 10 requires that for the purposes of the foregoing the worker must have available for his family housing considered as normal for national workers in the region where he is employed.[46]

Article 10 was considered in the case of *Netherlands v. Reed*[47] where the ECJ held that the term "spouse" in this provision referred to a marital relationship only and could not therefore be interpreted as requiring that the companion of a worker in a stable relationship must in certain circumstances be treated as a "spouse" for the purposes of Article 10.[48] This confinement of the application of Article 10 to parties to a valid civil marriage must be considered a major restriction on its usefulness, given the possible relationships which both exist and are regarded as socially acceptable outside the institution of marriage. However, the term "spouse" has in some ways been interpreted in the case law of the ECJ in a manner wider than might have been anticipated. In *Diatta v. Land Berlin*,[49] which concerned a Senegalese woman who resided in Germany apart from her French husband from whom she had separated with the intention of divorcing him, and who was refused an extension of her residence permit by the relevant German authorities on the grounds that she was no longer the spouse of a Community national, the Court held that Article 10 did not require that the member of a family to whom it applied must live permanently with the worker. The Court held that: "a requirement that the family must live under the same roof permanently cannot be implied."[50] More

---

[45]   Art. 10(2) of the Regulation.

[46]   Note however that Art. 10 also stipulates that this latter stipulation "must not give rise to discrimination between national workers and workers from the other Member States". The implications of this seem somewhat unclear. Does it mean, for example (as it seems to) that the requirement that the migrant worker have normal housing available for his or her family cannot be relied upon by the host State in order to disentitle family members to install themselves with the worker in any case where no such similar requirement is imposed of national workers before their family members may install themselves with them? If this is indeed the case, then the "housing considered as normal" requirement loses much of its force.

[47]   Case 59/85 [1986] E.C.R. 1283.

[48]   See, however, the findings of the Court in relation to the concept of an Art. 7(2) social advantage discussed below. Note also that the Court in *Reed* specifically reached its conclusions "in the absence of any indication of a general social development which would justify such a broad conclusion". Query therefore if this aspect of the judgment should be regarded as set in stone given the widespread evidence of changes in mores and re-evaluation of values across the Community.

[49]   Case 267/83 [1985] E.C.R. 567.

[50]   *ibid.,* para. 18. Note that the absence of any such requirement holds good not only for the spouse of the Community migrant worker, but also for other members of the family, such as children. (See Case C–413/99 *Baumbast and R. v. Secretary of the State for the Home Department* (judgment of the European Court of Justice of September 17, 2002) at para. 62 thereof, where the non-residence of a migrant worker's children with him was held not to affect their rights under Articles 10 and 12 of Regulation 1612/68.)

specifically, it held that: "the marital relationship cannot be regarded as dissolved so long as it has not been terminated by the competent authority. It is not dissolved merely because the spouses live separately, even where they intend to divorce at a later date."[51]

If anything, an even broader approach was evinced by the ECJ in *R. v. Immigration Appeal Tribunal and Surinder Singh ex parte Secretary of State for the Home Department*.[52] The facts of this case, previously outlined, are of particular interest here because they involved the additional complication that a decree nisi of divorce had been granted in 1987 to Mrs. Singh against her husband (the non-Community national in the relationship) – a development which had inspired the United Kingdom authorities to refuse to grant Mr. Singh indefinite leave to stay in the country as the spouse of a British citizen. The Court clearly did not view the grant of such a decree as having taken the case outside the scope of Community law (or, more specifically, as meaning that the case did not involve a spousal relationship), observing that:

"it is not alleged that Mr. and Mrs. Singh's marriage was a sham. Moreover, although the marriage was dissolved by a decree absolute of divorce delivered in 1989, that is not relevant to the question referred for a preliminary ruling, which concerns the basis of the right of residence of the person concerned during the period before the date of that decree."

Although indicative to some extent of the broad approach which the ECJ will adopt to the meaning of "spouse", the ruling in *Surinder Singh* also indicates that there are limits to the breadth of the concept. Thus, one important implication would appear to be that the act of going through a "sham" marriage for the purpose of availing themselves of the rights available to married couples will not make either party thereto a spouse within the meaning of Article 10. Further, it is possible to read the judgment as indicating a view on the part of the Court that had a decree *absolute* of divorce already been granted by the time of the decision to refuse him further permission to remain in the country, Mr. Singh would no longer have been regarded as a spouse for the purposes of Community law. In other words, it would seem that once a marriage is finally dissolved, a spouse will lose his or her Article 10 right to install him or herself with their erstwhile spouse in a Member State, in addition to the other rights. This is, of course, a serious matter for a third-country spouse because he or she will then be at the mercy of the domestic legal system, which (as in the case of *Diatta* and *Singh*) may wish to refuse the

---

[51] *ibid.*, para. 18.
[52] Case C–370/90 [1992] E.C.R. I–4265. The case involved Council Directive 73/148/EEC of May 21, 1973 on the Abolition of Restrictions on Movement and Residence Within the Community for Nationals of Member States With Regard to Establishment and the Provision of Services [1973] O.J. L172/14 rather than Regulation 1612/68 but no distinction has been drawn by the European Court of Justice between the concept of a "spouse" (which appears in both these measures) for the purposes of Regulation 1612/68 and Directive 73/148/EEC.

individual in question further residence rights and perhaps even to deport him or her.

It is submitted that there would appear to be a need for reform here. It scarcely seems acceptable that (i) a party to an intolerable marriage be prevented from bringing the relationship to a legal end by the fear that any such divorce will be accompanied with the individual in question being deported, or (ii) one party to a marriage be in effect empowered to threaten the other with loss of residence rights because divorce is accompanied by these consequences. These are issues which attracted the attention of the High-Level Panel on the Free Movement of Persons, which observed that:

> "the right of residence in the host Member State enjoyed by a third-country national who is the spouse of a Union citizen is subject to the durability of that person's marriage. In the event of divorce, the interested party may find him or herself, from one day to the next, deprived of the right to stay in the Member State where he/she was hitherto resident. The precariousness of this situation is hard to accept, in particular as it may be used to the disadvantage of such persons. It is not rare for them (most often women) to be subjected during marriage to the threat of divorce. Even in the event of the marriage being dissolved, Community law should continue to offer some legal protection to the spouse who is a third-country national, in particular with regard to his/her right of residence. The fact that the third-country national may have exercised certain rights in the Community during his/her marriage creates objective ties whose effects exceed the duration of the marriage. Such is the case in particular where there are common children or where the spouse has exercised his/her right to pursue a profession. Accordingly it is suggested not only that national authorities be invited to take into account this situation but also that the various Community provisions applicable to the right to remain, should be amended so as to recognize a right of residence for the divorced spouse who is a third-country national."[53]

The plight of divorcees has now been recognised, at least at the level of draft Community legislation[54] although, of course, whether this draft legislation will ultimately be adopted remains to be seen. It should, at any rate, be noted that even at present, the divorce of a migrant worker will not affect rights conferred by Regulation 1612/68 on his or her children, such as the right of residence or the right to pursue their education.[55] Another important issue concerning

---

[53] Report of the High-Level Panel on the Free Movement of Persons chaired by Mrs. Simone Veil presented to the Commission on March 18, 1997, pp.74–75.

[54] See Proposal for a European Parliament and Council Regulation Amending Council Regulation (EEC) 1612/68 of October 15, 1968 on Freedom of Movement for Workers Within the Community (COM(1998)394) at Article 1(9) thereof. See also the Proposal for a European Parliament and Council Directive Amending Directive 68/360/EEC on the Abolition of Restrictions on Movement and Residence Within the Community for Workers of Member States and Their Families (COM (1994) 394) at Article 1(4) thereof.

[55] Case C–413/99 *Baumbast and R. v. Secretary of the State for the Home Department* (judgment of the European Court of Justice of September 17, 2002) at paras 60 to 63.

Article 10 is the question of what constitutes dependence for the purposes of this provision. In *Centre Public d'Aide Sociale de Courcelles v. Lebon*,[56] it was held by the ECJ that the question of the existence of dependence is one of fact. According to the Court: "the person having that status is a member of the family who is supported by the worker and there is no need to determine the reasons for recourse to the worker's support or to raise the question whether the person concerned is able to support himself by taking up paid employment."[57]

Article 11 confers the right to take up employment on certain family members. It provides that where a national of a Member State is pursuing an activity as an employed or (somewhat curiously in a Regulation which otherwise concerns only workers) self-employed person in the territory of a Member State, his spouse and those of the children who are under the age of 21 years or dependent on him, shall have the right to take up any activity as an employed person throughout the territory of that same State *"even if they are not nationals of any Member State."* Thus, once again one finds a specific acknowledgment that a right conferred on family members by Regulation 1612/68 is to apply regardless of the fact that such persons may be third-country nationals. Two further points may be made about the Article 11 right to take up any activity as an employed person. The first is that this right has been held by the ECJ to cover any activity as an employed person – even those occupations subject to a system of administrative authorisation and to special legal rules governing their exercise. Hence in *Gül v. Regierungspräsident Düsseldorf*,[58] a case brought by a doctor of Cypriot nationality married to a British national who was a migrant worker in Germany, the ECJ held that Article 11 carried with it the right for a spouse to engage in the medical profession, provided that the spouse could show that he had the professional qualifications required by the host Member State for the exercise of the occupation in question.[59]

The second observation to be made about Article 11 is that the rights granted by Article 11 have been held to be linked to the rights which a migrant Community worker enjoys under Article 39 and Regulation 1612/68. This is significant, for Article 3(1) of Regulation 1612/68 requires non-discriminatory treatment of migrant Community workers by provisions laid down by law, regulation, administrative action or administrative practices of a Member State. The net effect of this is, as was held in *Gül*, that Article 11, where applicable, entitles spouses of Community migrant workers *regardless of their nationality* to the application in the same manner of the same provisions as are applied to nationals of the host State regarding access to and practice of their profession.[60]

---

[56] Case 316/85 [1987] E.C.R. 2811
[57] *ibid.*, para. 22.
[58] Case 131/85 [1986] E.C.R. 1573.
[59] *ibid.*, paras. 11 to 18.
[60] *ibid.*, paras. 19 to 26. This is the case whether the spouse's qualifications are recognised under

Article 12 of Regulation 1612/68 provides, *inter alia*, that the children of a national of a Member State who is or has been employed in the territory of another Member State shall be admitted to that State's general educational, apprenticeship and vocational training courses under the same conditions as the nationals of that State, if such children are residing in its territory. Article 12 has been expressly held by the ECJ to apply to children who are third country nationals.[61] It is a provision which has been broadly interpreted by the Court, which, in construing it, has had regard not only to the letter of Article 12, but also to the spirit underlying it.[62] In *Michel S*,[63] Article 12 was interpreted widely enough to be taken to be capable of referring to provision made under Belgian law to enable disabled persons to recover their ability to work, and in *Casagrande*,[64] widely enough to cover a secondary school grant, as a general measure intended to facilitate educational attendance. The scope of the provision *ratione personae* has also been broadly construed. Hence in *Gaal*,[65] the view was taken that Article 12 would apply to persons at an advanced level of education (in this case, university level), notwithstanding the fact that they were no longer dependent on their parents and were 21 years of age or older.[66] In *Echternach and Moritz*, where what was at issue was the refusal of the Dutch authorities to provide study grants to two German students, it was held that the child of a worker of a Member State who has been in employment in another Member State retains, on his family's return to his home country, the right to continue his education in the host State notwithstanding the fact that his migrant worker parent is no longer resident there. This is of interest in that it shows that the derivative rights of family members of a migrant worker may, under Article 12 of Regulation 1612/68, outlast the status of that individual under Community law as a worker for the purposes of Article 39 of the Treaty.[67]

---

the legislation of the host Member State or by virtue of Community legislation. See paras. 27 to 30.

61 Case C–413/99 *Baumbast and R. v. Secretary of the State for the Home Department* (judgment of the European Court of Justice of September 17, 2002) at para. 56 thereof. The Court drew inspiration in this regard from the fact that Article 10 of the Regulation applies, on its own terms, to descendants of Community workers "irrespective of their nationality".

62 See, *e.g.* Case C–413/99 *Baumbast and R. v. Secretary of the State for the Home Department* (judgment of the European Court of Justice of September 17, 2002) at para. 54 thereof.

63 Case 76/72 *Michel S v. Fonds National de Reclassement Handicapés* [1973] E.C.R. 457.

64 Case 9/74 *Casagrande v. Landeshauptstadt München* [1974] E.C.R. 773.

65 Case C–7/94 *Landesamt fürAusbildungsförderung Nordrhein-Westfalen v. Gaal* [1995] E.C.R. I–1031.

66 Contrast Article 11, which, on its own terms, applies only to those children of a migrant worker and his spouse who are under the age of 21 or are dependent on the migrant worker. In *Echternach and Moritz*, above, n.67, the Court had already confirmed that Art. 12 of Regulation 1612/68 applied to any form of education including university studies and vocational studies at a technical college.

67 Cases 389–390/87 *Echternach and Moritz v. Minister van Onderwijs en Wetenschappen* [1989] E.C.R. 723. (See also now in this respect Case C–413/99 *Baumbast and R. v.*

The extraordinary reach which Article 12 is capable of having was revealed in the recent finding of the European Court of Justice in *Baumbast* that:

> "the right conferred by Article 12 of Regulation No. 1612/68 on the child of a migrant worker to pursue, under the best possible conditions, his education in the host Member State necessarily implies that that child has the right to be accompanied by the person who is his primary carer and, accordingly, that that person is able to reside with him in that Member State during his studies. To refuse to grant permission to remain to a parent who is the primary carer of the child exercising his right to pursue his studies in the host Member State infringes that right."[68]

Factors leading the Court to this conclusion included the Court's view that Regulation 1612/68 had to be interpreted in the light of the requirement of respect for family life – as well as the Court's pragmatic conclusion that to refuse the right to remain in the host Member State to parents who were the carers of children during the period of their children's education might deprive

---

Secretary of the State for the Home Department (judgment of the European Court of Justice of September 17, 2002) at para. 52 et seq. in which it was established that the Article 12 right of the child to continue with his or her education in the host State is not confined to the situation of where such a continuation of the child's education is not possible in the worker's home Member State. Thus even where it would have been possible for the child to continue their education in the home Member State, the right to continue it in the host State is guaranteed by Article 12). The continuation of rights first obtained while the status of migrant worker still pertained is, however, exceptional. For once the relevant employment relationship has ended, and the person concerned returns to his or her Member State of origin, he or she loses the status of a worker within the meaning of Art. 39 of the Treaty. Hence he or she can not rely on Art. 7(2) of Regulation 1612/68 in order to obtain rights from the Member State in which he or she was employed. (See Case C–33/99 *Fahmi and Amado v. Bestuur van de Sociale Verzekeringsbank* [2001] E.C.R. I–2415, especially at paras. 39 to 51 of the Court's judgment). This case involved an unsuccessful attempt by a Community migrant worker who had returned to her own State to rely on Art. 7(2) to have her children's studies financed in the same conditions as those applied by her former host State to its own nationals. (See also Case C–389/99 *Rundgren* [2001] E.C.R. I–3731, especially at paras 32 to 35 of the Court's judgment; Case C–43/99 *Leclere and Deaconescu v. Caisse nationale des prestations familiales* [2001] E.C.R. I–4265 especially at paras 52 to 61 of the Court's judgment and Case C–85/96 *Sala v. Freistaat Bayern* [1998] E.C.R. I–2691, at para. 32 of the Court's judgment). In Case C–413/99 *Baumbast and R. v. Secretary of the State for the Home Department* (judgment of the European Court of Justice of September 17, 2002), Advocate General Geelhoed was clearly of the opinion that family members of a Community national migrant worker could no longer rely on Article 10 of Regulation 1612/68 once the worker lost his or her status as a worker. (See Paragraphs 83 to 86 of the Opinion of the Advocate General, delivered on July 5, 2001). As *Echternach and Moritz* itself demonstrates, however, the status of being a migrant worker may produce certain effects after the employment relationship has ended. Hence, for example, a person whose work has ended and who is now genuinely seeking work may still be classified as a worker – although a person seeking his or her first employment will not be regarded as coming within the concept. (See Case C–292/89 *R. v. Immigration Appeal Tribunal, ex parte Antonissen* [1991] E.C.R. I–745 and . Case C–278/94 *Commission v. Belgium* [1996] E.C.R. I–4307).

[68] Case C–413/99 *Baumbast and R. v. Secretary of the State for the Home Department* (judgment of the European Court of Justice of September 17, 2002) at para. 73.

those children of a right which was granted to them by the Community legislature.[69]

The foregoing was an important finding in its own right. However, this aspect of *Baumbast* is also notable in that it is an instance of the conferring of rights on persons who are two steps removed from the individual enjoying the original right of free movement. In this case the right was conferred neither on the worker, nor on the child of the worker, but rather on that parent of the worker's child who is the child's primary carer. Nor should the point be missed that in the light of this ruling, the conferring by Community law of rights on one category of third country nationals (*viz.*, the third-country national children of migrant workers) is now capable, under Community law, of giving rise to derivative rights on the part of others (*viz.*, third-country national parents of such children). This aspect of the *Baumbast* ruling is therefore a significant one on a number of levels.

15.(3)(a)(ii) Article 7(2) and third-country family members: a tale of unanticipated advantages

Apart from Articles 10, 11 and 12, a further Article of Regulation 1612/68 which has proven to be of relevance to workers' families has been – to a somewhat unanticipated degree – Article 7(2). Under Article 7(1), it is stipulated that a *worker who is a national of a Member State* may not, in the territory of another Member State, be treated differently from national workers by reason of his nationality in respect of any conditions of employment and work. Article 7(2) goes on to establish that such a worker "shall enjoy the same social and tax advantages as national workers." It can be seen from the italicised wording cited above that the primary benefit of Article 7(1) is intended to be conferred on workers who are nationals of a Member State. However, the very broad interpretation given by the ECJ to the concept of an Article 7(2) social advantage has resulted in this provision being of considerable value in so far as concerns the rights of migrant workers' family members, including third-country family members. Of critical importance here has been the fact that the Court has held that there is such a thing as an *indirect* social advantage, *i.e.* that a worker can gain a social advantage from something being done for his or her family member. This is of particular importance in that once an advantage to a migrant worker's family is classified as an indirect

---

[69] See paras 72 and 71 respectively of the Court's judgment. It is possible to see the Court's decision in this and other respects in *Baumbast* as a response to factors such as the increased instability and increased variety in family relationships and forms of cohabitation in Europe in recent times, as well as the increased significance of immigration of nationals of non-Member States. Indeed, all of these matters were referred to by Advocate General Geelhoed in his Opinion in *Baumbast* although they were not adverted to by the Court. (See paras 22 to 27 of the Advocate General's Opinion).

social advantage, the advantage must be enjoyed by his or her family on the same basis as it is enjoyed by the families of national workers.

The judicial discovery of the notion of an indirect social advantage has obviously been a major development in terms of improving the legal rights of the families of migrant workers. The Court initially showed some reluctance in recognising the concept. Hence, in the early case of *Michel S v. Fonds National de Reclassement Handicapés*,[70] a case examined above in another context, in which the mentally handicapped son of an Italian migrant worker sought to gain access to certain benefits provided under Belgian law, the Court held that the benefits referred to in Article 7 were benefits to the workers themselves and stated that "benefits reserved for the members of their families on the other hand, were excluded from the application of Article 7".[71] However, a very different approach to Article 7(2) was manifested in the subsequent ruling by the Court of Justice in *Cristini v. Societé Nationale des Chemins de Fer*.[72] This case concerned the entitlement of the Italian widow of an Italian worker in France to a reduction card issued by the French national railway company for rail fares for large families, something which had been refused to her on the ground of her nationality. On this occasion, the Court rejected the argument that the advantages prescribed by Article 7(2) were exclusively those connected with the contract of employment itself – and implicitly rejected too, its own previous approach in *Michel S*. The benefit to the worker in *Cristini* if, indeed, any can be said to have accrued at all, since the migrant worker himself was deceased by the time the disputed refusal to grant the benefit occurred, was an indirect one.[73] This approach of affording recognition to the concept of an indirect social advantage was further developed in *Inzirillo v. Caisse d'Allocations Familiales de l'Arrondissement de Lyon*[74] where the grant of a disability allowance for an adult handicapped son who had never worked in a host Member State of the Community was held to be an Article 7(2) social advantage for his migrant worker father.[75] Like *Cristini*, *Inzirillo* is of interest for present purposes because in cases such as these, Community law requires the worker to be a Community national, but

---

[70] Case 76/72 [1973] E.C.R. 457.

[71] The invocation of Art. 12 of Regulation 1612/68 by the plaintiff in this case was more successful, however. See *above*.

[72] Case 32/75 [1975] E.C.R. 1085.

[73] Note further the subsequent case of Case C–185/96 *Commission v. Greece* [1998] E.C.R. I–6601 where a range of special benefits provided for in Greek legislation for large families, including preferential treatment in the education, health and housing areas, were also held to constitute social advantages for the purposes of Art. 7(2).

[74] Case 63/76 [1976] E.C.R. 2057.

[75] Note in particular paras. 21 of the Court's judgment where it observes that "the matters covered by Art. 7(2) must be defined in such a way as to include every social and tax advantage, whether or not linked to a contract of employment, such as an allowance for handicapped adults which is awarded by a Member State to its own nationals under legislation which gives a legally protected right thereto."

not the spouse/child who is the direct recipient of the assistance.[76] Thus, it may be said that notwithstanding the fact that the primary beneficiaries of the provisions of Article 7(2) are intended to be workers who are Community nationals, third-country family members can benefit considerably under its provisions; this occurs notwithstanding the fact that this provision falls outside those provisions of the Regulation which are specifically directed at the worker's family.

The precise definition of a social advantage for the purposes of Article 7(2) has tended to be somewhat elusive,[77] but further light was shed both on the breadth of the concept and the potential of Article 7(2) to improve the lot of third-country family members in *Netherlands v. Reed*.[78] This case arose from the refusal of the Dutch authorities to grant a residence permit to the respondent, Florence Reed, an unmarried British national who was in a stable and long-term relationship with a British migrant worker in the Netherlands. According to the ECJ, the non-marital status of the relationship ruled out the possibility of reliance on Article 10 by Reed,[79] but an expansive interpretation of Article 7(2) by the Court came to the rescue. Under Dutch policy, an alien in a stable relationship with a Dutch national would have been permitted to reside in the Netherlands. The Court held that:

---

[76] It should be noted that subsequent case law of the ECJ has revealed that Community law does not require that the relevant spouse/child be resident in the territory of the Member State conferring the advantage in question. See Case C–185/96 *Meeusen v. Hoofddirectie van de Informatie Beheer Groep* [1999] E.C.R. I–3289.

[77] In Case 207/78 *Ministère Public v. Even* [1979] E.C.R. 2019, the ECJ stated somewhat vaguely that it followed "from all its provisions and from the objective pursued that the advantages which this regulation extends to workers who are nationals of other Member States are all those which, whether or not linked to a contract of employment, *are generally granted to national workers primarily because of their objective status as workers or by virtue of the mere fact of their residence on the national territory and the extension of which to workers who are nationals of other Member States therefore seems suitable to facilitate their mobility within the Community*", para. 22. Emphasis added. This formulation has been repeated in a number of other cases, such as *Hoeckx v. Openbaar Centrum voor Maatschappelijk Welzijn* [1985] E.C.R. 973. The words "by virtue of the mere fact of their residence on the national territory" are significant. Note the unfavourable attitude of Advocate General La Pergola in Case C–356/98 *Kaba v. Secretary of State for the Home Department* [2000] E.C.R. I– 2623 to the suggestion that advantages the grant of which has nothing to do with the status of an individual as a worker fall outside Art. 7(2). See para. 39 of the Advocate General's Opinion and see also the judgment of the ECJ in Case 59/85 *Netherlands v. Reed* [1986] E.C.R. 1283. The *Even* definition is one so wide that, as Craig and de Búrca point out, it could be argued to encompass even the right to vote, Craig and de Búrca, *EU Law* (3rd ed., Oxford University Press, 2002), p. 738. Wide as it is, *Even* itself is authority for the proposition that pensions granted for wartime military service do not come within its ambit. Further evidence that the concept of a social advantage is not endlessly elastic was provided in Case C–411/98 *Ferlini v. Centre Hospitalier de Luxembourg* [2000] E.C.R. I–8081, where equal treatment in the fixing of scales of fees for medical and hospital maternity care was not regarded as a social advantage by the ECJ, para. 45.

[78] Case 59/85 [1986] E.C.R. 1283.

[79] See above.

> "it must be recognised that the possibility for a migrant worker of obtaining permission for his unmarried companion to reside with him, where that companion is not a national of the host member-State, can assist his integration in the host State and thus contribute to the achievement of freedom of movement for workers. Consequently, *that possibility must also be regarded as falling within the concept of a social advantage for the purposes of Article 7(2) of Regulation 1612/68.*"[80]

In *Reed*, therefore, Article 7(2) was sufficiently broadly construed to be capable, in an appropriate case, of entitling a Community national migrant worker to have a partner from another State reside with him or her. It just so happened that on the facts, the nationality of the partner in *Reed*, i.e. Reed herself, was British. But had Reed been a third-country national it would have made no difference to the result in the case. *Reed* is therefore of interest for present purposes because it shows that there are circumstances in which Article 7(2) is capable of being invoked in order to benefit an unmarried partner of a Community worker – even where that partner is a third-country national. Indeed, it is the only provision of Regulation 1612/68 which is at present capable of having such an effect.[80a] The very considerable limitations of the case should, however, be noted. The rights conferred by Article 7(2) are conferred only to the extent that such rights are already enjoyed by host State nationals. Hence, in a host State – such as Ireland – where the host State's own nationals enjoy no *Reed*-style right to have unmarried partners reside with them, Article 7(2) would confer no such right either.[81] In other words, no generalised right of residence for unmarried partners from third countries can therefore be deduced from the judgment in *Reed*.[82]

---

[80] Para. 28 of the judgment. Emphasis added.

[80a] In the light of the ruling in *Baumbast*, an unmarried partner of a community migrant worker could also benefit under Art.12 of Regulation 1612/68, but such an individual would benefit by virtue of being the parent of, and primary carer for, the migrant worker's child rather than by virtue of being the migrant worker's partner. (See text above at n.68).

[81] Note, however, the right enunciated by the Supreme Court in *Fajujonu v. the Minister for Justice* [1990] 2 I.R. 151, whereby children holding Irish citizenship of an alien who has resided for an appreciable time in the State have the right to the company, care and parentage of their parents within a family unit. *Quaere* whether in Ireland, such a right could be asserted by migrant Community workers to be a social advantage within the meaning of Art. 7(2) and thus entitle them to have third-country national parents reside with them in Ireland. Hogan and Whyte have suggested that it is arguable that the reasoning in *Fajujonu* is also applicable to the childless marriage of an alien and a citizen "unless one is prepared to accept that a spouse is not constitutionally entitled to the society of his/her partner." (Hogan and Whyte, *The Irish Constitution – J.M. Kelly* (third edition, 1994) at p.1003.) Compare the recent decision of the ECJ in Case C–413/99 *Baumbast and R. v. Secretary of the State for the Home Department* (judgment of the European Court of Justice of September 17, 2002) regarding the scope of Article 12 of Regulation 1612/68, which is examined in the text *supra*. Note that at the time of writing the precise parameters of the *Fajujonu* ruling are being explored in further litigation before the Supreme Court. See report in *The Irish Times*, October 24, 2002.

[82] Contrast the right, examined in the text above, conferred by Article 12 of Regulation 1612/68 on the child of a migrant worker to be accompanied by the parent who is his primary carer.

The case law of the ECJ reveals certain other limits to the use to which Article 7(2) may be put by, *inter alia*, third-country nationals. A significant ruling in this regard is that of the Court in *Belgian State v. Taghavi*.[83] Noushin Taghavi was the Iranian spouse of an Italian migrant worker, both she and her husband being resident in Belgium. She applied for an allowance payable under Belgian law for handicapped persons. The difficulty was that Belgian law stipulated that the allowance was payable only to handicapped persons who were Belgian. Taghavi relied on the argument, *inter alia*, that the allowance in question constituted an Article 7(2) social advantage and that she should, therefore, be able to claim it. The response of the ECJ was to deny that national workers enjoyed any social advantage at all within the meaning of Article 7(2), rejecting the Commission's arguments to the contrary with the observation that:

> "suffice it to say in this connection that . . . a Belgian worker's spouse who is not a national of a Member State of the Community cannot claim the allowance in question. Accordingly, since there is no 'social advantage' for national workers, Article 7(2) of Regulation No. 1612/68 cannot apply."[84]

The ruling may have reflected a desire on the part of the Court to reverse what had been its approach in previous cases and to call a halt to the gradual widening of the scope of Article 7(2). In so far as this was the Court's intention, it seems arguable that a more satisfactory approach would have been for it to have done so by rejecting Taghavi's arguments on the basis that the handicapped person's allowance at issue was not granted on account of a person's status as a member of a worker's family.[85] Instead, it took the

---

This right of residence for the caring parent is a generalised one – *i.e.*, it applies across the territory of the European Union. Further, it is not derived from the worker's rights, but rather from those of the worker's child.

[83] Case C–243/91 [1992] E.C.R. I–4401.

[84] Para. 11 of the Court's judgment.

[85] The Court has previously adopted this approach in its application of Regulation 1408/71. See *Kermaschek v. Bundesanstalt für Arbeit* [1976] E.C.R. 1669 (although see more recently Case C–308/93 *Cabanis-Issarte* [1996] E.C.R. I–2097 and Case C–189/00 *Ruhr v. Bundeanstalt für Arbeit* [2001] E.C.R. I–8225). Indeed, in its conclusions in Taghavi concerning the non-applicability of Regulation 1408/71, the Court held that the allowance at issue in that case was "not granted on account of a person's status as member of a worker's family". However, no reliance was placed by the Court in *Taghavi* on any similar such conclusion concerning Art. 7(2) of Regulation 16/2/68. Such an approach would not have been without its own difficulties. It must be admitted that the approach of the ECJ generally has been to regard benefits as coming within the concept of an Art. 7(2) social advantage without regard to the issue of whether the conferring of these benefits is related to the status of the beneficiary. As Advocate General La Pergola observed in his Opinion in Case C–356/98 *Kaba v. Secretary of State for the Home Department* [2000] E.C.R. I 2623: "in *Reed*'s case the Court did in fact include in the list of social advantages a benefit granted, without further qualification, to the nationals of the host Member State and to the holder of an unlimited right of residence." The Advocate General also noted the broad scope of the right at issue in Case C–85/96 *Sala v. Freistaat Bayern* [1998] E.C.R. I–2691. (See Opinion of the Advocate General in *Kaba* at para. 39).

alternative approach of limiting the field of application of Article 7(2) by taking a narrow view of the notion of a "comparator" – a concept the application of which has been frequently problematic in the operation of the non-discrimination principle in Community law.[86] Many of the difficulties associated with the notion of the comparator stem from the difficulty of deciding just how broadly it should be defined. If, as sometimes happens, it is defined excessively narrowly, the effect will be that access to equality will be fenced off beyond the reach of an excessively large group of persons whose characteristics do not match those of the comparator. It may be argued that this is what happened in *Taghavi*, where the comparator for the purposes of Article 7(2) was defined as a Belgian national placed in very much the same situation as the migrant worker, including – crucially here – the factor that the nationality of the comparator's spouse is that of a Community Member State. From a policy standpoint, such an approach seems less than ideal in that it enables, as it did in *Taghavi*, host Member States in effect to emasculate Article 7(2) as a source of derivative rights for third-country nationals, and to reduce its effect as a stimulus to the free movement of labour[87] by the simple expedient of providing that particular benefits or advantages are to be enjoyed only by Community nationals.[88] Once this is done, then according to the logic of the Court in *Taghavi*, Article 7(2) will be effectively rendered toothless in so far as concerns its capacity to confer derived rights on third-country family members. Such an approach may sit well with a literal interpretation of the requirement of Article 7(2) that a migrant worker "enjoy the same social and tax advantages as national workers". But so too would giving a broader definition to the relevant comparator.[89]

The reasoning in *Taghavi* may be contrasted with the approach taken in the earlier case law of the ECJ.[90] In the earlier case of *Office national de l'emploi*

---

[86] See for some pertinent observations in this regard Fredman, "Combating Racism with Human Rights: The Right to Equality" in Fredman ed., *Discrimination and Human Rights: The Case of Racism* (Oxford University Press, 2001) 9, pp.16–18; and by the same writer "European Community Discrimination Law: A Critique" (1992) 21 I.L.J. 119 at pp.123–125. See also Barnard and Hepple "Substantive Equality" (2000) 59 C.L.J. 562 at pp.563–564.

[87] The *Taghavi* approach arguably creates a disincentive to the free movement of workers in that the result of such an approach may be that a migrant worker may be "induced not to remain in the Member State where he had established himself and found employment". See the arguments to this effect in para. 16 of the Opinion of Advocate General Van Gerven in *Taghavi* and para. 23 of Case 94/84 *Office national de l'emploi v. Deak* [1985] E.C.R. 1873.

[88] The law at issue in *Taghavi* made its benefits available only to Belgian nationals, a point of difficulty under Community law which appears to have been passed over in this case because Taghavi was not a Community national.

[89] *e.g.* comparing the rights of migrant workers who are married with those of nationals who are married without attaching any importance to the nationality of the spouse.

[90] And not only with the case law of the Court concerning Art. 7(2). Compare for example the case of Case C–249/96 *Grant v. South West Trains* [1998] E.C.R. I–621, in which the Court – unlike in *Taghavi* – did not simply insert the comparator (in that case, one of a different sex as opposed to one of a different nationality) into precisely the same situation as the plaintiff

v. Deak,[91] which concerned a Hungarian national living in Belgium with his
mother, an Italian migrant worker, the claimant was refused a special
unemployment benefit on the grounds of his Hungarian nationality. The Court,
in contrast to its later finding in *Taghavi,* held that Article 7 precluded a
Member State from such a denial of a benefit to a third-country family
member.[92] Deak's third-country nationality was specifically adverted to by the
Court as making no difference to its conclusions, which were reached in the
light of the careful regard paid by the Court both to the objective of freedom
of movement for workers within the Community and to the principle of equal
treatment laid down in Article 7 of Regulation.[93] As far as the principle of free
movement was concerned, the Court held that:

> "a worker anxious to ensure for his children the enjoyment of the social
> benefits provided for by the legislation of the Member States for the support of
> young persons seeking employment would be induced not to remain in the
> Member State where he had established himself and found employment if that
> State could refuse to pay the benefits in question to his children because of their
> foreign nationality."[94]

That result, held the Court, "would run counter to the objective of the principle
of freedom of movement for workers within the Community".[95] The Court
went on:

> "the principle of equal treatment laid down in Article 7 of Regulation No.
> 1612/68 for workers who are nationals of a Member State and indirectly, for
> members of their families applies without regard to the nationality of those
> family members. That is expressly confirmed by the wording of Article 11 of
> that Regulation, which provides that the spouse of a national of a Member State
> who is pursuing an activity as an employed or self-employed person in the
> territory of another Member State and those of his children who are under the
> age of 21 years or who are dependent on him have the right to take up any
> activity as an employed person throughout the territory of that same State,
> 'even if they are not nationals of any Member State'."[96]

However, as we have seen, a different view was to be taken by the Court of the
requirements of the principle of equal treatment in *Taghavi.*[97]

---

in that case. Although, see for arguments critical of that ruling in turn, see Carey "From
Obloquy to Equality: In the Shadow of Abnormal Situations" (2001) 20 Y.E.L. 79.
[91]   Case 94/84 [1985] E.C.R. 1873.
[92]   *ibid.,* para. 24.
[93]   *ibid.,* para. 25.
[94]   *ibid.,* para. 23.
[95]   *ibid.*
[96]   *ibid.,* para. 26.
[97]   In fairness, it should be pointed out that in his Opinion in *Taghavi,* Advocate General Van
Gerven, although he felt constrained to follow the approach of the Court in *Deak,* also
expressed his opinion that the view of the Court in that case – which he saw as having been
based on the principle of free movement – had gone further than had been required by the

Another more recent case in which the requirements of the principle of equal treatment have been held not to extend to the lengths sought by a third-country national seeking to rely on Article 7(2) has been *Kaba v. Secretary of State for the Home Department.*[98] Here, the ECJ had to deal with issues raised by the situation of a third-country national, a Yugoslav man, married to a French migrant worker in the United Kingdom who herself held a five-year residence permit. In a sparsely-reasoned judgment, the Court refused to hold that an individual in such a situation acquired through his marriage the derivative right to apply for indefinite leave to remain in the United Kingdom after only twelve months' residence there by virtue of Article 7(2) – even though spouses of United Kingdom nationals and persons "present and settled in the United Kingdom" acquired exactly this right under U.K. law, with four years' residence being required of the spouses of migrant workers.[99] The Court, while conceding that a condition was imposed here which was more easily met by national workers than by migrant workers,[100] adopted the approach that this was not a case of like situations being treated in an unlike manner, which would be a violation of the requirements of equal treatment, but rather was a case of unlike situations being treated in an unlike manner, which does not violate the requirements of equal treatment.[101] In so far as concerned the conditions under which leave to remain indefinitely was to be granted, the situation of migrant workers who did not enjoy an unconditional right of residence in a Member State was to be distinguished from that of persons who did. Hence, the Court held that:

> "the Member States are entitled to rely on any objective difference there may be between their own nationals and those of other Member States when they lay down the conditions under which leave to remain indefinitely in their territory is to be granted to the spouses of such persons.
>
> More particularly, the Member States are entitled to require the spouses of persons who do not themselves enjoy an unconditional right of residence to be resident for a longer period than that required for the spouses of persons who already enjoy such a right, before granting the same right to them."[102]

---

prohibition of discrimination in Art. 7(2) alone. Advocate General Van Gerven defined this as meaning: "that a worker who is a national of a Member State must enjoy the same social and tax advantages as national workers in the territory of other Member States. By the same token, a member of the family of a migrant worker who is a national of a Member State must be able to enjoy, in the territory of other Member States, the same advantages as members of the families of national workers."

98 Case C–356/98 [2000] E.C.R. I 2623.
99 *ibid.*, paras. 7 and 8.
100 Namely, the condition that the individual in question be present and settled in national territory, *ibid.*, para. 28.
101 See for a discussion the requirements of the principle of equality in Community law Tridimas, *The General Principles of EC Law* (Oxford University Press, 1999) chap. 2. Also, for recent developments in Equality Law, see above Kimber, Chap. 13.
102 See para. 31 of the Court's judgment. Note in this respect the observation by Castro Oliveira that a factor influencing the ECJ in this case may have been the fact that the spouse of the

The Court in *Kaba* appears to have been heavily influenced by the fact that as Community law stands at present, the right even of nationals of one Member State to reside in another Member State is not unconditional.[103] It seems that increasing, in the name of the principle of equal treatment reflected in Article 7(2), the derivative rights of third-country family members beyond the rights enjoyed by Community national migrant workers themselves, was simply a step too far for the Court.

Cases such as *Taghavi* and *Kaba* may reflect a desire on the part of the Court to impose some limits on the judicial transformation of Article 7(2) from a clause of legislation intended to secure equal treatment for migrant Community workers into a powerful legal device for imposing equality in relation to a huge range of matters between a far wider category of individuals than merely workers, in particular between third-country family members of migrant workers and host Member State nationals. Opinions may differ on the point at which it ceases to be appropriate to view migrant Community workers as indirectly benefiting from advantages conferred on family members. But agreement may be reached on one issue. No matter where that point is, the conferring of rights on third-country family members of Community migrant workers by means of the vehicle of Article 7(2) will always amount to no more than a derivative benefit of the primary goal of the securing of equality, in terms of social and taxation advantages, for the migrant worker him or herself. The securing of equal rights on a generalised basis for third-country family members of migrant Community workers has never been the primary objective of Article 7(2). And for better or for worse, at least as that Article is interpreted by the ECJ at present, it is an end which will not now be achieved by an expansive interpretation of Article 7(2). Perhaps the main value of decisions such as *Taghavi* and *Kaba* has been to illustrate this reality so graphically.

It may be noted in passing that the ability of adult children of migrant workers to rely on Article 7(2) is also limited as can be seen from *Centre Public d'Aide Sociale de Courcelles v. Lebon*,[104] in which the Court held that once a child of a Community national migrant worker has reached the age of 21 and is no longer dependent on the worker, a benefit to that child does not constitute a social advantage for the worker within the meaning of Article 7(2)

---

migrant worker applied for a more extensive right of residence than that conferred on the migrant worker himself. (A. Castro Oliveira, "Workers and Other Persons: Step-By-Step From Movement to Citizenship – Case Law 1995–2001" (2002) 39 C.M.L.Rev. 77 at 117.) The conclusions of the Court in the *Kaba* case are heavily criticised in S. Peers, "Dazed and Confused: Family Members' Residence Rights and the Court of Justice" (2001) 26 E.L. Rev. 76.

[103] *ibid.*, para. 30.

[104] Case 316/85 [1987] E.C.R. 2811. This case arose from litigation stemming from the refusal of the Belgian authorities to pay Marie-Christine Lebon, the daughter of a migrant worker, minimum means of subsistence known as the "minimex". The same form of payment was at issue more recently in Case C–184/99 *Grzelczyk v. Centre public d'aide sociale d'Ottignies-Louvain-la-Neuve* [2002] E.C.R. I–6153, which is examined elsewhere in this article.

of Regulation 1612/68.[105] This is obviously a ruling which severely limits the usefulness of Article 7(2) to adult children of migrant workers – including those having the nationality of a third country, who are likely to be in the most vulnerable legal position of this category of individual.

15.(3)(b) Abolition of restrictions on movement and residence within the community for workers of Member States and their families and Council Directive 68/360/EEC

Before turning to the topic of the legislative provision which has been made for third-country family members of persons other than workers, the relevance of Council Directive 68/360/EEC of October 15, 1968 on the Abolition of Restrictions on Movement and Residence Within the Community for Workers of Member States and their Families[106] merits at least brief mention. Broadly, this measure provides for the abolition of restrictions on the movement and residence of nationals of Member States taking up employment in another Member State and of the same members of their families to whom Regulation 1612/68 applies – which includes third-country family members. That this is so is confirmed by certain provisions of the Directive which refer specifically to such persons, or lay down special rules regarding them.

Hence, Article 3 of the Directive stipulates that Member States shall allow workers and their family members[107] to enter their territory simply on production of a valid identity card or passport. According to Article 3(2), no entry visa or equivalent document may be demanded "*save from Members of the family who are not nationals of a Member State. Member States shall accord to such persons every facility for obtaining any necessary visas.*" Member State discretion under Article 3 was given a restrictive reading in the *MRAX* case,[108] where the ECJ had regard both to the importance which it felt the Community legislature had attached to the protection of family life, and to the principle of proportionality. According to the Court, on a proper construction of Article 3, read in the light of the latter principle, a Member

---

[105] *ibid.*, para. 13. Curiously, in reaching this conclusion, the Court seemed to place reliance on age limits mentioned in Art. 10 of Regulation 1612/68. This is interesting because, as we have seen, the judgment in the *Reed* case was reached without the scope of Art. 7(2) being held to be limited in any way by reference to Art. 10. Thus, as already noted, it was held in that case that a social advantage might accrue to a Community national migrant worker by virtue of indirect benefits being conferred on a partner who did not come within the definition of a "spouse" for the purposes of Art. 10. Note the ruling in *Lebon* was handed down subsequent to that in *Reed*.

[106] [1968] O.J. Sp. Ed. L257/13 at p.485. For relatively recent reform proposals, see the Proposal for a European Parliament and Council Directive Amending Directive 68/360/EEC on the Abolition of Restrictions on Movement and Residence Within the Community for Workers of Member States and Their Families COM (1998) 394 final. [1998] O.J. C 344/12.

[107] In the sense in which the latter are provided for in Regulation 1612/68.

[108] Case C–459/99 *Mouvement contre le racisme, l'antisémitisme et la xénophobie (MRAX) v. Belgian State* (judgment of the European Court of Justice of July 25, 2002).

State is not permitted to send back at the border a third country national who is married to a national of a Member State and who attempts to enter its territory without being in possession of a valid identity card or passport, or, if necessary, a visa, where he is able to prove his identity and the conjugal ties and there is no evidence to establish that he represents a risk to the requirements of public policy, public security or public health within the meaning of the Directive. Rather, according to the Court, if Article 3(2) of Directive 68/360 was not to be denied its full effect, a visa would have to be issued without delay and, as far as possible, at the place of entry into the national territory.[109]

Article 4(3) of Directive 68/360 stipulates that for the issue of a residence permit (as opposed to entry to the Member State's territory, which is governed by Article 3), Member States may require the production by the members of a worker's family only of the document by which they entered the territory and a document proving their relationship.[110] Again, the level of discretion left to Member States under Article 4(3) has recently received a narrow construction. Reasoning by analogy with its own earlier case-law concerning Directive 68/360,[111] the ECJ came to the conclusion in *MRAX* that a Member State is not permitted either (a) to refuse to issue a residence permit, or (b) to issue an expulsion order against any third country national who is able to furnish proof of his identity and of his marriage to a national of a Member State, on the sole ground that he has entered the territory of the Member State concerned unlawfully. The Court also took a narrow view in *MRAX* of the discretion allowed under Article 4(3) to Member States in dealing with third-country spouses who remain in their territory for a period of time longer than that permitted in their visas. It held that a Member State may neither (a) refuse to issue a residence permit to; nor (b) issue an order expelling a third country national spouse on the sole ground that his or her visa expired before he applied for a residence permit.[112] Two reasons were offered for this view being taken. First, it was felt that an order of expulsion from national territory on the sole ground that a visa had expired would constitute a sanction manifestly disproportionate to the gravity of the breach of national law involved. Secondly,

---

[109] See para. 60 of the Court's judgment.

[110] This latter document must be issued by the competent authority of the State of origin or the State whence they came. Note that in cases coming within Article 10(1) and (2) of Regulation 1612/68, a document issued by the competent authority of the State of origin or the State whence they came, testifying that they are dependent on the worker or that they live under his roof in such a country, may also be required.

[111] One aspect of this case-law is that the view has been taken that the issue of a residence permit to a Member State national does not give rise to rights but merely constitutes proof of status (see Case C–363/89 *Roux v. Belgium* [1991] E.C.R. I–273). Another is that the use of expulsion orders to penalise failures to comply with legal formalities is regarded as a manifestly disproportionate sanction (Case 48/75 *Royer* [1976] E.C.R. 497). Both of these views are reflected in the outcome of *MRAX*.

[112] Paragraph 91 of the Court's judgment.

the Court noted that while Article 4(3) authorised Member States to demand, for the purposes of the issue of a residence permit, production of the document with which the person concerned entered the territory, it did not require that the document must still be valid.[113]

Apart from the foregoing provisions, Article 4(4) is also of note in that it specifically stipulates that "a member of the family who is not a national of a Member State shall be issued with a residence document which shall have the same validity as that issued to the worker on whom he is dependent."

15.(4) THIRD-COUNTRY FAMILY MEMBERS OF COMMUNITY NATIONALS WHO HAVE EXERCISED THEIR RIGHT OF ESTABLISHMENT UNDER ARTICLE 43 (EX 52) TEC OR THEIR RIGHT TO PROVIDE SERVICES UNDER ARTICLE 49 (EX 59) TEC

15.(4)(a) Abolition of Restrictions on Movement and Residence within the Community for Nationals of Member States with Regard to Establishment and the Provision of Services and Council Directive 73/148/EEC

It is not only third-country family members of migrant Community workers who benefit under Community law. Provision has also been made for the rights of third-country family members of Community nationals who have exercised their right of establishment under Article 43 (ex 52) TEC or their right to provide services under Article 49 (ex 59) TEC. This provision is made in Council Directive 73/148/EEC of May 21, 1973 on the Abolition of Restrictions on Movement and Residence within the Community for Nationals of Member States with Regard to Establishment and the Provision of Services.[114] The stipulations of Directive 73/148 strongly resemble those of Directive 68/360, and again, certain provisions of the Directive make clear the applicability of the Directive to third-country family members by referring specifically to them, or laying down special rules regarding them. Hence, Article 1 of the Directive requires that the Member States abolish restrictions on the movement and residence of, *inter alia*, the spouse and children under twenty-one years of age, "*irrespective of their nationality*", of Member State nationals exercising their establishment rights or free movement of service rights in another

---

[113] See Paragraphs 89 and 90 of the Court's judgment in *MRAX*. It should be noted that these findings did not exhaust the rights which the Court viewed such a third-country national married to a national of a Member State as enjoying. Such a third-country national who is refused a first residence permit, or whose expulsion has been ordered before the issue of the permit – including where he is not in possession of an identity document or where, requiring a visa, he has entered the territory of a Member State without one or has remained there after its expiry – benefits from the procedural guarantees afforded by Article 9 of Directive 64/221, according to the Court. (See paras. 100 to 104 of the Court's judgment.)

[114] [1973] O.J. L172/14.

Member State. The same goes for restrictions on the movement and residence of "the relatives in the ascending and descending lines of such nationals, which relatives are dependent on them, *irrespective of their nationality*."

Article 3 of Directive 73/148 contains a provision concerning visas and entry requirements which is effectively identical to that in Article 3 of Directive 68/360 which has already been examined above.[115] Article 4(3) mirrors almost word for word what Article 4(4) of Directive 68/360 provides in relation to residence documents. The similarity stretches beyond mere wording: concepts found in Directive 73/148 which are similar to those found in the measures examined above concerning free movement of workers tend to be given a similar definition by the ECJ.[116]

Focusing on the rights of residence of third-country family members of service providers, it should be noted that the Preamble to Directive 73/148 declares that "freedom to provide services entails that persons providing and receiving services should have the right of residence *for the time during which the services are being provided*."[117] In line with this, Article 4(2) of the Directive provides that "the right of residence for persons providing and receiving services *shall be of equal duration with the period during which the services are provided*."[118] In the light of this, it might have been thought surprising if a right of permanent residence for family members, including third-country family members, of Community national service providers could be regarded as implied in the provisions of Directive 73/148. The ECJ was confronted, however, in the recent landmark case of *Carpenter v. Secretary of State for the Home Department*,[119] with the question of whether such a right could be deduced either from the terms of Directive or from elsewhere in the body of Community law. The reference to the Court of Justice in *Carpenter* was made in the course of proceedings brought by Mrs. Mary Carpenter, the Filipino spouse of a United Kingdom national, arising from a decision by the U.K. Secretary of State to make a deportation order against her. Mrs. Carpenter's husband owned a business established in the U.K. which provided advertising services to advertisers established in other Member States of the European Community. Mrs. Carpenter, who had no right of residence in any Member State apart from any derivative rights which Community law might

---

[115] Hence the findings of the ECJ in Case C–459/99 *Mouvement contre le racisme, l'antisémitisme et la xénophobie (MRAX) v. Belgian State* (judgment of the European Court of Justice of 25 July, 2002) were also expressly applied by the Court in relation to the corresponding provisions of Directive 73/148 as well.

[116] *R. v. Immigration Appeal Tribunal and Surinder Singh ex parte Secretary of State for the Home Department* Case C–370/90 [1992] E.C.R. I–4265 which deals with the concept of "spouse" for the purposes of Directive 73/148 and which is examined in the text above.

[117] Clause 2 of the Preamble. Emphasis added.

[118] Emphasis added.

[119] Case C–60/00 Opinion of Advocate General Stix-Hackl delivered on September 13, 2001, judgment of the European Court of Justice delivered July 11, 2002.å

confer on her, maintained that since her husband's business required him to travel around in other Member States, providing and receiving services, and since he could do so more easily by virtue of the fact that she was looking after his children from his first marriage, her deportation would restrict her husband's right to provide and receive services.[120] The impugned decision by the United Kingdom authorities, by contrast, was based on the view that whereas Mr. Carpenter had the right to travel to other Member States to provide services and to be accompanied for that purpose by his spouse, nonetheless while resident in the United Kingdom, he could not be considered to be exercising any freedom of movement within the meaning of the Treaty.[121] In other words, the view was taken that his situation was a *Morson and Jhanjan*-type wholly internal one, of no concern to EC law.[122]

Advocate General Stix-Hackl, in her Opinion to the Court, rejected – correctly, it is submitted – the notion that the case involved a wholly internal situation.[123] However, any possibility of reliance by Mrs. Carpenter on Article 49 of the EC Treaty, was rejected by the Advocate General, who opined that:

> "as a national of the Philippines . . . Mrs. Carpenter cannot herself rely on the fundamental freedoms, and hence not on Article 49. Since she cannot rely on the freedom to provide services, she cannot derive any right of residence therefrom. The relevant provisions concerning the entry and residence of nationals of non-member countries are rather to be found in secondary law".[124]

Thereafter, the Advocate General's Opinion contained better tidings for Mrs. Carpenter. Advocate General Stix-Hackl held, perhaps somewhat surprisingly, given the wording of Directive 73/148, that this Directive, interpreted in the light of "primary law and fundamental rights, in particular the right to respect for family life" *could* be relied upon by the third-country spouse of a Community national, if the latter provided services from his own State to persons in other Member States, to obtain the right to reside with him or her.

---

[120] *ibid.*, para. 17 of the judgment.

[121] *ibid.*, para. 18.

[122] See *Morson and Jhanjan v. Netherlands* Cases 35 and 36/82 [1982] E.C.R. 3723 discussed in the text below. This view found support from the Commission, which saw a clear distinction between the situation of a spouse (such as Mrs. Carpenter) of a Member State national who merely provided services from his State of origin and that of a spouse of a national of a Member State who had left his Member State of origin and moved to another Member State in order to become established or work there, paras. 25 to 27.

[123] The issue of what constitutes a wholly internal situation is an interesting one, but does not concern us for the purposes of this chapter. See in particular paras. 59 to 75 of the Advocate General's opinion.

[124] *ibid.*, para. 38 of the Advocate General's opinion. Compare the initial reluctance of the ECJ in recognising the concept of an indirect social advantage for the purposes of Art. 7(2) of Regulation 1612/68; See Case 76/72 *Michel S v. Fonds National de Reclassement Handicapés* [1973] E.C.R. 457 discussed in the text above.

A person in the position of Mrs. Carpenter, therefore, should be entitled to succeed under the Directive.

The ECJ also reached a conclusion favourable to Mrs. Carpenter – but on grounds which were almost the opposite of those relied upon by the Advocate General. Although once again rejecting the assertion that facts such as those at issue in the case involved a wholly internal situation,[125] the Court concluded, on the basis of an analysis of the objectives and content of Directive 73/148, that the Directive governed only the conditions under which a Member State national and family members might leave that national's Member State of origin and enter and reside in *another* Member State for a period stipulated in the Directive.[126] Directive 73/148 did not, according to the Court, and contrary to the views expressed by Advocate General Stix-Hackl, govern the right of residence of family members of a service provider in his or her own Member State.

The Court then addressed the relevance of Article 49. First, the Court restated its view that Mr. Carpenter, a "significant proportion" of whose business consisted of cross-border services "carried on both within his Member State of origin for the benefit of persons established in other Member States, and within those States", was exercising the right to provide services guaranteed by Article 49 of the EC Treaty.[127]

Secondly, the Court expressed the view that a restriction was being imposed on the exercise of this right: it was clear that "the separation of Mr. and Mrs. Carpenter would be detrimental to their family life and, therefore, to the conditions under which Mr. Carpenter exercises a fundamental freedom", *i.e.* "to provide services". As far as the Court was concerned, "that freedom could not be fully effective if Mr. Carpenter were to be deterred from exercising it by obstacles raised in his country of origin to the entry and residence of his spouse."[128]

Thirdly, the Court turned to the question of whether such obstacles created by U.K. law could be justified. Here the Court deployed its own jurisprudence relating to fundamental rights:

> "A Member State may invoke reasons of public interest to justify a national measure which is likely to obstruct the exercise of the freedom to provide

---

[125] Case C–60/00 Opinion of Advocate General Stix-Hackl delivered on September 13, 2001; judgment of the European Court of Justice delivered July 11, 2002, paras 28–30.

[126] ibid., paras. 31 to 36. In the case of service providers, the relevant period is specified in Art. 4(2) of the Directive, which, as seen above, specifies a period of service of equal duration with the period during which the services are provided.

[127] *ibid.*, para. 37.

[128] *ibid.*, para. 39. In para. 38 of its judgment the Court recalled that the Community legislature had recognised *e.g.* in Regulation 1612/68 and Directive 68/360, the importance of ensuring the protection of the family life of nationals of the Member States in order to eliminate obstacles to the exercise of the fundamental freedoms guaranteed by the Treaty.

services only if that measure is compatible with the fundamental rights whose observance the Court ensures . . .

The decision to deport Mrs. Carpenter constitutes an interference with the exercise by Mr. Carpenter of his right to respect for his family life within the meaning of Article 8 of the Convention for the Protection of Human Rights and Fundamental Freedoms . . . which is among the fundamental rights which, according to the Court's settled case law, restated by the Preamble to the Single European Act and by Article 6(2) EU, are protected in Community law."[129]

Some such interference is permissible under Convention case law. The ECJ had regard to what the case law of the European Court of Human Rights required of such permissible interferences, namely, in particular, proportionality, and seemed to conclude that these requirements had not been met. A decision to deport Mrs. Carpenter, taken in circumstances such as those in the case at hand, the Court decided, did not strike a fair balance between the competing interests of the right of Mr. Carpenter to respect for his family life, and, on the other hand, the maintenance of public order and public safety.[130]

In the light of all this, the conclusion of the Court of Justice was that:

"Article 49 of the EC Treaty, read in the light of the fundamental right to respect for family life, is to be interpreted as precluding, in circumstances such as those in the main proceedings, a refusal, by the Member State of origin of a provider of services established in that Member State who provides services to recipients established in other Member States, of the right to reside in its territory to that provider's spouse, who is a national of a third country."[131]

Carpenter is a highly significant decision as regards the rights of third-country family members, since it appears to be the first time that any such derivative right for a third-country family member of a Community national, much less a right of permanent residence, has been implied from a Treaty article. It has been seen in the text above that the conferring of certain derivative rights on family members has previously been held by the ECJ to be required under particular provisions of Community secondary legislation.[132] Thanks to *Carpenter*, a similar possibility has now been discovered to exist in relation to Article 39 of the EC Treaty. Of course, there is no reason why Treaty provisions relating to the free movement of workers and freedom of establishment should not also be held capable of giving rise to such derivative

---

[129] *ibid.*, ara. 40 to 41. The Court specifically adverted to its own previous rulings in Case C–260/89 *ERT* [1991] E.C.R. I–2925 and Case C–368/95 *Familiapress* [1997] *E.C.R.* I–3689.

[130] Paras. 42 to 43 of the Court's judgment.

[131] *ibid.*, para. 46.

[132] *e.g.* Art. 7(2) of Regulation 1612/68. See *e.g.*, Case 32/75 *Cristini v. Societé Nationale des Chemins de Fer* [1975] E.C.R. 1085, overturning the previous approach of the Court of Justice, manifested in Case 76/72 *Michel S v. Fonds National de Reclassement Handicapés* [1973] E.C.R. 457. See for a case involving a derived right of residence under Art. 7(2) Case 59/85 *Netherlands v. Reed* [1986] E.C.R. 1283 discussed in the text above.

rights for third-country family members. Even should this be held to be the case, however, the effect should not be so dramatic as it will be in the field of free movement of services. This is not merely because the number of persons providing services to other Member States is likely to be vastly greater than that of the number of persons who establish themselves in another Member State or migrate for work purposes to another Member State. It is also because, as has been seen, permanent residence rights for family members of migrant workers and exercisers of the right of establishment have already been provided for by secondary legislation. Nonetheless, even in relation to these free movements, *Carpenter* is of potential significance: the point should not be missed that it is possible that a Treaty-based derivative right of permanent residence might expand beyond the scope of such rights, either in terms of the extent of the rights conferred or in terms of the kinds of family members held to come within such a right. And, of course, it is also possible that other derivative rights not provided for in the relevant secondary legislation might be held to exist. Perhaps a more tantalising question, however, and one with more far-reaching consequences for the extension of the right of permanent residence, is whether third-country family members of providers of goods will now be held to have the same entitlements as third-country family members of providers of services. One might well ask what logical justification exists, if any, for drawing a distinction between the two categories of person.

Obviously, at least for now, the finding in *Carpenter* remains of most direct concern to third-country family members of service providers. It follows from what has been said above that the precise dimensions of the right remain to be explored. To what family members of a service provider will the right of permanent residence be capable of accruing – for example, will it apply to parents or to children of the service provider? Or perhaps to divorced spouses (with or without rights of access to children)? Will service recipients, as well as providers, be held to be capable of benefiting from it? It is perhaps stating the obvious to note that only time and further developments in the jurisprudence of the ECJ can provide answers to these and the many other fascinating questions raised by the ruling in *Carpenter*.

15.(5) THIRD-COUNTRY FAMILY MEMBERS OF COMMUNITY NATIONALS WHO COME WITHIN DIRECTIVES 90/364/EEC, 90/365/EEC, 93/96/EEC, REGULATION 1251/70/EEC OR DIRECTIVE 75/34/EEC

With the passage of time, the process of expanding the number of *primary* addressees of Community free movement rights has gained considerable pace. Legislation has played a key role here with the adoption of measures which have conferred free movement rights on a range of persons well beyond that of providers or recipients of services and persons wishing to exercise a right of establishment or to work in another Member State.[133] Each such step has involved the simultaneous creation of a new category of derivative beneficiary. For such measures have also contained provisions relating to family members, including third-country family members, of their primary addressees. It is proposed to examine briefly here the relevant enactments in this regard.

15.(5)(a) Right of Residence for Persons With Sufficient Resources

Council Directive 90/364/EEC of June 28, 1990 on the Right of Residence,[134] sometimes referred to as the "Playboy Directive", was adopted so as to make provision for residence in any Member State for persons, as well as certain members of their families, who have sufficient resources to avoid them becoming an unreasonable burden on the public finances of the host Member State and who are covered by sickness insurance in respect of all risks in the host Member State. The family members covered are (a) the spouse of the holder of right of residence and their descendants who are dependents; and (b) dependent relatives in the ascending line of the holder of the right of residence and his or her spouse.[135] Third-country family members are clearly intended to be covered: Article 2(1) duplicates the provisions concerning the issue of a residence document to non-Member State nationals found in Article 4(3) of Directive 73/148 and Article 4(4) of Directive 68/360 by providing that a residence document must be issued to the third-country family member which is of the same validity as that issued to the Community national on whom the family member depends.

Article 2(2) echoes, and, indeed, is somewhat broader than, the provisions of Article 11 of Regulation 1612/68 by providing:

> "the spouse and the dependent children of a national of a Member State entitled to the right of residence within the territory of a Member State shall be entitled to take up any employed *or self-employed activity* anywhere within the territory of that Member State, *even if they are not nationals of a Member State*."[136]

15.(5)(b) Right of residence for employees and self-employed persons who have ceased their occupational activity

Provision was made for a generalised right of residence for ex-employees and ex-self-employed persons by Council Directive 90/365/EEC of June 28, 1990

---

[133] The case law of the ECJ interpreting EC Treaty provisions on citizenship play a more prominent role. (See judgment by the Court in Case C–413/99 *Baumbast and R. v. Secretary of the State for the Home Department* (judgment of the European Court of Justice of September 17, 2002). What the rights of third-country family members of migrant citizens would be remains as of yet an open question, however. (See para. 95 of the Court's judgment).

[134] [1990] O.J. L180/26.

[135] See Art. 1(2) of the Directive.

[136] In contrast to Regulation 1612/68, see Art. 10(1), provision to the effect that any such child's being under 21 years of age (as opposed to having to be dependent) would suffice to bring

on the Right of Residence for Employees and Self-Employed Persons Who
Have Ceased Their Occupational Activity.[137] Such persons must be in receipt
of an invalidity or early retirement pension, old-age benefits, a pension in
respect of an industrial accident or disease, which must be of an amount
sufficient to meet somewhat similar requirements to those laid down in
Directive 90/364 concerning resources. A similar requirement is also imposed
concerning sickness insurance. Exactly the same provisions are made
regarding the rights of family members – including third-country family
members – of employees and self-employed persons who have ceased their
occupational activity as are made in respect of the family members of persons
coming within Directive 90/364/EEC.[138] Somewhat surprisingly, the ECJ has
found that, notwithstanding the similarity in wording between the income
requirements in Directive 90/365 and the equivalent requirements in Directive
90/364, the Member States are not bound to apply them in an identical manner.
Hence in *Commission v. Italy,*[139] the ECJ declined to find Italy in breach of
Community law for having required a level of income in respect of relatives of
migrant retirees which was only one third of that required in respect of
beneficiaries of Directive 90/364.[140] On the other hand, the Court found that
Italy had violated the requirements of Directives 90/365 and 90/364 alike by
limiting the means of proof of facts such as the dependent status of family
members – in particular by requiring documents issued or certified by Member
State authorities.

15.(5)(c) Right of Residence for Students

The process of the putting into law of rights of residence for students and their
family members had a more tortuous legislative history than did the two 1990
Directives. These rights were originally provided for in Directive 90/366/EEC
of June 28, 1990 on the Right of Residence for Students[141] but this Directive
was annulled by the ECJ in *European Parliament v. Council of the European
Communities.*[142] The relevant provisions were then re-adopted in substance in

---

him or her within the scope of Art. 2(2) of Directive 90/364 was for some reason thought
superfluous. Spouses and dependent children coming within Art. 2(2) of Directive 90/364
would seemingly be well advised, therefore, not to engage in work or self-employed
activities which are sufficiently profitable to end their dependence on the Member State
national from whom they derive their rights.

137   [1990] O.J. L180/28.
138   See Arts. 1(2) and 2(2) of Directive 90/365.
139   Case C–424/98 [2000] E.C.R. I-4001.
140   See in particular paras 25 to 27 of the Court's judgment. It may be that the Court, in reaching
this conclusion, was concerned that the free movement of retirees would have been
endangered by a contrary holding, since the response on the part of Member States might
have been to "level down" the entitlements of retirees to those of beneficiaries under
Directive 90/364.
141   [1990] O.J. L180/30.
142   Case C–295/90 [1992] E.C.R. I-4193.

Council Directive 93/96/EEC of October 29, 1993 on the Right of Residence for Students.[143] Requirements as to sickness insurance, sufficient resources to avoid becoming a burden on the social assurance system and enrolment in a recognised educational establishment are all laid down by this Directive. These requirements must be met before a national of a Member State can come within its terms.[144] However, differences in the wording of these requirements in Directive 93/96/EEC and the similar requirements in Directives 90/364 and 90/365 have permitted the ECJ to adopt a liberal approach in relation to Directive 93/96 and to rule that Italy has violated this Directive, *inter alia*, by not allowing students who are accompanied by family members to assure the Italian authorities of the adequacy of their resources simply by making a declaration.[145]

Derived rights under Directive 93/96, however, are extremely limited in scope. The only family members who obtain a derivative right of residence in the case of a student are the student's spouse and children,[146] which seems an inordinately strict approach for the Community to have adopted.

As with the two 1990 Directives, the right of residence of all concerned (in other words, of both the student and his or her family members), lasts only as long as the addressees of the right fulfil the conditions set out by the Directive.[147] This is a particularly significant limitation, given that Article 2(1) of the Directive provides that the right of residence shall be restricted to the duration of the course of studies in question. On the other hand, exactly the same provisions are made in the 1993 Directive regarding the right of family members of students, including third-country family members, to engage in employed or self-employed activities as are made in respect of the family members of persons coming within the two 1990 Directives.[148] An identical

---

[143] [1993] O.J. L317/59.
[144] Directive 93/96, Art. 1.
[145] Case C–424/98 *Commission v. Italy* [2000] E.C.R. I-4001.
[146] *ibid.*
[147] See now, however, the approach of the European Court of Justice in Case C–184/99 *Grzelczyk v. Centre public d'aide sociale d'Ottignies-Louvain-la-Neuve* [2002] E.C.R. I-6153, which seems to indicate that such conditions will be interpreted in a manner broadly favourable to the right of residence of the student. *Grzelczyk* is also highly significant in that it confirmed (in so far as concerns students coming within the ambit of Directive 93/96) the approach of the Court in Case C–85/96 *Martínez Sala v. Freistaat Bayern* [1998] E.C.R. I-2691 that possession of the status of a legally resident migrant EU citizen suffices to entitle an applicant to equal treatment within the (ill-defined) material scope of the Treaty. *Quaere* how far this entitlement to equal treatment extends. (See generally on this topic the case note on *Grzelczyk* by Iliopoulou and Toner at (2002) 39 C.M.L.Rev. 609. See also A Castro Oliveira, *loc. cit.*, at p.80 thereof and pp.82 to 84 and C. Jacqueson, "Union Citizenship and the Court of Justice: Something New Under the Sun? Towards Social Citizenship" (2002) 27 E.L. Rev. 260.) See also in this respect the decision of the ECJ in *D'Hoop v. Office national de l'emploi* (judgment of the Court of July 11, 2002).
[148] *ibid.*, Art. 2(2).

requirement is also imposed on the Member State to issue a residence document to third-country family members within the meaning of the Directive.[149]

15.(5)(d) Regulation 1251/70 on the right of workers to remain in the territory of a Member State after having been employed in that state and Council Directive 75/34/EEC concerning the right of nationals of a Member State to remain in the territory of another Member State after having pursued therein an activity in a self-employed capacity

The provisions of Regulation (EEC) 1251/70 of the Commission of June 29, 1970 on the Right of Workers to Remain in the Territory of a Member State After Having Been Employed in that State,[150] and Council Directive 75/34/EEC of December 17, 1974 Concerning the Right of Nationals of a Member State to Remain in the Territory of Another Member State After Having Pursued Therein an Activity in a Self-Employed Capacity[151] are almost identical.

Regulation 1251/70 should be read in conjunction with Regulation (EEC) 1612/68 of the Council of October 15, 1968 on Freedom of Movement for Workers within the Community, for the 1970 Regulation is designed to give a right to remain permanently in the territory of a Member State to a national of another Member State who (a) at the time of termination of his or her activity, has reached the age laid down by the law of that Member State for entitlement to an old-age pension and who has been employed in that State for at least the last twelve months and resided there continuously for more than three years; or (b) having resided continuously in that other Member State for two years ceases to work there as an employed person due to permanent incapacity to work (except no condition as to length of residence is imposed if the incapacity results from an accident at work or an occupational disease entitling the worker to a pension for which an institution of the host State is responsible); or (c) after three years' continuous employment and residence in the territory of that State, works as an employed person in the territory of another Member State, while retaining his or her residence in the territory of the first State, to which he or she returns, as a rule, each day or at least once a week.[152]

For its part, Directive 75/34/EEC makes almost exactly similar provision in respect of nationals of other Member States who have pursued an activity there in a self-employed capacity rather than having worked there.[153] It should,

---

[149]   *ibid.*, Art. 2(1).
[150]   [1970] O.J. Sp. Ed. L142/24 at p.402.
[151]   [1975] O.J. L14/10.
[152]   See Art. 3 of the Regulation.
[153]   In drafting Directive 75/34, the Community legislature took the additional precaution of specifying that where the law of a Member State does not grant the right to an old-age

therefore, be read in conjunction with Directive 73/148 on the Abolition of Restrictions on Movement and Residence within the Community for Nationals of Member States with Regard to Establishment and the Provision of Services rather than Regulation 1612/68.

Of interest for present purposes is that the Regulation also applies to members of their families as defined in Article 10 of Regulation 1612/68, who, it will be remembered, can be third-country nationals.[154] The rights of such family members are set out in Article 3 of the 1970 Regulation. Briefly, Paragraph 1 of Article 3 provides that the members of a worker's family (within the meaning of the Regulation) who are residing with the worker in the territory of a Member State shall be entitled to remain there permanently if the worker has acquired the right to remain in the territory of that State under the 1970 Regulation, and to do so even after the worker's death. Paragraph 2 provides that if the worker dies during his working life and before having acquired the right to remain in the territory of the State concerned, members of his family shall be entitled to remain there permanently on condition that:

- the worker, on the date of his decease, had resided continuously in the territory of that Member State for at least two years; or

- his death resulted from an accident at work or an occupational disease; or

- the surviving spouse is a national of the State of residence or lost the nationality of that State by marriage to that worker.

The first indent of Article 3(2) has recently been considered by the ECJ in *Givane v. Secretary of State for the Home Department*,[155] a reference made in proceedings brought by the widow and children (all of Indian nationality) of a Portuguese man. He had moved to the United Kingdom in order to work as a cook in 1992 and had remained there for three years before interrupting his residence with a ten-month stay in India prior to returning to the United Kingdom where he died 21 months later. Leave to remain in the U.K. was subsequently refused to his family on the grounds that the deceased man had not resided continuously in the United Kingdom for the two years prior to his death. In proceedings stemming from this decision, the U.K. Immigration Appeal Tribunal referred questions to the ECJ which included the question of whether Article 3(2) of Regulation 1251/70 required a two-year period of residence to be established in the period *immediately prior* to a worker's death, or whether it might be established by a period of continuous residence which occurred at an *earlier* point in the worker's life. At the time of writing the ECJ

---

pension to certain categories of self-employed workers, the age requirement mentioned in the text above at (a) shall be considered as satisfied when the beneficiary reaches 65 years of age.

[154] Art. 1 of Regulation 1251/70.

[155] Case C–257/00 Opinion of Advocate General Alber delivered May 16, 2002.

has not delivered a judgment in this case. However, Advocate General Alber, who has come to the conclusion that a literal interpretation of the various language versions of Article 3(2) leads to no definite resolution of the issue, has proposed that a purposive consideration of this provision in the context of the rest of the Regulation should lead the Court to conclude that a two-year period of continuous residence immediately prior to death is not needed provided the worker had a previous two-year period of continuous residence and that there has not subsequently been an interruption of residence exceeding two years. Whether the Court will accept this relatively liberal interpretation to the rights of family members under Article 3(2) remains to be seen.

The rights conferred by Regulation 1251/70 on family members, including third-country family members, are obviously of considerable value. On the other hand, the fairly narrow scope *ratione personae* of Regulation 1251/1970 means that it has now to some extent been superceded by the much broader Directive 90/365. However, sight should not be lost of the fact that Regulation 1251/70 confers a permanent and unconditional right of residence, whereas the right of residence conferred by Directive 90/365 is conditional on the relevant beneficiaries having sufficient resources to avoid them becoming an unreasonable burden on the public finances of the host Member State and being covered by sickness insurance in respect of all risks in the host Member State.[156] Furthermore, it persists only as long as beneficiaries of the right fill these conditions.[157]

15.(6) Third-Country Family Members of Nationals of Non-EU States which have entered into Association Agreements with the Community (Including the Europe Agreements)

The final category of third-country family members whose rights under Community law are to be considered are third-country family members of nationals of non-EU States which have entered into association agreements with the Community. Third-country family members who fall into this category are, at least for the time being, in a somewhat unique category since the individual from whom their rights are derived (a) will not him or herself be a Community national, and (b) will not be in a position under Community law to be deemed, held, or considered equivalent to that of a Community national exercising a free movement right.[158] The extent of rights which are conferred

---

[156] Directive 90/365, Art.1.

[157] *ibid.*, Art. 3.

[158] It is true that family members of nationals of EEA States which are not in the EU derive their rights from an individual who is not a Community national, but the position of both the family member and the individual from whom the rights are derived is equivalent to that of Community nationals in a similar position.

on what we may call primary addressees of Community law,[159] as well as the extent of any derivative rights which are conferred on family members, will vary somewhat from agreement to agreement. It is proposed to look briefly at family rights under the following association agreements, which are the most significant in this regard.[160]

15.(6)(a) Europe Agreements

Europe Agreements are a form of Association Agreement which have been concluded with the Central and Eastern European Countries (CEECs) of Hungary, Poland, the Czech Republic, the Slovak Republic, Romania, Bulgaria, Estonia, Latvia, Lithuania and Slovenia, and are obviously important stepping stones on the road to enlargement of the EU. Each of the Europe Agreements with these countries contains a Title IV, which deals with the movement of workers, establishment and supply of services. In substance the contents of these Title IVs are the same. Freedom of establishment is provided for,[161] and provision is also made concerning free movement of services. Certain provisions are also made concerning free movement of workers. However, no right of *entry* into the Community is created for CEEC workers. Further, a right of *residence* is not created by the Europe Agreements (even for CEEC workers who are already present and working in the Member States). And even CEEC nationals who hold a residence permit in a Member State acquire neither the right *to a work permit* by virtue of the Europe

---

[159] Note that agreements between the Community and third countries are a source of Community law. See generally Hartley, *The Foundations of European Community Law* (4th ed., 1998), chap.6.

[160] See generally Hailbronner, *Immigration and Asylum Law and Policy of the European Union* (2000), p.212 et seq. See also Staples, *Rights Enjoyed by Third Country Nationals Under EC Association Agreements* (Paper presented at the Irish Centre for European Law conference on the rights of third country nationals in EC law held in Trinity College Dublin on November 25, 2000). Apart from the Association Agreements considered in the text, the EEC–Morocco Co-operation Agreement has featured prominently in the recent case law of the Court, with the rights of workers coming within the agreement having been considered by the Court of Justice both in Case C–33/99 *Fahmi and Amado v. Bestuur van de Sociale Verzekeringsbank* [2001] E.C.R. I–2415 and in Case C–416/96 *El-Yassini v. Secretary of State for the Home Department* [1999] E.C.R. I–1209.

[161] Without any provision being made for social rights or rights of family reunification. Note also Hailbronner's observations concerning the limited nature of the right of establishment. above, n.160, p.244 *et seq.*, and the recent decisions of the ECJ confirming the limited nature of this right: Case C–63/99 *R v. Secretary of State for the Home Department, ex parte Gloszczuk* [2001] E.C.R. I–6319; Case C–235/99 *R v. Secretary of State for the Home Department, ex parte Kondova* [2001] E.C.R. I–6427, Case C–257/99 *R v. Secretaty of State for the Home Department, ex parte Barkoci and Malik* [2001] E.C.R. 6557. These cases are examined in B. Bogusz, "Regulating the Right of Establishment for Accession State Nationals: 'Reinforcing the Buffer Zone' or Improving Labour Market Flexibility?" (2002) 27 E.L. Rev. 472. See more generally E. Guild, N. Rollason and R. Copeman-Hill, *A Guide to the Right of Establishment under the Europe Agreements* (Baileys, Shaw and Gillett, London, 1996).

Agreements,[162] nor the right *to move freely within that Member State or the Community generally.* One point that the Europe Agreements do provide for, however, is that CEEC workers who have been admitted to the labour market of a Member State shall not be discriminated against as regards working conditions,[163] a right which, it seems to Hailbronner, can be considered directly effective.

15.(6)(a)(i) Legal Position of Family Members

The Europe Agreements deal only with the family members of workers. In the light of what has just been said concerning the workers themselves, it scarcely comes as a surprise to discover that the rights conferred on family members are of a very limited kind. It *is* provided that legally resident spouses and children of workers who are lawfully employed in the territory of a Member State, (subject to certain exceptions)[164] are to have access to the labour market of that State for the duration of the period for which the worker him or herself is authorised to be employed.[165] However, this right is overshadowed by the failure of the Europe Agreements to create a right for the family members in question to install themselves with the worker in the host State, in other words, a right of family reunification. Furthermore, the right which is conferred by the Europe Agreements is confined to members of a very narrowly defined family, namely spouses and children, with family members of seasonal workers and workers admitted to the host State under a bilateral agreement being excluded.[166]

15.(6)(b) The EEC-Turkey Association Agreement

In so far as the conferring of rights on Turkish nationals and their families are concerned, the provisions of the EEC-Turkey Association Agreement[167]

---

[162] See, *e.g.* Art. 41(3) of the Poland Agreement which binds the Member States only to examine the possibility of granting work permits to Polish nationals who already have residence permits in the Member State concerned. Corresponding provisions are to be found in the other Europe Agreements.

[163] See, *e.g.* Art. 37(1) (first indent) of the Poland Agreement. See Hailbronner, above, n.160, p.243. Corresponding provisions are to be found in the other Europe Agreements.

[164] Seasonal workers or workers falling within the scope of bilateral agreements between States are excepted from this.

[165] See Art. 37(1) second indent of the Poland Agreement. Corresponding provisions are found in the other Europe Agreements.

[166] See, *e.g.* Arts. 37(1) and 41, respectively, of the Poland Agreement. Corresponding provisions are to be found in the other Europe Agreements. Note that the Europe Agreements also make provision concerning certain social benefits, *e.g.* that nationals from the relevant States enjoy the right to receive family allowances for legally resident members of their family. See, *e.g.* Art. 38(1) of the Poland Agreement. Again, corresponding provisions are to be found in the other Europe Agreements.

[167] The Agreement Establishing an Association Between the European Economic Community and Turkey [1973] O.J. C 113/2 was signed at Ankara on September 12, 1963. An Additional Protocol was signed at Brussels on November 23, 1970 [1973] O.J. C113/18.

concerning freedom of establishment and the freedom to provide services, do not appear to confer directly effective rights, since they are provisions which are in the nature of a programme.[168] In contrast, the rights of Turkish workers to gain access to Member State employment markets, as well as some associated residence rights of such workers, are governed by a measure which has direct effect: Council of Association Decision 1/80, which was adopted under the auspices the EEC-Turkey Association Agreement.[169] Decision 1/80 does not govern the first entry and residence in a Member State of a Turkish worker. However, once *Turkish* workers are given even temporary residence status in a Member State, Decision 1/80 becomes relevant. Community law is relevant, therefore, except as regards initial admission of Turkish workers to a Member State's territory and except as regards the conditions under which such workers take up their first employment,[170] both of which matters are within the competence of Member State legal systems to regulate.

15.(6)(b)(i) Legal position of family members of Turkish workers

Decision 1/80 does not confer any right on the family members of Turkish workers to install themselves with a worker in a Member State, *i.e.* family reunification rights. However, Article 7 of Decision 1/80 does provide for certain conditional rights concerning access to the employment market for such persons. It must be remembered that these rights are dependent on the family members in question being authorised to join a Turkish worker resident in a Member State.

Article 7 specifically provides that those members of the family of a Turkish worker, who has been duly registered as belonging to the labour force of a Member State, who are authorised to join him:

– shall be entitled – *subject to the priority to be given to workers of Member States of the Community* – to respond to any offer of employment *after they have been legally resident for at least three years in that Member State*;

– shall enjoy free access to any paid employment of their choice *provided that they have been legally resident there for at least five years.*[171]

Furthermore, under Article 7, children of Turkish workers *who have completed a course of vocational training in the host country* may respond to any offer of employment there, irrespective of the length of time they have been resident in

---

[168] See generally Peers, "Towards Equality: Actual and Potential Rights of Third-Country Nationals in the European Union" (1996) 33 C.M.L.Rev. 7. See also Staples, *op.cit.*, esp. at p.5 *et seq.*

[169] Namely Art. 12 of the EEC–Turkey Association Agreement and Art. 36 of the Additional Protocol taken together with Art. 7 of the Agreement.

[170] See Hailbronner, above n.160, p.224 and note the authorities cited by Staples, *op.cit.*, p.245 at n. 27.

[171] Emphasis added.

that Member State, *provided one of their parents has been legally employed in the Member State concerned for at least three years.*[172] It is not required that the parent in question should still work or even still be resident in the relevant host Member State in order for the child to avail of this right – merely that the parent in question has in the past been legally established there for at least three years.[173] The right comes into being independently of the ground on which a right to enter or stay was originally granted to the child of the worker. Hence, the fact that the right to enter or stay may have been originally given to the relevant child for the purposes of study rather than with a view to reuniting the family does not prevent the Article 7 right to respond to an offer of employment from arising.[174]

These are obviously far more limited rights than are enjoyed by, *e.g.* spouses of Community nationals, and subject to more restrictions, such as training requirements and a requirement to wait a number of years before the rights accrue. Furthermore, the ECJ has held that Member States may impose mandatory conditions on the enjoyment of the above rights, *e.g.* conditions to be met in order to prevent sham or fraud marriages such as restrictions on residence aimed at ensuring actual cohabitation of family members of Turkish workers in one household with the worker.[175] The greatest restriction of all,

---

[172] Emphasis added.

[173] Case C–210/97 *Akman v. Oberkreisdirektor des Rheinisch-Bergerischen-Kreises* [1998] E.C.R. I–7519.

[174] Case C–355/93 *Eroglu v. Land Bad Württenberg* [1994] E.C.R. I–5113. See in particular para. 22.

[175] Case C–351/95 *Kadiman v. Freistaat Bayern* [1997] E.C.R. I–2133 where the Court noted that "a Member State retains the power to subject a right of residence to conditions of such a kind as to ensure that the presence of the family member in its territory is in conformity with the spirit and purpose of the first para. of Art. 7 of Decision No. 1/80", quoted in the text above. See para. 33 of the Court's judgment and more generally paras. 24 to 44. In that case it was held to be legitimate for a Member State to subject the extension of a residence permit for a family member to the condition that the person concerned actually live with the worker for the period of three years mentioned in Art. 7(1), unless objective circumstances justified separation, *e.g.* the distance between the worker's residence and the place of employment of the member of his family. Specific reference was made to the risk of sham marriages by the Court in its judgment in upholding the Member States' right to adopt such provisions, para. 38. A less restrictive approach to conditions relating to residence has tended to be seen in relation to analogous provisions concerning family members of migrant Community workers, although the important difference is that the provisions here are Community law measures and come within the interpretive purview of the ECJ. Hence, the requirement under Art. 10(3) of Regulation 1612/68 that a worker must have available for his family housing considered as normal for national workers has been held to apply "solely as a condition under which each member of the worker's family is permitted to come and live with him and . . . once the family has been brought together, the position of the migrant worker cannot be different in regard to housing requirements from that of a worker who is a national of the Member State concerned." Case 249/86 *Commission v. Germany* [1989] E.C.R. 1263). See in particular para. 12. It is to be noted also that the Court has refused to read into Art. 10 any obligation on family members to live permanently with the worker Case 267/83 *Diatta v. Land Berlin* [1985] E.C.R. 567.

however, is that these rights are made dependent on the family members in question being authorised to join a Turkish worker resident in a Member State, whose own initial admission and initial terms of employment are at the discretion of the host Member State.[176]

---

[176] This Article is not concerned with social security matters. In so far as the reader is interested in these, see Staples, above n.160, at p.20 *et seq.* The main provisions of relevance here are Art. 39(1) of the Additional Protocol to the Ankara Agreement and the Council of Association Decision No. 3/80 on the Application of the Social Security Schemes of Member States in the European Communities to Turkish Workers and Members of their Families. In relation to Decision 3/80, see in particular Case C–262/96 *Sürül v. Bundesanstalt für Arbeit* [1999] E.C.R. I–2685.

BIBLIOGRAPHY

Barnard, *EC Employment Law* (2nd ed., Oxford University Press, 2000).
Barnard and Hepple, "Substantive Equality" (2000) 59 C.L.J. 562.
Barrett and Bernardeau, *Towards a European Civil Code* (Academy of European Law, Trier, 2002).
Carey "From Obloquy to Equality: In the Shadow of Abnormal Situations" (2001) 20 YEL 79.
Castro Oliveira, "Workers and Other Persons: Step-By-Step From Movement to Citizenship – Case Law 1995–2001" (2002) 39 C.M.L.Rev. 77.
Craig and de Búrca, *EU Law* (3rd ed., Oxford University Press, 2002)
Everson, "The Legacy of the Market Citizen" in Shaw and More, *New Legal Dynamics of European Integration* (Clarendon, 1995).
Fredman, "Combating Racism with Human Rights: The Right to Equality" in S. Fredman (ed.), *Discrimination and Human Rights: The Case of Racism* (Oxford University Press, 2001).
Fredman "European Community Discrimination Law: A Critique" (1992) 21 I.L.J. 119.
Hailbronner in *Immigration and Asylum Law and Policy of the European Union* (Kluwer Law International, 2000).
Hartley, *The Foundations of European Community Law* (4th ed., Oxford University Press, 1998.
Hogan and Whyte, *The Irish Constitution – J.M. Kelly* (3rd ed., 1994).
Ingoldsby, "Free Movement – A Department of Justice Perspective" in Hyland, *The Free Movement of Workers Within the European Union* (Irish Centre for European Law, 1999).
More, "The Principle of Equal Treatment: From Market Unifier to Fundamental Right" in Craig and Búrca, *The Evolution of EU Law* (Oxford University Press, 1999).
O'Leary, *The Evolving Concept of European Citizenship* (Kluwer, 1996).
Peers, "Dazed and Confused: Family Members' Residence Rights and the Court of Justice" (2001) 26 E.L. Rev. 76.
Staples, *Rights Enjoyed by Third Country Nationals Under EC Association Agreements* (Paper presented at the Irish Centre for European Law conference on the rights of third country nationals in EC law held in Trinity College Dublin on November 25, 2000).
Swann, *The Economics of the Common Market* (7th ed., Penguin, 1992).
Tridimas, *The General Principles of EC Law* (Oxford University Press, 1999).
Watson "Free Movement of Workers: A One-way Ticket?" (1993) 22 I.L.J. 68.
Weiler, *The Constitution of Europe* (Cambridge University Press, 1999).

SUBJECT INDEX